THE COMPUTER TUTOR

THE COMPUTER TUTOR

A Complete Masterclass
for Your Micro

Guild Publishing London

Volume Editor Maurice Geller

First published in Great Britain 1986 by
Orbis Book Publishing Corporation Ltd
A BPCC plc company
© Orbis Publishing 1983, 1984, 1985
Compilation © Orbis Book Publishing
Corporation Ltd 1986

This edition published 1986 by
Book Club Associates
by arrangement with
Orbis Book Publishing Corporation Ltd

Printed in England by Jarrold & Sons
ISBN 1-85155-047-X home
       1-85155-048-8 export

CONTENTS

Introduction

The question that all home computer owners ask themselves eventually is, 'where can I go next?' It is perfectly possible for anyone to use a computer – whether for doing the accounts or blasting Space Invaders out of the sky – with only the vaguest idea, if any, about how it works. But most enthusiasts find that the programs and games they've bought to begin with quickly become boring and inadequate. Rather than simply running pre-programmed software, they are soon ready to explore different applications, modify existing software and, of course, write programs of their own and gain a wider appreciation of the uses and working of the micro. THE COMPUTER TUTOR enables you to do all these things.

The book begins with a comprehensive, step-by-step guide to programming in BASIC. Giving a thorough grounding in the use of the language, it enables even a beginner to create computer programs successfully, and acts as a useful refresher and good practice guide for the more experienced. This guide is followed by a detailed examination of expert programming technique, designed to help the self-taught or novice programmer to write clear efficient programs and to discover many of the 'tricks of the trade' that make programming easier. A series of programming projects are included to build on and develop this material, increasing and refining the home computer user's knowledge not only of BASIC but also good programming practice.

There is a comprehensive course on machine code programming – the key to the real power of the microprocessor, allowing the programmer direct control over all the machine's functions. Covering both 6502 and Z80 operation codes, it leads to a full understanding of the fundamentals of programming.

The book assesses all the important computer languages, highlighting their strengths and weaknesses and looking at the factors that should be considered when choosing a particular language for any application. And there are full user's guides to LOGO, one of the best preparatory languages available, and PASCAL, a well-structured and efficient language that encourages good programming technique.

The volume considers all the principal software applications with a detailed look at different packages, so that the reader will understand their operation and methods and learn more about professional programming techniques. It also examines a full range of peripheral devices, the add-ons and attachments with which you can upgrade and expand your machine and the tasks you can accomplish with it. It is all aimed to help you move beyond the confines of your machine and truly make the most of your micro.

Maurice Geller

1 PROGRAMMING IN BASIC

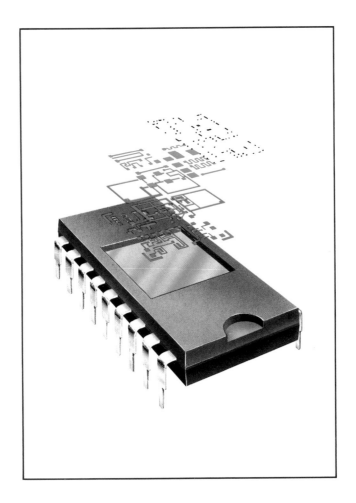

Widely available, versatile, easy to learn and easy to use,
BASIC is the standard language of microcomputing. Its
development represented the major breakthrough from
the complex syntax and functions of the early
programming languages.

SIMPLY OBEYING ORDERS

It is perfectly possible for anyone to use a computer — at home or at work — without knowing anything at all about how the computer works. Starting here, THE HOME COMPUTER COURSE begins a step-by-step series that explains, from the beginning, all you need to know to be able to create your own computer programs successfully.

Many people find that after a while, the pre-packaged programs and games they've bought for their computer start to become a little boring and they wonder if they can modify them or even write their own. But a computer can do nothing by itself. It must be given a list of instructions telling it in minute detail exactly what to do and how to go about achieving it. These instructions form what is called a *program* and the art of creating them is called *programming*.

There is nothing difficult about programming. You don't even have to be good at maths, unless, of course, you want to write programs to perform mathematical tasks. All you need to begin with is to understand BASIC.

Your First Language

Most home computers are provided with a built-in computer language called BASIC. As its name implies, it is designed to enable beginners to learn the rudiments of programming quickly and easily. Like any human language, BASIC has it own grammar, vocabulary and syntax, although the vocabulary is far smaller than that of English. BASIC uses a number of short English words that are easily recognisable and simple to learn. As a general-purpose language it is suitable for both the novice and the more experienced user.

But one drawback with the language is that over the years, different computer manufacturers have tended to include their own modifications. The result is that there are a large number of variations in BASIC, particularly regarding the commands for controlling the more recently developed aspects of the machine — such as colour, graphics and sounds. Any variations of BASIC which occur in the most popular computers are shown in the 'Basic Flavours' box in each lesson.

Because of the variations in BASIC from computer to computer, it is nearly impossible to write a BASIC program of any complexity that will run on every computer. Fortunately, however, the language has a common core, which is usually the same in all machines. We'll start by concentrating

on that core, and as the course progresses we will work steadily towards more complex programs.

The Initial Steps

Let's begin by writing a small program and seeing what happens. This one will show the computer apparently making a mistake. Switch on the computer and type in the program exactly as shown, including all the spaces. The <CR> at the end of each line is to remind you to hit Carriage Return. On your computer, this key may be labelled RETURN, ENTER or even ↵.

```
10 REM COMPUTERS NEVER MAKE
   MISTAKES<CR>
20 PRINT "TYPE IN A NUMBER"<CR>
30 INPUT A<CR>
40 LET A = A + 1<CR>
50 PRINT "I THINK THE NUMBER YOU TYPED
   WAS  ";<CR>
60 PRINT A<CR>
70 END<CR>
```

After you have typed it all in, type LIST<CR>. The program you just typed should reappear on the screen. LIST is an instruction to the computer to 'print' a listing of the program in memory. If the program appeared on the screen properly after typing LIST, we could try to RUN it. If you make a mistake when typing in the program, don't worry. After you have LISTed the program, simply retype any line containing a mistake. Don't forget the line number. Try typing

25 REM HERE IS ANOTHER 'REM' LINE<CR>

and then LIST the program again. To get rid of the line, type the line number alone, followed by <CR>. When you are satisfied the program has been typed correctly, you can 'run' it by typing RUN<CR>. Try this and you should see on the screen:

TYPE IN A NUMBER

Go ahead and type a number. Try 7. (Use numerals — the computer won't recognise 'seven' as 7 unless we specially program it to do so.) If you typed in 7, the screen should look like this:

I THINK THE NUMBER YOU TYPED WAS 8

Did the computer really make a mistake, or was it simply obeying orders? If we look at the program line by line we can see what each instruction made the computer do. Here's the first line:

10 REM COMPUTERS NEVER MAKE MISTAKES

REM stands for REMark. Anything appearing on the same line after REM is ignored by the computer. Remarks are a handy way of reminding yourself what the computer is doing. This particular REM is just a title — it does not tell us what the program is doing. We'll see how helpful properly written REMs are later in the course. Now let's look at:

20 PRINT "TYPE IN A NUMBER"

When BASIC gets to the word PRINT, the part that follows it is 'printed' on the computer screen. Notice that the sentence is enclosed in double quote marks. One of BASIC's rules is that the characters (letters) appearing inside double quote marks after a PRINT statement will appear on the screen exactly as they were typed in. We'll see another way of using PRINT in line 60. Next comes:

30 INPUT A

We'll skip this line for now and come back to it after looking at line 40.

40 LET A = A + 1

The letter A is used here as a variable. A variable is like a labelled box that can contain either a number or some characters. Instead of having to remember what's in the box, all we have to know is what the box is called in order to reference it. It's like saying "Pass me the box labelled B" instead of "Pass me the box containing the 15mm cheese-head screws".

In this line we have a 'box' called A. This box is called a variable, because the value of what we put in it can vary. We can assign virtually any value to a variable. A value was assigned to variable A in line 30, so let's see how it was done:

30 INPUT A

Using the word INPUT is one of the ways in BASIC of assigning (giving) a specific value to a variable. When the BASIC program gets to a line starting with INPUT it waits for something to be typed in from the keyboard. INPUT A lets the computer know that we have a variable called A and that whatever is typed in at the keyboard will be assigned to that variable. Typing 7<CR> at this point puts 7 in box A, or to use computer jargon, assigns the value 7 to variable A. Now that we know what a variable is, and one of the ways of assigning a value to it, let's look at line 40 again.

40 LET A = A + 1

The name of the variable to which a value is assigned always appears on the left of the equals sign. Here we are giving a new value to A. The statement means 'LET the new value of A equal the old value plus 1.' The old value of A was 7. We have now made it 7 + 1, so the new value is 8.

50 PRINT "I THINK THE NUMBER YOU TYPED
       WAS ";

This is our print statement again. It 'prints' the

character string (that is, the words or numbers you have typed) between the double quote marks. Notice the semi-colon at the end of the line. It helps to specify the positions at which things are printed on the screen. Later in the course we'll return to how the semi-colon is used in more detail. Now let's look at:

60 PRINT A

Here's another PRINT statement, but this time there are no quote marks around the A. We already know that the program will not print an actual A on the screen because we have seen that quote marks are needed to do that. Without the quotes, BASIC looks for a variable with the same label as the character after PRINT. If it finds one, it prints the value of the variable. (If it doesn't find one, it gives an error message!) This program already has a variable called A and so BASIC prints its value — what is it?

If you thought the answer was 7, remember that BASIC works through programs line by line,

The box below shows how 'variables' are used in BASIC. It also illustrates how the GOTO statement (see next page) is used to form a loop

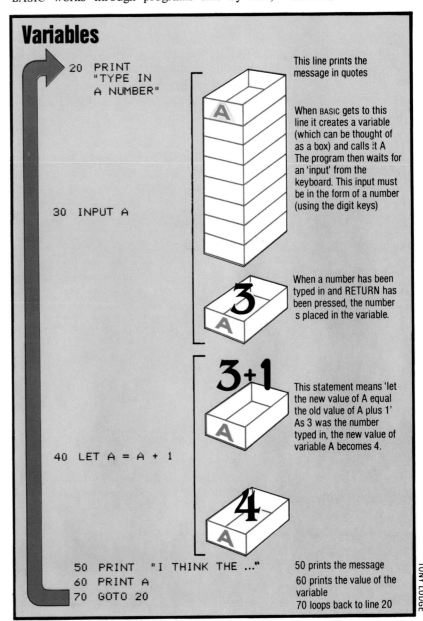

Variables

```
20  PRINT
    "TYPE IN
    A NUMBER"



30  INPUT A
```

This line prints the message in quotes

When BASIC gets to this line it creates a variable (which can be thought of as a box) and calls it A The program then waits for an 'input' from the keyboard. This input must be in the form of a number (using the digit keys)

When a number has been typed in and RETURN has been pressed, the number s placed in the variable.

```
40  LET A = A + 1
```

This statement means 'let the new value of A equal the old value of A plus 1' As 3 was the number typed in, the new value of variable A becomes 4.

```
50  PRINT  "I THINK THE ..."
60  PRINT A
70  GOTO 20
```

50 prints the message
60 prints the value of the variable
70 loops back to line 20

TONY LODGE

Basic Flavours

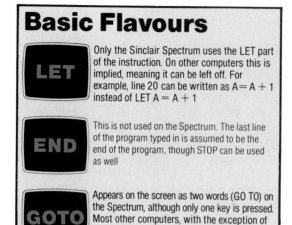

LET — Only the Sinclair Spectrum uses the LET part of the instruction. On other computers this is implied, meaning it can be left off. For example, line 20 can be written as A = A + 1 instead of LET A = A + 1

END — This is not used on the Spectrum. The last line of the program typed in is assumed to be the end of the program, though STOP can be used as well

GOTO — Appears on the screen as two words (GO TO) on the Spectrum, although only one key is pressed. Most other computers, with the exception of the BBC will accept the instruction typed as two words

following the order of the line numbers. By the time we got to line 60 the value of A had already been changed to 8, and that is what it will print. Finally we come to:

    70 END

The END statement tells BASIC that the end of the program has been reached. Some versions of BASIC insist that all programs should finish with END while others do not (see the 'Basic Flavours' box).

Notice that when you run the program it only 'works' once. To get it to go through once more you have to type RUN<CR> again. Now we'll look at a way of getting the program to work as many times as we want by using the GOTO statement.

Using GOTO

The same program but with an extra line is given below. If you have switched off the computer to take a break, type it in. Otherwise all you need to do is to type in lines 70 and 80. These are shown in blue in the listing below.

    10 REM COMPUTERS NEVER MAKE
       MISTAKES<CR>
    20 PRINT "TYPE IN A NUMBER"<CR>
    30 INPUT A<CR>
    40 LET A = A + 1<CR>
    50 PRINT "I THINK THE NUMBER YOU TYPED
       WAS " ; <CR>
    60 PRINT A<CR>
    70 GOTO 20<CR>
    80 END<CR>

After you have typed it all in and LISTed it, see if you can figure out what will happen before you try to RUN it. Then type RUN<CR> and, as in the first version of the program, you should see:

    TYPE IN A NUMBER

Type in any number (using the numeral keys) and hit RETURN. The computer will add 1 to the number and display it at the end of the message.

    I THINK THE NUMBER YOU TYPED WAS n

You will see that this is immediately followed by the TYPE IN A NUMBER message again. Entering another number and hitting return again makes the program cycle like this *ad infinitum*. The reason this happens can be found in line 70:

    70 GOTO 20

When BASIC reaches a GOTO statement, instead of continuing to the next line, it GOes TO the line number specified. Here it is directed back to line 20 and the whole program is run all over again. It goes on looping back like this forever. If you want to stop the program from running you'll find there's no way of getting out of the loop. The program just goes on and on waiting for your input.

As you would expect, there are ways of writing the program so that we can get out of it if we want to, and we'll look at one of these in the next instalment of this course. Meanwhile, we still have to stop the program. If your computer has a BREAK key, it can be used to stop the program from running. Typing RUN<CR> will start the program again.

Notice that we still have the END statement at the end of the program. The way we have written this program, with the GOTO 20 statement creating an endless loop, we never do get to the end, but some versions of BASIC insist that we always use an END at the end!

If you can't find a way of stopping the program, try hitting the RESET key. That is almost certain to halt the program. Then try to LIST it again. If you get a list, you will be able to 'edit' the program in the exercises below. If you do not get a list, it means the RESET on your computer destroys the program in memory and you will then have to type the whole thing in again.

Exercises

These questions are carefully graded and are designed to be fun. Working through exercises is one of the best ways of checking that you have understood the material presented and are making genuine progress.

Before starting the exercises, try changing a few of the lines to see the effect on the way the program runs. You can't possibly do the computer any harm even if you make mistakes or hit the wrong keys. To change a line, type in the program and then check the result by LISTing it. The whole program will appear on the screen again. Type the number of the line you want to change followed by the new line. Try this:

    10 REM COMPUTERS SOMETIMES MAKE
       MISTAKES<CR>

then type LIST again. Notice how the first line has been changed. If you want to get rid of everything in the line, just type the line number followed by <CR>. Try:

    10<CR>
       LIST

Line 10 should have disappeared. Put line 10 back in by typing out the whole line again — not forgetting the line number!

■ Rewrite the program so that the computer really does print out the number typed in. Hint: taking out one whole line should do the trick.

■ Retype line 70 so that the program goes to line 80. LIST the program. RUN the program. Why didn't it run the same way as before?

■ Change line 60 so that the computer prints an A on the screen instead of the value of variable A.

■ Rewrite line 60 so that the computer prints the value of variable A once again. Remove line 10 (the REM line) completely. RUN the program. Does it run any differently?

■ Put in a new REMark on line 25. New lines can be added by simply typing the new number followed by the new statement. Put in a remark on line 25 to remind you what will happen next — it could be something like 'expects an input from the keyboard'. After you have typed the new line and

hit <CR>, LIST the program again and check that your new remark appears in the right place.

■ Rewrite the program so that it multiplies the number you type in by 10. You'll need to change line 50 to print something like THE NUMBER YOU TYPED MULTIPLIED BY 10 IS. This time we will not want to add to the value of the old variable, we'll wants to multiply it by 10. BASIC uses the * sign to mean 'multiply'. (Don't use an X because BASIC only recognises it as a letter, not as a multiplication sign.)

We have now covered quite a lot of ground. We have seen how to write comments, which BASIC calls REMarks, how to PRINT character strings on the screen, how to PRINT the value of a variable on the screen, and how to make the program GOTO a specified line number.

Next we'll see how to get out of a loop by using an IF-THEN statement. We'll find out how to get the program to 'perform' for us a specified number of times instead of looping forever. And we'll also see how to slow the program down to make the computer look as if it's really having to think.

And Then There Was BASIC

Today, BASIC is the world's most popular programming language. Computer languages were invented to allow the human operator to communicate more easily with the machine, and BASIC is one of the easiest to learn and use. It consists of instructions in simple English combined, where necessary, with the mathematical symbols found on a typewriter keyboard.

BASIC is a quick language to master. Within a few minutes of unpacking a microcomputer you can be writing simple programs. It was devised in 1965 at Dartmouth College, New Hampshire, with the express purpose of simplifying existing languages. The inventors were two teachers, Thomas Kurtz and John Kemeny. The universal use of BASIC has meant slight variations in the language have crept in. But the core of BASIC remains common to all manufacturers.

A program is a sequence of instructions which the computer executes to perform a specified task. The task might be to produce a monthly financial forecast, or to move a Space Invader across the television screen. The program appears as a series of numbered lines. Each line contains one instruction and the number allows the computer to obey the commands in the right order. Commands are quickly learnt and even the most complicated

BASIC has taken the mystique out of programming and made computing accessible to everyone

program uses nothing more than combinations and repetitions of the elementary commands.

Most computers arrive from the manufacturers with BASIC built in. Computers can also be programmed in 'machine code' (described as a 'low' level language because it is close in structure to the logic found in the electronic circuits). BASIC is a 'high' level language as it is nearer to everyday English. There are many other high level languages devised for more technical and specialised applications, but BASIC is the best introduction to them all. It's a simple and powerful language.

TO THE POINT

Here we consider the crucial importance that ordinary punctuation marks take on in writing computer programs.

In our first BASIC listing, on page 8, you may have noticed the semi-colon at the end of line 50. The function of this punctuation mark in BASIC was not explained at the time, but is nevertheless very important. It is used in almost all versions of BASIC to concatenate printed sections ('concatenate' means 'join together'). Lines 50 and 60 on page 8 were:

```
50 PRINT "I THINK THE NUMBER YOU TYPED
   WAS ";
60 PRINT A
```

Line 50 printed the words inside the double quote marks. Line 60 printed the value of the variable A. Putting in the semi-colon caused the value of variable A to be printed directly after the words within quotes in line 50. If no semi-colon had been used, it would have been printed on the line following the words.

The program below has been designed to illustrate some of the useful properties of the semicolon as it is used in BASIC. Try typing it in and running it. From now on, we will omit the <CR> reminder at the end of each line to indicate that you should press the RETURN key. This next program allows you to enter a range of temperatures in Centigrade (also known as Celsius) and have them converted automatically to their equivalents in Fahrenheit.

```
10 REM PROGRAM TO CONVERT DEGREES C TO F
20 PRINT "ENTER THE LOWEST TEMPERATURE"
30 INPUT L
40 PRINT "ENTER THE HIGHEST TEMPERATURE"
50 INPUT H
60 FOR X = L TO H
70 LET F = X * 9 / 5 + 32
80 PRINT X," IN CENTIGRADE IS " F;"
   IN FARENHEIT"
90 NEXT X
100 END
```

Enter this program, LIST it to check that it has been entered correctly, and then RUN it. First you will be asked to enter the lowest temperature. Try typing in −5. Then you will be asked to enter the highest temperature. Try typing in 10. The program will convert all temperatures at one degree

intervals from −5 to 10 degrees Centigrade to their Fahrenheit equivalents. You should get a 'printout' on the screen looking something like:

```
-6  IN CENTIGRADE IS 21.2 IN FARENHEIT
-5  IN CENTIGRADE IS 23 IN FARENHEIT
-4  IN CENTIGRADE IS 24.8 IN FARENHEIT
```

Notice that the columns are not very even because of the decimal points, but that each value in Centigrade is printed with its equivalent in Fahrenheit on a single line. After you have run the program a few times, re-type line 80 just as it is, but substitute commas wherever we have printed semi-colons. RUN the program again. As you can see, the printout becomes a complete mess.

To see why this happened, let's try a very simple program to compare the effect of commas compared with the effect of semi-colons. Type NEW<CR>. Then enter:

```
10 REM COMPARE ; WITH ,
20 PRINT "THIS LINE USES SEMI-COLONS"
30 PRINT "H";"E";"L";"P"
40 PRINT "THIS LINE USES COMMAS"
50 PRINT "H", "E", "L", "P"
60 END
```

When BASIC prints line 30 it will appear on the screen as HELP, whereas line 50 will appear as H E L P. See the 'Basic Flavours' box for variations between different machines. The comma has many uses in BASIC, but in PRINT statements it has the effect of making the individual items appear on the screen (or on a paper printout) spaced out, usually by between 8 and 16 spaces depending on the version of BASIC. If the PRINT statement is used without either commas or semi-colons, the items will be printed out on separate lines.

Apart from illustrating BASIC's use of the semicolon, our temperature conversion program also revises several statements covered in the first two parts of the Basic Programming course. Lines 30 and 50 set variables L and H to the values for the lowest and highest temperatures we want to convert. Line 60 is the first part of a FOR-NEXT loop. It seems to differ from the FOR-NEXT loop we have encountered so far by using letters instead of numbers. In fact, there is no difference. The letters we are using here, L and H, are variables with numeric values corresponding to the values typed in at the INPUT L and INPUT H stage of the program. If, as suggested earlier, you entered −5 and 10, the statement FOR X = L TO H is therefore equivalent to FOR X = −5 TO 10.

Line 80 in effect says: PRINT the value of X (which starts at the lowest temperature and increments by 1 each time up to the highest temperature) followed directly on the same line (that's why we used the semi-colon) by the words in quotes, followed directly again (another semi-colon) by the value of F. If you look carefully at F, you will see that it is the current value of the Centigrade temperature, converted into Fahrenheit by multiplying it by nine, dividing it by five and then adding 32. The NEXT X line ensures that we go through the conversions until the upper limit in the FOR-NEXT loop has been reached.

Before going on to look at a more sophisticated variation on the PRINT statement, it is worth taking a second look at line 70 in our temperature conversion program:

```
70 LET F = X * 9 / 5 + 32
```

This line assigns a value to the variable F (which stands for Fahrenheit). The program first takes the value of X (the temperature in Centigrade), multiplies it by 9, divides that by 5 and then adds 32. The way this formula would be presented in an ordinary arithmetic book is $F = C \times 9 \div 5 + 32$. BASIC uses * for multiplication, / for division, + for addition and − for subtraction.

In ordinary arithmetic, and in BASIC too, the order in which arithmetical operations are carried out is important. Multiplication always has top priority, followed by division, followed by addition, followed by subtraction. If parts of an arithmetic expression are enclosed in round brackets, they must be evaluated first. If you want an addition to be performed first, before a multiplication, the addition part must be enclosed in brackets. For example, if you wanted to know how much money you had in your current account plus your savings account in dollars, you might express it in part of a program like this:

```
D = (C + S) * 1.5
```

If your current account has £600 (C) and your savings account has £1,300 (S) and there are 1.5 dollars to the pound, you will want to add the pounds first (C + S) and then multiply by 1.5 to convert to dollars. Without the brackets, the value of your savings account would first be multiplied by 1.5 and then the value of your current account would be added to the result — not what you wanted at all! Always be sure to check that the arithmetic parts will be calculated in the right order.

Print Using

In order to look at a final refinement to our temperature conversion program, try typing it in again and RUNing it. Enter, say, −10 as the value for the lowest temperature and 10 as the value for the highest. As we have already seen, the printout on the screen is very ragged. This is because of the semi-colons used in line 80 in order to concatenate (run together) all the parts being printed, instead of printing them on separate lines. Which is fine, except that the space taken up by the figures —

both the Centigrade and the Fahrenheit ones — varies. This has the effect of pulling the columns out of alignment and making the printout look untidy.

Almost all versions of BASIC have a special PRINT feature called PRINT USING. It allows the appearance of the printed numbers or words to be 'formatted' or tidied up. If you want to print the value of X and that value is known in advance to range from, say, −99 to 99, the figures can be printed out correctly aligned by using PRINT USING "###";X. The three 'hash' signs allow up to three digits, or two digits preceded by a minus sign, to be printed. If more than three digits are entered, they will not be printed out correctly. If, however, only two digits are entered (or only one) they will be positioned correctly. If decimal points are required, they can be included in the appropriate position within the hash signs. For example, the statement can take the form PRINT USING "###.##";X. Use one 'hash' sign for each digit. All the decimal points will line up automatically.

Modify the original program by changing line 80 and adding lines 82, 84 and 86:

```
80 PRINT USING "###";X;
82 PRINT " IN CENTIGRADE IS ";
84 PRINT USING "###.##";F;
86 PRINT " IN FAHRENHEIT"
```

LIST the program again and then RUN it. All the columns should now be lined up perfectly.

We will find out how to 'save' programs, so that they do not need to be re-typed every time, in the next instalment of the course.

Exercises

■ Try entering a 'lowest temperature' of −1000. Why doesn't the program work this time? How would you modify the PRINT USING statement in line 80 to make it work?

■ Alter line 84 so that only whole numbers (no decimal fractions) are printed.

■ Write a program to convert a range of figures in pounds to dollars, using an exchange rate of $1.50 to the £.

Basic Flavours

PRINT USING
This facility is not available on the Commodore 64, Oric, Spectrum, ZX81 or BBC Micro. However, the BBC can limit the number of decimal places to be printed, and this is achieved by using the following instruction:
@%=131594

COMMA
The use of a comma between print fields will separate the items to be printed by inserting a set number of spaces, and this varies depending upon which computer is being used. On the BBC and Commodore 64 this is set at 10 spaces, with 16 on the Dragon, Spectrum and ZX81. The Oric uses only four spaces

ROUTINE MATTERS

We introduce the subroutine, a feature of BASIC **that saves repetition and keeps programs neat and manageable.**

What we have done so far is to type in programs, run them, made modifications to them and then cleared the memory (using the NEW command) when we wanted to enter new programs. When we have needed to run the old program again, it has been necessary to type the whole thing in again.

To save this repetitious work, all versions of BASIC are provided with a command that allows any program to be stored on cassette tape. The program below can be saved on tape by using the simple command SAVE followed by a file name. The program calculates the number of tiles needed to tile a room.

```
10 REM THIS PROGRAM CALCULATES THE
   NUMBER OF TILES
20 REM NEEDED TO TILE A ROOM
30 PRINT "ENTER SIDE OF TILE IN MM"
40 INPUT A1
45 LET T=0
50 REM LINE 60 FINDS AREA OF TILE
60 LET A2 = A1 * A1
70 PRINT "ENTER THE NUMBER OF WALLS"
80 REM W SETS LIMIT FOR LOOP
```

```
90 INPUT W
100 FOR X = 1 TO W
110 PRINT "LENGTH OF WALL NO."; X; "IN METRES"
120 REM D IS DIMENSION OF WALL
130 INPUT D
140 REM IT IS CONVERTED TO MM
150 REM IN THE SUBROUTINE
160 GOSUB 380
170 REM LINE 190 SETS L TO
180 REM LENGTH OF WALL IN MM
190 LET L = D2
200 PRINT "HEIGHT OF WALL NO."; X; "IN METRES"
210 REM LINES 230 TO 250 SET H
220 REM TO HEIGHT OF WALL IN MM
230 INPUT D
240 GOSUB 380
250 LET H = D2
260 REM LINE 270 SETS A3 TO AREA OF WALL
270 LET A3 = L * H
280 REM S (SUB-TOTAL) IS AREA OF WALL DIVIDED
290 REM BY AREA OF TILE
300 LET S = A3/A2
310 REM T (TOTAL) HAS THE NEW SUB-TOTAL
320 REM ADDED EACH TIME THRU THE LOOP
330 LET T = T + S
340 NEXT X
350 REM PRINT THE TOTAL
360 PRINT T
370 END
380 LET D2 = D * 1000
390 RETURN
```

Having typed in the program, all you need to do to save it on cassette tape is to use the SAVE command. First, of course, the cassette recorder must be set up in accordance with the instructions in your computer's handbook. The SAVE command is extremely easy to use. Just type SAVE followed by a file name in double quotation marks. A file name is the name given to a file, and a file, in computer terms, is like a file in a filing cabinet — a program or set of data that can be stored away or retrieved when required. It is best to use a file name that will remind you of the function of the program. Since our program calculates the number of tiles needed to tile a room, we could call it "TILES". Once the cassette recorder is set up, insert a blank tape to hold the program.

Cassette decks with a remote control socket can usually have the motor controlled directly by the computer. Otherwise, set the recorder in the record mode and then put it in the pause mode. Type in the SAVE command, including the file name. Set the recorder running by releasing the pause control and then hit RETURN.

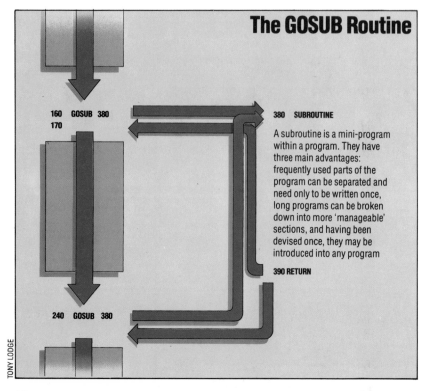

The GOSUB Routine

160 GOSUB 380
170

380 SUBROUTINE

A subroutine is a mini-program within a program. They have three main advantages: frequently used parts of the program can be separated and need only to be written once, long programs can be broken down into more 'manageable' sections, and having been devised once, they may be introduced into any program

390 RETURN

240 GOSUB 380

TONY LODGE

To test that the program has been recorded correctly, erase the computer's memory by typing NEW‹CR›. Rewind the cassette, put it into the play mode and then load the program back into the computer using the LOAD command. LOAD must be followed by the file name of the file wanted. Type LOAD "TILES" and then hit RETURN.

After the program has been loaded into the computer, a message on the screen such as READY or OK indicates that the load has been completed. LIST the program and check that it is the same as the one you typed in.

THE GOSUB STATEMENT

GOSUB is a statement that diverts the flow of a program to a subroutine. A subroutine is like a separate mini-program or program-within-a-program. In the program used to illustrate it here, the subroutine is very simple. It is included to show the principle, although other ways could easily have been devised to produce the same results without using a subroutine.

Our program calculates the number of tiles needed to tile a room by finding out the area of the tiles used. It then asks for the length and height of each wall to be entered. It works out the area of the wall after the length and height has been converted from metres to millimetres. The number of tiles needed is found by dividing each wall's area by the area of a tile and adding the results. The conversion of wall length and height into millimetres is done in the subroutine, which simply multiplies the length or height (in metres) by 1000 to find the equivalent in millimetres.

Subroutines have three advantages. Frequently used parts of programs can be separated off and only need to be written once — no matter how often the operation is required. They allow long and complex programs to be broken down into more manageable and easily understood units or sections. Finally, subroutines can be re-used in any program where its function is appropriate.

In our program, the subroutine starts at line 380 and consists of only one statement: LET D2 = D * 1000. This takes D, the wall dimension (length or height) and multiplies it by 1000 to convert from metres to millimetres. The result is assigned to variable D2.

The instruction that forces the program to go to the subroutine is GOSUB. It occurs first in line 160. Variable D was assigned the value of the length of the wall in line 130. Line 160 forces the program to go to the subroutine, where variable D2 is given the value of D multiplied by 1000. The RETURN instruction in line 390 is needed to make the program return from the subroutine to the main program. Subroutines always return to the line after the GOSUB statement, in this case, to line 170.

The next occurrence of GOSUB is in line 240, which 'calls' the same subroutine. This time, the subroutine RETURNs to line 250. Although this program uses only one subroutine, it is possible to use as many as are needed. In every case, the GOSUB statement will have to include the line

number of the appropriate subroutine. Notice that the END statement occurs in line 370, before the subroutine. END indicates the end of the main program and also serves to stop the program from running on through the subroutines after it has been completed.

Although this program is a little longer than previous programs in this course, it is really no more complex. Try and follow it through, line by line, and see what is happening at each stage. Apart from GOSUB and subroutines this program introduces only one new concept — longer variable names.

It may be helpful to draw boxes with the variable names written on them and to write in the values at each stage.

Line 300: LET S = A3/A2 will sometimes give a number with a decimal fraction. Try running the program and entering the tile size as 110mm and the wall length and height as 2.3 and 1.8 metres respectively, using just one wall. You should get an answer of 342.149 tiles. Since tiles are never sold in units of less than one, this answer is not completely appropriate. What we will look at next are some of the ways of getting an appropriate answer in whole numbers.

Exercises

■ See what happens if you enter the size of the tile as 0mm. You should get an error message at the end of the run. Why is this? Why don't you get a similar error message when you enter the length of one of the walls as 0 metres? Hint: multiplying by zero and dividing by zero are not the same thing — try it on your calculator!

■ The program only works for square tiles. See if you can change lines 30 to 60 to find the area of rectangular tiles (just as we found the area of rectangular walls later in the program).

■ Add a statement at line 355 to increase the total number of tiles by five per cent to allow for wastage. Multiplying a number by 105/100 will increase it by five per cent.

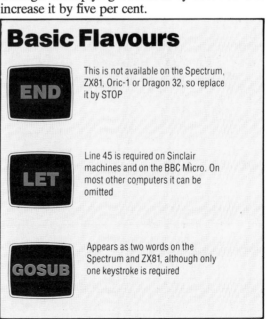

Basic Flavours

END This is not available on the Spectrum, ZX81, Oric-1 or Dragon 32, so replace it by STOP

LET Line 45 is required on Sinclair machines and on the BBC Micro. On most other computers it can be omitted

GOSUB Appears as two words on the Spectrum and ZX81, although only one keystroke is required

CHRISTMAS IN BASIC

We write a program that brings together all the topics covered so far and introduces several new and powerful commands for dealing with data.

The purpose of the program is to calculate the number of days remaining until Christmas. If you look at the program listing, you will see that it starts with a list of the variables used. This practice is certainly not essential, but is advisable as it can make your programs much easier to understand when you come to look at them later. Some versions of BASIC allow variables to have long names, DAY for example, rather than the single letters we have been using. If you are lucky enough to have a BASIC that allows long variable names, choose meaningful names. DAY, MONTH or DAYNUM are much better than A, X or D. If you have no choice in the matter because your BASIC does not allow long variable names, listing the variables at the top of the program makes it almost as 'readable'.

When the program is run, the first thing that will appear on the screen will be the PRINT statements starting at line 230. These state briefly what the program will do and then prompt the user to type in the date in the form shown, using commas to separate the day, month and year.

The first unfamiliar statement will be in line 300. This is a DIMension statement. It is used to set the number of items or elements allowed in the array labelled X. An array, sometimes called a subscripted variable, is like an ordinary variable except that the box contains several compartments. In line 300 we are creating a variable called X with 13 compartments inside the box. We shall return to the subject of arrays and the DIM statement in more detail later in the course.

310 INPUT D, M$, Y

This line is an ordinary INPUT statement except that it expects three inputs. D is a numeric variable that will contain today's date. Y is another numeric variable for the year. M$ is slightly different. It is called a 'string variable' and this is indicated by the $ (dollar) sign. A string variable accepts characters from the keyboard as well as numbers. If, for example, we type 23, JANUARY, 1983, variable D will be assigned the value 23, variable M$ will be assigned the character string JANUARY and variable Y will be assigned the value 1983.

330 GOSUB 560 REM 'NO OF MONTH' ROUTINE

This statement instructs the program to branch to the subroutine starting at line 560. Note, also that a REMark has been inserted on the same line. If there is room on the line, it is not always necessary to put REMs on a new line. This particular subroutine is only used by the main program once, and strictly speaking could just as easily have been incorporated into the main program. Making it into a subroutine just keeps this part separate from the rest of the program.

When the program was originally written, a number was used for the month and this part of the program was not needed. Later it was decided to allow the month to be entered as a typed word spelled out in full. In order to convert the spell-out month into its equivalent number, the extra program now forming this subroutine was written separately. The only change needed to the main (original) program was to add a single GOSUB statement. This subroutine illustrates the ease with which programs can be built up in blocks and linked together using the GOSUB and RETURN statements.

The subroutine itself is very simple, but illustrates how clever BASIC is at manipulating character strings. Suppose we had entered JANUARY as the month part of the INPUT statement. Variable M$ would then be assigned the character string JANUARY. The first line of the subroutine is:

560 IF M$ = "JANUARY" THEN LET M = 1

This statement compares the contents of M$ with the characters inside the double quotation marks. If they are the same (as they are in this case) the line goes on to set the value of numeric variable M to 1. Do not confuse variable M with variable M$. They are different. Only one can contain a string variable, the one with the $ sign! After checking to see if M$ is the same as the string JANUARY, the program moves to the next line and checks to see if the contents of M$ are the same as FEBRUARY. It is not, so M is not set to 2. Only where the match is correct will variable M be set to a value, and that value is the same as the number of the month — 1 for January, 3 for March and so on.

On getting to line 680 BASIC RETURNs to the main program, to the line after the GOSUB statement. This is line 340. It contains a REM but no comment. It is inserted simply to space out the program and to make it easier to read.

Lines 350 to 370 are a FOR—NEXT loop. This increments the value of I, starting with 1 and counting up to 13. The variable I is used as the subscript of the array X in line 360. It should be examined carefully.

360 READ X (I)

READ is a new statement we have not encountered before. READ is always used with a corresponding DATA statement. The DATA statement for this line is in line 510:

DATA 31, 28, 31, 30, 31, 30, 31, 31, 30, 31, 30, 25, 0

These numbers, except for the last two, are the numbers of days in each month of the year. The two lines are equivalent to 13 separate LET statements

LET X(1) = 31
LET X(2) = 28
LET X(3) = 31
LET X(4) = 30
LET X(5) = 00
LET X(6) = 00
LET X(7) = 31
LET X(8) = 31
LET X(9) = 30
LET X(10) = 31
LET X(11) = 30
LET X(12) = 25
LETX(13)=0

The loop set up in line 350 makes I count up from 1 to 13 so we were able to substitute X(I) for X(1), X(2), X(3) etc.

Before returning to this program, let's consider a far simpler small program:

10 READ A, B, C
20 LET D = A + B + C
30 PRINT D
40 DATA 5, 10, 20

Here, the READ statement in line 10 reads the first item of DATA in line 40 and 'writes' its value into the first variable. In other words, it assigns the value 5 to variable A. READ then reads the next item of data and puts it in the next variable. This program makes A = 5, B = 10 and C = 20. It then adds these and assigns the result to variable D. This result, 35, is then PRINTed in line 30.

Back to the 'Christmas' program. The first time round the loop starting in line 350, the value of I is set out to 1. Line 360 is therefore equivalent to READ X(1). The corresponding data item in line 510 is 31 (the first item). Consequently X(1) is set to 31.

The second time round the loop, I becomes 2 so line 360 is equivalent to READ X(2). The next data item in the DATA line is 28. This means that X(2) is set to 28. In this way all 13 'compartments' in the subscripted variable X are filled up with the number of days in each month; except for the 12th compartment, which has only 25 days in it, and the 13th, which has 0. (Can you see why?)

390 GOSUB 750 REM 'LEAP YEAR' ROUTINE

This line directs the program to a subroutine that checks if the year entered is a leap year or not.

```
100 REM   LIST OF VARIABLES
110 REM
120 REM   D = TODAY'S DATE
130 REM   M$ = NAME OF MONTH
140 REM   Y = YEAR
150 REM   I = INDEX 1
160 REM   X = ARRAY FOR DAYS IN EACH MONTH
170 REM   R = REMAINING DAYS
180 REM   M = NO. OF MONTH
190 REM   L = INDEX 2
200 REM   Z = INT. VALUE OF Y/4
210 REM
220 REM
230 PRINT "THIS PROGRAM CALCULATES"
240 PRINT "THE NUMBER OF DAYS REMAINING"
250 PRINT "UNTIL CHRISTMAS"
260 PRINT
270 PRINT "ENTER TODAY'S DAY,MONTH,YEAR"
280 PRINT "E.G. 12,JULY,1984"
290 PRINT
300 DIM X(13)
310 INPUT D,M$,Y
320 REM
330 GOSUB 560  REM 'NO OF MONTH' ROUTINE
340 REM
350 FOR I = 1 TO 13
360 READ X(I)
370 NEXT I
380 REM
390 GOSUB 750  REM  'LEAP YEAR' ROUTINE
400 REM
410 LET R = X(M) - D
420 FOR L = M TO 11
430 LET M = M + 1
440 LET R = R + X(M)
450 NEXT L
460 REM
470 IF R = 1 THEN GOTO 500
480 PRINT "THERE ARE";R;"DAYS LEFT UNTIL CHRISTMAS"
490 GOTO 520
500 PRINT "THERE IS 1 DAY LEFT UNTIL CHRISTMAS"
510 DATA 31,28,31,30,31,30,31,31,30,31,30,25,0
520 END
530 REM
540 REM
550 REM
560 IF M$ = "JANUARY" THEN LET M = 1
570 IF M$ = "FEBRUARY" THEN LET M = 2
580 IF M$ = "MARCH" THEN LET M = 3
590 IF M$ = "APRIL" THEN LET M = 4
600 IF M$ = "MAY" THEN LET M = 5
610 IF M$ = "JUNE" THEN LET M = 6
620 IF M$ = "JULY" THEN LET M = 7
630 IF M$ = "AUGUST" THEN LET M = 8
640 IF M$ = "SEPTEMBER" THEN LET M = 9
650 IF M$ = "OCTOBER" THEN LET M = 10
660 IF M$ = "NOVEMBER" THEN LET M = 11
670 IF M$ = "DECEMBER" THEN LET M = 12
680 RETURN
690 REM
700 REM
710 REM
720 REM NOTE: THIS ROUTINE DOES NOT CHECK
730 REM        FOR LEAP YEARS AT THE END OF
740 REM        EACH CENTURY
750 LET Y = Y / 4
760 LET Z = INT(Y)
770 IF Y - Z = 0 THEN GOTO 790
780 RETURN
790 LET X(2) = X(2) + 1
800 RETURN
```

```
750 LET Y = Y/4
760 LET Z = INT(Y)
770 IF Y–Z = 0 THEN GOTO 790
780 RETURN
790 LET X(2) = X(2) + 1
800 RETURN
```

A leap year is defined as one which is wholly divisible by the number 4. If it is a century, it must also be divisible by 400 to qualify as a leap year. To keep it simple, we have not attempted to check the century, only the divisibility by 4.

Line 750 sets Y to the old value of Y (the year) divided by 4. The new Y will be a whole number if the year is exactly divisible by 4. Otherwise it will have a decimal fraction.

Line 760 uses the function INT to find the 'integer' value of Y. Integer means whole number. While having no effect on integers, the INTeger function will round down fractional numbers to the nearest whole number. The number to be rounded down is placed in brackets after INT. Alternatively, a variable name can be put in the brackets. So LET Z = INT(496.25) would set Z to 496.

Line 770 subtracts Z from Y and checks to see if the result is 0. If it is, it means the year is a leap year (as there was no decimal fraction in the new Y). If that is the case, the program branches to line 790 using GOTO. Line 790 adds 1 to the second item in the array (the second item was 28, the number of days in an ordinary February).

If the result of the subtraction in line 770 was not zero, X(2) is left as it is and the subroutine RETURNs to the main program, to line 400.

Line 400 is another REM used just to space out the program to aid readability. The next line that actually does something is 410, where R is the variable holding the number of remaining days. It is set here to the number of days in the month entered minus the day entered. If we had entered, for example, 12, FEBRUARY, 1983, D would be equal to 12 and M would be 2. Therefore X(M) would be the same as X(2) and the second item in the X array is 28 (it would not have had 1 added to it as 1983 is not a leap year). Consequently R will be set to 28 − 12, i.e. 16, the number of days remaining in the current month, February.

Line 420 starts another loop. This one is designed to increment the value of M. Can you see why we say FOR L = 1 TO 11 rather than FOR L = 1 TO 12? If M was 2 because we had entered the month as FEBRUARY, line 430 will increment it to 3. Line 440 then sets R, the number of days remaining, to the old R plus X(M). The latter is now equivalent to X(3) since M has been incremented by 1. The value of X(3) is 31, the number of days in March. Line 440 therefore sets the new value of R to 16 + 31 (16 was the result of subtracting 12 from 28). The next time round the loop, M is incremented to 4 and the number of days in April, X(4), is added to the old value of R. The variable R therefore becomes 16 + 31 + 30.

The last circuit through the loop occurs when L = 11, and X(12)'s value, 25, is added to R.

What happens to the loop if a December date is input, so that M = 12? Because of the discrepancy in the limits, some machines skip the loop entirely, while others execute it once, so that X(13) is added to R. X(13) has been set to 0 to give the correct result.

```
470 IF R = 1 THEN GOTO 500
```

This line simply checks if there is only one day remaining to Christmas so that we get a grammatically correct sentence on the screen. If R is not 1, there must be more than one day remaining, so the PRINT statement in line 480 will be grammatically correct.

So that's all there is to it. The version of BASIC we have used should run on most computers (see the 'Basic Flavours' box) except possibly for the 'leap year' subroutine. BASIC is very inconsistent in the way it uses LET. If lines like IF M$ = "SEPTEMBER" THEN LET M = 9 do not work on your computer, the subroutine can be rewritten like this:

```
560 IF M$ = "JANUARY" THEN GOTO 900
570 IF M$ = "FEBRUARY" THEN GOTO 910
580 IF M$ = "MARCH" THEN GOTO 920
:
900 LET M = 1
905 RETURN
910 LET M 3 2
915 RETURN
920 LET M = 3
925 RETURN 925
(. . . and so on)
```

This solution is more space-consuming and less easy to follow with all its GOTOs and RETURNs. However, it does demonstrate that there are usually several ways of solving every problem.

Basic Flavours

READ DATA These commands are not available on the ZX81, so delete lines 300, 350 – 370 and 510. Add:
```
10 DIM X(13)
20 FOR K = 1 TO 13
30 PRINT "INPUT ITEM NO.";K
40 INPUT X(K)
50 NEXT K
60 STOP
```
RUN the program and enter the data. Delete lines 10–60 and SAVE the program, which also saves the contents of the array. After LOADing the program in future, use GOTO 100 rather than RUN, thus preserving variables

INPUT The ZX81 requires an INPUT command for each item, so add 285 PRINT "WHEN PROMPTED", and:
```
310 PRINT "INPUT DAY"
312 INPUT D
```
with similar lines for month and year

REM On the BBC Micro, Commodore 64 and Vic-20, REM statements at the end of a program line must be preceded by a colon(:)

BRAVING THE ELEMENTS

Here we introduce subscripted variables. Unlike their simple counterparts, these can contain any number of elements.

In our earlier program for calculating the number of days to Christmas we encountered a new type of variable called a 'subscripted' variable. These differ from ordinary or 'simple' variables in that they can have any number of compartments or elements within the box. Simple variables recognise two letters or letters followed by a digit from 0 to 9 (some versions of BASIC allow whole words to be used as variable names). A, B, B1, C3 and R2 are all simple variables. Subscripted variables look like this: A(6), B(12) or X(20). The subscript is the number in brackets. The examples we have given would be read as: 'A sub six', 'B sub twelve' and 'X sub twenty'.

If we think of a simple variable as being a box with a name or label on it, we can think of a subscripted variable as a box containing a specified number of internal elements. If we want a variable with 12 elements, we create it initially using the BASIC DIM statement, like this: DIM A(12). Any letter of the alphabet may be used.

Assigning values to simple variables is straightforward, using either LET or INPUT statements, like LET A = 35, LET B1 = 365 or INPUT C3. Values can be entered in the elements of a subscripted variable in the same way. Let's see how we would assign values to a subscripted array. ('Array' is an alternative name for a set of subscripted variables.) For example:

```
10 DIM A(5)
```

creates a subscripted variable with five elements. We can now assign a value to each element:

```
20 LET A(1) = 5
30 LET A(2) = 10
40 LET A(3) = 15
50 LET A(4) = 20
60 LET A(5) = 100
```

To find out how these variables differ from simple variables, let's assign values to a few simple variables:

```
70 LET X = 5
80 LET Y = 6
90 LET Z = 7
```

Try entering all these on your computer and then check the contents of each variable using the PRINT command. Many of the statements in BASIC also function as commands. After you have entered the statements above, check them by

LISTing them and then type RUN. Now you can type PRINT X<CR>. You should see 5 instantly displayed on the screen. Next type PRINT Y. The computer will respond to this PRINT command by displaying 6 on the screen. If you want to check the elements in the subscripted variable, type PRINT A(1) to find out the value of the first element in the array. The computer should respond by printing 5 on the screen. Try PRINTing the values of A(3) and A(5).

The important difference between subscripted variables and ordinary variables is that the subscript can itself be a variable. To see what this means, type PRINT A(X). The screen will respond with the figure 100. Why?

Look at the list you have typed in and check the value of variable X. It is 5. A(X) is equivalent to A (the value of variable X) and this is equivalent to A(5). Typing PRINT A(X) is therefore exactly equivalent to typing PRINT A(5). What value would you expect if you typed PRINT A(Y − X)? Before actually trying it, see if you can work out the answer.

Assigning Values

If there are only a few simple variables, the LET statement is the simplest way of assigning values to them. Subscripted variables may well have a large number of elements in the array, so let's see what the alternative methods of entering the values are:

```
10 DIM A(5)
20 PRINT "INPUT THE VARIABLES"
30 INPUT A(1)
40 INPUT A(2)
50 INPUT A(3)
60 INPUT A(4)
70 INPUT A(5)
```

This method is just as tiresome to type in as using LET statements, though it would certainly work. If we know exactly how many variables there are (in this case there are five) it is easier to use a FOR-NEXT loop, like this:

```
10 DIM A(5)
20 FOR X = 1 TO 5
30 INPUT A(X)
40 NEXT X
```

This program would expect five values to be typed on the computer keyboard when the program was run. The RETURN key would have to be pressed after each figure had been entered. If we know beforehand what the values in the variable are, it is easier to enter them using a READ statement together with a DATA statement, like this:

```
10 DIM A(5)
20 FOR X = 1 TO 5
30 READ A(X)
40 NEXT X
50 DATA 5, 10, 15, 20, 100
```

Try this short program, and then test the contents of the array using the PRINT command (that is, use PRINT after the program has been RUN. For example, PRINT A(1)‹CR› and PRINT A(5). Now we can add a few lines to the program to print the elements in the array for us automatically:

```
60 FOR L = 1 TO 5
70 PRINT A(L)
80 NEXT L
90 END
```

RUN this program and check that the correct values are printed on the screen. Then retype line 50 using five different DATA items. Remember that the numbers in a DATA statement must be separated from each other using commas, but there must be no comma before the first number or after the last one.

The simplest way to assign values is to use READ and DATA statements. If the values will be different every time the program is run, using the INPUT statement inside a FOR-NEXT loop is probably the best way. If the total number of elements in the array is fixed, the number can be used as the upper limit in the FOR statement.

Let's use all we have learnt so far to build a short but powerful program. Suppose we wanted to sort some numbers into ascending order. Before setting out to write the program, the first thing to do is to figure out how to solve the problem in a logical way. When the way to solve the problem seems clear, write down the steps one after the other using clear, short English sentences.

Suppose we start with five numbers: 4, 9, 2, 8, 3. Sorting these into ascending order is a trivial problem. We just scan along the line and notice which is the smallest, and put it on the left, and then repeat the process for the remaining digits.

The computer, however, needs a very precise set of instructions, so we shall have to think very clearly about what steps are required. Here's one approach: Compare the first digit with the second digit. If the first digit is bigger than the second one, swap them. If the first digit is smaller than the second one, leave their positions unchanged.

Compare the second digit with the third digit. If the second digit is smaller than the third one, leave their position unchanged.

Repeat the process of comparing pairs of digits until the last pair of digits has been compared.

If there were no swaps, all the numbers must be in order. If there were any swaps, go back to the beginning and repeat the process.

If you think about this process, you will see that it will indeed sort any group of numbers into ascending numeric order. Look at what would happen to our original set of numbers as each pair of digits is compared:

```
4 9 2 8 3
4 2 9 8 3
4 2 8 9 3
4 2 8 3 9
```

All the pairs have now been compared and swapped where necessary. Since at least one swap took place, go back to the beginning and repeat the process:

```
4 2 8 3 9
2 4 8 3 9
2 4 3 8 9
2 4 3 8 9
```

There were still swaps, so go back to the beginning and repeat:

```
2 4 3 8 9
2 3 4 8 9
2 3 4 8 9
```

There were no swaps, last time through, so every number must be smaller than the number to its right. The numbers must be in ascending order and the operation can be terminated.

Using subscripted variables allows a sort routine like this to be implemented easily in BASIC, because the subscript itself can be a variable. If our original five numbers were the values in an array; so that A(1) = 4, A(2) = 9, A(3) = 2, A(4) = 8 and

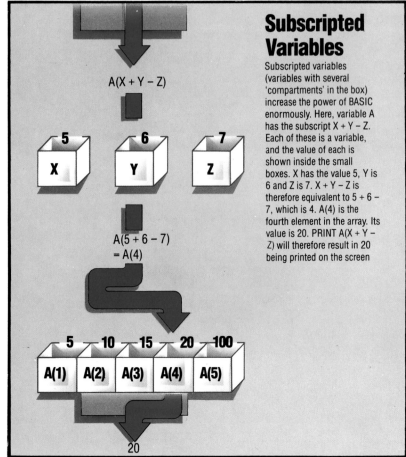

Subscripted Variables

Subscripted variables (variables with several 'compartments' in the box) increase the power of BASIC enormously. Here, variable A has the subscript X + Y − Z. Each of these is a variable, and the value of each is shown inside the small boxes. X has the value 5, Y is 6 and Z is 7. X + Y − Z is therefore equivalent to 5 + 6 − 7, which is 4. A(4) is the fourth element in the array. Its value is 20. PRINT A(X + Y − Z) will therefore result in 20 being printed on the screen

A(5) = 3, then if X has the value 1, A(X) will be the contents of A(1), which is 4. A(X + 1) will be the contents of A(2), which is 9, and so on.

Look at the program and see if you can see exactly what is going on. Line 20 sets variable N to the number of numbers we want to sort. Let's assume we want to sort five numbers: when the program is run we will type in 5 and then hit RETURN.

Line 30 is the DIMension statement. If N is 5, it sets the size of the array to 5. This line is equivalent to DIM A(5).

Lines 40 to 60 are a FOR-NEXT loop that allows us to type in the five numbers. Most versions of BASIC prompt the user with a question mark on the screen. RETURN will have to be pressed after each number has been entered. The numbers may be more than one digit, and may include decimal fractions.

Line 90 sets the variable S to 0. This variable is being used as a 'flag'. Later in the program, A is tested to see if it is 1 or not. It is only ever set to 1 if two numbers have been swapped, as we shall see in line 240. We shall investigate the use of 'flags' in more detail later in the course.

Line 100 sets up the limits for a loop; in this case from 1 to 4 (because N is 5 so N — 1 is 4). The first time through the loop, L is 1 so A(L) in line 110 will be A(1) or the first element in the array and A(L + 1) will be A(2), the second element in the array. The next time round the loop, L will be incremented to 2, so A(L) will be equivalent to A(2) and A(L + 1) will be equivalent to A(3). Line 110 tests to see if A(L) is greater than the number immediately to its right in the array. The sign for 'greater than' is ›.

If the first number is bigger than the next one, the program branches to a subroutine that swaps the numbers. If the first number is not bigger than the next one, there is no branch to the subroutine and BASIC simply continues to the next line, which is the NEXT L statement. After the loop has been repeated four times, it stops the program and goes to line 130 which tests the 'swap' flag, S, to see if it has been set or not. If it has been set (in the 'swap' subroutine), the program branches back to line 90 to repeat the comparison process. If S is not 1 it means no swap took place, so all the numbers are

in order. The rest of the program simply prints them out.

The swap subroutine needs a temporary variable to store one of the numbers to be swapped. After the two numbers have been swapped in lines 210, 220 and 230, the 'swap' flag S is set to 1 and then the program RETURNs to the main program.

```
10 PRINT "HOW MANY NUMBERS DO YOU WANT
   TO SORT?"
20 INPUT N
30 DIM A(N)
40 FOR X = 1 TO N
45 PRINT "NEXT NUMBER"
50 INPUT A(X)
60 NEXT X
70 REM
80 REM SORT ROUTINE
90 LET S = 0
100 FOR L = 1 TO N — 1
110 IF A(L) › A(L + 1) THEN GOSUB 200
120 NEXT L
130 IF S = 1 THEN 90
140 FOR X = 1 TO N
150 PRINT "A(";X;") = ";A(X)
160 NEXT X
170 END
180 REM
190 REM
200 REM SWAP SUBROUTINE
210 LET T = A(L)
220 LET A(L) = A(L + 1)
230 LET A(L + 1) = T
240 LET S =1
250 RETURN
```

Exercises

■ Extend the program to find the average value of the numbers input. The average is equal to the sum of items divided by the total number of items. The simplest way to do this is to insert a GOSUB just before the END statement in line 170. The subroutine should read each of the elements in the array and add the values to a 'sum' variable. After all the elements have been added, the sum should be divided by the number of elements. The sum is most easily derived by using the number of elements as the upper limit of a FOR-NEXT loop.

■ Change one line in the program so that the numbers will be sorted in descending order.

■ This exercise is directed mainly at owners of the TI99/04A which does not like having variables used as subscripts in subscripted variables. TI BASIC does, however, accept statements such as DIM A(12). Rewrite the program so that the INPUT statement expects an exact number of numbers to be input, 12, say. This will avoid the problem of using a variable name as a subscript. Lines 100 and 110 will also have to be changed. The swap subroutine will not work in TI BASIC for the same reason. This will have to be changed too.

■ A tough one. Our way of sorting numbers is by no means the only way to do it. See if you can think up an alternative method.

Basic Flavours

If this program is to be run on the ZX81 or Spectrum, line 130 must be amended to read: 130 IF S=1 THEN GOTO 90

This statement is not available on the ZX81 and Spectrum, so use STOP instead

In assignment statements, such as 90 LET S= 0, the word LET is optional on most machines but not on the ZX81 and Spectrum.

ORGANISE YOUR PROGRAM

We sort a program using built-in functions to rearrange information, to illustrate how relatively complex programs can be broken down into simple sub-programs or subroutines that can be written and tested separately.

Apart from the advantage of being separately testable, the use of subroutines allows the development of the program to follow a logical progression. There are many approaches to writing a program in BASIC. One of the commonest is 'trial and error': you sit down at the computer and start entering lines of BASIC without having thought out carefully what is required to make the program work. This method leads to badly structured programs that will often not work the first time. If the structure of the program is not clear, it is not easy to find the mistakes or 'bugs'.

A much better approach is to sit down with a notebook and work out the structure of the program first, in steps of ever-increasing refinement, until a correct and working program can be written. To illustrate this approach we'll take the following problem.

Let's write a program that will input a number of names, the forename followed by surname. Now reverse the order of each name so that the surname comes first, followed by a comma and a space, and by the forename. It will then sort the names into alphabetical order and print them out.

For example, if the names BILL JONES and FRED ASHTON were entered (in that order), the program would print out:

ASHTON, FRED
JONES, BILL

Before even attempting to write a program to do this, first write down the desired input and output in the most general terms:

Step 1
Input names in random order, first name first
Output names in alphabetical order, surnames first

This simply clarifies what we want to be done. This is an essential first step to a properly organised program. The next step is to refine the stages in the first step and make sure that the program still works. Do not, at this stage, get into too much detail. Simply write down in a little more detail, the stages involved:

Step 2

Find out number of names to be input
Enter names
Reverse names
Sort names
Print names

Look at the above list and check that it will work. Can you see anything wrong with it? Are there any flaws in the logic? If not, you are ready to go on to the next stage of refinement.

The stages we arrived at in Step 2 are small enough and simple enough to be written separately as small sub-programs. Sub-programs are called subroutines in BASIC. Let's give the subroutines names to make them easier to identify. Subroutine 1, to find out the number of names to be input, can be called FINDNUM. Subroutine 2, to enter the names, can be called ENTER. Subroutine 3, to reverse the names, can be called REVERSE. Subroutine 4, to sort the names, can be called SORT. Finally, Subroutine 5, to print the names can be called PRINTNAMES.

Step 3.1 FINDNUM
Prompt the user to input required number
Get the required number N
Use N to set up string array
Step 3. 2 ENTER
If number of names is less than N,
prompt user to input another name
Add name to string array
Step 3.3 REVERSE
Find length of string (name)
Find 'space' in string
Put characters in string up to 'space'
into temporary string variable
Put characters in string from 'space' to
end into another temporary variable
Add comma space to end of variable
Assign second followed by first
temporary variables to original string
Step 3. 4 SORT
Compare first item in array with next item
If first item is bigger than next one
(i.e. higher in the alphabet), swap
Compare second item with third
Swap, if necessary
Repeat until all pairs are compared
Go back to beginning of array and
repeat comparison of pairs until no swaps
have taken place

This sort routine is of course exactly the same as the one used earlier in this chapter. The 'swap' part will be dealt with as a subroutine called from within the SORT subroutine.

Step 3.5 PRINTNAMES

Print each item in the array until all items have been printed

Each of the steps needed to build this program has now been worked out in a reasonable amount of detail. The SORT routine has only been sketched roughly since it was dealt with fully in the last instalment of the course. And SWAP, which is 'called' from within this subroutine, has been left out completely. Let's now see how easy it is to convert programs worked out in English into a program in BASIC.

Step 4
1. FINDNUM

The three lines in Step 3.1 translate directly into BASIC statements. The user is prompted by a PRINT statement, the number is found by using an INPUT statement and the array is dimensioned by using the DIM statement:

```
PRINT "HOW MANY NAMES DO YOU WISH TO
    ENTER?"
INPUT N
DIM A$ (N)
RETURN
```

The variable N now contains the maximum number of names to be entered. The DIM statement dimensions a string array. String variables contain strings of alphanumeric characters instead of numbers. A string variable name always ends with a 'dollar' sign. A$ alone could only contain one string. DIM A$ (N) creates an array that can contain 'N' strings. Subscripted variables have been dealt with earlier in the course.

The RETURN statement transfers control back to the main program at the line following the subroutine call. Values assigned to variables in the subroutine will be 'carried back' to the main program and can be used elsewhere in the program, even in other subroutines.

2. ENTER

As long as the number of names entered is less than N, the user needs to be prompted to enter a name and this name must be added to the string array. This calls for creating a FOR-NEXT loop; we know that the first name in the array will be its first element, and that the last one will be the Nth, so:

```
FOR X = 1 TO N
PRINT "ENTER NAME"
INPUT A$(X)
NEXT X
RETURN
```

That should suffice to enter all the names into the array. But sharp readers will have spotted what happens when we come to reverse the order of the first and last names in the REVERSE subroutine. Each element (name) in the array will have to be pulled out again, then reversed, and then put back in the array. Rather than complicate and lengthen

the program by doing that, it would be simpler to call the REVERSE subroutine from within the ENTER subroutine after each name has been typed in. The name can then be reversed before it is assigned to the array. To do that, we just have to add one line, thus:

```
FOR X = 1 TO N ·
PRINT "ENTER NAME"
INPUT A$(X)
GOSUB [REVERSE]
NEXT X
RETURN
```

All the names in the array will now be in reversed order (surname first, followed by forename) and will therefore be ready for sorting.

3. REVERSE

To reverse the order of names, we need to know where the 'space' is separating the first name from the surname. When we know where the space is, we can use various functions to pull out parts of the string and assign those parts to other strings. Functions in BASIC are commands that perform a predefined operation on the value following the function name. This part is always in brackets. Many functions are 'built in' but it is also possible to define your own. A typical 'built in' function is SQR ( ). This function 'returns' the square root of the value inside the brackets. So: LET A = SQR (9): PRINT A will print a 3.

REVERSE uses the functions LEN (to find the length of the string), INSTR (to locate the position of the space), LEFT$ (to remove a specified number of characters from the left of the string) and

Programs Within A Program

The main program this time is very short. All the real work is done in the sub-programs (called subroutines in BASIC). Each of the steps needed to make the program work are separated and written as short 'mini-programs'. These are then simply linked together by the main program.

When the program is run, each time a GOSUB statement is encountered, the program branches to the specified subroutine line number and that section of the program is then executed. The end of the subroutine is indicated by the RETURN statement. On reaching this, the program returns to the point immediately after the GOSUB that called the subroutine.

Subroutines can be 'nested' within subroutines. The ENTER subroutine calls another subroutine called REVERSE, and SORT sometimes calls another subroutine called SWAP.

Breaking down a problem into separate subroutines linked by a simple main program makes the development and testing of programs far easier

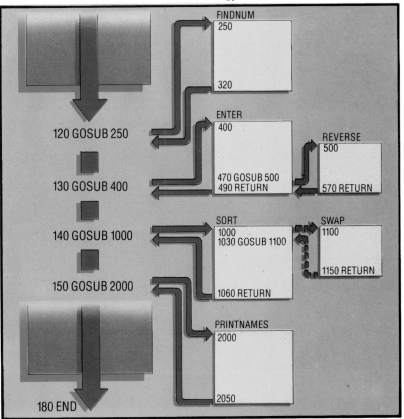

RIGHT$ (to remove a specified number of characters from the right of the string). We will not discuss in detail exactly how these functions work at the moment. We will take a more comprehensive look at functions in BASIC in the next part of the course.

4. SORT

SORT, and the SWAP subroutine called from within it, follow closely the routines used last time.

5. PRINT NAMES

This is very straightforward:

```
FOR Q = 1 TO N
PRINT A$(Q)
NEXT Q
RETURN
```

Now all that remains is to write the main program. It's as simple as this:

```
REM MAIN PROGRAM
GOSUB [FINDNUM]
GOSUB [ENTER]
GOSUB [SORT]
GOSUB [PRINT]
END
```

We have put the 'names' of the subroutines in square brackets. A few BASICS are able to call subroutines by name, but most have to use line numbers. When the program is actually written out, the appropriate line numbers are inserted in place of the subroutine names. Appropriate REMs and PRINT messages are also added.

Exercises

Now that we have covered almost all of the most important features of BASIC, it is time to check your progress by working through these exercises. They range in difficulty from the very easy to the moderately difficult.

■ **Variables** Put a circle around the expressions below that are valid numeric variables, and draw a cross through the expressions that are not valid variable names at all. Leave the valid string variable names unmarked.

A B6 2Z D$ 15 X$ A12 D9 Q81 Q5 6F H$

■ **Arithmetic 1** Write a short program to assign the value 6 to variable B and then PRINT the value of B.

■ **Arithmetic 2** Write a short program to assign the value 5 to variable A, 7 to variable B and 9 to variable C. Add the values of these three variables and assign the sum to variable D. PRINT the value of variable D.

■ **Arithmetic 3** Look at these lines of BASIC and then work out what the value of C will be.

```
LET C = 5 + 4 * 3
PRINT C
```

```
10 REM   THIS PROGRAM SORTS NAMES
20 REM    INTO ALPHABETICAL ORDER
30 PRINT "FIRST DECIDE HOW MANY"
40 PRINT "NAMES YOU WANT TO ENTER"
50 PRINT "THEN ENTER THE NAMES IN"
60 PRINT "FIRSTNAME(SPACE)LASTNAME"
70 PRINT "ORDER."
80 REM
90 REM   THIS IS THE MAIN PROGRAM
100 PRINT
110 PRINT
120 GOSUB 250
130 GOSUB 400
140 GOSUB 1000
150 GOSUB 2000
160 REM
170 REM   END OF MAIN PROGRAM
180 END
250 REM   SUBROUTINE TO FIND NO. OF
260 REM   NAMES TO BE ENTERED
270 PRINT "HOW MANY NAMES DO YOU"
280 PRINT "WISH TO ENTER?"
290 PRINT
300 INPUT N
310 DIM A$(N)
320 RETURN
400 REM   SUBROUTINE TO ENTER NAMES
410 PRINT "ENTER NAME IN THIS FORM:"
420 PRINT "FIRSTNAME(SPACE)LASTNAME(CR)"
430 PRINT "E.G. JILL THOMPSON"
440 FOR X = 1 TO N
450 PRINT "ENTER NAME"
460 INPUT A$(X)
470 GOSUB 500
480 NEXT X
490 RETURN
500 REM   SUBROUTINE TO REVERSE ORDER OF NAMES
510 LET L = LEN(A$(X))
520 LET S = INSTR(A$(X)," ")
530 LET C$ = LEFT$(A$(X),S - 1)
540 LET F$ = RIGHT$(A$(X),L - S)
550 LET F$ = F$ + ", "
560 LET A$(X) = F$ + C$
570 RETURN
1000 REM   SORT ROUTINE
1010 LET S = 0
1020 FOR P = 1 TO N - 1
1030 IF A$(P) > A$(P + 1) THEN GOSUB 1100
1040 NEXT P
1050 IF S = 1 THEN GOTO 1000
1060 RETURN
1100 REM   SWAP SUBROUTINE
1110 LET T$ = A$(P)
1120 LET A$(P) = A$(P + 1)
1130 LET A$(P + 1) = T$
1140 LET S = 1
1150 RETURN
2000 REM   PRINT SUBROUTINE
2010 PRINT
2020 FOR Q = 1 TO N
2030 PRINT A$(Q)
2040 NEXT Q
2050 RETURN
```

■ **Arithmetic 4** What result will be printed in this program?

```
LET A = 3
LET B = 2
LET C = 9
LET D = 4
LET E = (A + B) * (C - D)
PRINT E

LET E = 5
LET E = E * E
PRINT E
```

■ **Comparisons 1** What value of X will be required for the PRINT message to be printed?

```
70 LET A = 5
80 LET B = X
90 LET R = B - A
100 IF R = 0 THEN GOTO 120
110 GOTO 10
120 PRINT "CONGRATULATIONS! YOU HAVE WON"
999 END
```

■ **Comparisons 2** What is the smallest value of X that will make the program jump to line 300?

```
250 IF X > 6 * 100 THEN GOTO 300
```

■ **Comparisons 3** What is the smallest value of Z that will make the program jump to the 'congratulations' message?

```
340 IF Z < 10000 THEN GOTO 500
350 IF Z >= 10000 THEN GOTO 520
:
:
500 PRINT "YOUR SCORE IS TOO LOW. TRY AGAIN"
510 GOTO 600
520 PRINT "CONGRATULATIONS. YOU ARE NOW A
MASTER"
530 GOTO 700
```

■ **Print 1** Assume that the value of T is 50. Write a PRINT statement that will print THE VALUE OF T IS 50. Hint: Put the 'message' in double quotes, use a semi-colon and the variable name.

■ **Print 2** Look at the following short program and complete the PRINT statement so that the program will print a score message like this:

SORRY, BUT YOUR SCORE OF 175 IS TOO LOW

Complete the line so that the actual value of the score can vary each time.

```
620 REM VARIABLE S IS THE SCORE SO FAR
620 IF S <= 500 THEN GOTO 640
630 GOTO 700
640 PRINT "SORRY"
```

■ **Print 3** What message will be printed when the program is run?

```
200 LET A$= "THE HOME COMPUTER COURSE ?"
210 LET B$ = "HOW DO YOU LIKE ";
220 PRINT B$
230 PRINT A$
```

■ **Input 1** INPUT is one way of assigning a value to a variable. If the following program is run, which key will need to be pressed for the program to print out an answer of 12?

```
60 INPUT N
70 LET N = N * 2
80 PRINT N
```

■ **Input 2** What will be printed here?

```
100 PRINT "PLEASE TYPE YOUR NAME"
110 INPUT N$
120 PRINT "HI ";N$;"I'M YOUR COMPUTER"
```

Basic Flavours

This program will not run on the Atari 400 and 800 because their string handling is so different from that of other machines

On the ZX81 and Spectrum replace line 310 by:
310 DIM A$ (N,30)
This creates a string array called A$ that has N elements, each of them 30 characters long.

In line 1050 the command GOTO 1000 comes immediately after the word THEN. In this case, most computers allow you to omit the word GOTO; so line 1050 might be written
1050 IF S=1 THEN 1000

INSTR

This command is not available on the ZX81, Spectrum, Commodore 64, Vic-20 and Oric-1. On the Commodore machines and the Oric-1 delete line 520 and replace it by:
```
515 LET S= 0
520 FOR P=1 TO L
523 IF MID$(A$(X),P,1)=" " THEN LET S=P
524 IF S=P THEN LET P=L
525 NEXT L
```
On the Spectrum and ZX81 delete lines 510 to 560, and replace them by:
```
510 LET D$=A$(X)
520 LET L=LEN D$
530 LET S =0
540 FOR P=1 TO 1
550 IF D$(P)=" " THEN LET S=P
560 IF S=P THEN LET P=L
570 NEXT P
580 LET C$=D$( TO S-1)
590 LET F$=D$(L-S)
600 LET A$(X)=F$+", "+C$
610 RETURN
```

None of these commands is available on the Spectrum or ZX81. Their equivalents in Sinclair BASIC are:
LEFT$(Z$,N)   replace by Z$(TO N)
RIGHT$(Z$,N)   replace by
               Z$(LEN(Z$)-N+1 TO)
MID$(Z$,P,N)   replace by
               Z$(P TO P+N-1)

FULLY FUNCTIONAL

There are built-in-functions in BASIC, which means that a lot of the programming has already been done for you. Knowing how to use them adds power to your computing.

Suppose you wanted to calculate the square root of a number in one of your programs. There are a number of ways this could be done. The crudest and least satisfactory way would be to create a table of square root values and to use this to give you the value wanted for a particular number. You probably learnt how to do this in school. An alternative method is to use the square root 'function', built in to most versions of BASIC. Here, the arithmetic of the operation is taken care of by BASIC without the programmer having to worry about it. Let's see how it works:

```
10 REM THIS PROGRAM FINDS THE SQUARE ROOT
20 REM OF A NUMBER
30 PRINT "INPUT THE NUMBER YOU WANT TO"
40 PRINT "FIND THE SQUARE ROOT OF"
50 INPUT N
60 LET A = SQR(N)
70 PRINT "THE SQUARE ROOT OF ";N;" IS ";A
80 END
```

Type in this short program and see that it does indeed give you the square root of any number you type in. Let's look at the rules of how to use this 'square root' function.

A 'function' in BASIC is generally a command word (SQR in this case) followed by brackets that enclose the expression to be operated on. In this program, N is the number input from the keyboard. It is the number we want the square root of. Line 60 says 'let the square root of N be assigned to the variable A'. Line 70 prints out the value of A.

The expression inside the brackets is called the 'argument' of the function and does not always have to be a variable: it is equally possible to use actual numbers. Type this in and see what happens when you run it:

```
10 PRINT SQR(25)
20 END
```

You will see that this works just as well. Similarly, we can use more complex arguments inside the brackets. Try this one:

```
10 LET A = 10
20 LET B = 90
30 LET C = SQR(A+B)
40 PRINT C
50 END
```

This little program can be shortened by combining lines 30 and 40 like this:

```
10 LET A = 10
20 LET B = 90

30 PRINT SQR(A+B)
40 END
```

The way to think of functions is as short programs built in to BASIC that are available for the programmer to use at any time. Most versions of BASIC have quite a large number of functions as well as the facility of allowing the programmer to define new ones for use within a program. Later, we will see how this is done. Here we will look at a few more of the commonly available functions. They come in two varieties: numeric functions, in which the argument (the part inside the brackets) is a number, numeric variable or numeric expression, and string functions, in which the argument is a character string or expression made up from character strings. First we'll look at a few of the numeric functions.

Previously, on page 14, we used a program that calculated the number of tiles needed to tile a room. A small 'bug' in this program was that the answer could well involve fractions of a tile. 988.24 could represent a possible result of running this program. At times like this we want a way of rounding the answer to the nearest whole number. Whole numbers are referred to mathematically as 'integers' and one of the functions in BASIC will 'return' the integer part of any number. Here's how it works:

```
10 PRINT "INPUT A NUMBER CONTAINING A
   DECIMAL FRACTION"
20 INPUT N
30 PRINT "THE INTEGER PART OF THE NUMBER
   IS ";
40 PRINT INT(N)
50 END
```

If this program is run and the number you input is 3.14, the program will print on the screen:

```
THE INTEGER PART OF THE NUMBER IS 3
```

Of course, if we are dealing with tiles, we would then need to add 1 to the answer, to make sure that we bought more than the required amount, not less.

On other occasions, we may want to find the 'sign' of a number to see if it is negative, zero or positive. To do this, most BASICs incorporate a SGN function. Try this:

```
10 PRINT "INPUT A NUMBER"
20 INPUT N
30 LET S = SGN(N)
40 IF S = −1 THEN GOTO 100
```

```
50 IF S = 0 THEN GOTO 120
60 IF S = 1 THEN GOTO 140
100 PRINT "THE NUMBER WAS NEGATIVE"
110 GOTO 999
120 PRINT "THE NUMBER WAS ZERO"
130 GOTO 999
140 PRINT "THE NUMBER WAS POSITIVE"
150 GOTO 999
999 END
```

If you look at the values 'returned' by the SGN function to S in line 30 (these are tested in lines 40, 50 and 60) you will see that there are three possible values. −1 is returned if the argument in the brackets was a negative number, 0 if the argument was zero and 1 if the argument was a positive number. Using the SGN function in line 30 saves several lines of programming. We could have written:

```
IF N < 0 THEN LET S = -1
IF N = 0 THEN LET S = 0
IF N > 0 THEN LET S = 1
```

The action performed by a BASIC function can always be achieved through normal programming; using a function just saves time, space and programming effort.

Here are a few more numeric functions. ABS returns the 'absolute' value of a number. The absolute value of a number is the same as its real value with the sign removed. Thus, the absolute value of −6 is 6. Try this:

```
10 LET X = -9
20 LET Y = ABS(X)
30 PRINT Y
40 END
```

MAX finds the maximum value of two numbers. Thus:

```
10 LET X = 9
20 LET Y = 7
30 LET Z = X MAX Y
40 PRINT Z
50 END
```

MIN is similar to MAX but finds the smaller of two numbers. Try this:

```
10 PRINT "INPUT A NUMBER"
20 INPUT X
30 PRINT "INPUT ANOTHER NUMBER"
40 INPUT Y
50 LET Z = X MIN Y
60 PRINT Z
70 END
```

Notice that these latter two functions have two arguments instead of one, and they don't need to be enclosed in brackets. Most BASICs also have a number of other numeric functions, including LOG to find the logarithm of a number, TAN to find the tangent, COS to find the cosine and SIN to find the sine. We will look at some of the ways these 'trigonometrical' functions can be used later.

BASIC also has several built-in functions that operate on character strings. We used some of these in our name-sorting program (page 23) but at the time did not look closely at how they worked. Now we will look at these and a few other string functions in more detail.

One of the most useful string functions is LEN. This counts the number of characters in a string enclosed in double quotation marks or the number of characters assigned to a string variable. Try this:

```
10 LET A$ = "COMPUTER"
20 LET N = LEN(A$)
30 PRINT "THE NUMBER OF CHARACTERS IN THE
   STRING IS ";N
40 END
```

Why would we ever need to know how many characters there are in a string variable? To see why, enter and run this short program designed to build a 'name triangle'. It prints first the first letter of a word, then the first and second letter and so on until the whole word is printed.

```
5 REM PRINTS A 'NAME TRIANGLE'
10 LET A$ = "JONES"
20 FOR L = 1 TO 5
30 LET B$ = LEFT$(A$,L)
40 PRINT B$
50 NEXT L
60 END
```

Now run this program. Can you figure out what the printout will be? It should look like this:

```
J
JO
JON
JONE
JONES
```

This short program uses the LEFT$ function to extract characters from a string. LEFT$ takes two arguments. The first specifies the string and the second (which comes after a comma) specifies the number of characters to be extracted from the string, starting from the left of the string. A$ has been assigned the string "JONES" so LEFT$(A$,1) would 'return' the letter J. LEFT$(A$,2) would return the letters JO. The short program above uses an index, L, that ranges from 1 to 5, so that the second argument in the LEFT$ function goes up from 1 to 5 each time through the loop. We knew exactly how many characters there were in the word we wanted to print (JONES), so it was easy to decide that 5 should be the upper limit in the FOR-NEXT loop. But what would we do if we did not know beforehand how many characters there would be in the loop?

This is where the LEN function comes in. LEN takes a string (in double quotes) or a string variable as its argument. Here are a few examples to show how it works:

```
10 REM PROGRAM TO TEST THE 'LEN' FUNCTION
20 PRINT LEN("COMPUTER")
30 END
```

The program should print 8 when it is run. It has counted the number of characters in the word COMPUTER and returned this value. Let's do the same thing in a slightly different way:

```
10 REM FINDING THE LENGTH OF A STRING
20 LET A$ = "COMPUTER COURSE"
30 LET L = LEN(A$)
40 PRINT L
50 END
```

If this program is run, the computer should print 15 on the screen. There are 15 characters in this string, not 14. Don't forget that the space between the two words is a character as far as the computer is concerned. Now let's apply the LEN function in a modification of our earlier program to print out a 'triangular name':

```
10 REM THIS PROGRAM PRINTS A 'NAME
      TRIANGLE'
20 PRINT "TYPE IN A NAME"
30 INPUT A$
40 LET N = LEN(A$)
50 FOR L = 1 TO N
60 LET B$ = LEFT$(A$,L)
70 PRINT B$
80 NEXT L
90 END
```

Each time this loop is executed, the value of L increments from 1 up to N (which is the length of the name in the string). If you input the name SIMPSON, line 40 will be equivalent to LET N = LEN ("SIMPSON"), so N will be set to 7. The first time through the loop, line 50 will set L to 1 and line 60 will be equivalent to LET B$=LEFT$ ("SIMPSON",1) so B$ will be assigned one character from the string, starting from the left. This character is S.

The second time through the loop, L will be set to 2 so line 60 will be equivalent to LET B$ = LEFT$ ("SIMPSON",2). This will take the first two characters from the string and assign them to string variable B$. B$ will therefore contain SI.

The LEN function found that there were 7 characters in the string SIMPSON and assigned this value to variable N, so the last time through the loop B$ will be assigned all seven characters from the string and the whole string will be printed.

Note that LEFT$ has a companion function, RIGHT$, which takes characters from the right of the string variable in exactly the same way.

Finally, we will look at one more string function, also used in the name-sorting program. This is INSTR; it is used to find the location of the first occurrence of a specified string (called a 'sub-string') within a string. In the name-sorting program, INSTR was used to locate the position of the space between the first name and surname. Here's how it works:

```
10 LET A$ = "WATERFALL"
20 LET P = INSTR(A$,"FALL")
30 PRINT P
40 END
```

Before entering and running the program, see if you can anticipate what value will be printed for P. Remember, INSTR locates the starting position of the first occurrence of the 'sub-string' within the string. If the string is WATERFALL, the starting position of the sub-string FALL will be 6 — the F in FALL is the sixth letter in WATERFALL. Some BASICS do not use INSTR, but have a similar function called INDEX instead. Here's how to use INSTR (or INDEX) to locate a space within a string:

```
10 REM FINDING THE POSITION OF A SPACE IN A
      STRING
20 LET A$ = "HOME COMPUTER"
30 LET P = INSTR(A$," ")
40 PRINT P
50 END
```

Notice that the second argument in the INSTR function (line 30) is " ". The quotes enclose a space — the character to be searched for. The program will print 5 as the value of P since the space is in the fifth position in the string. Work out what would be printed if line 30 were changed to:

```
LET P = INSTR(A$,"C")
```

Lastly, a handy function used with the PRINT statement. See what happens when you run this program:

```
10 PRINT "THIS LINE IS NOT INDENTED"
20 PRINT TAB(5); "THIS LINE IS INDENTED"
30 END
```

Can you see what happened? The second line was printed starting five places in from the left margin. TAB is analogous to the tabulator on a typewriter. Here is another short program using the TAB function:

```
10 REM  USING THE TAB FUNCTION
20 PRINT "ENTER THE TAB VALUE"
30 INPUT  T
40 LET W$ = "TABULATION"
50 PRINT TAB(T);W$
60 END
```

Now you can go back to the name-sorting program on page 136 and see how some of those functions were used there.

Exercises

■ **Loops 1** What will be printed when this program is run?

```
10 LET A = 500
20 FOR L = 1 TO 50
30 LET A = A −1
40 NEXT L
50 PRINT "THE VALUE OF A IS ";A
```

■ **Loops 2** What will you see on the screen if this program is run?

```
10 REM
20 REM THIS IS A TIMING LOOP
30 REM SEE HOW LONG IT TAKES
40 REM
```

Basic Flavours

On the Spectrum and ZX81 functions such as TAB, LEN, CHR$ can be used without brackets, so that TAB(30), for example, can be written TAB 30

None of these commands is available on the Spectrum or ZX81; their equivalents in Sinclair BASIC are:
LEFT$(Z$,N)   replace by Z$(TO N)
RIGHT$(Z$,N)   replace by Z$(LEN(Z$)−N+1 TO)

MID$(Z$,P,N)   replace by Z$(P TO P+N−1)
When N=1 in a MID$() command then the Sinclair equivalent is very much simpler than the above:
MID$(Z $,P,1)   replace by Z$(P)

This is not available on the Spectrum, ZX81, Commodore 64, Vic 20, and Oric-1, but you can write a sub-routine to replace it. Suppose that a program line is:
20 LET P=INSTR(A$,"FALL")
Replace it by:
20 LET X$=A$: LET Z$="FALL":GOSUB 9930:LET P=U
9929 STOP
9930 LET U=0:LET X=LEN(X$): LET Z=LEN(Z$)
9940 FOR W=1 TO X−Z+1
9950 IF MID$(X$,W,Z)=Z$ THEN LET U=W
9960 IF U=W THEN LET W=X−Z+1
9970 NEXT W
9980 RETURN
On the Spectrum and ZX81 replace line 9950 by:
9950 IF X$(W TO W+Z−1)=Z$ THEN LET U=W

```
50 PRINT "START"
60 FOR X = 1 TO 5000
70 NEXT X
80 PRINT "STOP"
90 END
```

■ **Loops 3** What result will be printed if the following program is run and you type in the number 60 when asked?

```
10 PRINT "THINK OF A NUMBER AND TYPE IT IN"
20 INPUT N
30 LET A = 100
40 FOR L = 1 TO N
50 LET A = A + 1
60 NEXT L
70 PRINT "THE VALUE OF A IS NOW ";A
80 END
```

■ **Loops 4** What will happen if this program is run?

```
10 PRINT "I LIKE BASIC"
20 GOTO 10
30 END
```

■ **Loops 5** What will you see on the screen if this program is run?

```
10 FOR Q = 1 TO 15
20 PRINT "I'M FEELING LOOPY"
30 NEXT Q
40 END
```

■ **Read-Data 1** What result will be printed?

```
10 READ X
20 READ Y
30 READ Z
40 PRINT "WE'RE TESTING THE 'READ' STATEMENT"
50 DATA 50,100,20
60 PRINT X + Y +Z
```

■ **Read-Data 2** What will be printed on the screen if this program is run?

```
100 FOR L = 1 TO 10
110 READ X
120 PRINT "X = ";X
130 NEXT L
140 DATA 1,2,3,5,7,11,13,17,19,23
```

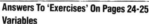

Answers To 'Exercises' On Pages 24-25
Variables
(A) (B6) X (D$) X X$ (A12) (D9) (Q81) (Q5) X H$

Arithmetic 1
10 LET B = 6
20 PRINT B
Arithmetic 2
10 LET A = 5
20 LET B = 7
30 LET C = 9
40 LET D = A + B + C
50 PRINT D
Arithmetic 3
17
Arithmetic 4
25
25
Comparisons 1
5
Comparisons 2
601 (integers are assumed)
Comparisons 3
10000
Print 1
PRINT "THE VALUE OF T IS ";T
Print 2
640 PRINT "SORRY, BUT YOUR SCORE OF ";S;" IS TOO LOW"
Print 3
This was a deliberate mistake.
The semi-colon at the end of the line will cause a syntax error at run time. The program should read:
200 LET A$= "THE COMPUTER TUTOR?"
210 LET B$= "HOW DO YOU LIKE"
220 PRINT B$;A$

and the result would then have been:
HOW DO YOU LIKE THE COMPUTER TUTOR?
Input 1
6
Input 2
PLEASE TYPE YOUR NAME
HI (YOUR NAME) I'M YOUR COMPUTER

Note that the answers to 'Variables' will differ for some machines, which do not allow more than one alphabetic character (i.e., no numeric suffix)

LEAVING IT TO CHANCE

Continuing our look at BASIC functions, we come to RND, which produces random — or nearly random — numbers for use in games or statistical programs.

Now that we have seen how several of BASIC's functions work we shall look at one of the most commonly used — the RND function. RND is used to generate random numbers. It is also used in games whenever there is an element of chance.

Unfortunately, RND is one of the most variable 'words' in BASIC. Our description of it may differ from the way it is implemented in your home micro. Let's, therefore, clarify the differences between BASIC used in the Basic Programming course and your BASIC.

Most of our programs are based on Microsoft BASIC (or MBASIC). Microsoft is an American company and their BASIC was one of the first made widely available. BASIC is a language with no official standard, but Microsoft's version is as near to a standard as there is. Many other versions are modelled on Microsoft's, and the company has been commissioned to produce versions for several popular computers.

The chief difference between MBASIC and most of the more recent versions is that home computers now have powerful graphics capabilities that were not available when MBASIC was developed. Other versions of BASIC generally include a number of graphics commands and statements. To get the most from your computer, you will want to use its graphics capabilities to the full, and this will require a careful study of the owner's manual.

Of the various BASICs supplied with popular home computers, Sinclair BASIC (used in the ZX81 and Spectrum) and BBC BASIC probably differ most from MBASIC. Texas Instruments' version (used in the TI99/4A) also has a number of significant differences. As far as possible, we point out how to modify our programs in the 'Basic Flavours' boxes and you should refer to these if you have any problems running the programs.

As mentioned previously, the RND function differs from version to version. Check in your BASIC manual to see how it has been implemented in your version. We are illustrating its use in a very simple dice game. As with previous programs we have done most of the work in subroutines. This technique has the advantage of making the

programs more readable, easier to write and easier to debug.

The main program starts with the statement RANDOMIZE in line 20. Most, but not all, versions of BASIC need this statement to 'reseed' the RND function. It is actually quite hard to get computers to produce genuinely random numbers. Without this reseeding operation, the same sequence of supposedly random numbers would be produced each time by the RND function. Line 50 then calls a subroutine that uses RND to assign a random number to the variable D. The form we have used is:

```
320 LET D = INT(10 * RND)
```

This is the line most likely to need changing when you enter the program. Details of how different versions of RND work are given in 'Basic Flavours', so let's see what's happening in this Microsoft BASIC. The RND uses an expression (in brackets, as is usual with functions) as an option to alter slightly the sequence of numbers generated. With no expression — for example LET A = RND — the value of A will be a number between 0 and 1. We do not want a number smaller than 1 so we multiply the number by 10. This can be done like this: LET A = 10 * RND. If, for the sake of argument, RND had returned the value 0.125455, the value of A would now be 1.25455.

To eliminate the fractional part of the number and retain only the integer portion, we use the INT (integer) function like this: LET A = INT(10 * RND). Some versions of BASIC allow the upper limit of the random numbers generated to be specified in the expression used in the brackets after RND. For example, Dragon BASIC will print a whole number in the range 1 to 6 in response to: PRINT RND(6).

Since our Microsoft BASIC cannot do this, we check to see if the numbers returned are greater than 6 or less than 1 as such numbers are of no use in a dice game. This is done in lines 330 and 340:

```
330 IF D > 6 THEN GOTO 320
340 IF D < 1 THEN GOTO 320
```

If D is outside the limits 1 to 6, the GOTOs make the program jump back and try again.

Having chosen a random value for D between 1 and 6, the dice throw subroutine RETURNs to the main program. This prints the message YOUR SCORE IS A, followed by a picture of a dice. Notice how the appropriate picture of a side is selected. It is done in the SELECT subroutine. For example, if the dice (and therefore D) is a 1, line 410 calls the subroutine starting at line 530 thus:

```
410 IF D = 1 THEN GOSUB 530
```

This subroutine is nothing more than a series of PRINT statements designed to produce crude graphics on the screen. Your BASIC may well have much better screen graphics, and if this is the case it would be better to substitute the appropriate graphics statements in place of our subroutines.

Once the program has chosen a dice for you at random, it will then repeat the process to select and display a dice for the computer. The part of the program that decides who has won has been incorporated in the main program; it could just as well have been written as a subroutine, but this would hardly be worth it since it is only four lines long. Line 200 compares M (my dice) with C (computer's dice) to see if they are equal. If they are, the words IT'S A DRAW are assigned to the string variable S$. Line 210 tests to see if M is greater than C. If it is, it assigns the words YOU HAVE WON to S$. Line 220 tests to see if M is less than C. If it is, it assigns the words THE COMPUTER HAS WON to S$. Line 240 simply prints the result and the game is over. Although this program is rather long, it is essentially very simple. It uses only one function, RND, has no loops, no subscripted variables and nothing more complicated than a few IF . . . THEN statements.

Given that the RND function is so variable, and that some versions of BASIC (Microsoft's, for example) require the RANDOMIZE statement to generate a new sequence of random numbers, is there any way we could generate truly random (i.e. unpredictable) numbers without using these functions? Several techniques are available.

One of the functions we have not looked at so far is INKEY$ (pronounced 'inkey-string'). Each time the word INKEY$ is encountered, the program inspects the keyboard to see if a key has been pressed. The program does not wait for a character to be input as it does when the command INPUT is used. So the command INKEY$ is usually placed in a loop. The program then continually scans the keyboard, waiting for something to be input. There is usually a test within the loop to terminate it, if an appropriate character has been input. This makes it possible to write a program to form a counting loop that will terminate when a specific character has been typed in. What would happen if we used this program?

```
10 PRINT "HIT THE SPACE-BAR"
20 FOR X = 0 TO 1
30 LET R = R + 1
40 LET A$ = INKEY$
50 IF A$ = "   " THEN GOTO 80
60 LET X = 0
70 NEXT X
80 FOR Q = 0 TO 1
90 IF R < 10 THEN GOTO 130
100 LET Q = 0
110 LET R = R / 10
120 NEXT Q
130 PRINT INT (R)
140 END
```

Would R be a random number? It should be, so let's look at the program and see why.

Line 10 prints the prompt HIT THE SPACE-BAR. Before we have time to respond to this prompt, the program has entered the FOR X = 0 TO 1 loop in line 20. 0 and 1 may seem like strange limits for the loop, but we will see how this structure is used shortly. Line 30 assigns the value 1 to variable R the first time through the loop. Line 40 assigns whatever character is typed in on the keyboard to the string variable A$ in line 40. This is done using the INKEY$ function. If you were to hit the letter R, R would be assigned to A$. Line 50 tests A$ to see whether it is a space (this is represented in BASIC as a space between double quote marks thus "   "). If A$ is a space, the program branches using the GOTO statement, but if A$ is not a space, the program continues to the next line.

This is line 60, which says LET X = 0. Now X is the index of the loop. The NEXT X statement in line 70 causes the program to return to the beginning of the loop in line 20. Since X has been reset to 0, the loop repeats it. In this way the FOR X = 0 TO 1 loop will be repeated indefinitely, as long as the IF A$ =

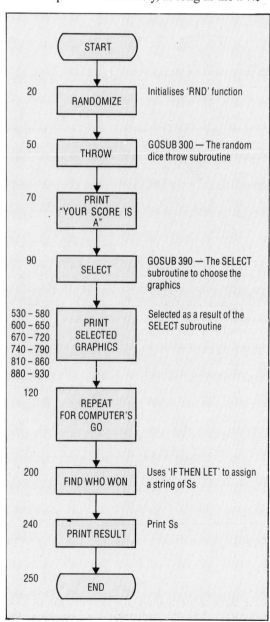

	START	
20	RANDOMIZE	Initialises 'RND' function
50	THROW	GOSUB 300 — The random dice throw subroutine
70	PRINT "YOUR SCORE IS A"	
90	SELECT	GOSUB 390 — The SELECT subroutine to choose the graphics
530 – 580 600 – 650 670 – 720 740 – 790 810 – 860 880 – 930	PRINT SELECTED GRAPHICS	Selected as a result of the SELECT subroutine
120	REPEAT FOR COMPUTER'S GO	
200	FIND WHO WON	Uses 'IF THEN LET' to assign a string of Ss
240	PRINT RESULT	Print Ss
250	END	

Program Flow
The flowchart shows the main actions performed by the program in simplified form. Corresponding line numbers are given on the left and short explanatory notes on the right. This is not a full flowchart as many of the 'decisions' and branches in the program are not shown

" " test fails.

If at some stage the space bar is pressed, A$ will be assigned the character representing a space, and so the program will branch to line 80 and the loop will not be repeated.

But what will happen while the loop is repeating? Line 30 increments the value of R at each repetition of the loop. The first time through, R would be set to 1, the second time through it would be set to 1 + 1 and so on. When the loop has been broken out of by the test on A$, we could read R to see what we had counted up to.

Computers, however, operate very quickly and so R could be in the hundreds by the time we press the space bar. What would we do if we wanted values of R only between 1 and 10? Line 80 sets up another loop to enable us to test R and divide it by 10 if it is larger than 10. As long as R is larger than 10, the test in line 90 will fail, the value of Q will be reset to 0 and the loop will be repeated. Line 110 divides the value of R by 10 and a result is not printed out until the value of R has been reduced to a figure of less than 10. Line 30 ensures that the value of R can never be 0.

In theory, then, this program should produce a random number varying between 1 and 9 inclusive. But does it? The INT statement ensures that the decimal fractions have been removed, therefore the possible values of R would be 1,2,3,4,5,6,7,8,9. The average of these numbers is 5 (because their sum is 45, and 45 ÷ 9 = 5). Try it and see. You could do this by running the program a number of times, noting the value of R each time and then calculating the average. Alternatively, you could add some lines to the program to make it run, say, 100 times, adding the value of R to another variable S and then dividing S by 100.

When we tried this, we found that the average value of R was well below 5 and so the numbers could not have been random. It is instructive to consider why this could be.

The problem is that although BASIC is fast, it is not fast enough. The first loop lets the value of R increment until it reaches hundreds, or even thousands, before we press the space bar. Unless you make a deliberate effort to vary the amount of time elapsing between seeing the HIT THE SPACE-BAR prompt and actually pressing it, chances are you will press it after a fairly regular lapse of time. In this time, the value of R will probably have increased to several hundred.

The divisions that take place to reduce the value of R to a figure below 10 do not take place until after the space bar has been pressed. This means that R will almost always be in the low hundreds before the divisions take place and so the final value of R will tend to be low.

Is it possible to write a routine that overcomes this problem? The answer is yes, if we can make the counting process fast enough for our reaction time to the HIT THE SPACE-BAR prompt to be truly unpredictable. The solution is to make the test for the 'greater than upper limit' part of the first loop. Consider this program:

```
10 REM   GAME OF DICE -- MAIN PROGRAM
20 RANDOMIZE
30 REM    YOUR THROW
40 REM   GOSUB 'THROW' ROUTINE
50 GOSUB 300
60 LET M = D
70 PRINT "YOUR SCORE IS A"
80 REM   GOSUB 'SELECT' ROUTINE
90 GOSUB 390
100 PRINT
110 REM   COMPUTER'S THROW
120 REM    GOSUB 'THROW' ROUTINE
130 GOSUB 300
140 LET C = D
150 PRINT "THE COMPUTER'S SCORE IS A"
160 REM   GOSUB 'SELECT' ROUTINE
170 GOSUB 390
180 PRINT
190 REM   WHO WON?
200 IF M = C THEN LET S$ = "DRAW"
210 IF M > C THEN LET S$ = "YOU WON"
220 IF M < C THEN LET S$ = "COMPUTER WON"
230 REM   PRINT RESULT
240 PRINT S$
250 END
260 REM
270 REM
280 REM
290 REM
300 REM   RANDOM DICE THROW SUBROUTINE
310 REM
320 LET D = INT(10*RND)
330 IF D > 6 THEN GOTO 320
340 IF D < 1 THEN GOTO 320
350 RETURN
360 REM
370 REM
380 REM
390 REM   SELECT SUBROUTINE
400 REM
410 IF D = 1 THEN GOSUB 530
420 IF D = 2 THEN GOSUB 600
430 IF D = 3 THEN GOSUB 670
440 IF D = 4 THEN GOSUB 740
450 IF D = 5 THEN GOSUB 810
460 IF D = 6 THEN GOSUB 880
470 RETURN
480 REM
490 REM
500 REM
510 'GRAPHICS' SUBROUTINES
520 REM
530 PRINT "|        |"
540 PRINT "|        |"
550 PRINT "|        |"
560 PRINT "|   *    |"
570 PRINT "|        |"
580 PRINT "|        |"
590 RETURN
600 PRINT "|        |"
610 PRINT "|        |"
620 PRINT "|     *  |"
630 PRINT "|        |"
640 PRINT "| *      |"
650 PRINT "|        |"
660 RETURN
670 PRINT "|        |"
680 PRINT "|        |"
690 PRINT "|     *  |"
700 PRINT "|   *    |"
710 PRINT "| *      |"
720 PRINT "|        |"
730 RETURN
740 PRINT "|        |"
750 PRINT "|        |"
760 PRINT "| *    * |"
770 PRINT "|        |"
780 PRINT "| *    * |"
790 PRINT "|        |"
800 RETURN
810 PRINT "|        |"
820 PRINT "|        |"
830 PRINT "| *    * |"
840 PRINT "|   *    |"
850 PRINT "| *    * |"
860 PRINT "|        |"
870 RETURN
880 PRINT "|        |"
890 PRINT "|        |"
900 PRINT "| *    * |"
910 PRINT "| *    * |"
920 PRINT "| *    * |"
930 PRINT "|        |"
940 RETURN
```

```
 5 LET R = 0
10 PRINT "HIT THE SPACE-BAR"
20 FOR X = 0 TO 1
30 LET R = R + 1
40 IF R > 9 THEN LET R = 1
50 IF INKEY$ = "   " THEN GOTO 80
60 LET X = 0
70 NEXT X
80 PRINT R
```

In this program, R can never be less than 1 or greater than 9. By the time the space bar is pressed (and recognised by the INKEY$ function in line 50), R will have a value somewhere between 1 and 9 inclusive.

This program was tested 1,000 times and found an average value for R of 5.014. Since a perfect average would be 5 and the error is only 0.28% high, this suggests that the program does indeed generate a random number very close to the theoretical average. The point is, of course, that even when a program appears reasonable on paper, there may be unforeseen flaws in it. Actual testing is well worth while.

Some readers will have noticed that these random number programs could be shortened by using various GOTO statements in place of the FOR . . . NEXT loop. Our reason for avoiding GOTO statements will become clearer in future parts of the Basic Programming course.

Basic Flavours

On the BBC Micro and the Oric-1, delete line 20, and replace line 320 by:

```
320 LET D = INT(10*RND(1))
```

On the Vic-20 and the Commodore 64, replace line 20 by:

```
20 LET X = RND(−TI)
```

and replace line 320 by:

```
320 LET D = INT(10*RND(1))
```

On the Spectrum, the word RANDOMIZE is abbreviated on the keyboard to RAND, but it will appear on the screen as RANDOMIZE

On the Oric-1 and the Lynx, replace INKEY$ by KEY$.
On the Vic-20 and the Commodore 64, replace line 40 by:

```
40 GET A$
```

Then replace line 50 by:

```
50 GET A$: IF A$="   " THEN GOTO 80
```

On the BBC Micro, replace INKEY$ by INKEY$(10). The number in brackets is the time in hundredths of a second during which the system will wait for a keypress; so for fast response use a low number, and vice versa

Exercises

■ **RND Function** Modify the last program in the text to give a random number in the range 1 to 6 (inclusive).

■ **Loop And Average** Add lines to the last program in the text to make it repeat 100 times and produce an average of the 100 results.

■ **Replace With Subroutine** Replace lines 50 and 130 in the main program (the random dice throw subroutine) with a GOSUB calling your 'random number generator' in the first exercise.

■ **INKEY$** Using the INKEY$ function, how would you write a program to read any key typed at the keyboard and print: THE KEY YOU HIT WAS: * as a result (* represents the key you pressed).

■ **Timing Loop** Write a timing loop (a 'counting' loop) and use the INKEY$ function to find how big the value of a variable becomes after 10 seconds (you'll need to use a watch). Write the program so that the final printout reads: THE VALUE OF R AFTER 10 SECONDS IS: * (* represents the value of R).

■ **IF-THEN Tests** Write a simple game program in which the computer generates a random number between 1 and 100 (inclusive) and the player has to guess what the number is. The player has five tries. Each time, the program responds with the messages YOUR GUESS IS TOO LARGE, YOUR GUESS IS TOO SMALL, or YOU ARE RIGHT, CONGRATULATIONS, or NO MORE GOES. YOU LOSE!

Answers To 'Exercises' On pages 28-29
Loops 1
THE VALUE OF A IS 450
Loops 2
START
STOP
Loops 3
THE VALUE OF A IS NOW 160
Loops 4
I LIKE BASIC
I LIKE BASIC
I LIKE BASIC
:
:
Until you RESET or BREAK the program
Loops 5
I'M FEELING LOOPY
(15 times)
Read-Data 1
WE'RE TESTING THE READ STATEMENT
170
Read-Data 2
X=1
X=2
:
:
X=23

ANOTHER DIMENSION

One-dimensional arrays, as we have seen, store a collection of data that have something in common. Two-dimensional arrays are used for tables and charts.

So far we have considered two types of variables, simple variables and subscripted variables. Simple variables are like memory locations where numbers (or character strings) can be stored and manipulated by referring to the variable 'label'. Simple variables can store just one value or string and have 'simple' variable names — N, B2, X, Y3 are examples. Subscripted variables, sometimes called one-dimensional arrays, can store a whole list of values or strings. The number of values or strings that can be held is specified at the beginning of the program using the DIM statement. For example, DIM A(16) establishes that the array labelled A can contain 16 separate values. It should be noted, however, that many BASICs accept A(0) as the first element, so that DIM A(16) actually defines 17 elements. These 'locations' are referred to by using the appropriate subscript. PRINT A(1) will print the first element in the array; LET B = A(12) assigns the value in the 12th element in the array to variable B; LET A(3) = A(5) assigns the value of the fifth element to the third element.

Sometimes, however, we need to be able to manipulate data that is best presented as tables or charts. Such data could range from tables of football results to a breakdown of sales by item and department in a store. As an example of a typical table of data, consider this breakdown of household expenditure over a one year period:

	RENT	PHONE	ELECTR.	FOOD	CAR
JAN	260.00	25.10	41.50	161.30	50.55
FEB	260.00	35.40	43.75	145.90	46.20
MAR	260.00	29.05	50.70	151.20	43.40
APR	260.00	26.20	44.60	155.30	49.20
MAY	260.00	19.30	39.80	150.95	48.30
JUN	260.00	20.45	32.60	147.65	52.30
JUL	260.00	30.50	26.10	150.35	58.40
AUG	260.00	29.50	22.40	148.05	61.20
SEP	260.00	28.25	24.45	148.60	59.45
OCT	260.00	31.15	34.50	154.90	23.50
NOV	260.00	31.05	39.50	160.05	45.95
DEC	260.00	28.95	42.20	210.60	51.25

Arranging the information in this way allows it to be manipulated in a number of ways relatively simply. It is easy, for example, to find the total expenditure in March by simply adding up all the figures in the row for March. It is just as easy to find the total expenditure for the year on the telephone or the car by adding up the vertical columns. Similarly, it is easy to find monthly or yearly averages. This table is called a two-dimensional

array. It has 12 rows and five columns.

Two-dimensional arrays such as this can also be represented in BASIC in much the same way as single-dimension arrays. The difference is that the variable now needs two subscripts to reference any location.

If we were writing a BASIC program using this table of information, the simplest thing would be to treat the whole table as a single two-dimensional array. Just as with ordinary subscripted arrays, we give it a variable name. Let's call it A (for 'Array'). Again, as with ordinary subscripted arrays, it will need to be DIMensioned. As there are 12 rows and five columns, it is dimensioned thus: DIM A(12,5). The order in which the two subscripts are put is important; the convention is that rows are specified first and columns second. Our table above has 12 rows (one for each month) and five columns (one for each of the five categories of expenditure), it is therefore a 12-by-5 array.

The DIM statement serves two essential functions. It sets aside enough memory locations in the computer's memory for the array, and it allows each of the locations to be specified by the variable name followed, in brackets, by the row and column positions. The DIM statement DIM X(3,5), for example, would create a variable X able to represent an array with three rows and five columns.

Look at the table and assume that the information has been entered as the elements in a two-dimensional array labelled A. Find the values present in A(1,1), A(1,5), A(2,1), A(3,3) and A(12,3).

It is possible to enter a table of information as an array in part of a program by using LET statements, for example.

```
30 LET A(1,2) = 25.1
40 LET A(1,3) = 41.5
50 LET A(1,4) = 161.30
     :
     :
610 LET A(12,5) = 51.25
```

But this is clearly a laborious way of doing things. A far simpler method is to use either READ and DATA statements or the INPUT statement with nested FOR...NEXT loops. Let's see how it could be done using the READ statement:

```
10 DIM A(12,5)
20 FOR R = 1 TO 12
30 FOR C = 1 TO 5
40 READ A(R,C)
50 NEXT C
60 NEXT R
70 DATA 260, 25.1, 41.5, 161.3, 50.55, 260, 35.4,
```

43.75
80 DATA 145.9, 46.2, 260, 29.05, 50.7, 151.2, 43.4, 260
90 DATA 26.2, 44.6, 155.3, 49.2, 260, 19.3, 39.8, 150.95
100 DATA 48.3, 260, 20.45, 32.6, 147.65, 52.3, 260, 30.5
110 DATA 26.10, 150.35, 58.4, 260, 29.5, 22.4, 148.05, 61.2, 260
120 DATA 28.25, 24.45, 148.6, 59.45, 260, 31.15, 34.5
130 DATA 154.9, 23.5, 260, 31.05, 39.5, 160.05, 45.95
140 DATA 260, 28.95, 42.2, 210.6, 51.25
150 END

There are a number of important points to note about this program. The first is that the DIM statement is right at the beginning of the program. A DIM statement should be executed only once in a program and so it is usual to place it near the beginning or before any loops are executed. The second point to note is that there are two FOR...NEXT loops, one to set the 'row' part of the subscript and one to set the 'column'. These two loops do not follow one after the other; they are 'nested' one inside the other. Notice the limits chosen. FOR R = 1 TO 12 will increment the value for the row from one to 12; FOR C = 1 TO 5 will increment the value for the column from one to five.

Right in the middle of the nested loop is the READ statement. The crucial part of the program is:

```
20 FOR R = 1 TO 12
30 FOR C = 1 TO 5
40 READ A(R,C)
50 NEXT C
60 NEXT R
```

The first time through, after lines 20 and 30 have been executed, the values of R and C will both be one, so line 40 will be equivalent to READ A(1,1). The first item of data in the DATA statement is 260, so this value will be assigned to the first row and the first column of the array. The choice of eight elements to each DATA statement is purely arbitrary.

After that has happened, the NEXT C statement sends the program back to line 30 and the value of C is incremented to two. Line 40 is now equivalent to READ A(1,2) and the next item of data, 25.1, will be assigned to the first row and the second column of the array. This process is repeated until C has been incremented to 5. After that, the NEXT R statement in line 60 returns the program to line 20 and R is incremented to two. Line 30 will set C to one again and so now line 40 will be equivalent to READ A(2,1).

Nesting loops in this way is very useful, but care is needed. Each loop must be nested completely within another loop and the order of the NEXT statements must be carefully observed. Notice how the first loop, FOR R, has the second NEXT statement. When there are two loops, one nested inside the other, the first loop is called the outer loop and the second is called the inner loop. The whole of the inner loop will always be completed before the index of the outer loop is incremented. It is possible to nest loops to as many 'depths' as required by the program, but such programs can become complex and difficult to follow and debug. It is bad programming practice to put branching instructions inside loops and GOTOs are to be avoided.

Let's look at the DATA statements. Notice that commas are used to separate data items, but there must be no comma before the first data item or after the last. We have inserted spaces between each data item, but this is not normal. Mistakes when entering the data are easy to make and difficult to spot later. As many DATA statements as required may be used. Each new line needs to start with a DATA statement. The data is read in one item at a time, starting from the beginning of the first DATA statement and working through until all the items have been read. Be sure that the number of data items is correct or you will get an error message when the program is run.

The program presented so far does not actually do anything except convert appropriate data into a two-dimensional array. After the program has been entered and RUN, nothing will apparently happen and all you will see on the screen will be the BASIC prompt. To test that the data is correctly placed, try a few PRINT commands. (A command in BASIC is a keyword that can be immediately executed without having to be within a program and does not therefore need a line number. Examples are LIST, RUN, SAVE, AUTO, EDIT and PRINT). PRINT A(1,1) <CR> should cause the number 260 to appear on the screen. What will be printed by the following commands?

```
PRINT A(12,1)
PRINT A(1,5)
PRINT A(5,1)
PRINT A(5,5)
```

To make the program do something useful, it will need to be extended. As it stands it forms an adequate basis for a 'main program'. To use it as part of a larger, more useful program, modules can be written as subroutines to be called by GOSUBs inserted at suitable points before the END statement.

In the early stages of designing a household accounts program, it is best to start with a simple written description of the general requirements. We might decide that we want to be able to have totals and averages calculated for monthly expenditure or by category (electricity, for example). We can work out the details of how to derive these results at a later stage. If there is a choice to be made within the program about which subroutines we wish to be executed we will probably want to be prompted by a 'menu' which will direct control to the appropriate subroutines as a result of our response. An early sketch of the program at this stage might look like this:

```
MAIN PROGRAM
(DATA ENTRY)
MENU
(SELECT SUBROUTINES)
END
```

A little further refinement may show that we will need subroutines to calculate totals for months or for categories (MONTHTOTAL and CATTOTAL), average monthly expenditure (MONTHAV) and average yearly expenditure by category (CATAV). The reason for using one-word names for these subroutines is to help us to plan the program without having to worry about details such as line numbers at this stage. On reflection we may decide that even the main menu selection part of the program should be dealt with as a subroutine in order to keep the main part of the program as a separate module. The next stage of refinement of the program will look like this:

```
MAIN PROGRAM (DATA ENTRY)
    MENU (CALL SUBROUTINE)
END

**SUBROUTINES**

1 MENU
2 TOTALS
3 AVERAGES

(2) TOTALS
4 MONTHTOTAL
5 CATTOTAL

(3) AVERAGES
6 MONTHAV
7 CATAV
```

This sketch of the program shows that the MENU subroutine will give us a choice of either TOTALS or AVERAGES. Both of these will themselves be subroutines. The TOTALS subroutine will give a further choice of MONTHTOTAL or CATTOTAL. These will be the subroutines that perform the actual calculations.

The AVERAGES subroutine will give a choice of MONTHAV or CATAV, and again these will be subroutines to perform the appropriate calculations. At this stage it should be possible to see whether our 'program' will do what we want, without doing any actual coding (detailed program writing in BASIC). If we can be satisfied that 'so far so good', we are ready to tackle the writing of the modules (subroutines) themselves. The only change needed to the main program will be a subroutine call before the END statement, so we could add:

```
145 GOSUB **MENU**
```

Note that we are still using 'names' for subroutines rather than line numbers. Many languages, PASCAL, for example, allow sub-programs to be called by name, but most versions of BASIC do not and actual line numbers are needed instead. However, these 'details' can be incorporated later.

Let's see how the MENU subroutine could be written (line numbers have been omitted and you can add appropriate ones if you wish to implement this program).

```
REM THE **MENU** SUBROUTINE
PRINT "WOULD YOU LIKE T(OTALS) OR
    A(VERAGES)?"
PRINT "TYPE EITHER A OR T"
INPUT L$
IF L$ = "T" THEN GOSUB *TOTALS*
IF L$ = "A" THEN GOSUB *AVERAGES*
RETURN
```

Note that we are marking the subroutines called by enclosing them within *——* marks. You will have to use line numbers instead. These can be inserted when you are in a position to know what they are.

Suppose you type T for TOTALS. The program will then call the TOTALS subroutine. This will then present another menu and could look like this:

```
REM THE **TOTALS** SUBROUTINE
PRINT "WOULD YOU LIKE TOTALS FOR"
PRINT "M(ONTH) OR C(ATEGORY)?"
PRINT "TYPE EITHER M OR C"
INPUT L$
IF L$ = "M" THEN GOSUB *MONTHTOTAL*
IF L$ = "C" THEN GOSUB *CATTOTAL*
RETURN
```

Suppose you selected M for MONTHTOTAL. Let's see how we could write a module to calculate the total expenditure for any month in the year.

```
REM THE **MONTHTOTAL** SUBROUTINE
REM THIS CALCULATES TOTAL EXPENDITURE FOR
REM ANY MONTH
PRINT "SELECT MONTH"
PRINT "1-JAN 2-FEB 3-MAR 4-APR 5-MAY"
PRINT "6-JUN 7-JUL 8-AUG 9-SEP"
PRINT "10-OCT 11-NOV 12-DEC"
PRINT "TYPE A NUMBER FOR THE MONTH"
LET T = 0
INPUT M
FOR C = 1 TO 5
LET T = T + A(M,C)
NEXT C
PRINT "THE TOTAL EXPENDITURE FOR MONTH"
PRINT "NUMBER ";M;" IS ";T
RETURN
```

The number representing the month is typed in and the INPUT statement assigns the number to the variable M (MONTH). M is used to specify the 'row' subscript of the two-dimensional array A. The FOR-NEXT loop increments the value of C (column) from one to five so the first time through the loop, if we had selected three for March, the LET statement would be equivalent to LET T = T + A(3,1). The next time round it would be equivalent to LET T = T + A(3,2) and so on.

As practice we'll leave you to write the other subroutines, or try out the other exercises. Two-dimensional arrays are ideal for any program that involves tables of data, be they statistical, financial or any other quantity.

Answers to Exercises On Page 33

RND Function

```
40 IF R >6 THEN LET R = 1
```

Loop And Average

```
5 FOR L = 1 TO 100
:
80 LET T = T + R
90 NEXT L
100 LET A = T/100
110 PRINT A
120 END
```

Replace With Subroutine

Delete lines 5, 80, 90, 100, and 110 in the solution above. Change lines 10 to 70 to (say) 1000 to 1070. Check that line 40 is as in the RND Function solution above. Then add 1080 RETURN. Incorporate the result into the main program. Change lines 50 and 130 in the main program to read 50 GOSUB 1000 and 130 GOSUB 1000.

INKEYS

```
10 PRINT "TYPE ANY KEY"
20 LET A$ = INKEY$
30 IF A$ ="" THEN GOTO 20
40 PRINT "THE KEY YOU HIT WAS";A$
50 END
```

Timing Loop

```
5 PRINT "HIT THE SPACE-BAR AFTER 10
    SECONDS"
10 FOR L = 0 TO 1
20 LET R = R + 1
30 IF INKEY$ = "   " THEN GOTO 60
40 LET L = 0
50 NEXT L
60 PRINT "THE VALUE OF R AFTER 10 SECONDS IS
    ";R
70 END
```

IF…THEN

```
10 GOSUB 1000
20 PRINT "GUESS THE NUMBER"
30 FOR G = 1 TO 5
40 INPUT N
50 IF N >R THEN GOTO 110
60 IF N <R THEN GOTO 130
70 IF N = R THEN GOTO 150
80 NEXT G
90 PRINT "NO MORE GOES. YOU LOSE!"
100 GOTO 500
110 PRINT "YOUR GUESS IS TOO LARGE"
120 GOTO 80
130 PRINT "YOUR GUESS IS TOO SMALL"
140 GOTO 80
150 PRINT "YOU ARE RIGHT,
    CONGRATULATIONS".
500 END
1000 REM **RANDOM SUBROUTINE**
(Insert your subroutine here.)
1020 RETURN
```

Exercises

■ **Assigning Values** Write a program that assigns values to the elements ('Petrol', 'Service' etc.) of the matrix (see illustration below). Next, write a subroutine that asks for a month, and an expense heading, and prints the contents of the box thus specified. Finally, write a subroutine that finds the sum of each column, and places the result in the bottom box, does the same across the rows, and then calculates the grand total, which it stores in the lower right box.

■ **Bugs** The following program would not run properly and would produce an error message. There are two mistakes. Find them and make appropriate corrections.

```
●10 DIM A(3,4)
20 FOR R = 1 TO 3
30 FOR C = 1 TO 4
40 READ A(R,C)
50 NEXT C
60 NEXT R
70 FOR X = 1 TO 3
90 FOR Y = 1 TO 4
100 PRINT A(Y,X)
110 NEXT Y
120 NEXT X
130 DATA 2,4,6,8,10,12,14,16,18,20,22
140 END
```

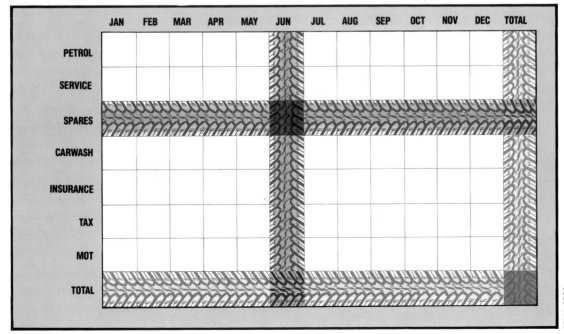

Car Expenses
The picture shows a grid of 8 × 13 squares. The rows represent different elements of the cost of running a car, and the columns represent the different months of the year. Follow the exercise on 'Assigning Values' to calculate the yearly cost of running a car

TONY LODGE

KEEPING CONTROL

All versions of BASIC feature 'control structures' that govern the flow of a program. Some machines, however, offer a wide range of alternatives, with subtle differences.

We have now covered almost all of the more important aspects of the BASIC language. In this section we will present an overview of the topics we have covered so far, deal with a few interesting asides and give some pointers to where we shall go next.

First the overview: a high-level language such as BASIC provides the user with a set of instructions that are translated internally into a form the computer can understand. Any computer program can be written using just two simple patterns, called 'constructs'. These are 'sequence' constructs and 'control structures' of which only two are essential in BASIC: IF . . . THEN . . . ELSE and WHILE . . . DO. Most other computer languages provide considerably more.

The sequence construct allows the task to be broken down into a set of sub-tasks that perform the main task when executed in sequence. The size of the sub-tasks depends on the language; in BASIC the sub-tasks are represented by the statements written on each line, and the sequence is represented by the line numbers. Thus, if the task is to multiply the value assigned to a variable by 10, the sequence we could use might be:

```
110 INPUT N
120 LET N = N * 10
130 PRINT N
```

In addition to sequence constructs, we also need control structures. These are constructs that alter the order of execution of statements in a program.

The simplest control structure provided by BASIC is GOTO. This is an unconditional jump (or branch) that re-directs the execution of the program to a specified line number without a test or condition having to be satisfied. GOSUB is also an unconditional branch, but the program will always RETURN to the point immediately after the GOSUB and its use in structured programming is perfectly acceptable.

The IF . . . THEN . . . ELSE control structure is available in BASIC. It takes the form of the IF . . . THEN statement and has the following syntax ('syntax' is the computer jargon for 'form'):

IF (specified condition) is true THEN execute specified statement (ELSE) execute the next statement

Note that in standard BASIC, the ELSE part of IF . . . THEN . . . ELSE is implied. In some BASIC dialects and

in certain other languages, PASCAL for example, ELSE forms part of the statement.

IF . . . THEN . . . ELSE (IF . . . THEN in BASIC) performs one of two sub-tasks depending on whether a certain condition is true or not. Consider the following program, which is designed to find the square roots of numbers input from the keyboard unless a 'flag' value of −9999 is input (in order to terminate the program):

```
10 PRINT "INPUT A NUMBER"
20 INPUT N
30 IF N = −9999 THEN GOTO 70
40 LET S = SQR(N)
50 PRINT "THE SQUARE ROOT OF ";N;" IS ";S
60 GOTO 10
70 END
```

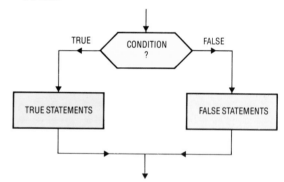

The IF . . . THEN . . . ELSE Control Structure
If the condition is True, the True statements will be executed. If the condition is False, the False statements will be executed

What line 30 is really saying here is 'IF it is true that N = −9999 THEN go to the end of the program ELSE (if it is not true that N = −9999) execute the next line of the program to find the square root'.

The other essential control structure (WHILE . . . DO) is not directly available in BASIC, but it can easily be simulated. WHILE . . . DO is a type of 'do-loop' and it means 'repeat a statement or set of statements WHILE a specified condition is true' or 'WHILE a condition is true DO something'.

WHILE . . . DO always tests the condition before the statements are executed, so if the test fails first time through, the statements (called the body of the loop) are not executed. As an example, consider a games program that prompts the player to 'PRESS SPACE-BAR WHEN READY'. This part of the program could be written (in 'pseudo-language' or simplified English) as:

```
WHILE space-bar is not pressed
DO scan keyboard
start game
```

In BASIC this could be written:

```
250 PRINT "PRESS SPACE-BAR WHEN READY"
260 IF INKEY$ < > "  " THEN GOTO 260
270 GOSUB *START*
```

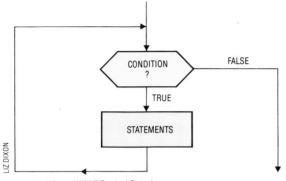

The DO . . . WHILE Control Structure
The loop is repeated as long as the condition is True. The statements may never be executed (if the initial condition is False)

Line 260 says IF INKEY$ is not equal to (< >) a space (" ") THEN go back and check the keyboard again. A slightly more elegant way of writing it would be:

```
250 PRINT "PRESS SPACE-BAR WHEN READY"
260 FOR X = 0 TO 1 STEP 0
270 IF INKEY$ = "  " THEN LET X = 2
280 NEXT X
290 GOSUB *START*
```

In this program fragment the loop (to scan the keyboard) is executed only if the space-bar has not been pressed. If the space-bar has been pressed (i.e. INKEY$ = " ") then the program exits from the FOR . . . NEXT loop to line 290, which is the call to the START subroutine. (NB. We are using 'labels' or names for subroutines. Many versions of BASIC cannot call subroutines by name and you will have to use line numbers instead of labels.)

We haven't encountered STEP before, and this is perhaps an unusual application for it. When using a FOR . . . NEXT loop, STEP allows the 'index' to be incremented in units other than one. FOR I = 1 TO 10 STEP 2 will cause I to have the value 1 on the first pass of the loop, followed by 3, 5, 7 and 9. The next increment (to 11) will exceed the limit of 10 so the loop will be finished. It is even possible to have the index counting backwards. For I = 10 TO 1 STEP−1 will cause I to count from 10 down to 1. Using STEP 0 is really a clever trick that ensures that the loop

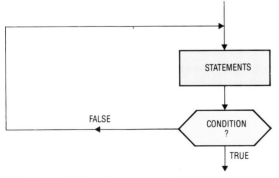

The REPEAT . . . UNTIL Control Structure
The loop is repeated until the condition becomes True. The statements will always be executed at least once

will never finish unless X is 'artificially increased' — as in the case of our IF . . . THEN statement.

Another useful control structure, again not directly available in BASIC but easily simulated, is REPEAT . . . UNTIL. Here the condition test comes after the main body of the loop, so the statement or statements in the main body will always be repeated at least once. Look at this 'random number generator':

```
10 PRINT "HIT THE SPACE-BAR"
20 FOR X = 0 TO 1 STEP 0
30 LET R = R + 1
40 IF R > 9 THEN LET R = 1
50 IF INKEY$ = "  " THEN LET X = 2
60 NEXT X
70 PRINT "THE VALUE OF R IS  ";R
```

Here, the main body (incrementing the value of R) is always executed at least once since the test to branch out of the loop (IF INKEY$ = " ") does not come until after the increment statement (LET R = R + 1).

Yet another non-essential but useful control structure is that usually called CASE. In BASIC, the CASE structure is implemented using either ON . . . GOTO or ON . . . GOSUB. This is how it works. ON . . . GOTO is a multiple-branching statement that incorporates several IF . . . THEN conditional tests into a single statement. Consider a program fragment that converts the numbers 1 to 7 into the words for the seven days of the week:

```
1050 IF D = 1 THEN GOTO 2020
1060 IF D = 2 THEN GOTO 2040
1070 IF D = 3 THEN GOTO 2060
1080 IF D = 4 THEN GOTO 2080
1090 IF D = 5 THEN GOTO 3000
2000 IF D = 6 THEN GOTO 3020
2010 IF D = 7 THEN GOTO 3040
2020 PRINT "MONDAY"
2030 GOTO*END*
2040 PRINT "TUESDAY"
2050 GOTO*END*
2060 PRINT "WEDNESDAY"
2070 GOTO*END*
2080 PRINT "THURSDAY"
2090 GOTO*END*
3000 PRINT "FRIDAY"
3010 GOTO*END*
3020 PRINT "SATURDAY"
3030 GOTO*END*
3040 PRINT "SUNDAY"
3050 GOTO*END*
```

A more compact way of achieving the same object in BASIC is to use ON . . . GOTO like this:

```
1050 ON D GOTO 2020,2040,2060,2080,
     3000,3020,3040
```

ON . . . GOSUB works the same way, except that the value of the variable determines which subroutine is branched to. Here is a slight modification of the dice program (see page 32) using ON . . . GOSUB to select the appropriate graphics for the dice selected by the RND function:

DECIMAL	BINARY	CHARACTER
32	0 0 1 0 0 0 0 0	= (space)
33	0 0 1 0 0 0 0 1	= !
34	0 0 1 0 0 0 1 0	= "
35	0 0 1 0 0 0 1 1	= #
36	0 0 1 0 0 1 0 0	= $
37	0 0 1 0 0 1 0 1	= %
38	0 0 1 0 0 1 1 0	= &
39	0 0 1 0 0 1 1 1	= '
40	0 0 1 0 1 0 0 0	= (
41	0 0 1 0 1 0 0 1	=)
42	0 0 1 0 1 0 1 0	= *
43	0 0 1 0 1 0 1 1	= +
44	0 0 1 0 1 1 0 0	= ,
45	0 0 1 0 1 1 0 1	= -
46	0 0 1 0 1 1 1 0	= .
47	0 0 1 0 1 1 1 1	= /
48	0 0 1 1 0 0 0 0	= 0
49	0 0 1 1 0 0 0 1	= 1
50	0 0 1 1 0 0 1 0	= 2
51	0 0 1 1 0 0 1 1	= 3
52	0 0 1 1 0 1 0 0	= 4
53	0 0 1 1 0 1 0 1	= 5
54	0 0 1 1 0 1 1 0	= 6
55	0 0 1 1 0 1 1 1	= 7
56	0 0 1 1 1 0 0 0	= 8
57	0 0 1 1 1 0 0 1	= 9
58	0 0 1 1 1 0 1 0	= :
59	0 0 1 1 1 0 1 1	= ;
60	0 0 1 1 1 1 0 0	= <
61	0 0 1 1 1 1 0 1	= =
62	0 0 1 1 1 1 1 0	= >
63	0 0 1 1 1 1 1 1	= ?
64	0 1 0 0 0 0 0 0	= @
65	0 1 0 0 0 0 0 1	= A
66	0 1 0 0 0 0 1 0	= B
67	0 1 0 0 0 0 1 1	= C
68	0 1 0 0 0 1 0 0	= D
69	0 1 0 0 0 1 0 1	= E
70	0 1 0 0 0 1 1 0	= F
71	0 1 0 0 0 1 1 1	= G
72	0 1 0 0 1 0 0 0	= H
73	0 1 0 0 1 0 0 1	= I
74	0 1 0 0 1 0 1 0	= J
75	0 1 0 0 1 0 1 1	= K
76	0 1 0 0 1 1 0 0	= L
77	0 1 0 0 1 1 0 1	= M
78	0 1 0 0 1 1 1 0	= N
79	0 1 0 0 1 1 1 1	= O
80	0 1 0 1 0 0 0 0	= P
81	0 1 0 1 0 0 0 1	= Q
82	0 1 0 1 0 0 1 0	= R
83	0 1 0 1 0 0 1 1	= S
84	0 1 0 1 0 1 0 0	= T
85	0 1 0 1 0 1 0 1	= U
86	0 1 0 1 0 1 1 0	= V
87	0 1 0 1 0 1 1 1	= W
88	0 1 0 1 1 0 0 0	= X
89	0 1 0 1 1 0 0 1	= Y
90	0 1 0 1 1 0 1 0	= Z
91	0 1 0 1 1 0 1 1	= [
92	0 1 0 1 1 1 0 0	= \
93	0 1 0 1 1 1 0 1	=]
94	0 1 0 1 1 1 1 0	= ^
95	0 1 0 1 1 1 1 1	= _
96	0 1 1 0 0 0 0 0	= `
97	0 1 1 0 0 0 0 1	= a
98	0 1 1 0 0 0 1 0	= b
99	0 1 1 0 0 0 1 1	= c
100	0 1 1 0 0 1 0 0	= d
101	0 1 1 0 0 1 0 1	= e
102	0 1 1 0 0 1 1 0	= f
103	0 1 1 0 0 1 1 1	= g
104	0 1 1 0 1 0 0 0	= h
105	0 1 1 0 1 0 0 1	= i
106	0 1 1 0 1 0 1 0	= j
107	0 1 1 0 1 0 1 1	= k
108	0 1 1 0 1 1 0 0	= l
109	0 1 1 0 1 1 0 1	= m
110	0 1 1 0 1 1 1 0	= n
111	0 1 1 0 1 1 1 1	= o
112	0 1 1 1 0 0 0 0	= p
113	0 1 1 1 0 0 0 1	= q
114	0 1 1 1 0 0 1 0	= r
115	0 1 1 1 0 0 1 1	= s
116	0 1 1 1 0 1 0 0	= t
117	0 1 1 1 0 1 0 1	= u
118	0 1 1 1 0 1 1 0	= v
119	0 1 1 1 0 1 1 1	= w
120	0 1 1 1 1 0 0 0	= x
121	0 1 1 1 1 0 0 1	= y
122	0 1 1 1 1 0 1 0	= z
123	0 1 1 1 1 0 1 1	= {
124	0 1 1 1 1 1 0 0	=	
125	0 1 1 1 1 1 0 1	= }
126	0 1 1 1 1 1 1 0	= ~

ASCII
Here is a complete list of the ASCII values between 32 and 126, their binary equivalents, and the characters they represent. The meaning attached to values outside this range varies considerably from machine to machine

```
390 REM SELECT SUBROUTINE
400 REM USING ON...GOSUB
410 ON D GOSUB 530,600,670,740,810,880
470 RETURN
```

Although your version of BASIC probably contains many statements and functions we have not covered, most will be extensions to the 'basic' BASIC designed to take advantage of particular features of your machine. Many of these will relate to graphics features built into the hardware — instructions such as PAINT, PAPER, INK, BEEP and CIRCLE. These tend to be 'machine specific' and so we have not included them in our course, though we will be giving you more details in other articles.

Before ending the basic part of our BASIC course, however, there are some loose ends to tie up — a discussion of the ASCII character set, together with a couple of functions for helping manipulate characters, and a way of defining new functions (or functions not included in your version of BASIC).

Several methods of representing letters of the alphabet and other characters such as numbers and punctuation marks in digital form have been devised over the years. One of the first was Morse code, which uses combinations of dots and dashes to represent characters. From the computer's point of view, Morse code suffers from the disadvantage of using different numbers of bits for different letters — between one and six dots and dashes for each character. Other attempts at making a more regular and systematic character code (e.g. the Baudot code, which uses five bits to represent up to 32 characters) have fallen by the wayside and the almost universal system now in use is the ASCII code (American Standard Code for Information Interchange).

The ASCII code uses one byte to represent the 94 printable characters, the 'space' and a number of control 'characters'. Eight bits could give 256 unique combinations (2^8), but this is far more than is needed to represent the characters of a standard typewriter or computer keyboard, so only seven are used, allowing for 128 unique combinations. (The eighth bit is usually wasted but is sometimes used to specify an alternative set of foreign language or graphics characters.) The binary and decimal ASCII codes for the standard range of characters are given in the table.

As you can see from the table, the ASCII code for the letter A is 65 and for B is 66. The codes for the lower case letters a and b are 97 and 98. Every lower case letter has an ASCII code value larger by 32 than its upper case equivalent. This constant 'offset' makes it easy to convert lower case letters in character strings into upper case letters, and vice-versa. To do this we will need two further functions not used so far in the Basic Programming course — ASC and CHR$.

The ASC function takes a printable character and returns its ASCII code equivalent, so PRINT ASC("A") would print the number 65 on the screen; PRINT ASC("b") would print 98.

The CHR$ function does the opposite; it takes a number, assumes it is an ASCII code and returns the character it represents. Thus PRINT CHR$(65) would print A, while PRINT CHR$(98) would print b. The CHR$ and ASC functions are widely used, along with LEFT$, RIGHT$ and MID$ in programs making heavy use of character strings. Here's a short program that accepts a character from the keyboard, checks to see if it is upper case and converts it to upper case if it is not:

```
10 REM LOWER TO UPPER CASE CONVERTER
20 PRINT "INPUT A CHARACTER"
30 INPUT C$
40 LET C = ASC(C$)
50 IF C > 90 THEN LET C = C -32
60 PRINT CHR$(C)
```

We shall see more of this type of string manipulation throughout the rest of this book.

Finally, in this round-up, a look at functions you may not have in your version of BASIC. Almost all versions of the language allow the programmer to create new functions, and these are almost as easy to use as built-in functions. The DEF statement signals to BASIC that a new function is being defined. Here's how to define a function to calculate the volume of a sphere (the formula is $V = \frac{4}{3}\pi r^3$, where r is the radius of the sphere and π (pi) is the constant approximately equal to 3.14159):

```
10 REM FUNCTION TO CALCULATE VOLUME OF A
   SPHERE
20 DEF FNV(X) = 4 * 3.14159 * X * X * X/3
30 PRINT "INPUT RADIUS OF SPHERE"
40 INPUT R
50 PRINT "THE VOLUME OF A SPHERE OF RADIUS
   ";R;" IS"
60 PRINT FNV(R)
70 END
```

This way of defining a function is fairly straightforward, but let's look at the line in detail:

```
DEFines   function identifier
   ↓             ↓
20 DEF FNV(X) = 4* 3.14159 * X * X * X/3
       ↑    ↑
FuNction   dummy variable
```

When the function is defined, the letters FN are followed by an identifying letter — V in the case of the function above — and this must then be followed by a 'dummy variable'. This dummy variable must also be used in the function definition on the right of the equals sign. When the function is used in a program, any numeric variable can be used in place of the dummy variable in the definition.

At a further point in the program above it would be equally possible to use the 'volume of a sphere' function like this:

```
 999 LET A = 66
1000 LET B = FNV(A)
1010 PRINT B
```

```
1020 LET C = 5
1030 LET D = B + FNV(C)
1040 PRINT D
1050 LET G = FNV(16)
1060 PRINT G
```

Some BASICS allow multiple variables to be used in the defined function. Thus, a function to find the average of two numbers could be written:

```
110 DEF FNA(B,C) = (B + C )/ 2
110 INPUT "ENTER TWO NUMBERS";B,C
120 LET A = FNA(B,C): REM THE 'AVERAGE'
    FUNCTION
130 PRINT "THE AVERAGE OF ";B;" AND ";C;" IS ";A
```

Notice that line 110 above combines the equivalent of two separate statements in one. Most BASICS will automatically print words appearing in double quotation marks following the INPUT statement, so this line is equivalent to:

```
110 PRINT "ENTER TWO NUMBERS"
115 INPUT A,B
```

Line 120 also manages to get the equivalent of two statements in one line by using the colon (:) separator. Statements that would normally belong on separate lines may be written on one line

provided each 'stand-alone' statement is separated from the preceding one by a colon. This can help to save space in long programs, but its use is not to be encouraged as it makes programs less readable and mistakes more likely.

We have now covered all the main points of the BASIC language. However, good programming practice is more than just a question of knowing your way around a particular language.

In the next chapter of this book what we shall be looking at are the techniques that enable you to build upon this knowledge and produce good — and *efficient*— computer programs.

Basic Flavours

DEF FN(A,B)

On the Oric-1, the Vic-20, the Dragon-32 and the Commodore 64 you cannot write more than one variable inside the brackets.

ASC( )

On the Spectrum and the ZX81, replace:

ASC(A$) by CODE A$

and replace:

CHR$(65) by CHR$ 65

CHR$( )

If the argument is an expression, it must be put in brackets. Simple arguments — like A$ and 65 — do not need brackets, however.

ON... GOSUB

ON... GOTO

These statements are not available on the ZX81, Spectrum or Lynx.

INPUT" "

On the BBC Micro replace

INPUT "ANY MESSAGE";MS$

by

INPUT "ANY MESSAGE",MS$

DEF FN

On the BBC Micro you must define functions at the end of the program after the word END or STOP, not at the beginning as in the example given. In this case, as in many others, BBC BASIC is more powerful than standard BASIC, so consult your manual for more information.

2 PROGRAMMING TECHNIQUE

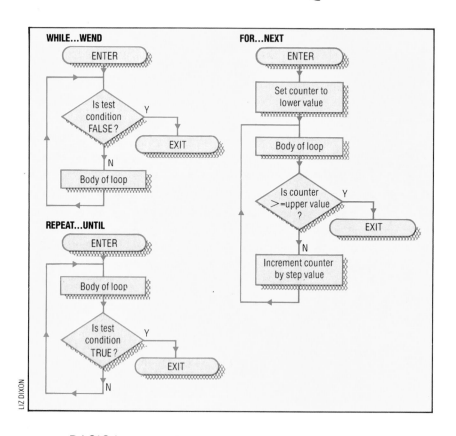

BASIC is easy to learn and to use, but it is not a very structured language, so the writing of bad, unclear or inefficient code can easily become a habit. A grounding in proper technique will greatly enhance your skills and add new dimensions to your BASIC programs.

TRICKS OF THE TRADE

Most people teach themselves programming by using the manual that comes with their computer. This is a good enough way to get started, but it often means you never learn to write efficient programs nor discover the tricks of the trade that make programming easier. We introduce a chapter which is designed to give you insights into the techniques used by good programmers.

Good programming is developed through experimentation and experience. The novice programmer, often solving problems through enormous enthusiasm and sheer effort, is gradually transformed into a technician with an awareness of short-cuts and rule-of-thumb methods that achieve the desired results. Eventually, the programmer will develop the simple clarity and direct approach of the expert. But there is no reason why the personal progress of a home computer programmer cannot be hastened by learning from the mistakes of others who have taken the same path. The lessons are there for the learning, and everyone's programming can benefit from them. Our course begins with a discussion of some of the more helpful hints that can aid a beginner.

Programming is a problem-solving process, and a great part of it should be carried out in the mind and with a pencil and paper long before a line of code is written. The stages in this process are well-known: a clear comprehensive statement of the problem in practical terms, followed by repeated re-statement of the problem with increasing precision, until it is formulated with as much detail and accuracy as possible. This description nearly always contains or implies the essential solution, which must then be expounded in greater and more practical detail so that it becomes a working method. In programming, only the last stage should involve coding, and that should be a straightforward realisation of the preceding stages. When the coding stage overlaps the real problem-solving, poor solutions and bad code result.

Solutions are often known as *algorithms*, processes of computation analysed in logical stages. The efficiency of a program depends mainly upon that of its algorithm, and this is judged in terms of its 'completeness' and its 'correctness'. These two commonsense qualities refer to the program's theoretical and practical ability to cope with the foreseeable range of input conditions, and to the consistency of its internal logic. Needless to say, it's much easier to recognise their absence than to demonstrate their presence, but every program must be subjected to this judgement, and the earlier

in its development the better.

Solutions must be *reliable*, as well as complete and correct. Not only must they handle their prescribed range of problems, but they must also deal predictably and safely with conditions outside their range. This usually means having the ability to recognise potential error conditions, and being able to stop operating with all the data intact, as well as displaying some useful status message. It is difficult to judge whether code is sufficiently reliable, as a program that isn't reliable is easier to recognise than one that is. Experience leads to better judgement.

Making programs reliable and robust is a worthy aim that nearly always conflicts directly with an equally desirable goal — keeping them *economical*. Everything costs money, even if it's only the time you spend writing programs for fun. There always comes a moment when you have to decide between continuing to work on a program that's nearly 'bombproof', and abandoning it to start a fresh project. Even if your time is unlimited, the computer's memory and operating speed are not. It's quite possible to surround the central algorithm with so much precautionary code and error-trapping that protecting against crashes can take more time than solving the original problem.

TESTING AND DEBUGGING

Solving analytical and logical problems in theory is enormously important, but programs are meant to perform a task. Once the first syntax and logical errors have been dealt with it's time to begin *testing*. This is so familiar an idea that it hardly seems to merit statement, never mind emphasis. But it is, in fact, a much misunderstood process. In anything but trivial programs there are usually far too many possible combinations of input conditions for exhaustive trials, so tests must be devised to put as much strain as possible on what are likely to be the most vulnerable (and what are expected to be the strongest) parts of the program. Generating comprehensive test conditions is not a simple matter and takes time and money. The professional approach to testing is that there are no perfect programs, only bad tests.

Successful tests reveal a program's inadequacies, and should do so in a logical fashion so that *debugging* takes as little time as possible. Like testing, debugging is an essential process that regularly fails to be achieved precisely because it embodies the same human failings that make it necessary in the first place. A program bug should be approached as another problem to be solved, exactly as described earlier — statement, analysis, algorithm, testing — but it is most often treated as a casual pest to be swatted, poisoned or crushed, with

Bar Charts
The colours and depths of the bars forming the chart are easily adjusted in the program by changing the values of the control variables

predictably disastrous consequences for its surroundings.

As these development stages are completed, so familiarity and satisfaction combine to convince the programmer that the program works now, will always work and will never need changing, and anyway the code is a model of clarity. But programmers, not programs, need documentation. No program is self-explanatory, and there are always reasons for wanting to change working programs. Like any other mechanism, they need *maintenance*, and maintenance means manuals. Programs should be internally documented (using REM lines) for the programmer's benefit, and externally documented with accompanying literature for the sake of the user — even if the user is the programmer.

All of these lessons once had to be learned by mainframe programmers, and have been ignored and painfully rediscovered by microcomputer programmers. Taken together they comprise a programming 'structure', a unified approach to problem-solving far more comprehensive than a book of cautionary tales about avoiding GOTOs or embracing WHILE...WEND. Efficient programs are written by efficient programmers on a basis of structured experience and logical thinking. This chapter aims to encourage both.

```
399 REM************************
400 REM*   3-D BAR CHARTS      *
401 REM************************
500 GOSUB 1500:        REM INITIALISE
720 YY=22:XX=2:        REM ORIGIN COORDS
760 GOSUB 3200:        REM DRAW AXES
800 FOR E=LT-1 TO 0 STEP -1
820 OC=XX+E*DB:OL=YY-E*DB
840 GOSUB 2200:        REM INPUT DATA
900 FOR D=1 TO NN
920 HT=DT(D)
940 X0=OC+(D-1)*(BB+LT*DB):Y0=OL-HT-DB
960 GOSUB 4000:        REM PRINT BAR
980 NEXT D
1000 NEXT E
1100 XP=10:YP=23:GOSUB 3500
1120 PRINT"THREE-DIMENSIONAL HISTOGRAM"
1200 A$=INKEY$:IF A$="" THEN GOTO 1200
1400 END
1499 REM************************
1500 REM*   INITIALISE   S/R      *
1501 REM************************
1520 CL$=CHR$(147):  REM CLEAR SCREEN
1540 PRINT CL$
1560 PO$=CHR$(19):    REM HOME CRSR
1580 RT$=CHR$(13):    REM <RETURN>
1600 BB=2:DB=1:       REM BAR DIMENSIONS
1620 SW=40:SD=25:     REM SCREEN DIM'S
1640 HB=SD-DB:        REM MAX BAR HEIGHT
1660 DIM B$(HB+DB)
1680 FOR K=1 TO SD:PO$=PO$+RT$:NEXT K
1800 DIM DT(SW)
1900 GOSUB 2400:      REM BUILD BAR
2100 LT=4:            REM DEPTH FACTOR
2190 RETURN
2199 REM************************
2200 REM* INPUT DATA ARRAY S/R  *
2201 REM************************
2220 READ NN
2240 FOR Z=1 TO NN:READ DT(Z):NEXT Z
2310 DATA 6,12,10,4,7,8,10
2320 DATA 5,7 ,8 ,8,6,7
2330 DATA 6,7 ,4 ,8,5,3,9
2340 DATA 5,11,6 ,4,11,6
2390 RETURN
2399 REM************************
2400 REM* BUILD WHOLE BAR S/R   *
2401 REM************************
2500 TC$=CHR$(158):   REM SIDES=YELLOW
2520 FC$=CHR$(31):    REM FRONT=BLUE
2540 RV$=CHR$(18):    REM REVERSE ON
2560 NL$=CHR$(146):   REM REVERSE OFF
2580 CR$=CHR$(29):    REM CURSOR RIGHT
2600 CH$=CHR$(32):    REM SPACE CHAR.
2620 C1$=CHR$(169):   REM "▼"  CHAR.
2640 C2$=RV$+C1$:     REM "◢"  CHAR.
2680 FOR K=1 TO SW
2700 SP$=SP$+CH$
2720 RC$=RC$+CR$
2740 FF$=FF$+CH$
2760 NEXT K
2800 TL$=SP$+"/"
```

Structure
Modular, and reasonably self-explanatory

Documentation
This routine is obviously crucial, but is entirely unexplained

Variable Names
Well commented, but not very meaningful

Completeness/Correctness
Does this work for all values? Does it produce the right output in all cases — when a value is less than zero, for example?

Error Trapping
No checksum, no scaling, nor error handling

Documentation
Good: no 'magic numbers', no mysterious control characters, everything translatable

```
2820 BL$=SP$+NL$+C1$
2840 FL$=LEFT$(FF$,BB)
2900 L$=TC$+C2$+RV$+RIGHT$(TL$,BB)
2920 FOR K=1 TO DB
2940 B$(K)=LEFT$(RC$,DB-K)+L$+LEFT$(SP$,K-1)
2960 NEXT K
3000 L$=FC$+RV$+FL$+TC$+RIGHT$(TL$,DB)
3020 FOR K=DB+1 TO HB
3040 B$(K)=L$
3060 NEXT K
3100 L$=FC$+RV$+FL$+TC$
3120 FOR K=1 TO DB
3140 B$(HB+K)=L$+RIGHT$(BL$,DB+2-K)
3160 NEXT K
3190 RETURN
3199 REM************************
3200 REM*    DRAW    AXES    S/R  *
3201 REM************************
3300 PRINT TC$:         REM SET COLOUR
3320 FOR Y=2 TO YY-1
3340 XP=XX-1:YP=Y:GOSUB 3500:PRINT"!"
3360 XP=XX+YY-Y:GOSUB 3500:PRINT"/"
3380 NEXT Y
3400 YP=YY
3420 FOR X=XX-1 TO SW-1
3440 XP=X:GOSUB 3500:PRINT"-"
3460 NEXT X
3490 RETURN
3499 REM************************
3500 REM* PUT CRSR  @ XP,YP S/R  *
3501 REM************************
3600 PRINT LEFT$(PO$,YP)TAB(XP-1);
3620 RETURN
3999 REM************************
4000 REM* PRINT PARTIAL BAR S/R  *
4001 REM************************
4100 FOR V=1 TO HT
4120 XP=X0:YP=Y0+V-1
4140 GOSUB 3500:        REM PLACE CRSR.
4160 PRINT B$(V)
4180 NEXT V
4200 FOR V=1 TO DB
4220 XP=X0:YP=Y0+HT+V-1:GOSUB 3500
4240 PRINT B$(HB+V)
4260 NEXT V
4490 RETURN
READY.
```

Curate's Egg

This program to display three-dimensional bar charts is an annoying mixture of good and bad style: the internal documentation is good where it exists and the structure is modular, but the program is not self-explanatory, there is no error-trapping, and no user documentation

Basic Flavours

This program is written in Microsoft BASIC, and should run unchanged on micros with a 40×25 screen display. The screen dimensions are initialised in line 1620. The control character values initialised in subroutines 1500 and 2400 are for the Commodore 64; consult the ASCII chart in your manual for other machines

STYLE COUNSEL

Documenting a program involves much more than adding comments to it or writing user instructions. A well-documented program has sufficient information to indicate what it is meant to be doing, and how it is meant to be doing it. We show how a simple program, in BASIC and PASCAL, can be given suitable documentation.

Consider Listing 1 of our program, on page 46. It is clearly a great mystery; what it does is anyone's guess. Apart from saying that it 'inputs two numbers, multiplies them with two other numbers, adds the two results together and prints the answer', there is very little evidence of the precise task that the code performs. Now look at the second version of the program (Listing 2). All is revealed. Yet no comments have been added, no program titles or REMark lines inserted and no external documents have been produced.

It is worth taking a detailed look at the differences between these two versions. First of all, the meaningless numbers of the first listing have been replaced by names (AYEAR and AMONTH). Numbers whose values do not change while the program is running are called *constants*. Some languages, such as PASCAL, have a special notation for constants (in Listing 2, the two constants are defined separately from the variables), while other languages, like BASIC, do not. (Lines 10 and 20 of the BASIC program use variables to define the constants.) Giving names to constants is really only worthwhile if they are going to be used frequently, otherwise comments in the program would serve the purpose just as well.

The second crucial difference is that all the confusing variable names have been given longer, intelligible names. The ones that we chose here (NYEARS to replace A, ageinsecs instead of e, and so on) were picked because they are each less than 10 characters long, and the first two characters distinguish them from each other. The reason for this last requirement is explained shortly.

Generally, it is good practice to give your variables names that are related to the role they play in the program. For example, you could call a loop counter LOOP (instead of the usual J or I), and the first and last values of the counter could be put into constants or variables with appropriate names. Thus, a loop reading like this:

```
FOR J = 1 TO 10 ... NEXT J
```

could look like this:

```
FOR LOOP = FIRST TO TENTH ... NEXT LOOP
```

Long variable names do, of course, take longer to type in and use up more memory, but they do have

the advantage of making programs easier to understand and speed up the debugging process. If your language uses only the first two characters of a name to distinguish between them, make sure that the names you choose differ in the first two characters. Thus, two long variable names (say CODENO and COMP) may look different to the programmer, but be indistinguishable to the computer.

Another major difference between the listings is that the second uses long and meaningful prompts for its input and adds a sensible explanation to its output (the PRINT lines in BASIC, the write lines in PASCAL). This achieves two very important things. The first is that it makes the program more readable. Even if the variables were single letters, the program would still make a lot more sense than previously. The second, and more important, benefit is that it makes the program accessible, even to someone who has never seen it before.

PROGRAM LAYOUT

PASCAL users will already be aware of the advantages of laying out a program neatly on the screen. Very simple features — like indenting lines, leaving blank lines and using a mixture of upper and lower case — can turn an impenetrable mass of symbols into a tidy and legible piece of logic. Formatting a program for the screen or the printer really comes into its own when your programs use loop constructs (FOR...NEXT, WHILE...WEND, REPEAT...UNTIL) and especially when loops are nested inside other loops.

Having said this, it is a lamentable fact that most BASICS give very little option about how you lay out the program. In this respect, the compiled languages like PASCAL are far more flexible in that they are usually written with a text editor (or word processor). On the other hand, editing a BASIC program is generally a rather crude affair (unless, like Microsoft's MBASIC, your interpreter will take an ASCII version of the program and 'tokenise' it to turn it into a runnable program). Worse still, many BASICS will take the programs you write and reformat them to remove indentation! Some, on the other hand, will add indentation for you. The BBC Micro is quite good at this, but you have to remember to give it the LISTO command. Most PASCAL systems will include a formatter and they are generally very useful. However, for the sake of your own clarity of thought, it is a good idea to devise some formatting conventions, within the limits of your language.

Comments are, of course, the main way of documenting your programs within the programs themselves. Again conventions vary from language to language. BASIC uses the REM statement. The word REM must appear at the front of your comment and then the interpreter will ignore everything it finds up to the next end-of-statement marker (: or (cr)). In other languages (PASCAL, PL/1, PROLOG, etc.) comments are bracketed by /* and */ (sometimes { and }), and anything between the marks is ignored by the compiler. An advantage of this system is that comments can run over more than one line. The disadvantage is that, if you forget the second */, the rest of your program is taken to be a comment and will be ignored!

Use comments wherever you feel some explanation may be needed: when you are defining constants, initialising variables, beginning a program, beginning a new procedure (subroutine), defining a function, or writing some code that isn't readily understood because of its complexity. Comments need not be long or wordy, and often just a reminder is needed. When you are trying to understand the logic of last year's adventure program, large blocks of general comment that break up the code and do not give enough detail can be more of a hindrance than a help, so keep comments short and to the point. Put them before tricky sections of code, and only put them inside the code when their presence is not likely to interfere with reading the logical structure of the program. Our final program (Listing 3) shows some examples as guidelines.

External documentation, in the form of handbooks and written specifications, is the hardest and most tedious to produce. For programmers, studies have shown that written documentation is usually only consulted as a last resort. However, when it is used, it can save a lot of effort. If your program is not too long and is well documented internally, it is unlikely that you will ever find a need for external *program* documentation. *User* documentation is another matter and will be discussed later in the series. Nonetheless, it is often useful to have some written documentation to hand when it comes to revising an old program or to debugging a new one. One of the ways in which the so-called 'fifth generation' languages aim to improve programmer productivity is by generating the documentation automatically. This will be achieved by using information from the design phase of a program's development. Not surprisingly, one of the best ways to document your own programs is to use this same trick.

Keep a file on your programs as you write them. Put into it all the notes you make as you design the program, including drafts of algorithms and flowcharts. Most importantly, keep the final version of the flowchart you have used to write the code from. If you have a printer, keep a listing of the finished program. Note that, in our completed version of the program, the first comment includes the program name and a date. Whenever you modify a program, change the date on it so that you know that it is the latest version.

Properly Documented

Listing 1

BASIC

```
(a)  10 INPUT A,B
     20 C=A*31536000
     30 D=B*2592000
     40 E=C+D
     50 PRINT E
```

PASCAL

```
(b)  program abcde (input,output);
     var a,b,c,d,e:integer;
     begin
     read(a,b);
     c:=a*31536000;
     d:=b*2592000;
     e:=c+d;
     writeln(e);
     end.
```

Listing 2

BASIC

```
(a)  10 AYEAR=31536000
     20 AMONTH=2592000
     30 PRINT"Enter your age (years then months separated by a comma) ";
     40 INPUT NYEARS,NMONTHS
     50 YSECS=NYEARS*AYEAR
     60 MSECS=NMONTHS*AMONTH
     70 AGEINSECS=YSECS+MSECS
     80 PRINT"Your age in seconds is (approximately) ";AGEINSECS
```

PASCAL

```
(b)  program ageinseconds (input,output);
     const
        ayear=31536000;
        amonth=2592000;
     var
        nyears,nmonths,ysecs,msecs,ageinsecs:integer;
     begin
        write('Enter your age (years then months separated by a comma) ');
        read(nyears,nmonths);
        ysecs:=nyears*ayear;
        msecs:=nmonths*amonth;
        ageinsecs:=ysecs+msecs;
        writeln('Your age in seconds is (approximately) ',ageinsecs);
     end.
```

Listing 3

BASIC

```
(a)  10 REM "AGEINSECONDS"  June 1984
     20 REM INPUTs age in years and months (y,m) and
     30 REM uses an approximate conversion (month = 30 days)
     40 REM to give age in seconds.
     50 REM
     60 AYEAR=31536000:REM          seconds in 365 days
     70 AMONTH=2592000:REM          seconds in 30 days
     80 PRINT"Enter your age (years then months separated by a comma) ";
     90 INPUT NYEARS,NMONTHS
    100 REM age in secs is (age in years * secs in year) plus
                    (months since last birthday * secs in month)
    110 YSECS=NYEARS*AYEAR
    120 MSECS=NMONTHS*AMONTH
    130 AGEINSECS=YSECS+MSECS
    140 PRINT"Your age in seconds is (approximately) ";AGEINSECS
```

PASCAL

```
(b)  program ageinseconds (input,output);
     /*   June 1984
          reads age in years and months (y,m) and uses an
          approximate conversion (month = 30 days) to give
          age in seconds.                                  */
     const
        ayear=31536000;      /* seconds in 365 days */
        amonth=2592000;      /* seconds in 30 days  */
     var
        nyears,nmonths,ysecs,msecs,ageinsecs:integer;
     begin
        write('Enter your age (years then months separated by a comma) ');
        read(nyears,nmonths);
        /* age in secs is (age in years * secs in year) plus
           (months since last birthday * secs in month)     */
        ysecs:=nyears*ayear;
        msecs:=nmonths*amonth;
        ageinsecs:=ysecs+msecs;
        writeln('Your age in seconds is (approximately) ',ageinsecs);
     end.
```

PLAN OF ACTION

Our examination of programming techniques has so far concentrated on documentation, and the need to make each section of a program clear and understandable. Here we look at the wider implications of program design and consider the questions that should be asked before any code is written.

Program design is seen by those involved — the designer/programmer and the user — as a grand and formal exercise in applied problem-solving. Unfortunately, the problems to be solved are always assumed to be of the technical programming kind — how to format the screen, how to make this loop faster, where to fit everything into RAM, and so on — whereas the real problems are present from the start of the project, and are usually created at the first meeting of the user and the 'expert'. Users are rarely very clear about the true nature of their problems — they hope the expert will tell them what the problem is and how to solve it — and experts very often think they know the problem and the solution before the user even begins to state it. The result is bad initial communication, leading to an incomplete description of the problem and the user's requirements. Working from this specification is bound to produce an unsatisfactory system that the user may be pressurised into accepting.

For home computing projects the programmer is usually also the designer (or 'systems analyst') and the consumer. This should mean that communication problems are lessened considerably. Nonetheless, as a combined user/designer, you should always make the effort to explain problems, solutions and requirements to yourself as clearly as if you were talking to another person.

Let's consider an imaginary user and his problem: he's a keen aircraft modeller who also owns a cassette-based microcomputer. He wants to store fairly detailed descriptions of materials used in the construction of each model that he makes so that when working on later models he can search his records for previous use of this kind of glue, or that type of joint. What the designer must therefore get from the user is a clear statement of the following:

■ The program function. This can start off as a vague statement of intent such as 'It should store my model records', but it must be refined by the designer's persuasion and interrogation into something more like a requirement specification,

such as 'It should store my descriptions of the model and its construction and materials, as typed in at the keyboard, and display them when I type in the model's name, or some aspect of its construction.' This states the user's needs rather more clearly, and points to some of the specific programming tasks involved (storing, searching, indexing, retrieving, etc.).

■ How the program will be used. Some of the physical details of typical usage may be clear from the function description, but these may not be complete. For example, the user may not want the model details displayed on the screen because he works in a shed without a television set. In this case, a 'hard copy' print-out of selected details may be required.

■ What it will look like — input and output formats. The professional programmer will often use pre-printed charts representing the screen to draw each display that the user will see during input/output phases. Such elaborations are not often necessary for home use, although high resolution graphics may be an exception to this. Screen formats are a very important aspect of the *user interface* — the interactions between user and machine — and deserve the sort of close attention and discussion that is sometimes given to more obviously ergonomic aspects of computing, such as the positioning of keyboards and monitors, height of the table, and levels of illumination, etc.

■ How it should be organised — file and program formats. The user may feel that he needs to store at least 100 aircraft descriptions, and anything less will be useless. On the other hand, he may only ever build half a dozen more or less standard models. The size of a program's data files has serious implications for their format and access methods. A serial scan through six model descriptions on cassette taking, say, five minutes may be quite acceptable to the user, whereas waiting for 100 to be searched would be out of the question. A solution might be to put the program and description index file on one tape, and the descriptions themselves on 20 other tapes classified by aircraft type, for example.

The size of the program itself can also become a problem: if the text input section requires a complex text editor, if the program is fat with menus and heavy with significant messages, if the file-handling sections employ complicated searching and indexing routines, then the program may have to be split into several separate programs in order to fit into the available RAM.

■ What it should do — special procedures and calculations. In the model aircraft example, these

Describe, Define, Design
If the typical software development team of user, designer and programmer had set out to solve the problem of moving heavy loads around gardens, this is what they might have produced. Bad communication — between expert and non-expert, and amongst experts — is still a major problem facing all design teams

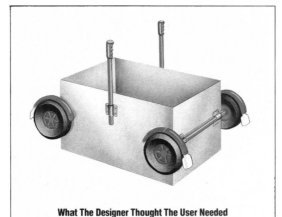

What The Designer Thought The User Needed

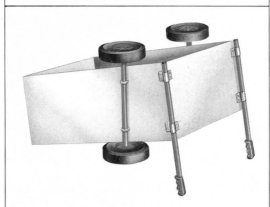

What The Programmer Thought The Designer Meant

What They Finally Sold To The User

What The User Really Wanted

STEVE CROSS

are unlikely to arise but they often do so when other problems are considered. There may be 20 perfectly good and equivalent ways of going through a particular process but the user may well insist on one and only one of these.

Getting this wrong makes the user immediately dissatisfied with the program. The designer may be tempted away from the user's preferred method by the greater efficiency of other methods, but any advantage is quickly lost if the user won't use the program! Discovering the user's procedures can be very helpful when it comes to designing calculations. Why invent a formula for calculating wing-loadings, for example, if you can simply ask the model maker how he does it?

With all this information noted down, the job of translating the specification into a program can begin. A useful approach to take is to design the user-program dialogue first, then the data files and then the processes that control it all. The word 'dialogue' is taken to mean the two-way communication of information that goes on between the user and the program. This does not simply consist of the input of model aircraft details and their subsequent display but also includes every prompt, message and menu that the program produces and every input, command or selection that the user enters. It is also important to fix the style of dialogue at this stage. For the aircraft program a choice between menu and command-driven interactions might be appropriate. The decisions taken here will have a considerable effect on the structure of the overall program. The contents and format of the dialogue must be considered in detail, but the reward for this effort is that all the data manipulated by the program should now be specified. This means that the storage space required for error messages and prompts can be calculated and, most importantly, the files can now be designed.

For the model aircraft program, where files will contain large blocks of text and will be very lengthy, splitting the file up onto several tapes so that each can be searched more quickly may be the best solution. If it warrants the effort, the data may be compressed by a coding algorithm before it is written to tape, and then decoded on reading.

By this time, the necessary functions will be apparent. There will be routines to allow the data text to be added and edited, to file the newly input text (these should update any indexes used by the system), to accept component names, to search for and display descriptions, etc. All these must be presented as options to the user, and they must all be able to deal with invalid data.

At this stage it is advisable for the user to make a careful check on the design to ensure that it performs as it should. If all is well, the program can now be coded. Of course, this is easier said than done, and the act of turning the design into an efficient working program may well reveal further problems.

PRIMITIVE PARTS

An algorithm is a series of instructions that describe how some process may be performed. A knitting pattern is an algorithm; so is a recipe; and so is a computer program. We discuss how an understanding of the principles of algorithms can improve your programming.

An algorithm describes a process either in terms of other processes that have already been defined, or in terms of processes that are so basic that they do not need to be defined. Thus, in a recipe, one instruction may be 'prepare a bechamel sauce', where a bechamel sauce recipe (algorithm) has been given elsewhere in the cookbook. Another instruction may be 'bring the mixture to the boil', where the operation of bringing something to the boil is assumed to be fully understood by the user. In programming terms, algorithms are constructed from instructions that either use algorithms (procedures, routines, functions) written elsewhere in the program, or ones built into the language (commands such as PRINT and DIM, or maths functions like LOG and TAN).

Here we take a look at how algorithms are constructed from other algorithms and *primitive* processes. The primitives at the disposal of a programmer are the commands and functions in the language. From these, algorithms are written that can do small things (move a sprite, say, or accept a number as an input). These algorithms are then used to build more general algorithms (updating the game display, or controlling a menu system), and these algorithms are in turn used as parts of larger ones again until the whole program, viewed as a single algorithm, is written in terms of lower-level algorithms. This concept is the basis of what is known as *structured* or *modular* programming and is a subject we will return to later in the course.

DESIGNING ALGORITHMS

An algorithm has an input and an output. This is just to say that, as a process, the algorithm will work on some initial data to produce a result. This initial data is passed to the algorithm from outside in the guise of 'parameters', which remain constant for any particular use of the algorithm but may change between different uses. Passing parameters will be familiar to even a novice programmer since the simple program:

```
10 PRINT "Hello World!"
```

passes the parameter 'Hello World!' to the algorithm called by the PRINT command. Similar examples are FNA(P), TAN(P), LEFT$(P$,5) and POKE P,5, where P, P$ and 5 are all parameters. In the same way, an algorithm's results are passed back as parameters. If the programming language being used has local variables (e.g. PASCAL and C) then the parameters would normally be passed with a procedure call, as in:

```
procedure(parameter1,parameter2,etc.);
```

It is an essential first step in designing an algorithm to consider the contents of the input and output parameters, their types (integer, floating point, real, string, etc.) and their magnitudes and ranges.

When the input and output of the algorithm have been defined, the next step is to form ideas as to how one can be transformed into the other. Unfortunately, there is no 'cookbook' method for creating these transformations as they require creativity and ingenuity. However, there are several ways of helping the process along.

The most obvious and most often overlooked is to borrow the algorithm from somewhere else. At the simplest level, the in-built functions of a programming language provide many useful algorithms, such as string-handling, trigonometric functions, input/output, and (possibly) sorting and matrix manipulation. Apart from this, the algorithm needed may already exist in another of your programs. The code for this could be incorporated in the new program (creating your own library of algorithms is extremely useful). In addition, there are published collections of algorithms that are often available from public libraries. *The Art of Computer Programming, Vol I: Fundamental Algorithms* by D. E. Knuth, although heavy going, is highly recommended.

Programs published in the computer magazines are well worth scrutinising for routines that may be of use. Finally, there are algorithms that are used in other pertinent domains, and although they were never meant for computing they are extremely useful. The accountancy section of the local library will be full of books containing formulae for calculating balances and depreciation. A little research among these could make writing an accounts program a lot easier and the result is likely to be a lot more reliable. The same is true for other disciplines: engineering, electronics, maths, etc.

Whether adapting an existing algorithm, or creating one from scratch, there are certain criteria that must be applied to each instruction it contains. These are *definiteness* and *effectiveness*. Definiteness means that the instruction should not be ambiguous in any way. Ambiguity is easy to introduce at an early stage when the algorithm is being written down in English. Words like 'and' and 'or' in English are very different from the AND and OR of Boolean logic. For example, if the algorithm was meant to select all the names in a list that begin with an 'A' *and* all those beginning with 'B', you could easily write code like:

IF FIRSTLETTER="A" AND FIRSTLETTER="B" THEN

which is wrong because a logical OR is needed!

The criterion of effectiveness is a demand that the program should not contain impossible instructions. An instruction is said to be effective if it can be done with a pencil and paper in a finite time. This means that instructions like 'let X equal the highest prime number' are not effective (there isn't a highest prime number).

GENERAL CONSIDERATIONS

There are also criteria to judge the algorithm as a whole. An algorithm must *terminate*. The algorithm that follows does not terminate (even though its instructions are definite and effective) and if this was coded into a program it would endlessly loop:

step 1 let I equal 1
step 2 if I > 3 then exit
step 3 goto step 1

Telling whether an algorithm will terminate is not always easy, but, in general, algorithms that involve loops test for a particular condition before they terminate (e.g. if I > 3 in our example), and it is necessary to check that it is possible to meet that condition.

Efficiency, generality and *elegance* are ways of judging between different algorithms. Efficiency is usually judged in terms of time and memory use. The two are usually quite compatible — fast code may need relatively little space, but bear in mind that this need not be so. Having found an algorithm, it can be 'tuned' for efficiency by changing its details. A calculation will be noticeably faster and will use less memory if, for example, integer rather than floating point arithmetic is used. Alternatively, a completely different algorithm for doing the same thing could be found.

Generality is the ability of an algorithm to cope with many different situations apart from the one for which it was designed. It is worth while, in the long run, to attempt to make all algorithms as general as possible. If a program called for a yes/no response several times, it would be worth writing a routine that prompts the user with 'please type y or n', accepts the input, checks whether it is 'y' or 'n', reprompts if it is neither and otherwise returns the appropriate response. However, the routine could be made more general if it could be fed with different prompts and potential replies, so it could be used in many different situations. Elegance means finding algorithms that are both simple and ingenious. In all cases it is more sensible to find efficient, general algorithms rather than elegant ones.

Another important aspect of algorithms is the flow of control and of data within them and how this can be represented with flow charts. This is the subject of the next instalment in this series.

Pyramids And Primitives
The block-structure diagram on the left clearly shows the nesting of a program's algorithms, while the procedure flow diagram on the right emphasises the articulations and process levels of the same program. The most 'primitive' algorithms are the most deeply nested, and the lowest in the hierarchy

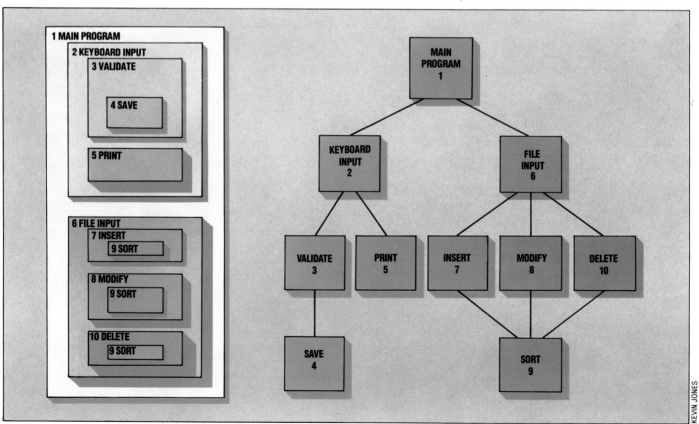

KEVIN JONES

LOOP LINES

Flowcharts are an important technique in program design, but the commonplace notation is not always sufficiently precise, especially when dealing with loop structures. We consider various ways of classifying loops, and introduce a new flowchart symbol — the iteration box.

Iteration, or looping, is one of the essential structures of any programming language. Earlier in the course, we said that a loop was used in an algorithm whenever a decision switched the flow of control onto a path that brought it back, eventually, to the same initial decision. This adequately describes the structure: the repeated performance of a body of code. However, it doesn't define it in all its many forms. Since loops are such an essential primitive structure, comprising probably 60 per cent of all processor activity, it is extremely useful to look at them in more detail. We will pay particular attention to their effect on general program/algorithm structure, and to the various ways in which they are constructed and classified.

Loops are often divided into two classes, depending on their similarity to the two high-level language loop structures, REPEAT...UNTIL and WHILE...ENDWHILE; both types are used in PASCAL, and the REPEAT loop is implemented in BBC and Oric BASIC. The two types differ in their positioning of the loop exit test: in a REPEAT loop the test comes at the end of the loop body, whereas in a WHILE loop it comes at the start. This means that the body of a REPEAT loop, once entered, will always be executed at least once, whereas that of a WHILE loop need not be. This first difference can be seen quite clearly in the flowchart diagram.

Another way of classifying loops is according to whether the variable that acts as the loop counter is used in the loop exit test, or whether some other test condition controls the loop exit. This is less clearly seen in a flowchart of the conventional linear kind. In fact, the kind of 'commonsense' flowchart that we have become familiar with portrays loops in an unhelpful way. In these flowcharts, a loop looks exactly the same as a simple branch, and it is often necessary to examine the algorithm in detail to distinguish between them.

A clearer notation, called the 'iteration box', exists, which clearly marks the start of a loop, and eliminates the loop/branch confusion. It consists of three linked boxes: the first box shows the initialisation of the counter, the second shows the incrementing of the counter, and the third contains

the loop exit test. REPEAT and WHILE loops can both be shown in this form, but differ in the flow of control through the boxes, while the test box indicates whether the loop is counter-controlled or not. These points can be clearly seen in the diagram.

In a REPEAT loop the flow of control is 'initialise-body-test-body-test', whereas a WHILE loop goes 'initialise-test-body-test-body'. This can be seen in the way that the control lines leave and re-enter the iteration box, with the body of the loop 'dangling' from them.

Loop Classification

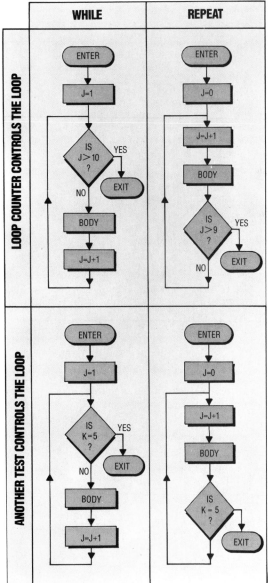

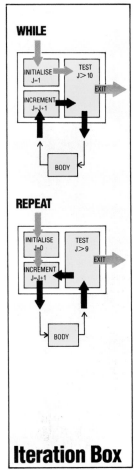

Iteration Box

DECISIVE MOVES

We continue our look at how to improve our use of flowcharts in the planning stages of program development. Here, we show you how compound decisions can be broken down into simple components, and look at the use of 'decision tables' in the more complex cases.

Programmers often want to use compound decisions in their programs such as:

IF AGE > 12 AND AGE < 20 THEN STATUS= "TEENAGER"

Algorithms with instructions like this are easier to understand if the compound decision is broken down into its component decisions.

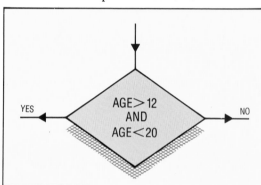

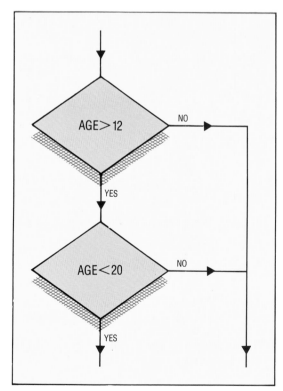

We have represented our BASIC example in diagrammatic form to show how the compound version is less satisfactory than the simple version. Our second example (below), consisting of three component decisions, makes the flow of logic through the decision boxes far more intelligible than its compound counterpart. It also makes clear a similarity with the rules of Boolean logic, which enable the construction of complex circuits out of a combination of simple logic gates.

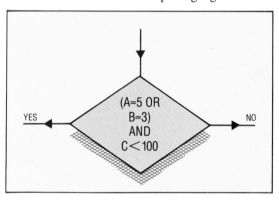

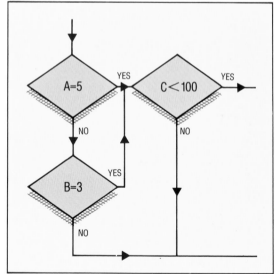

In the examples we have used, all the decisions have been binary ones, yet it is quite common for an algorithm to involve decisions with more than two possible outcomes. If we are reading an input from the keyboard that represents a selection from a menu, we would then want to branch to one of a number of different subroutines to take the requested action. To do this, most programming languages provide multiple branching constructs such as CASE..OF..in PASCAL and ON...GOTO and ON...GOSUB in BASIC. The rules for binary decisions also apply to multiple decisions: only one route may be taken out of the decision box and all exits must be well labelled, with all possible routes being mutually exclusive and covering all possibilities. A multiple decision may be drawn, as in our example, with a set of exit paths leading from the same decision box. However, it is rare to see this and, more often, the decision will be broken down into binary decisions, as shown.

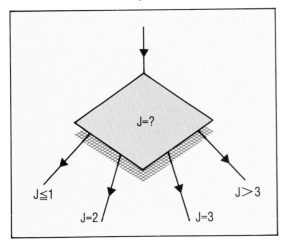

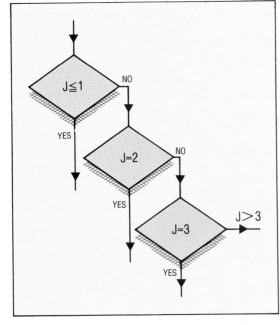

All multiple decisions can be represented as a set of binary decisions in this way.

THE DECISION TABLE

As an alternative to flowcharts, especially where there may be many multiple decisions, we can recommend the use of decision tables. We give an example of such a table, which represents a set of rules for making decisions. The table has four main sections: text describing the conditions for the rules, text describing the actions to be taken, a grid showing how the conditions fit into the rules, and a grid showing which actions are appropriate to each rule. In the 'conditions/rules' grid, values of variables appear in the cells, while in the 'actions/rules' grid below it, a tick indicates what action should be performed and a value acts as an input parameter for that action. Rule 4, for

CONDITIONS		RULES							
		1	2	3	4	5	6	7	8
FIRE BUTTON PRESSED		✓	✗	✗	✓	✓	✗	✓	✗
GAME LEVEL		1	1	2	2	1	1	2	2
PLAYER LEVEL		NOVICE	NOVICE	NOVICE	NOVICE	EXPERT	EXPERT	EXPERT	EXPERT
ACTIONS									
ALIEN EVASIVE ACTION						✓	✓	✓	✓
RANDOM BLASTER SHIELDS				✓	✓			✓	✓
REDUCE ENERGY LEVEL BY		1%	1%	2%	2%	2%	2%	4%	4%

example, reads as: 'If the fire button is pressed and the game level is 2 and the player level is novice, then activate random blaster shields and reduce energy level by two per cent.'

Decision tables also serve to combine simple decisions into compound decisions and, in simpler forms than the one given here, are exactly equivalent to the truth tables used for predicting the output of logic gates.

One final point about the use of flowcharts. Wherever possible, restrict your flowcharts to one page. It can be irritating and time consuming leafing through many pages of paper. If your algorithm becomes too large, try and break it down into smaller algorithms. Remember that each algorithm can be used as a single instruction in some other algorithm. In this way, each routine in a program could be written as a single process box in a flowchart of the whole program, even if that routine uses other routines that in turn use others, and so on.

Inevitably something will go wrong now and then and a need will arise for a flowchart to continue beyond one page. If this happens, divide the flowchart at a suitable point (a decision, say) and use a circle with an identifying symbol inside it to point to the place where the flow of control continues on the next page (represented by another circle with the same symbol inside it, as shown below). If control returns to the main program, use the circles again to point back. Another solution is to view the missing portion as a separate algorithm, refer to it in a process box and represent it with its own separate flowchart.

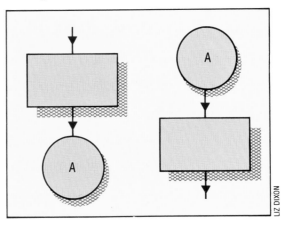

PIECES OF THE PUZZLE

The most efficient way to create programs in any language is to use 'modular structuring'. Some languages, such as PASCAL, encourage this approach, while BASIC users need to discipline themselves to adopt the technique. We show you how your programming will be greatly enhanced using modules of code as your basic components.

A module is a piece of code that performs a particular function. The points of entry and exit, known as the module's 'interfaces', must be precisely defined, and the processes that occur between these interfaces should be entirely independent of the rest of the program. Once a module has been written, it can be treated as a 'black box'. Data may pass in and out of the module's interfaces, but what goes on inside can be left to itself.

Modules can be joined together to build up a program without the writer having to worry about how they perform their tasks. A stock of modules can be built up by a programmer to be used when needed, and programmers can pass modules on to be used in another writer's programs. But in order to take advantage of modular structured programming, we need to take careful note of the flow of control and the flow of data when we write the modules.

To ensure that all your modules behave in the same way with respect to the flow of control, a very simple rule should be followed: all modules should have a single entry point and a single exit. What this means in practice is that the flow of control within the module has to be carefully designed so that it starts at one place and, no matter how much it loops and branches, it reaches the same exit by all possible routes.

Modules correspond to the algorithms we have been looking at in previous instalments of the course. 'Structured' languages, such as PASCAL, allow the programmer to create subroutines that may be called by name, and which use their own variables. Such languages encourage a programmer to enter or leave a routine (called a 'procedure') by single entry and exit points.

In BASIC, using the GOSUB . . . RETURN combination, a subroutine can be called from the main program and, after the subroutine has been carried out, control will return to the line immediately after the GOSUB command. However, there is no restriction on which line the GOSUB sends control to. Two different GOSUBs may send control to different lines of a subroutine with a single RETURN, and the result might be completely different in each case. Similarly, there is no restriction on how many RETURN statements may be used in a subroutine.

This means that the BASIC programmer must be self-disciplined. You should start by making sure that all GOSUBs to the same subroutine point to the same line number, and that every subroutine has only one RETURN in it. It is best to get in the habit of marking the first line of each subroutine with a REM statement giving it a title, and use that line as the entry point. Make the RETURN the last line of the subroutine. This is not essential but it makes things much clearer.

THE GOTO RULE

Extra care should be taken with the GOTO command, which can play havoc with program structure. The rule here is: only use a GOTO to send control to a line *within* the same subroutine. This avoids the potential danger of skipping over a RETURN or passing control to the wrong RETURN. There are times when it is necessary to leave a routine without executing every line. In this case you should GOTO the line with RETURN on it, and there should be no problems.

Using GOTO within loops is even more dangerous. If control jumps out of a loop, BASIC cannot know this and assumes that the rest of the program is the body of that loop! The safety rule is: when in the body of a loop, never GOTO a line outside the body of that loop. If a loop needs to be terminated early, set the loop counter or test variable to the terminal value and GOTO the test line (the line with NEXT or WHILE in it). As with the RETURN statement, put NEXT or WHILE on a line of its own to make this easier. Keeping track of the structure of a program is a lot simpler if GOTOs are avoided as much as possible.

Branches are the most likely place for control to go astray, so try not to allow any decisions to send control out of a subroutine unless it is with a proper call to another subroutine. Remember that each subroutine has a single exit point, so make sure that it is possible to follow the flow of control through every branch to that point. Drawing a flow chart for the routine makes this easy to check. Setting a flag can often reduce the need for GOTOs in routines involving loops and branches.

We can think of data passing in and out of modules, just as we did for algorithms (see page 49). So that modules can be used independently of each other, you must design them so that the only influence they have on each other is through the data that passes between them. The main program passes data to a module and, when the module has been executed, any result that has been generated

is passed back.

Data moves around programs inside variables and the freedom of movement of a variable is called its 'scope'. Many programming languages can restrict the scope of a variable to particular subroutines. In PASCAL, the variables used in a particular subroutine (procedure) must be 'declared' for that procedure. Variables declared for the main program are *global* and may be used anywhere in the program (including within any of its modules). Variables declared within a particular procedure, however, are *local* to that procedure and can only be used there.

Local variables can have the same names as global ones and using one does not affect the value of the other. Using a language that supports local variables allows us to write subroutines without having to worry about how the variables used in the routine might affect variables in other routines. Unfortunately, very few versions of the BASIC language support local variables, which means that if we wish to write independent

subroutines we must somehow simulate the effect of having local variables.

The simplest way to do this is to adopt naming conventions that distinguish variables that do different jobs. Some conventions already exist and are widely used by programmers. Using I, J and K as loop counters and index values is very common, a practice that has been adopted from mathematics.

Having described a program with a flowchart, it is a simple matter to number the subroutines involved, or to give them some other kind of code. Any global variables that need to be made local to a particular subroutine can then be suffixed by this code to make them unique. Thus, routine number 5 may use the local variables SUM5 and TOTAL5 to distinguish them from SUM12 and TOTAL12 in routine number 12. Be careful though that the BASIC you are using doesn't look only at the first two characters! Variables that are used to pass values between subroutines and those used only in the main program need not be coded.

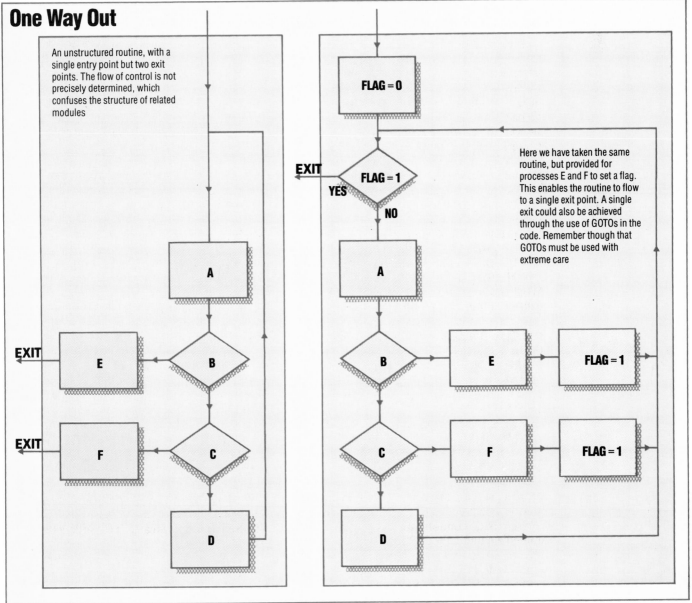

One Way Out

An unstructured routine, with a single entry point but two exit points. The flow of control is not precisely determined, which confuses the structure of related modules

Here we have taken the same routine, but provided for processes E and F to set a flag. This enables the routine to flow to a single exit point. A single exit could also be achieved through the use of GOTOs in the code. Remember though that GOTOs must be used with extreme care

LIZ DIXON

TOP SECRET

Our course on program design has so far shown how programs may be constructed from small, largely independent units called modules. We have looked in detail at how such building blocks are designed, and here we show you how to use them in the development of a complete program.

When building a program, it is a good idea to develop an overall structure, consisting of a base level of general-purpose routines that are used by other routines of increasing specialisation on higher levels, all under the direction of a single control module at the top. This 'pyramid' structure will allow us to use a design method called 'program refinement' or 'top-down design'.

Top-down design, as its name suggests, entails designing the topmost control program first. We describe its functions in terms of calls to 'lower' level routines and, for the time being, we need not worry too much about how these lower-level modules will work. Once this is done, we move down a level and describe the workings of each routine called by the top-level module. Each routine is described in terms of the routines it must call, and this process is repeated level by level until we reach the lowest level. At that stage, the functions performed by the routine we are describing are so simple that they may be defined by using the programming language itself.

As an example, let us look at the design of a 'Hangman' game. Instead of the player trying to guess a word selected by the program, as is the case with most computer versions of the game, we want the program to guess a word that we have chosen. One way of achieving this, without giving the program a long list of English words, is to enter data on the likelihood of particular letter sequences occurring.

```
100 REM Initialise variables and arrays


500 REM *****Control Routine***********
510 REM
520 GOSUB 1000:REM Title & Help screens
530 GOSUB 2000:REM Set up Board
540 GOSUB 4000:REM Find word length
from player
550 GOSUB 8000:REM Select data set and
load it
560 GOSUB 3000:REM Guess a letter
570 GOSUB 4500:REM Check guess with
player
580 GOSUB 5000:REM Update the board
590 IF GAME_NOT_OVER THEN 560: REM
guess again until game is over
600 IF WIN THEN GOSUB 10000 ELSE
GOSUB 11000:REM Give appropriate
```

```
ending for win or lose
610 GOSUB 6000:REM ask the player for
another game
620 IF ANOTHER THEN 530:REM if
another then start again
630 GOSUB 7000:REM say goodbye and stop
640 END
```

We know before we start that certain things must be done: variables need to be initialised, arrays must be dimensioned, the 'board' display has to be set up and updated as necessary, and routines must be written that keep the score, that make guesses, and that end the game.

Our first attempt at designing the control routine has a simple REM statement to indicate that variables and arrays must be initialised – we can fill in all the necessary details at a later stage. The control routine itself is simply a pair of loops. The outer loop (line 620) tests to see whether the user is signalling the end of a session, while the inner loop (line 590) tests to see if the game has ended.

Should we need to test the control routine, we must set up dummy subroutines to match the GOSUBs. Each GOSUB in the control routine should have a REM statement to explain its function and should start at a convenient line number – preferably one that is a round figure, such as 1000 or 5000. It is a good idea to ensure that routines with similar functions are given standardised line numbers; this will make life easier when routines are moved from one program to another. For example, game instructions might be contained in a subroutine that begins at line 1000, while a GOSUB 7000 program line will always end a game by calling a standard routine.

Our initial control routine is kept short and simple. It will fit onto the screen and therefore is easier to understand and debug than a program that extends over several screens. The three variables, GAME NOT OVER, WIN and ANOTHER, are all flags that are set in the various subroutines called by the control routine and are used here to determine whether the control program works in the way we intend. It should be quite easy to spot any errors in logic in this simple control routine.

At this stage it is necessary to look at the program's structure with a critical eye – we need to ensure that the program behaves as it should in all circumstances. We can also start to make improvements in the program design; for example, we might like to make the instructions available at any stage of the game and it might also be a good idea to keep a record of how many games the computer or player has won and a list of words that beat the program. Any or all of these changes can be made at this stage.

The next step is to specify each of the

subroutines called by the control program. Our listings show how two of these routines might look. The first (beginning at line 4000) simply prompts the user for a number between 1 and 20 (the word length). It uses a general-purpose subroutine that is assumed to exist at line 51000, which will take a string specified in PROMPT$, print it and then accept a number input by the user. If this number is not an integer that falls between the limits set by MIN% and MAX%, an error message will be given and the user will be asked to input a new number. This subroutine may easily be used in other programs, and a library of such general-purpose modules may be built up for use in later projects.

```
4000 REM Discover word length from
player
4010 REM
4020 PROMPT$="How many letters are
there in your word ?"
4030 MIN%=1
4040 MAX%=20
4050 GOSUB 51000:REM input an integer
between MIN% & MAX%
4060 WORDLEN%=RESP%:REM RESP% is used by
the subroutine at 51000 to pass back
the response
4070 RETURN

8000 REM select data set and load it
8010 REM
8020 IF WORDLEN%>7 THEN FILE_L%=8
              ELSE FILE_L%=WORDLEN%
8030 FILENO_L$=STR$(FILE_L%)
8040 FILENAME$="TABLE"+FILENO_L$
8050 GOSUB 9000:REM OPEN, READ & CLOSE
the file with the likelihood data for
the appropriate word length.
8060 RETURN
```

The other routine (beginning at line 8000) uses local variables (FILE L% and FILENO L$). We have assumed that the data needed to guess a letter is in eight sets of tables that give the likelihood of finding any particular letter next to any other. As we want only one set of data in RAM at any time, we must build up a string in FILENAME$ to hold the

name of the data file, and then call the subroutine at line 9000 to read the file.

In many cases, we will find that our program will move directly from one routine to another. However, we will usually want to create an extra routine that calls each of the other two in turn. This may seem like an unnecessary complication, but it allows us to keep a tight control over the program's 'flow' and it has the added bonus of keeping program modules separate so that they may be easily added to other programs.

This use of subroutines that are transportable from one program to another does involve extra work, and care must be taken when designing the routines so that they are suitable for use in a wide variety of circumstances. This may often be achieved simply by replacing constants with variables. It is important that all subroutines should be well documented. The documentation should specify the exact purposes of the routine, giving details of the variables used, the values expected as input and output, and any side-effects (moving the cursor position, changing the memory map, closing files, and so on).

A standard layout is also very helpful; you should make sure that all line numbers have a fixed interval, the titles and comments are restricted to a set number of lines at the beginning of the routine, and that RETURN is always on the last line. Be sure to note the first and last line number of each routine. When a library routine is required, make sure that the program has an appropriate gap in its line numbers and then MERGE the subroutine into the program. If your micro has no MERGE command, it may be possible to use a text editor to combine programs that have been SAVEd in ASCII format rather than the usual 'tokenised' form. If this is not possible, your library subroutines will need to be typed in each time they are used. However, the fact that they will not need to be redesigned should make the extra work worthwhile.

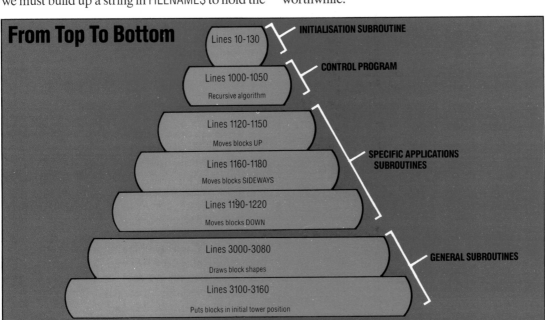

From Top To Bottom

INITIALISATION SUBROUTINE — Lines 10-130

CONTROL PROGRAM — Lines 1000-1050 Recursive algorithm

SPECIFIC APPLICATIONS SUBROUTINES —
Lines 1120-1150 Moves blocks UP
Lines 1160-1180 Moves blocks SIDEWAYS
Lines 1190-1220 Moves blocks DOWN

GENERAL SUBROUTINES —
Lines 3000-3080 Draws block shapes
Lines 3100-3160 Puts blocks in initial tower position

LIZ DIXON

Top-down Programming
This diagram illustrates the principle of top-down programming. For our example we have used a Towers of Hanoi game. This is a simple puzzle designed to illustrate the technique of recursion, in which different-sized blocks are moved between piles according to certain rules. The line numbers in the diagram refer to the BBC listing. Towers of Hanoi program that appears on page 475. The line numbers in the diagram refer to the BBC listing.

The first layer of the structure represents the initialisation program, which must be completed before the rest of the program can be executed. The CONTROL PROGRAM in our diagram represents the recursive algorithm, which performs the calculations and calls the other subroutines as necessary. The SPECIFIC APPLICATIONS SUBROUTINES (lines 1120 to 1220), are used to move the block shapes from pile to pile in the display. The final two sections of the diagram, GENERAL SUBROUTINES, represent the last two sections of the program that are used to format the initial display and create the design for the blocks.

FAULT LINES

The detection and correction of errors is an important aspect of program design. Problems may be caused by typing errors, but faulty logic or a misconception of the program's function can have more serious results. We examine potential trouble-spots — at the interfaces between subroutines and between the program and its user.

There are many potential sources of error at each stage of a program's creation, from its specification, through design and coding, to the testing. Errors are often introduced at the specification and design stages if little thought is given to the nature of the problem and insufficient care is taken to ensure that the program does exactly what it is supposed to do. We can reduce the chances of these mistakes occurring by following the structured design methods that were outlined earlier in this chapter. Further errors are likely to arise as the design is translated into code — poor typing can introduce bugs, as anyone who

has ever misspelt a variable name knows only too well! — and even testing and debugging can cause other mistakes when a correction to one fault itself leads to others.

But it is at the interfaces — between routines and between the program and its user — that most errors are to be found. Particular care should be taken to ensure that any values passed across these interfaces are of the correct data type and fall within the range required by the program. Values may be checked either within the routine that passes them or in the routine that accepts them; the process of checking values as they pass between routines is known as 'firewalling'.

To ensure that values output by a routine are in an appropriate range and are of the right data type, checks should be carried out if the output depends on a value entered by a user or read from a file. Values that are entered into a routine should always be checked. Subroutines can be designed to give a well-defined set of outputs, but human beings do not operate so methodically and tend to have a wide range of different responses to any given prompt, so stringent checks must be placed in any routines that accept data from users. Similarly, files of data may be corrupted or misread, so checks should be placed in all file-handling routines.

Errors do not often cause programs to crash. When they do, it is because the program has broken a rule of the language (using an operator illegally, for example, as in RESULT = FIRST$ + SECOND$) or a rule of the operating system (opening too many files at the same time, say). The following code would appear to be a perfectly legitimate program:

```
10 FOR COUNTER=1 TO 10
20    SUM=SUM+1
30    PRINT COUNTER, SUM
40    GOTO 10
50 NEXT COUNTER
```

However, it is a non-terminating algorithm and will crash the system because of the way the language works. In this case, the language (BASIC) uses the 'stack' to keep track of FOR...NEXT loops, adding to the stack each time a new loop is started. In this program, line 50 (with the NEXT command that would decrement the stack) is never reached, and so the stack gradually fills up until eventually a 'stack overflow' message is generated and the interpreter stops the program. Errors such as this are usually easily spotted, but if they appear in rarely used sections of code thorough testing may be needed to uncover them.

A more insidious type of error is one that allows

Error Checklist
A logical structured approach is the essence of error avoidance and debugging; the following error checklist (from an idea by G J Myers in 'The Art Of Software Testing') is an abbreviated example of such an approach

Variables
1 Are all variable names unique, bearing in mind that many interpreters use only the first two characters of any name?
2 Have any variables (especially loop counters or subroutine parameters) been re-used while their contents are still significant?
3 Are array subscripts within bounds, and are they whole numbers?
4 Do array subscripts start at element zero or element one?

Calculations
1 Do calculations yield string or numeric results, and are the results assigned to string or numeric variables?
2 Does any calculation result in a number too small or too large for the computer to handle? Can this cause a 'divide by zero' error?
3 Can rounding errors be significant?
4 Are all operations in an expression executed in the correct logical order, as opposed to the order imposed by the precedence of arithmetic operators?

Comparisons
1 Are strings always compared only with strings, and numbers with numbers?
2 Does it matter if a test string is wholly or partly upper-or lower-case?
3 Are strings of unequal length being compared, and does the difference in length matter more or less than differences in characters?
4 Are Boolean and comparison operators being mixed properly? A>B OR C is not the same as A>B OR A>C, for example.
5 Does the precedence of Boolean and comparison operators affect the execution of any comparison expression?

Control
1 Do loops and algorithms terminate whatever the state of the variables?
2 Do loops and routines have only one entry and exit point each?
3 When an IF...THEN statement fails, does control pass to the next program statement or the next program line?
4 What happens if none of the test conditions in a multiple branch statement is satisfied?

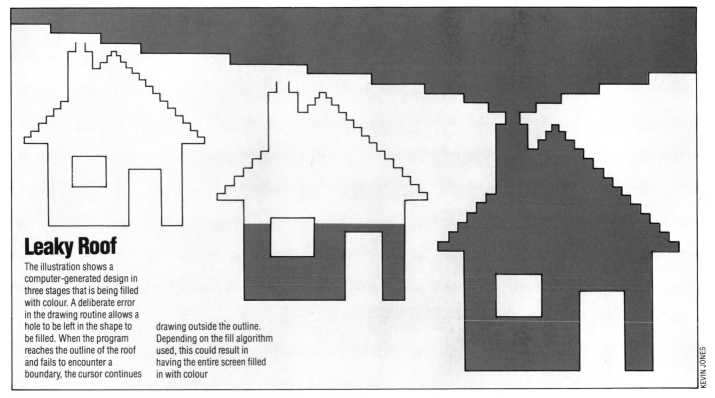

Leaky Roof

The illustration shows a computer-generated design in three stages that is being filled with colour. A deliberate error in the drawing routine allows a hole to be left in the shape to be filled. When the program reaches the outline of the roof and fails to encounter a boundary, the cursor continues drawing outside the outline. Depending on the fill algorithm used, this could result in having the entire screen filled in with colour

KEVIN JONES

a program to run normally, but invalidates the results. As an example, we have chosen to look at a fill pattern that draws a shape on the screen, then fills it with colour. Fill routines look for the boundaries of the shape. When a boundary is reached, the computer turns the cursor around and continues drawing until it reaches another boundary. For a fill routine to work, the boundaries must be well-defined and complete. In other words, there cannot be an open space in the shape's outline or the fill routine will spill the colour out beyond the boundaries.

The versions of the BASIC language used by most home micros make error-handling relatively easy, producing clear and concise error messages and allowing a crashed program to be continued after variable values have been altered at the keyboard — a useful facility when a program is being debugged. Most BASIC dialects will allow the use of a command such as ON ERROR GOTO to transfer the flow of control to a special error-handling routine and thus deal with otherwise 'fatal' bugs. This is done by including a program line such as:

```
30 ON ERROR GOTO 20000: REM error-handling
routines
```

near the start of the program. Any error will then cause the program to act as though the GOTO 20000 command had been encountered. ON ERROR will usually also set two variables; the first of these stores an error number that indicates the type of error that has occurred, and the other simply holds the line number at which the mistake was encountered. The names given to these variables and the resulting error numbers will vary from machine to machine, so the manual must be consulted. Once an error has occurred, program flow is diverted to line 20000, the error is identified from the number held in the relevant variable and the appropriate action is taken.

A well-written program will not have more than one ON ERROR routine. Such a routine will not be able to deal with syntax errors, memory shortages, stack overflows, etc. The best that this facility can offer is an orderly shutdown of the system, ensuring that all files are CLOSEd and that the user knows exactly what has happened.

Some errors, such as a division by zero, which could be handled by such a routine, should in fact be dealt with in a different manner. There are several reasons for this:

● The ON ERROR GOTO command and the subsequent jump back to the main program constitute an extra entry to and exit from a routine. This violates the structured programming principle that routines should have only one entry and one exit point.

● The proper place to protect against a division by zero is in the routine that does the division. It is bad practice to design algorithms that may crash the system. If the extra error-checking involved slows the program to an unacceptable degree, the routine should be redesigned so that this hazard doesn't arise.

● Error-handling routines rapidly become complicated IF...THEN...ELSE chains with multiple exits. They are inevitably restricted by the line numbering of the rest of the program and so must be rewritten whenever any routine using them is redesigned. They are particularly difficult to design, test and debug, and any mistake in such a routine can introduce far-reaching problems by diverting the flow of control in unforeseen ways.

THE HUMAN FACTOR

An important aspect of program design is the 'man-machine interface' — the part of the program that deals with the transfer of information from user to program and vice versa. Here, we investigate the factors to be considered when designing this interface.

Computer programming was for many years a mysterious topic that was understood only by professionals who were prepared to devote much time and effort to the subject. Before the advent of the microcomputer with its typewriter-style keyboard, programs were often entered one byte at a time via switches on the computer's front panel, or by punching holes in tapes on a teletype console.

Today's user is, by contrast, a pampered creature. Manufacturers no longer expect the computer owner to struggle with machine code, and the phrase 'user-friendly' was coined to indicate that micros may be used and programmed by anyone, regardless of experience. In 1982, the Alvey Committee, in a report entitled *A Programme for Advanced Information Technology*, identified the man-machine interface (MMI) as one of the four main areas of research and development, together with software engineering, very large scale integrated circuit (VLSI) design and knowledge-based systems.

In any application, the interaction between computer and user, where data or instructions are passed between the two, is of paramount importance. This 'dialogue' is conducted through the computer's input/output (I/O) devices, with the keyboard serving as the main source of input and the display screen providing the output. Joysticks, paddles, mice, touch screens and other devices may also be used for input, while the computer can utilise a printer, sound (or speech) generator or even a robot to express the output.

In addition to any constraints imposed by the I/O devices used, the dialogue between user and machine is influenced by software. For example, the computer's operating system (OS) controls many details of the screen and keyboard operation. The rate at which keys repeat when held down, and the delay between repetitions, is set by the operating system, which also buffers keystrokes to allow the computer to store characters that have been entered faster than they can be displayed. This is very important as it affects the speed at which the user may enter information into the computer. The buffer size is critical and should be known by the user — the CP/M operating system, for example, buffers a

single keystroke; many home machines buffer 10 strokes or more.

But keystroke buffers may cause problems. An experienced user who is working with a menu-driven system may know in advance that the menu choices he requires are 2 from the main menu, 5 from the next menu, then 3, 4, 6, etc. Because he is familiar with the system, he types his choices at great speed. With a 10-character buffer, the user will end up where he wanted to go because the keystrokes will all be 'remembered' in the correct sequence. With a one-character buffer, the time taken to display the second menu may be longer than the time taken to type the sequence. Thus, instead of selecting choice number 5 from this menu, then 3 and so on, choice number 6 alone is made (because this is the only character held in the buffer) and the system stops there.

But a large buffer can also lead to problems. A menu program that takes a long time to react to a keypress (this may occur if the choice leads to a file being read) may cause the user to think that nothing is happening. The natural response is to try the last choice entered, then press an assortment of keys until there is a response. This

CP/M

may lead to the program attempting to process the spurious characters held in the buffer; the results may be surprising!

'Garbage collection', which involves clearing the computer's memory registers to free working space is another source of problems. This can make a program appear to 'hang' for long periods, during which the user may again try to take corrective action. Garbage collection is likely to cause problems in large programs that do a lot of string handling. Some versions of BASIC allow the programmer to force a garbage collection; it is a good idea to do this at frequent intervals — but the user should be given a 'please wait' message as the computer will appear to be doing nothing while garbage collection is being dealt with.

The way that a programming language handles input and output will influence the design of the interface between computer and user. The superior string-handling facilities of BASIC will lead to more sophisticated use of strings in the human-computer dialogue than is allowed by languages like PASCAL. BASICS that have built-in commands for cursor addressing will encourage better screen layouts than those that do not. The same holds true for BASICS with graphics commands. BASIC is well supplied with input/output commands — INPUT and PRINT are fine for simple programs. But for real control of input (the kind needed to produce a form containing protected input fields, for example) try experimenting with GET$, INKEY$, INPUT$() and similar commands. PRINT USING is an extremely versatile command for formatting output; it is invaluable for aligning decimal points and for justifying columns of text.

Micronet 800 'Log-on'

USER PSYCHOLOGY

The user is the most unpredictable element in any man-machine system. Like any other component, though, the user has certain performance characteristics that must be understood before the interface is designed.

People share with computers the basic characteristic of being 'information processors'. However, human beings have inherent limitations on the amount of new information they can hold in 'working memory' — it has been reckoned that for most types of information around seven different items may be held in the brain at one time. The size of these items depends on how meaningful or well structured they are. If the information to be remembered consists of random characters, each item will consist of no more than a single character. But if the characters are not random but form

common surnames, each item remembered could be an entire name. Increasing the structure of the information in this way increases the user's ability to remember and make use of it.

There are several ways of helping people to structure information when using computers. One method is to relate data to familiar, well-understood structures — this is the way that the Lisa-style 'desk-top' metaphor works. Similarly, a financial spreadsheet package may be organised to look like a book with pages, indexes, etc. Another method is to train the user to understand unfamiliar structures. By repeatedly showing examples, and explaining topics in depth, the program itself may be used to teach the user how the information should be structured. The

Apple Macintosh

drawback with training of this type is that it is expensive in both time and effort. Detailed instructions, 'help' screens and 'signposts' may provide a type of on-line training, but these can be difficult to use efficiently.

Finally, presenting information in recognisable patterns can help the user to understand the program. This can be done by using colour or layout to lead the eye to the desired information. To understand what this means, consider colour-coding as it is used in Prestel and similar videotext programs. On a typical page, the heading and 'footer' will be set in blocks of the same colour; there will be a single background colour, and text will be displayed in two other colours, with alternate paragraphs in each colour. Key words may be highlighted by using yet another colour. The purpose of this is to allow the user to select only the information required and to ignore whole sections of the page if these sections contain information of no immediate value. Colour-coding can be confusing if it is over-used, however, and tests have shown that people may waste time reading and re-reading paragraphs to try to understand the significance of an entirely arbitrary colour change! A good rule of thumb is: never use more than four colours at once.

Three Degrees
These photographs of microcomputer operating systems illustrate three varying degrees of user-friendliness. In the first photograph, a new user is attempting to communicate with the CP/M operating system. CP/M has no built-in 'help' features, so requires a thorough knowledge of commands before it can be used properly. Our second example is a menu-driven system — the 'Log-on' menu for Micronet 800 on the BBC Micro. Options are clearly numbered, and the user makes his selection by entering the appropriate number from the menu. The screen does not offer a great deal of information, so the user must understand the options before he can make use of them. Our final photograph shows the Apple Macintosh operating system, which provides visual clues and graphic displays, as well as simple, easily understood menus

GUIDELINES

As more memory becomes available on microcomputers, the techniques used to guide the user through the workings of a program can become more sophisticated. Here we discuss the design and implementation of general-purpose 'help' routines that may be incorporated into your own programs.

Memory is now cheap. The next generation of home computers, which may have a *minimum* of 128 Kbytes of RAM, will leave most of us with far more memory than even our most ambitious programs will ever require. Throughout the history of computing, a shortage of memory has been the major excuse for failing to provide users with sufficient instructions, sensible error messages or on-line help. Now there is no excuse.

There are three main user aids that can be provided within a program: instructions, 'help' pages and 'signposts'. Instructions take two forms. They can be given in a single block at the beginning of the program, or they may be supplied as required throughout the program (as prompts for user input, for instance). Ideally, both should be available to the user.

In their simplest form, instructions may simply be a page — or several pages — of text explaining in clear English how to use the program. The text can be held in strings or DATA statements within the program, and will be displayed when required by a call to a subroutine written for this purpose. At the start of the main program, the user is asked if instructions are needed; if they are, the subroutine is called. Thereafter, other routines that accept user input should be tailored so that a specified

input ('?' is common, or you could use 'I') triggers a call to the instructions subroutine. It is a good idea to create a standard 'display instructions' command, and modify any library input routines to accept it. Don't forget to modify any prompts used in your routines so that 'Press any key for more...' becomes 'Press any key for more (or "I" for instructions)'. This will give you a standard format that will be used in all your programs.

But instructions need not be text-only. Diagrams may be included, and the instruction routines can be developed to give examples and allow the user to practise and learn. Such instruction routines are common in programs that run scientific experiments — here the user may be required to perform a specified task to a particular level of skill before being allowed to progress to the main program. Such 'teaching' routines are not easy to develop because they must simulate the

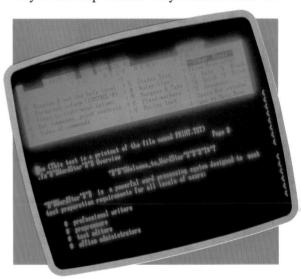

behaviour of the rest of the program, as well as evaluating the user's performance. It is well worth the attempt, however, as designing this type of routine will give an indication of the problems that the main program will present to the user.

In a similar fashion, 'help' pages may be called up to explain the operation of particular parts of the program. This facility is found in many systems, where it is available to explain the use of commands — the Unix operating system, for example, allows the entire user manual to be accessed as on-line help! Providing help in your own programs need be no more difficult than supplying instructions: at each appropriate point, simply allow the user to enter a help request instead of the usual input — when this happens the program should call the relevant help routine. A complex program is likely to require a large

Words Of Advice
Micropro Wordstar provides a top-selling example of command-driven software with 'on-line help'. The on-screen help menu can be abbreviated or removed by the user, but an enormously detailed Help file structure is always available at a single keypress

number of help pages, so again a general help routine is desirable. This may require the user to input a number to identify the particular help page required. On disk-based systems, the help pages may be held on disk as separate files. The help routine will then create the appropriate file name from the user's input, read in the file and display it on the screen.

Both help and instructions routines may well take up more than just a single page of information. If this is the case, your display routine should be designed in such a way that the user is able to move backwards and forwards through the pages at will. You should also ensure that the user can leave the routine at any stage and return to the exact point at which the main program was left — it

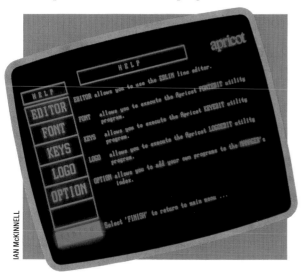

IAN McKINNELL

program such commands onto function keys and display a single-line message to show each key's function. It is always good practice to display a

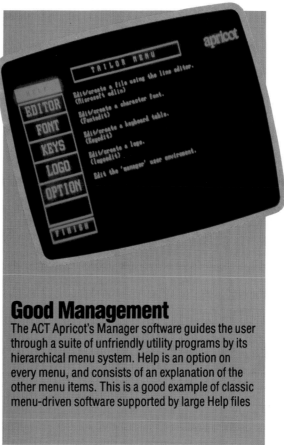

Good Management
The ACT Apricot's Manager software guides the user through a suite of unfriendly utility programs by its hierarchical menu system. Help is an option on every menu, and consists of an explanation of the other menu items. This is a good example of classic menu-driven software supported by large Help files

is very frustrating to go through 10 pages of redundant information each time the instructions are required! If a prompt had been given, it will now have been lost so it must be repeated. The help routine should set a flag that tells the calling routine that it must go back to the last instruction before the help call, first clearing the flag.

A common metaphor for user interactions with complex programs is to think of the user navigating through a tangled network of logic. The newcomer to the program will not understand its structure and can easily become disoriented and lost. Thus 'signposts' are needed to guide the user. A menu is the clearest example; this operates like a road sign that shows the possible exits from a junction. Systems such as Apple's Macintosh and Lisa work in a similar way, using icons instead of menu options.

Some directions are more important than others. In a command-based system, there may be dozens of possible commands. However, not all of these will be relevant or even possible at a given point in the program. If the number of options is small, it is useful to display a line or two to explain what they are. Some options — such as QUIT — must be available at all times, so it is a good idea to keep these on permanent display. UNDO, SAVE and other application-specific commands may also be constantly available. A common technique is to

signpost that indicates the way out of a program — this instils confidence in first-time users, whose major concern is often to find the emergency exit!

Some experimental systems have been developed that can monitor a user's performance and adjust the level of help given accordingly. Commercial programs with this feature are still a long way off, but it is possible to use simple techniques to achieve at least a part of this goal. If the user is asked to give his or her name each time the program is run, then a file can be kept of users and their skill levels. These levels can be calculated (from the number of times a particular user has run the program, say, or from the highest score achieved if the program in question is a game) and updated at the end of the program run. As the skill level increases, the type of help and signposting supplied will change, becoming briefer and less intrusive. The user might also be asked to choose the level of help required, as in the Wordstar word processing package. Ideally, both alternatives would be used.

Incorporating help can be a valuable guide to improving a program's performance. Once a help routine has been designed (such as the one provided here) it is a simple matter to modify it to record which help pages were used and how often they were needed. This gives a clear indication of the trouble-spots in the program.

CHOICE OPTIONS

In any complex program there will be points at which the user will need to branch to one of a number of available options. The menu system lays out the list of choices at certain specified stages for the user to select from; a command system allows the user to choose from a range of options at any time. We consider both techniques.

Menus may be simple lists of numbered items or they may be screens full of elaborate icons, but the principle behind their use is the same. A menu is used when the program reaches a multi-way branch in its logic; the user is asked to choose which route to take from a list of available options displayed on the screen. Menu-based programs tend to be tree structures: the user enters the tree at the 'root' and is guided by the menu options towards one of the 'leaves', where the information or function is to be found.

The major advantage of this approach is that the user needs little or no knowledge of the program structure because the route is well 'signposted' all the way. However, more experienced users find the job of navigating their way through a chain of menus tedious for often-repeated tasks. Novices, too, may have difficulty with the tree structure; correcting a wrong decision involves working back through all the menus to the point at which the mistake was made, re-entering the correct option, and then continuing from there. Prestel is a particularly 'deep' structure of this type, and users frequently encounter this problem. Menus need not form a tree at all — they may be organised into a network by using loops. However, this tends to increase the risk of getting lost within the program structure and so is not suitable for novice users.

Designing a menu system can be difficult, although the actual programming is relatively easy. The main problem is that the entire program must be clearly specified before any code is written. (This is good practice anyway, but is not always straightforward.) Adding new functions at a late stage can involve changing several menus earlier in the program, and this may require major restructuring. When the program is designed, all menu logic should be included in a single routine that calls the routines at the 'leaves' when these are reached. The menu routine can thus be seen as a more complex form of the normal control routine, with all internal branching controlled by the user. This keeps the design tidy, and serves to separate the control logic from the functional parts of the program, allowing each to be developed and debugged independently.

Program flow will now follow a set pattern. For each menu along the route, the menu logic routine passes a set of user prompts to a routine that puts them into 'slots' in a menu 'frame'. The slots will probably contain a screen header message that displays a title and any other necessary information about the menu, a 'footer' that explains how to make the choice (with sufficient space for the user's response), and the menu options themselves. In general, the most effective menu layout has up to eight options displayed in a column, with the response code (number, letter, mnemonic, etc.) at the left of each item.

The menu routine calls an input routine, perhaps passing to it the conditions that must be specified for a legal input, and accepts in return the user's response. It then interprets this response (typically a single keypress) and either passes control to the next menu or calls the appropriate application routine if it is the last menu in the chain. Once the routine has been executed, the menu from which it was called might be redisplayed, or control could pass to some other part of the program (the root menu, perhaps).

Menus require a lot of text for headers, footers and prompts, but much of this will be repeated for each menu 'frame'. The explanation of how to choose a menu option (the 'help' command), an option offering an exit to the root menu, and other recurring choices may all be required by several different menus. If this is the case, space may be saved and the logic made clearer if all prompts are held in a string array (or on a random access disk file), from which they may be called by their index number. Design the menu display routine to accept references to this array and to display the appropriate headers, footers, prompts, etc.

A command-driven system is one that has a range of commands available to the user at any stage in the program. Each command goes straight to a subroutine that performs the required function. This system must be designed to inspect all input to ascertain whether it is data or a program command. The difference is usually signalled by the user pressing a particular key before each command input. The Control key is often used for this purpose. A word processor, for example, might accept the word 'save' as just one more word of text, but interpret it as a storage command if the Control key was pressed before the word was typed.

In a command-driven system, the 'tree' is very shallow and broad, and a single routine, acting as the control program, is used to direct the user to the required subroutine. This 'command interpreter' has four main tasks. The first is simply

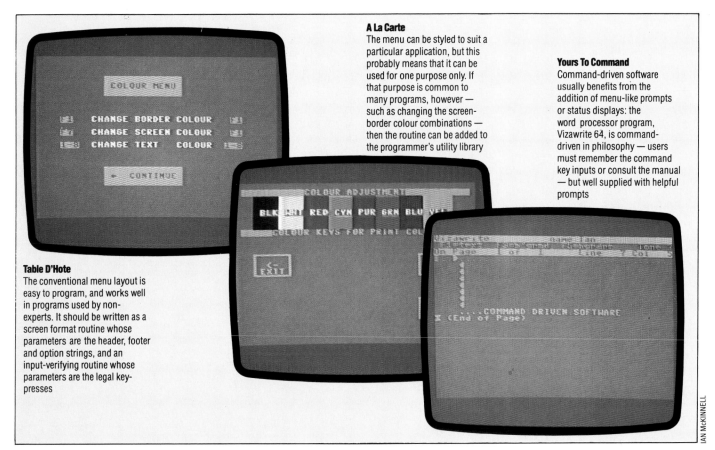

A La Carte
The menu can be styled to suit a particular application, but this probably means that it can be used for one purpose only. If that purpose is common to many programs, however — such as changing the screen-border colour combinations — then the routine can be added to the programmer's utility library

Yours To Command
Command-driven software usually benefits from the addition of menu-like prompts or status displays: the word processor program, Vizawrite 64, is command-driven in philosophy — users must remember the command key inputs or consult the manual — but well supplied with helpful prompts

Table D'Hote
The conventional menu layout is easy to program, and works well in programs used by non-experts. It should be written as a screen format routine whose parameters are the header, footer and option strings, and an input-verifying routine whose parameters are the legal key-presses

to wait for an input. The second is to 'parse' this input — the interpreter must separate the input line into its functional units. The third task is to interpret the command by preparing the appropriate subroutine call. (What is the routine's address? Are there parameters to be passed?) Finally, it must actually call the routine to be executed. When control returns, the interpreter goes back to its first job — waiting!

The format of a command may be extremely elaborate, and some command languages are similar to a simplified form of English. An example of a command language is the Unix shell, where the typical command format is:

```
Command + optional parameter list
e.g. L
or L −1
```

Here, the Unix command L lists a file directory, while L −1 (where −1 is an optional parameter) lists a file directory in 'long' format.

The parser must be able to recognise the various parts of the command line. Unix keeps things simple (in most cases) by taking the first word as the command and recognising parameters by a preceding minus sign. Command language parameters are not for the use of the command interpreter itself, but are required by the subroutines that the interpreter calls. Routines used in the command system should ideally adopt a standard format for input parameters. If this is done, the command interpreter can pass the parameters in the form in which they were entered (as strings, perhaps).

It is obviously much easier to create a command interpreter than to write a menu system. Experienced users tend to prefer command systems, as these are faster and more flexible than menu-driven programs. Most operating systems are command driven, which is unfortunate for novice users as such systems provide no signposting facilities and the on-line help routines (if there are any) require some knowledge of the system. In addition, the sheer number of commands and optional parameters in a typical command system means that even those reasonably familiar with the system will require help facilities or need to consult the operating manual frequently.

Beginners hate commands and experts hate menus. This problem is virtually insoluble, although some hybrid systems exist that can be quite effective. For example, the Wordstar word processing program is basically a command-driven system, but it can appear to the user to be a menu system. The commands are control codes (some with parameters) and the user runs the system entirely with these. The menus that appear on the screen use these commands as mnemonics for selecting options so that, as the novice uses the menus to run the program, the commands are learnt at the same time. The help level may be set to permit the menus to be dispensed with once the user is sufficiently proficient to find them a nuisance. The Wordstar menu system is only two levels deep, however; this approach would be more difficult to implement with more complex systems.

Two Into Three
There are usually many ways of solving the same problem — these displays show different ways of allowing the user to change the screen, border and text colours on a Commodore 64

LENDING LIBRARY

It is extremely useful to develop techniques that make more efficient use of the time and effort spent in programming. We discuss one such method — creating libraries of routines that can be merged into programs — and list the sort of details that must be taken into account when programmers share the task of coding.

Following the structured design methods that we have already described in this course may seem like a long-winded approach — but it does, in fact, save time (not only in the coding but especially in the debugging of a program). This is because programs that are created at the keyboard tend to have unnecessarily complicated structures and algorithms, which means that they take longer to write, are more prone to error and, because they are more difficult to follow, take much more effort to test and debug. Planning the program in advance simplifies the structure and the algorithms and thus leads to fewer coding errors and easier testing and debugging.

Most importantly, designing ahead saves the programmer from writing a control or file structure that is later found to be inadequate (perhaps not enough space in a field in the file has been allowed for). Problems like this, which are fundamental to the way the program works, can lead to major portions of it needing to be rewritten.

Those with a 'proper' typewriter-style keyboard may like to invest some time in learning to touch-type. Apart from this, though, there is little that may be done to increase the speed at which program lines are entered at the keyboard. However, the process of coding programs may be greatly speeded up in several ways. The first is the simplest: invent, adopt and use a number of 'conventions' when coding. Such measures include: using particular types of name for local variables to differentiate them from main program variables; beginning each subroutine at lines ending in 00; ending each subroutine with RETURN on a line of its own; starting each type of subroutine in a particular block of lines (file-handling routines between 9000 and 9999, utilities at 50000 onwards, and so on).

The benefits of using these conventions are numerous: you don't have to hunt for the menu routines because you know that they are always in the same place; you don't have to worry about whether you have used the same variable name in the main program and in a subroutine — because its name will indicate it is a local variable.

PROGRAM LIBRARIES

Such coding techniques are also useful when libraries of programs are created. A well-organised library of subroutines can save as much as half of the coding time on a large program. The

Uniform System
Libraries of subroutines are useless without a uniform documentation system accompanying them. This is especially true for cassette users — inspecting the contents of an undocumented cassette by loading and listing each program is a thankless task

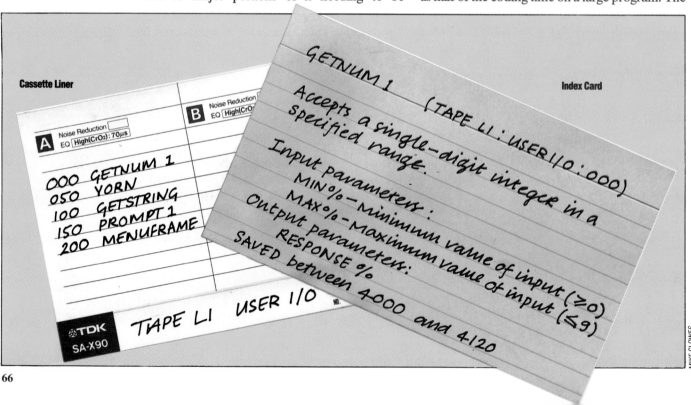

MIKE CLOWES

best way to start such a library is to go through existing programs and take out all the subroutines that are well written and have some general applicability (I/O routines, date routines, upper to lower case conversion, and so on). Each routine should be saved as a separate file, and these should be grouped together according to function (if they are to be stored on tape then each function group should be stored on a separate cassette) with meaningful file names to identify them. Keep a card index or a database of the file names, together with a description of what each routine does.

Needless to say, it is important to ensure that all library routines are thoroughly tested and debugged. They will be used in programs for which they were not specifically designed, so make sure that they will trap any illegal input values. You should also ensure that any values output from the library routines will not cause problems to the program that uses them. Make each routine as efficient as possible and include as much internal documentation as is necessary for you to understand the routine's function at a later date. Add to the collection as the need arises — there is no point in adding new routines 'on spec' as experience shows that this is largely wasted effort. Don't forget to number the lines of the library routines according to the convention established (this will save on RENUMbering when the routines are merged into a new program). Useful library routines may be found in computer magazines, which often publish routine listings as well as complete programs (and these can be cannibalised to obtain the useful subroutines).

To make use of a library like this, it is necessary to have a way of merging routines together to form a complete program. For those using compiled languages, a 'link-loader' or similar program is usually supplied; this takes compiled modules and joins them to make an executable program. For BASIC programmers, unless a compiler is available, the easiest way to achieve this is to use a combination of RENUMber and MERGE commands. To merge a library routine into the new program, first load the program, decide where the library routine will go and make sure there is a large enough block of unused line numbers for it to fit in. If necessary, RENUMber the library routine so that it will go into the space allotted to it. Then use the MERGE command to join the two programs; check that everything works as it should and SAVE the new program with the library routine in place.

GROUP EFFORTS

It is often the case that home computer users work together in groups to write programs — either at school or in their user clubs. Most of what has been said about program design and programmer efficiency is particularly relevant to such team efforts. In fact, most of these ideas and the concept of structured programming were developed in order to split the workload of commercial programming projects. Thus, a number of different programmers could work on different

MERGE

● The Spectrum has the straightforward version of the command: it merges the named file with the program in memory; the incoming line overwrites the existing line in the event of a line number collision.

● With the BBC Micro *SPOOL command you can create ASCII versions of the program files, then write a BASIC program (or use a word processor) to access these files, one program line at a time. Merge the two files into a third ASCII file, and convert it into a program using the *EXEC command.

● On the Commodore: OPEN 1,1:CMD1:LIST:PRINT #1:CLOSE 1 creates on tape an un-named ASCII file of the program in memory. LOAD the other program, and add to it a routine to INPUT and print the ASCII file lines on screen. Stop the program and RETURN over the screen, thus merging the two programs

parts of the same program at the same time to produce a working program.

For BASIC programmers to work like this, it is essential to agree on the conventions to be used when coding. Assuming that a design has been agreed on, the programmer of an individual module needs to know:

1) What the files will be and how they will be organised.
2) What conventions have been agreed for naming variables. The most important variables, such as arrays that are used throughout the program, should be named in advance. A convention should be agreed for naming local variables. Variables that are passed between modules should either be named in advance or a way of ensuring that each is unique should be devised — adding the module number of the originating module as a suffix, for instance.
3) What library routines are available to the group, the format of each of these, how their variables are named, what they do, and how well tested and debugged they are.
4) How error-handling routines are organised (for instance, whether each routine copes with its own errors or whether the routines set an error 'flag', which is then dealt with by the control routine).
5) The exact function of any module that is being written.
6) The exact range and type of data that each individual module will accept as input and return as output.

This implies a lengthy planning stage with many meetings to agree strategy, followed by a short programming stage. Testing — including the testing of group-produced programs — will be dealt with later in the chapter. Before that we will concentrate on the design of programs that will run faster and use less memory.

FINE TUNING

Our chapter on program design has so far concentrated on 'structured' programming methods. Using the techniques we have suggested will make your programs easier to design and debug, but will do nothing to make them run any faster. Here we consider ways to increase program execution speed.

Structured programming and good program layout are techniques that make programs easier to use, but do not improve program efficiency. To make programs run faster and use less memory space, it is often necessary to sacrifice clarity in a program's design. So we should bear in mind, when 'tuning up' a piece of code, that almost anything that is done to make it faster will invariably make it more difficult to read, understand and debug.

The inherent slowness of interpreted languages like BASIC means that there will be times when programs will run at an unacceptable pace and must be speeded up. The most efficient way of speeding up a BASIC program is to compile it. However, very few micros support a true BASIC compiler — there are disk- and cassette-based compilers on the market, but most of them support only integer BASIC, and may require special formatting of your program before compilation. Compiling is a slow process, especially during program development, and especially when the system is cassette-based. The compiler will occupy user memory, and the more comprehensive its facilities, the more RAM it will take from the user program area. In general on home micros, compiling is recommended only for fully tested and debugged programs.

File accesses slow programs down more than any other single cause. In a program that frequently reads from and writes to disk or tape (a database program, say) delays are inevitable. Access to a record in a random access file on a floppy disk takes an average of about a quarter of a second. Access to data in serial files takes longer (and varies with the length of the file) and tape accesses are considerably longer. If these delays are causing problems, it may be possible to reduce the number of accesses by reading in more data at once and storing it in RAM, and by 'saving up' updates to files until the end of the session. Interactive programs often cause problems because the user is left staring at a screen for several seconds. A partial solution here is to re-organise the program so that files are read and written while the user is busy doing something else (reading a screenful of instructions, for instance).

Another cause of slowness is real arithmetic. Real numbers are ones with decimal places (integers are whole numbers). Because of the decimal part, fetching a real number from memory and performing an arithmetical operation on it requires many more machine cycles than doing the same for an integer. In programs with a lot of arithmetic, it pays to replace all the variables involved with integer variables (e.g. SUM should be replaced by SUM%). Savings of around 20 per cent can be achieved for even moderately numerical programs and 'number-crunching' applications stand to gain by as much as 50 per cent.

Designing a faster algorithm is one of the best ways of speeding a program up. Some sources of algorithms have already been recommended in this course. Try these, and be on the lookout for those published in computer magazines. Otherwise, devising algorithms is a matter of creativity and insight. BASICs usually have a wealth of inbuilt functions (such as INSTR, SGN, LOG, and so on) that are very fast. This speed is a result of their being written in machine code and using the best algorithms available. It is often worth checking the manual again to see what inbuilt functions are offered before coding your own version. User-defined functions, implemented with the command DEF FN, also run quickly. This command is most useful in programs with repeated calculations or a repeated sequence of string manipulations, where it can replace a subroutine call, which is much slower.

Writing routines in machine code generally makes them run faster. This is because interpreted languages translate program lines into machine

Micro Compilers

BBC Micro Turbo Compiler Salamander, 17 Norfolk Road; Brighton BN1 3AA. 0273 771942	Cassette	£9.95
Commodore 64 DTL-BASIC Compiler Dataview Wordcraft Ltd, Radix House, East Street, Colchester CO1 2XB. 0206 86914	Cass/Disk	£14.95
Spectrum Softek FP Softek IS, Combined FP and IS, Softek International, 12/13 Henrietta St, London WC2. 01-240 1422	Cass Cass Cass	£19.95 £9.95 £24.95

code as they are encountered while the program is running (they do not do it particularly efficiently, either). Writing in machine code avoids this translation process. Unfortunately, writing Assembly language programs is much more difficult than writing BASIC, and the cost in time and effort may not be worth the eventual saving. However, some programs — those using animated graphics, for instance — would not work as intended if they were written in BASIC alone.

There are many other ways of making smaller savings in processing speed. Use a variable instead of an actual number (e.g. MAX rather than 267.5) for faster access to values, especially in loops. Use different letters to start variable names, and spread these initial letters evenly throughout the alphabet. Use multiple statement lines (if that is possible) and create a sizeable interval between line numbers (such as 10). With FOR . . . NEXT loops, if the interpreter permits, leave off the loop counter variable (for example, use NEXT rather than NEXT LOOP). Inside a loop, try to avoid calculating the same value over and over again. Instead, calculate it outside the loop and incorporate it as a variable.

SAVING SPACE

Integer arithmetic not only saves time, it also saves space. Where it may take four or five bytes to store a real number, it need take only two to store an integer. This represents a major saving, especially where large arrays are involved. Other improvements to the speed of a program will also save space: using inbuilt or user-defined functions saves code, as does writing in Assembly language and using multiple statement lines. Compiling tends to *increase* the size of smaller programs and only saves space for large ones.

Removing REM statements is an obvious space-saver, and using shorter strings of text for prompts also helps. Putting large blocks of text into files that are stored outside the program keeps them out of the way when they are not needed (instructions and 'help' files are the biggest burdens). Remove as many spaces as is legal within a line, and use shorter line numbers and shorter variable names. If an array needs to be dimensioned but its exact size is not known, don't just guess a convenient round number. Instead, leave it until the information needed is on hand and then dimension it with a variable, like this:

```
10 INPUT"How many instances are in this
     category?";INSTANCES%
20 DIM ARRAY%(INSTANCES%)
```

This is called 'dynamic dimensioning' and it is something that BASIC offers and most other languages don't — so make the most of it!

Another technique involves increasing BASIC's memory allocation in RAM. This can be done by using commands like HIMEM. What these commands usually do is to change the area in RAM that is available to BASIC programs and variables. The normal use for this is to store machine code programs in a safe place where they won't be overwritten, but the same command can be used to access extra space from that normally reserved for the screen memory. If it does not matter what is appearing on the screen, then this is a good way to get an extra kilobyte of RAM. If it is not possible to change HIMEM, the screen memory can still often be used by PEEKing and POKEing directly to the memory locations reserved for it.

If all else fails and the program simply will not fit in the space available, many BASICS have a CHAIN command that allows one program to pass control to another. Some BASICS allow use of the COMMON command; this passes particular variables and their current values to the next program. CHAIN on home micros (if it exists at all) is usually a very simple command that enables all or none of the variables from the first program to be passed to the second.

If programs are written in a structured way, the individual subroutines should be capable of being written and tested independently. Their execution can also be individually timed. Write a simple timer like this one:

```
100 REM Use this first section to set any variables
105 REM that the routine will need (don't forget
110 REM to dimension arrays and fill them with
115 REM realistic data too if the routine uses any).
120 REM This program is in BBC BASIC and TIME
125 REM is a pseudo-variable that holds a value in
130 REM hundredths of a second, generated by the
135 REM system clock
200 START=TIME
210 GOSUB 2000:REM The routine being timed is
     called here.
220 FINISH=TIME
230 PRINT "Execution took"; (FINISH-START)/100;
     "seconds."
240 END
```

With this routine it is possible to experiment with different algorithms and other ways of increasing speed.

How To Be Quick

● Weigh carefully the demands of good style against the need for speedy, sometimes incomprehensible, code.

● Compile when you can; define functions and procedures if you can't.

● Avoid file accesses.

● Avoid absolute real numbers. Initialise variables and use integer arithmetic, if your micro allows it.

● Design your algorithms carefully and learn from the example of others.

● Consider the advantages and disadvantages of machine code. While it may be fast, it takes longer to write and to debug.

● Condense your code, and remove your REMs once you have a working version.

ROUTINE CHECK UP

Our examination of programming techniques should certainly have provided plenty of ideas for program design and development. In this final part, we discuss the methods that may be used to test a finished program.

One of the great advantages of programming in an interpreted language like BASIC is that code can be tested as it is being written. The programmer can, at any time, type RUN and see what happens. On most machines, it is a simple matter to 'break' into a running program, PRINT the values of key variables, change these values and then CONTinue. All this means that most of the more obvious mistakes will have been spotted and corrected. Yet this kind of *ad hoc* debugging is not a substitute for testing, which must be done when the program is in its complete and final form.

Validation testing aims to ensure that a program will do exactly what it is meant to do. For any legal set of input data it must produce the correct output, and for any illegal input it must take the appropriate actions. A simple way to test a program might seem to be to give it a sample of every legal input and then check that the results are as expected. For almost every program, this will be impossible, however. Even a program that takes two integers, adds them and prints the result would need to be tested for every possible integer value! Yet this is only part of the problem, as every *illegal* value would need to be tested, too.

Another possibility might be to look at every 'path' through the program. A particular path can be found by following one route through a control flow diagram (flowchart) from beginning to end. Each branch on the way allows for alternate paths and each loop adds more. Figure 1 shows a simple program that is a loop containing a number of IF...THEN statements. There are four paths within the body of the loop and the loop is executed 10 times. This means that the number of unique routes from 'start' to 'finish' is 1,398,100 — a staggering number for what would probably amount to a dozen lines of code. Clearly, testing this way would be out of the question.

So, if exhaustive data testing does not work and exhaustive logic testing does not work, what does? The surprising answer is that nothing does. There is no way to test completely a reasonably complex program in a realistic time. Partly for this reason, testing follows the law of diminishing returns — the number of errors found per unit of effort decreases with each extra unit. So, the time to stop is when the effort of doing it outweighs the cost of the program's (as yet undetected) faults.

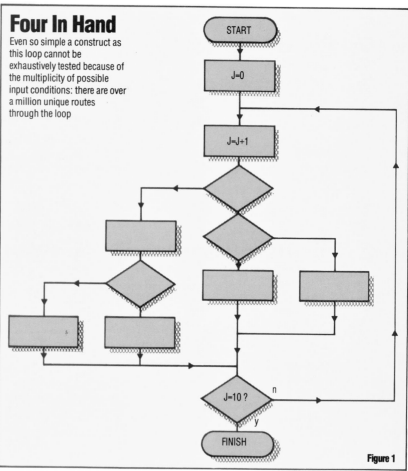

Four In Hand

Even so simple a construct as this loop cannot be exhaustively tested because of the multiplicity of possible input conditions: there are over a million unique routes through the loop

START
J=0
J=J+1
J=10 ? n y
FINISH

Figure 1

However, despite these drawbacks, it is worth devising some method of testing. A reasonable assumption is that if a machine will operate correctly on one datum of a particular type it will operate correctly on all data of the same type. So, if a subroutine works for one positive integer within its range, it should work for all positive integers in that range. This leads us to a type of testing known as 'equivalence class testing'. The idea is to develop a set of test cases that are each representative of a class of cases that should all behave in the same way. Thus, if a piece of code checks that an input is in the range 1 to 100, we should test for inputs that are less than the lowest value expected, greater than the highest value, and within the expected range (value <1; value >100; and $1=<$ value $=<100$).

Examining every logic path can also be simplified to invoking each point of entry to all routines (although ideally there should only be one for each) and, inside each routine, covering each possible outcome of every decision branch. In figure 2 we have a routine for adjusting bonus points in a game. It takes the input parameters

Just Testing
A complete set of hand-calculated test data for the example illustrated in the flowcharts might look like this:

LEVEL	INPUT HITS	BONUS	OUTPUT BONUS
6	10	200	1300
4	10	550	2300
7	10	550	3950
4	10	200	800
7	10	200	1400
1	20	2500	2600
1	20	550	550
6	5	200	300
6	50	200	300
4	5	2500	2600
7	50	2500	2600
4	50	550	550
7	5	550	550

BONUS,LEVEL and HITS and returns a (possibly new) value for BONUS.It might be written thus:

```
6030 IF LEVEL>2 AND HITS=10 THEN
     BONUS=BONUS*LEVEL
6040 IF LEVEL=6 OR BONUS>2000 THEN
     BONUS=BONUS+100
```

To cover the outcome of each conditional expression, we need to consider the inputs to each that would cause an output of 'yes' or 'no'. In both decisions we are looking at the effects of two variables combined by a logical operator (AND and OR). This means that we have to take the combined values of the variables and not their individual values into consideration. To see why, consider what would happen if we tested values for LEVEL of 4 and 1 and for HITS of 10, 5 and 20 in the first decision. When LEVEL=4, the three values of HITS are tested but when LEVEL=1 they are not. This is a case of part of a decision 'masking' another part. So that we can test each part separately, it is best to simplify compound decisions.

Looking at figure 3, we can see that with four binary decisions there are 2^4 (=16) possible outcomes and we must cover them all. A start is to list the conditions for a yes or no outcome for each decision like this:

	1	2	3	4
yes	LEVEL>2	HITS=10	LEVEL=6	BONUS>20000
no	LEVEL=2	HITS<10	LEVEL<6	BONUS=2000
	LEVEL<2	HITS>10	LEVEL>6	BONUS<2000

These can then be used to derive the values for representative test data. For instance, for the path taking the route adfi (see figure 3), LEVEL must be greater than 2 and equal to 6, HITS must be not equal to 10 and BONUS may be any value (because it is not involved). The values LEVEL=6, HITS=20 and BONUS=150 would exercise this path — as would many others, of course. The route abehj could be tested with LEVEL=4, HITS=10 and BONUS=600 (don't forget we are talking about the *input* value of BONUS that may later be multiplied with LEVEL).

Equally importantly, the results that should be produced by each set of test data should be calculated before the test run so that the results can be compared. The input data on their own will merely test whether the program runs. To test that it is doing what it should, the output must be calculated (by hand) beforehand. A complete set of test cases for this example is shown (left).

Equipped with a method of 'exercising' our software, we now need a way of tackling a large program so that the complexity does not become overwhelming. It is here that another benefit of structured programming is felt. Programs written as a collection of independent modules arranged in a hierarchy allow us to test each module individually. Because the modules are arranged in this way, we can start with the topmost module and work down, testing each individual module only when all of those above it have been tested, and we

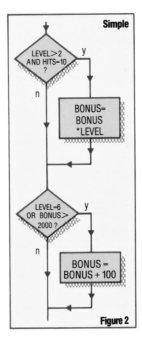

Simple

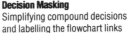

Figure 2

Decision Masking
Simplifying compound decisions and labelling the flowchart links makes systematic testing easier

Compound

Figure 3

can use already-tested modules to provide data for those lower in the structure.

The module being tested will have above it (unless it is the first one), a fully tested *driver* module. The modules below it, known as *stubs*, are, so far, untested and therefore unreliable, so they are simulated by short pieces of code that simply return the appropriate test data when called by the module being tested. This arrangement is sometimes known as a *test harness* and it is a framework into which module routines can be put for testing. Figure 4 shows the principle. Modules 1, 2 and 3 have already been tested while modules 5, 6 and 7 are simulated.

One final point must be stressed. Testing is an important part of the program's life cycle and, as such, deserves to be well documented. It pays to keep records of the test data derived for a routine so that, if it shows a bug later, the same tests will not have to be repeated, or the testing can be examined for where it was inadequate.

Top-Down Testing
Testing is made much simpler by the top-down approach, since each module can be tested as it is written, both in isolation and in association with other tested modules. The behaviour of unwritten modules can be simulated by writing 'stubs' — code that artificially generates examples of the module's predicted output

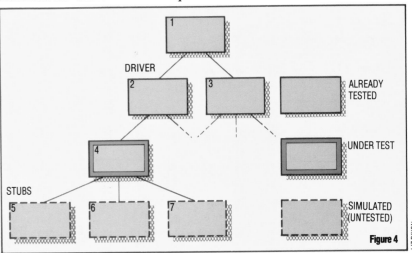

DRIVER

ALREADY TESTED

UNDER TEST

STUBS

SIMULATED (UNTESTED)

Figure 4

LIZ DIXON

3 PROGRAMMING PROJECTS

The best way to build on and develop expertise in
programming analysis, design and construction is, of
course, by creating programs of your own. It's an added
bonus when the programming projects in question result
in the generation of some very useful and
entertaining software.

ROLL CALL

Programs that are built in to home computers and provide editing facilities or other programming aids are known as 'utilities'. We begin this chapter by examining a range of utility programs for the more popular home computers and developing our own BASIC utilities.

The range of utilities featured on home micros varies considerably: some computers have only a simple editor, as in the Sinclair Spectrum, while other machines feature more extensive facilities. The BBC Micro, for example, includes the TRACE and RENUMber commands: the former causes the line number of each BASIC statement to be displayed as the line is being executed, and the latter automatically renumbers the lines of a BASIC program. Both of these facilities are immensely useful in program development and debugging. But whatever is provided with your machine, it is invariably helpful to have additional utilities, and there is a wide range of commercially available programs to choose from.

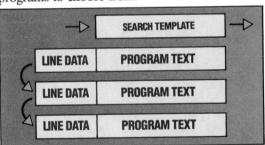

Utility programs are generally written in Assembly language, partly because of the speed of machine code and partly because it is not easy for a BASIC program to alter itself without crashing the computer. However, we will begin by looking at some simple utilities that can be writen in BASIC. In this way, we can concentrate our attention on what a utility program has to do, without having to consider other complicating details, such as the role of the computer's operating system and the BASIC interpreter.

Although it is difficult for a BASIC program to alter itself, there is no problem in creating a BASIC program that inspects another BASIC program. The utility program we give here, in versions for the Spectrum and the BBC Micro, searches through a BASIC program for the name of a variable or function, and prints the line numbers where the name is found.

Both programs begin by finding where the program text starts in the computer's memory. Then they go through the program line by line,

skipping over those sections that cannot include a name and extracting all the names. The final step involves comparing each extracted name with the name the program was asked to find.

When the program starts its search of a new line of BASIC text, it first notes the line number, which in both cases is stored in two bytes, and the line's length (the number of bytes it occupies). In the BBC Micro, the line length is contained in one byte, and is the total number of bytes in the line from the line number to the end-of-line marker (ASCII code 13). In the Spectrum, the line length is stored in two bytes, and represents the number of bytes from the character following the length bytes to the end-of-line marker (thus not including the line number and line length bytes in its total).

In both versions of the program, we ignore all the REM statements and anything that is enclosed in quotes, as we will not normally have any program variables in these character strings. The BBC Micro allows you to include hexadecimal numbers in a program, prefixed by the character &. We need to make sure that our program does not mistake these hexadecimal numbers for variable names, and therefore we need to make the program skip over any strings preceded by an &. For example, we do not want our program to mistake the hex number A0 in &A0 as the variable name 'A0'.

In the Spectrum, numbers are stored in a program as the ASCII characters for the digits of the number, followed by the ASCII code byte 14, and then five bytes containing the binary equivalent of the number. Our program needs to be able to skip over the number code and the five byte binary equivalent.

Having tested for these conditions, the program proceeds to inspect the current line for any names. In both programs, a name is defined as beginning with a letter, followed by another letter or a digit. The BBC Micro version allows integer variables (distinguished by a % character after the name) and the underscore character, and both versions allow string variables, which are followed by a $ character.

The name of an array, a function or (in the BBC Micro) a procedure will be followed by an open bracket — (. Strictly speaking, this is not part of the name, but is used by the programs to distinguish these from simple variables.

There are further complications in the Spectrum program. In particular, Spectrum BASIC does not distinguish between upper- and lower-case for characters in a variable name. Thus, FRED, Fred or FRed are all treated as the same variable name. The Spectrum program, therefore, converts

Searching Hi And Lo
On the BBC Micro and the Spectrum a program line begins with three or four bytes dedicated to the line number and the length of the line. This is followed by the tokenised BASIC text. When the program encounters the line it records the line number and calculates the start address of the next line from the length of the current line. It then 'slides' the search template along the program text until it meets end-of-line, end-of-program, a REM token or a successful match

all letters to upper-case before it starts its matching. The Spectrum will also allow spaces to be included in variable names, but these can lead to problems and we advise against their use.

Spectrum BASIC does not make the strict distinction found in most other BASIC dialects between string variables and string arrays — in fact, a Spectrum string variable is more like a character array. Since we can have, for example, T$ and T$(i), referring to a string and part of the same string, the program does not attempt to distinguish between simple string variables and string arrays. This is not a real limitation, however, as Spectrum BASIC does not allow you to have a string variable and array with the same name.

To use our utility program, first type it in and save it, and then merge it with the program you want searched, using the MERGE command on the Spectrum or the method described in Chapter 37 of the User Guide for the BBC Micro. Invoke the search routine with RUN 9000 (Spectrum) or GOTO 30000 (BBC Micro), and type in the name you want to find when asked for it. If you want an array name, add an open bracket at the end of the name.

Finally, as an exercise, you may like to use the principles described here to write a program that tells you which lines in a program contain a call to a specified subroutine. On the opposite page we have supplied a full listing of this program for the Commodore 64.

Spectrum

```
9000 INPUT "Name to search for? "; LINE T$
9010 FOR i=1 TO LEN (T$)
9020 IF T$(i)>="a" AND T$(i)<="z" THEN
LET T$(i)=CHR$ (CODE (T$(i))-32)
9030 NEXT i
9040 LET TokenforREM=234
9050 LET Quote=34
9060 LET Newline=13
9070 LET Underscore=95
9080 LET Number=14
9090 LET PROG=23635
9100 LET Textpointer=PEEK (PROG)+256*PEEK (PROG+1)
9110 LET Lineno=256*PEEK (Textpointer)+PEEK (Textpointer+1)
9120 IF Lineno>=9000 THEN STOP
9130 LET Textpointer=Textpointer+2
9140 LET Textlength=PEEK (Textpointer)+256*PEEK (Textpointer+1)
9150 LET Textpointer=Textpointer+2
9160 LET Nextline=Textpointer+Textlength
9170 IF PEEK (Textpointer)=Newline THEN
LET Textpointer=Textpointer+1: GO TO 9110
9180 IF PEEK (Textpointer)<>TokenforREM
THEN GO TO 9220
9190 REM Skip over REM line
9200 LET Textpointer=Nextline
9210 GO TO 9110
9220 IF PEEK (Textpointer)<>Quote THEN
GO TO 9280
9230 REM Skip anything between quotes, but stop at end of line in case of unmatched quote
9240 LET Textpointer=Textpointer+1
9250 IF PEEK (Textpointer)=Newline THEN
LET Textpointer=Textpointer+1: GO TO 9110
9260 IF PEEK (Textpointer)<>Quote THEN
GO TO 9240
9270 LET Textpointer=Textpointer+1
9275 GO TO 9170
9280 IF PEEK (Textpointer)<>Number THEN
GO TO 9320
9290 REM Skip 5-byte binary number
9300 LET Textpointer=Textpointer+6
9305 GO TO 9170
9310 REM First character of name must be upper or lower case letter
9320 IF PEEK (Textpointer)>=CODE ("A") AND PEEK (Textpointer)<=CODE ("Z") THEN
LET c$=CHR$ (PEEK (Textpointer)): GO TO 9370
9330 REM Use upper case instead of lower case
9340 IF PEEK (Textpointer)>=CODE ("a") AND PEEK (Textpointer)<=CODE ("z") THEN
LET c$=CHR$ (PEEK (Textpointer)-32): GO TO 9370
9350 LET Textpointer=Textpointer+1
9360 GO TO 9170
9370 LET n$=""
9380 LET n$=n$+c$
9390 LET Textpointer=Textpointer+1
9400 REM Letter, digit or underscore after first character of name
9410 IF PEEK (Textpointer)>=CODE ("A") AND PEEK (Textpointer)<=CODE ("Z") THEN
LET c$=CHR$ (PEEK (Textpointer)): GO TO 9380
9420 REM Use upper case instead of lower case
9430 IF PEEK (Textpointer)>=CODE ("a") AND PEEK (Textpointer)<=CODE ("z") THEN
LET c$=CHR$ (PEEK (Textpointer)-32): GO TO 9380
9440 IF PEEK (Textpointer)>=CODE ("0") AND PEEK (Textpointer)<=CODE ("9") THEN
LET c$=CHR$ (PEEK (Textpointer)): GO TO 9380
9450 IF PEEK (Textpointer)=Underscore THEN GO TO 9380
9460 REM End with $ for string variable
9470 IF PEEK (Textpointer)=CODE ("$") THEN LET n$=n$+"$": LET Textpointer=Textpointer+1: GO TO 9500
9480 REM ( if array or function
9490 IF PEEK (Textpointer)=CODE ("(") THEN LET n$=n$+CHR$ (PEEK (Textpointer)):
LET Textpointer=Textpointer+1
9500 IF n$=t$ THEN PRINT n$;" IN LINE ";Lineno
9520 GO TO 9170
```

BBC Micro

```
30000 INPUT "Name to search for";
TARGET$
30010 TokenforREM=244
30020 Quote=34
30030 Hex=38
30040 Newline=13
30050 Underscore=95
30060 Textpointer=PAGE
30070 Textpointer=Textpointer+1
30080 Lineno=256*?Textpointer+?(Textpointer+1)
30090 IF Lineno>=30000 THEN END
30100 Textpointer=Textpointer+2
30110 Linelength=?Textpointer
30120 Endline=Textpointer+Linelength-3
30130 Textpointer=Textpointer+1
30140 IF ?Textpointer=Newline THEN GOTO 30070
30150 IF ?Textpointer<>TokenforREM THEN GOTO 30180
30160 REM Skip over REM line
30170 Textpointer=Endline:GOTO 30070
30180 IF ?Textpointer<>Quote THEN GOTO 30240
30190 REM Skip anything between quotes, but stop at end of line in case of unmatched quote
30200 Textpointer=Textpointer+1
30210 IF ?Textpointer=Newline THEN GOTO 30070
30220 IF ?Textpointer<>Quote THEN GOTO 30200
30230 Textpointer=Textpointer+1
30235 GOTO 30140
30240 IF ?Textpointer<>Hex THEN GOTO 30300
30250 REM Skip hex number, to avoid confusion with variable names
30260 Textpointer=Textpointer+1
30270 IF ?Textpointer>=ASC("0") AND ?Textpointer<=ASC("9") THEN GOTO 30260
30280 IF ?Textpointer>=ASC("A") AND ?Textpointer<=ASC("F") THEN GOTO 30260
30285 GOTO 30140
30290 REM First character of name must be upper or lower case letter
30300 IF ?Textpointer>=ASC("A") AND ?Textpointer<=ASC("Z") THEN GOTO 30330
30310 IF ?Textpointer>=ASC("a") AND ?Textpointer<=ASC("z") THEN GOTO 30330
30320 GOTO 30130
30330 Name$=""
30340 Name$=Name$+CHR$(?Textpointer)
30350 Textpointer=Textpointer+1
30360 REM Letter, digit or underscore after first character
30370 IF ?Textpointer>=ASC("A") AND ?Textpointer<=ASC("Z") THEN GOTO 30340
30380 IF ?Textpointer>=ASC("a") AND ?Textpointer<=ASC("z") THEN GOTO 30340
30390 IF ?Textpointer>=ASC("0") AND ?Textpointer<=ASC("9") THEN GOTO 30340
30400 IF ?Textpointer=Underscore THEN GOTO 30340
30410 REM End with $ for string variable, % for integer variable
30420 IF ?Textpointer=ASC("$") THEN Name$=Name$+CHR$(?Textpointer):Textpointer=Textpointer+1:GOTO 30450
30430 IF ?Textpointer=ASC("%") THEN Name$=Name$+CHR$(?Textpointer):Textpointer=Textpointer+1
30440 REM ( if array, procedure or function
30450 IF ?Textpointer=ASC("(") THEN Name$=Name%+CHR$(?Textpointer):Textpointer=Textpointer+1
30460 IF Name$=TARGET$ THEN PRINT Name$;" IN LINE ";Lineno
30470 GOTO 30140
30480 END
```

CALLING COMMODORE

The variable search program can easily be converted to work on the Commodore 64. The Commodore 64 program is, in fact, a little simpler because there are not so many special cases to allow for.

Many of the variable names in the Commodore version of the program have to be abbreviated to avoid including a BASIC keyword. For example, NEWLINE cannot be used as a variable name because it starts with NEW, and TEXTPOINTER cannot be used either because it includes INT.

The changes near the beginning of the program are necessary because of the differences in the way a line of BASIC is stored in the computer's memory. In the BBC Micro and the Spectrum, a line of BASIC in the internal format begins with a two-byte line number, with the high order byte coming first, and one or two bytes for the length of the line. In the Commodore 64 a line of BASIC begins with a two-byte pointer to the start of the next line and a two-byte line number, with the low order byte coming first in both.

We still have to skip REM lines and strings inside quotes, but we do not have to look for any other special cases that might cause confusion, like the hexadecimal numbers on the BBC Micro or the hidden binary form of numbers on the Spectrum.

The section of the program that actually picks out the variable names looks for a letter of the alphabet first, then letters or digits, and at the end it looks for a $ or % sign indicating a string or integer variable and a (, indicating a function or array. The Commodore 64 does not allow the underscore character that can be included in variable names on the BBC Micro and the Spectrum.

Although the Commodore 64 can display both upper and lower case letters, the difference is only in the form of the character as it appears on the screen, and not in the internal code for the character. Thus, the program only needs to look for upper case letters in a variable name.

The Commodore 64 version of the program is used in the same way as the BBC Micro and Spectrum versions. Type in the search program and SAVE it, then LOAD the program to be searched and append the search program to it. You can then search the program by "RUN 30000", and typing in the variable name when the program asks for it, ending the name with "(" if you want to find an array name.

There is a simple method of joining two SAVEd programs on the Commodore 64, provided the line numbers in the first program are all less than the line numbers in the second program. The method uses two of the pointers in page zero: TXTTAB, at addresses 43 and 44, which hold the address where the BASIC program starts, and VARTAB, at addresses 45 and 46. A BASIC program ends with a byte containing zero that marks the end of the last line of the program, then two more zero bytes that mark the end of the program. The address in VARTAB is normally the byte following the last of these zeros. To join two programs together, first LOAD the program with the lowest line numbers, then type:

PRINT PEEK(45), PEEK(46)

If the first number is between two and 255 subtract two from it and POKE the result into address 43. If it is zero or one, POKE 254 or 255 into address 43 and POKE one less than the result of PEEK(46) into address 44. You can then LOAD the second program, and finally type:

POKE 43,1 : POKE 44,8

This will put the normal value back into the 'start of BASIC' pointer and the programs will now be joined together.

Commodore 64 Search Utility

```
30000 INPUT "NAME TO SEARCH FOR"; T$
30010 RE=143
30020 QUOTE=34
30030 NL=0
30040 TEXTPTR=2049
30050 NXTLINE=PEEK(TEXTPTR)+256*PEEK(TEXTPTR+1)
30070 TEXTPTR=TEXTPTR+2
30080 LINENO=PEEK(TEXTPTR)+256*PEEK(TEXTPTR+1)
30085 IF LINENO>=30000 THEN END
30090 TEXTPTR=TEXTPTR+2
30140 IF PEEK(TEXTPTR)=NL THEN TEXTPTR=TEXTPTR+1:GOTO 30050
30150 IF PEEK(TEXTPTR)<>RE THEN GOTO 30180
30160 REM SKIP OVER REM LINE
30170 TEXTPTR=NXTLINE:GOTO 30050
30180 IF PEEK(TEXTPTR)<>QUOTE THEN GOTO 30300
30190 REM SKIP ANYTHING IN QUOTES,STOP AT END OF LINE IN CASE OF UNMATCHED
      QUOTE
30200 TEXTPTR=TEXTPTR+1
30210 IF PEEK(TEXTPTR)=NL THEN TEXTPTR=TEXTPTR+1:GOTO 30500
30220 IF PEEK(TEXTPTR)<>QUOTE THEN GOTO 30200
30230 TEXTPTR=TEXTPTR+1
30235 GOTO30140
30290 REM FIRST CHARACTER OF NAME MUST BE LETTER
30300 IF PEEK(TEXTPTR)>=ASC("A") AND PEEK(TEXTPTR)<=ASC("Z") THEN GOTO 30330
30310 TEXTPTR=TEXTPTR+1
30320 GOTO30140
30330 NAME$=""
30340 NAME$=NAME$+CHR$(PEEK(TEXTPTR))
30350 TEXTPTR=TEXTPTR+1
30360 REM LETTER OR DIGIT AFTER FIRST CHARACTER
30370 IF PEEK(TEXTPTR)>=ASC("A") AND PEEK(TEXTPTR)<=ASC("Z") THEN GOTO 30340
30390 IF PEEK(TEXTPTR)>=ASC("0") AND PEEK(TEXTPTR)<=ASC("9") THEN GOTO 30340
30410 REM END WITH $ FOR STRING VARIABLE, % FOR INTEGER VARIABLE
30420 IF PEEK(TEXTPTR)=ASC("$") THEN NAME$=NAME$+"$":TEXTPTR=TEXTPTR+1
      :GOTO30450
30430 IF PEEK(TEXTPTR)=ASC("%") THEN NAME$=NAME$+"%":TEXTPTR=TEXTPTR+1
30440 REM ( IF ARRAY OR FUNCTION
30450 IF PEEK(TEXTPTR)=ASC("(") THEN NAME$=NAME$+"(":TEXTPTR=TEXTPTR+1
30460 IF NAME$=T$ THEN PRINT NAME$;" IN LINE";LINENO
30470 GOTO 30140
30480 END
```

ROOM FOR MANOEUVRE

Simple utility programs such as the variable search and replace program can be written entirely in BASIC, using only information about how individual lines of BASIC are stored. For more complicated utilities, however, we need greater detail and therefore must resort to machine code.

In order to operate our variable search program, we merged it with the program to be searched. With this method, the only information from the operating system that we had to supply was the address where the BASIC program starts; the end of the program being searched was found by testing for the lowest line number in the utility program.

The utility that we are creating is a variable replace program. This is a very useful program to have on file. If you had used a variable name throughout a program only to find it was illegal, imagine how much time such a program would save. Similarly, you might have written a program you wanted someone else to use in which the variable names were not easy to decipher. Here we explain the necessary theory for the machine code and in the next instalment we will publish the listings.

SPACE IN MEMORY

In this exercise, we need to put the utility program in a separate section of memory from the program it is working on. We must also find a different method of locating the end of the BASIC program, and a means of accommodating two BASIC programs in the computer at the same time.

The three computers that we are looking at — the BBC Micro, Commodore 64 and Sinclair Spectrum — use a set of pointers to tell the operating system and the BASIC interpreter where to locate BASIC programs and variables, etc. Unfortunately, the details are different in the three machines.

On the BBC Micro, there are four important pointers: PAGE and TOP, which hold the beginning and end address of the BASIC program; LOMEM, which holds the start address of the BASIC variables; and HIMEM, which holds the end address of the BASIC area. These four pointers are stored as built-in BASIC variables, and we can read or alter their values by simple BASIC statements. If we have a BASIC program in memory and we wish to add another, we change PAGE to a value higher than TOP — using the command OLD to reset TOP and LOMEM — and can then add the new program without affecting the original program. We change from one program to another by giving new values

to both PAGE and HIMEM and using the command OLD.

Once we have the utility program running, the values of the pointers refer to the utility program; to enable the utility to find the start and end of the program it is to work on, we need to copy the original values into an area of memory that will not be altered when we change programs. Another method of finding the end of a program is to use the end marker that the BASIC interpreter puts in. This is simply a byte holding a value of 128 or more, immediately following the carriage return character at the end of the last line of the program. This byte, and the one following, will be interpreted as the HI and LO bytes of the next line number. Since the HI byte of this number is 128 or more, this will give a line number of 32768 (256×128) or more. As the highest valid line number is 32767, we can be sure that we have found the end of program marker and not just another line number.

The Commodore 64 uses seven pointers, stored in zero page memory, to indicate various parts of the BASIC program area. TXTTAB, at addresses 43 and 44, points to the start of the BASIC program; VARTAB, ARYTAB, STREND, FRETOP and FRESPC, at addresses 45 to 54, point to various sections of the variable table; and MEMSIZ, at addresses 55 and 56, points to the end of the BASIC area. It is possible to change these pointers in order to create a separate area in which to run a BASIC program by use of the POKE command. However, a short machine code program is recommended as it is more direct, and reduces the chances of crashing the computer with a typing mistake.

In the Commodore 64, the end of a BASIC program is indicated by two bytes containing zeros immediately following the zero byte marking the end of the last line of the program. Following the chain of pointers at the beginning of each line of the program until we find a pointer of zero will indicate the end of the program.

FOR THE SPECTRUM

Creating this utility is rather more complicated on the Spectrum. Instead of a separate area for the BASIC program, there is a single, continuous block of memory that includes not only the BASIC program and variables, but also all the workspace areas used by the operating system and the BASIC interpreter. With this layout of the memory it is difficult, if not impossible, to have two BASIC programs in the main working area, so we will make a copy of our program above RAMTOP and work on it there. This still leaves the problem of recovering the program and fitting it into the main program area after it has been altered, and we will need a machine code program to do this for us.

The Spectrum manual gives a great deal of information about the way a BASIC program is stored and what the various areas of memory are used for. However, because of the large number of different sections in the working area, and the way these areas can move around, it is difficult to write utility programs without using machine code subroutines from the ROM. If you want to do any

serious utility programming on the Spectrum, a valuable reference work is *The Complete Spectrum ROM Disassembly*, by Dr Ian Logan and Dr Frank O'Hara. This explains how all the ROM routines work.

Two of the most important subroutines in the ROM for use in utility programs are the routines that open up or reclaim space in the working area, and we will be looking at these when we come to the variable search and replace program.

Try experimenting with BASIC. (You may need once or twice to refer to Chapter 4 on machine code.)

You can try altering the contents of a program during execution but you should save the program first, as a system crash is a common result. Use the Monitor program (see page 138), which allows you to inspect and alter the contents of memory. This can inspect and alter itself under your command. Insert some extra REM lines at the start of the program and try these suggestions on them first:

■ Find the start of BASIC text area (see page 128), and inspect the Monitor program in memory until you can identify program lines.

■ Change the values of the bytes after a REM token, then quit the program and list the altered line.

■ Try putting a value greater than 127 into a REM line — again, quit and list: you may be surprised.

■ Alter the line number bytes of a line — this produces unpredictable results, especially if the new number is out of sequence with its neighbours.

■ You can alter the line length bytes — try decreasing the indicated length first — but you

should insert a new end-of-line marker at the indicated byte.

■ On the Commodore 64 you can change the link address bytes: try replacing one line's link address by the link address of the succeeding line, and then list the program.

■ If you're feeling more ambitious, consult your manual and explore the variables' storage area. This usually begins in the memory map where the BASIC text area ends. There are up to six different variable types, each with its own storage format: numeric variables, numeric arrays, integer variables, integer arrays, string variables and string arrays. String and integer variable formats are the simplest, being essentially straightforward representations of the data and the variable name; numeric array data is the most complicated.

■ You can try changing token values in program lines: this will change the command word. If you do this via the Monitor program to a line that it is currently executing, you will be introducing a potentially massive paradox into the interpreter

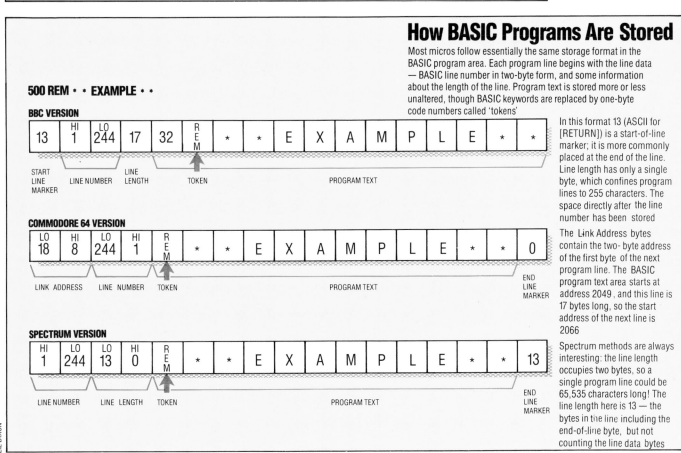

How BASIC Programs Are Stored

Most micros follow essentially the same storage format in the BASIC program area. Each program line begins with the line data — BASIC line number in two-byte form, and some information about the length of the line. Program text is stored more or less unaltered, though BASIC keywords are replaced by one-byte code numbers called 'tokens'

500 REM * * EXAMPLE * *

BBC VERSION

| 13 | HI 1 | LO 244 | 17 | 32 | R E M | * | * | E | X | A | M | P | L | E | * | * |

START LINE MARKER | LINE NUMBER | LINE LENGTH | TOKEN | PROGRAM TEXT

In this format 13 (ASCII for [RETURN]) is a start-of-line marker; it is more commonly placed at the end of the line. Line length has only a single byte, which confines program lines to 255 characters. The space directly after the line number has been stored

COMMODORE 64 VERSION

| LO 18 | HI 8 | LO 244 | HI 1 | R E M | * | * | E | X | A | M | P | L | E | * | * | 0 |

LINK ADDRESS | LINE NUMBER | TOKEN | PROGRAM TEXT | END LINE MARKER

The Link Address bytes contain the two-byte address of the first byte of the next program line. The BASIC program text area starts at address 2049, and this line is 17 bytes long, so the start address of the next line is 2066

SPECTRUM VERSION

| HI 1 | LO 244 | LO 13 | HI 0 | R E M | * | * | E | X | A | M | P | L | E | * | * | 13 |

LINE NUMBER | LINE LENGTH | TOKEN | PROGRAM TEXT | END LINE MARKER

Spectrum methods are always interesting: the line length occupies two bytes, so a single program line could be 65,535 characters long! The line length here is 13 — the bytes in the line including the end-of-line byte, but not counting the line data bytes

LIZ DIXON

NAME CALLING

Having looked in more detail at the way a BASIC program is stored, we can now extend the variable search program to include a facility to replace one variable name by another. Here we look at the BBC Micro and the Commodore 64 versions; in the next section we will develop the same program for the Spectrum.

Our variable replace program is a more demanding utility than the simple search for variable names that we developed on pages 73 to 75. For this reason we need to add a machine code

program. The BBC Micro's 6502 CPU and the Commodore 64's 6510 CPU have the same Assembly language, so it is a good idea to look at them together.

Our first task is to find a method of holding two separate programs in the computer at the same time. As we have already explained, we can do this on the BBC Micro by altering the built-in BASIC variables PAGE and HIMEM. On the Commodore 64, we need a machine code program to alter the various pointers in zero page memory. The first part of the Assembly language listing, beginning at the label SWITCH, will do this for us.

The routine SWITCH will enable us to accommodate two BASIC programs: one beginning at address 800 hex (the usual place for a BASIC program); and the other beginning at address 9000 hex. SWITCH begins by looking at the pointer TXTTAB to see which of the program areas is current, and then changes the pointer values to make the other program area current.

TXTTAB is changed to point to the start of the new program area, then FRETOP and MEMSIZ must point to the byte after the last byte of the new program area, while FRESPC points to the end of the new program area. The program then searches down the chain of link address pointers (see page 76) to find the end of the BASIC program, using VARTAB as the temporary pointer. When it finds the two zero link address bytes that mark the end of the program, it increments the previous pointer twice and copies the result into ARYTAB and STREND. In this way VARTAB, ARYTAB and STREND all point to the byte immediately after the BASIC program.

The main changes to the BASIC program that we need to make are the extra subroutines at lines 30500 and 30600. The first of these finds the end of the BASIC program, using the length of line bytes in the BBC version and the next line pointers in the Commodore 64 version.

The subroutine at line 30600 actually makes the change in the variable names. When the old and new variable names are the same length, the new name can simply be written over the old. Where the old and new variable names have different lengths, the procedure is a little more complicated. In this case, the program must either make extra space, or close up any unneeded space in the program it is changing, and make corresponding changes to the variables it uses to keep track of its position in the program being altered. It must also change the length of line byte in the BBC version and the next line pointers in the Commodore 64 version.

Intelligent Copy
The replace routine has to move large sections of the BASIC program up and down in memory when it inserts new variable names of different lengths. In this it encounters the four possible conditions of the source and destination addresses. If it always copies from the start of the source block then, when the head of the destination block overlaps the tail of the source block, the copying will overwrite some of the source data. An 'intelligent' copy routine will detect this case and avoid corruption by copying this source block from the tail first. A 'dumb' copy always copies from the head of the source block

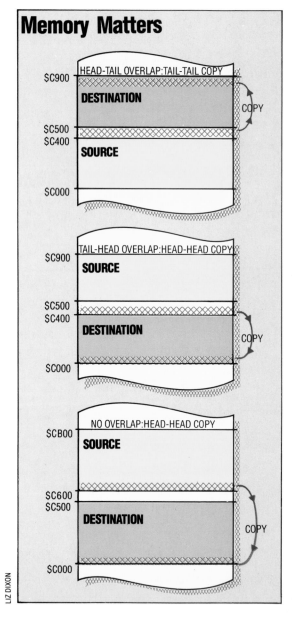

Memory Matters

HEAD-TAIL OVERLAP:TAIL-TAIL COPY

$C900

DESTINATION

COPY

$C500
$C400

SOURCE

$C000

TAIL-HEAD OVERLAP:HEAD-HEAD COPY

$C900

SOURCE

$C500
$C400

DESTINATION

COPY

$C000

NO OVERLAP:HEAD-HEAD COPY

$CB00

SOURCE

$C600
$C500

DESTINATION

COPY

$C000

LIZ DIXON

The program also uses machine code subroutines to open or close up space. Although this could be done in BASIC, it would be unacceptably slow in even a medium-size program, with thousands of bytes to be moved every time.

There are two machine code routines: UP to make extra space; and DOWN to close up unneeded space. Details of the block of program to be moved are passed to the machine code through the memory locations CURR, LAST and DIFF.

For the subroutine UP, the following memory locations need to be initialised:

CURR: address of bottom of block to be moved
LAST: one less than address of top of block to be moved
DIFF: number of bytes to be freed

and for DOWN they need to be initialised as:

CURR: address of top of block to be moved
LAST: one less than address of bottom of block to be moved
DIFF: number of bytes to be reclaimed

Note that the two subroutines start at opposite ends of the block to be moved and make the moves in opposite directions. This is to avoid the data being overwritten before it has been moved.

To use the BBC version of the variable replace program, you first need to type in (or LOAD) and RUN the Assembly language program to put the machine code into memory. Then LOAD the program to be altered and type in:

P% = PAGE

This passes the start address of the program to the variable replacement program. Then set PAGE to a value above LOMEM, and LOAD and RUN the variable replacement program. You can get back to the altered program with:

HIMEM = PAGE — 1
PAGE = P%

To use the Commodore 64 version of the program you also need to get the machine code into memory; either with the BASIC loader program or by assembling the source code. If you assemble the source code, or load the machine code directly as machine code, you will need to POKE zeros into addresses 36864, 36865 and 36866. This is equivalent to NEWing the alternate program area.

After loading the machine code, SYS 49152 will change from one program area to the other. If you forget where you are, you can find out with PRINT PEEK (44), which will give 8 for the normal program area and 144 for the alternate program area.

Once you have the machine code in the computer, you can LOAD the program to be altered into the normal program area and the variable replacement program into the alternate program area, then RUN the variable replacement program.

C64 Switch And Copy

```
10 ADDR=49152
20 FOR LINE=1000 TO 1180 STEP 10
30 S=0
40 FOR ADDR = ADDR TO ADDR+7
50 READ BYTE
60 POKE ADDR,BYTE
70 S=S+BYTE
80 NEXT ADDR
90 READ CHECKSUM
100 IF S<>CHECKSUM THEN PRINT"DATA ERROR IN
    LINE";LINE:END
110 NEXT LINE
120 POKE36864,0:POKE36865,0:POKE36866,0
1000 DATA162,0,164,44,192,8,208,9,787
1010 DATA160,160,32,72,192,169,144,208,1137
1020 DATA7,160,144,32,72,192,169,8,784
1030 DATA162,1,134,43,133,44,134,45,696
1040 DATA133,46,160,0,177,45,170,200,931
1050 DATA177,45,224,0,208,240,201,0,1095
1060 DATA208,236,230,45,208,2,230,46,1205
1070 DATA136,16,247,165,45,133,47,133,922
1080 DATA49,165,46,133,48,133,50,96,720
1090 DATA134,51,132,52,134,55,132,56,746
1100 DATA202,136,134,53,132,54,96,160,967
1110 DATA0,177,251,164,255,145,251,160,1403
1120 DATA0,196,251,208,2,198,252,198,1305
1130 DATA251,165,253,197,251,208,234,165,1724
1140 DATA254,197,252,208,228,96,164,255,1654
1150 DATA177,251,160,0,145,251,230,251,1465
1160 DATA208,2,230,252,165,253,197,251,1558
1170 DATA208,236,165,254,197,252,208,230,1750
1180 DATA96,0,0,0,0,0,0,0,96
```

BBC Copy

```
10 MODE 7
20 HIMEM=HIMEM-&100
30 CURR = &70
40 LAST = &74
50 DIFF = &78
60 FOR PASS = 1 TO 2
70 P%=HIMEM
80[ OPT 1
90 .UP    LDY #0
100 .UP1  LDA (CURR),Y
110       LDY DIFF
120       STA (CURR),Y
130       LDY #0
140       CPY CURR
150       BNE UP2
160       DEC CURR+1
170 .UP2  DEC CURR
180       LDA LAST
190       CMP CURR
200       BNE UP1
210       LDA LAST+1
220       CMP CURR+1
230       BNE UP1
240       RTS
250 .DOWN LDY DIFF
260       LDA (CURR),Y
270       LDY #0
280       STA (CURR),Y
290       INC CURR
300       BNE DOWN1
310       INC CURR+1
320 .DOWN1 LDA LAST
330       CMP CURR
340       BNE DOWN
350       LDA LAST+1
360       CMP CURR+1
370       BNE DOWN
380       RTS
390]
400 NEXT PASS
410PRINT~UP,~DOWN
```

Variable Replacement

Commodore 64
Make the following changes to the program on page 700:

```
30005 INPUT "REPLACE BY"; RS
30006 CURR = 251
30007 LAST = 253
30008 DI = 255
30035 GOSUB 30500
30036 IF ERR THEN PRINT "CAN'T FIND END OF
      PROGRAM": END
30060 IF NXTLINE = 0 THEN END
30065 CURRLINE = TEXTPTR
delete line 30085
30460 IF NAMES = T$ THEN GOSUB 30600
30465 IF ERR THEN PRINT "NO ROOM AT LINE";
LINENO: END
```

BBC Micro
Make the following changes to the program on page 665:

```
30005 INPUT "Replace by"; REPLACEMENTS$
30006 CURR = &70
30007 LAST = &74
30008 DIFF = &78
30055 GOSUB 30500
30056 IF Outofroom THEN PRINT "Can't find end
      of program": PRINT "PAGE in wrong place?":
      END
30060 Textpointer = P%
30070 IF Lineno > 32767 THEN END
30105 Lengthbyte = Textpointer
30460 IF Name$ = Target$ THEN GOSUB 30600
30465 IF Outofroom THEN PRINT "No room at
      line"; Lineno: END
```

ALL CHANGE

To implement the variable replace program on the Spectrum, we must use a different method from the BBC and Commodore versions. Instead of having the utility program in a different area of memory from the program it is working on, the variable replace program is merged onto the end.

As the variable replace program scans through the program it makes a copy of the altered version in an area above RAMTOP. The altered version is then copied back to the main program area by a machine code program that adjusts the amount of space available if the length of the program has been changed, so that the new version fits into the BASIC text area.

The first part of the BASIC program is similar to the variable search program (see page 74). There are some extra variables, including Altprog, which points to the start of the area reserved for the copy of the program, and Altpointer, which keeps track of where the next byte in the altered program should go. The main changes involve copying the program, instead of just reading it. The copying is done by the subroutine at line 9800, which copies

Automatic Writing

The Z80 LDIR and LDDR op-codes are block transfer instructions using automatic increment or decrement: the HL register is initialised to point to the start of the source block, DE must point to the start of the destination, and BT must contain the number of bytes in the block. LDIR and LDDR then copy the source byte to the destination byte, automatically increment or decrement HL and DE, and decrement BC until it reaches zero, when the copy is deemed complete. Notice that LDIR is a 'dumb' copy (see page 78) — the programmer's intelligence is assumed

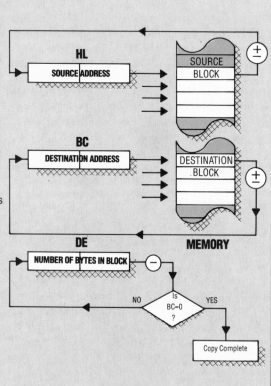

KEVIN JONES

Variable Replace Program

```
9000 INPUT "Name to search for? "; LINE
t$
9005 INPUT "Replace by?"; LINE r$
9010 FOR i=1 TO LEN (t$)
9020 IF t$(i)>="a" AND t$(i)<="z" THEN
LET t$(i)=CHR$ (CODE (t$(i))-32)
9030 NEXT i
9040 LET TokenforREM=234
9050 LET Quote=34
9060 LET Newline=13
9070 LET Underscore=95
9080 LET Number=14
9090 LET PROG=23635
9100 LET Textpointer=PEEK (PROG)+256*PEE
K (PROG+1)
9102 LET Altprog=46000
9105 LET Altpointer=Altprog
9110 LET Lineno=256*PEEK (Textpointer)+P
EEK (Textpointer+1)
9111 PRINT lineno
9120 IF Lineno>=9000 THEN  GO TO 9600
9130 LET q=2: GO SUB 9800
9135 LET Lengthaddr=Altpointer
9140 LET Nextline=Textpointer+2+PEEK (Te
xtpointer)+256*PEEK (Textpointer+1)
9150 LET q=2: GO SUB 9800
9160 LET Byte=PEEK (Textpointer): LET q=
1: GO SUB 9800
9170 IF Byte=Newline THEN· GO TO 9110
9180 IF Byte<>TokenforREM THEN  GO TO 92
20
9190 REM Copy REM  unaltered
9200 LET q=Nextline-Textpointer: GO SUB
9800
9210 GO TO 9110
9220 IF Byte<>Quote THEN  GO TO 9280
9230 REM Copy anything between quotes, b
ut stop at end of line in case of unmatc
hed quote
9235 LET q=1
9240 IF PEEK (Textpointer+q-1)=Newline T
HEN  GO SUB 9800: GO TO 9110
9250 IF PEEK (Textpointer+q-1)=Quote THE
N  GO SUB 9800: GO TO 9160
9260 LET q=q+1
9270 GO TO 9240
9280 REM Copy 5-byte binary number
9290 IF Byte=Number THEN  LET q=5: GO SU
B 9800: GO TO 9160
9310 REM First character of name must be
 upper or lower case letter
9320 IF Byte>=CODE ("A") AND Byte<=CODE
("Z") THEN  LET c$=CHR$ (Byte): GO TO 93
70
9330 REM Use upper case instead of lower
 case
9340 IF Byte>=CODE ("a") AND Byte<=CODE
("z") THEN  LET c$=CHR$ (Byte-32): GO TO
 9370
9360 GO TO 9160
9370 LET n$=""
9380 LET n$=n$+c$
9400 REM Letter, digit or underscore aft
er first character of name
9410 IF PEEK (Textpointer)>=CODE ("A") A
ND PEEK (Textpointer)<=CODE ("Z") THEN
LET c$=CHR$ (PEEK (Textpointer)): LET Te
xtpointer=Textpointer+1: GO TO 9380
9420 REM Use upper case instead of lower
 case
9430 IF PEEK (Textpointer)>=CODE ("a") A
ND PEEK (Textpointer)<=CODE ("z") THEN
LET c$=CHR$ (PEEK (Textpointer)-32): LET
 Textpointer=Textpointer+1: GO TO 9380
9440 IF PEEK (Textpointer)>=CODE ("0") A
ND PEEK (Textpointer)<=CODE ("9") THEN
LET c$=CHR$ (PEEK (Textpointer)): LET Te
xtpointer=Textpointer+1: GO TO 9380
9450 IF PEEK (Textpointer)=Underscore TH
EN  LET c$=CHR$ (PEEK (Textpointer)): LE
T Textpointer=Textpointer+1: GO TO 9380
9460 REM End with $ for string variable
9470 IF PEEK (Textpointer)=CODE ("$") TH
EN  LET n$=n$+"$": LET Textpointer=Textp
ointer+1: GO TO 9500
9480 REM ( if array or function
9490 IF PEEK (Textpointer)=CODE ("(") TH
EN  LET n$=n$+CHR$ (PEEK (Textpointer)):
 LET Textpointer=Textpointer+1
```

```
9500 IF n$=t$ THEN  LET n$=r$
9505 LET Altpointer=Altpointer-1
9510 FOR p=1 TO LEN (n$)
9520 POKE Altpointer,CODE (n$(p))
9530 LET Altpointer=Altpointer+1
9540 NEXT p
9550 IF n$<>r$ THEN  GO TO 9160
9560 LET LengthLow=PEEK (Lengthaddr)+LEN
 (r$)-LEN (t$)
9570 IF LengthLow>255 THEN  LET Lengthlo
w=LengthLow-256: POKE Lengthaddr+1,1+PEE
K (Lengthaddr+1)
9580 POKE Lengthaddr,LengthLow
9590 GO TO 9160
9599 REM Prepare to move altered program
 back to main program area
9600 LET Oldlength=Textpointer-(PEEK (PR
OG)+256*PEEK (PROG+1))
9610 LET Newlength=Altpointer-Altprog
9620 POKE 45060,Newlength-256*INT (Newle
ngth/256)
9630 POKE 45061,INT (Newlength/256)
9660 POKE 45056,Textpointer-256*INT (Tex
tpointer/256)
9670 POKE 45057,INT (Textpointer/256)
9680 IF Oldlength=Newlength THEN  RANDOM
IZE USR (45084)
9690 IF Oldlength<Newlength THEN  LET X=
Newlength-Oldlength
9700 IF Oldlength>Newlength THEN  LET X=
Textpointer-(Oldlength-Newlength)
9710 POKE 45058,X-256*INT (X/256)
9720 POKE 45059,INT (X/256)
9730 IF Oldlength<Newlength THEN  RANDOM
IZE USR 45062
9740 IF Oldlength>Newlength THEN  RANDOM
IZE USR 45074
9800 FOR p=Textpointer TO Textpointer+q-
1
9810 POKE Altpointer,PEEK (p)
9820 LET Altpointer=Altpointer+1
9830 NEXT p
9840 LET Textpointer=p
9850 RETURN
9900 SAVE "REPLACE" LINE 9910: SAVE "REP
MC"CODE 45064,37: STOP
9910 CLEAR 45055: LOAD "REPMC"CODE
```

Machine Code Loader

```
10 CLEAR 45055
20 LET a=45062
30 FOR l=1000 TO 1040 STEP 10
40 LET s=0
50 FOR a=a TO a+7
60 READ b
70 POKE a,b
80 LET s=s+b
90 NEXT a
100 READ c
110 IF s<>c THEN  PRINT "DATA ERROR IN
LINE ";l: STOP
120 NEXT l
1000 DATA 42,0,176,237,75,2,176,205,913
1010 DATA 85,22,24,10,42,0,176,237,596
1020 DATA 91,2,176,205,229,25,33,176,937
1030 DATA 179,237,91,83,92,237,75,4,998
1040 DATA 176,237,176,207,255,0,0,0,1051
```

Replace Assembly Program

```
0000          MKROOM EQU   $1655
0000          RCLAM1 EQU   $19E5
0000          T0     EQU   $B000
0000          T1     EQU   $B002
0000          T2     EQU   $B004
0000          ALTPRG EQU   $B3B0
0000          PROG   EQU   $5C53
B006                 ORG   $B006
B006 2A00B0   UP     LD    HL, (T0)
B009 ED4B02B0        LD    BC, (T1)
B00D CD5516          CALL  MKROOM
B010 180A            JR    COPY
B012 2A00B0   DOWN   LD    HL, (T0)
B015 ED5B02B0        LD    DE, (T1)
B019 CDE519          CALL  RCLAM1
B01C 21B0B3   COPY   LD    HL, ALTPRG
B01F ED5B535C        LD    DE, (PROG)
B023 ED4B04B0        LD    BC, (T2)
B027 EDB0            LDIR
B029 CF              RST   8
B02A FF              DB    $FF
```

the number of bytes specified by q, and updates the pointers to the old and new programs.

Variable names are copied by the code starting at line 9500, and, if the variable name has been changed, the two bytes at the beginning of the line that hold the length of the line are altered to reflect the change in length.

After the whole program has been altered and copied to the new area, the BASIC program calculates the values needed by the machine code for copying back the altered program, and then POKEs these values into the memory locations where the machine code expects to find them.

If the new and old programs are the same length, the new program can be copied into the same space that is occupied by the old program. In this case, the only information needed by the machine code program is the program's length.

If the new program is longer than the old program, we have to make extra space in the program area by moving up the variable replace routine, which we want to keep. The extra space is made by calling the ROM subroutine, MAKE-ROOM, at address 1655 hex. When MAKE-ROOM is called, the HL register pair must contain the address after the place where space is to be made, and the BC register pair must hold the length of the space needed. The value required for HL is just the final value of the variable Textpointer, and the value for BC is the difference between the old and the new lengths.

If the new program is shorter than the old, we have to move the variable replace program down. We can do this by using the ROM subroutine RECLAIM-1 at address 19E5 hex. When RECLAIM-1 is called, the HL register pair must hold the address of the first byte to be left alone, and the DE register pair must contain the address of the first byte to be reclaimed. The value required for HL is again the final value of the variable Textpointer, and the value required for DE is calculated by subtracting the difference between the old and new lengths from Textpointer.

The altered program is copied back to the main program area by the block move instruction LDIR (LoaD with Increment and Repeat). The start address of the altered program area is loaded into HL, the start address of the main program area into DE, the length of the altered program into BC, and then the LDIR instruction moves the whole of the altered program, byte to byte.

The last two lines in the Assembly language program use another ROM routine, at address 8. This is the 'report' routine that prints an error message and other comments. The routine is called by the RST 8 instruction, and the report produced is specified by the byte following the RST 8 instruction. The value of the byte is one less than the report number, so FF hex, or -1, gives the OK or Program finished report; 0 gives NEXT without FOR, and so on. The machine code program ends with RST8, instead of the usual RET instruction, to avoid returning to the BASIC program that has been moved.

SPIRIT OF ADVENTURE

Adventure gaming is an extremely popular pastime among home computer users. But playing a game is only half the fun; writing your own adventure is an enjoyable and creative activity. We begin an extensive programming project in which we take you through all the stages of building up an adventure game.

Adventure game playing became popular in the early 1970s when the game Dungeons and Dragons was devised. In this game, the players take on the roles of various characters within an imaginary world designed by the Dungeonmaster. This imagined world generally consists of an intricate maze of rooms, containing objects and perils, which the players have to negotiate. Generally, the aim of the game is to escape from the maze, usually rescuing someone or something

along the way. Mainframe programmers were the first to apply the game to computers, constructing complex labyrinths for other mainframe users to wander through. The advantage of computer-based Dungeons and Dragons was that the Dungeonmaster and the players did not have to be present at the same time, allowing individuals to play whenever they wished. Since then the Dungeons and Dragons type of game has widened its scope and appeal considerably — Essex University's Multi-User Dungeon is an excellent example of how sophisicated some have become.

Some adventure games are purely text-based, whereas others make use of colour and graphics to provide screen images. However, some critics argue that the addition of graphics uses up valuable memory space that could otherwise be used to add intricacies to the game's structure. They also point out that a computer graphic picture of a scene or location is no match for one's

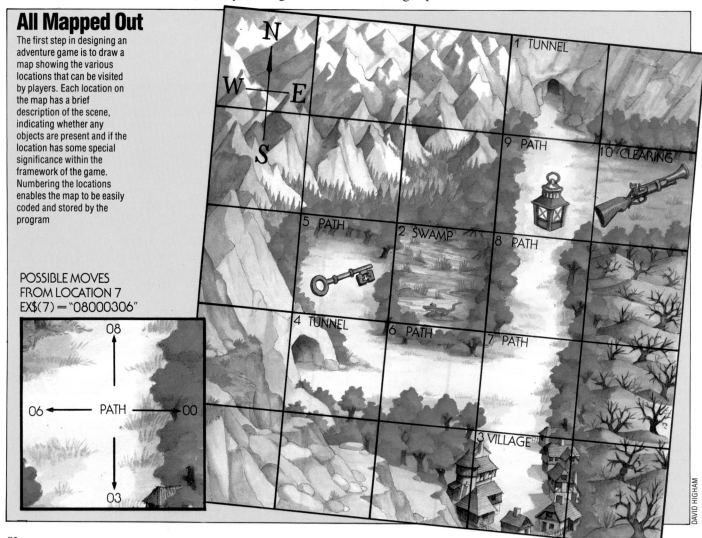

All Mapped Out

The first step in designing an adventure game is to draw a map showing the various locations that can be visited by players. Each location on the map has a brief description of the scene, indicating whether any objects are present and if the location has some special significance within the framework of the game. Numbering the locations enables the map to be easily coded and stored by the program

POSSIBLE MOVES
FROM LOCATION 7
EX$(7) = "08000306"

own imagination conjuring up a picture based on a textual description. However, the rise in the popularity of adventure games is almost certainly attributable to the enhanced visual appeal that graphics give, and, although some recent micro games use only simple pictures to enhance the text, others attempt to make the game visual.

In our programming project we shall be looking at the techniques involved in programming an adventure game. During the project, you will be given sections of a listing to an adventure game called Digitaya, which will build into a complete program. In this game, the player is cast as an 'electronic' agent given the task of descending into a microcomputer to locate and rescue the mysterious Digitaya from the clutches of the machine. There are many dangers and difficulties along the way and you have to use all your knowledge of computers to good effect to escape unharmed. The program is, as far as possible, written in 'standard' BASIC, with 'Flavours' given where appropriate. Therefore, provided you have sufficient memory capacity, the program will run on your computer. As we are going to discuss the various programming techniques in detail, it would be difficult not to give away many of the secrets of the game, and this would spoil, to some extent, the pleasure of playing it when it is complete. We will, therefore, construct a shorter game called Haunted Forest, in parallel with Digitaya, which will demonstrate the techniques and algorithms used to build the larger game.

MAKING A MAP

The starting point for the design of our adventure game is to construct a map of the fantasy world that we are imagining. On this map, we mark out the various locations within the world, the position of any objects to be found, and signify those locations that are considered 'special'. Most locations on the map will simply allow the player to move in and out of them, and pick up or drop any objects that are there. Special locations may be perilous (a swamp or a place where a dragon lurks), or they may require a series of special actions to be performed before you can enter into, or exit from, them.

The best way to begin making a map is to consider roughly how many locations are needed for the game. Haunted Forest has 10 locations and was designed on a five by five grid (as shown in the illustration), whereas Digitaya has nearly 60 locations and was originally designed using a 10 by 10 grid.

The grid squares are initially unnumbered and the designer starts by filling in locations on the map. On the Haunted Forest map there is a path, two tunnels, a swamp, a clearing and a village. The positions of several objects are also marked at the bottom of the squares where they are located. Those locations marked with an asterisk (*) are 'special' and will be treated in a different way to the rest of the locations.

Once the layout has been finalised we can number each location. The only special consideration we have taken into account in choosing the location number is that all the special locations have been numbered first. The order in which the others are numbered is not important, but once numbers have been selected it is important that they are not changed later.

PROGRAMMING THE MAP DATA

The first programming task is to convert the information in the map into data for the program. There are many ways of doing this, but what we will do here is use two one-dimensional arrays to hold the map data. The first array, LN$(), holds descriptions of each location. For example, for location 7, LN$(7) will contain 'on a path'. When the data is used later in the program to describe a location it will be prefixed by the words 'You are'.

The second array, EX$(), holds data about the possible moves that can be made out of a location. Both of our games limit themselves to four directions: North, East, South and West. EX$() provides information about the location number to be moved to for each of the four directions. The data is held as a string made up of eight digits. The location number for each direction is entered in the order NESW, using a two-digit number for each direction.

For example, location 7 has exits to the North, South and West, but none to the East. The first two digits of EX$(7) are 08 (not just 8), which shows that location 8 is to the North. The second pair of digits, 00, indicates that there is no exit in this direction (East). The digit pairs 03 and 06 represent the locations found to the South and West of location 7. Using this system, up to 39 locations could be specified; if more than this were required then the data for EX$() would have to be entered as groups of three digits.

The three objects in the Haunted Forest are read into another array — IV$(,). This two-dimensional array keeps track of the position of each object as it is moved around the forest. Each object has a description and its starting location on the map. For example, IV$(C,1) may be GUN, and its position at the start of the game is given by IV$(C,2), As the objects are carried around during the game the position members of the array will be updated accordingly.

At the end of the map data in both of our listings there is another item of data. This is a 'checksum' and is given to ensure that the direction data has been typed in correctly. This is done by calculating a running total of the data values, which is compared against the checksum. If these are not the same then a mistake has been made and the program will stop running. You will notice that in Digitaya two checksums are used. This is because the total sum of all the direction data is too large to be held easily in one checksum, so a total for the left-hand and right-hand four digits is calculated separately. In the next stage of the project, we will design routines to handle and display the map data assembled here.

Digitaya

```
6090 REM **** READ ARRAY DATA S/R ****
6100 REM ** READ INVENTORY **
6110 DIM IV$(8,2),IC$(4)
6120 FOR C =1TO8
6130 READ IV$(C,1),IV$(C,2)
6140 NEXT C
6150 :
6160 REM ** READ LOCATION & EXIT DATA **
6170 DIM LN$(55),EX$(55)
6180 C1=0:C2=0:REM INITIALISE CHECKSUMS
6190 FOR C=1TO54
6200 READ LN$(C),EX$(C)
6210 C1=C1+VAL(LEFT$(EX$(C),4))
6220 C2=C2+VAL(RIGHT$(EX$(C),4))
6230 NEXT C
6240 READ CA:IFCA<>C1THEN PRINT"CHECKSUM ERROR":ST
OP
6250 READ CB:IFCB<>C2THEN PRINT"CHECKSUM ERROR":ST
OP
6260 RETURN
6270 REM **** INVENTORY DATA ****
6280 DATA ADDRESS NUMBER,45,KEY,34,LASER SHIELD,25
6290 DATA TICKET TO THE TRI-STATE,26,DATA CREDIT C
ARD,28
6300 DATA DIGITAYA,30,CODE BOOK,19,BUFFER ACTIVATI
NG DEVICE,13
6310 :
6320 REM **** LOCATION & EXIT DATA ****
6330 DATA IN THE TV OUTLET,00000000
6340 DATA IN THE USER PORT,00090100
6350 DATA IN THE CASSETTE PORT,00110000
6360 DATA IN THE JOYSTICK PORT,00130000
6370 DATA IN A TRI-STATE DEVICE,00170000
6380 DATA IN THE ARITHMETIC & LOGIC UNIT,00310016
6390 DATA AT THE GATEWAY TO MEMORY,00490000
6400 DATA ON THE I/O HIGHWAY,09000001
6410 DATA ON THE I/O HIGHWAY,10000802
6420 DATA ON THE I/O HIGHWAY,11000900
6430 DATA ON THE I/O HIGHWAY,12001003
6440 DATA ON THE I/O HIGHWAY,13531100
6450 DATA ON THE I/O HIGHWAY,14001204
6460 DATA ON THE I/O HIGHWAY,15001300
6470 DATA ON THE I/O HIGHWAY A SIGN SAYS 'S OUT H'
,00001400
6480 DATA IN THE DATA REGISTER,00061700
6490 DATA ON AN 8 LANE HIGHWAY,16001805
6500 DATA ON AN 8 LANE HIGHWAY,17001900
6510 DATA ON AN 8 LANE HIGHWAY,18002000
6520 DATA ON AN 8 LANE HIGHWAY,19292100
6530 DATA ON AN 8 LANE HIGHWAY,20282200
6540 DATA ON AN 8 LANE HIGHWAY,21272300
6550 DATA ON AN 8 LANE HIGHWAY,22262400
6560 DATA ON AN 8 LANE HIGHWAY,23250000
6570 DATA IN THE CHARACTER MATRIX,26360024
6580 DATA HIGH IN THE MEMORY,27352523
6590 DATA IN THE MIDDLE OF MEMORY,28342622
6600 DATA IN THE MIDDLE OF MEMORY,29332721
6610 DATA LOW IN THE MEMORY,00542820
6620 DATA IN THE ACCUMULATOR'S LAIR,00000600
6630 DATA IN A LONG CORRIDOR,00420006
6640 DATA IN AN INDEX REGISTER,31000000
6650 DATA LOW IN THE MEMORY,54403428
6660 DATA IN THE MIDDLE OF MEMORY,33393527
6670 DATA HIGH UP IN MEMORY,34383626
6680 DATA IN THE CHARACTER MATRIX,35370025
6690 DATA IN A RANDOM VECTOR TABLE,00000000
6700 DATA HIGH IN MEMORY OVERLOOKING A HIGHWAY,390
03735
6710 DATA IN THE MIDDLE OF MEMORY,40003834
6720 DATA IN MEMORY - TO THE EAST IS A GATEWAY,410
03933
6730 DATA LOW IN MEMORY,00004054
6740 DATA IN A CORRIDOR,00430031
6750 DATA IN A CORRIDOR,00440042
6760 DATA IN A CORRIDOR,00004543
6770 DATA IN THE ADDRESS REGISTER,00004600
6780 DATA ON A 16 LANE HIGHWAY,45004700
6790 DATA ON A 16 LANE HIGHWAY,46004800
6800 DATA ON A 16 LANE HIGHWAY,47004900
6810 DATA ON A 16 LANE HIGHWAY A LARGE GATE LOOMS
TO THE WEST,48005007
6820 DATA ON A 16 LANE HIGHWAY,49005100
6830 DATA ON A 16 LANE HIGHWAY,50005200
6840 DATA ON A 16 LANE HIGHWAY,51000000
6850 DATA IN A VECTOR TO MEMORY,00290012
6860 DATA LOW IN MEMORY,00413329
6870 REM ** CHECKSUM DATA **
6880 DATA 100169,103973
```

Haunted Forest

```
6000 REM **** READ OBJ & MAP DATA ****
6010 DIM IV$(3,2),LN$(10),EX$(10),IC$(2)
6020 FOR C=1 TO 3
6030 READ IV$(C,1),IV$(C,2)
6040 NEXT C
6050 :
6060 FOR C=1 TO 10
6065 READ LN$(C),EX$(C)
6070 CC=CC+VAL(EX$(C)):REM CHECKSUM TOTAL
6080 NEXT C
6090 :
6100 READ CD:IFCD<>CC THENPRINT"CHECKSUM ERROR":STOP
6110 :
6120 REM ** OBJECT DATA **
6130 DATA GUN,10,LAMP,9,KEY,5
6140 :
6150 REM ** MAP DATA **
6160 DATA NEAR A TUNNEL ENTRANCE,00000900
6170 DATA IN A SWAMP,00000000
6180 DATA IN A VILLAGE,07000000
6190 DATA NEAR A TUNNEL ENTRANCE,05060000
6200 DATA ON A PATH,00020400
6210 DATA ON A PATH,02070004
6220 DATA ON A PATH,08000306
6230 DATA ON A PATH,09000702
6240 DATA ON A PATH,01100800
6250 DATA IN A CLEARING,00000009
6260 REM ** CHECKSUM DATA **
6270 DATA 32253121
6280 RETURN
```

STORY LINE

The adventure games that we are designing in this programming project are text-based — when the player enters a new location, the description and the possible exits must be printed to the screen. Here, we develop a utility that will allow us to format output to the screen.

As Digitaya and Haunted Forest are both text-based adventures, they use words to describe locations and events. Passing this information to the screen using PRINT statements can be inelegant. For example, a PRINT statement that exceeds the length of one screen line will carry onto the next line, often splitting in two words that fall across the end of the screen line. A laborious way to get around this problem would be to consider each PRINT statement in the program individually and 'manually' format the output so that words on the ends of lines were not split. If there were just a few occasions on which this had to be done then it would not be too much of a chore, but in an adventure game program this would have to be done a lot. The alternative is to design a routine that formats output for us. To use such a routine we should be able to pass the sentence we want to format to the routine via a string variable, and the routine should take care of the formatting and output.

Digitaya and Haunted Forest both use a special routine to format their output, so before we continue to describe the game programming itself, let's look at how this routine works. Here is the listing from the Haunted Forest game.

```
5500 REM **** FORMAT OUTPUT S/R ****
5510 LC=0:     REM CHAR/LINE COUNTER
5520 OC=1:     REM OLD COUNT INITIAL VALUE
5530 OW$="":   REM OLD WORD  INITIAL VALUE
5540 LL=40:    REM LINE LENGTH
5550 SN$=SN$+" DUMMY "
5560 PRINT
5570 FOR C=1 TO LEN(SN$)
5580 LC=LC+1
5590 IF MID$(SN$,C,1)=" " THEN GOSUB5800
5600 NEXT C
5605 PRINT
5610 RETURN
5620 :
5800 REM ** END OF LINE CHECK S/R **
5810 NW$=MID$(SN$,OC,C-OC+1):REM NEW WORD
5820 IF LC<LL THENPRINTOW$;:GOTO5840
5830 PRINTOW$:LC=LEN(NW$)
5840 OC=C+1:OW$=NW$
5850 RETURN
```

The routine first of all searches through the sentence, passed to it by the variable SN$, for a space character. Whenever a space is found, the subroutine at line 6020 is called. This subroutine carries out several important tasks. Using OC to indicate the beginning of a word (initially, OC is set to 1), and C to keep track of the current character under examination, the word encountered before the space can be isolated using MID$ and stored in NW$ (for 'New Word'). Before the contents of NW$ are output to the screen, they will be transferred to OW$.

A line counter, LC, is used to count how many characters have been used so far on any given line, and this is checked at line 6040 to ensure that it is less than the permitted line length, LL. If this is the case, then OW$ is PRINTed, followed by a semi-colon to ensure that any output that follows will continue on the same line. If LC does exceed LL then, again, OW$ is PRINTed, but this time omitting the semi-colon (and thus, any output that follows

Formation Display
The screen formatting routine used by Haunted Forest and Digitaya allows any screen output to be formatted so that word breaks do not occur. By using variables OW$ and NW$ the routine 'looks' one word ahead of the word about to be printed. If the next word were to exceed the designated line length, the semi-colon suppressing a carriage return is ommited, causing a new line to be started

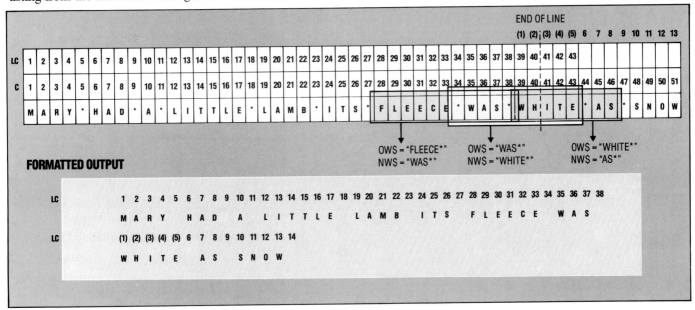

FORMATTED OUTPUT

will start on a new line). In addition, the line counter, LC, is reset to the length of the new word.

Now let's see how this subroutine works in practice. The routine scans through the sentence to be formatted, searching for a space. When a space is found, the characters between it and the last space found are designated as forming a new word. The routine is, effectively, looking ahead one word from that which is being PRINTed. The routine checks if the maximum wordlength has been exceeded when the new word is added to the screen line. If so, the routine causes a new line to be started. Thus, word splits over the end of the lines are avoided. The addition of " DUMMY " to the end of the sentence is important, as this provides a last word to be stored in NW$. The spaces around " DUMMY " are significant: the former marking it as a separate word and the latter providing a final space to be detected by the routine.

Let's take as our example, the sentence 'Mary had a little lamb its fleece was white as snow.' The screen width we will use is 40 characters wide. If the sentence were unformatted, the word 'white' would be split in two, with the letters 'ite' starting a new line. The formatting routine, however, takes the sentence two words at a time. If we consider the two words preceeding 'white', then 'fleece' would be stored in OW$ and 'was' in NW$. Having checked that the counter, LC, does not exceed 40, OW$ is PRINTed, followed by a semi-colon; 'was' is then transferred from NW$ to OW$ and the routine continues to scan the sentence, and finds the word 'white'. At this stage, the counter LC exceeds 40, indicating that 'white', falls over a line break. In this situation, OW$ (now containing the word 'was') is still PRINTed but without a semi-colon. In addition, the counter LC is reset to the number of characters in this word. The word 'white' is transferred to OW$, for subsequent PRINTing on a new line.

TESTING THE ROUTINE

In order to test the routine, we will use it format and display the initial description of the story. We can assemble a sentence of up to 248 characters, using the variable SN$, and call the formatting subroutine. Type in the following lines:

```
1000 REM **** STORY SO FAR S/R ****
1010 SN$="WELCOME TO THE HAUNTED FOREST"
1020 GOSUB5500:REM FORMAT
1030 PRINT
1040 SN$="AS YOU AWAKE FROM A DEEP SLEEP, THE "
1050 SN$=SN$+"FOREST FLOOR FEELS SOFT AND DRY. "
1060 SN$="YOU DO NOT KNOW HOW YOU CAME TO BE HERE "
1070 SN$=SN$+"BUT KNOW THAT YOU MUST FIND THE "
1080 SN$=SN$+"VILLAGE ON THE EDGE OF THE WOOD TO "
1090 SN$=SN$+"REACH SAFETY."
1100 GOSUB5500:REM FORMAT
1110 PRINT
1120 SN$="YOU LOOK AROUND, TRYING TO GET YOUR BEARINGS."
1130 GOSUB5500:REM FORMAT
1140 PRINT:PRINT"PRESS ANY KEY TO START"
1150 GET A$:IF A$="" THEN 1150
1160 PRINTCHR$(147):REM CLEAR SCREEN
1170 RETURN
```

We then need to call the 'Story So Far' subroutine using these lines:

```
205 GOSUB 1000: REM STORY SO FAR
990 END
```

Digitaya Listings

```
1110 GOSUB1250:REM STORY SO FAR
1270 END

1290 REM **** STORY SO FAR ****
1300 SN$="WELCOME TO 'DIGITAYA'"
1310 GOSUB5880:REM FORMAT
1320 PRINT
1330 SN$="AS THE MACHINE HUMS QUIETLY. YOU LOOK AROUND."
1340 SN$=SN$+" TO THE NORTH AND SOUTH STRETCHES A WIDE HIGHWAY."
1350 SN$=SN$+" YOUR MISSION IS TO FIND THE MYSTERIOUS DIGITAYA"
1360 SN$=SN$+" AND CARRY IT TO SAFETY THROUGH ONE OF THE OUTPUT PORTS."
1370 SN$=SN$+".. BUT WHICH ONE ?"
1380 GOSUB5880
1390 PRINT:PRINT"PRESS A KEY TO START"
1400 GETA$:IFA$=""THEN1400
1410 PRINTCHR$(147):REM CLEAR SCREEN
1420 RETURN

5880 REM **** FORMAT PRINTING S/R ****
5890 LC=0:   REM CHAR/LINE COUNTER
5900 OC=1:   REM OLD COUNT
5910 OW$="":REM OLD WORD
5920 LL=40:REM SCREEN LINE LENGTH
5930 SN$=SN$+" DUMMY "
5940 PRINT
5950 FOR C=1 TO LEN(SN$)
5960 LC=LC+1
5970 IF MID$(SN$,C,1)=" " THENGOSUB6020
5980 NEXTC
5990 PRINT
6000 RETURN
6010 :
6020 REM **** END OF LINE CHECK S/R ****
6030 NW$=MID$(SN$,OC,C-OC+1)
6040 IF LC<LL THENPRINTOW$;:GOTO6060
6050 PRINTOW$:LC=LEN(NW$)
6060 OC=C+1:OW$=NW$
6070 RETURN
```

Basic Flavours
Spectrum:
For the Digitaya listing, make the following changes to the Formatting Routine:

Replace SN$ by S$, OW$ by O$, NW$ by N$
```
5920 LET LL=32: REM SCREEN LENGTH LINE
5970 IF S$(C TO C)=" " THEN GOSUB 6020
6030 LET N$=S$ (OC TO C)
```

In the Story So Far subroutine, replace $SN by $S

```
1400 IF INKEY$="" THEN 1400
1410 CLS
```

For the Haunted Forest listing, replace the same string variable names, and change these lines:

```
5540 LET LL=32: REM SCREEN LINE LENGTH
5590 IF S$ (C TO C)=" " THEN GOSUB 5800
5810 LET N$=S$ (OC TO C)
```
and
```
1150 IF INKEY$="" THEN 1150
1160 CLS
```

BBC Micro:
For the Story So Far subroutine, the following changes must be made to Digitaya:

```
1095 MODE 1
1400 A$=GET$
1410 CLS
```

and Haunted Forest:

```
1160 CLS
```

ON LOCATION

So far in our adventure game programming project, we have developed a map of the locations that form the basis of a game and written a utility routine that formats output to the screen. We are now in a position to design routines that describe locations within the game and allow the player to move between locations.

The basic description of each location is held in the array LN$() (see page 83) and can be accessed simply by specifying the number of the location arrived at. In Haunted Forest, the position held by the player at any given time is stored in the variable P, and, therefore, the description of that location is stored in LN$(P). When the location data was first designed the description's final grammatical context was kept in mind; the description always being phrased in such a way that it could be prefixed by 'You are...'. For a given location, P, the description can be formatted and output to the utility developed in the last instalment, by combining 'You are' with the description held for that location in the array LN$(). Line 2010 in the Haunted Forest listing shows this.

In addition to the basic description of the location arrived at, the player will also want to know if any objects are present. The objects used in the game are stored — together with their initial positions in the inventory — in a two-dimensional array, IV$(,). For example, IV$(N,1) holds the description of the Nth object in the inventory, and IV$(N,2) holds its position. If we wish to determine whether or not there is an object at a particular location we must search through the inventory, checking each object's position against the number of the location that is being described. As there are only three objects in Haunted Forest and eight objects in Digitaya, a simple linear search using a FOR...NEXT loop can be implemented.

Lines 2040-2080 show the search loop used in Haunted Forest. The second column of the inventory array is scanned for a match with the current location, P. When a match is found, then the corresponding description is added to the sentence that describes the objects. As more than one object may be present in any one location, we must allow for the construction of a sentence where a list of objects is given, each separated by a comma. By using SP$, initially as a null string, and later as a comma, we can insert the correct punctuation between each item. A flag, F, initially set to zero, is set to one to signal the fact that an object match has been found during the search. If the flag remains at zero at the end of the search,

then no objects are present, and this fact can be output to the player — as in line 2090 of Haunted Forest.

```
2000 REM **** DESCRIBE LOCATION ****
2010 SN$="YOU ARE "+LN$(P):GOSUB5500
2020 SN$="YOU SEE "
2030 REM ** CHECK INVENTORY FOR OBJ **
2040 F=0:SP$=""
2050 FOR I=1 TO 3
2060 IF VAL(IV$(I,2))<>P THEN 2080
2070 SN$=SN$+SP$+"A "+IV$(I,1):F=1:SP$=", "
2080 NEXT I
2090 IF F=0 THEN SN$=SN$+"NO OBJECTS"
2100 GOSUB5500:REM FORMAT OUTPUT
2110 RETURN
```

The data containing details of the possible exits from each location is held in the array EX$(). Each string value is made up of eight digits. By subdividing these eight digits into groups of two, we obtain — working from left to right — the

A Room With A View
The details of the locations in our adventure game are held in three string arrays, which contain object names and whereabouts (V$), location exits (EX$) and descriptions (LN$). EX$ (34), for example, might contain the eight-digit number 33390027, showing that location 34 connects to locations 33,39 and 27 by its north, east and west exits respectively. LN$(34) contains 'The Middle Of Memory', which describes location 34. IV$(2,2) contains the number 34, showing that IV$(2,1) — The Key — is in location 34. Given the current location number the program assembles this information into a description

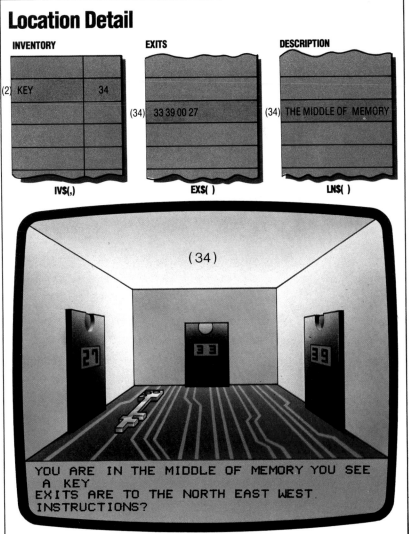

Location Detail

INVENTORY   EXITS   DESCRIPTION

(2) KEY   34

(34) 33 39 00 27

(34) THE MIDDLE OF MEMORY

IV$(,)   EX$( )   LN$( )

(34)

```
YOU ARE IN THE MIDDLE OF MEMORY YOU SEE
A KEY
EXITS ARE TO THE NORTH EAST WEST.
INSTRUCTIONS?
```

KEVIN JONES

numbers of the locations lying to the north, east, south and west of the current location. In order to determine which exits are possible, the program first splits the eight-digit string into the four numbers that describe which location lies in each direction.

```
2300 REM **** DESCRIBE EXITS S/R ****
2310 EX$=EX$(P)
2320 NR=VAL(LEFT$(EX$,2))
2330 EA=VAL(MID$(EX$,3,2))
2340 SO=VAL(MID$(EX$,5,2))
2350 WE=VAL(RIGHT$(EX$,2))
```

If there is no exit in a given direction, the value assigned is zero — and this is a great help with the description of the exits. A preliminary check must be made to see if any exits are possible before starting to construct the sentence 'There are exits to the...'. This can be done by performing a logical OR on all four direction variables, and this will only produce a zero result if all four direction variables are zero. If this is not the case, then the routine continues to test each direction variable in turn. If the variable is non-zero then the corresponding direction is added to the sentence.

```
2355 IF(NR OR EA OR SO OR WE)=0 THEN RETURN
2360 PRINT:SN$="EXITS ARE TO THE "
2370 IF NR <>0 THEN SN$=SN$+"NORTH "
2380 IF EA <>0 THEN SN$=SN$+"EAST "
2390 IF SO <>0 THEN SN$=SN$+"SOUTH "
2400 IF WE <>0 THEN SN$=SN$+"WEST "
2410 GOSUB 5500:REM FORMAT
2415 PRINT
2420 RETURN
```

Now that we have developed routines that describe each location, we can develop procedures that will allow the player to do things within the world we have created. In a future instalment of the project, we shall be considering more detailed algorithms that analyse instructions. For now, we will deal with the movement instructions the player can issue by simply entering a one word direction command, such as 'NORTH' or 'SOUTH'. If such an instruction is passed to a movement subroutine as the variable NN$, then the movement routine is as follows:

```
3500 REM **** MOVE S/R ****
3510 MF=1:REM SET MOVE FLAG
3520 DR$=LEFT$(NN$,1)
3530 IF DR$<>"N"ANDDR$<>"E"ANDDR$<>"S"ANDDR$<>"W"
     THEN GOTO3590
3540 IF DR$="N"AND NR<>0 THEN P=NR:RETURN
3550 IF DR$="E"AND EA<>0 THEN P=EA:RETURN
3560 IF DR$="S"AND SO<>0 THEN P=SO:RETURN
3570 IF DR$="W"AND WE<>0 THEN P=WE:RETURN
3580 PRINT:PRINT"YOU CAN'T "; IS$
3585 MF=0:RETURN
3590 REM ** NOUN NOT DIRECTION **
3600 PRINT"WHAT IS ";NN$;" ?"
3610 MF=0:RETURN
```

This routine actually uses only the first letter of the direction command passed to it. It begins by checking that the command is, in fact, a direction. If so, the direction specified in the command is acted upon. After ensuring that there is an exit in that direction, P — the variable that keeps track of the player's position — is changed to the value of NR, EA, SO or WE.

Before we can use the subroutines that we have developed here, however, we need to tie them all together to form a repeating loop. The flowchart

shows the logical structure of this main calling loop. Although this is not the final structure of the main program loop it serves to demonstrate the aspects of the program covered so far. To use the subroutines given here, insert the following lines, which form a part of the main loop.

```
200 GOSUB6000:REM READ ARRAY DATA
210 P=INT(RND(TI)*10+1):REM START POINT
230 REM **** MAIN LOOP STARTS HERE ****
240 MF=0:REM MOVE FLAG
245 PRINT
250 GOSUB2000:REM DESCRIBE POSITION
255 GOSUB2300:REM DESCRIBE EXITS
260 PRINT:INPUT"INSTRUCTIONS"; IS$
```

Also include the following lines in the main calling loop:

```
270 NN$=IS$:GOSUB 3500:REM MOVE
280 GOTO 230:REM RESTART MAIN LOOP
```

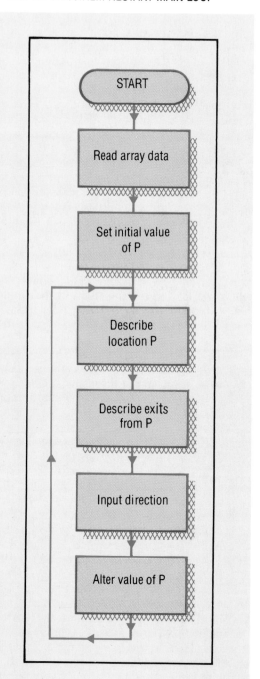

SPECTRUM VARIATIONS

Because the Spectrum holds all string arrays as fixed-length strings, problems arise when we wish to print out an element of a string array as part of a larger sentence. When dimensioning an array on the Spectrum, the last number in the statement defines the length of each element in the array. For example, DIM a$(3,2,20) dimensions a three-by-two element array, with each element having a fixed length of 20 characters. If we assign an element in the array to a string with less than 20 characters, then the difference is made up by adding spaces to the end of the string. This wastes precious space in memory. Therefore, to insert Spectrum string-array variables into sentences, we must first of all remove any trailing spaces. Spectrum users should type in the following routine to do this in the Haunted Forest listing:

```
7000 REM **** SPECTRUM TRUNCATE ****
7010 FOR I=LEN(A$) TO 1 STEP -1
7020 IF A$(I TO I)<>" " THEN LET N=I:LET I=1
7030 NEXT I
7040 LET S$=S$+A$(TO N)
7050 RETURN
```

For the Digitaya listing, type in these same commands, but use line numbers 8500 to 8550.

This routine truncates A$, removing any trailing spaces, before adding it to S$. Remember that S$ is the string variable used to assemble a sentence for formatting. To use this routine, we must pass the string-array element (to be incorporated into the sentence) to the variable A$, and then call the subroutine. Therefore, we must make the following alterations to Spectrum versions of Haunted Forest and Digitaya:

Haunted Forest:
```
2010 LET S$="YOU ARE ":A$=L$(P):GOSUB7000:
     GOSUB 5500
2070 LET S$=S$+P$+"A ": A$=V$(I,1):
     GOSUB7000:LET F=1:LET P$=", "
```

Digitaya:
```
1450 LET S$="YOU ARE ":A$=L$(P):
     GOSUB8500:GOSUB5880
1500 IF VAL(V$(I,2))=P THEN LET S$=S$+P$+"A "
     :A$=V$(I,1):GOSUB8500:LET F=1:LET P$=" "
```

Digitaya Listing

The structure of Digitaya is similar to Haunted Forest. Add the following lines to the listings given so far in the project:

```
1100 GOSUB6090:REM READ ARRAY DATA
1210 PRINT:INPUT"INSTRUCTIONS";IS$
1120 P=47:REM START POINT
1130 :
1140 REM **** MAIN LOOP STARTS HERE ****
1150 :
1160 MF=0:PRINT
1170 GOSUB1440:REM DESCRIBE POSITION
1180 GOSUB1560: REM LIST EXITS
```

Also include these lines:

```
1220 NN$=IS$:GOSUB 2000:REM MOVE
1230 GOTO 1140:REM RESTART MAIN LOOP
```

Describe Location And Exits
```
1440 REM **** DESCRIBE POSITION S/R ****
1450 SN$="YOU ARE "+LN$(P):GOSUB5880
1460 SN$="YOU SEE "
1470 REM ** SEARCH FOR OBJECT **
1480 F=0:SP$=""
1490 FOR I=1TO8
1500 IF VAL(IV$(I,2))=P THEN SN$=SN$+SP$+"A
     "+IV$(I,1):F=1:SP$=" "
1510 NEXTI
1520 IF F=0 THENSN$=SN$+"NO OBJECTS"
1530 GOSUB5880:REM FORMAT
1540 RETURN
1550 :
1560 REM **** LIST EXITS S/R ****
1570 EX$=EX$(P)
1580 NR=VAL(LEFT$(EX$,2))
1590 EA=VAL(MID$(EX$,3,2))
1600 SO=VAL(MID$(EX$,5,2))
1610 WE=VAL(RIGHT$(EX$,2))
1620 IF(NR OR EA OR SO OR WE)=0THEN RETURN
1630 PRINT:SN$="EXITS ARE TO THE "
1640 IF NR<>0 THEN SN$=SN$+"NORTH "
1650 IF EA<>0 THEN SN$=SN$+"EAST "
1660 IF SO<>0 THEN SN$=SN$+"SOUTH "
1670 IF WE<>0 THEN SN$=SN$+"WEST "
1675 GOSUB 5880:REM FORMAT
1680 PRINT:RETURN
```

Move To Subroutine
```
2000 REM **** MOVE S/R ****
2010 MF=1:REM MOVE FLAG SET
2020 DR$= LEFT$(NN$,1)
2030 IFDR$<>"N"ANDDR$<>"E"ANDDR$<>"S"ANDDR$<>
     "W"TH EN2100
2040 IF DR$="N" AND NR<>0 THEN P=NR:RETURN
2050 IF DR$="S" AND SO<>0 THEN P=SO:RETURN
2060 IF DR$="E" AND EA<>0 THEN P=EA:RETURN
2070 IF DR$="W" AND WE<>0 THEN P=WE:RETURN
2080 PRINT"YOU CANT ";IS$
2090 MF=0:RETURN
2100 REM NOUN NOT OK
2110 PRINT"WHAT IS ";NN$;" ?"
2120 MF=0:RETURN
```

Basic Flavours

Spectrum:
Throughout both games listings, replace EX$() with E$(), EX$ with X$, SN$ with S$, IS$ with T$, LN$() with L$(), NN$ with R$, SP$ with P$, DR$ with D$. For the Digitaya listing, substitute the following lines:

```
1580 LET NR=VAL(X$(TO 2))
1590 LET EA=VAL(X$(3 TO 4))
1600 LET SO=VAL(X$(5 TO 6))
1610 LET WE=VAL(X$(7 TO))
2020 LET D$=R$(TO 1)
```

For the Haunted Forest listing, substitute the following lines:

```
210 RANDOMISE:P=INT(RND(1)*10+1)
2320 LET NR=VAL(X$(TO 2))
2330 LET EA=VAL(X$(3 TO 4))
2340 LET SO=VAL(X$(5 TO 6))
2350 LET WE=VAL(X$(7 TO))
3520 LET D$=R$(TO 1)
```

BBC Micro:
Substitute the following line in the Haunted Forest listing:

```
210 P=RND(10)
```

TAKING ORDERS

Up to this point in our adventure game programming project, we have discussed methods of map making, formatting output and moving around the adventure world. Now we need to look at how the program analyses and obeys instructions given to it by the player.

Adventures are usually constructed so that the player can move from location to location, picking up and dropping objects along the way. A set of commands allows the player to perform these simple tasks. The commands we have used are:

GO (direction)	To move between locations
TAKE (object)	To pick up an object
DROP (object)	To put down an object
LIST	To list the objects carried
LOOK	To redisplay the description of the current location
END	To end the game

Variations on these may also be available, such as MOVE instead of GO, or GET instead of TAKE. Part of the fun of playing an adventure game is to determine what words the game will accept. For example, a player might try the command SWIM when in a dry location. If the program responds by telling the player that he cannot swim *here*, then the player could reasonably assume that there are locations where swimming *is* allowed. (Alternatively, the programmer might just want the player to think that!)

The number of commands accepted by a game varies according to the complexity of the game and the amount of effort the programmer has made to cover every eventuality. The most important thing for the designer to do is to make sure the program does not crash if a player tries to enter a command that is not catered for. A failsafe routine that prints 'I don't understand' may be all that's required, bearing in mind that some flexibility should be added so that players can enter commands in different ways. For example, it would be annoying for a program that accepts the command TAKE LAMP to respond to the command TAKE THE LAMP with 'I don't understand'. Adding flexibility will be discussed at greater length later. For the moment, we need to look at the type of instructions that might be given during the game, and devise a routine that will break these down into a form that can be easily interpreted.

COMMAND SPLITTING

No matter what the instruction is, it is very likely that it will be phrased in the *imperative* — such as, GO SOUTH TOWARDS THE RIVER or KILL THE ALIEN. The advantage of this sentence structure is that it is easy to break down: the verb always comes as the first word in the sentence, the object of the verb follows this, and finally there may be some form of qualification of the action. A first stage in the analysis of a command is to separate the verb from

Chequered Flags

Flags are used widely in programs that have a modular construction. Conditions that involve branches in program control can be tested for within a module but branching on the result of such a test can be delayed until a return to the main program section is made. By setting a variable to a pre-determined value when the test is made, the value of the variable can later be tested within the main program section. Variables used to indicate conditions in this way are termed 'flags'. The flowchart shows the main program loop, as constructed so far, for Haunted Forest. The flag F indicates whether or not a command has a valid format and is set during the 'split command' subroutine. The subroutine used to identify and execute normal commands uses two flags: VF is used to signal that the verb part of the command has been correctly recognised. If, in executing a command, the player moves to a new location, the fact that a move is to be made is signalled by MF. When MF is tested within the main program loop, a value of 1 indicates that the loop should branch back to describe the new location to which the player has moved

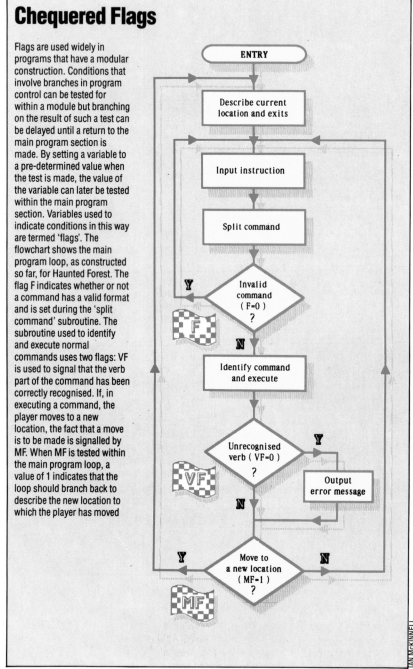

the rest of the sentence. This task can be easily achieved by scanning through the sentence one character at a time, using MID$, until a space is found. The part of the sentence that lies to the left of the space is the verb, and can be assigned to the variable VB$. The part of the sentence to the right can be assigned to a second variable, NN$. This subroutine is used in Haunted Forest to split the instruction assigned to the variable IS$:

```
2500 REM **** SPLIT COMMAND S/R ****
2510 IF IS$="LIST" OR IS$="END" THEN VB$=IS$:F=1:RETURN
2515 IF IS$="LOOK" THEN VB$=IS$:F=1:RETURN
2520 F=0
2530 LS=LEN(IS$)
2540 FOR C=1 TO LS
2550 A$=MID$(IS$,C,1)
2560 IF A$<>" " THEN 2590
2570 VB$=LEFT$(IS$,C-1):F=1
2580 NN$=RIGHT$(IS$,LS-C):C=LS
2590 NEXT C
2600 :
2610 IF F=1 THEN RETURN
2620 PRINT:PRINT"I NEED AT LEAST TWO WORDS"
2630 RETURN
```

Before the routine attempts to split up the sentence, it first checks to make sure that the command is not one of the three possible single-word instructions — that is, LIST, LOOK or END. If it is a single-word command, then the complete instruction is assigned to VB$, and the routine is exited. If the command is not one of these, then the routine enters a FOR...NEXT loop and begins to scan for the first space. Two techniques used within this loop need special mention. Both relate to the fact that it is extremely bad programming style to perform a conditional jump out of a FOR...NEXT loop without passing through the NEXT statement. Instead, to signal the fact that some condition has been met — in this particular case, that a space has been found — a flag, F, is set to one. Secondly, when the first space has been found, it is a waste of time to continue scanning through the rest of the sentence.

The loop can be neatly terminated at this point by setting the loop counter, C, to its upper limit, LC. Consequently, when the program again reaches NEXT, it will pass on to the following instruction, rather than loop back to the FOR statement. Once the loop has been correctly terminated, then the status of the flag, F, can be tested. A flag value of one indicates that the sentence consists of more than one word, and all that remains to do at this stage is to return to the main loop. If the flag is not one, then the command has only one word and is not one of the single-word commands tested for earlier. In this case, a message stating that two words are required is printed before returning for another command.

NORMAL COMMANDS

For the main part of the program, the player will simply move from location to location and pick up or drop objects that may be found. Therefore, for the majority of locations, the commands GO, TAKE, DROP, LIST, LOOK, END — and their variants — are sufficient to allow the player to do this. Only in unusual circumstances will the player wish to use other more specialised commands. For example, there is little point in using the command KILL if

there is nothing present to kill. We can, however, devise a program structure where, on the majority of occasions, only the six commands associated with movement and objects are tested for. When the player enters a new location, the program can test to see if it is one that has been designated 'special' in some way. If this is the case, then any new command requirements can be dealt with by a specific command subroutine for that particular location. Therefore, the main calling loop to our program should do the following:

1) Describe the location and list the exits.
2) Determine whether the location is 'special'.
3) Ask for a command and, if the location is not special, scan the list of normal commands.

There must also be a facility in the main loop to distinguish between a command that causes a move to a new location and one that does not. In the first case, the loop needs to go back to the beginning of the loop to describe the new location and decide whether or not it is special. In the second case, it is necessary only to loop back to ask for a new command. The simplest way to implement this is to use a 'move flag', MF, which is normally set to zero. If a command involves movement then this flag is set to one. The status of MF can be tested at the end of the main loop and the appropriate jump made. Add the following lines to Haunted Forest:

```
270 GOSUB2500:REM SPLIT INSTRUCTION
275 IF F=0 THEN 260:REM INVALID INSTRUCTION
280 GOSUB3000:REM NORMAL COMMANDS
290 IF VF=0 THENPRINT:PRINT"I DONT UNDERSTAND"
300 IF MF=1 THEN 240:REM NEW LOCATION
310 IF MF=0 THEN 260:REM NEW INSTRUCTION

3000 REM **** NORMAL COMMANDS S/R ****
3010 VF=0:REM VERB FLAG
3020 IF VB$="GO" OR VB$="MOVE" THENVF=1:GOSUB3500
3030 IF VB$="TAKE" OR VB$="PICK"THEN VF=1:GOSUB3700
3040 IF VB$="DROP" OR VB$="PUT"THEN VF=1:GOSUB3900
3050 IF VB$="LIST" OR VB$="INVENTORY"THEN VF=1:GOS
     UB4100
3055 IF VB$="LOOK" THEN VF=1:MF=1:RETURN
3060 IF VB$="END" OR VB$="FINISH" THEN VF=1:GOSUB4
     170
3070 RETURN
```

In the first routine, another flag, VF, is used to indicate whether or not the verb has been understood and obeyed. Only when the verb has been isolated is VF set to one. We can insert a failsafe 'I don't understand' statement in the main loop by testing the status of VF. If VF remains zero then the verb in the command has not been recognised by the analysis routine, and the statement is displayed.

In the next instalment of the project, we will deal with subroutines for picking up, dropping and listing objects. For now, we can add a short END command subroutine to our group of normal commands:

```
4170 REM **** END GAME S/R ****
4180 PRINT:PRINT"ARE YOU SURE (Y/N) ?"
4190 GET A$:IF A$<>"Y" AND A$<>"N" THEN 4190
4200 IF A$="N" THEN RETURN
4210 END
```

The LOOK command is also straightforward. To redescribe the current position, we simply need to set the 'move flag', MF, to one and return to the main program loop. Setting MF will cause the main program to loop back to the beginning, thus calling the routines that describe a location and its exits. As the value of the location variable, P, is not changed by the LOOK command, the same location will be described. This command is useful if, after the player has performed a series of actions, the original description of the current location has moved off the screen.

ADDING FLEXIBILITY

When issuing movement commands, the player may type in different forms of the same instruction. For example, GO NORTH, MOVE NORTH and GO TOWARDS THE NORTH are asking the same thing. Although it is not vital for an adventure game program to recognise all of these forms, it makes playing the game more interesting if a number of different instruction formats are legal. The three movement commands we just gave have a common structure: they all start with a movement verb, and the direction required is a discrete word. It is possible, therefore, to design a routine that will search the part of the sentence coming after the verb for the direction. The routine scans this part of the sentence for spaces, isolating each word in turn and comparing it with

the four direction words sought until a match is found.

```
3630 REM **** SEARCH FOR DIRECTION S/R ****
3640 NN$=NN$+" ":LN=LEN(NN$):C=1
3645 FOR I=1 TO LN
3650 IF MID$(NN$,I,1)<>" " THEN NEXT I:RETURN
3655 W$=MID$(NN$,C,I-C):C=I+1
3660 IF W$="NORTH" OR W$="EAST" THEN NN$=W$:I=LN
3665 IF W$="SOUTH" OR W$="WEST" THEN NN$=W$:I=LN
3670 NEXT I
3675 RETURN
```

In the last instalment of the project we developed a movement routine. To add this new routine to the movement routine we need simply to add the following line:

```
3505 GOSUB3630:REM SEARCH FOR DIRECTION
```

It is worth noting that this routine will not obey instructions such as GO IN A NORTHERLY DIRECTION, since the direction word cannot be isolated by the routine. It would be possible to design a routine that worked on the principle of scanning groups of four and five letters, comparing each group with the four possible direction words. However, such a routine would have a long execution time. On the other hand, our program will accept GO NORTHWARDS, as the movement routine finally uses the first letter of the second part of the sentence, NN$. In this case, the N in NORTHWARDS would be accepted as N for NORTH.

Digitaya Listings

```
1220 GOSUB1700:REM ANALYSE INSTRUCTIONS
1225 IF F=0 THEN 1210:REM INVALID INSTRUCTION
1230 GOSUB 1900:REM NORMAL INSTRUCTIONS
1240 IF VF=0 THENPRINT"I DON'T UNDERSTAND"
1250 IF MF=1 THEN 1160:REM NEW POSITION
1260 IF MF=0 THEN 1210:REM NEW INSTRUCTION

1700 REM **** ANALYSE INSTRUCTION S/R ****
1705 F=0:REM ZERO FLAG
1710 IFIS$="END" OR IS$="LIST" THEN VB$=IS$:F=1:
     RETURN
1720 IF IS$="LOOK" THEN VB$=IS$:F=1:RETURN
1730 :
1740 REM ** SPLIT INSTRUCTION **
1750 VB$="":NN$="":REM ZERO VERB AND NOUN
1770 LS=LEN(IS$)
1780 FOR C=1TO LS
1790 A$=MID$(IS$,C,1)
1800 IF A$=" " THEN VB$=LEFT$(IS$,C-1):NN$=RIGHT$(I
     S$,LS-C):F=1:C=LS
1810 NEXT
1830 IF F=0 THEN PRINT:PRINT"I NEED AT LEAST TWO
     WORDS"
1840 RETURN
1850 :
1900 REM **** NORMAL ACTIONS S/R ****
1910 VF=0
1920 PRINT
1930 IF VB$="GO"ORVB$="MOVE"THENVF=1:GOSUB2000
1940 IF VB$="TAKE"ORVB$="PICK"THEN VF=1:GOSUB2140
1950 IF VB$="DROP"ORVB$="PUT"THENVF=1:GOSUB2360
1960 IF VB$="LIST"ORVB$="INVENTORY"THENVF=1:
     GOSUB2540
1965 IF VB$="LOOK" THEN VF=1:MF=1:RETURN
1970 IF VB$="END"ORVB$="FINISH"THENVF=1:GOSUB2610
1980 RETURN

2015 GOSUB8600:REM SEARCH FOR DIRECTION

2610 REM **** END GAME S/R ****
2620 PRINT:PRINT"ARE YOU SURE (Y/N) ?"
2630 GETA$:IFA$<>"Y"AND A$<>"N"THEN2630
2640 IFA$="N"THEN RETURN
2650 END

8600 REM **** SEARCH FOR DIRECTION S/R ****
8610 NN$=NN$+" ":LN=LEN(NN$):C=1
8620 FORI=1 TO LN
8630 IF MID$(NN$,I,1)<>" " THEN NEXT I:RETURN
8640 W$=MID$(NN$,C,I-C):C=I+1
8650 IF W$="NORTH" OR W$="EAST" THEN NN$=W$:I=LN
8660 IF W$="SOUTH" OR W$="WEST" THEN NN$=W$:I=LN
8670 NEXT I
8680 RETURN
```

Basic Flavours

Spectrum:
In both programs, use I$ for IS$, B$ for VB$, and R$ for NN$ throughout.
Replace the following lines in Digitaya:

```
1790 LET A$=I$(C TO C)
1800 IF A$="" THEN LET B$=I$(TO C-1):LET R$=I$
     (LEN(I$)-LS+C+1 TO):LET F=1:LET C=LS
2630 LET A$=INKEY$:IF A$<>"Y"
     AND A$<>"N" THEN 2630
8630 IF R$(I TO I)<>"" THEN NEXT I:RETURN
8640 LET W$=R$(C TO I-1):LET C=I+1
```

Replace these lines in Haunted Forest:

```
2550 LET A$=I$(C TO C)
2570 LET B$=I$(TO C-1):LET F=1
2580 LET R$=I$(LEN(I$)-LS+C+1 TO):LET C=LS
3650 IF R$(I TO I)<>"" THEN NEXT I:RETURN
3655 LET W$=R$(C TO I-1):LET C=I+1
4190 LET A$=INKEY$:IF A$<>"Y" AND
     A$<>"N" THEN GOTO 4190
```

BBC Micro:
Replace this line in Digitaya:

```
2630 REPEAT:A$=GET$:UNTIL A$="Y" OR
     A$="N"
```

and this line in Haunted Forest:

```
4190 REPEAT:A$=GET$:UNTIL A$="Y" OR
     A$="N"
```

TAKE YOUR PICK

The first thing we did in this project was draw up a map of the imaginary adventure world of our game (see page 82). On this map, we positioned objects that will be of use to the player. Here we show you how to develop the routines needed to allow players to pick up and carry the objects around.

In the last part of the project we looked at command analysis and designated a group of 'normal' commands (see page 91). Included in this group were the commands TAKE and DROP, together with their variations PICK and PUT. Once the appropriate command has been recognised we can construct the routines that obey the command. We will first consider TAKE.

To understand the methods employed by the TAKE routine, let's recap on the way that the program keeps track of objects within the adventure world. In the first section of the project we designed DATA statements for each location that contained location descriptions, the names of objects present and information about the possible exits. After the data is read in, the array IV$(,) (used to store the object data for Haunted Forest) has the following contents:

N	IV$(N,1)	IV$(N,2)
1	GUN	10
2	LAMP	9
3	KEY	5

The first column of the array holds the object name, while the second contains its initial location number on the adventure world map. During the description of any location, the second column of this array is scanned to see if any of the objects are at the player's current location, P. When the player wishes to take an object from a location, using a command of the format TAKE THE OBJECT, several factors must be considered:

• Is the object in the command valid; in other words, does it appear in the inventory array, IV$(,)?
• Is the object present at the player's current location?
• Does the player already have the full quota of objects allowed by the game's rules?

If all of these considerations can be answered satisfactorily then the player may take the object. This involves adding the object description to the player's personal object array, IC$(), and deleting the position marker from the relevant entry in IV$(,). Note that the object name does not have to be deleted. If we use a position marker of −1 for each object that has been picked up and carried,

then such objects will not appear in location descriptions. It would be rather odd to pick up the GUN from location 10, move to location 9 and then back to location 10, finding on your return that the GUN was still there. Thus the array IV$(,) keeps a record of the positions of all objects *not* being carried by the player. The flowchart for the TAKE routine shows the simple logic that must be applied.

```
3700 REM **** TAKE S/R ****
3710 GOSUB 5300:REM IS OBJECT VALID
3720 IF F=0 THEN SN$="THERE IS NO "+W$:GOSUB5500:
     RETURN
3730 OV=F:GOSUB5450:REM CHECK INVENTORY
3740 IF HF=1 THEN SN$="YOU ALREADY HAVE THE "+IV$
     (F,1):GOSUB5500:RETURN
3750 :
3755 REM ** IS OBJECT HERE ? **
3760 IF VAL(IV$(F,2))<>P THEN SN$=IV$(F,1)+" IS
     NOT HERE":GOSUB5500:RETURN
```

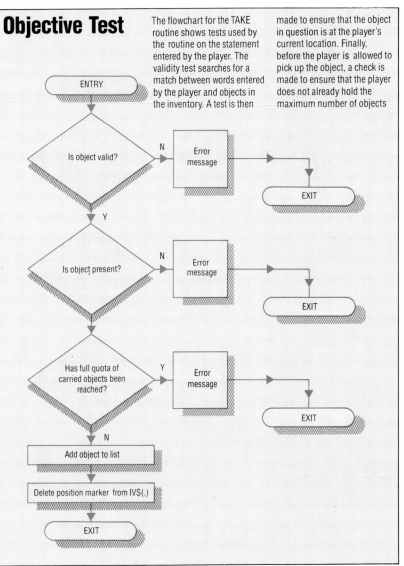

Objective Test

The flowchart for the TAKE routine shows tests used by the routine on the statement entered by the player. The validity test searches for a match between words entered by the player and objects in the inventory. A test is then made to ensure that the object in question is at the player's current location. Finally, before the player is allowed to pick up the object, a check is made to ensure that the player does not already hold the maximum number of objects

The Big Match

```
10REM **** MATCH AN OBJECT DEMO ****
40MODE 5:COLOUR 2:DIM V$(3)
60FOR I=1 TO 3:READ V$(I):NEXT I
90A$="THE":B$="KNIFE":C$="KNI"
.95S$="  "
110M$=A$:GOSUB 1000:REM MATCH 'THE'
130M$=B$:GOSUB 1000:REM MATCH 'KNIFE'
150M$=C$:GOSUB 1000:REM MATCH 'KNI'
160END
1000REM **** MATCH S/R ****
1010CLS:F=0:LW=LEN(M$)
1030FOR J=1 TO 3:LI=LEN(V$(J))
1042X=1:Y=6:GOSUB2000:PRINT S$
1045X=1:Y=6:GOSUB2000:PRINT V$(J)
1047FOR I=1 TO LI-LW+1
1050X=1:Y=5:GOSUB2000:PRINT S$
1060X=I:Y=5:GOSUB2000:PRINT M$
1070IF MID$(V$(J),I,LW)=M$ THEN F=I:I=LI:J=3
1075FOR D=1 TO 300:NEXT D,I:REM DELAY
1086IF F<>0 THEN GOSUB 2500
1087NEXT J:RETURN
2000REM **** POSITION CURSOR AT X,Y ****
2010PRINT TAB(X,Y);:RETURN
2500REM **** MATCH FOUND ****
2502COLOUR 1:X=F:Y=6:GOSUB2000:PRINT M$
2505FOR K=1 TO 5:X=1:Y=10:GOSUB2000:PRINT S$
2508FOR D=1 TO 500:NEXT:REM DELAY
2510X=1:Y=10:GOSUB2000:PRINT "MATCH FOUND"
2512FOR D=1 TO 500:NEXT D,K:REM DELAY
2520A$=GET$:COLOUR 2:RETURN
3000REM **** INVENTORY DATA ****
3005DATA"SMALL FORK","RED DOOR","LARGE KNIFE"

  10 REM ** SPECTRUM MATCH **
  40 INK 6:DIM V$(3,20)
1070 IF V$(J,I TO I+LW-1)=M$ THEN F=I:I=LI:J=3
2010 PRINT AT (Y,X);:RETURN
2502 INK 2:X=F:Y=6:GOSUB2000:PRINT S$
2520 A$=INKEY$:IF A$="" THEN 2520
2525 INK 6:RETURN

  10 REM ** CBM 64 MATCH **
  40 PRINT CHR$(158):DIM V$(3)
  50 DN$=CHR$(17): FOR K=1 TO 5:DN$=DN$+DN$:NEXT:
     DN$=CHR$(19)+DN$
2010 PRINT LEFT$(DN$,Y)TAB(X);:RETURN
2502 PRINTCHR$(28):X=F:Y=6:GOSUB2000:PRINT S$
2520 GETA$:IF A$="" THEN 2520
2525 PRINT CHR$(158):RETURN
```

The validity test subroutine designed for use with the TAKE routine scans the statement entered a word at a time, trying to find a match with an entry in the inventory. This short program illustrates the way in which the validity routine searches through the inventory for a match. Three objects are held in the inventory for this demonstration and the program tries to match the words 'THE', 'KNIFE' and 'KNI'. Whenever a match is found, the program waits for a keypress before continuing

```
3770 :
3780 REM ** ADD OBJECT TO LIST **
3790 A=0
3800 FOR J=1 TO 2
3810 IF IC$(J)="" THEN IC$(J)=IV$(F,1):AF=1:J=2
3820 NEXT J
3830 :
3840 REM ** FULL QUOTA **
3850 IF AF=0 THEN PRINT"YOU ALREADY HAVE TWO
     OBJECTS":RETURN
3860 :
3870 SN$="YOU TAKE THE "+IV$(F,1):GOSUB5500
3880 IV$(F,2)="-1":REM DELETE INVENTORY ENTRY
3890 RETURN
```

Let's now look at each of the three tests separately.

THE VALIDITY TEST

The most important and complicated of the three tests is the *validity test*. In its simplest form this could be a routine that just took the second part of the split command and compared it with each of the components of the inventory array, IV$(,). However, if this was the case, the TAKE command would be limited to the rigorous structure of TAKE OBJECT. Even variations such as TAKE THE GUN would be unacceptable as the routine would attempt to match THE GUN with the inventory, rather than just GUN. To allow flexibility in the command structure of TAKE we must develop a more sophisticated method of comparing the second part of the command given with the object inventory.

The most obvious method of increasing flexibility is to divide the second part of the command given into its constituent words and then compare each in turn with the object inventory. While overcoming the problem outlined earlier, this method too has its flaws. If, for example, we wanted to use a two-word description of an object such as LARGE KNIFE, then the command TAKE THE LARGE KNIFE would not give a match using this method. The routine would compare the words THE, LARGE and KNIFE separately with the inventory list. This problem can be overcome by making the routine even more sophisticated. Instead of searching for an exact match, a routine could be designed that would scan each object description in the inventory for the command word under examination, moving through the object name letter by letter until a match was found or the end of the object name was reached. The screen shots show how this is done.

One advantage of looking for a match between command and inventory in this way is that shortened versions of the object word can be given in the command. In the above example, the command TAKE THE KNI would also make the correct match, assuming that there were no other object names in the inventory prior to LARGE KNIFE with the combination of letters KNI. If this were the case, then an incorrect match would be made with the earlier entry in the inventory. Problems of this type are part of the price that must be paid for the greater flexibility of the routine. Most incorrect matching problems can be eliminated by careful selection of object names. If two object names must contain the same group of characters, or if one name is a substring of another — such as BULL and BULLET — then the shorter of the two names should be placed earlier in the inventory array. In addition, different object descriptions that contain the same words, such as LARGE KNIFE should not be used.

```
5300 REM **** VALID OBJECT S/R ****
5310 NN$=NN$+" ":LN=LEN(NN$):C=1:F=0
5315 FOR K=1 TO LN
5320 IF MID$(NN$,K,1)<>" " THEN NEXT K:RETURN
5325 W$=MID$(NN$,C,K-C):C=K+1
5330 LW=LEN(W$)
5335 FOR J=1 TO 3
5340 LI=LEN(IV$(J,1)):REM LENGTH OF OBJECT
5350 FOR I=1 TO LI-LW+1
5360 IF MID$(IV$(J,1),I,LW)=W$ THEN F=J:I=LI:J=3:K
=LN
5370 NEXT I,J,K
5380 RETURN
```

Having found a match, the routine sets the variable F to the inventory array element that corresponds to the object in the command. If no match is found, then the value of F will remain zero, indicating that no such object exists in the game.

IS THE OBJECT PRESENT?

Once the array number of the object has been established by the validity test subroutine, the location of the object can easily be checked against the current location variable, P. The object to be picked up is in IV$(F,1) and its location is in IV$(F,2). Line 3760 of the TAKE routine in Haunted Forest checks this value against that of P. However, the error message generated — 'OBJECT is not here' — may not be strictly correct. The object may be present in the current location, but held by the player. Thus, a check should be made to see if the player is carrying the object in question before the error message is made. If so, a different error message (such as 'You already have the OBJECT') can be output. The following subroutine checks the main inventory and sets a flag, HF, to one if the object is being carried by the player. This condition is indicated by a −1 in the relevant element of the array.

```
5450 REM **** IS OBJECT HELD S/R ****
5460 HF=0
5470 IF IV$(OV,2)="-1" THEN HF=1
5480 RETURN
```

CHECKING THE PLAYER'S LIST

These two related tasks of checking to see if the player's list is full and adding to the list can be combined. Using the array IC$() to hold the objects carried, a FOR...NEXT loop can be used to locate the first free space in the array so that the new object may be entered. In the rules of Haunted Forest, a player may carry two objects only at any one time. Thus, the FOR...NEXT loop used is executed twice only. If a free space is found then the new object name is entered; if not then a message to the effect that the player is already carrying two objects is output to the screen.

The final task is to delete the position marker of the object just picked up from the inventory. This is simply done by setting IV$(F,2) to −1.

THE LIST COMMAND

Now that the player has the ability to pick up objects, we can include another command. It is often useful for the player to be able to see what objects are being carried. For example, if the player comes across a locked door he may have

forgotten that he picked up a key 20 moves before. Allowing the player to list the objects carried serves as a useful memory jogger. The code required is simple: a FOR...NEXT loop is used to display the contents of the player's object inventory, IC$().

```
4100 REM **** LIST CARRIED INVENTORY ****
4110 PRINT"OBJECTS HELD:"
4120 FOR I=1 TO 2
4130 PRINT" ";IC$(I),
4140 NEXT I
4150 RETURN
```

Digitaya Listings

```
2140 REM **** TAKE S/R ****
2145 IV$(4,1)="TICKET TO TRI-STATE"
2150 GOSUB5730:REM IS OBJECT VALID
2160 IF F=0 THEN PRINT"THERE IS NO ";W$:RETURN
2170 REM ** IS OBJECT ALREADY TAKEN ? ****
2180 OV=F:GOSUB5830
2190 IFHF=1 THEN SN$="YOU ALREADY HAVE THE "+IV$(F
,1):GOSUB5880:RETURN
2200 :
2210 REM ** IS OBJECT HERE **
2220 IF VAL(IV$(F,2))<>P THENSN$=IV$(F,1)+" IS NOT
 HERE":GOSUB5880:RETURN
2230 :
2240 REM ** ADD OBJECT TO LIST **
2250 AF=0:FOR J=1 TO 3
2260 IFIC$(J)="" THENIC$(J)=IV$(F,1):AF=1:J=4
2270 NEXTJ
2280 :
2290 REM ** CHECK FOR FULL QUOTA **
2300 IF AF=0THENPRINT"YOU ALREADY HAVE 4 OBJECTS":
RETURN
2310 :
2320 SN$="YOU TAKE THE "+IV$(F,1):GOSUB5880
2330 IV$(F,2)="-1":REM DELETE POSITION ENTRY
2340 RETURN

5730 REM **** VALID OJECT S/R ****
5740 NN$=NN$+" ":LN=LEN(NN$):F=0:C=1
5745 FOR K=1 TO LN
5750 IF MID$(NN$,K,1)<>" " THEN NEXTK:RETURN
5755 W$=MID$(NN$,C,K-C):C=K+1:LW=LEN(W$)
5760 FORJ=1 TO 8
5770 LI=LEN(IV$(J,1)):REM LENGTH OBJECT
5780 FORI=1TO LI-LW+1
5790 IFMID$(IV$(J,1),I,LW)=W$THENF=J:I=LI:J=8:K=LN
5800 NEXT I,J,K
5810 RETURN
5820 :
5830 REM **** IS OBJECT HELD S/R ****
5840 HF=0
5850 IFIV$(OV,2)="-1"THEN HF=1
5860 RETURN

2540 REM **** LIST INVENTORY S/R ****
2550 PRINT"OBJECTS HELD:"
2560 FORI=1TO4
2570 PRINT" ";IC$(I)
2580 NEXTI
2590 RETURN
```

Basic Flavours

Spectrum:

For the Haunted Forest listing make the following changes:

Replace SN$ by S$, IV$(,) by IC$() by I$() and NN$ V$(,), by R$.

5320 IF R$(K TO K)<>" " THEN NEXT K:RETURN
5325 LET W$=R$(C TO K−1)
5360 IF V$(I TO I+LW−1)=W$ THEN LET F=J: LET I=LI:LET J=3:LET K=LN

For the Digitaya listing, replace the same string variable names and make the same changes listed above, but for lines 5750, 5755 and 5790 respectively.

SPECIAL ASSIGNMENT

In the last section of our adventure game project we designed routines to enable the player to pick up objects. Now we must develop the corresponding routines that allow the player to drop any objects he may be carrying. We also look at the first of the 'special' locations.

The DROP subroutine bears many similarities to the TAKE routine described on page 93. Indeed, we can use the same object checking routines that were developed for use with the TAKE command. Three checks on the object are made during the TAKE routine. The first is designed to test whether or not the second part of the command phrase contains a valid object. This is done by checking each word of the command phrase systematically against the object names in the inventory array — IV$(,). If a match is found then a variable, F, is set, giving the position of the matched object within the array. This validity check must also be used in the DROP routine to establish whether the object exists and, if it does, to determine its position in the inventory.

The second check used in the TAKE routine is also used in the DROP routine; this tests whether the player holds the object specified in the command in the inventory of carried objects — IC$(). Obviously, a player cannot drop an object that he is not carrying! The third test used in the TAKE routine checks to ensure that the object to be picked up is at the player's current location, as determined by the position variable, P. However, as the object to be dropped must be held by the player, its position will not appear in the main inventory, and this third test is, therefore, not needed by the DROP routine.

Assuming that both tests result in a favourable outcome, then the following changes must be made to both the main and the player's inventories:

1) The position of the object to be dropped will now be specified by F. The current position, P, must be entered in the main inventory array in position IV$(F,2).

2) The object description must be deleted from the player's personal inventory of objects carried, IC$(). This is best done by searching through the array until the appropriate object is found and replacing it with a null string.

The logic of the DROP routine is shown in the flowchart. Here is the listing for the routine in the Haunted Forest game:

```
3900 REM **** DROP S/R. ****
3910 GOSUB5300:REM VALID OBJECT
3920 IF F=0 THEN SN$="THERE IS NO "+W$:GOSUB5500:
RETURN
3930 :
3940 REM ** IS OBJECT IN CARRIED INVENTORY **
3950 OV=F:GOSUB5450
3960 IF HF=0 THEN SN$="YOU DO NOT HAVE THE "+IV$
(F,1):GOSUB5500:RETURN
3970 :
3980 REM ** DROP OBJECT **
3990 SN$="YOU DROP THE "+IV$(F,1):GOSUB5500
4000 IV$(F,2)=STR$(P):REM MAKE ENTRY IN INVENTORY
4010 :
4020 REM ** DELETE OBJECT FROM CARRIED INVENTORY
**
4030 FOR J=1TO2
4040 IF IC$(J)=IV$(F,1) THEN IC$(J)="":J=2
4050 NEXT J
4060 RETURN
```

It can be seen that one of the major advantages of programming in modules is that the same routines can be accessed for different purposes. By using a system of flags, decisions can be made within short

Drop It!

The logic of the DROP routine is similar to that of the TAKE routine (see page 93), but only the validity of the object and its presence in the player's inventory need be checked before the DROP command is executed. The main inventory is then updated to show a new location for the object, and the object name is deleted from the player's inventory

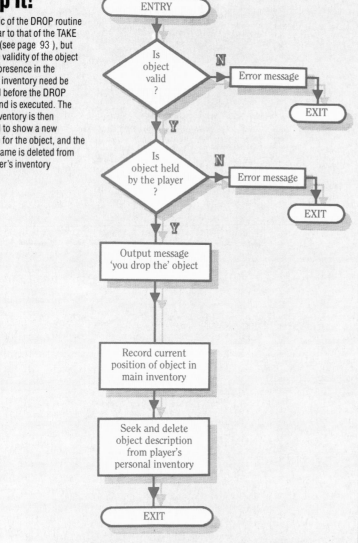

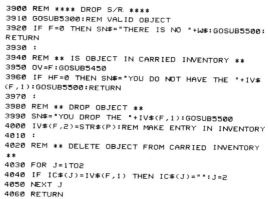

subroutines that are not acted upon until control is returned to the routine that called the subroutine. A good example of the use of this type of program structure is the validity test described earlier. This subroutine is called by both the TAKE and DROP routines. In each case, the subroutine makes a decision as to the validity of the object part of the command phrase. However, the flow of the program is not altered until a RETURN is effected to either the TAKE or DROP routines. Only after returning is the value of the flag, F, set by the validity test subroutine and the appropriate branch made. One criticism of this technique is that we are effectively testing the same condition twice — once to set the flag value, and again to test the value of the flag. Although this is true, the added flexibility and ease of debugging achieved by employing this technique usually outweighs the slightly longer execution time that results.

SPECIAL LOCATIONS

We are now at the point in our project where we have completed the programming of the game's skeleton; that is, the programming that allows the player to carry objects and move around in the adventure world. We can now move on to the next phase of design in which we consider the 'special' locations where objects are put to use, perils are met and where the player's ingenuity and skill are tested.

Before we look in detail at the programming of the routines for one of the special locations in the Haunted Forest, let's consider the additions to be made to the main program loop in order to detect special locations. These two lines must be inserted into the listing:

```
257 GOSUB2700:REM IS P SPECIAL ?
258 IF SF=1 THEN 300:REM NEXT INSTRUCTION
```

Line 257 calls a subroutine to see if the current location is special. If this is the case then a 'special flag', SF, is set to one. This means that when control is eventually returned to the main program loop, the part of the main loop dealing with instructions can be avoided. The subroutine that decides whether the current location is special or not is:

```
2700 REM **** IS P SPECIAL S/R ****
2705 SF=0:REM UNSET SPECIAL FLAG

2716 REM ** OTHER SPECIAL LOCATIONS **
2720 ON P GOSUB4590,4690,4790,4590
2730 RETURN
```

You will recall that, when we designed the original map for the Haunted Forest, we numbered the four special locations first (see page 82). We can, therefore, simplify the selection of the appropriate subroutine for each special location by making use of the ON. . . GOSUB command. As can be seen by the way it is used in line 2720, this command is followed by a series of line numbers, and the appropriate line number is selected according to the value of P. If P is one, for example, the command will GOSUB to the first line number from the list; if P is two, then the second line number will be used for the GOSUB call, and so on.

There are four line numbers, one for each of the special locations in Haunted Forest. If P exceeds four, then control simply passes to the following line. If each of the four subroutines that can be called from line 2720 sets an SF flag, then the fact that P was a special location can be flagged. If no routine is called, the SF flag will remain set at zero, indicating that P is just an ordinary location. The ON. . . GOSUB command is clearly an economical alternative to a series of IF. . . THEN statements testing the value of a variable and branching to different subroutines accordingly.

THE TUNNEL ENTRANCE

Two of the special locations in the Haunted Forest are the two entrances to a tunnel (locations 1 and 4). To deal with the simple scenario of the player wishing to enter the tunnel, we need to construct carefully a routine that handles the normal commands and allows the player to enter the tunnel or retreat back down the path.

```
4590 REM **** TUNNEL ENTRANCE S/R ****
4600 SF=1
4605 SN$="YOU HAVE ARRIVED AT THE MOUTH OF A LARGE
TUNNEL":GOSUB5500
4610 SN$="YOU CAN ENTER THE TUNNEL OR RETREAT
ALONG THE PATH":GOSUB5500
4620 :
4625 PRINT:INPUT"INSTRUCTIONS";IS$
4630 GOSUB2500:REM SPLIT INSTRUCTION
4635 IF F=0 THEN 4625:REM INVALID INSTRUCTION
4637 GOSUB3000:REM NORMAL INSTRUCTIONS
4640 IF MF=1 THEN RETURN:REM PLAYER RETREATS
4645 IF VF=1 THEN 4625:REM INSTRUCTION OBEYED
4650 REM ** NEW INSTRUCTIONS **
4655 IF VB$="ENTER" THEN GOSUB 4700:RETURN
4660 IF VB$="RETREAT" AND P=4 THEN MF=1:P=6:RETURN
4665 IF VB$="RETREAT" AND P=1 THEN MF=1:P=9:RETURN
4667 SN$="I DON'T UNDERSTAND":GOSUB5500:GOTO 4625
```

The routine starts by setting SF to one to indicate that a special location has been reached. After displaying a message on the screen, describing the tunnel entrance and the options open to the player, an instruction is asked for. Once again, rather than re-inventing the wheel each time we wish to analyse an instruction, we can take advantage of the modular construction of the program to call up the 'split instruction' and 'normal command' subroutines developed for use in the TAKE and DROP routines. By considering carefully the states of the various flags set by these two subroutines, we can transfer control within our new routine as required. Let's consider these flags individually.

The F flag set by the 'split instruction' routine indicates whether the instruction passed to it has a valid format. If the instruction is a one-word command not recognised by the routine, then F takes the value zero — in which case we will want to loop back to get another instruction.

The MF flag is set by the 'normal command' routine if a description of a location is required — this happens when a GO or LOOK command is issued. A RETURN to the main program loop will allow the new location to be moved to, in the former case, or the same location to be described and the special routine re-entered, in the latter case.

The VF flag is also set by the 'normal command' routine. A value of one indicates that the instruction was recognised and obeyed, in which case we should loop back for the next instruction. If VF<>1 then the command is not one of the normal commands. Having dealt with the normal command possibilities we can add new commands to this routine. In this case, two such instructions are included: ENTER, to go into the tunnel, and RETREAT, to move one location away from the tunnel entrance. As this routine is designed to work for both entrances to the tunnel, the RETREAT command must take account of which end of the tunnel the player is negotiating — this is indicated by P taking the value 1 or 4. P can, therefore, be reset accordingly before leaving the routine so that a change of location is made on re-entry to the main program loop.

The special perils that await the adventure player once inside the tunnel are the subject of the next instalment.

Digitaya Listings

```
1190 GOSUB2670:REM IS P SPECIAL
1200 IF SF=1 THEN 1250:REM NEXT LOOP

2360 REM ** DROP S/R **
2370 GOSUB5730:REM IS OBJECT VALID
2380 IF F=0 THEN PRINT"THERE IS NO ";W$:RETURN
2390 :
2400 REM ** IS OBJECT HELD ? **
2410 OV=F:GOSUB5830
2420 IFHF=0THENPRINT"YOU DO NOT HAVE THE ";IV$(F,1
):RETURN
2430 :
2440 REM ** DROP OBJECT **
2450 SN$="YOU DROP THE "+IV$(F,1):GOSUB5880
2460 IV$(F,2)=STR$(P):REM UPDATE OBJ POSITION
2470 :
2480 REM ** DELETE FROM HELD OBJ LIST **
2490 FORJ=1TO4
2500 IF IC$(J)=IV$(F,1)THENIC$(J)="":J=4
2510 NEXTJ
2520 RETURN

2670 REM **** IS P SPECIAL S/R ****
2680 SF=0:REM UNSET SPECIAL FLAG

2710 ON P GOSUB 2850,2960,3450,3830,4180,4550,5150
2720 RETURN

2850 REM **** TV OUTLET S/R ****
2860 SF=1
2870 SN$="YOU HAVE ENTERED THE TV OUTLET AND THERE
 IS NO ESCAPE."
2880 SN$=SN$+"YOU ARE DOOMED FOREVER TO BE A TV CH
AT SHOW HOST"
2890 GOSUB 5880:REM FORMAT PRINT
2900 PRINT
2910 PRINT"WELCOME TO THE SHOW......
2920 FORJ=1TO500:NEXTJ
2930 GOTO 2910
2940 END

3830 REM **** JOYSTICK PORT ****
3840 SF=1
3850 SN$="A USER WITH RED-RIMMED EYES ZAPS HIS LAS
ER AT YOU REPEATEDLY."
3860 GOSUB5880:REM FORMAT
3870 :
3880 REM ** INSTRUCTIONS **
3890 RD=RND(TI):IF RD>.65THEN 4110:REM HIT
3900 PRINT:INPUT"INSTRUCTIONS";IS$
3910 GOSUB1700:GOSUB1900:REM ANALYSE INSTRUCTION
3920 IFMF=1THENMF=0:PRINT"YOU CAN'T MOVE...YET":GO
TO3880
3930 IFVF=1THEN3880:REM NEXT INSTRUCTION
3940 IFVB$<>"USE"THENPRINT"I DON'T UNDERSTAND":GOT
O3880
3950 GOSUB5730:REM IS OBJECT VALID
3960 IFF=0THENPRINT"THERE IS NO ";NN$:GOTO3880:REM
 NEXT INSTRUCTION
3970 :
3980 REM ** IS OBJECT LASER SHIELD **
3990 IF F=3 THEN4020:REM OK
4000 SN$="YOUR "+IV$(F,1)+" IS NO USE":GOSUB5880:G
OTO3880
4010 :
4020 OV=3:GOSUB5830:REM IS LASER SHIELD CARRIED
4030 IFHF=0THENSN$="YOU DO NOT HAVE THE "+IV$(3,1)
```

```
:GOSUB5880:GOTO3880
4040 :
4050 REM ** SAVED **
4060 SN$="YOU USE THE LASER SHIELD TO PROTECT YOUR
SELF. A BLAST KNOCKS"
4070 SN$=SN$+" YOU OUT OF THE JOYSTICK PORT AND BA
CK INTO THE MACHINE."
4080 GOSUB5880:REM FORMAT
4090 P=INT(RND(TI)*40+7):MF=1:RETURN
4100 :
4110 REM ** HIT **
4120 SN$="YOU ARE HIT BY THE LASER AND YOU ARE ONL
Y DIMLY AWARE THAT"
4130 SN$=SN$+" YOUR ATOMS HAVE BEEN DISTRIBUTED TO
 THE FOUR CORNERS"
4140 SN$=SN$+" OF THE UNIVERSE"
4150 GOSUB5880:REM FORMAT
4160 END

5150 REM **** GATEWAY TO MEMORY S/R ****
5160 SF=1
5170 SN$="AN USHER GREETS YOU BUT TELLS YOU THAT Y
OU CANNOT BE ADMITTED"
5180 SN$=SN$+" UNLESS YOU GIVE AN ADDRESS":GOSUB58
80
5190 REM ** INSTRUCTIONS **
5200 PRINT:INPUT"INSTRUCTIONS";IS$
5210 GOSUB1700:GOSUB1900:REM ANALYSE
5220 IF MF=1 THEN RETURN:REM MOVE OUT
5230 IF VF=1 THEN 5200:REM NEXT INSTRUCTION
5240 IF VB$<>"GIVE"THENPRINT"I DON'T UNDERSTAND":G
OTO 5200
5250 :
5260 GOSUB5730:REM IS OBJECT VALID
5270 IFF=0THENPRINT"THERE IS NO ";W$:GOTO5200:REM
NEXT INSTRUCTION
5280 :
5290 REM ** IS OBJECT ADDRESS **
5300 IF F=1 THEN5330:REM OK
5310 PRINT"HE NEEDS YOUR ADDRESS":GOTO5200
5320 :
5330 OV=1:GOSUB5830:REM IS ADDRESS CARRIED
5340 IF HF=1 THEN 5370
5350 SN$="YOU DON'T HAVE THE "+IV$(1,1):GOSUB5880:
GOTO5200
5360 :
5370 REM ** OK PASS THROUGH **
5380 SN$="THE USHER LOOKS AT YOUR ADDRESS AND ALLO
WS YOU TO PASS"
5390 SN$=SN$+" THROUGH":GOSUB5880
5400 P=40:MF=1:RETURN
```

Basic Flavours

Spectrum:

In both programs use these alternatives for the variable names: S$ for SN$, R$ for NN$, V$(,) for IV$(,), I$() for IC$(), T$ for IS$, B$ for VB$. Substitute the following lines in the Haunted Forest listing:

```
2720 IF P=1 THEN GOSUB4590
2722 IF P=2 THEN GOSUB4690
2724 IF P=3 THEN GOSUB4790
2726 IF P=4 THEN GOSUB4590
```

Substitute the following lines in the Digitaya listings:

```
2710 IF P=1 THEN GOSUB2850
2711 IF P=2 THEN GOSUB2960
2712 IF P=3 THEN GOSUB3450
2713 IF P=4 THEN GOSUB3830
2714 IF P=5 THEN GOSUB4180
2715 IF P=6 THEN GOSUB4550
2716 IF P=7 THEN GOSUB5150
3890 LET RD=RND(1)
4090 LET P=INT(RND(1)*40+7)
```

BBC Micro:

Substitute the following lines in the Digitaya listings:

```
3890 RD=RND(1)
4090 P=RND(40)+7
```

GHOST APPEARANCE

In the last part of our adventure game project, we started to look at the special locations used in the Haunted Forest game, concentrating on the decision presented to the player to enter the tunnel. Now we look at the rest of the tunnel routine and design a subroutine to produce random ghosts to haunt the forest.

In the last instalment, we discussed the special locations that have a tunnel entrance: at these locations the player is given the opportunity either to enter the tunnel or retreat back down the path that led to the entrance. If the player elects to enter the tunnel, then a new subroutine is called at line 4655. Let's now look at the subroutine that handles the option where the player goes into the tunnel. This subroutine is written according to certain rules laid down by the game's designer. To begin with, the player can pass through the tunnel only if he is carrying the lamp; and, in addition, the player must light the lamp to see the way forward.

As the player must be able to issue instructions while inside the tunnel, the subroutine should begin with a sequence that accepts an instruction input and splits this up for processing. We can allow the player to use some of the normal input instructions — such as TAKE, DROP, LIST or END — but here we must be careful. As far as the location pointer, P, is concerned, the player is still at the mouth of the tunnel and, therefore, able to GO in certain permitted directions. Consequently, we must suppress the GO instructions while we are inside the tunnel.

On returning from the 'normal commands' subroutine, if a GO command has been issued the 'move flag' (MF) will be set, and the value of P will have changed. This effect can be negated by simply restoring P to the value it had before the 'normal commands' subroutine was called.

Having handled normal commands satisfactorily, we can move on to deal with the specialised commands necessary for this particular situation. A RETREAT command can be used to allow the player to return to the tunnel entrance he came through. The only other command that we will allow is LIGHT, or a variation, USE. If the instruction issued is neither of these commands, the routine will output a catch-all I DON'T UNDERSTAND message before looping back for another instruction.

If the command is LIGHT or USE, then we have to make several checks before obeying the command:

1. Is the specified object a valid object?
2. Is the specified object held by the player?
3. Is the specified object the lamp?

If the answer to all these questions is 'yes', then the player will be allowed to pass through to the other end of the tunnel, as all the conditions for passing through the tunnel have been met. These object checks may seem familiar. They are, in fact, almost identical to those used in the TAKE and DROP routines (see page 92). Therefore, we can use previously written subroutines to carry out these checks.

```
4700 REM ** ENTER TUNNEL **
4705 SN$="YOU ENTER THE TUNNEL BUT IT IS TOO DARK
TO "
4710 SN$=SN$+" FIND YOUR WAY.":GOSUB5500
4725 PRINT:INPUT"INSTRUCTIONS";IS$
4730 GOSUB2500:REM SPLIT INSTRUCTION
4732 :
4735 IF F=0 THEN 4725:REM INVALID INSTRUCTION
4740 OP=P:GOSUB3000:REM NORMAL INSTRUCTIONS
4745 IF MF=1THEN SN$="IT IS SO DARK THAT YOU CAN O
NLY SEE":P=OP
4747 IF MF=1THENSN$=SN$+" THE TUNNEL ENTRANCE":GOS
UB5500:MF=0:GOTO4725
4750 IF VF=1 THEN 4725:REM INSTRUCTION OBEYED
4755 IF VB$="RETREAT" AND P=4 THEN MF=1:P=6:RETURN
4760 IF VB$="RETREAT" AND P=1 THEN MF=1:P=9:RETURN
4762 IFVB$<>"USE"ANDVB$<>"LIGHT"THEN SN$="I DON'T
UNDERSTAND"
4765 IFVB$<>"USE"ANDVB$<>"LIGHT"THEN GOSUB5500:GOT
O4725
4777 :
4780 REM ** SEARCH FOR LAMP **
4790 GOSUB5300:REM VALID OBJECT ?
4795 OV=F:GOSUB5450:REM IS OBJECT HELD ?
4797 IF F=0 THEN SN$="THERE IS NO "+W$:GOSUB5500:G
OTO4725
4800 IF HF=0 THEN SN$="YOU DO NOT HAVE THE "+IV$(F
,1):GOSUB5500:GOTO4725
4810 REM ** IS OBJECT LAMP ? **
4815 IF F<>2 THEN SN$="THE "+IV$(F,1)+" IS NO USE"
:GOSUB5500:GOTO4725
4835 REM ** SUCCESS **
4840 SN$="YOU USE THE LAMP TO LIGHT YOUR WAY THROU
GH THE TUNNEL"
4845 SN$=SN$+" AND EVENTUALLY EMERGE FROM THE EXIT
.":GOSUB5500
4850 IF P=1 THEN MF=1:P=4:RETURN
4855 IF P=4 THEN MF=1:P=1:RETURN
```

SUPERNATURAL EVENTS

In addition to having special locations, such as the tunnel entrances, we can also program random events or perils into our adventure game. Up to this point in the development of our Haunted Forest game we have not mentioned ghosts, nor do they appear on the adventure world map for the game (see page 82). Instead, the ghosts randomly appear to the player as he moves around the forest, and they can be fended off only by taking a bizarre form of action. Before we look in detail at the 'ghosts' routine, let's consider how we can incorporate the routines to generate random appearances into the main program structure. The main program loop calls a subroutine at line 2700 to test whether or not a new location is special in some way. This is also the best place to incorporate the following piece of code to decide whether the program should generate random spooks:

```
2707 REM ** RANDOM GHOST **
2710 IF P>4 AND RND(1)<0.1 THEN GOSUB 4290:RETURN
```

Line 2710 first of all ensures that the current location has not already been designated as special, since ghosts appearing in the middle of special routines could make life very complex. If the location is ordinary then, using the RND command, there is a 1-in-10 chance that the program will produce a ghost. RND commands generate 'pseudo-random' numbers — so called because the pattern of numbers generated from power-up is predictable. To make the sequence less predictable, we use the RND command with a negative operand in the case of the BBC Micro and Commodore 64, and the RANDOMISE command for the Spectrum (see 'Basic Flavours').

```
207 R=RND(-1)
```

If the 'ghosts' routine is called, then we enter another special scenario in which the player is confronted by the ghostly apparition. The routine follows the usual procedure: it generates an initial message, asks for an instruction and splits the instruction into the verb and the rest of the sentence. Normal commands are dealt with by the standard subroutine, but, again, the GO command is suppressed — a message informs the player that, being transfixed with terror, he cannot move.

SAFETY NET

New commands can be dealt with at this stage. In common with the other special location handling routines, the quality of the finished game depends upon how much programming effort is put into designing these routines. Any command not directly useful in the routine can be dealt with by the I DON'T UNDERSTAND safety net. With additional programming effort, however, we can handle commands that might be expected of the player, but which will not help the situation. An example of this approach is used in the 'ghosts' routine.

If a player is confronted with a ghost, his first thought might be to FIGHT or KILL the ghost (if you can kill ghosts!). The 'ghosts' routine deals with these two commands by calling a special subroutine. This subroutine simply displays a message that these instructions do not assist the player, but does so in a way that is substantially more attractive than simply reporting I DON'T UNDERSTAND.

```
4290 REM **** RANDOM GHOST S/R ****
4295 SF=1:GC=0
4300 SN$="YOU FEEL A COLD SENSATION RUNNING THE LE
NGTH"
4305 SN$=SN$+" OF YOUR SPINE. SUDDENLY A WHITE APP
ARITION"
4310 SN$=SN$+" APPEARS FROM OUT OF THE TREES AND"
4315 SN$=SN$+" MOVES TOWARDS YOU":GOSUB5500:REM FO
RMAT
4320 :
```

```
4325 SN$="THE GHOST MOVES CLOSER":GOSUB5500
4330 GC=GC+1:IF GC>4 THEN GOSUB4455:REM
4335 PRINT:INPUT"INSTRUCTIONS";IS$
4340 GOSUB2500:REM SPLIT INSTRUCTION
4345 IF F=0 THEN 4325:REM NEXT INSTRUCTION
4350 OP=P:GOSUB3000:REM ANALYSE INSTRUCTION
4355 IF MF=1 AND VB$="GO"THEN GOSUB4400:GOTO 4325
4357 IF MF=1 AND VB$="LOOK" THEN GOSUB2000:GOSUB23
00:GOTO4325
4360 IF VF=1 THEN 4325:REM NEXT INSTRUCTION
4365 REM ** NEW INSTRUCTION WORDS **
4370 IF VB$="KILL" OR VB$="FIGHT" THEN GOSUB4425:G
OTO 4325
4375 :
4385 IF VB$="SING" THEN GOSUB4500:RETURN
4390 SN$="I DON'T UNDERSTAND":GOSUB5500:GOTO4325
4395 :
4400 REM ** ATTEMPT TO MOVE **
4405 SN$="YOU ARE TRANSFIXED WITH TERROR AND CANNO
T"
4410 SN$=SN$+" MOVE...YET":MF=0:GOSUB5500:P=OP
4415 RETURN
4420 :
4425 REM ** FIGHT OR KILL **
4430 SN$="THE GHOST IS A BEING OF THE
SUPERNATURAL"
4435 SN$=SN$+" AND LAUGHS AT YOUR FEEBLE ATTEMPTS"
4440 SN$=SN$+" TO INJURE HIM":GOSUB5500
4445 RETURN
4450 :
4455 REM ** DEATH **
4460 SN$="THE PAIN IN YOUR CHEST BECOMES UNBEARABL
E"
4465 SN$=SN$+" AND YOU SLUMP ONTO THE LEAFY FOREST
FLOOR.":GOSUB5500
4470 SN$="YOUR SPIRIT RISES FROM YOUR INERT BODY"
4475 SN$=SN$+" AND YOU FLOAT AWAY INTO THE MIST TO
JOIN"
4480 SN$=SN$+" THE OTHER TORMENTED SOULS OF THE"
4485 SN$=SN$+" HAUNTED FOREST.":GOSUB5500
4490 END
```

STING IN THE TAIL

If any of the normal commands, or commands that are of no use to the player, are issued, the routine will obey them if possible and loop back for the next instruction. There is a sting in the tail of this routine, because a count is kept of the number of instructions issued by the player while being confronted by the ghost. If more than four instructions are issued, then the ghost moves in to kill the player. The only way that the player can escape is to SING a song. If the player elects to sing, he is given a choice of three songs, one of which (randomly chosen) will appease the ghost. If, however, the wrong tune is chosen, the player's spirit will join the army of tormented souls who have lost their way in the Haunted Forest:

```
4500 REM ** SING **
4505 SN$="YOU KNOW THREE SONGS. WHICH ONE WILL YOU
CHOOSE ?":GOSUB5500
4510 SN$="1) THE THEME FROM 'GHOSTBUSTERS'":GOSUB5
500
4515 SN$="2) 'THERE'S A GHOST IN MY HOUSE'":GOSUB5
500
4520 SN$="3) 'WAY DOWN UPON THE SWANEE RIVER'":GOS
UB5500
4525 PRINT:INPUT"MAKE YOUR CHOICE";C$
4530 IF VAL(C$)>3 OR VAL(C$)<1 THEN PRINT:PRINT"IN
VALID":GOTO4525
4535 CR=INT(RND(1)*3)+1
4537 IF CR<>VAL(C$) THEN GOSUB4542:REM WRONG TUNE
4540 GOSUB4565:REM CORRECT
4542 REM **** WRONG TUNE S/R ****
4545 SN$="THE GHOST HAS A PARTICULAR HATRED OF"
4550 SN$=SN$+" THAT TUNE AND LUNGES AT YOU.":GOSUB
5500
4555 GOSUB 4455:REM DEATH
4560 :
4565 REM ** CORRECT TUNE **
4570 SN$="THE GHOST IS APPEASED BY YOUR RENDITION
OF THE TUNE"
4575 SN$=SN$+" AND VAPOURISES INTO THIN AIR":GOSUB
5500
4580 RETURN
```

GHOSTS BY LIZ DIXON

Digitaya Listings

```
2690 IF P=37 THEN2780:REM VECTOR TABLE
2700 IF P>7 THEN 2750:REM RANDOM BUG

2740 REM ** RANDOM BUG **
2750 RA=RND(TI)
2760 IF RA<0.05THEN GOSUB 5420:REM BUG
2770 RETURN
2780 REM ** VECTOR TABLE **
2790 SF=1
2800 SN$="YOU ARE MOVED AT HIGH SPEED TO A NEW LOC
ATION":GOSUB5880
2810 FORJ=1TO1000:NEXT:REM PAUSE
2820 P=INT(RND(TI)*40+7)
2830 MF=1:RETURN

4550 REM **** ALU ****
4560 SF=1
4570 RN=INT(RND(TI)*3+1)
4580 IF RN=1 THEN CD$="AND"
4590 IF RN=2 THEN CD$="OR"
4600 IF RN=3 THEN CD$="NOT"
4610 SN$="MOUNTED ON THE WALL THERE ARE THREE BUTT
ONS MARKED"
4620 SN$=SN$+" 'AND', 'OR' AND 'NOT'. ACCESS CAN B
E GAINED TO THE"
4630 SN$=SN$+" ACCUMULATOR BY PRESSING THE CORRECT
 BUTTON"
4640 GOSUB5880:REM FORMAT
4650 :
4660 REM ** INSTRUCTIONS **
4670 PRINT:INPUT"INSTRUCTIONS";IS$
4680 GOSUB1700:GOSUB1900:REM ANALYSE
4690 IF MF=1THEN RETURN:REM MOVE OUT
4700 IF VF=1THEN 4670:REM NEXT INSTRUCTION
4710 IFVB$="USE"OR VB$="PRESS"THEN4740
4720 PRINT"I DON'T UNDERSTAND":GOTO4670
4730 :
4740 REM ** VALID COMMAND **
4750 IF VB$="PRESS"THEN 4930
4760 REM ** COMMAND IS 'USE' **
4770 GOSUB5730:REM IS OBJECT VALID
4780 IFF=0THENPRINT"THERE IS NO ";NN$:GOTO4670:REM
 NEXT INSTRUCTION
4790 :
4800 REM ** IS OBJECT CODE BOOK **
4810 IF F=7 THEN4850:REM OK
4820 SN$="YOUR "+IV$(F,1)+" IS OF NO USE":GOSUB588
0
4830 GOTO4670:REM NEXT INSTRUCTION
4840 :
4850 OV=7:GOSUB5830:REM IS CODE BOOK HELD
4860 IFHF=1THEN4900:REM OK HELD
4870 SN$="YOU DO NOT HAVE THE "+IV$(7,1)
4880 GOSUB5880:GOTO4670:REM NEXT INSTRUCTION
4890 :
4900 SN$="YOU OPEN THE CODE BOOK AND FIND THE WORD
 '"+CD$+"' WRITTEN INSIDE"
4910 GOSUB5880:GOTO4670:REM NEXT INSTRUCTION
4920 :
4930 REM ** COMMAND IS PRESS **
4940 IFNN$="AND"OR NN$="OR"OR NN$="NOT"THEN4970
4950 SN$="THERE IS NO "+NN$:GOSUB5880:GOTO4670:REM
 NEXT INSTRUCTION
4960 :
4970 REM ** RIGHT OR WRONG **
4980 IFNN$=CD$ THEN GOSUB5100:RETURN
4990 GOSUB5010:RETURN
5000 :
5010 REM ** WRONG S/R **
5020 SN$="WRONG, A TRAP DOOR OPENS AND YOU FIND YO
URSELF BACK"
5030 SN$=SN$+" BACK IN MAIN MEMORY"
5040 GOSUB5880:REM FORMAT
5050 IF RN=1 THEN P=39
5060 IF RN=2 THEN P=35
5070 IF RN=3 THEN P=29
5080 MF=1:RETURN
5090 :
5100 REM ** RIGHT S/R **
5110 SN$="THE GATEWAY TO THE ACCUMULATOR SWINGS OP
EN AND"
5120 SN$=SN$+" YOU PASS THROUGH":GOSUB5880
5130 P=30:MF=1:RETURN

5420 REM **** RANDOM BUG ****
5430 SF=1
5440 SN$="A LARGE AND UGLY BUG APPEARS FROM BEHIND
 A CHIP"
5450 SN$=SN$+" AND LUNGES TOWARDS YOU":GOSUB5880
5460 :
5470 REM ** INSTRUCTIONS **
5480 PRINT:INPUT"INSTRUCTIONS";IS$
5490 GOSUB1700:GOSUB1900:REM ANALYSE
5500 IFMF=1THENMF=0:PRINT"YOU CAN'T MOVE...YET!":GO
TO5480
5510 IF VF=1THEN5480:REM NEXT INSTRUCTION
5520 IF VB$="KILL"ORVB$="FIGHT"THEN5550
5530 PRINT"I DON'T UNDERSTAND":GOTO5480
5540 :
5550 REM ** COMAND IS FIGHT/KILL **
5560 RA=RND(TI)
5570 IFRA<0.5 THEN GOSUB5600
5580 GOSUB5670:RETURN
5590 :
5600 REM **** KILLED BY S/R ****
5610 SN$="YOU FIGHT WITH THE BUG. IT SHOWERS YOU W
ITH SPURIOUS"
5620 SN$=SN$+" ERRORS AND THEY EAT INTO YOUR BRAIN
."
5630 SN$=SN$+" FINALLY YOU CAN TAKE NO MORE AND YO
UR HEAD EXPLODES."
5640 GOSUB5880
5650 END
5660 :
5670 REM **** YOU KILL S/R ****
5680 SN$="YOU FIGHT WITH THE BUG AND THOUGH IT IS
A HARD STRUGGLE"
5690 SN$=SN$+" YOU EVENTUALLY IRON IT OUT AND SURV
IVE.":GOSUB5880
5700 RETURN
```

Basic Flavours

Spectrum

In both programs, replace SN$ with S$, IS$ with T$, IV$(,) with V$(,), VB$ with B$, CD$ with C$ and NN$ with R$.

Replace these lines in the Haunted Forest listing:

```
207 RAND
4815 IF F< >2 THEN LET S$="THE":LET
     A$=V$(F,1):GOSUB7000
4816 IF F< >2 THEN LET S$=S$+" IS NO
     USE":GOSUB5500:GOTO4725
```

Replace these lines in the Digitaya listing:

```
2750 LET RN=RND(1)
2820 LET P=INT(RND(1)*40+7)
4570 LET RN=INT(RND(1)*3+1)
4820 LET SN$="YOUR ":LET A$=V$(F,1):GOSUB
     8500
4825 LET SN$=SN$+" IS OF NO USE": GOSUB
     5880
5560 LET RA=RND(1)
```

BBC Micro:

Replace these lines in the Haunted Forest listing:

```
207 RND(—TIME)
4535 CR=RND(3)
```

Replace these lines in Digitaya listing:

```
2750 RN=RND(1)
2820 P=RND(40)+7
4570 RN=RND(3)
5560 RA=RND(1)
```

SCREEN ROUTINES

Although most adventure games are text-based, some take advantage of the large memory and colourful graphics now available on home micros to create relevant screen displays. We present the first of three pieces in which we design sample screens for our adventure game for the BBC Micro, Commodore 64 and the Spectrum.

In this instalment, we will consider how the graphics facilities of the BBC Micro can be used to create screen displays for adventure games. The game that we have been developing, which we have called Digitaya, is a text-based adventure game. That is to say, it uses words to describe the imaginary surroundings in which the player is placed. A text-based adventure, for example, would simply display the message 'You are in the throne room' to conjure up a setting, while a graphic adventure would attempt to draw a room with a throne.

The screens that we will design here display two locations of particular interest in Digitaya: namely, the entrance to the joystick port and the Arithmetic and Logic Unit. The number of such screens is often limited by the amount of memory available; the commands required to produce each display take up memory space that would otherwise be available to increase the complexity of the plot.

ALU SCREEN DESIGN

Before we can start to design a screen for the BBC Micro, we must answer several questions:
1) How much memory do I have available?
2) How many colours do I need?
3) What standard of resolution is required?
All these questions can, in fact, be combined into one: 'What mode shall I use?'. Higher resolution and a wider range of colours mean that valuable RAM is taken up by the screen area. In our design, we shall use mode 1, which gives us four colours, a 40 by 25 screen and medium resolution. We should set the mode to be used by inserting the following line at the beginning of the program:

1095 MODE 1

Having decided on the mode, we can then sketch out what our screen is to look like, pencilling in suitable co-ordinates as we go. The design chosen here scrolls the upper-case letters A, L and U onto the screen. In the game, the player must press one of three buttons — marked AND, OR and NOT — and these must also be moved onto the display.

Additional features include a thin border around the edge of the screen and a tapering foreground. Our rough design looks like this:

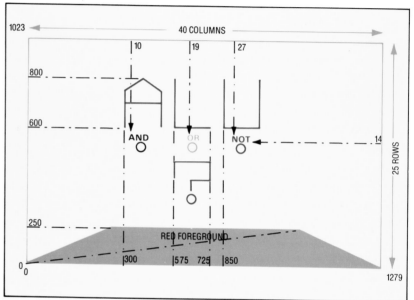

Each letter is formed by MOVEing to a start point and then using PLOT 1 to draw the shape of the letter as a series of lines relative to the start point. By designing the letters in this way they can be moved around the screen simply by changing the initial MOVE command. We can also rub out letters by redrawing the letter shape in the same position, but specifying Exclusive-OR plotting by using GCOL 3.

The buttons are formed by redefining a character. In this case, CHR$(240) is redefined by the procedure button to become the shape shown on the right. Notice that CHR$(240) is assigned to the variable button$ for use in the main part of the routine. The buttons and labels can be simply positioned by PRINTing them at co-ordinates specified by the TAB command.

The foreground is created using the triangular fill primitives provided by the PLOT 85 command. This command joins the point specified to the last two points previously plotted and then fills the resulting triangle with colour. The quadrilateral shape of the foreground can be drawn and filled by two such fill primitives.

The code for the screen display forms a subroutine of the special routine designed to deal with the ALU location in the game. The command A$=GET$, at line 7560, waits for a keypress before restoring the original foreground colour, clearing the screen and RETURNing to the main ALU routine to continue with the game. To call this graphic subroutine, the following line should also

Mode D'Emploi
In a BBC Micro program various 'trade-off' decisions must be made. In this program, Mode 1 gives the necessary resolutions, but at the expense of a 20 Kbyte screen memory

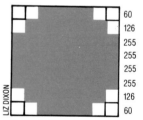

On The Button
In the ALU picture for the BBC Micro a button shape is required to represent the three choices, AND, OR and NOT, available to the player. In the absence of a CIRCLE command or special PET-type graphics characters we must redefine an existing BBC character. Using an 8 by 8 grid we can design a shape and represent it using 8 decimal numbers. CHR$(240) can then be redefined using the VDU 23 command:

VDU 23, 240, 60, 126, 255, 255, 255, 255, 126, 60

be inserted in the main program:

```
4565 GOSUB 7000: REM ALU PICTURE S/R
```

JOYSTICK PORT SCREEN

In Digitaya, if a player strays into the joystick port location, then he or she is in danger of being hit by a laser beam. The design of our screen display, therefore, involves drawing a joystick port with laser beams emanating from its centre. The joystick port is drawn using several full stop characters PRINTed to the top left corner of the screen, and a typical D-type surround is then drawn using high resolution graphics and PLOT statements. Notice that after MOVEing to the start position, all of the succeeding PLOT statements that create the port surround are PLOT 1 commands — which means they draw relative to the last point plotted. This is extremely convenient, because if shapes are drawn using a series of relative commands then, if it is decided to move the position of the whole shape, only the first MOVE statement has to be altered.

The foreground consists of a rectangular block of colour, once again drawn using two triangular fill primitives. To give an impression of depth, a series of converging lines is drawn over this, using a FOR . . . NEXT loop (lines 8170-8200). The loop sets up values of X from 0 to 1280 — the width of the screen in graphics units. A series of lines is drawn to the bottom of the screen, the start point on the horizon for each point increasing as X increases. However, the step of 32, used between consecutive lines at the bottom of the screen, is reduced to a step of 4 at the horizon (by dividing each X value by 8 in the MOVE command that defines the start point of each line).

The laser beam effect is produced by drawing a line from the centre of the joystick port to a randomly-chosen point on the horizon, in a random colour. The line is subsequently rubbed out — without disturbing the background — by plotting the same line in the Exclusive OR plotting mode, set by GCOL 3. The drawing and rubbing out of lines is placed within a REPEAT. . . UNTIL loop, together with a test to see if a key is pressed on the keyboard. Use of INKEY$, instead of GET$, allows program execution to continue while it is testing for a keypress within the loop. This loop is terminated when a key is pressed, the screen is then cleared, the original text colour restored and program control handed back to the main joystick port routine. To call this graphics subroutine the following line should be inserted:

```
3845 GOSUB 8000:REM JOYSTICK PORT PICTURE
```

Taking Some Stick
In both the joystick port and the ALU screens extensive use is made of the relative plotting facility since it permits easy erasure and movement of whole graphics shapes. Another plotting option is used to DRAW and FILL solid blocks of hi-res colour

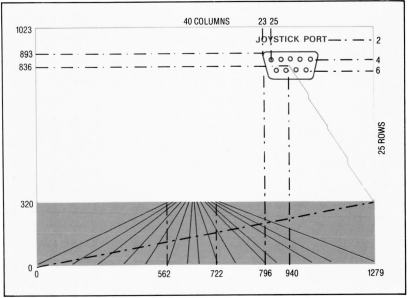

KEVIN JONES

ALU Screen

```
7000 REM **** ALU SCREEN S/R ****
7010 CLS
7015 REM ** CURSOR OFF **
7017 VDU23,1,0;0;0;0;
7020 REM ** BORDER **
7030 GCOL 0,1
7040 MOVE 0,0
7050 DRAW 0,1023
7060 DRAW 1279,1023
7070 DRAW 1279,0
7080 DRAW 0,0
7090 :
7100 REM ** PATH **
7110 MOVE 1279,0
7120 PLOT 85,500,250
7130 PLOT 85,800,250
7140 REM ** LETTER A **
7150 GCOL 3,2
7160 FORX=0 TO 300 STEP 10
7170 FOR I=1 TO 2
7180 PROCletter_a
7190 NEXT I,x
7200 PROCletter_a
7210 :
7220 REM ** LETTER L **
7230 FOR Y=300 TO 590 STEP 10
7240 FOR I=1 TO 2
7250 PROCletter_l
7260 NEXT I,Y
7270 PROCletter_l
7280 :
7290 REM ** LETTER U **
7300 FOR X=1280 TO 850 STEP -10
7310 FOR I=1 TO 2
7320 PROCletter_u
7330 NEXT I,X
7340 PROCletter_u
7350 :
7360 REM ** BUTTONS **
7370 PROCbutton
7380 COLOUR3
7390 PRINT TAB(11,15)button$
7400 COLOUR1
7410 PRINT TAB(20,15)button$
7420 COLOUR2
7430 PRINT TAB(28,15)button$
7440 REM ** COMMANDS **
7450 COLOUR3
7460 PRINT TAB(10,14)"AND"
7470 COLOUR2
7480 PRINT TAB(19,14)"OR"
7490 COLOUR2
7500 PRINT TAB(27,14)"NOT"
7510 :
7520 MOVE 575,400
7530 PROCq_mark
7540 :
7550 REM ** WAIT FOR KEY **
7560 A$=GET$
7562 REM ** CURSOR ON **
7564 VDU23,1,1;0;0;0;
7566 COLOUR3:CLS
7570 RETURN
7580 :
7590 DEF PROCletter_a
7600 MOVE X,600
7610 PLOT 1,0,150
7620 PLOT 1,75,50
7630 PLOT 1,75,-50
7640 PLOT 1,0,-150
7650 PLOT 0,0,80
7660 PLOT 1,-150,0
7670 ENDPROC
7680 :
7690 DEF PROCletter_l
7700 MOVE 725,Y
7710 PLOT 1,-150,0
7720 PLOT 1,0,200
7730 ENDPROC
7740 :
7750 DEF PROCletter_u
7760 MOVE X,800
7770 PLOT 1,0,-200
7780 PLOT 1,150,0
7790 PLOT 1,0,200
7800 ENDPROC
7810 :
7820 DEF PROCbutton
7830 VDU 23,240,60,126,255,255,255,126,60
7840 button$=CHR$(240)
7850 ENDPROC
7860 :
7870 DEF PROCq_mark
7880 PLOT 1,0,60
7890 PLOT 1,150,0
7900 PLOT 1,0,-70
7910 PLOT 1,-75,0
7920 PLOT 1,0,-50
7930 PLOT 0,-8,-30
7940 PLOT 1,16,0
7950 PLOT 1,0,-16
7960 PLOT 1,-16,0
7970 PLOT 1,0,16
7980 ENDPROC
8000 REM **** JOYSTICK PORT PICTURE ****
8010 :
8020 REM ** CURSOR OFF **
8030 VDU23,1,0;0;0;0;
8040 CLS
8050 REM ** BORDER **
8060 GCOL 0,1
8070 MOVE 0,0
8080 DRAW 0,1023
8090 DRAW 1279,1023
8100 DRAW 1279,0
8110 DRAW 0,0
8120 :
8130 REM ** HORIZON **
8140 PLOT 85,1279,319
8150 PLOT 85,0,319
8160 GCOL0,2
8170 FOR X= 0 TO 1280 STEP 32
8180 MOVE 562+X/8,320
8190 DRAW X,0
8200 NEXT X
8210 :
8220 REM ** JOYSTICK **
8230 COLOUR 2
8240 PRINTTAB(23,2)"JOYSTICK PORT"
8250 PRINTTAB(25,4)". . . . ."
8260 PRINTTAB(25,6)" . . . ."
8270 GCOL 0,2
8280 MOVE 796,893
8290 PLOT 1,288,0
8300 PLOT 1,4,-4
8310 PLOT 1,4,-4
8320 PLOT 1,0,-4
8330 PLOT 1,-4,-4
8340 PLOT 1,-30,-81
8350 PLOT 1,-4,-4
8360 PLOT 1,-4,-4
8370 PLOT 1,-218,0
8380 PLOT 1,-4,4
8390 PLOT 1,-4,4
8400 PLOT 1,-30,81
8410 PLOT 1,-4,4
8420 PLOT 1,0,4
8430 PLOT 1,4,4
8440 :
8450 REM ** SHOOT **
8460 REPEAT
8470 A$=INKEY$(10)
8480 X=RND(1279):Y=320
8490 GCOL 3,RND(3)
8500 FOR I=1 TO 2
8510 MOVE 940,836
8520 DRAW X,Y
8530 NEXT I
8540 UNTIL A$<>"":REM WAIT FOR KEYPRESS
8550 :
8560 REM ** CURSOR BACK ON **
8570 VDU23,1,1;0;0;0;
8575 COLOUR3:CLS
```

DRAWING PICTURES

We continue with our look at the design of two graphic screens for our Digitaya game. These screens depicted two locations of importance — the ALU and the joystick port. We now look at the design of these screens for the Sinclair Spectrum.

The design of the ALU screen involves the scrolling of the letters A, L and U down to the centre of the screen using high resolution graphics. On the BBC Micro, this scrolling was performed by drawing the letter from a specified start point using relative drawing commands, then rubbing it out, moving the start point and repeating the whole procedure (see page 102). The same idea can be used in the Spectrum version.

The Spectrum's DRAW command allows relative drawing only — that is, starting from the last point specified — but this is ideally suited to this particular scrolling application. By PLOTting an initial start point and then carrying out a series of DRAW commands to create the shape of the letter, we can easily move the entire letter design around the screen by simply changing the co-ordinates of the point initially PLOTted. Rubbing out can be accomplished by drawing the same shape in the same position, but with all the colours inverted. This effect is turned on by using INVERSE 1, and turned off again with INVERSE 0. Thus, for each position that the letter takes up, we shall draw it twice: once with INVERSE 0, to make the shape appear, and again with INVERSE 1 to rub it out.

If we take the example of the letter A, which scrolls on from the left, we can place all these instructions within a FOR . . . NEXT loop. This loop increases the value of the x co-ordinate of the initially-plotted point for the shape. Nested inside this loop is a second FOR . . . NEXT structure that simply carries out the drawing commands twice. The last value of x is 55, which denotes the final resting position of the letter on the screen. Obviously, we do not want to rub out the final version of the letter, so a test is inserted to ensure that the letter will be erased (by switching to INVERSE 1) only if the x co-ordinate is less than 55. The principles discussed here are also applied to the other two letters to make L scroll up the screen and U scroll on from the right.

ALU ROUGH DESIGN

When designing a graphic screen it is important to rough out a design on paper and make an initial estimate of the co-ordinate values that each shape on the screen will have. In addition, any letters that

have to be PRINTed to the screen should also be positioned, in terms of rows and columns. The screen shot shows such a design, with the screen dimensions in graphics and character units.

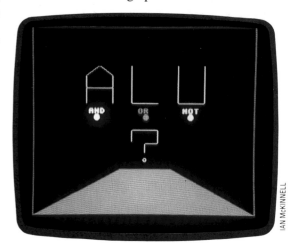

IAN McKINNELL

The words AND, OR and NOT are positioned on the screen using the PRINT AT r,c command: r being the number of rows from the top of the screen, and c indicating the number of columns from the left hand margin. The buttons are drawn using CIRCLE x,y,r where the co-ordinates of the centre and the length of the radius are specified.

On completion of the drawing routines, the program waits for a keypress before resetting the INK and PAPER to the original colours and clearing the screen. It then RETURNs to the main ALU routine. The keypress is tested by INKEY$; if no key is pressed then the test is simply repeated.

To call this subroutine, the following line should be inserted into the Digitaya program:

    4565 GOSUB 7000:REM ALU PICTURE S/R

THE JOYSTICK PORT

The joystick port screen is designed to shoot laser beams from the centre of a joystick connector socket. The pins for the socket are full stop characters PRINTed to the screen and the D-type surround is drawn using high resolution graphics. To give the picture a sense of depth, a series of tapering lines is drawn in the foreground. The start point for each line is on the horizon line, and is selected by a PLOT command. The end of each line is at the bottom of the screen. The lines are spaced at one-unit intervals on the horizon, and widen to seven units at the bottom of the screen.

The fact that Spectrum BASIC's DRAW command is relative makes the routine slightly more complex than if we were able to specify an absolute end point. If the x co-ordinate of the start point of the left-most line is 111, then we have to make a calculation based on this to find the relative offset to the end point. The FOR ... NEXT loop in lines 8030-8060 shows this calculation, which is based on the step-length at the bottom of the screen and the start point on the horizon.

As before, it is useful to rough out the dimensions and co-ordinates of the design on paper before starting to write the code. The screen shot shows such a design:

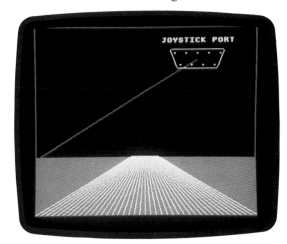

The laser beams are drawn from the joystick port by moving to a point at the centre of the port and then DRAWing a line to a random point on the horizon, using a randomly-selected INK colour. By repeating the procedure with INVERSE 1, we can rub out the line, making the beam appear for only a short interval (creating a lightning effect). However, when the line is rubbed out a problem occurs. Because the beam is drawn from a point at the centre of the port, it crosses the previously drawn graphics that depict the port itself. When the line is rubbed out, gaps appear in the joystick port graphics, and so it is necessary, when rubbing out the line, to redraw them.

Even though the end of any line drawn from the joystick port stops just short of the horizon line, the horizon is also affected. Because of the way the Spectrum controls colour, the portion of the horizon nearest the point where the beam ends takes on the same colour as that used to draw the line. This is because the Spectrum can support only one INK and one PAPER colour within any one character cell; any graphics already present within the cell take on the foreground colour of the new INK colour used in the cell. Therefore, in addition to redrawing the joystick port, the horizon line must also be redrawn after a beam line is erased. The routine continues to fire laser beams until a keypress is made, at which point program control is RETURNed to the main joystick port routine, after having reset the normal INK and PAPER colours.

The following line should be inserted in the main program to call this subroutine:

3845 GOSUB 8000:REM JOYSTICK PORT PICTURE

Implementing these two graphic screens on the Commodore 64 will be the subject of the next instalment in the project.

ALU Screen

```
7000 REM **** alu picture s/r ****
7010 INK 6: PAPER 0: CLS
7015:
7017 REM **** letter A ****
7020 FOR x=0 TO 55 STEP 5
7030 INVERSE 0
7040 FOR i=1 TO 2
7050 PLOT x,100
7060 DRAW 0,30
7070 DRAW 15,20
7080 DRAW 15,-20
7090 DRAW 0,-30
7095 DRAW 0,20
7096 DRAW -30,0
7110 IF x<55 THEN   INVERSE 1
7115 NEXT i
7120 NEXT x
7130:
7140 REM **** letter L ****
7150 FOR y=100 TO 150 STEP 5
7152 INVERSE 0
7155 FOR i=1 TO 2
7160 PLOT 113,y
7170 DRAW 0,-50
7180 DRAW 30,0
7190 IF y<150 THEN   INVERSE 1
7200 NEXT i
7210 NEXT y
7220:
7230 REM **** letter U ****
7240 FOR x=225 TO 170 STEP -5
7250 INVERSE 0
7260 FOR i=1 TO 2
7270 PLOT x,150
7280 DRAW 0,-50
7290 DRAW 30,0
7300 DRAW 0,50
```

```
7310 IF x>170 THEN   INVERSE 1
7320 NEXT i
7330 NEXT x
7340:
7350 REM **** buttons ****
7360 PRINT AT 10,7;"AND"
7370 PRINT AT 10,15;"OR"
7380 PRINT AT 10,22;"NOT"
7390 INK 3: CIRCLE 70,80,5
7400 INK 4: CIRCLE 128,80,5
7410 INK 5: CIRCLE 185,80,5
7420:
7430 REM **** q mark ****
7435 INK 6
7440 PLOT 113,45
7450 DRAW 0,15
7460 DRAW 30,0
7470 DRAW 0,-20
7480 DRAW -15,0
7490 DRAW 0,-7
7500 FOR r=6 TO 0 STEP -2
7510 CIRCLE 128,23,r
7520 NEXT r
7530: ′
7540 IF INKEY$="" THEN   GO TO 7540
7550 INK 0: PAPER 7: CLS
7560 RETURN
```

Joystick Port Screen

```
8000 REM **** jstick port pic s/r ****
8010 INK 6: PAPER 0: CLS
8020 REM **** foreground ****
8030 FOR n=1 TO 31
8040 PLOT 112+n,50
8050 DRAW 7*n-112,-50
8060 NEXT n
8070:
8080 REM **** horizon ****
```

```
8085 INK 6: INVERSE 0
8090 PLOT 0,50
8100 DRAW 255,0
8110:
8120 REM **** port ****
8130 PRINT AT 1,18;"JOYSTICK PORT"
8140 PRINT AT 3,20;". . . . ."
8150 PRINT AT 5,21;". . . . ."
8160 PLOT 158,152
8170 DRAW 75,0
8180 DRAW 1,-1
8190 DRAW 1,-1
8200 DRAW 0,-1
8210 DRAW -1,-1
8220 DRAW -10,-25
8230 DRAW -2,-2
8240 DRAW -52,0
8250 DRAW -2,2
8260 DRAW -10,25
8270 DRAW -1,1
8280 DRAW -1,1
8290 DRAW 0,1
8300 DRAW 1,1
8310:
8320 REM **** shoot ****
8340 INK RND*7
8350 LET x=RND*255-194
8360 LET y=-86
8365 INVERSE 0
8367 FOR i=1 TO 2
8370 PLOT 194,136
8380 DRAW x,y
8385 INVERSE 1
8387 NEXT i
8390:
8400 REM **** test for key ****
8410 IF INKEY$="" THEN   GO TO 8080
8415 INVERSE 0
8420 INK 0: PAPER 7: CLS
8430 RETURN
```

SCREEN PLAY

We have now designed screen displays for two special locations in the Digitaya adventure, for the Spectrum and BBC Micro. Here, we look at designing and programming these displays on the Commodore 64.

The designs of the adventure screens for the BBC Micro and the Spectrum were similar: both computers have high-resolution graphics and easy PRINT formatting in BASIC. The differences lay mainly in the screen dimensions and BASIC dialect words that handle high-resolution plotting. Designing similar screens for the Commodore 64, however, requires a radically different approach. The 64 does have high-resolution facilities, but effectively these are available only to the machine code programmer, as no BASIC commands are provided to handle high-resolution, and performing the relevant PEEKs and POKEs in BASIC to produce high-resolution displays is so slow as to make it unusable in this application. Instead, we must adapt the relatively easy-to-use facilities offered by the Commodore 64.

Graphics characters can be used to build up large letters or other displays by combining different characters. Sprites are a convenient method of introducing high-resolution shapes to the normal Commodore screen. PET characters can be positioned on the screen using either a series of PRINT statements or by POKEing the relevant character code to the screen. We shall demonstrate both methods.

JOYSTICK PORT SCREEN

Lines 8020 to 8170 of the Joystick Screen listing are concerned with reading in the data for the two sprites used in this routine. The first, sprite 0, is

defined by the first 63 numbers in the group of DATA statements between lines 8450 and 8497, and represents the joystick port (shown in the diagram). Sprite data is usually positioned high in the BASIC program area, but with a large BASIC program this data stands a good chance of being overwritten. An alternative location is the cassette buffer area between locations 832 and 1022, where the data for up to three sprites can be held. This routine stores its sprite data in this safe area.

Sprite 0 is stretched to twice its original width to produce the final displayed shape by setting bit 0 of the horizontal expansion register in line 8170. Notice that all the registers controlling the attributes of sprites, such as colour, position and expansion, are related to the start address for the video control chip (VIC). Remembering that the horizontal expansion register has the address VIC+29 is much easier than memorising its actual memory location (53277). Some sprite attributes require a whole register for each sprite — for example, the X and Y co-ordinate registers — but where the eight bits independently control a function for the eight available sprites, attributes can be controlled by setting and unsetting the appropriate bit in a single register. Sprite 1 is defined by the remaining 13 numbers in the DATA statements and represents an object to be fired out of the joystick port.

Since the 'solid' part of sprite 1 is small (it represents a projectile), it is quicker and easier to enter the 63 bytes of data that define it in two stages. Firstly, POKE 63 zeros into the defining area, and then READ and POKE in the few numbers that define the shape. In this way, we can dispense with the large number of zeros that would otherwise be required as data.

Lines 8190 to 8220 are concerned with the construction of strings constituted from a series of PET graphics characters. LE$ forms a horizontal line the width of the screen by combining 40 of the special PET characters on the front right of the C key. DW$ is a series of cursor-down characters. LS$ and RS$ are groups of left and right diagonals (on the front right of the N and M keys) that are used to form a herringbone pattern in the foreground. This pattern introduces depth and perspective to the scene.

Shoot-Em-Up!
The joystick port's 'shooting' action is accomplished on the 64 through the use of a sprite defined as a projectile. The outlines are set by POKEing zeros into the defining area, then the solid areas are READ from DATA statements and poked into the correct sprite locations

PROJECTILE — SPRITE 1

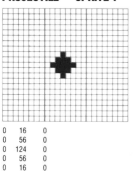

0	16	0
0	56	0
0	124	0
0	56	0
0	16	0

Sprite Stretching
The values listed for the joystick port sprite are READ from DATA statements and poked into the appropriate sprite locations. As designed, the joystick port is too compressed, but it can be stretched horizontally (as shown) by changing the value of the horizontal expansion register

JOYSTICK PORT — SPRITE 0

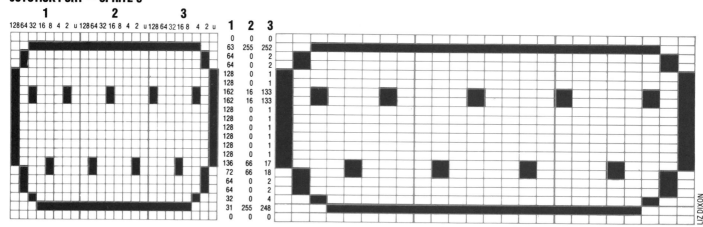

The 'Shoot' routine at line 8310 chooses a random point at the bottom of the screen and directs sprite 1 down to it, the process repeating until the player presses a key. The screen colours are reset to normal, the screen is cleared and the sprites are turned off before returning to the main program. To use this subroutine with Digitaya, the following line should be inserted:

3845 GOSUB 8000:REM JOYSTICK PORT PICTURE

The other listing provides a graphics display for the ALU location in Digitaya and demonstrates different methods of displaying characters on the screen. Lines 7040 to 7090 read a number of DATA statements and POKE the values straight into the screen area. The corresponding location in the colour area is also POKEd with the colour code for the character. In this example the colour code is 2, causing characters to be displayed in red.

A rather unusual trick is used to cause the large letters ALU to scroll down the screen. The first line of graphics character codes that go to make up the letters ALU are POKEd to the second line on the screen. The subroutine at line 7680 is then called, causing the screen to scroll down one line. The second line of codes can then be POKEd into the same screen area as the first, and the subroutine is called again. Repeating this for each of the eight lines of code makes the letters ALU appear to scroll from the top of the screen.

Two other methods of presenting character data to the screen are demonstrated. Characters can be PRINTed directly, as at lines 7130 and 7140, or read as a data string to be PRINTed, as is the case with the question mark design at lines 7170 and 7590 to 7670. This second method allows ease of design within the DATA statements.

To use this routine add the following line:

4565 GOSUB 7000: ALU PICTURE

Letter Writing
The ALU location for Digitaya is created from three PET low-resolution graphics characters, as shown. The large letters formed appear to scroll down from the top of the screen into their resting position

	PET Graphics Character	Screen Codes Normal	Screen Codes Reverse
☐		32	160
▨		105	233
▨		95	223

LIZ DIXON

ALU Screen

```
7000 REM **** ALU PICTURE S/R ****
7010 VIC=53248:CS=55296:SC=1024
7020 PRINT CHR$(147):REM CLEAR SCREEN
7030 POKE VIC+32,0:POKE VIC+33,0:REM SET SCREEN/BORD
7040 CC=0
7050 FOR J=1 TO 8:GOSUB7680:REM SCROLL
7060 FOR I=47 TO 72
7070 READ A:CC=CC+A:POKE SC+I,A:POKE CS+I,2
7080 NEXT I,J
7090 READ CS:IF CS<>CC THEN PRINT"CHECKSUM ERROR":STOP
7100 GOSUB7680:REM SCROLL
7110 PRINTCHR$(158):REM TEXT YELLOW
7120 FOR I=1 TO 8:PRINT:NEXT I:REM MOVE DOWN
7130 PRINTTAB(9)"AND"SPC(7)"OR"SPC(8)"NOT"
7140 PRINTTAB(10)"0"SPC(9)"0"SPC(9)"0"
7150 PRINTCHR$(28):REM TEST RED
7160 REM ** QUESTION MARK **
7170 FOR I=1 TO 9:READ Q$:PRINTTAB(16)Q$:NEXT I
7180 REM **** AWAIT KEY AND RESET ****
7190 GET A$:IF A$="" THEN 7190
7200 POKE VIC+32,14:POKE VIC+33,6:REM SCREEN/BORD
7210 PRINTCHR$(154):REM LT BLUE TEXT
7220 PRINTCHR$(147):REM CLEAR SCREEN
7230 RETURN
7240 REM **** SCREEN DATA ****
7250 REM ** ROW 1 **
7260 DATA 160,32,32,32,32,160,32,32,32
7270 DATA 95,160,160,160,160,105
7280 DATA 32,32,32,32,95,160,160,160,160,105
7290 REM **ROW 2 **
7300 DATA 160,32,32,32,32,160,32,32,32
7310 DATA 160,223,32,32,32,32,32,32,32
7320 DATA 160,223,32,32,233,32,32,160
7330 REM ** ROW 3 **
7340 DATA 160,32,32,32,32,160,32,32,32
7350 DATA 160,32,32,32,32,32,32,32,32
7360 DATA 160,32,32,32,32,160
7370 REM ** ROW 4 **
7380 DATA 160,160,160,160,160,160,32,32,32,32
7390 DATA 160,32,32,32,32,32,32,32,32
7400 DATA 160,32,32,32,32,160
7410 REM ** ROW 5 **
7420 DATA 160,32,32,32,32,160,32,32,32
7430 DATA 160,32,32,32,32,32,32,32,32
7440 DATA 160,32,32,32,32,160
7450 REM ** ROW 6 **
7460 DATA 233,105,32,32,95,223,32,32,32
7470 DATA 160,32,32,32,32,32,32,32,32
7480 DATA 160,32,32,32,32,160
7490 REM ** ROW 7 **
7500 DATA 32,233,105,95,223,32,32,32,32
7510 DATA 160,32,32,32,32,32,32,32,32
7520 DATA 160,32,32,32,32,160
7530 REM ** ROW 8 **
7540 DATA 32,32,233,223,32,32,32,32,32,32
7550 DATA 160,32,32,32,32,32,32,32,32
7560 DATA 160,32,32,32,32,160
7570 DATA 14463:REM CHECKSUM
7580 REM ** QUESTION MARK DATA **
7590 DATA " ????? "
7600 DATA "?    ?"
7610 DATA "?      ?"
7620 DATA "     ??"
```

```
7630 DATA "   ?   "
7640 DATA "   ?   "
7650 DATA "   ?   "
7660 DATA "       "
7670 DATA "   •   "
7680 REM **** SCROLL SCREEN S/R ****
7690 POKE 218,160
7700 PRINTCHR$(19);CHR$(17);CHR$(157);CHR$(148)
7710 RETURN
```

Joystick Port Screen

```
8000 REM **** JOYSTICK PICTURE S/R ****
8010 PRINTCHR$(147):REM CLEAR SCREEN
8020 S0=832:S1=S0+64:REM SPR DATA START ADDR
8030 CC=0:VIC=53248:REM START OF VIC CHIP
8040 FOR I=S0 TO S0+62:READ A:CC=CC+A:POKE I,A:NEXT
8050 FOR I=S1 TO S1+62:POKE I,0:NEXT I
8060 FOR I=S1+25 TO S1+37:READ A:CC=CC+A:POKE I,A:NEXT I
8065 READ CS:IF CS<>CC THEN PRINT"CHECKSUM ERROR":STOP
8070 POKEVIC+33,0:POKEVIC+32,0:REM SET SCREEN/BORDER
8080 REM ** SET SPRITE POINTERS **
8090 POKE 2040,S0/64:POKE 2041,S1/64
8100 REM ** SET VIC SPRITE CONTROL REGS **
8110 POKE VIC+39,7:REM SET SPR 0 COLOUR
8120 POKE VIC+40,7:REM SET SPR 1 COLOUR
8130 POKE VIC,65:REM SET SPR 0 X COORD
8140 POKE VIC+1,70:REM SET SPR 0 Y COORD
8150 POKE VIC+2,74:REM SET SPR 1 X COORD
8160 POKE VIC+3,70:REM SET SPR 1 Y COORD
8170 POKE VIC+29,1:REM EXPAND SPR 0 HORIZ
8190 LE$="":FOR I=1 TO 40:LE$=LE$+CHR$(195):NEXT I
8200 DW$="":FOR I=1 TO 25:DW$=DW$+CHR$(17):NEXT I
8210 LS$="":FOR I=1 TO 11:LS$=LS$+CHR$(206)+" ":NEXT I
8220 RS$="":FOR I=1 TO 11:RS$=RS$+CHR$(205)+" ":NEXT I
8230 PRINTCHR$(158):REM TEXT YELLOW
8240 PRINTCHR$(19):PRINT TAB(2)"JOYSTICK PORT"
8250 PRINTCHR$(154):REM TEXT LT BLUE
8260 PRINTCHR$(19):LEFT$(DW$,17):LE$
8270 PRINT CHR$(145);
8280 PT$=LEFT$(LS$,19)+LEFT$(RS$,21)
8290 PT$=PT$+RIGHT$(LS$,19)+RIGHT$(RS$,21)
8300 FOR I=1 TO 3:PRINT PT$:NEXT I
8305 POKE VIC+21,3:REM TURN ON SPR 0 & 1
8310 REM ** SHOOT **
8320 YB=240:Y1=70
8330 X1=74:X=INT(RND(1)*150)+24
8340 G=2*(X-X1)/(YB-Y1)
8350 FOR Y=Y1 TO YB STEP 2
8360 X1=X1+G:POKE VIC+2,X1:POKE VIC+3,Y
8370 NEXT Y
8380 GET A$:IF A$="" THEN 8330
8390 REM ** RESET SCREEN **
8400 POKE VIC+21,0:REM TURN SPRITES OFF
8410 POKE VIC+32,14:POKEVIC+33,6:REM RESET SCREEN/BORD
8420 PRINT CHR$(147):REM CLEAR SCREEN
8430 RETURN
8440 REM **** SPRITE DATA ****
8450 DATA 0,0,0,63,255,252,64,0,2,64,0,2
8460 DATA 128,0,1,128,0,1,162,16,133,162,16,133
8470 DATA 128,0,1,128,0,1,128,0,1,128,0,1
8480 DATA 128,0,1,128,0,1,136,66,17,72,66,18
8490 DATA 64,0,2,64,0,2,32,0,4,31,255,248
8495 DATA 0,0,0,16,0,0,56,0,0,124,0,0,56,0,0,16
8497 DATA 3701:REM CHECKSUM
```

SINK OR SWIM

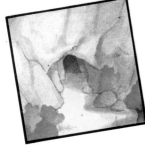

As our adventure game programming project approaches its conclusion, we analyse the design of the last two special locations in Haunted Forest — the swamp and the village — and complete the listing for our Digitaya adventure.

Two special locations in Haunted Forest are still to be dealt with: the swamp and the village. Let us start by looking at the swamp location. As with all special locations it is important to decide on a storyline for the special location before starting to program. This story can be as complex or as simple as the programmer sees fit, but he must bear in mind that a very complex plot at each location can make for a great deal of programming effort and eat large holes in the computer's residual memory.

THE SWAMP

The storyline for the swamp is as follows:

As the player enters the swamp he starts to sink. The player can use all the 'normal commands' available, but cannot leave the swamp.
Instead, the player must elect to swim if he is to leave the swamp.
The player can swim only if he carries less than two objects, as these weigh him down.
If the player is carrying two objects, then he must drop one if he is not to sink.
All objects dropped in the swamp are lost for good and cannot be recovered later.

```
4870 REM **** SWAMP S/R ****
4875 SF=1
4880 SN$="YOU START TO SINK INTO THE SWAMP.":GOSUB
5500
4885 PRINT:INPUT"INSTRUCTIONS";IS$
4890 GOSUB2500:REM SPLIT INSTRUCTION
4895 IF F=0 THEN 4885:REM INVALID
4900 GOSUB3000:REM NORMAL INSTRUCTIONS
4910 IF VB$="LOOK" THENGOSUB2000:GOTO4885
4915 IF VB$="DROP"THEN IV$(F,2)="-2":REM OBJ LOST
FOREVER
4917 IF VF=1 THEN 4885:REM NORMAL COMMAND
4920 REM ** NEW COMMANDS **
4925 IF VB$<>"SWIM"THEN SN$="I DON'T UNDERSTAND":G
OSUB5500:GOTO4885
4930 REM ** SWIM **
4932 F=0
4935 FOR I=1 TO 2
4940 IF IC$(I)<>""THEN F=F+1
4950 NEXT I
4955 IF F<2 THENGOSUB5035:RETURN:REM SWIM AWAY
4960 GOSUB 5000:RETURN:REM TWO OBJS HELD
5000 REM **** TWO OBJECTS HELD S/R ****
5010 SN$="THE OBJECTS ARE WEIGHING YOU DOWN AND YO
U ARE SINKING.":GOSUB5500
5012 PRINT:INPUT"INSTRUCTIONS";IS$
5015 GOSUB2500:REM SPLIT INSTRUCTION
5020 IF VB$<>"DROP" THENGOSUB5080:REM SINK
5025 GOSUB3900:IV$(F,2)="-2":REM DROP OBJ
5030 IF HF=0 OR F=0 THEN 5080:REM SINK
5035 REM **** SWIM AWAY ****
5040 SN$="YOU CAN NOW SWIM THROUGH THE SWAMP. WHIC
H WAY WILL YOU GO?":GOSUB5500
5050 EX$(2)="00080605":GOSUB2300:REM DEFINE AND DI
SPLAY EXITS
```

```
5055 PRINT:INPUT"INSTRUCTIONS";IS$
5060 GOSUB2500:REM SPLIT INSTRUCTION
5062 IF F=0 THEN 5055:REM INVALID
5065 GOSUB3500:REM MOVE
5067 EX$(2)="00000000":REM ZERO EXIT DATA
5070 RETURN
5075 :
5080 REM **** SINK S/R ****
5085 SN$="YOU SINK INTO THE SWAMP AND DROWN":GOSUB
5500
5090 END
```

Lines 4870-4917 allow normal commands to be dealt with, using the standard subroutines previously designed. If the player elects to drop an object immediately on entering the swamp this will be dealt with by the DROP routine. However, this routine reinstates the dropped object's position in the main inventory IV$(,), using the current value of the location counter, P. This in turn means that, as far as the program is concerned, the dropped object now resides at the swamp location. If we want to lose all trace of an object dropped in the swamp, then, in the case of a player wanting to drop an object here, we must amend the relevant entry in IV$(,).

Remember that IV$(F,2) holds the position of object F. Normally this is either the location number, or -1 if the object is carried by the player. To make the object appear to vanish from the game entirely we need to make IV$(F,2) incapable of being interpreted as a location or of indicating that the player holds the object. In line 4915, IV$(F,2) takes the value -2, F having already had the relevant object designated to it by the DROP routine.

If the player elects to SWIM, the program is allowed to fall through to line 4930. Here, the player's personal inventory is checked to determine how many objects are being carried. If the count is less than two then the program calls the SWIM AWAY subroutine, which allows the player to leave the swamp. If the player is carrying two objects he is given the opportunity to drop one; if he fails to take this course of action he sinks.

The SWIM AWAY routine allows the escaping player to specify the direction in which he wishes to swim. The exit data given for the swamp in the original DATA statements is 00000000, indicating that there are no exits from the swamp. Line 5050 redefines the exit data and calls the subroutine that describes the exits. The player is then allowed to select one exit and thus leave the swamp. Note that the exit data for the swamp is zeroed at the end of this routine, so that if the player re-enters the swamp later there won't be any exits.

THE VILLAGE

The village provides the escape route from the haunted forest, although the player still has to

carry out several tasks before he is allowed to leave the adventure. The storyline for the village location is:

The village is surrounded by a high, apparently unscalable wall.
The gate through the wall is guarded.
To get into the village the player must first kill the guard, using the gun.
The player then has to unlock the gate with the key to escape from the forest.

The village routine actually consists of two parts: first, the guard peril has to be negotiated and, second, the gate has to be unlocked. It is not difficult to envisage a scenario where the player, carrying the gun, arrives at the village and kills the guard, only to find that a key is needed to open the gate. If the player does not have the key, then he will need to leave the village location in search of it. If on the player's return the same description of the village location is given — i.e. that a guard is present — this will not be consistent. A particular feature of the game should be encountered and dealt with only once. If the guard is killed, then that 'characteristic' of the village must be removed.

This is not as difficult as it sounds. A flag can be used to denote whether or not the guard is alive or dead. The variable GF is used for this purpose — its initial value is zero indicating a live guard. If the player kills the guard, then GF is set to 1. The value of GF can be tested on entering the village location to determine whether the guard peril still exists or not. Having killed the guard, the player moves forward to the gate. Instructions can be split and dealt with using the standard subroutines that we have already. If the player has the key and uses it to unlock the gate then he has successfully completed the adventure.

```
5100 REM **** VILLAGE S/R ****
5102 SF=1
5105 SN$="THE VILLAGE IS SURROUNDED BY A TALL WALL
.":GOSUB5500
5106 IF GF<>0 THEN GOSUB5190:RETURN:REM GATE
5107 SN$="A GUARD IS AT THE ENTRANCE GATE TO THE V
ILLAGE":GOSUB5500
5115 PRINT:INPUT"INSTRUCTIONS";IS$
5120 GOSUB2500:IF F=0 THEN 5115:REM INVALID
5125 GOSUB3000:REM NORMAL INSTRUCTIONS
5130 IF VB$="LOOK"THEN GOSUB2000:REM DESCRIBE
5135 IF VB$="GO" AND MF=1 THEN RETURN
5140 IF VF=1 THEN 5115:REM NEXT INSTRUCTION
5145 IF VB$<>"KILL"THENSN$="I DON'T UNDERSTAND":GO
SUB5500:GOTO5115
5150 REM ** KILL **
5155 SN$="WHAT WILL YOU USE TO KILL THE GUARD?":GO
SUB5500
5160 SN$="ENTER OBJECT OR <I> FOR INSTRUCTION":GOS
UB5500
5162 INPUT IS$:IF IS$="I" THEN 5115
5165 GOSUB2500:REM SPLIT
5167 IF F=0 THEN 5160:REM INVALID
5170 GOSUB5300:IF F=0 THEN SN$="THERE IS NO "+W$:G
OSUB5500:GOTO5160
5172 OV=F:GOSUB5450:REM IS OBJECT HELD
5174 IF HF=0 THEN SN$="YOU DO NOT HAVE THE "+IV$(F
,1):GOSUB5500:GOTO5160
5175 IF F<>1 THEN SN$="THE "+IV$(F,1)+" IS NO USE"
:GOSUB5500:GOTO5160
5180 SN$="YOU KILL THE GUARD":GOSUB5500:GF=1
5185 :
5190 REM **** LOCKED GATE S/R ****
5195 SN$="YOU MOVE FORWARD AND TRY TO OPEN THE GAT
E TO THE VILLAGE"
5200 SN$=SN$+" BUT THE GATE IS LOCKED AND WILL NOT
MOVE":GOSUB5500
5205 PRINT:INPUT"INSTRUCTIONS";IS$
5210 GOSUB2500:IF F=0 THEN 5205:REM INVALID
5215 GOSUB3000:REM NORMAL INSTRUCTIONS
5220 IF VB$="LOOK"THEN GOSUB2000:REM DESCRIBE
5225 IF VB$="GO" AND MF=1 THEN RETURN
5230 IF VF=1 THEN 5205:REM NEXT INSTRUCTION
5232 IF VB$="USE"THEN 5240
5234 IF VB$="UNLOCK"THENSN$="HOW?":GOSUB5500:GOTO5
205
5235 SN$="I DON'T UNDERSTAND":GOSUB5500:GOTO5205
5240 GOSUB5300:REM VALID OBJECT
5242 OV=F:GOSUB5450:REM IS OBJ CARRIED
5244 IF F=0 THEN SN$="THERE IS NO "+W$:GOSUB5500:G
OTO5205
5246 IF HF=0 THEN SN$="YOU DO NOT HAVE THE "IV$(F,
1):GOSUB5500:GOTO5205
5248 IF F<>3 THEN SN$="THE "+IV$(F,1)+" IS NO USE"
:GOSUB5500:GOTO5205
5250 REM ** THROUGH GATE AND SAFE **
5255 SN$="YOU UNLOCK THE GATE, AND DISGUISING YOUR
SELF IN THE DEAD"
5260 SN$=SN$+" GUARD'S CLOTHES, WALK UNNOTICED THR
OUGH THE VILLAGE"
5265 SN$=SN$+" AND THE SAFETY OF THE OUTSIDE WORLD
.":GOSUB5500
5270 END
```

So that we can call these two special location routines, we must amend line 2720 of the subroutine that decides whether or not a location is special. Make this change:

```
2720 ON P GOSUB4590,4870,5100,4590
```

Basic Flavours

Spectrum:
In the Haunted Forest listing, replace SN$ by S$, IS$ by T$, VB$ by B$, IV$(,) by V$(,), EX$() by X$() and IC$() by I$().
Substitute the following lines:

```
2720 IF P=1 THEN GOSUB 4590
2722 IF P=2 THEN GOSUB 4870
2724 IF P=3 THEN GOSUB 5100
2726 IF P=4 THEN GOSUB 4590

4937 LET A$=IC$(1):GOSUB7000
4940 IF A$<>"" THEN LET F=F+1

5175 IF F<>1 THEN LET S$="THE"
     :LET A$=V$(F,1):GOSUB7000
5177 IF F<>1 THEN LET S$=S$+ "IS NO
     USE":GOSUB5500:GOTO5160

5248 IF F<>3 THEN LET S$="THE"
     :LET A$=V$(F,1): GOSUB7000
5249 IF F<>3 THEN LET S$=S$+
     "IS NO USE":GOSUB5500:GOTO5205
```

In the Digitaya listing, replace SN$ by S$, IS$ by I$, VB$ by B$, IV$(,) by V$(,) and IC$() by I$().
Substitute the following lines:

```
3650 LET S$="YOUR ":LET A$=V$(F,1):
     GOSUB7000
3655 LET S$=S$+" IS USELESS, THE
     FORCE INCREASES"

4520 LET V$(4,2)=STR$(RND(1) (INT
     *40+8)
```

BBC Micro:
In the Haunted Forest listing substitute this line:

```
190 LET GF=0
```

In the Digitaya listing substitute the following line:

```
4520 IV$(4,2)=RND(40)+8
```

Digitaya Listing

```
2960 REM **** USER PORT S/R ****
2970 SF=1
2980 SN$="ESCAPE IS AT HAND BUT THE DDR BOOKING CL
ERK"
2990 SN$=SN$+" BARS YOUR WAY. HE TELLS YOU THAT HE
 HAS BEEN INSTRUCTED TO"
3000 SN$=SN$+" ACCEPT INPUTS ONLY. HOWEVER HE DOES
 TAKE ALL MAJOR"
3010 SN$=SN$+" CREDIT CARDS."
3020 GOSUB 5880:REM FORMAT PRINT
3030 :
3040 PRINT:INPUT"INSTRUCTIONS";IS$
3050 GOSUB1700:REM ANALYSE INSTRUCTIONS
3060 GOSUB1900:REM NORMAL ACTIONS
3070 IF MF=1 THEN RETURN:REM MOVE OUT
3080 IF VF=1 THEN3040:REM NEXT INSTRUCTION
3090 IF VB$<>"GIVE" THENPRINT"I DON'T UNDERSTAND":
GOTO3040
3100 :
3110 REM ** INSTRUCTION IS GIVE **
3120 GOSUB5730:REM IS OBJECT VALID
3130 IFF=0THENPRINT"THERE IS NO ";NN$:GOTO3040:REM
 NEXT INSTRUCTION
3140 :
3150 REM ** IS OBJECT CREDIT CARD **
3160 IF F<>5THENPRINT"HE ONLY ACCEPTS CREDIT CARDS
":GOTO3040
3170 :
3180 REM ** IS CARD CARRIED **
3190 OV=5:GOSUB5830
3200 IFHF=0THENPRINT"YOU DO NOT HAVE THE ";IV$(5,1
):GOTO 3040
3210 :
3220 SN$="THE CLERK TAKES THE CARD AND SAYS 'THAT
WILL DO NICELY, SIR'"
3230 GOSUB5880:REM FORMAT PRINT
3240 SN$="YOU ARE ALLOWED TO PASS THE BARRIER AND
ENTER THE USER PORT"
3250 GOSUB5880:REM FORMAT PRINT
3260 :
3270 REM ** IS DIGITAYA CARRIED **
3280 OV=6:GOSUB5830
3290 IF HF=1 THEN 3380:REM SUCCESS
3300 :
3310 REM ** FAILURE **
3320 SN$="WELL DONE YOU HAVE SUCCEEDED IN ESCAPING
 FROM THE CLUTCHES"
3330 SN$=SN$+" OF THE MACHINE, BUT HAVE FAILED IN
YOUR MISSION"
3340 SN$=SN$+" TO BRING BACK THE MYSTERIOUS DIGITA
YA"
3350 GOSUB5880:REM FORMAT PRINT
3360 END
3370 :
3380 REM ** SUCCESS **
3390 SN$="CONGRATULATIONS, YOU HAVE SUCCEEDED IN Y
OUR MISSION"
3400 SN$=SN$+" TO RESCUE THE WONDEROUS DIGITAYA FR
OM THE"
3410 SN$=SN$+" CLUTCHES OF THE MACHINE."
3420 GOSUB5880:REM FORMAT PRINT
3430 END
3440 :
3450 REM **** CASSETTE PORT S/R ****
3460 SF=1
3470 SN$="YOU FEEL AN IRRESISTIBLE FORCE PULLING
YOU TOWARDS"
3480 SN$=SN$+" PERMANANENT MAGNETIC SUSPENSION"
3490 GOSUB5880:REM FORMAT
3500 NS=0:REM START COUNTING INSTRUCTIONS
3510 REM ** INSTRUCTIONS **
3520 NS=NS+1:IFNS>3THEN3770:REM SUCKED OUT
3530 PRINT:INPUT"INSTRUCTIONS";IS$
3540 GOSUB1700:REM ANALYSE INSTRUCTIONS
3550 GOSUB1900:REM NORMAL ACTIONS
3560 IFMF=1THENMF=0:PRINT"YOU CAN'T MOVE...YET":GO
TO3510
3570 IFVF=1THEN3510:REM NEXT INSTRUCTION
3580 IFVB$<>"USE"THENPRINT"I DON'T UNDERSTAND":GOT
O3510
3590 REM ** INSTRUCTION IS USE **
3600 GOSUB5730:REM IS OBJECT VALID
3610 IFF=0THENPRINT"THERE IS NO ";NN$:GOTO3510
3620 :
3630 REM ** IS OBJECT BUFFER ACTIVATOR **
3640 IF F=8 THEN3680:REM OK
3650 SN$="YOUR "+IV$(F,1)+" IS USELESS, THE FORCE
INCREASES"
3660 GOSUB 5880:GOTO3510:REM NEXT INSTRUCTION
3670 :
3680 OV=8:GOSUB5830:REM IS BUFF ACT HELD
3690 IFHF=0THENSN$="YOU DON'T HAVE THE "+IV$(8,1):
GOSUB5880:GOTO3510
3700 :
3710 REM ** SAVED **
3720 SN$="YOU USE THE BUFFER ACTIVATOR TO COUNTER
THE PULL"
3730 SN$=SN$+" INTO MAGNETIC OBLIVION. THE FORCE S
UBSIDES"
3740 GOSUB5880:REM FORMAT
3750 RETURN
3760 :
3770 REM ** SUCKED OUT **
3780 SN$="THE FORCE BECOMES TOO STRONG AND YOU ARE
 PULLED OUT"
3790 SN$=SN$+" THROUGH THE CASSETTE PORT INTO MAGN
ETIC NOTHINGNESS."
3800 GOSUB 5880:REM FORMAT
3810 END
4180 REM **** TRI-STATE DEVICE S/R ****
4190 SF=1
4200 SN$="A LARGE SIGN SAYS 'I/O THIS WAY' BUT AS
YOU MOVE TOWARDS IT"
4210 SN$=SN$+" A TICKET COLLECTOR SHOUTS 'TICKETS
PLEASE'"
4220 GOSUB5880:REM FORMAT
4230 :
4240 REM ** INSTRUCTIONS **
4250 PRINT:INPUT"INSTRUCTIONS";IS$
4260 GOSUB1700:GOSUB1900:REM ANALYSE
4270 IFMF=1 THEN RETURN
4280 IFVF=1THEN4240:REM NEXT INSTRUCTION
4290 IFVB$<>"GIVE"ANDVB$<>"OFFER"THENPRINT"I DON'T
 UNDERSTAND":GOTO4240
4300 REM ** INSTRUCTION IS GIVE **
4310 GOSUB5730:REM IS OBJECT VALID
4320 IFF=0THENPRINT"THERE IS NO ";NN$:GOTO4240:REM
 NEXT INSTRUCTION
4330 :
4340 REM ** IS OBJECT TICKET **
4350 IF F=4 THEN4400:REM OK
4360 SN$="THE TICKET COLLECTOR SHAKES HIS HEAD AND
 SAYS"
4370 SN$=SN$+" 'I CANNOT ACCEPT THIS "+IV$(F,1)
4380 GOSUB5880:GOTO4240:REM NEXT INSTRUCTION
4390 :
4400 OV=4:GOSUB5830:REM IS TICKET HELD
4410 IFHF=0THENPRINT"YOU DO NOT HAVE THE TICKET":G
OTO4240
4420 :
4430 REM ** OK **
4440 SN$="THE TICKET COLLECTOR ACCEPTS YOUR TICKET
 AND ALLOWS YOU"
4450 SN$=SN$+" TO PASS THE BARRIER."
4460 GOSUB5880:REM FORMAT
4470 REM ** DEL TICKET FROM LIST **
4480 F=0
4490 FORJ=1TO4
4500 IF IC$(J)=IV$(4,1)THENIC$(J)="":J=4
4510 NEXT J
4520 IV$(4,2)=STR$(INT(RND(TI)*40+8)):REM REALLOCA
TE TICKET POSITION
4530 P=15:MF=1:RETURN
```

THE HAUNTED FOREST

We round up our adventure game programming project with a full listing of the Haunted Forest game. In showing how this program was created, we have demonstrated all the basic principles involved in the design of an adventure game. The full listing given here will help you tie together all the component routines we have given.

Haunted Forest is a short adventure game designed to demonstrate some of the basic programming techniques of adventure game programming. Of necessity, the game is limited in both storyline and the number of options open to the player. The construction of Haunted Forest shows how an adventure game program can be built around a simple framework, the basis of which is a map showing all the different locations and their relationships to each other within the adventure world. Whether the game has 16 or 600 locations, it must still be designed using the map as a basis. In addition, objects and special 'perils' can be marked on the map. It is obviously important that the overall storyline and the major perils have been worked out in some detail before programming begins. Often, drawing out the adventure world map on squared paper is the best way to rationalise and form ideas for the rules of the game. Once a final concept has been arrived at, then programming can begin.

Normally the first task is to recode the two-dimensional pictorial map as array elements. In the system used by Haunted Forest, the location data is stored in two one-dimensional arrays, holding a location description and a coded list of the exits available from that location. Objects present in the game are held in a two-dimensional array, indicating a description of the object and the location it resides at. At this stage, we have a simple database representing the adventure world, and simple handling routines can be developed to allow the player to move around the various locations and pick up or drop objects. The specific rules relating to the way the game is played are — at this stage — largely undefined, apart from equipping the game with the objects needed to enable the player to negotiate the hazards presented by the game's special scenarios.

This version of the program was written for the Commodore 64 but will run on most machines that support Microsoft-type BASIC dialects. Minor amendments may be necessary with regard to random number generation and screen clearing. We also give detailed 'Basic Flavours' for the BBC Micro. Because of the Spectrum's peculiar string

array handling, however, Spectrum flavours are too numerous to list here. You must refer back to past issues for these. To assist you in collating Spectrum flavours, we do include a conversion table for the string variable names, which are used in all the Spectrum flavours given previously.

Because an adventure game relies on the player 'discovering' perils and hidden procedures in order to negotiate the adventure world, a detailed look at how a game is constructed inevitably 'gives away' the game's scenario. In showing the full internal workings of the Haunted Forest game, therefore, we have of necessity revealed the details of that game's scenario. Our Digitaya game was provided throughout the series in tandem with the Haunted Forest to provide you with an adventure to play without knowing the scenario. We will list Digitaya in the next section.

Conversion Table For Spectrum String Variables		
Microsoft	**Spectrum**	**Purpose Of Variables**
LN$()	L$()	Location description
EX$()	E$()	Exits
IC$()	I$()	Objects held by player
IV$(,)	V$(,)	Objects in game
SN$	S$	Holds sentence for formatting
OW$	O$	'Old word' in format routine
NW$	N$	'New word' in format routine
EX$	X$	Exits from current location
IS$	I$	Current instruction
DR$	D$	Direction specified by instruction
NN$	R$	Non-verb part of instruction
VB$	B$	Verb part of instruction
CD$	C$	Code word

Basic Flavours

BBC Micro:
The following lines should be subtituted in the Haunted Forest listing:

207 RND (–TIME)
210 P=RND (10)

1160 CLS

4190 REPEAT:A$=GET$:UNTIL A$="Y" OR A$="N"
4535 CR=RND(3)

6067 CC=0

The Final Listing

```
130 REM ** HAUNTED **
140 REM ** FOREST **
180 :
200 GOSUB6000:REM READ ARRAY DATA
205 GOSUB 1000:REM STORY SO FAR
207 R=RND(-1)
210 P=INT(RND(TI)*10+1):REM START POINT
220 :
230 REM **** MAIN LOOP STARTS HERE ****
240 MF=0:REM MOVE FLAG
245 PRINT
250 GOSUB2000:REM DESCRIBE POSITION
255 GOSUB2300:REM DESCRIBE EXITS
257 GOSUB2700:REM IS P SPECIAL ?
258 IF SF=1 THEN 300:REM NEXT INSTRUCTION
260 PRINT:INPUT"INSTRUCTIONS";IS$
270 GOSUB2500:REM SPLIT INSTRUCTION
275 IF F=0 THEN 260:REM INVALID INSTRUCTION
280 GOSUB3000:REM NORMAL COMMANDS
290 IF VF=0 THENPRINT:PRINT"I DONT UNDERSTAND"
300 IF MF=1 THEN 240:REM NEW LOCATION
310 IF MF=0 THEN 260:REM NEW INSTRUCTION
320 :
990 END
1000 REM **** STORY SO FAR S/R ****
1010 SN$="WELCOME TO THE HAUNTED FOREST"
1020 GOSUB5500:REM FORMAT
1030 PRINT
1040 SN$="AS YOU AWAKE FROM A DEEP SLEEP, THE "
1050 SN$=SN$+"FOREST FLOOR FEELS SOFT AND DRY. "
1060 SN$=SN$+"YOU DO NOT KNOW HOW YOU CAME TO BE HERE "
1070 SN$=SN$+"BUT KNOW THAT YOU MUST FIND THE "
1080 SN$=SN$+"VILLAGE ON THE EDGE OF THE WOOD TO "
1090 SN$=SN$+"REACH SAFETY."
1100 GOSUB5500:REM FORMAT
1110 PRINT
1120 SN$="YOU LOOK AROUND, TRYING TO GET YOUR BEARINGS."
1130 GOSUB5500:REM FORMAT
1140 PRINT:PRINT"PRESS ANY KEY TO START"
1150 GET A$:IF A$="" THEN 1150
1160 PRINTCHR$(147):REM CLEAR SCREEN
1170 RETURN
1180 :
2000 REM **** DESCRIBE LOCATION ****
2010 SN$="YOU ARE "+LN$(P):GOSUB5500
2020 SN$="YOU SEE "
2030 REM ** CHECK INVENTORY FOR OBJ **
2040 F=0:SP$=""
2050 FOR I=1 TO 3
2060 IF VAL(IV$(I,2))<>P THEN 2080
2070 SN$=SN$+SP$+"A "+IV$(I,1):F=1:SP$=", "
2080 NEXT I
2090 IF F=0 THEN SN$=SN$+"NO OBJECTS"
2100 GOSUB5500:REM FORMAT OUTPUT
2110 RETURN
2120 :
2299 :
2300 REM **** DESCRIBE EXITS S/R ****
2310 EX$=EX$(P)
2320 NR=VAL(LEFT$(EX$,2))
2330 EA=VAL(MID$(EX$,3,2))
2340 SO=VAL(MID$(EX$,5,2))
2350 WE=VAL(RIGHT$(EX$,2))
2353 :
2355 IF(NR OR EA OR SO OR WE)=0 THEN RETURN
2360 PRINT:SN$="EXITS ARE TO THE "
2370 IF NR <>0 THEN SN$=SN$+"NORTH "
2380 IF EA <>0 THEN SN$=SN$+"EAST "
2390 IF SO <>0 THEN SN$=SN$+"SOUTH "
2400 IF WE <>0 THEN SN$=SN$+"WEST "
2410 GOSUB 5500:REM FORMAT
2415 PRINT
2420 RETURN
2430 :
2500 REM **** SPLIT COMMAND S/R ****
2510 IF IS$="LIST" OR IS$="END" THEN VB$=IS$:F=1:RETURN
2515 IF IS$="LOOK" THEN VB$=IS$:F=1:RETURN
2520 F=0
2530 LS=LEN(IS$)
2540 FOR C=1 TO LS
2550 A$=MID$(IS$,C,1)
2560 IF A$<>" " THEN 2590
2570 VB$=LEFT$(IS$,C-1):F=1
2580 NN$=RIGHT$(IS$,LS-C):C=LS
2590 NEXT C
2600 :
2610 IF F=1 THEN RETURN
2620 PRINT:PRINT"I NEED AT LEAST TWO WORDS"
2630 RETURN
2650 :
2700 REM **** IS P SPECIAL S/R ****
2705 SF=0:REM UNSET SPECIAL FLAG
2707 REM ** RANDOM GHOST **
2710 IF P>4 AND RND(1)<0.1 THEN GOSUB 4290:RETURN
2715 :
2716 REM ** OTHER SPECIAL LOCATIONS **
2720 ON P GOSUB4590,4870,5100,4590
2730 RETURN
2735 :
3000 REM **** NORMAL COMMANDS S/R ****
3010 VF=0:REM VERB FLAG
3020 IF VB$="GO" OR VB$="MOVE" THENVF=1:GOSUB3500
3030 IF VB$="TAKE" OR VB$="PICK"THEN VF=1:GOSUB3700
3040 IF VB$="DROP" OR VB$="PUT"THEN VF=1:GOSUB3900
3050 IF VB$="LIST" OR VB$="INVENTORY"THEN VF=1:GOSUB4100
3055 IF VB$="LOOK" THEN VF=1:MF=1:RETURN
3060 IF VB$="END" OR VB$="FINISH" THEN VF=1:GOSUB4170
3070 RETURN
3080 :
```

```
3500 REM **** MOVE S/R ****
3505 GOSUB3630:REM SEARCH FOR DIRECTION
3510 MF=1:REM SET MOVE FLAG
3520 DR$=LEFT$(NN$,1)
3530 IF DR$<>"N"ANDDR$<>"E"ANDDR$<>"S"ANDDR$<>"W"THENGOTO3590
3540 IF DR$="N"AND NR<>0 THEN P=NR:RETURN
3550 IF DR$="E"AND EA<>0 THEN P=EA:RETURN
3560 IF DR$="S"AND SO<>0 THEN P=SO:RETURN
3570 IF DR$="W"AND WE<>0 THEN P=WE:RETURN
3580 PRINT:PRINT"YOU CAN'T "+IS$
3585 MF=0:RETURN
3590 REM ** NOUN NOT DIRECTION **
3600 PRINT"WHAT IS ";NN$;" ?"
3610 MF=0:RETURN
3620 :
3630 REM **** SEARCH FOR DIRECTION S/R ****
3640 NN$=NN$+" ":LN=LEN(NN$):C=1
3645 FOR I=1 TO LN
3650 IF MID$(NN$,I,1)<>" " THEN NEXT I:RETURN
3655 W$=MID$(NN$,C,I-C):C=I+1
3660 IF W$="NORTH" OR W$="EAST" THEN NN$=W$:I=LN
3665 IF W$="SOUTH" OR W$="WEST" THEN NN$=W$:I=LN
3670 NEXT I
3675 RETURN
3700 REM **** TAKE S/R ****
3710 GOSUB 5300:REM IS OBJECT VALID
3720 IF F=0 THEN SN$="THERE IS NO "+W$:GOSUB5500:RETURN
3730 OV=F:GOSUB5450:REM CHECK INVENTORY
3740 IF HF=1 THEN SN$="YOU ALREADY HAVE THE "+IV$(F,1):GOSUB5500:RETURN
3750 :
3755 REM ** IS OBJECT HERE ? **
3760 IF VAL(IV$(F,2))<>P THEN SN$=IV$(F,1)+" IS NOT HERE":GOSUB5500:RETURN
3770 :
3780 REM ** ADD OBJECT TO LIST **
3790 AF=0
3800 FOR J=1 TO 2
3810 IF IC$(J)="" THEN IC$(J)=IV$(F,1):AF=1:J=2
3820 NEXT J
3830 :
3840 REM ** FULL QUOTA **
3850 IF AF=0 THEN PRINT"YOU ALREADY HAVE TWO OBJECTS":RETURN
3860 :
3870 SN$="YOU TAKE THE "+IV$(F,1):GOSUB5500
3880 IV$(F,2)="-1":REM DELETE INVENTORY ENTRY
3890 :
3895 :
3900 REM **** DROP S/R ****
3910 GOSUB5300:REM VALID OBJECT
3920 IF F=0 THEN SN$="THERE IS NO "+W$:GOSUB5500:RETURN
3930 :
3940 REM ** IS OBJECT IN CARRIED INVENTORY **
3950 OV=F:GOSUB5450
3960 IF HF=0 THEN SN$="YOU DO NOT HAVE THE "+IV$(F,1):GOSUB5500:RETURN
3970 :
3980 REM ** DROP OBJECT **
3990 SN$="YOU DROP THE "+IV$(F,1):GOSUB5500
4000 IV$(F,2)=STR$(P):REM MAKE ENTRY IN INVENTORY
4010 :
4020 REM ** DELETE OBJECT FROM CARRIED INVENTORY **
4030 FOR J=1TO2
4040 IF IC$(J)=IV$(F,1) THEN IC$(J)="":J=2
4050 NEXT J
4060 RETURN
4070 :
4100 REM **** LIST CARRIED INVENTORY ****
4110 PRINT"OBJECTS HELD:"
4120 FOR I=1 TO 2
4130 PRINT" ";IC$(I)
4140 NEXT I
4150 RETURN
4160 :
4170 REM **** END GAME S/R ****
4180 PRINT:PRINT"ARE YOU SURE (Y/N) ?"
4190 GET A$:IF A$<>"Y" AND A$<>"N" THEN 4190
4200 IF A$="N" THEN RETURN
4210 END
4220 :
4290 REM **** RANDOM GHOST S/R ****
4295 SF=1:GC=0
4300 SN$="YOU FEEL A COLD SENSATION RUNNING THE LENGTH"
4305 SN$=SN$+" OF YOUR SPINE. SUDDENLY A WHITE APPARITION"
4310 SN$=SN$+" APPEARS FROM OUT OF THE TREES AND"
4315 SN$=SN$+" MOVES TOWARDS YOU":GOSUB5500:REM FORMAT
4320 :
4325 SN$="THE GHOST MOVES CLOSER":GOSUB5500
4330 GC=GC+1:IF GC>4 THEN GOSUB4455:REM
4335 PRINT:INPUT"INSTRUCTIONS";IS$
4340 GOSUB2500:REM SPLIT INSTRUCTION
4345 IF F=0 THEN 4325:REM NEXT INSTRUCTION
4350 OP=P:GOSUB3000:REM ANALYSE INSTRUCTION
4355 IF MF=1 AND VB$="GO"THEN GOSUB4400:GOTO 4325
4357 IF MF=1 AND VB$="LOOK" THEN GOSUB2000:GOSUB2300:GOTO4325
4360 IF VF=1 THEN 4325:REM NEXT INSTRUCTION
4365 REM ** NEW INSTRUCTION WORDS **
4370 IF VB$="KILL" OR VB$="FIGHT" THEN GOSUB4425:GOTO 4325
4375 :
4385 IF VB$="SING" THEN GOSUB4500:RETURN
4390 SN$="I DON'T UNDERSTAND":GOSUB5500:GOTO4325
4395 :
4400 REM ** ATTEMPT TO MOVE **
4405 SN$="YOU ARE TRANSFIXED WITH TERROR AND CANNOT"
4410 SN$=SN$+" MOVE...YET":MF=0:GOSUB5500:P=OP
4415 RETURN
4420 :
4425 REM ** FIGHT OR KILL **
4430 SN$="THE GHOST IS A BEING OF THE SUPERNATURAL"
4435 SN$=SN$+" AND LAUGHS AT YOUR FEEBLE ATTEMPTS"
4440 SN$=SN$+" TO INJURE HIM":GOSUB5500
4445 RETURN
4450 :
4455 REM ** DEATH **
4460 SN$="THE PAIN IN YOUR CHEST BECOMES UNBEARABLE"
4465 SN$=SN$+" AND YOU SLUMP ONTO THE LEAFY FOREST FLOOR.":GOSUB5500
```

KEVIN JONES

```
4470 SN$="YOUR SPIRIT RISES FROM YOUR INERT BODY"
4475 SN$=SN$+" AND YOU FLOAT AWAY INTO THE MIST TO JOIN"
4480 SN$=SN$+" THE OTHER TORMENTED SOULS OF THE"
4485 SN$=SN$+" HAUNTED FOREST.":GOSUB5500
4490 END
4495 :
4500 REM ** SING **
4505 SN$="YOU KNOW THREE SONGS. WHICH ONE WILL YOU CHOOSE ?":GOSUB5500
4510 SN$="1) THE THEME FROM 'GHOSTBUSTERS'":GOSUB5500
4515 SN$="2) 'THERE'S A GHOST IN MY HOUSE'":GOSUB5500
4520 SN$="3) 'WAY DOWN UPON THE SWANEE RIVER'":GOSUB5500
4525 PRINT:INPUT"MAKE YOUR CHOICE";C$
4530 IF VAL(C$)>3 OR VAL(C$)<1 THEN PRINT:PRINT" INVALID":GOTO4525
4535 CR=INT(RND(1)*3)+1
4537 IF CR<>VAL(C$) THEN GOSUB4542:REM WRONG TUNE
4540 GOSUB4565:RETURN:REM CORRECT
4542 REM **** WRONG TUNE S/R ****
4545 SN$="THE GHOST HAS A PARTICULAR HATRED OF"
4550 SN$=SN$+" THAT TUNE AND LUNGES AT YOU.":GOSUB5500
4555 GOSUB 4455:REM DEATH
4560 :
4565 REM ** CORRECT TUNE **
4570 SN$="THE GHOST IS APPEASED BY YOUR RENDITION OF THE TUNE"
4575 SN$=SN$+" AND VAPOURISES INTO THIN AIR":GOSUB5500
4580 RETURN
4585 :
4590 REM **** TUNNEL ENTRANCE S/R ****
4600 SF=1
4605 SN$="YOU HAVE ARRIVED AT THE MOUTH OF A LARGE TUNNEL":GOSUB5500
4610 SN$="YOU CAN ENTER THE TUNNEL OR RETREAT ALONG THE PATH":GOSUB5500
4620 :
4625 PRINT:INPUT"INSTRUCTIONS";IS$
4630 GOSUB2500:REM SPLIT INSTRUCTION
4635 IF F=0 THEN 4625:REM INVALID INSTRUCTION
4637 GOSUB3000:REM NORMAL INSTRUCTIONS
4640 IF MF=1 THEN RETURN:REM PLAYER RETREATS
4645 IF VE=1 THEN 4625:REM INSTRUCTION OBEYED
4650 REM ** NEW INSTRUCTIONS **
4655 IF VB$="ENTER" THEN GOSUB 4700:RETURN
4660 IF VB$="RETREAT" AND P=4 THEN MF=1:P=6:RETURN
4665 IF VB$="RETREAT" AND P=1 THEN MF=1:P=9:RETURN
4667 SN$="I DON'T UNDERSTAND":GOSUB5500:GOTO 4625
4700 REM ** ENTER TUNNEL **
4705 SN$="YOU ENTER THE TUNNEL BUT IT IS TOO DARK TO"
4710 SN$=SN$+" FIND YOUR WAY.":GOSUB5500
4725 PRINT:INPUT"INSTRUCTIONS";IS$
4730 GOSUB2500:REM SPLIT INSTRUCTION
4732 :
4735 IF F=0 THEN 4725:REM INVALID INSTRUCTION
4740 OP=F:GOSUB3000:REM NORMAL INSTRUCTIONS
4745 IF MF=1THEN SN$="IT IS SO DARK THAT YOU CAN ONLY SEE":P=OP
4747 IF MF=1THENSN$=SN$+" THE TUNNEL ENTRANCE":GOSUB5500:MF=0:GOTO4725
4750 IF VF=1 THEN 4725:REM INSTRUCTION OBEYED
4755 IF VB$="RETREAT" AND P=4 THEN MF=1:P=6:RETURN
4760 IF VB$="RETREAT" AND P=1 THEN MF=1:P=9:RETURN
4762 IFVB$<>"USE"ANDVB$<>"LIGHT" THEN SN$="I DON'T UNDERSTAND"
4765 IFVB$<>"USE"ANDVB$<>"LIGHT" THEN GOSUB5500:GOTO4725
4777 :
4780 REM ** SEARCH FOR LAMP **
4790 GOSUB5300:REM VALID OBJECT ?
4795 OV=F:GOSUB5450:REM IS OBJECT HELD ?
4797 IF F=0 THEN SN$="THERE IS NO "+W$:GOSUB5500:GOTO4725
4800 IF HF=0 THEN SN$="YOU DO NOT HAVE THE "+IV$(F,1):GOSUB5500:GOTO4725
4810 REM ** IS OBJECT LAMP ? **
4815 IF F<>2 THEN SN$="THE "+IV$(F,1)+" IS NO USE":GOSUB5500:GOTO4725
4835 REM ** SUCCESS **
4840 SN$="YOU USE THE LAMP TO LIGHT YOUR WAY THROUGH THE TUNNEL"
4845 SN$=SN$+" AND EVENTUALLY EMERGE FROM THE EXIT.":GOSUB5500
4850 IF P=1 THEN MF=1:P=4:RETURN
4855 IF P=4 THEN MF=1:P=1:RETURN
4860 :
4870 REM **** SWAMP S/R ****
4875 SF=1
4880 SN$="YOU START TO SINK INTO THE SWAMP.":GOSUB5500
4885 PRINT:INPUT"INSTRUCTIONS";IS$
4890 GOSUB2500:REM SPLIT INSTRUCTION
4895 IF F=0 THEN 4885:REM INVALID
4900 GOSUB3000:REM NORMAL INSTRUCTIONS
4910 IF VB$="LOOK" THENGOSUB2000:GOTO4885
4915 IF VB$="DROP"THEN IV$(F,2)="-2":REM OBJ LOST FOREVER
4917 IF VF=1 THEN 4885:REM NORMAL COMMAND
4920 REM ** NEW COMMANDS **
4925 IF VB$<>"SWIM" THEN SN$="I DON'T UNDERSTAND":GOSUB5500:GOTO4885
4930 REM ** SWIM **
4932 F=0
4935 FOR I=1 TO 2
4940 IF IC$(I)<>"" THEN F=F+1
4950 NEXT I
4955 IF F<2 THENGOSUB5035:RETURN:REM SWIM AWAY
4960 GOSUB 5000:RETURN:REM TWO OBJS HELD
5000 REM ** TWO OBJECTS HELD S/R **
5010 SN$="THE OBJECTS ARE WEIGHING YOU DOWN AND YOU ARE SINKING.":GOSUB5500
5012 PRINT:INPUT"INSTRUCTIONS";IS$
5015 GOSUB2500:REM SPLIT INSTRUCTION
5020 IF VB$<>"DROP" THENGOSUB5080:REM SINK
5025 GOSUB3900:IV$(F,2)="-2":REM DROP OBJ
5030 IF HF=0 OR F=0 THEN 5080:REM SINK
5035 REM **** SWIM AWAY ****
5040 SN$="YOU CAN NOW SWIM THROUGH THE SWAMP. WHICH WAY WILL YOU GO?"
     :GOSUB5500
5050 EX$(2)="00080605":GOSUB2300:REM DEFINE AND DISPLAY EXITS
5055 PRINT:INPUT"INSTRUCTIONS";IS$
5060 GOSUB2500:REM SPLIT INSTRUCTION
5062 IF F=0 THEN 5055:REM INVALID
5065 GOSUB3500:REM MOVE
5067 EX$(2)="00000000":REM ZERO EXIT DATA
5070 RETURN
5075 :
5080 REM **** SINK S/R ****
5085 SN$="YOU SINK INTO THE SWAMP AND DROWN":GOSUB5500
5090 END
5100 REM **** VILLAGE S/R ****
5102 SF=1
```

```
5105 SN$="THE VILLAGE IS SURROUNDED BY A TALL WALL.":GOSUB5500
5106 IF GF<>0 THEN GOSUB5190:RETURN:REM GATE
5107 SN$="A GUARD IS AT THE ENTRANCE GATE TO THE VILLAGE":GOSUB5500
5115 PRINT:INPUT"INSTRUCTIONS";IS$
5120 GOSUB2500:IF F=0 THEN 5115:REM INVALID
5125 GOSUB3000:REM NORMAL INSTRUCTIONS
5130 IF VB$="LOOK"THEN GOSUB2000:REM DESCRIBE
5135 IF VB$="GO" AND MF=1 THEN RETURN
5140 IF VF=1 THEN 5115:REM NEXT INSTRUCTION
5145 IF VB$<>"KILL"THENSN$="I DON'T UNDERSTAND":GOSUB5500:GOTO5115
5150 REM ** KILL **
5155 SN$="WHAT WILL YOU USE TO KILL THE GUARD?":GOSUB5500
5160 SN$="ENTER OBJECT OR (I) FOR INSTRUCTION":GOSUB5500
5162 INPUT IS$:IF IS$="I" THEN 5115
5165 GOSUB2500:REM SPLIT
5167 IF F=0 THEN 5160:REM INVALID
5170 GOSUB5300:IF F=0 THEN SN$="THERE IS NO "+W$:GOSUB5500:GOTO5160
5172 OV=F:GOSUB5450:REM IS OBJECT HELD
5174 IF HF=0 THEN SN$="YOU DO NOT HAVE THE "+IV$(F,1):GOSUB5500:GOTO5160
5175 IF F<>1 THEN SN$="THE "+IV$(F,1)+" IS NO USE":GOSUB5500:GOTO5160
5180 SN$="YOU KILL THE GUARD":GOSUB5500:GF=1
5185 :
5190 REM **** LOCKED GATE S/R ****
5195 SN$="YOU MOVE FORWARD AND TRY TO OPEN THE GATE TO THE VILLAGE"
5200 SN$=SN$+" BUT THE GATE IS LOCKED AND WILL NOT MOVE":GOSUB5500
5205 PRINT:INPUT"INSTRUCTIONS";IS$
5210 GOSUB2500:IF F=0 THEN 5205:REM INVALID
5215 GOSUB3000:REM NORMAL INSTRUCTIONS
5220 IF VB$="LOOK" THEN GOSUB2000:REM DESCRIBE
5225 IF VB$="GO" AND MF=1 THEN RETURN
5230 IF VF=1 THEN 5205:REM NEXT INSTRUCTION
5232 IF VB$="USE" THEN 5240
5234 IF VB$="UNLOCK"THENSN$="HOW?":GOSUB5500:GOTO5205
5235 SN$="I DON'T UNDERSTAND":GOSUB5500:GOTO5205
5240 REM ** VALID OBJECT **
5242 OV=F:GOSUB5450:REM IS OBJ CARRIED
5244 IF F=0 THEN SN$="THERE IS NO "+W$:GOSUB5500:GOTO5205
5246 IF HF=0 THEN SN$="YOU DO NOT HAVE THE "IV$(F,1):GOSUB5500:GOTO5205
5248 IF F<>3 THEN SN$="THE "+IV$(F,1)+" IS NO USE":GOSUB5500:GOTO5205
5250 REM ** THROUGH GATE AND SAFE **
5255 SN$="YOU UNLOCK THE GATE, AND DISGUISING YOURSELF IN THE DEAD"
5260 SN$=SN$+" GUARD'S CLOTHES, WALK UNNOTICED THROUGH THE VILLAGE"
5265 SN$=SN$+" AND THE SAFETY OF THE OUTSIDE WORLD.":GOSUB5500
5270 END
5289 :
5300 REM **** VALID OBJECT S/R ****
5310 NN$=NN$+" ":LN=LEN(NN$):C=1:F=0
5315 FOR K=1 TO LN
5320 IF MID$(NN$,K,1)<>" " THEN NEXT K:RETURN
5325 W$=MID$(NN$,C,K-C):C=K+1
5330 LW=LEN(W$)
5335 FOR J=1 TO 3
5340 LI=LEN(IV$(J,1)):REM LENGTH OF OBJECT
5350 FOR I=1 TO LI-LW+1
5360 IF MID$(IV$(J,1),I,LW)=W$ THEN F=J:I=LI:J=3:K=LN
5370 NEXT I,J,K
5380 RETURN
5390 :
5450 REM **** IS OBJECT HELD S/R ****
5460 HF=0
5470 IF IV$(OV,2)="-1" THEN HF=1
5480 RETURN
5490 :
5500 REM **** FORMAT OUTPUT S/R ****
5510 LC=0:     REM CHAR/LINE COUNTER
5520 OC=1:     REM OLD COUNT INITIAL VALUE
5530 OW$="":   REM OLD WORD  INITIAL VALUE
5540 LL=40:    REM LINE LENGTH
5550 SN$=SN$+" DUMMY "
5560 PRINT
5570 FOR C=1 TO LEN(SN$)
5580 LC=LC+1
5590 IF MID$(SN$,C,1)=" " THEN GOSUB5800
5600 NEXT C
5605 PRINT
5610 RETURN
5620 :
5800 REM ** END OF LINE CHECK S/R **
5810 NW$=MID$(SN$,OC,C-OC+1):REM NEW WORD
5820 IF LC<LL THENPRINTOW$;:GOTO5840
5830 PRINTOW$:LC=LEN(NW$)
5840 OC=C+1:OW$=NW$
5850 RETURN
6000 REM **** READ OBJ & MAP DATA ****
6010 DIM IV$(3,2),LN$(10),EX$(10),IC$(2)
6020 FOR C=1 TO 3
6030 READ IV$(C,1),IV$(C,2)
6040 NEXT C
6050 :
6060 FOR C=1 TO 10
6065 READ LN$(C),EX$(C)
6070 CC=CC+VAL(EX$(C)):REM CHECKSUM TOTAL
6080 NEXT C
6090 :
6100 READ CD:IFCD<>CC THEN PRINT"CHECKSUM ERROR":STOP
6110 :
6120 REM ** OBJECT DATA **
6130 DATA GUN,10,LAMP,9,KEY,5
6140 :
6150 REM ** MAP DATA **
6160 DATA NEAR A TUNNEL ENTRANCE,00000900
6170 DATA IN A SWAMP,00000000
6180 DATA IN A VILLAGE,07000000
6190 DATA NEAR A TUNNEL ENTRANCE,05060000
6200 DATA ON A PATH,00020400
6210 DATA ON A PATH,02070004
6220 DATA ON A PATH,00000306
6230 DATA ON A PATH,09000702
6240 DATA ON A PATH,01100800
6250 DATA IN A CLEARING,00000009
6260 REM ** CHECKSUM DATA **
6270 DATA 32253121
6280 RETURN
```

DIGITAYA

This is the final instalment of our adventure game programming project series. We give here the complete listing of Digitaya, a larger game given in tandem with the Haunted Forest.

The structure of Digitaya has many similarities to that of Haunted Forest, but the game is on a much larger scale. The original layout for Digitaya involved a map of 100 locations, on which was drawn the internal layout of a computer, complete with memory, data bus, processor and much of the other hardware found inside an average home computer. The player's task is to track down the mysterious Digitaya, who is held captive somewhere inside the machine. You must negotiate many hazards, such as the joystick port, vector table and random program bugs, using your knowledge of a computer's internal layout to rescue Digitaya.

Digitaya uses similar routines to those of the Haunted Forest to carry out the mundane functions of the game, such as moving from location to location, picking up and dropping objects and looking around. However, special routines have been added to this skeletal structure to cater for the game's special perils and pitfalls.

When playing an adventure game it is often advisable to map out your route with pencil and paper as you move around the adventure world. The primary task of the successful adventure game player is to get inside the mind of the game's creator. Recreating the map of locations used in the game is often a good step towards this goal. Digitaya is designed on a flat grid, but don't expect all adventure maps to exist in only two dimensions. Three-dimensional maps are quite feasible within the kind of program structure outlined in the project. A game could also be conceived that existed in four dimensions, the fourth dimension being time. Such a game, built on a constantly shifting map, would probably defeat all but the most skilled and experienced adventure gamers.

The listing given is for the Commodore 64, although the program will run on most machines that have a Microsoft-type BASIC. Detailed flavours are given for the BBC Micro.

Some REM statements can be removed from the listing to reduce the typing effort, but to ensure the program works correctly remove them only from the end of the program lines that include other code. Lines that contain only REMs are usually subroutine titles and their line numbers are used in the GOSUB calls. Removing such lines is likely to result in an UNDEFINED STATEMENT error.

Basic Flavours
Spectrum:
Due to the unusual way in which the Spectrum handles string arrays and variables, flavours for Digitaya are too numerous to give here. You should refer to past issues. However, to help you recode the listing, we detail the main points to look for. First, the Spectrum allows only single-character string variables. All the variable names that require conversion are given in a table on page 997.

The Spectrum also allows only fixed-length string arrays, the length of each array element being set by the DIM statement. This can cause problems if, say, a string array is dimensioned so that each element is 20 characters long. If a 15-character string is then assigned to an array element, the remaining five characters in the element are filled with space characters. We need to strip off spaces from the array element, for example, before adding it to any sentence we are constructing. The variable A$ is used to pass the array element to the subroutine and should be assigned before making the subroutine call. To illustrate its use consider this example:

Microsoft version:

```
3650 SN$="YOUR"+IV$(F,1)+"IS USELESS, THE
     FORCE INCREASES"
```

Spectrum version:

```
3650 LET S$="YOUR ":A$=IV$(F,1):GOSUB
     8500: LETS$=S$+" IS USELESS, THE FORCE
     INCREASES"
```

The only other problem is screen clearing. In the Commodore version this is achieved using PRINT CHR$(147). Simply replace these statements with CLS.

BBC Micro
The following lines should be substituted in the Digitaya listing:

```
1400   A$=GET$
1410   CLS
2630   REPEAT:A$=GET$:UNTIL A$="Y" OR
       A$="N"
2750   RA=RND(1)
2820   P=RND(40)+7
3890   RD=RND(1):IF RD>.65 THEN 4110:REM
       HIT
4090   P=RND(40)+7
4520   IV$(4,2)=STR$(RND(40)+7):REM
       REALLOCATE TICKET POSITION
4570   RN=RND(3)+1
5560   RA=RND(1)
```

ADVENTURE GAME

The Digitaya Adventure

```
1030 REM ** 'DIGITAYA' **
1040 REM ** A COMPUTER **
1050 REM ** ADVENTURE GAME **
1090 :
1100 GOSUB6090:REM READ ARRAY DATA
1110 GOSUB1290:REM STORY SO FAR
1120 P=47:REM START POINT
1130 :
1140 REM **** MAIN LOOP STARTS HERE ****
1150 :
1160 MF=0:PRINT
1170 GOSUB1440:REM DESCRIBE POSITION
1180 GOSUB1560: REM LIST EXITS
1190 GOSUB2670:REM IS P SPECIAL
1200 IF SF=1 THEN 1250:REM NEXT LOOP
1210 PRINT:INPUT"INSTRUCTIONS";IS$
1220 GOSUB1700:REM ANALYSE INSTRUCTIONS
1225 IF F=0 THEN 1210:REM INVALID INSTRUCTION
1230 GOSUB 1900:REM NORMAL INSTRUCTIONS
1240 IF VF=0 THENPRINT"I DON'T UNDERSTAND"
1250 IF MF=1 THEN 1160:REM NEW POSITION
1260 IF MF=0 THEN 1210:REM NEW INSTRUCTION
1270 END
1280 :
1290 REM **** STORY SO FAR ****
1300 SN$="WELCOME TO 'DIGITAYA'"
1310 GOSUB5880:REM FORMAT
1320 PRINT
1330 SN$="AS THE MACHINE HUMS QUIETLY. YOU LOOK AROUND."
1340 SN$=SN$+" TO THE NORTH AND SOUTH STRETCHES A WIDE HIGHWAY."
1350 SN$=SN$+" YOUR MISSION IS TO FIND THE MYSTERIOUS DIGITAYA"
1360 SN$=SN$+" AND CARRY IT TO SAFETY THROUGH ONE OF THE OUTPUT
     PORTS."
1370 SN$=SN$+".. BUT WHICH ONE ?"
1380 GOSUB5880
1390 PRINT:PRINT"PRESS A KEY TO START"
1400 GETA$:IFA$=""THEN1400
1410 PRINTCHR$(147):REM CLEAR SCREEN
1420 RETURN
1430 :
1440 REM **** DESCRIBE POSITION S/R ****
1450 SN$="YOU ARE "+LN$(P):GOSUB5880
1460 SN$="YOU SEE "
1470 REM ** SEARCH FOR OBJECT **
1480 F=0:SP$=""
1490 FOR I=1TO8
1500 IF VAL(IV$(I,2))=P THEN SN$=SN$+SP$+"A "+IV$(I,1):F=I:SP$="  "
1510 NEXTI
1520 IF F=0 THENSN$=SN$+"NO OBJECTS"
1530 GOSUB5880:REM FORMAT
1540 RETURN
1550 :
1560 REM **** LIST EXITS S/R ****
1570 EX$=EX$(P)
1580 NR=VAL(LEFT$(EX$,2))
1590 EA=VAL(MID$(EX$,3,2))
1600 SO=VAL(MID$(EX$,5,2))
1610 WE=VAL(RIGHT$(EX$,2))
1620 IF(NR OR EA OR SO OR WE)=0THEN RETURN
1630 PRINT:SN$="EXITS ARE TO THE "
1640 IF NR<>0 THEN SN$=SN$+"NORTH "
1650 IF EA<>0 THEN SN$=SN$+"EAST "
1660 IF SO<>0 THEN SN$=SN$+"SOUTH "
1670 IF WE<>0 THEN SN$=SN$+"WEST "
1675 GOSUB 5880:REM FORMAT
1680 PRINT:RETURN
1690 :
1700 REM **** ANALYSE INSTRUCTION S/R ****
1705 F=0:REM ZERO FLAG
1710 IFIS$="END" OR IS$="LIST" THEN VB$=IS$:F=1:RETURN
1720 IF IS$="LOOK" THEN VB$=IS$:F=1:RETURN
1730 :
1740 REM ** SPLIT INSTRUCTION **
1750 VB$="":NN$="":REM ZERO VERB AND NOUN
1770 LS=LEN(IS$)
1780 FOR C=1TO LS
1790 A$=MID$(IS$,C,1)
1800 IF A$=" " THEN VB$=LEFT$(IS$,C-1):NN$=RIGHT$(IS$,LS-C):F=1:C=LS
1810 NEXT
1820 IF F=0 THEN PRINT:PRINT"I NEED AT LEAST TWO WORDS"
1840 RETURN
1850 :
1900 REM **** NORMAL ACTIONS S/R ****
1910 VF=0
1920 PRINT
1930 IF VB$="GO"ORVB$="MOVE"THENVF=1:GOSUB2000
1940 IF VB$="TAKE"ORVB$="PICK" THEN VF=1:GOSUB2140
1950 IF VB$="DROP"ORVB$="PUT"THENVF=1:GOSUB2360
1960 IF VB$="LIST"ORVB$="INVENTORY"THENVF=1:GOSUB2540
1965 IF VB$="LOOK" THEN VF=1:MF=1:RETURN
1970 IF VB$="END"ORVB$="FINISH"THENVF=1:GOSUB2610
1980 RETURN
1990 :
2000 REM **** MOVE S/R ****
2010 MF=1:REM MOVE FLAG SET
2015 GOSUB8600:REM SEARCH FOR DIRECTION
2020 DR$= LEFT$(NN$,1)
2030 IFDR$<>"N"ANDDR$<>"E"ANDDR$<>"S"ANDDR$<>"W"THEN2100
2040 IF DR$="N" AND NR<>0 THEN P=NR:RETURN
```

```
2050 IF DR$="S" AND SO<>0 THEN P=SO:RETURN
2060 IF DR$="E" AND EA<>0 THEN P=EA:RETURN
2070 IF DR$="W" AND WE<>0 THEN P=WE:RETURN
2080 PRINT"YOU CANT ";IS$
2090 MF=0:RETURN
2100 REM NOUN NOT OK
2110 PRINT"WHAT IS ";NN$;" ?"
2120 MF=0:RETURN
2130 :
2140 REM **** TAKE S/R ****
2145 IV$(4,1)="TICKET TO TRI-STATE"
2150 GOSUB5730:REM IS OBJECT VALID
2160 IF F=0 THEN PRINT"THERE IS NO ";NN$:RETURN
2170 REM ** IS OBJECT ALREADY TAKEN ? ****
2180 OV=F:GOSUB5830
2190 IF HF=1 THEN SN$="YOU ALREADY HAVE THE "+IV$(F,1):GOSUB5880
     :RETURN
2200 :
2210 REM ** IS OBJECT HERE **
2220 IF VAL(IV$(F,2))<>P THENSN$=IV$(F,1)+" IS NOT HERE":GOSUB5880
     :RETURN
2230 :
2240 REM ** ADD OBJECT TO LIST **
2250 AF=0:FOR J=1TO4
2260 IFIC$(J)=""THENIC$(J)=IV$(F,1):AF=1:J=4
2270 NEXTJ
2280 :
2290 REM ** CHECK FOR FULL QUOTA **
2300 IF AF=0THENPRINT"YOU ALREADY HAVE 4 OBJECTS":RETURN
2310 :
2320 SN$="YOU TAKE THE "+IV$(F,1):GOSUB5880
2330 IV$(F,2)="-1":REM DELETE POSITION ENTRY
2340 RETURN
2350 :
2360 REM ** DROP S/R **
2370 GOSUB5730:REM IS OBJECT VALID
2380 IF F=0 THEN PRINT"THERE IS NO ";NN$:RETURN
2390 :
2400 REM ** IS OBJECT HELD ? **
2410 OV=F:GOSUB5830
2420 IFHF=0THENPRINT"YOU DO NOT HAVE THE ";IV$(F,1):RETURN
2430 :
2440 REM ** DROP OBJECT **
2450 SN$="YOU DROP THE "+IV$(F,1):GOSUB5880
2460 IV$(F,2)=STR$(P):REM UPDATE OBJ POSITION
2470 :
2480 REM ** DELETE FROM HELD OBJ LIST **
2490 FORJ=1TO4
2500 IF IC$(J)=IV$(F,1)THENIC$(J)="":J=4
2510 NEXTJ
2520 RETURN
2530 :
2540 REM **** LIST INVENTORY S/R ****
2550 PRINT"OBJECTS HELD:"
2560 FORI=1TO4
2570 PRINT"   ";IC$(I)
2580 NEXTI
2590 RETURN
2600 :
2610 REM **** END GAME S/R ****
2620 PRINT:PRINT"ARE YOU SURE (Y/N) ?"
2630 GETA$:IFA$<>"Y"AND A$<>"N"THEN2630
2640 IFA$="N"THEN RETURN
2650 END
2660 :
2670 REM **** IS P SPECIAL S/R ****
2680 SF=0:REM UNSET SPECIAL FLAG
2690 IF P=37 THEN2780:REM VECTOR TABLE
2700 IF F>7 THEN 2750:REM RANDOM BUG
2710 ON P GOSUB 2850,2960,3450,3830,4180,4550,5150
2720 RETURN
2730 :
2740 REM ** RANDOM BUG **
2750 RA=RND(TI)
2760 IF RA<0.05THEN GOSUB 5420:REM BUG
2770 RETURN
2780 REM ** VECTOR TABLE **
2790 SF=1
2800 SN$="YOU ARE MOVED AT HIGH SPEED TO A NEW LOCATION":GOSUB5880
2810 FORJ=1TO1000:NEXT:REM PAUSE
2820 P=INT(RND(TI)*40+7)
2830 MF=1:RETURN
2840 :
2850 REM **** TV OUTLET S/R ****
2860 SF=1
2870 SN$="YOU HAVE ENTERED THE TV OUTLET AND THERE IS NO ESCAPE."
2880 SN$=SN$+"YOU ARE DOOMED FOREVER TO BE A TV CHAT SHOW HOST"
2890 GOSUB 5880:REM FORMAT PRINT
2900 PRINT
2910 PRINT"WELCOME TO THE SHOW....."
2920 FORJ=1TO500:NEXTJ
2930 GOTO 2910
2940 END
2950 :
2960 REM **** USER PORT S/R ****
2970 SF=1
2980 SN$="ESCAPE IS AT HAND BUT THE DDR BOOKING CLERK"
2990 SN$=SN$+" BARS YOUR WAY. HE TELLS YOU THAT HE HAS BEEN
     INSTRUCTED TO"
3000 SN$=SN$+" ACCEPT INPUTS ONLY. HOWEVER HE DOES TAKE ALL MAJOR"
3010 SN$=SN$+" CREDIT CARDS."
3020 GOSUB 5880:REM FORMAT PRINT
3030 :
```

115

```
3040 PRINT:INPUT"INSTRUCTIONS";IS$
3050 GOSUB1700:REM ANALYSE INSTRUCTIONS
3060 GOSUB1900:REM NORMAL ACTIONS
3070 IF MF=1 THEN RETURN:REM MOVE OUT
3080 IF VF=1 THEN3040:REM NEXT INSTRUCTION
3090 IF VB$<>"GIVE" THENPRINT"I DON'T UNDERSTAND":GOTO3040
3100 :
3110 REM ** INSTRUCTION IS GIVE **
3120 GOSUB5730:REM IS OBJECT VALID
3130 IFF=0THENPRINT"THERE IS NO ";NN$:GOTO3040:REM NEXT INSTRUCTION
3140 :
3150 REM ** IS OBJECT CREDIT CARD **
3160 IF F<>5THENPRINT"HE ONLY ACCEPTS CREDIT CARDS":GOTO3040
3170 :
3180 REM ** IS CARD CARRIED **
3190 OV=5:GOSUB5830
3200 IFHF=0THENPRINT"YOU DO NOT HAVE THE ";IV$(5,1):GOTO 3040
3210 :
3220 SN$="THE CLERK TAKES THE CARD AND SAYS 'THAT WILL DO NICELY,
     SIR'"
3230 GOSUB5880:REM FORMAT PRINT
3240 SN$="YOU ARE ALLOWED TO PASS THE BARRIER AND ENTER THE USER
     PORT"
3250 GOSUB5880:REM FORMAT PRINT
3260 :
3270 REM ** IS DIGITAYA CARRIED **
3280 OV=6:GOSUB5830
3290 IF HF=1 THEN 3380:REM SUCCESS
3300 :
3310 REM ** FAILURE **
3320 SN$="WELL DONE YOU HAVE SUCCEEDED IN ESCAPING FROM THE
     CLUTCHES"
3330 SN$=SN$+" OF THE MACHINE, BUT HAVE FAILED IN YOUR MISSION"
3340 SN$=SN$+" TO BRING BACK THE MYSTERIOUS DIGITAYA"
3350 GOSUB5880:REM FORMAT PRINT
3360 END
3370 :
3380 REM ** SUCCESS **
3390 SN$="CONGRATULATIONS, YOU HAVE SUCCEEDED IN YOUR MISSION"
3400 SN$=SN$+" TO RESCUE THE WONDEROUS DIGITAYA FROM THE"
3410 SN$=SN$+" CLUTCHES OF THE MACHINE.
3420 GOSUB5880:REM FORMAT PRINT
3430 END
3440 :
3450 REM **** CASSETTE PORT S/R ****
3460 SF=1
3470 SN$="YOU FEEL AN IRRESISTIBLE FORCE PULLING YOU TOWARDS"
3480 SN$=SN$+" PERMANANENT MAGNETIC SUSPENSION"
3490 GOSUB5880:REM FORMAT
3500 NS=0:REM START COUNTING INSTRUCTIONS
3510 REM ** INSTRUCTIONS **
3520 NS=NS+1:IFNS>3THEN3770:REM SUCKED OUT
3530 PRINT:INPUT"INSTRUCTIONS";IS$
3540 GOSUB1700:REM ANALYSE INSTRUCTIONS
3550 GOSUB1900:REM NORMAL ACTIONS
3560 IFMF=1THENMF=0:PRINT"YOU CAN'T MOVE...YET":GOTO3510
3570 IFVF=1THEN3510:REM NEXT INSTRUCTION
3580 IFVB$<>"USE"THENPRINT"I DON'T UNDERSTAND":GOTO3510
3590 REM ** INSTRUCTION IS USE **
3600 GOSUB5730:REM IS OBJECT VALID
3610 IFF=0THENPRINT"THERE IS NO ";NN$:GOTO3510
3620 :
3630 REM ** IS OBJECT BUFFER ACTIVATOR **
3640 IF F=8 THEN3680:REM OK
3650 SN$="YOUR "+IV$(F,1)+" IS USELESS, THE FORCE INCREASES"
3660 GOSUB 5880:GOTO3510:REM NEXT INSTRUCTION
3670 :
3680 OV=8:GOSUB5830:REM IS BUFF ACT HELD
3690 IFHF=0THENSN$="YOU DON'T HAVE THE "+IV$(8,1):GOSUB5880:GOTO3510
3700 :
3710 REM ** SAVED **
3720 SN$="YOU USE THE BUFFER ACTIVATOR TO COUNTER THE PULL"
3730 SN$=SN$+" INTO MAGNETIC OBLIVION. THE FORCE SUBSIDES"
3740 GOSUB5880:REM FORMAT
3750 RETURN
3760 :
3770 REM ** SUCKED OUT **
3780 SN$="THE FORCE BECOMES TOO STRONG AND YOU ARE PULLED OUT"
3790 SN$=SN$+" THROUGH THE CASSETTE PORT INTO MAGNETIC NOTHINGNESS."
3800 GOSUB 5880:REM FORMAT
3810 END
3820 :
3830 REM **** JOYSTICK PORT ****
3840 SF=1
3850 SN$="A USER WITH RED-RIMMED EYES ZAPS HIS LASER AT YOU
     REPEATEDLY."
3860 GOSUB5880:REM FORMAT
3870 :
3880 REM ** INSTRUCTIONS **
3890 RD=RND(TI):IF RD>.65THEN 4110:REM HIT
3900 PRINT:INPUT"INSTRUCTIONS";IS$
3910 GOSUB1700:GOSUB1900:REM ANALYSE INSTRUCTION
3920 IFMF=1THENMF=0:PRINT"YOU CAN'T MOVE...YET":GOTO3880
3930 IFVF=1THEN3880:REM NEXT INSTRUCTION
3940 IFVB$<>"USE"THENPRINT"I DON'T UNDERSTAND":GOTO3880
3950 GOSUB5730:REM IS OBJECT VALID
3960 IFF=0THENPRINT"THERE IS NO ";NN$:GOTO3880:REM NEXT INSTRUCTION
3970 :
3980 REM ** IS OBJECT LASER SHIELD **
3990 IF F=3 THEN4020:REM OK
4000 SN$="YOUR "+IV$(F,1)+" IS NO USE":GOSUB5880:GOTO3880
4010 :
4020 OV=3:GOSUB5830:REM IS LASER SHIELD CARRIED
```

```
4030 IFHF=0THENSN$="YOU DO NOT HAVE THE "+IV$(3,1):GOSUB5880
     :GOTO3880
4040 :
4050 REM ** SAVED **
4060 SN$="YOU USE THE LASER SHIELD TO PROTECT YOURSELF. A BLAST
     KNOCKS"
4070 SN$=SN$+" YOU OUT OF THE JOYSTICK PORT AND BACK INTO THE
     MACHINE."
4080 GOSUB5880:REM FORMAT
4090 P=INT(RND(TI)*40+7):MF=1:RETURN
4100 :
4110 REM ** HIT **
4120 SN$="YOU ARE HIT BY THE LASER AND YOU ARE ONLY DIMLY AWARE
     THAT"
4130 SN$=SN$+" YOUR ATOMS HAVE BEEN DISTRIBUTED TO THE FOUR CORNERS"
4140 SN$=SN$+" OF THE UNIVERSE"
4150 GOSUB5880:REM FORMAT
4160 END
4170 :
4180 REM **** TRI-STATE DEVICE S/R ****
4190 SF=1
4200 SN$="A LARGE SIGN SAYS 'I/O THIS WAY' BUT AS YOU MOVE
     TOWARDS IT"
4210 SN$=SN$+" A TICKET COLLECTOR SHOUTS 'TICKETS PLEASE'"
4220 GOSUB5880:REM FORMAT
4230 :
4240 REM ** INSTRUCTIONS **
4250 PRINT:INPUT"INSTRUCTIONS";IS$
4260 GOSUB1700:GOSUB1900:REM ANALYSE
4270 IFMF=1 THEN RETURN
4280 IFVF=1THEN4240:REM NEXT INSTRUCTION
4290 IFVB$<>"GIVE"ANDVB$<>"OFFER"THENPRINT"I DON'T UNDERSTAND"
     :GOTO4240
4300 REM ** INSTRUCTION IS GIVE **
4310 GOSUB5730:REM IS OBJECT VALID
4320 IFF=0THENPRINT"THERE IS NO ";NN$:GOTO4240:REM NEXT INSTRUCTION
4330 :
4340 REM ** IS OBJECT TICKET **
4350 IF F=4 THEN4400:REM OK
4360 SN$="THE TICKET COLLECTOR SHAKES HIS HEAD AND SAYS"
4370 SN$=SN$+" 'I CANNOT ACCEPT THIS "+IV$(F,1)
4380 GOSUB5880:GOTO4240:REM NEXT INSTRUCTION
4390 :
4400 OV=4:GOSUB5830:REM IS TICKET HELD
4410 IFHF=0THENPRINT"YOU DO NOT HAVE THE TICKET":GOTO4240
4420 :
4430 REM ** OK **
4440 SN$="THE TICKET COLLECTOR ACCEPTS YOUR TICKET AND ALLOWS YOU"
4450 SN$=SN$+" TO PASS THE BARRIER."
4460 GOSUB5880:REM FORMAT
4470 REM ** DEL TICKET FROM LIST **
4480 F=0
4490 FORJ=1TO4
4500 IF IC$(J)=IV$(4,1)THENIC$(J)="":J=4
4510 NEXT J
4520 IV$(4,2)=STR$(INT(RND(TI)*40+8)):REM REALLOCATE TICKET
     POSITION
4530 P=15:MF=1:RETURN
4540 :
4550 REM **** ALU ****
4560 SF=1
4570 RN=INT(RND(TI)*3+1)
4580 IF RN=1 THEN CD$="AND"
4590 IF RN=2 THEN CD$="OR"
4600 IF RN=3 THEN CD$="NOT"
4610 SN$="MOUNTED ON THE WALL THERE ARE THREE BUTTONS MARKED"
4620 SN$=SN$+" 'AND', 'OR' AND 'NOT'. ACCESS CAN BE GAINED TO THE"
4630 SN$=SN$+" ACCUMULATOR BY PRESSING THE CORRECT BUTTON"
4640 GOSUB5880:REM FORMAT
4650 :
4660 REM ** INSTRUCTIONS **
4670 PRINT:INPUT"INSTRUCTIONS";IS$
4680 GOSUB1700:GOSUB1900:REM ANALYSE
4690 IF MF=1THEN RETURN:REM MOVE OUT
4700 IF VF=1THEN 4670:REM NEXT INSTRUCTION
4710 IFVB$="USE"OR VB$="PRESS"THEN4740
4720 PRINT"I DON'T UNDERSTAND":GOTO4670
4730 :
4740 REM ** VALID COMMAND **
4750 IF VB$="PRESS"THEN 4930
4760 REM ** COMMAND IS 'USE' **
4770 GOSUB5730:REM IS OBJECT VALID
4780 IFF=0THENPRINT"THERE IS NO ";NN$:GOTO4670:REM NEXT INSTRUCTION
4790 :
4800 REM ** IS OBJECT CODE BOOK **
4810 IF F=7 THEN4850:REM OK
4820 SN$="YOUR "+IV$(F,1)+" IS OF NO USE":GOSUB5880
4830 GOTO4670:REM NEXT INSTRUCTION
4840 :
4850 OV=7:GOSUB5830:REM IS CODE BOOK HELD
4860 IFHF=1THEN4900:REM OK HELD
4870 SN$="YOU DO NOT HAVE THE "+IV$(7,1)
4880 GOSUB5880:GOTO4670:REM NEXT INSTRUCTION
4890 :
4900 SN$="YOU OPEN THE CODE BOOK AND FIND THE WORD '"+CD$+"'
     WRITTEN INSIDE"
4910 GOSUB5880:GOTO4670:REM NEXT INSTRUCTION
4920 :
4930 REM ** COMMAND IS PRESS **
4940 IFNN$="AND"OR NN$="OR"OR NN$="NOT"THEN4970
4950 SN$="THERE IS NO "+NN$:GOSUB5880:GOTO4670:REM NEXT INSTRUCTION
4960 :
4970 REM ** RIGHT OR WRONG **
```

```
4980 IFNN$=CD$ THEN GOSUB5100:RETURN
4990 GOSUB5010:RETURN
5000 :
5010 REM ** WRONG S/R **
5020 SN$="WRONG, A TRAP DOOR OPENS AND YOU FIND YOURSELF BACK"
5030 SN$=SN$+" BACK IN MAIN MEMORY"
5040 GOSUB5880:REM FORMAT
5050 IF RN=1 THEN P=39
5060 IF RN=2 THEN P=35
5070 IF RN=3 THEN P=29
5080 MF=1:RETURN
5090 :
5100 REM ** RIGHT S/R **
5110 SN$="THE GATEWAY TO THE ACCUMULATOR SWINGS OPEN AND"
5120 SN$=SN$+" YOU PASS THROUGH":GOSUB5880
5130 P=30:MF=1:RETURN
5140 :
5150 REM **** GATEWAY TO MEMORY S/R ****
5160 SF=1
5170 SN$="AN USHER GREETS YOU BUT TELLS YOU THAT YOU CANNOT BE
     ADMITTED"
5180 SN$=SN$+" UNLESS YOU GIVE AN ADDRESS":GOSUB5880
5190 REM ** INSTRUCTIONS **
5200 PRINT:INPUT"INSTRUCTIONS";IS$
5210 GOSUB1700:GOSUB1900:REM ANALYSE
5220 IF MF=1 THEN RETURN:REM MOVE OUT
5230 IF VF=1 THEN 5200:REM NEXT INSTRUCTION
5240 IF VB$<>"GIVE"THENPRINT"I DON'T UNDERSTAND":GOTO 5200
5250 :
5260 GOSUB5730:REM IS OBJECT VALID
5270 IFF=0THENPRINT"THERE IS NO ";NN$:GOTO5200:REM NEXT INSTRUCTION
5280 :
5290 REM ** IS OBJECT ADDRESS **
5300 IF F=1 THEN5330:REM OK
5310 PRINT"HE NEEDS YOUR ADDRESS":GOTO5200
5320 :
5330 OV=1:GOSUB5830:REM IS ADDRESS CARRIED
5340 IF HF=1 THEN 5370
5350 SN$="YOU DON'T HAVE THE "+IV$(1,1):GOSUB5880:GOTO5200
5360 :
5370 REM ** OK PASS THROUGH **
5380 SN$="THE USHER LOOKS AT YOUR ADDRESS AND ALLOWS YOU TO PASS"
5390 SN$=SN$+" THROUGH":GOSUB5880
5400 P=40:MF=1:RETURN
5410 :
5420 REM **** RANDOM BUG ****
5430 SF=1
5440 SN$="A LARGE AND UGLY BUG APPEARS FROM BEHIND A CHIP"
5450 SN$=SN$+" AND LUNGES TOWARDS YOU":GOSUB5880
5460 :
5470 REM ** INSTRUCTIONS **
5480 PRINT:INPUT"INSTRUCTIONS";IS$
5490 GOSUB1700:GOSUB1900:REM ANALYSE
5500 IFMF=1THENMF=0:PRINT"YOU CAN'T MOVE...YET":GOTO5480
5510 IF VF=1THEN5480:REM NEXT INSTRUCTION
5520 IF VB$="KILL"ORVB$="FIGHT"THEN5550
5530 PRINT"I DON'T UNDERSTAND":GOTO5480
5540 :
5550 REM ** COMAND IS FIGHT/KILL **
5560 RA=RND(T1)
5570 IFRA<0.5 THEN GOSUB5600
5580 GOSUB5670:RETURN
5590 :
5600 REM **** KILLED BY S/R ****
5610 SN$="YOU FIGHT WITH THE BUG. IT SHOWERS YOU WITH SPURIOUS"
5620 SN$=SN$+" ERRORS AND THEY EAT INTO YOUR BRAIN."
5630 SN$=SN$+" FINALLY YOU CAN TAKE NO MORE AND YOUR HEAD
     EXPLODES."
5640 GOSUB5880
5650 END
5660 :
5670 REM **** YOU KILL S/R ****
5680 SN$="YOU FIGHT WITH THE BUG AND THOUGH IT IS A HARD STRUGGLE"
5690 SN$=SN$+" YOU EVENTUALLY IRON IT OUT AND SURVIVE.":GOSUB5880
5700 RETURN
5710 :
5720 :
5730 REM **** VALID OJECT S/R ****
5740 NN$=NN$+" ":LN=LEN(NN$):F=0:C=1
5745 FOR K=1 TO LN
5750 IF MID$(NN$,K,1)<>" " THEN NEXTK:RETURN
5755 IN$=MID$(NN$,C,K-C):C=K+1:LW=LEN(W$)
5760 FORJ=1 TO 8
5770 LI=LEN(IV$(J,1)):REM LENGTH OBJECT
5780 FORI=1TO LI
5790 IFMID$(IV$(J,1),I,LW)=W$THENF=J:I=LI:J=8:K=LN
5800 NEXT I,J,K
5810 RETURN
5820 :
5830 REM **** IS OBJECT HELD S/R ****
5840 HF=0
5850 IFIV$(OV,2)="-1"THEN HF=1
5860 RETURN
5870 :
5880 REM **** FORMAT PRINTING S/R ****
5890 LC=0:  REM CHAR/LINE COUNTER
5900 OC=1:  REM OLD COUNT
5910 OW$="":REM OLD WORD
5920 LL=40:REM SCREEN LINE LENGTH
5930 SN$=SN$+" DUMMY "
5940 PRINT
5950 FOR C=1 TO LEN(SN$)
5960 LC=LC+1
5970 IF MID$(SN$,C,1)=" " THENGOSUB6020
5980 NEXTC
5990 PRINT
6000 RETURN
6010 :
6020 REM **** END OF LINE CHECK S/R ****
6030 NW$=MID$(SN$,OC,C-OC+1)
6040 IF LC<LL THENPRINTOW$;:GOTO6060
6050 PRINTOW$:LC=LEN(NW$)
6060 OC=C+1:OW$=NW$
6070 RETURN
6080 :
6090 REM **** READ ARRAY DATA S/R ****
6100 REM ** READ INVENTORY **
6110 DIM IV$(8,2),IC$(4)
6120 FOR C =1TO8
6130 READ IV$(C,1),IV$(C,2)
6140 NEXT C
6150 :
6160 REM ** READ LOCATION & EXIT DATA **
6170 DIM LN$(55),EX$(55)
6180 C1=0:C2=0:REM INITIALISE CHECKSUMS
6190 FOR C=1TO54
6200 READ LN$(C),EX$(C)
6210 C1=C1+VAL(LEFT$(EX$(C),4))
6220 C2=C2+VAL(RIGHT$(EX$(C),4))
6230 NEXT C
6240 READ CA:IFCA<>C1THEN PRINT"CHECKSUM ERROR":STOP
6250 READ CB:IFCB<>C2THEN PRINT"CHECKSUM ERROR":STOP
6260 RETURN
6270 REM **** INVENTORY DATA ****
6280 DATA ADDRESS NUMBER,45,KEY,34,LASER SHIELD,25
6290 DATA TICKET TO TRI-STATE,26,DATA CREDIT CARD,28
6300 DATA DIGITAYA,30,CODE BOOK,19,BUFFER ACTIVATING DEVICE,13
6310 :
6320 REM **** LOCATION & EXIT DATA ****
6330 DATA IN THE TV OUTLET,00000000
6340 DATA IN THE USER PORT,00090100
6350 DATA IN THE CASSETTE PORT,00110000
6360 DATA IN THE JOYSTICK PORT,00130000
6370 DATA IN A TRI-STATE DEVICE,00170000
6380 DATA IN THE ARITHMETIC & LOGIC UNIT,00310016
6390 DATA AT THE GATEWAY TO MEMORY,00490000
6400 DATA ON THE I/O HIGHWAY,09000001
6410 DATA ON THE I/O HIGHWAY,10000802
6420 DATA ON THE I/O HIGHWAY,11000900
6430 DATA ON THE I/O HIGHWAY,12001003
6440 DATA ON THE I/O HIGHWAY,13531100
6450 DATA ON THE I/O HIGHWAY,14001204
6460 DATA ON THE I/O HIGHWAY,15001300
6470 DATA ON THE I/O HIGHWAY A SIGN SAYS 'S OUT H',00001400
6480 DATA IN THE DATA REGISTER,00061700
6490 DATA ON AN 8 LANE HIGHWAY,16001805
6500 DATA ON AN 8 LANE HIGHWAY,17001900
6510 DATA ON AN 8 LANE HIGHWAY,18002000
6520 DATA ON AN 8 LANE HIGHWAY,19292100
6530 DATA ON AN 8 LANE HIGHWAY,20282200
6540 DATA ON AN 8 LANE HIGHWAY,21272300
6550 DATA ON AN 8 LANE HIGHWAY,22262400
6560 DATA ON AN 8 LANE HIGHWAY,23250000
6570 DATA IN THE CHARACTER MATRIX,26360024
6580 DATA HIGH IN THE MEMORY,27352523
6590 DATA IN THE MIDDLE OF MEMORY,28342622
6600 DATA IN THE MIDDLE OF MEMORY,29332721
6610 DATA LOW IN THE MEMORY,00542820
6620 DATA IN THE ACCUMULATOR'S LAIR,00000600
6630 DATA IN A LONG CORRIDOR,00420004
6640 DATA IN AN INDEX REGISTER,31000000
6650 DATA LOW IN THE MEMORY,54403428
6660 DATA IN THE MIDDLE OF MEMORY,33393527
6670 DATA HIGH UP IN MEMORY,34383626
6680 DATA IN THE CHARACTER MATRIX,35370025
6690 DATA IN A RANDOM VECTOR TABLE,00000000
6700 DATA HIGH IN MEMORY OVERLOOKING A HIGHWAY,39003735
6710 DATA IN THE MIDDLE OF MEMORY,40003834
6720 DATA IN MEMORY - TO THE EAST IS A GATEWAY,41003933
6730 DATA LOW IN MEMORY,00004054
6740 DATA IN A CORRIDOR,00430031
6750 DATA IN A CORRIDOR,00440042
6760 DATA IN A CORRIDOR,00004543
6770 DATA IN THE ADDRESS REGISTER,00004600
6780 DATA ON A 16 LANE HIGHWAY,45804700
6790 DATA ON A 16 LANE HIGHWAY,46004800
6800 DATA ON A 16 LANE HIGHWAY,47004900
6810 DATA ON A 16 LANE HIGHWAY A LARGE GATE LOOMS TO THE WEST
     ,48005007
6820 DATA ON A 16 LANE HIGHWAY,49005100
6830 DATA ON A 16 LANE HIGHWAY,50005200
6840 DATA ON A 16 LANE HIGHWAY,51000000
6850 DATA IN A VECTOR TO MEMORY,00290012
6860 DATA LOW IN MEMORY,00413329
6870 REM ** CHECKSUM DATA **
6880 DATA :00169,103973
8599 :
8600 REM **** SEARCH FOR DIRECTION S/R ****
8610 NN$=NN$+" ":LN=LEN(NN$):C=1
8620 FORI=1 TO LN
8630 IF MID$(NN$,I,1)<>" " THEN NEXT I:RETURN
8640 W$=MID$(NN$,C,I-C):C=I+1
8650 IF W$="NORTH" OR W$="EAST" THEN NN$=W$:I=LN
8660 IF W$="SOUTH" OR W$="WEST" THEN NN$=W$:I=LN
8670 NEXT I
8680 RETURN
```

4 MACHINECODE

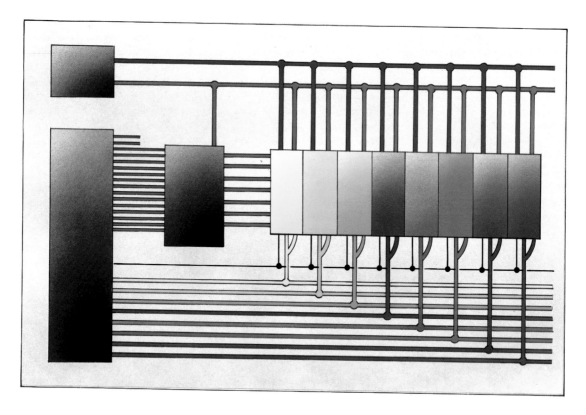

As their experience grows and the programming projects
they tackle become more adventurous, most users quickly
discover the limitations of BASIC. Programming in
Machine Code, by contrast, imposes very few constraints
and offers a massive increase in speed and efficiency.

INTRODUCING FIRST CONCEPTS

Machine code programming is the key to the real power of the microprocessor, allowing the programmer direct control over all the machine's functions. This first part of a comprehensive course, covering both 6502 and Z80 operation codes, will lead to a full understanding of the fundamentals of computer programming.

Machine code is a programming language, and it looks like this:

    INSTK: SBC $D9FA,X;Outport flag value

or like this:

    DE23 FD FA D9

or like this:

    11011110 00100011 11111101 11111010 11011001

Sometimes it looks like this:

    1240 LET ACC=ACC−FLAG (X)

and sometimes like this:

    PERFORM FLAG-ADJUST THROUGH LOOP1

It's all code of a sort, and since it's destined for a computing machine it's called *machine code*. To the machine it doesn't actually *look* like anything at all, being simply a pattern of voltage levels or a current of electricity.

What we usually mean when we say machine code is Assembly language, and the first example we gave in this article is an instruction in 6502 Assembly language. The point of giving all the other examples was to demonstrate that there is no specific machine language as such, only a number of different ways of representing a sequence of electrical events, and representing them in ways that we find more or less easy to understand. So the first thing to learn about machine code (or Assembly language – we won't worry about the distinction for the moment), is that it's just another programming language. However, the programming must always come before the language: whether you write your programs in IBM Assembler, Atari BASIC, or Venusian PsychoBabble, you have to solve the programming problem in your mind before you touch a keyboard. The programming language in which you then express your solution will obviously influence the form of the final program. Indeed you may choose among various possible languages precisely to make the coding of your program easier, or shorter, or more readable. But the solution must always come first: content must

precede form.

In that case, why call it machine code, and why bother to use it at all? We give the language this name because its instruction set corresponds exactly with the set of 'primitive' or fundamental operations that a particular microprocessor can perform. We use the machine code when it is important to direct the operation of the microprocessor exactly, step-by-step, rather than allowing a program language interpreter to control it in a more general way.

The commonest reason for wanting to use it is speed: if your program addresses the processor more or less directly, then you avoid the relatively lengthy business of program translation. In other words, by cutting out the middleman you save time. Program execution time, that is. The actual coding, testing, debugging, modification and maintenance of a machine code program is likely to take at least twice as long as the same operations would on a high-level language program. The unfriendliness and intractability of machine code stimulated the development of languages such as COBOL and BASIC.

If the set of machine code instructions is the set of processor operations, then what are these operations, and what does the processor do? In the simplest terms the Central Processing Unit (CPU) of a computer is a switch that controls the flow of current in a computer system between and among the components of that system. Those components are the memory, the Arithmetic Logic Unit (ALU), and the Input/Output devices. When you press a key on the keyboard, you are inputting some information; in the machine, however, you are simply generating a pattern of voltages in the keyboard unit. The CPU switches that pattern from the keyboard to part of the memory, then switches a corresponding pattern from elsewhere in memory to the screen so that a character pattern appears on the screen. To you this process may seem like operating a typewriter, but in a typewriter there is a mechanical connection between hitting a key and printing a character, whereas in a computer that linkage exists only because the CPU switches the right voltage patterns from place to place. Sometimes pressing a key doesn't cause a single character to appear on the screen: the keypress may destroy an asteroid, or save a program, or delete a disk file, or print a letter. The operation depends on how and where the CPU switches the electric current.

In this simplistic view the CPU is at the heart of the system, and all information (or electrical current) must pass through it from one component to another. In fact, the CPU and the system are more complicated than that, but it's not a misleading view. You can think of the CPU as a master controller that sets lesser switches throughout the system to control the flow of electricity, and thus controls the flow of information indirectly, rather than routing all information physically through itself.

The effects of the CPU's switching operations can be classified for our purposes as: arithmetic operations, logical operations, memory operations, and control operations. These operations are all the results of switching information through different paths in the system and in the CPU, and to the CPU they all seem like the same sort of thing.

Arithmetic operations are really the most important feature of the machine. The CPU can add two numbers together, or subtract one from the other. Subtraction is achieved by representing one of the numbers as a negative number and adding that negative number to the other number; 7+5=12 really means:

(plus 7) added to (plus 5) equals (plus 12).

7−5=2 really means:

(plus 7) added to (minus 5) equals (plus 2).

Multiplication and division are regarded as repeated additions or subtractions, so the CPU can be programmed to simulate these processes as well. If the CPU can cope with the four rules of arithmetic, then it can cope with any mathematical process. It is well to remember, however, that all its mathematical potential relies on the ability simply to add two numbers.

Logical operations for our present purposes can be described as the ability to compare two numbers: not merely in terms of relative size, but also in terms of the pattern of their digits. It's easy to see that seven is bigger than five because we can take five away from seven and still have a positive result. The CPU has the ability to do that sort of comparison, and it can also compare 189 with 102 and recognise that both numbers have the same digit in the hundreds column. It may not seem a very useful ability as yet, but its use will become more evident later.

The CPU can perform essentially two memory operations: it can copy information from a memory location into its own internal memory, and it can copy information from its internal memory to another memory location. By doing these two things one after another it can therefore copy information from any part of memory to any other part of memory. For the memory to be any use, the CPU must be able to do both these things, and these two operations are all it needs for complete management of the memory.

Control operations are really decisions about the sequence in which the CPU performs the other operations we have described here. It's not important at the moment to understand them any better than that: if you accept that the CPU can make decisions about its own operation, then that is sufficient at this stage.

So the CPU can do arithmetic, it can compare numbers, it can move information around in memory, and it can decide its own sequence of operations. This is a simple list of procedures, and yet it completely descibes or specifies an ideal computing machine! If the CPU can do those four things, then by doing them in the right sequences it can perform any computable task. The right sequence, of course, is the computer program for the particular task, and that's where we as programmers come in. If the CPU had the ability to generate its own operation sequences, then there would be no need for us.

You may not be convinced that the four types of operation we have described are a sufficient description of a conceptual computer, so let's think about a BASIC program in terms of the general operations performed. What are these fundamental operations? In any program you have variables, which are simply the names of places in memory where information is stored. Most programs perform some sort of arithmetic upon some of these variables. Having done the arithmetic, a program will often compare two pieces of information and as a result will execute one set of instructions or another. Information usually comes into a program from the user at the keyboard, and goes out to the user via the screen.

Except for the sentence about input and output, this description contains no more than the four elemental CPU operations put into different words. And, if you accept for the moment that to the CPU all Input/Output devices are just special areas of memory, then the picture of the ideal computer executing actual programs is complete. Consequently, the execution of a program can be described as a directed flow of information into, around, and out of the computer; you supply some information via the keyboard, that information is manipulated by your program, and some information appears on the screen.

If the idealised computer is just a CPU and some memory, then before going any further we should investigate computer memory: what is it, and how does it work?

Imagine a simple electrical circuit consisting of a battery, a switch, and a light bulb: if the switch is closed the light goes on, and stays on until the battery runs down or until the switch is opened. Then the condition of the light bulb — ON or OFF — is a piece of information, and the whole circuit is a memory device recording that information. Suppose now that the switch is placed at the entrance to a factory, and the light is placed in the Manager's office. When the first employee arrives at the factory, he or she closes the switch at the entrance, and the Manager in the office can see that the light is on and therefore knows that someone has turned up for work. The Manager doesn't have to be in the office when the light goes on; he or she can look at the light bulb at any time to find out whether someone has arrived. The information that someone has turned up for work is stored in the circuit.

That's almost exactly how information is stored in computer memory: all information reduces to the presence or absence of electricity in a circuit. Naturally there's more to it than that, so let's improve the management information system. Suppose we have four separate switch/bulb circuits (the four switches in a row at the door, and the four bulbs in a corresponding row in the office), so that closing the leftmost switch illuminates the leftmost bulb, and so on. Now imagine that every employee is told to close the switches in a unique way, so that when Catherine arrives she closes the first and second switches and opens the third and fourth; Richard closes the fourth switch and opens all the others; Bobby closes the first and third and opens the second and fourth; and so on for all the employees. The lights in the office now show the Manager which of the employees has turned up for work.

Suppose that the OFF position of each switch is labelled 0, and the ON position is labelled 1: therefore Catherine has to set the switches 1100 (first two switches ON, third and fourth OFF), Richard has to make the pattern 0001 (fourth switch ON, the others OFF) and Bobby has to set 1010 (first and third ON, the other two OFF). If the Manager reads each light bulb as 1 if it's ON, and 0 if it's OFF, then both the employees and the Manager will be speaking the same identification language. '0001' means 'Richard' to both people.

How many unique patterns of switches are there? Each switch can be in one of two positions, and there are four switches, so there are $2 \times 2 \times 2 \times 2 = 16$ different patterns. Let's consider all the possibilities:

0000, 0001, 0010, 0011, 0100, 0101, 0110, 0111, 1000, 1001, 1010, 1011, 1100, 1101, 1110, 1111

Try as you like, you can't make any more patterns than these, and there are 16 of them.

Notice how quickly we've moved from the concrete picture of light bulbs in a room, to the abstract matter of patterns of 1's and 0's. If we can abstract a little further we can turn these patterns into numbers.

Think about counting and writing down as you count. You can count from nought to nine very easily because each of those numbers has a unique name and a symbol to represent it. But what do you write down after nine? You have a name, ten, for that number, but no separate symbol to represent it. Therefore you must re-use some of the other symbols: 10, 11, 12, and so on until 99, when you run out of possibilities again, so the next number has three columns (100). This seems trivial, but you may remember how difficult it was when you learned it at school: all that squared paper with Hundreds Tens and Units written at the top of each sum? You now know that the number 152 means "1 in the Hundreds, 5 in the Tens, 2 in the Units", or $100+50+2=152$.

Counting works like this because we have ten digits $(0,1,2,3,\ldots,9)$ which we arrange to represent all possible numbers.

How does counting work, however, if there are only two digits: 0 and 1? We can count to 1 easily, but how can we represent the next number? We have run out of unique digits, so we must re-use what we have (just as we did when counting with ten digits), and write the next number as 10. Now we know that the next number is called 'two', so in this system 10 represents the number two. The next number as we count is three, and we must write that as 11. Then what? We've run out of two-digit combinations, so the next number, four, must be represented as 100; five must be 101, six is 110, and seven is 111. Here, we are counting in decimal numbers (nought, one, two, etc), but we're writing these down in binary numbers $(0,1,10,11,100,101,\ldots)$.

In the same way as a decimal number such as 152 means: $(1 \times 100)+(5 \times 10)+(2 \times 1)$, the binary number 101 means: $(1 \times 4)+(0 \times 2)+(1 \times 1)$. Instead of having hundreds, tens, and units columns for our numbers, we must use columns marked: fours, twos, and units. In a decimal number the value of a digit is multiplied by ten for every column it moves to the left; in a binary number the value of a digit is multiplied by two for every column it moves to the left.

So that's the binary system: just a different way of representing numbers. If you know Roman numerals you don't find it hard to accept that there are VII dwarfs in *Snow White*; so why not write 111 dwarfs? The actual number of dwarfs is not changed by the way we represent it, but it is a good idea to say the binary number as 'binary one one one', and to write it as '111 b' so that you don't confuse it with a decimal representation.

Now we can return to our original analogy of how the factory workers switch patterns, and decide on a method of making these a little easier to use. The most sensible thing to do is to treat these patterns as four-digit binary numbers. This means that Catherine's signal is 1100 binary, which is 12 decimal. Richard's signal is 0001 binary (1 decimal), and Bobby's signal is 1010 binary (10 decimal). When the Manager looks at a pattern of lights in the office, he or she can read it as a binary number, convert it to its decimal equivalent, and look down the list of employees to see who that number corresponds to. Thus we can say that information is stored in the current of electricity, and the switches make it meaningful.

Our analogy has given a simple picture of how information is represented in a computer: to the computer it's just patterns of voltages (i.e. lights are ON or OFF), but we humans find it easier to consider those patterns as binary numbers. It's all a matter of representation. If you now think of 1010 as the code meaning 'Bobby', then you may start to see how all of this relates to machine code itself. What we will be examining next is the way in which binary numbers are used to represent information inside your home computer.

Speeding Ahead
These three short programs, one for ZX Spectrum, one for the BBC Micro and the other for the Commodore 64, demonstrate the difference in speed of operation between BASIC and Machine Code by displaying either the entire character set (Commodore and BBC), or colour blocks (Spectrum), on the screen

Spectrum

```
1 REM*****************************
10 REM***SPECTRUM M/C CODE****
11 REM* DO NOT LIST LINE 1    *
12 REM* AFTER RUNNING PROG    *
13 REM*****************************
99 REM*****************************
150 LET PTR=23635:LET SA=PEEK
(PTR)+(256*PEEK(PTR+1))+7
200 BORDER 2
350 DATA 1,0,3,17,0,88,33,0,0,
237,176,201
400 FOR X=0 TO 11
500 READ MC
600 POKE SA+X,MC
700 NEXT X
1000 LET OFFSET=0
1100 FOR X=0 TO 1 STEP 0
1200 POKE SA+7,OFFSET
1300 LET DUMMY=USR SA
1400 LET OFFSET=OFFSET+13
1500 IF OFFSET>=256 THEN LET
OFFSET=OFFSET-256*INT(OFFSET/256)
1600 NEXT X
1700 STOP
1799 REM*****************************
1800 REM*SAVE PROG BEFORE RUN*
1801 REM*SAVE PROG BEFORE RUN*
1802 REM*****************************
```

BBC Micro

```
100 REM*******************************BBC**********************
                                  ***************************
149 REM*************************BBC************************
150 REM*     BBC M/C CODE DEMO      *
151 REM*************************************************
200 MODE 4:*TV 254
300 GOSUB 30000
700 FOR P=1920 TO 6079
800 K=K+1:IF K>2679 THEN K=1920
900 ?(HIMEM+P)= (K+47232)
1000 NEXT P
1100 PRINT TAB(13);"THAT WAS BASIC"
1200 INPUT" HIT RETURN FOR MACHINE CODE
VERSION ",A$:CLS
1300 FOR L=0 TO 15:FOR B=0 TO 255 STEP L
1400 ?(SA)=LS:?(SA+1)=HS
1500 ?(FA)=LF:?(FA+1)=HF
1600 DUMMY=USR(PSTRT)
1700 VDU 30
1800 NEXT B,LP
1900 STOP
30000 REM*****MC LOADER S/R****
30010 K=1919:PSTRT=PAGE+8:VSTR=HIMEM+192
0
30020 HS=INT(VSTR/256):LS=VSTR-256*HS:LF
=LS+56:HF=HS+2:SA=114:FA=116
30100 DATA 50,169,32,197,112,48,4,240,2,
133,112,165,112,32,227,255
30110 DATA 230,114,208,2,230,115,165,116
,197,114,208,7,165,117
30120 DATA 197,115,208,1,96,230,112,169,
128,197,112,208,224
30130 DATA 169,32,133,112,208,218,96,96,
96
30150 READ ZZ
30160 FOR BY=PSTRT TO PSTRT+ZZ
30170 READ MC:?(BY)=MC
30180 NEXT BY
30200 RETURN
30299 REM*******************************
30300 REM*    SAVE BEFORE RUNNING !! *
30301 REM*******************************
30399 REM*******************************
30400 REM*DO NOT LIST LINE 100 AFTER*
30401 REM*     RUNNING PROGRAM !!    *
30402 REM*******************************
```

Commodore 64

```
99 REM *****************************
100 REM*COMMODORE M/C CODE DEMO *
101 REM*****************************
200 PRINT CHR$(147)      :REM CLEAR SCREEN
300 PRINT "      THIS WON'T TAKE LONG"
400 GOSUB 60000
500 PRINT CHR$(147);CHR$(5)  :REM CLS AND
WHITE
600 CC=0
700 FOR P=SM TO FM
800 POKE P,CC:POKE P+OF,CL
900 CC=CC+1:IF CC>255 THEN CC=0
1000 NEXT P
1100 PRINT TAB(13);"THAT WAS BASIC"
1200 INPUT" HIT RETURN FOR MACHINE CODE
VERSION ";A$
1300 FOR LP=1 TO 9:FOR B=0 TO 255 STEP L
P
1400 POKE SA,LS:POKE SA+1,HS
1500 POKE FA,LF:POKE FA+1,HF
1600 POKE BA,B:POKE CH,0
1700 SYS AA
1800 NEXT B,LP
1900 STOP
60000 REM*****MC LOADER S/R****
60010 SM=256*PEEK(648):OF=55296-SM:FM=SM
+999:BD=53280:SC=BD+1:CS=8:CB=6:CL=0
60020 POKE BD,CB:POKE SC,CS
60030 LS=0:HS=PEEK(648):LF=232:HF=HS+3:S
A=251:FA=253:BA=250:CH=2
60100 DATA 850,885,169,0,170,165,250,133
,2,165,2,129,251
60110 DATA 230,251,208,2,230,252,165,253
,197,251,208,7,165,254
60120 DATA 197,252,208,1,96,230,2,208,22
9,240,223
60150 READ AA,ZZ
60160 FOR BY=AA TO ZZ
60170 READ MC:POKE BY,MC
60180 NEXT BY
60200 RETURN
60299 REM*******************************
60300 REM* SAVE THIS BEFORE RUNNING IT*
60301 REM*******************************
```

PAGED MEMORY

As the next step towards understanding the fundamentals of machine code programming, we must examine the way computers organise and manage their memory. Here, we look at the constraints imposed on both memory pagination and the operation of the CPU by the machine's use of the binary system.

In the first part of our chapter on Machine Code we gave an analogy of the way in which a computer stores information in the form of electric current. We used the example of a factory where each worker had an individual switch pattern that lit up four light bulbs in the manager's office, thus identifying who was at work. This showed how information (i.e. the name of the person who is working) could be represented by using a flow of electricity.

In our example, we found that by using four switches and bulbs we could represent the numbers from 0 to 15. In other words, there were only 16 possible patterns. However, if we had used eight switches and bulbs instead, then we could have made 256 unique patterns (2×2×2×2×2×2×2×2=256) and, therefore, have been able to count from 0 to 255.

In your home computer, memory is arranged in individual banks of eight switches, and each of those eight-switch banks is called a *byte*. In general, the CPU handles information one byte at a time, which means, in effect, that it can only add, compare, and store numbers between 0 and 255. This might seem to limit its arithmetical capabilities, but that isn't the case. If you think about doing a sum like 63951 + 48770 = ? then you will see that you actually manipulate the individual digits one at a time. Similarly, the CPU can perform arithmetic on large numbers using one byte at a time.

Because it has eight switches, a byte is a place where an eight-digit binary number can be stored. Each of these binary digit positions is called a *bit* — the smallest possible unit of information. A bit in a byte is either ON or OFF, a binary digit is either 1 or 0.

It's often important to talk about individual bits in a byte, so the convention is to number the bits 0 to 7 from right to left in the byte. If a byte contains the binary number 00000001, then we say that bit0 is 1, or that bit0 is ON, or that bit0 is SET; all the other bits are 0, or OFF, or CLEAR. Thus in the binary number 01001000: bit3 is SET, bit6 is SET, bit4 is OFF, bit7 is 0, bit0 is CLEAR, and so on. In a byte, bit0 is also called the Least Significant Bit (LSB), and bit7 the Most Significant Bit (MSB).

Computer memory, then, can be conceived as a long strip of squared paper, eight squares wide, and thousands of squares long: each row of eight squares is a byte, each square is a bit in a byte. Memory is useless if you can't locate items in it, so each of the bytes has an identifying label called its *address*; the address isn't written anywhere on the paper (or in the byte), it's simply the number of the byte in memory, counting from the start of memory. The first byte, therefore, has the address 0, the next byte has address 1, the next has address 2, and so on. If you want to write something in byte43, then you start at the bottom of the memory (at byte0) and count through the bytes until you reach byte43.

When you get there nothing will identify that byte as byte43 except for its position — you've counted forward from byte0, you've reached 43, so this must be byte43. The bytes of memory are actually minuscule banks of eight-transistor devices (one device per bit, eight devices per byte) etched into the chips inside your machine, and they are identical·in everything except their physical position.

However, there is one drawback to this method. This system of memory addressing would be fine if there were only a few hundred bytes. The CPU can count from 0 to 100 in fractions of a millisecond; but computers have thousands of bytes, and counting from 0 to 20000 must take some appreciable time, even for a microprocessor. The way a computer overcomes this problem is by dividing memory into *pages*, just as books are.

If we continue to think of computer memory as a strip of squared paper thousands of squares long and eight squares wide, we can imagine cutting that strip on the boundary of every 100 bytes (i.e. cut across the boundary between byte99 and byte100, cut across the boundary of byte199 and byte200, byte 299 and byte 300, and so on). Each of the strips of paper between the cuts is now a page of 100 bytes. Page0 starts at byte0 and continues to byte99; page1 starts at byte100 and continues to byte199, page2 is byte200 to byte299, etc. Now to find any byte, say byte3518, we don't have to count 3518 bytes from the start of memory because we can see from the address that this byte must be on page 35. Therefore, we need only count 35 pages from the bottom of memory, and then count the bytes from the bottom of that page until we reach byte18 on the page, which must be byte3518. Try it with a strip of squared paper if you haven't followed this.

This system of paged memory is convenient because we can look at the address of any byte, and split it into two parts — the digits from the hundred column leftwards are the page number of the byte, and the digits from the tens column to the right are the number of bytes counted from the bottom of that page. In the example above we have actually split the address 3518 into two numbers: page number 35, and byte number 18 on that page. We call 18 an *offset*, or *page offset*, because it is the number by which you must offset (or increase) the address of the bottom byte on the page in order to reach the byte in question.

The computer, however, doesn't count in decimal, as we do — it counts in binary. The paging system depends upon being able to find the page and the offset by simply inspecting the address of the byte. The decimal address 99 is represented by 01100011 in binary, and 100 decimal is 01100100 binary; decimal 199 is 11000111, and decimal 200 is 11001000 binary. We can see, from these examples, that there's no simple way of looking at the binary numbers and telling page from page, as we can so easily do with the decimal equivalents. The reason for this is the choice of page size.

We chose 100 as the page size precisely because it's a meaningful number in the decimal system (it's a power of 10). If we are to count in binary, however, then we must choose a page size to suit *that* system. The page size used by our computers is 256, so that page0 starts with byte0 and continues to byte255; page1 starts with byte256 and continues to byte511, and so on. To see why this is convenient we must write these addresses in binary:

```
Page 0:byte00000000 — byte11111111
Page 1:byte100000000 — byte111111111
```

As you can see, we can count in binary from 0 to 255 in an eight-bit number; the next number — 256 — requires nine bits, and with nine bits we can count up to 511. The next number — 512 — requires ten bits, and with ten bits we can count up to 1023; and so on. We now see that if the page size is 256 and we count in binary, then the offset is the rightmost eight bits, and the page number is given by the bits from bit8 leftwards.

This may be puzzling since we have already stated that the CPU can handle only single bytes, and a byte contains only eight bits. Therefore, you may ask, what good is it to talk about nine- and 10-bit numbers? The answer is that all addresses in memory are treated as two-byte numbers, and the CPU deals with them one byte at a time. If we rewrite the page boundaries as two-byte numbers this system becomes more clear:

```
Page  0 starts at 00000000 00000000
        ends  at 00000000 11111111
Page  1 starts at 00000001 00000000
        ends  at 00000001 11111111
Page 10 starts at 00000010 00000000
        ends  at 00000010 11111111
```

```
Page 11 starts at 00000011 00000000
        ends  at 00000011 11111111
```

and so on.

Now we can see that when the CPU fetches information from, or puts information into, a byte in memory, that byte will be identified by a two-byte address. The first, or leftmost, byte of the two gives the page number, while the second, or rightmost, byte gives the offset.

On page 125, we provide programs that convert from decimal into binary, as well as hexadecimal numbers. The latter are used extensively in machine code, and will be fully discussed later in the course.

Paged Addressing
Paged addressing divides memory into imaginary blocks or pages of 256 bytes. All addresses are then expressed as two-byte numbers: one byte gives the page number, the other gives the offset from the start of that page

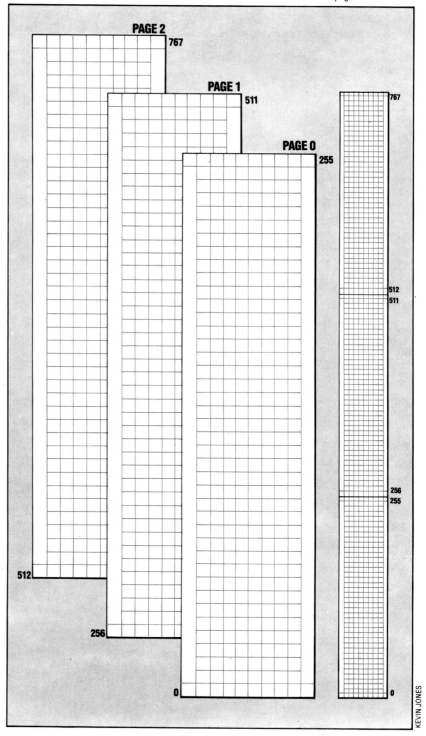

Number Cruncher

The three programs presented here, for the BBC Microcomputer, Spectrum and Commodore, accept decimal numbers, and deliver in return their binary equivalent

Commodore 64

```
10 REM*********COMMODORE**********
40 S$="=          ":X$="0123456789ABCDEF"
50 REM    S$ CONTAINS 9 SPACES
60 PRINT CHR$(147)          :REM CLEAR SCREEN
70 PRINT "          TO DISPLAY DECIMAL NUMBER
S"
80 PRINT "     AND THEIR BINARY EQUIVALEN
TS"
90 PRINT:PRINT "     *******ENTER 0 TO QUI
T********":PRINT
100 FOR K=1 TO 1
110 FOR L=1 TO 1
120 INPUT"TYPE ANY POSITIVE WHOLE NUMBER
";A$
130 NU=VAL(A$)
140 IF NU=0 THEN PRINT "PROGRAM EXIT":ST
OP
150 IF INT(NU)<>ABS(NU) THEN L=0
160 IF NU>65535 THEN PRINT NU;" IS TOO B
IG":L=0
170 NEXT L
200 NM=NU:H$="":GOSUB 2000
210 PRINT NU;TAB(5);N$
220 IF RIGHT$(A$,1)="+" THEN GOSUB 4000
230 PRINT H$:PRINT:PRINT
240 K=0:NEXT K
250 END
300 END
1000 REM******BINARY BYTE S/R*******
1010 B$=""
1020 FOR D=8 TO 1 STEP-1
1030 N1=INT(N/2)
1040 R=N-2*N1
1050 B$=MID$(STR$(R),2)+B$
1060 N=N1
1070 NEXT D
1080 RETURN
2000 REM****BINARY CONVERSION S/R***
2010 IF NM<256 THEN N=NM:GOSUB 1000:N$=S
$+B$:RETURN
2020 HI=INT(NM/256):LO=NM-256*HI
2030 N=HI:GOSUB 1000:N$="= "+B$
2040 N=LO:GOSUB 1000:N$=N$+" "+B$
2050 RETURN
3000 REM****HEX BYTE S/R*********
3010 HB=INT(N/16):LB=N-HB*16
3020 B$=MID$(X$,HB+1,1)+MID$(X$,LB+1,1)
3030 RETURN
4000 REM****HEX CONVERSION S/R******
4010 IF NM<256 THEN N=NM:GOSUB 3000:H$="
= "+B$:RETURN
4020 HI=INT(NM/256):LO=NM-256*HI
4030 N=HI:GOSUB 3000:H$="= "+B$
4040 N=LO:GOSUB 3000:H$=H$+" "+B$
4050 RETURN
```

BBC Micro

Copy the Commodore list with the following changes:

```
60 CLS:@%=5
210 PRINT TAB(0);NU;TAB(5);N$;
1050 B$=STR$(R)+B$
```

This program does not use the BBC's number representation facilities for the sake of compatibility of format with the other machines: you may be able to rewrite it in a shorter form.

Spectrum

```
10 REM*******SPECTRUM*********":LET X$="0
123456789ABCDEF"
40 LET S$="=          "
50 REM    S$ CONTAINS 9 SPACES
60 CLS
70 PRINT "  TO DISPLAY DECIMAL N
UMBERS"
80 PRINT " AND THEIR BINARY EQUI
VALENTS"
90 PRINT:PRINT " *******ENTER 0
TO QUIT********":PRINT
100 FOR K=1 TO 1
110 FOR L=1 TO 1
120 INPUT"TYPE ANY POSITIVE WHOL
E NUMBER ";A$
130 LET NU=VAL(A$)
140 IF NU=0 THEN PRINT "PROGRAM
EXIT":STOP
150 IF INT(NU)<>ABS(NU) THEN LET
L=0
160 IF NU>65535 THEN PRINT NU;"
IS TOO BIG":LET L=0
170 NEXT L
200 LET NM=NU:LET H$="":GOSUB 20
00
210 PRINT NU;TAB(5);N$;
220 IF A$(LEN A$)="+" THEN GOSUB
4000
230 PRINT H$:PRINT:PRINT
240 LET K=0:NEXT K
300 END
1000 REM**BINARY BYTE S/R**
1010 LET B$=""
1020 FOR D=8 TO 1 STEP-1
1030 LET N1=INT(N/2)
1040 LET R=N-2*N1
1050 LET B$=STR$(R)+B$
1060 LET N=N1
1070 NEXT D
1080 RETURN
2000 REM**BINARY CONVERS S/R**
2010 IF NM<256 THEN LET N=NM:GOS
UB 1000:LET N$=S$+B$:RETURN
2020 LET HI=INT(NM/256):LET LO=N
M-256*HI
2030 LET N=HI:GOSUB 1000:LET N$=
"= "+B$
2040 LET N=LO:GOSUB 1000:LET N$=
N$+" "+B$
2050 RETURN
3000 REM***HEX BYTE S/R******
3010 LET HB=INT(N/16):LET LB=N-H
B*16
3020 LET B$=X$(HB+1)+X$(LB+1)
3030 RETURN
4000 REM***HEX CONVERS S/R****
4010 IF NM<256 THEN LET N=NM:GOS
UB 3000:LET H$="=     "+B$:RETURN
4020 LET HI=INT(NM/256):LET LO=N
M-256*HI
4030 LET N=HI:GOSUB 3000:LET H$=
"= "+B$
4040 LET N=LO:GOSUB 3000:LET H$=
H$+" "+B$
4050 RETURN
```

If you input a number with a "+" on the end, for example: 6435+, then in addition to its decimal and binary representation, its hex representation will also be displayed.

MEMORY MONITOR

The hexadecimal number system appears to be a complicated and cumbersome alternative to our everyday decimal, but it is in fact an extremely useful and easily understood way of dealing with memory addresses and their contents when faced with the limitations of an eight-bit byte system of memory.

At this point in the Machine Code course, it's worth returning to the question of number representation. We are already familiar with the decimal (or denary) number system which we use most of the time, and we've investigated the binary system (see page 121). It is well to remember that both the decimal and binary systems are simply alternative expressions of the same concept — number. Most human beings, for example, have the same number of fingers per hand. You may say that the number is five, and someone else may call it *fünf*, or *cinq*, or *pente*; but a moment's empirical investigation will show that you're all talking about the same quantity or number — it is only your representation systems that are different. Different but equivalent. There is a one-to-one correspondence between all numbers expressed in English and all numbers expressed in any other language, and there is internal consistency in all these systems. Arithmetic yields the same results irrespective of the language used to describe the individual components of an arithmetic expression.

Different number systems are exactly similar to different languages. The number of fingers on a normal human hand is not changed by being called *fünf* or five, neither is it altered by being written 5 or 101b (the b here showing that 101 is to be interpreted as a binary number). The only reasons for choosing one system or the other are either custom or convenience.

We find it convenient to use decimal representation at first because it is the number system most commonly used around us. But it is not the only system. Digital clocks, for example, use a bizarre system of arithmetic: part decimal, part modulo 60 (there are 60 minutes in an hour and 60 seconds in a minute), and part modulo 24 (24 hours in a day). Before 1971 British money was reckoned in units of 12 (pence in a shilling) and 20 (shillings in a pound). Learning to use this system took years of agonised schooling — how many people ever really learned how to express shillings and pence as decimal fractions of a pound?

When talking about computers, we find it instructive to begin by talking about binary numbers because they so closely model the computer's electrical operations, being simply sequences of on-off switch states. If we only ever wanted to talk about single-byte numbers, then binary might serve as a complete alternative to decimal — translating eight-bit binary into decimal becomes surprisingly easy with a little practice. Unfortunately, memory addresses in particular and useful numbers in general are usually too large to be fitted into one byte, so computer programmers and engineers over the years have felt the need for a number system with the logical convenience of binary, as well as the range of decimal. Two systems have been used for these reasons: hexadecimal and octal. The first, now standard in microcomputing, is usually called *hex*, and is based on the number 16. Octal, based on 8, has been widely used in mainframe computing, but is increasingly being replaced by the hex system.

USING HEX NUMBERS

In looking at decimal and binary representation, we have seen two consequences follow from the choice of number base: the base is the number of unique digits needed in the system, and it is the multiplicative factor in the positional notation. For instance, there are ten unique digits in decimal (0–9), and the value of a decimal digit is multiplied by ten each time it shifts leftwards in a decimal number.

Hexadecimal, therefore, requires 16 unique digits, and they are the digits 0–9 and the letters A–F. Counting in hex is simply a matter of working through the single digits and then re-using them in positional notation. The hex number after 9, therefore, is A (decimal 10); next is B; next C; and so on until F (decimal 15). That exhausts the single digits, so the hex number after F is 10 (say this as: 'one-zero hex'), which corresponds to 16 decimal. From this we can see how the single digits are used, and that the value of the columns in a multi-digit hex number increases by a factor of 16 with leftward movement. In a decimal number we call the columns: Units, Tens, Hundreds and Thousands. By comparison, in a hex number the columns are: Units, Sixteens, Two-Hundred-and-Fifty-Sixes and Four-Thousand-and-Ninety-Sixes. By comparing the changes in the binary column with the changes in the hex column, you should be able to see the major advantage of hex numbers: the range of a four-bit binary number is exactly that of a single-digit hex number (i.e. 0 to 15 decimal). Some examples should make this clear:

Decimal	Binary	Hex
0	00000000	0
1	00000001	1
2	00000010	2
3	00000011	3
. . . .		
7	00000111	7
8	00001000	8
9	00001001	9
10	00001010	A
11	00001011	B
12	00001100	C
13	00001101	D
14	00001110	E
15	00001111	F
16	00010000	10
17	00010001	11
. . . .		
24	00011000	18
25	00011001	19
26	00011010	1A
27	00011011	1B
. . . .		
31	00011111	1F
32	00100000	20
33	00100001	21

The range of a single eight-bit byte number, therefore, is eight binary digits, or two hex digits:

0 to 255	in decimal
00000000 to 11111111	in binary
0 to FF	in hex

To convert a hex number into binary, therefore, you simply express each hex digit as a four-bit binary number. If a single-byte number is expressed as a two-digit hex number, then the leftmost hex digit corresponds to the four leftmost binary bits, while the rightmost hex digit corresponds to the four rightmost binary digits. Splitting a byte like this gives us two 'nybbles' (a nybble is half a byte). The leftmost nybble, corresponding to the leftmost hex digit, is called the upper or most significant nybble; and the rightmost nybble is called the lower or least significant nybble. Here is an example:

```
          Upper    Lower
          Nybble   Nybble
            ↓        ↓
  206   =  1100     1110   =  C E
   ↑         ↑                 ↑
decimal   binary equivalent  hex equivalent
```

It is important to make ourselves as familiar as possible with the hexadecimal number system, for the simple reason that it makes eight-bit byte manipulation much easier than if we were using binary. Convincing yourself of this requires a little practice, not just with number examples, but particularly with memory addresses and the contents of memory bytes. Once this becomes important — and very soon it will — you'll wonder how you ever managed in decimal.

We give programs in this instalment of the Machine Code course, for the BBC Micro, Commodore 64, and the Spectrum, that allow us to look at the contents of specified bytes in memory. These 'Mempeek' programs, as we have called them, ask you first to state the 'Start Address' (i.e. specify the first byte number) and then to give the number of bytes to be looked at. If, for example, you wished to specify byte1953 as your beginning point and request that the contents of the four following bytes be displayed, then the screen will show the decimal number 1953 in the leftmost column, and then list the contents of byte1953, byte1954, byte1955 and byte1956 in the next four columns.

Bear in mind that if the machine shows that byte1956 contains the decimal number 175, what we mean is that in one of the memory chips, an area that the machine calls byte1956 carries a pattern of eight voltage levels. If 0 volts is represented by 0, and 5 volts by 1, then byte1956 carries the voltage pattern 10101111. This we choose to interpret as a binary number, and its decimal equivalent is 175.

It is vital to remember that we use an imprecise kind of shorthand most of the time that we talk about computers; and expanding it into physical description is always salutary, and should help to avoid confusion.

The contents of a byte displayed on the screen are not the 'actual' contents. What we see are character data that have been assigned to the voltage patterns of the bytes. This means that having interpreted the voltage patterns as binary numbers, and having converted the binary to decimal numbers, we are going one step further and converting decimal numbers into characters according to ASCII — the American Standard Code for Information Interchange. This character data is displayed in the last column of the display. This is an internationally recognised code implemented in most computers, which substitutes decimal numbers between 0 and 127 for all the characters on a keyboard (historically, a teleprinter keyboard). In this code the decimal number 65 means the upper-case character 'A', 66 means 'B', 67 means 'C', and so on. Among the non-alphabetic characters, 32 means a space character, 42 means an asterisk, 13 means the Return key, and so on.

The printable ASCII characters start at number 32 and finish at number 127. Codes outside that range are undefined, or not printable, or specific to particular machines. Because of this, when we run the Mempeek programs, the monitor prints a dot to represent any byte containing a number out of range. In the next instalment of the course, we will provide a comprehensive ASCII character set for the values between 0 and 127.

An investigation of the ASCII character set is particularly useful as background to a full understanding of machine code for two important reasons. Firstly, it reinforces the point that how you interpret memory contents is entirely a matter of choice. You can say that a byte contains a number, or an address, or a coded character, or an instruction, or whatever you like. In any case it will be data waiting to be interpreted. Secondly, it does give a rather more understandable view of memory, especially those parts of it which do actually contain character data, some of it used by the machine's Operating System, and some of it used by you.

Operating System data includes all the Error and Prompt messages — READY, for example, or NONSENSE IN BASIC, or START TAPE THEN PRESS RETURN — anything that it is capable of saying to the user has to be ASCII coded and stored in memory. You may never have thought of that, and it's a revealing insight into a computer's limitations as an 'intelligent' machine. Our intelligence is obviously different: we don't memorise messages like that, we simply frame a thought and then generate an appropriate combination of words to express it.

Memory Maps

A memory map is a simple schematic representation of the use to which memory is being put, showing the parameters of specific areas. Some areas of memory are always used for the same purpose. On the Commodore 64, for example, bytes 0 to 1024 are used by the BASIC Operating System as a Work Area. Other areas of memory have varied uses depending upon the program size and state. The boundaries between these areas can be either *fixed* (shown in our diagrams below as solid lines) or *floating* (shown as broken lines). Fixed boundaries never alter, while floating boundaries are for those areas of memory that fluctuate according to need. In the Commodore memory map, the Screen RAM boundaries are fixed (at bytes 1024 to 2048), while the boundaries of the memory area where the BASIC Variables are kept fluctuate according to how many variables are being used at any given time.

The Mempeek programs on page 129 can be used to locate the current positions of the floating boundaries in the memory of your machine. The Commodore has six floating boundary pointers (also called System Variables). An example is given in the panel below explaining how the contents of a pair of bytes are used to calculate the required memory address. BBC BASIC has four System Variables to determine, and the Spectrum has five.

It must be remembered that a memory map is a static representation of something that is forever changing while the machine is in use. Each of the floating boundaries is subject to change at any time. We give ideas, on the next page, of how you can extend the Mempeek programs to observe variations in the pointer values.

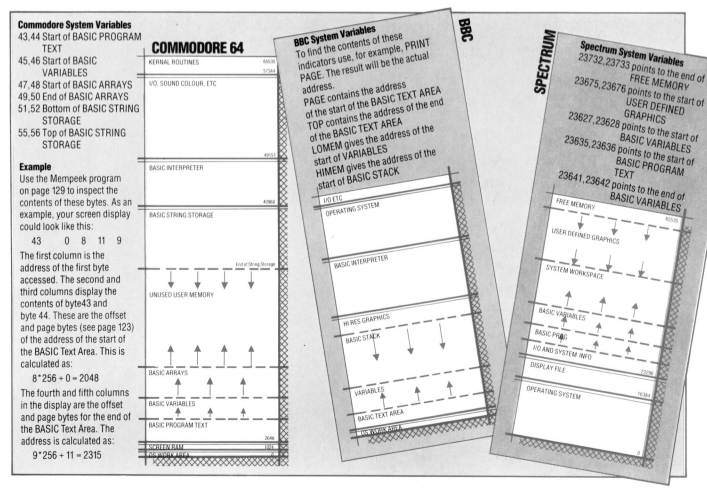

Commodore System Variables
43,44 Start of BASIC PROGRAM TEXT
45,46 Start of BASIC VARIABLES
47,48 Start of BASIC ARRAYS
49,50 End of BASIC ARRAYS
51,52 Bottom of BASIC STRING STORAGE
55,56 Top of BASIC STRING STORAGE

Example
Use the Mempeek program on page 129 to inspect the contents of these bytes. As an example, your screen display could look like this:

43   0   8   11   9

The first column is the address of the first byte accessed. The second and third columns display the contents of byte43 and byte 44. These are the offset and page bytes (see page 123) of the address of the start of the BASIC Text Area. This is calculated as:

8*256 + 0 = 2048

The fourth and fifth columns in the display are the offset and page bytes for the end of the BASIC Text Area. The address is calculated as:

9*256 + 11 = 2315

COMMODORE 64

KERNAL ROUTINES — 65535 / 57344
I/O, SOUND COLOUR, ETC
BASIC INTERPRETER — 49151
— 40960
BASIC STRING STORAGE
End of String Storage
UNUSED USER MEMORY
BASIC ARRAYS
BASIC VARIABLES
BASIC PROGRAM TEXT — 2048
SCREEN RAM — 1024
OS WORK AREA — 0

BBC System Variables
To find the contents of these indicators use, for example, PRINT PAGE. The result will be the actual address.
PAGE contains the address of the start of the BASIC TEXT AREA
TOP contains the address of the end of the BASIC TEXT AREA
LOMEM gives the address of the start of VARIABLES
HIMEM gives the address of the start of BASIC STACK

BBC

I/O ETC
OPERATING SYSTEM
BASIC INTERPRETER
HI RES GRAPHICS
BASIC STACK
VARIABLES
BASIC TEXT AREA
OS WORK AREA

SPECTRUM

Spectrum System Variables
23732,23733 points to the end of FREE MEMORY
23675,23676 points to the start of USER DEFINED GRAPHICS
23627,23628 points to the start of BASIC VARIABLES
23635,23636 points to the start of BASIC PROGRAM TEXT
23641,23642 points to the end of BASIC VARIABLES

FREE MEMORY — 65535
USER DEFINED GRAPHICS
SYSTEM WORKSPACE
BASIC VARIABLES
BASIC PROG
I/O AND SYSTEM INFO
DISPLAY FILE — 23296
OPERATING SYSTEM — 16384
— 0

BBC Micro

```
7 REM******************************
                    MEMPEEK 1   *
8 REM*     BBC
9 REM******************************
20 MODE 7
30 *TV 255
40 CLS
50 REPEAT
100 INPUT"START ADDRESS ",SA
200 INPUT"NUMBER OF BYTES (0 TO QUIT)",B
N
250 PRINT "****************************
**********"
300 FOR B%=SA TO (SA+BN-1) STEP 4
350 H$="":@%=6
400 PRINT TAB(0);B%;TAB(8);
450 @%=4
500 FOR C=0 TO 3
550 PK%=?(B%+C):PK$="."
600 PRINT PK%;
650 IF PK%=13 THEN PK$=CHR$(124)
700 IF (PK%>31) AND (PK%<128) THEN PK$=C
HR$(PK%)
750 H$=H$+PK$
800 NEXT C
850 PRINT TAB(32);H$
900 NEXT B%
950 UNTIL BN=0
1000 REM*************************
```

Spectrum

```
7 REM******************************
8 REM*    SPECTRUM    MEMPEEK 1    *
9 REM******************************
30 DIM H$(4)
50 FOR L=0 TO 1 STEP 0
100 INPUT"START ADDRESS ";SA
200 INPUT"NUMBER OF BYTES (0 TO
QUIT)";BN
250 PRINT "*********************
*********"
300 FOR B=SA TO (SA+BN-1) STEP 4
350 LET H$="...."
400 PRINT B;TAB 7;
500 FOR C=0 TO 3
550 LET PK=PEEK(B+C)
600 PRINT PK;" ";
650 IF (PK>31) AND (PK<128) THEN
LET H$(C+1)=CHR$ PK
700 IF PK=13 THEN LET H$(C+1)="
"
800 NEXT C
850 PRINT TAB 26;H$
900 NEXT B
950 IF BN=0 THEN LET L=2
1000 NEXT L
1050 REM*********************
**************
```

Using Mempeek

When you enter the Mempeek program into your machine, make sure that you SAVE it and check it carefully before you RUN it, because typing errors in this sort of program can lead to unrecoverable crashes.

The program will first ask you for a start address, and then the number of bytes that you wish to examine. Both should be positive whole numbers in the range 0 to 65535. Inputting 0 as the number of bytes will cause the program to end (quit). Suppose you wish the start address to be byte 230. The screen display might look like this:

```
START ADDRESS? 230
NUMBER OF BYTES (0 TO QUIT) ? 8
**********************************

230   193   32   65   49   . A1
234   129   64   93   98   .@]b

START ADDRESS?
```

The leftmost column gives the decimal address of the first byte, the next four columns give the decimal contents of the four bytes from that address on, and the last column gives the character representation of the bytes' contents (where this is possible), and '.' otherwise.

You might like to begin by just 'wandering around' in memory with this program, noting any interesting addresses, and then try to find where in memory the Operating System stores its error messages and BASIC keywords. Your User Manual may help you with this.

Once you've found the pointers that define the boundaries of the various areas of memory, you can try adding some REM lines to the program, and see what effect that has on pointer values. Then add some lines at the start of the program to do some string manipulation, and again, see what effect that has on the pointers and on the contents of the Variable Storage Area.

For example:

```
3 DIM Z$(254)
4 LET X$=""
5 FOR M=1 TO 255.LET X$=X$+"*":NEXT M
```

Commodore 64

```
7 REM******************************
8 REM*     COMMODORE MEMPEEK 1    *
9 REM******************************
30 PRINT CHR$(147)        :REM CLEAR SCREEN
40 PRINT CHR$(142)        :REM UPPER CASE
50 FOR LP=0 TO 1 STEP 0
100 INPUT"START ADDRESS ";SA
200 INPUT"NUMBER OF BYTES (0 TO QUIT)";B
N
250 PRINT "****************************
**********"
300 FOR B=SA TO (SA+BN-1) STEP 4
350 H$=""
400 PRINT B;TAB(8);
500 FOR C=0 TO 3
550 PK=PEEK(B+C):PK$="."
600 PRINT TAB(8+5*C);PK;
650 IF PK=0 THEN PK$=CHR$(122)
700 IF (PK>31) AND (PK<128) THEN PK$=CHR
$(PK)
750 H$=H$+PK$
800 NEXT C
850 PRINT TAB(32);H$
900 NEXT B
950 IF BN=0 THEN LP=1
1000 NEXT LP
1050 REM********************
```

TEXTUAL ANALYSIS

Before going on to investigate how machine code programs work, it is salutary to look at how BASIC programs are stored (in the BASIC Text Area of memory) and implemented (using the BASIC Interpreter program). This will serve as a reference point later when we come to discuss the way machine code operates in memory.

When you type or LOAD a BASIC program into the computer, you probably imagine that the computer is an empty vessel doing nothing until your instructions arrive. In fact, from the moment that the power is turned on, the computer is constantly running a sophisticated program of its own — the Operating System. This is a program, or set of programs, permanently burned into some of the ROM chips inside the machine. Its purpose is to make the machine work: it puts a display on the screen, it communicates with the printer and the disk drives, it scans the keyboard for keypresses, and so on. To the O.S. everything that comes into the machine is just data to be processed by its own programs.

One of these programs is called the BASIC Interpreter, and its purpose is to inspect the text of BASIC programs, and to implement their instructions. Everything in a BASIC program, therefore, is just data for the Interpreter program to process. When you type in a program, the Operating System recognises it as such because each new line begins with a valid line number. With some exceptions every character of that program line is stored in its own byte of the BASIC Program Text Area of memory. When you type RUN, the Operating System hands over control to the BASIC Interpreter, which — like any program — goes to work on processing its data (the contents of the BASIC Text Area).

The Interpreter does not change your program in any way, but simply interprets and implements it. And because the Interpreter obeys commands without question, it is quite possible to instruct it to look at the contents of any area of memory. If your program happens to allow you to inspect memory and you use it to inspect the Text Area, that's no paradox to the Interpreter. It just follows instructions if it can, and reports SYNTAX ERROR or OVERFLOW ERROR or something similar if it can't. It has neither the reasoning nor the vocabulary to issue error messages such as: TEMPORAL PARADOX or PHILOSOPHICAL DISCONTINUITY.

The Operating System stores your BASIC program character-by-character, with the exception of the BASIC keywords. Whenever it

recognises the letters (or characters, or numbers, or voltage patterns) that make up a BASIC keyword, the Operating System replaces that word by a single-byte code number, called a *token*. This saves memory space — RESTORE, for example, would otherwise use up seven bytes — and means that the Interpreter's job of translating the BASIC program is much easier to perform.

Different machines use different token conventions, but, in general, token codes are numbers greater than 127. The ASCII codes for the printable characters (shown in the table on page 131) are all in the range 32 to 127. Therefore, any byte in the BASIC Text Area containing a number bigger than 127 must be a token byte put there by the Operating System. When the Interpreter encounters such a byte it simply implements the appropriate built-in subroutine.

The question arises, however, of why, when you LIST a program, you don't see unprintable characters, but rather the BASIC keywords, etc.? The answer is that during a LIST the Operating System inspects each byte of the Text Area, and whenever it finds a byte having a value greater than 127 it treats it as a token. Somewhere in memory is stored a complete list of the ASCII representations of BASIC keywords and the value of a token will point to that position. It's just the same as if the Interpreter were using the token's value to locate its implementation subroutine. And consequently, the Operating System puts the keyword rather than the token on the screen during a LIST. You can demonstrate this to yourself on a Commodore 64 very easily. (It's less straightforward on the BBC and Spectrum.) In lower-case mode, type:

```
100 rem*******h*********
```

Now LIST 100, and you should see:

```
100 rem*******left$*********
```

On the Commodore machines, the ASCII value of 'H' in lower-case mode is 200 so when the O.S. found a value of 200 in that particular byte during the LIST, it interpreted it as the token for the keyword LEFT$. If you now type:

```
100 rem"*******H**************"
```

and LIST 100, you'll see:

```
100 rem"*******H**************"
```

This demonstrates that it is important to remember that some printable characters, usually graphics characters, do have ASCII codes greater than 127, and they will be recognised as such, provided they're in quotes. If not, they will be treated as tokens.

We are now at a point where we can begin to investigate how a BASIC program line is stored in memory. Computers differ in detail, but in general the first three or four bytes of a BASIC program line in the Text Area will contain the program line number and some information about the length of the line (see the panel). The line number that you attach to the line when you type it in is stored (although not as its ASCII equivalent — that would mean that line 61030 would require five bytes just to store its line number). Instead, the number is always stored in two-byte integer form. In this form, the numbers from 0 to 255 (which can be stored in one eight-bit byte, remember) are stored as a zero-byte followed by the byte containing the number. Numbers greater than 255 are stored exactly as paged addresses (see page 36): the value of the first byte is multiplied by 256, and added to the value of the second byte. 1000, for example, would be stored as 3,232 (3*256 + 232 = 1000). These two bytes are always in the same position in any line stored in the Text Area (although whether they are always the first two bytes or whatever depends upon the machine).

The information about the length of the line is placed in a single byte in the BBC and two bytes in the Spectrum. This represents simply the number of bytes in the line (including the two bytes for the line number and the line-length byte itself). If you know the address of the first byte of a BASIC program line in memory, and you add to it the contents of the line-length byte, then you will have the address of the first byte of the next program line. Since the biggest number expressible in one byte is 255, the maximum length of a BASIC program line on the BBC is, therefore, 255 characters. You might use the Mempeek program on page 129 to establish whether that is the limit of the number of *characters* you can type into a program line, or whether it is the limit of the length of the line as it is stored in the Text Area.

On the Commodore the line-length byte is replaced by two bytes called the *link address*. This is simply the actual address in two-byte form of the first byte of the next program line.

It's interesting to note that in the BBC and the Spectrum the next-line Start Address is calculated from the present address plus the line-length (which is slow but saves a byte); whereas on the Commodore the next address is stored as such

Conversion Chart
The American Standard Code for Information Interchange gives a standard character code value for the numbers 0-127. The codes 0-31 do not return printable characters, but are used to send control signals to peripherals such as the screen and the printer. The meaning of these codes, therefore, varies greatly from one machine to another — as the chart shows. Some machines, in particular the Commodore and the Spectrum in our chart, leave many codes unused (signified here by a ●). The codes 32-127 return the printable characters, and the standard ASCII codes in this range are common (with minor variations) to most computers. Your User Manual will give ASCII codes for your machine

ASCII CODE	ASCII	COMMODORE	SPECTRUM	BBC Micro
0	NUL — Does nothing	●	●	Null
1	SOH — Start heading	●	●	Next character to printer
2	STX — Start of text	●	●	Enable printer
3	ETX — End of text	●	●	Disable printer
4	EOT — End of transmission	●	●	Separate text/graphics cursors
5	ENQ — Enquire	White clr.key	●	Join text/graphics cursors
6	ACK — Acknowledge	●	PRINT	Enable VDU drivers
7	BEL — Ring bell	●	EDIT	Make short beep
8	BS — Backspace	Disables CBM key	Cursor left	Backspace cursor
9	HT — Horizontal tab	Enables CBM key	Cursor right	Forwardspace cursor
10	LF — Line feed	●	Cursor down	Cursor down
11	VT — Vertical tab	●	Cursor up	Cursor up
12	FF — Form feed	●	Delete key	Clear text area
13	CR — Carriage return	RETURN	ENTER	Return
14	SO — Shift out	L/case on	Number	Page mode on
15	SI — Shift in	●	●	Page mode off
16	DLE — Data link escape	●	INK	Clear graphics area
17	DC1 — Device control 1	Cursor down	PAPER	Def text colour
18	DC2 — Device control 2	Reverse on	FLASH	Def graphics colour
19	DC3 — Device control 3	Cursor home	BRIGHT	Def logical colour
20	DC4 — Device control 4	Delete key	INVERSE	Restore default log.clr
21	NAK — Negative acknowledge	●	OVER	Disable VDU drivers
22	SYN — Synchronous idle	●	AT	Select screen mode
23	ETB — End of transmission block	●	TAB	Reprogram display character
24	CAN — Cancel	●	●	Def graphics window
25	EM — End of medium	●	●	Plot m,x,y
26	SUB — Substitute	●	●	Restore default windows
27	ESC — Escape	●	●	Null
28	FS — File separator	Red clr.key	●	Def text window
29	GS — Group separator	Cursor right	●	Def graphics origin
30	RS — Record separator	Green clr.key	●	Move text cursor
31	US — Unit separator	Blue clr.key	●	Move text cursor to x,y

ASCII CODE	ASCII	ASCII CODE	ASCII
32	Space	80	P
33	!	81	Q
34	"	82	R
35	#	83	S
36	$	84	T
37	%	85	U
38	&	86	V
39	'	87	W
40	(	88	X
41	)	89	Y
42	★	90	Z
43	+	91	[
44	,	92	
45	–	93	]
46	.	94	^
47	/	95	
48	0	96	
49	1	97	a
50	2	98	b
51	3	99	c
52	4	100	d
53	5	101	e
54	6	102	f
55	7	103	g
56	8	104	h
57	9	105	i
58	:	106	j
59	;	107	k
60	<	108	l
61	=	109	m
62	>	110	n
63	?	111	o
64	@	112	p
65	A	113	q
66	B	114	r
67	C	115	s
68	D	116	t
69	E	117	u
70	F	118	v
71	G	119	w
72	H	120	x
73	I	121	y
74	J	122	z
75	K	123	{
76	L	124	!
77	M	125	}
78	N	126	"
79	O	127	Delete

(which uses an extra byte but is fast). This demonstrates that there's no *right* way to build a computer, there's only the individual designer's way. It is also a good example of the sorts of things that computer designers must take into consideration. They know that they have a fundamental choice between designing a machine that is slow but inexpensive, or one that is fast but expensive. Similarly, when writing a BASIC program on machines with limited memory (the unexpanded Vic-20 and ZX81 are good examples), you have to decide how to trade speed of execution against efficiency of memory usage.

Finally, notice that in the Text Area there will be a line-start or line-end marker for each line of the BASIC program. On the BBC Micro each line starts with a byte containing 13 (ASCII for Carriage Return), whereas this ends a Spectrum line. The Commodore BASIC line ends with a zero-byte (ASCII for " ").

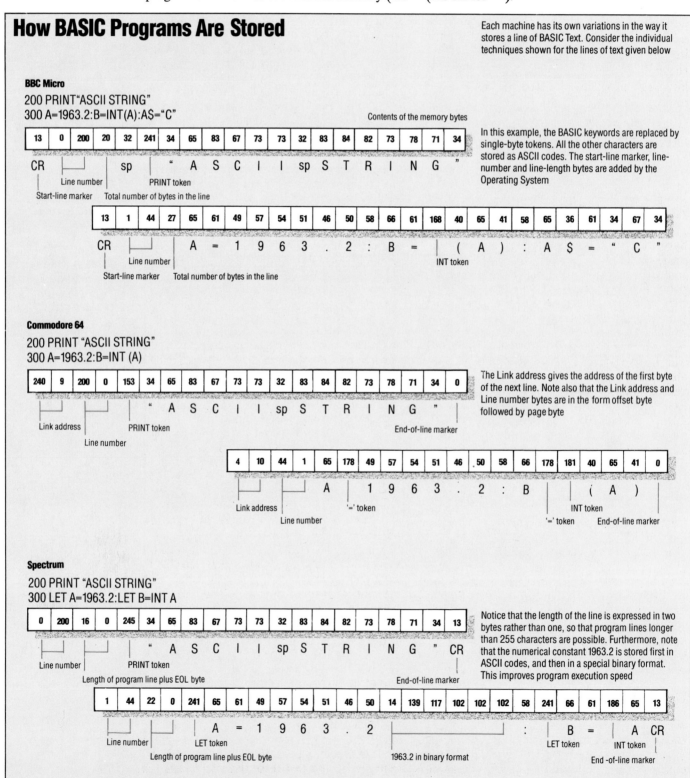

How BASIC Programs Are Stored

Each machine has its own variations in the way it stores a line of BASIC Text. Consider the individual techniques shown for the lines of text given below

BBC Micro

```
200 PRINT"ASCII STRING"
300 A=1963.2:B=INT(A):A$="C"
```

Contents of the memory bytes

| 13 | 0 | 200 | 20 | 32 | 241 | 34 | 65 | 83 | 67 | 73 | 73 | 32 | 83 | 84 | 82 | 73 | 78 | 71 | 34 |

CR   sp   "   A   S   C   I   I   sp   S   T   R   I   N   G   "

Line number / Start-line marker / Total number of bytes in the line / PRINT token

In this example, the BASIC keywords are replaced by single-byte tokens. All the other characters are stored as ASCII codes. The start-line marker, line-number and line-length bytes are added by the Operating System

| 13 | 1 | 44 | 27 | 65 | 61 | 49 | 57 | 54 | 51 | 46 | 50 | 58 | 66 | 61 | 168 | 40 | 65 | 41 | 58 | 65 | 36 | 61 | 34 | 67 | 34 |

CR   A   =   1   9   6   3   .   2   :   B   =   (A   )   :   A $ =   "   C   "

Line number / Start-line marker / Total number of bytes in the line / INT token

Commodore 64

```
200 PRINT "ASCII STRING"
300 A=1963.2:B=INT (A)
```

| 240 | 9 | 200 | 0 | 153 | 34 | 65 | 83 | 67 | 73 | 73 | 32 | 83 | 84 | 82 | 73 | 78 | 71 | 34 | 0 |

"   A   S   C   I   I   sp   S   T   R   I   N   G   "

Link address / Line number / PRINT token / End-of-line marker

The Link address gives the address of the first byte of the next line. Note also that the Link address and Line number bytes are in the form offset byte followed by page byte

| 4 | 10 | 44 | 1 | 65 | 178 | 49 | 57 | 54 | 51 | 46 | 50 | 58 | 66 | 178 | 181 | 40 | 65 | 41 | 0 |

A   1   9   6   3   .   2   :   B   (A   )

Link address / Line number / '=' token / INT token / '=' token / End-of-line marker

Spectrum

```
200 PRINT "ASCII STRING"
300 LET A=1963.2:LET B=INT A
```

| 0 | 200 | 16 | 0 | 245 | 34 | 65 | 83 | 67 | 73 | 73 | 32 | 83 | 84 | 82 | 73 | 78 | 71 | 34 | 13 |

"   A   S   C   I   I   sp   S   T   R   I   N   G   "   CR

Line number / PRINT token / Length of program line plus EOL byte / End-of-line marker

Notice that the length of the line is expressed in two bytes rather than one, so that program lines longer than 255 characters are possible. Furthermore, note that the numerical constant 1963.2 is stored first in ASCII codes, and then in a special binary format. This improves program execution speed

| 1 | 44 | 22 | 0 | 241 | 65 | 61 | 49 | 57 | 54 | 51 | 46 | 50 | 14 | 139 | 117 | 102 | 102 | 102 | 58 | 241 | 66 | 61 | 186 | 65 | 13 |

A   =   1   9   6   3   .   2   :   B   =   A   CR

Line number / LET token / Length of program line plus EOL byte / 1963.2 in binary format / LET token / INT token / End-of-line marker

ASSEMBLY LINES

In this part of the Machine Code course, we summarise the main conventions used when dealing with memory, particularly: lo-hi addressing, tokenisation, and the importance of context. We also introduce some differences between Assembly language programs for the 6502 and Z80 microprocessors.

When you RUN a program, the first thing that the Operating System does is to inspect the Start of BASIC Text pointers in order to determine where in memory the program to be executed resides. But to do this, the Operating System has to store the pointers' addresses, so why doesn't the OS simply store the addresses to which they point?

The main reason is flexibility. The Operating System, you will remember, is a permanent program resident in the ROM, and any data that it contains (such as memory addresses) is similarly permanent. Suppose that different versions of the computer are released over a period of time, and that, although it was convenient to have the Start of BASIC Text at byte2048 in Version 1, it becomes necessary to relocate it at byte4096 in Version 2. This will mean that the later machine will not be able to use the Operating System of the earlier version because of the different locations of the BASIC Text Area. Furthermore, new ROMs would have to be developed for each new version of the machine, which is expensive; and software written for one version may not be able to be run on the other. If, however, the Operating System ROMs contain only the pointer addresses, then the same ones can be used for all versions of the machine and only the pointer contents need be changed from model to model. The location of the pointers themselves can remain constant because the Operating System requires a relatively small block of memory for workspace and data storage (typically about 1,000 bytes). Fixing the position of this block — usually the first four pages of memory — and designing or re-designing the system around it does not greatly constrain the design team. On the other hand, having the location of, say, the BASIC Text Area fixed (a block of 3,000 to 40,000 bytes) is a severe restriction.

STANDARD PRACTICE

It is conventional to store addresses in pointers in what is called *lo-hi* form. If byte43 and byte44, for example, are to point to the address 7671 (page 29, offset 247), then byte43 will contain 247 (the offset or lo byte of the address), while byte44 will contain 29 (the page or hi byte of the address).

This may seem confusing but it is convenient for the microprocessor. It is also logical in that the lo byte of the address is stored in the lo byte of the pointer, and correspondingly the address hi byte in the pointer hi byte.

If we repeat the above example using hex rather than decimal numbers, the great advantage of the hexadecimal system can be seen (from now on addresses and other numbers will always be written in hex prefixed by '$'). The pointer bytes are $2B and $2C, and the address to which they point is $1DF7. Therefore, $2B contains F7 (the address lo byte), while $2C contains $1D (the address hi byte). Notice that when the address is in hex the rightmost two hex digits are the lo byte, and the leftmost two digits are the hi byte, which makes much better sense than using decimal numbers.

It's worth remarking that the BBC and Spectrum are unusual in storing program line numbers as two-byte numbers in hi-lo rather than lo-hi form. It's true that these are program parameters rather than byte addresses, but they work against the usual convention, nonetheless.

Another convention of memory addressing is that pointers, although they are two-byte quantities, are often referred to by the address of the lo byte alone. We might say, for example, that byte43 in the Commodore 64 points to the Start of BASIC Text. It is understood here, however, that byte43 and byte44 together are the pointers.

Other things to consider include tokens (see page 76). The significance of these for machine code programmers is two-fold: they represent multi-character English commands (such as PRINT or RESTORE) by single-byte numerical codes; and they use offsets as well. A BASIC command is one word, but executing it is not a single operation for the Operating System. The command PRINT, for example, requires that the data to be printed be found in memory or evaluated, and then sent character-by-character to the screen in ASCII code. These various tasks are carried out by a subroutine of the BASIC interpreter program. When the interpreter encounters the PRINT token in a program line it uses the value of that token to locate and then execute the corresponding subroutine.

Suppose there are only three commands in our version of BASIC: INPUT, PRINT, and STOP; and these are assigned the tokens: $80, $81, and $82 respectively. Furthermore, let's say that the interpreter subroutines that execute these commands start at bytes $D010, $EA97, and $EC00 respectively, and that these three addresses are stored in lo-hi form in the six bytes from $FA00 to

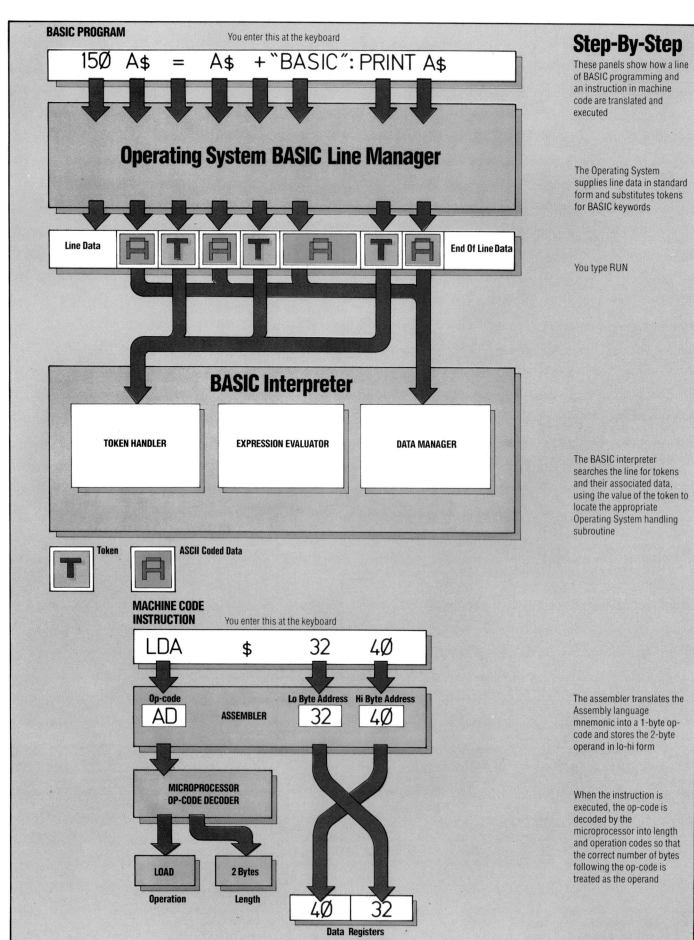

BASIC PROGRAM
You enter this at the keyboard

15Ø A$ = A$ + "BASIC": PRINT A$

Operating System BASIC Line Manager

Line Data | A T A T A T A | A T A | End Of Line Data

BASIC Interpreter

TOKEN HANDLER | EXPRESSION EVALUATOR | DATA MANAGER

T Token   A ASCII Coded Data

MACHINE CODE
INSTRUCTION
You enter this at the keyboard

LDA $ 32 4Ø

Op-code   ASSEMBLER   Lo Byte Address   Hi Byte Address
AD   32   4Ø

MICROPROCESSOR
OP-CODE DECODER

LOAD | 2 Bytes
Operation | Length

4Ø | 32
Data Registers

Step-By-Step

These panels show how a line of BASIC programming and an instruction in machine code are translated and executed

The Operating System supplies line data in standard form and substitutes tokens for BASIC keywords

You type RUN

The BASIC interpreter searches the line for tokens and their associated data, using the value of the token to locate the appropriate Operating System handling subroutine

The assembler translates the Assembly language mnemonic into a 1-byte op-code and stores the 2-byte operand in lo-hi form

When the instruction is executed, the op-code is decoded by the microprocessor into length and operation codes so that the correct number of bytes following the op-code is treated as the operand

KEVIN JONES

$FA05, giving us a table of three two-byte pointers. Now when our imaginary interpreter encounters a token — $81, for example — it proceeds to subtract $80 from it, multiplies the result by two, and adds that to $FA00. The final result in this case is $FA02, which is the lo byte of the pointer to the PRINT subroutine. If a token other than $81 had been encountered, then the algorithm described would have returned the pointer address for the corresponding subroutine. In this way the BASIC command PRINT is replaced by a token, $81, which is an offset to a table of pointers that direct the interpreter to the relevant part of its own program.

That's a measure of the 'distance' between BASIC, a so-called high-level language, and machine-code, the low-level language. BASIC looks comprehensible to us because it uses English language code words, algebraic logic and numbers and strings. When we replace the words by tokens, and the rest by ASCII codes, it begins to look a lot more like something a microprocessor can handle — and, as we've seen with tokens, that's almost exactly the case.

The final thing to consider about memory manipulation is the idea of *context*. We've seen in the BASIC Text Area the widespread use of codes — ASCII codes to represent characters and numbers, tokens to represent commands, and (in the Spectrum) special binary codes to represent numeric date (see page 132). All of these codes reduce to binary numbers in the range 00000000 to 11111111 ($00 to $FF, 0 to 255 decimal) contained in single bytes of memory, and interpreted according to their context. In the BASIC Text Area of the Commodore 64, for example, the BASIC program line:

200 rem*******left$*********

might have three bytes containing the decimal number 200 — once in the link address lo byte, once in the line number lo byte, and once in the token representation of 'left$'. Each byte looks the same as the others, yet means something different. It is only your expectations that tell you how to interpret that value in different places.

This is really where we came in, at the start of the Machine Code course. Then we said that everything stored in a computer is in some sort of machine code. Some of this was familiar (like ASCII codes), some unfamiliar (such as tokens), and some as yet unexplained (such as machine code programs). So let's now start looking at machine code programs themselves.

OPERATION CODES

Programs in machine code are sequences of bytes located anywhere in memory that are a mixture of instructions to the microprocessor, and data for the microprocessor to operate upon. As with all other bytes of memory, it is only the context that can separate the data bytes from the instruction bytes, so we must first consider the format of machine code program instructions.

A machine code instruction begins with a code that identifies the operation to be performed. This is called the *op-code,* or *opc,* and may be one or two bytes in length. The op-code may be a self-sufficient instruction requiring no data, but more usually it is followed by one or two bytes of data. A single byte of data is likely to be a numerical constant or an ASCII code, while two bytes of data following an op-code are always an address (always stored in lo byte/hi byte form). With the above definition we immediately come upon differences between microprocessors: the BBC Micro uses a MOS Tech 6502A, the Commodore 64 uses a MOS Tech 6510 (very similar to the 6502A, so in future we'll talk generally about the 6502 only), and the Spectrum has the Zilog Z80A. MOS Tech and Zilog developed their microprocessors at about the same time — the early 1970s — following the release by Intel of the first microprocessor in 1971. Both the 6502 and Z80 therefore share a design philosophy, but they differ sharply in detail. In particular, Z80 machine codes are completely different from 6502 machine codes. Thus, for example, 6502 op-codes are always one byte long, and may be followed by one or two data bytes or by none; but Z80 op-codes can be two bytes long, followed by one or two data bytes or by none.

When sent to the microprocessor, an op-code is decoded by the CPU's internal program into operation and length codes, and it is this latter information that enables the microprocessor to interpret the bytes following the opc. For example, to the 6502 the sequence of hex bytes:

A9 0E 8D 01 4E 60 44 52 41 54

represents three instructions, followed by four bytes of ASCII codes. This could be re-written as:

```
A9 0E
8D 01 4E
60
44
52
41
54
```

showing that the first instruction is opc A9, which is always followed by one data byte; the next instruction is opc 8D, which is always followed by two data bytes; while the next is opc 60 which requires no data and causes program execution to branch, so that the following data bytes are not examined by the processor at all. If the microprocessor is sent the first byte, A9, when it is expecting to receive an opc, then everything will function smoothly thereafter. The information in each opc will ensure that the correct number of data bytes for each opc is picked up by the processor, and the following byte will be treated as the next opc. If, however, the processor is expecting an opc and is sent the second byte, 0E, then it will treat this as an opc, with the result that the sequence will be interpreted thus:

```
0E 8D 01
4E 60 44
52
```

meaning: opc 0E, which takes two data bytes; then opc 4E, which also takes two data bytes; then opc 52, which isn't a legal opc, causing the equivalent of a syntax error in the processor. This demonstrates how an initial misunderstanding generates a series of gross logical errors in the program execution.

This also clearly shows some other important points about machine code: it really *is* unfriendly to the user (at least, in the beginning) in that it is difficult to read and write; it is highly sequential with nothing but the order differentiating one instruction from the next; and it is literal as only a machine can be, obeying wrong instructions as readily as it will correct ones, and rejecting only syntax errors.

Some of the unfriendliness can be avoided by writing alphabetic mnemonics instead of the numeric op-codes while the program is being developed, and only resorting to op-codes when the program is actually loaded into memory. These mnemonics constitute the processor Assembly language, and translating them into numerical op-codes is called assembly or assembling. Notice that there is a direct one-to-one correspondence between the set of Assembly language mnemonics, and the set of op-codes: although Assembly language is a higher-level language than machine code, the difference is minimal.

If we rewrite the machine code fragment above in 6502 Assembly language, then it looks like this:

```
0000 A9 0E      LDA #$0E
0002 8D 01 4E   STA $4E01
0005 60         RTS
```

while the same sequence of operations in Z80 Assembly language looks like this:

```
0000 3E 0E      LD A, $0E
0002 32 01 4E   LD ($4E01),A
0005 C9         RET
```

The first column shows the hex address in memory of the first byte of the line — the opc A9 in the 6502 list, for example, is in byte0; the page byte 4E in both lists is in byte4, and so on. The next column may contain one, two or three bytes, and shows the machine code listing. The third column starts with an Assembly language mnemonic, and shows the Assembly language version of the machine code. Don't bother trying to puzzle it all out now, it's enough that you've seen an Assembly language list, and can observe the differences and similarities between the Z80 and 6502 versions. You might also notice that the address in the second line appears in conventional lo-hi form in machine code, but 'normal' hi-lo form in Assembly language.

In the next instalment of the course we'll start to examine op-codes in detail, and take a look at the architecture of the microprocessor.

Hexadecimal Convertor

To convert the Mempeek program of page 129 so that byte contents are displayed in hexadecimal rather than decimal, make the following changes:

BBC Micro

Add:
```
3000 DEF PROCHXPRINT(DECNUM)
3100 LOCAL X$
3200 X$="0123456789ABCDEF"
3300 HB=INT(DECNUM/16):LB=DECNUM-HB*16
3400 B$=MID$(X$,HB+1,1)+MID$(X$,LB+1,1)+"    "
3500 PRINT B$;
3600 ENDPROC
```
and change line 600 to:
```
600 PROCHXPRINT(PK%)
```

Spectrum

Add:
```
10 LET X$="0123456789ABCDEF"
3000 REM******HEX BYTE S/R*******
3100 LET HB=INT (PK/16): LET LB=PK-HB*16
3200 LET B$=X$(HB+1)+X$(LB+1)+"    "
3300 PRINT B$;
3400 RETURN
```
and change line 600 to:
```
600 GOSUB 3000
```

Commodore 64

Add:
```
10 LET X$="0123456789ABCDEF"
3000 REM******HEX BYTE S/R*******
3100 HB=INT(PK/16):LB=PK-HB*16
3200 B$=MID$(X$,HB+1,1)+MID$(X$,LB+1,1)+"    "
3300 PRINT B$;
3400 RETURN
```
and change line 600 to:
```
600 GOSUB 3000
```

These changes will cause the contents of the memory to be displayed in hexadecimal. The start address and number of bytes should still be entered in decimal.

BYTE BY BYTE

At this stage in the Machine Code chapter we follow the full procedure of program development — from defining the initial task through its Assembly language interpretation to the machine code itself — and provide a BASIC program that enables you to enter and observe the results of the code thus created.

Throughout the course of this chapter, we have seen how BASIC program lines are reduced on entry to tokens followed by ASCII data. From this we realised that BASIC, although it is certainly a high-level language, isn't all that high-level: it consists essentially of sequences of instructions, and each instruction consists of a command word (immediately replaced by a token, which is itself only one level above a machine op–code) followed by the data for that command. The fact that the command words and their data (variables, numbers or strings) are closer to natural language, and that the instructions are visibly separated by line numbers or colons, makes a BASIC program look very much more high-level to us than it appears to the BASIC interpreter. It follows, therefore, that machine code should need only a little cosmetic work to make it reasonably comprehensible to our eyes.

The machine code 'cosmetic' that we use is Assembly language, in which alphabetic mnemonics like LDA and ADC stand for the single-byte op-codes that the microprocessor actually understands, and in which alphanumeric symbols such as LABEL1 and TFLAG can be used instead of memory addresses and numeric data. The microprocessor does not understand Assembly language, so before a program can be executed it must be translated into machine code — either by a program called an assembler, or manually by the programmer. The point of Assembly language is that it is machine code in translation. By simply substituting opcodes for mnemonics, and numbers for symbols, it can be turned directly into executable code. But it is much more comprehensible to human eyes than machine code could ever be, and is therefore extremely useful in program development. We shall always write programs in Assembly language, and hardly ever concern ourselves with the machine code equivalent until the very last stages of developing a program. But it's worth doing both at the moment for the sake of interest and for complete clarity, remembering that, in general, Assembly language will do everything we want.

The microprocessor can perform many different operations, but essentially it can only manipulate the contents of memory. It does this by acting directly on computer memory — the RAM and ROM chips that comprise tne computer system — or by working through its own internal memory, which consists of *registers*. These are several bytes of memory physically located inside the microprocessor chip, which have certain special functions, but are otherwise indistinguishable from any other bytes of memory.

ACCUMULATOR REGISTER

The most important of the microprocessor registers is called the *accumulator*. It is connected directly to the Arithmetic and Logic Unit, and so is used more often than any of the other registers. In order to use it we must be able to put information into it, a process which is called 'Loading the Accumulator'. Using Assembly language, we say that the 6502 does this by performing the LDA operation, and in the Z80 by the operation of LD A. Taking information *from* the accumulator is as essential as loading it, and in 6502 Assembly language this is achieved by the STA (STore the Accumulator contents) operation. The Z80, however, regards both loading and storing as different cases of the same thing — i.e. data transfer. Therefore, taking information from the accumulator register is also done by the LD A operation, but in a different format — as we'll see later in this article.

Suppose, then, that we want to write an Assembly language program that will copy the contents of one byte of memory into the next byte of memory. Let's start by copying byte$09FF into byte$0A00. Immediately, we can express this in Assembly language as:

6502	Z80
LDA $09FF	LD A,($09FF)
STA $0A00	LD ($0A00),A

Notice that we're copying the contents of byte$09FF into byte$0A00, without knowing what those contents are: it's vital to get this clear from the outset. Byte$09FF may contain any number from $00 to $FF, and all our program does is load that number into the accumulator, then transfer it from the accumulator to byte$0A00. The 6502 version of Assembly language does not make it clear that LDA refers to the *contents* of $09FF, but it does distinguish unequivocally between loading (LDA) and storing (STA). The Z80 version does not make this latter distinction in its opcodes, but its instruction format is always:

OPCODE DESTINATION, (SOURCE)

This version encloses memory addresses in brackets when it means 'the contents of', which reinforces the vital distinction between the address of a byte and what it contains.

The Assembly language program we have given is logically complete, but we shall execute it as a subroutine, so it needs the equivalent of the RETURN command (to refer the program back from the subroutine) to complete it. The opcodes are RTS in 6502, and RET in Z80.

If we are to use this subroutine, we must first translate it into machine code, then store the code somewhere in memory, and cause the microprocessor to execute it. We can use the Monitor program (on page 139) for the latter two tasks; but before that we must first do the translation and decide where the code is to go. This is an unfamiliar decision to BASIC programmers, who never have to think where a BASIC program will be stored — they just type it and RUN it. The storage decisions are made for the programmer by the system designers, and implemented by the operating system.

A machine code program can be stored and executed anywhere in memory, but some places are better than others. The safe places differ from machine to machine, hence the different versions of the program that follow:

6502

Location Address	Machine Code	Assembly Language
COMMODORE 64		
$0350	AD 56 03	LDA $0356
$0353	8D 57 03	STA $0357
$0356	60	RTS
BBC MICRO		
$0070	AD 76 00	LDA $0076
$0073	8D 77 00	STA $0077
$0076	60	RTS

Z80

Location Address	Machine Code	Assembly Language
16K SPECTRUM		
$7FA0	3A A6 7F	LD A,($7FA6)
$7FA3	32 A7 7F	LD ($7FA7),A
$7FA6	C9	RET
48K SPECTRUM		
$FFA0	3A A6 FF	LD A,($FFA6)
$FFA3	32 A7 FF	LD ($FFA7),A
$FFA6	C9	RET

Notice that each version of the program copies its own last byte into the byte that comes after it. The Spectrum 48K program, for example, copies the contents of $FFA6 into $FFA7. Notice also that addresses appear in hi-lo form in Assembly language (for our benefit), but lo-hi form in the machine code translation. A special note should be made that in Z80 the mnemonic is LD in both the first and second instructions, but that the opcodes differ: 3A for the data transfer to the accumulator, and 32 for the transfer from the accumulator.

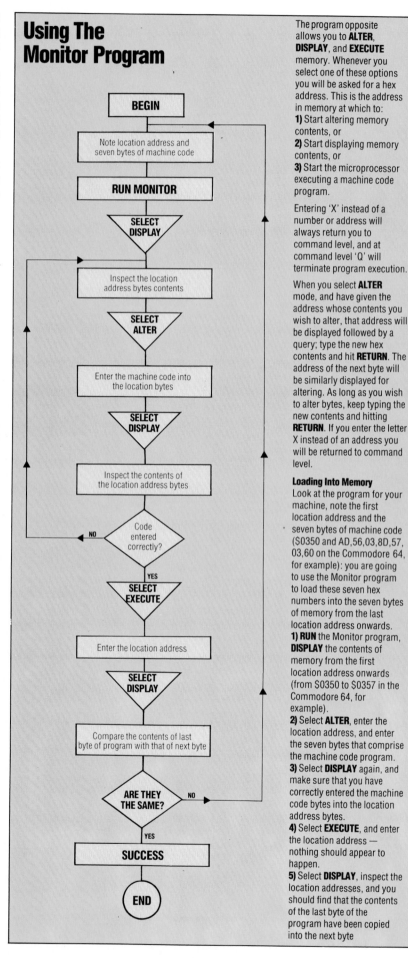

Using The Monitor Program

BEGIN

Note location address and seven bytes of machine code

RUN MONITOR

SELECT DISPLAY

Inspect the location address bytes contents

SELECT ALTER

Enter the machine code into the location bytes

SELECT DISPLAY

Inspect the contents of the location address bytes

Code entered correctly? — NO

YES

SELECT EXECUTE

Enter the location address

SELECT DISPLAY

Compare the contents of last byte of program with that of next byte

ARE THEY THE SAME? — NO

YES

SUCCESS

END

The program opposite allows you to **ALTER**, **DISPLAY**, and **EXECUTE** memory. Whenever you select one of these options you will be asked for a hex address. This is the address in memory at which to:
1) Start altering memory contents, or
2) Start displaying memory contents, or
3) Start the microprocessor executing a machine code program.

Entering 'X' instead of a number or address will always return you to command level, and at command level 'Q' will terminate program execution.

When you select **ALTER** mode, and have given the address whose contents you wish to alter, that address will be displayed followed by a query; type the new hex contents and hit **RETURN**. The address of the next byte will be similarly displayed for altering. As long as you wish to alter bytes, keep typing the new contents and hitting **RETURN**. If you enter the letter X instead of an address you will be returned to command level.

Loading Into Memory
Look at the program for your machine, note the first location address and the seven bytes of machine code ($0350 and AD,56,03,8D,57, 03,60 on the Commodore 64, for example): you are going to use the Monitor program to load these seven hex numbers into the seven bytes of memory from the last location address onwards.
1) **RUN** the Monitor program, **DISPLAY** the contents of memory from the first location address onwards (from $0350 to $0357 in the Commodore 64, for example).
2) Select **ALTER**, enter the location address, and enter the seven bytes that comprise the machine code program.
3) Select **DISPLAY** again, and make sure that you have correctly entered the machine code bytes into the location address bytes.
4) Select **EXECUTE**, and enter the location address — nothing should appear to happen.
5) Select **DISPLAY**, inspect the location addresses, and you should find that the contents of the last byte of the program have been copied into the next byte

Spectrum Monitor Program

```
48 REM++++++++++++++++++++
49 REM+                    +
50 REM+   HCAC MONITOR 1   +
51 REM+ ----SPECTRUM------ +
52 REM+ SAVE THIS PROGRAM  +
53 REM+ BEFORE YOU RUN IT  +
54 REM+                    +
55 REM++++++++++++++++++++
100 GOSUB 1000   :REM *INIT*
200 CLS
300 PRINT " ** HCAC MONITOR 1 CO
MMANDS **"
400 FOR P=1 TO LT:PRINT O$(P):NE
XT P
500 FOR Z=0 TO 1 STEP 0
550 GOSUB 2000   :REM *INPUT*
600 GOSUB (4500+CM*500)
650 NEXT Z
700 STOP
750 REM++++END MAIN PROG++++
1000 REM*****INIT  S/R******
1050 LET LT=4:DIM C$(LT):DIM O$(
LT,24):DIM X$(16)
1100 LET X$="0123456789ABCDEF"
1150 LET C$="ADGQ":LET C1=-48:LE
T C2=10-CODE(C$(1))
1200 LET O$(1)="      A - ALTER
 MEMORY"
1220 LET O$(2)="      D - DISPLA
Y MEMORY"
1240 LET O$(3)="      G - EXECUT
E M/CODE"
1260 LET O$(4)="      Q - EXIT
 PROGRAM"
1300 RETURN
2000 REM*****INPUT S/R******
2100 FOR P=0 TO 1 STEP 0
2150 PRINT:PRINT"COMMAND ??"
2190 IF INKEY$<>"" THEN GO TO 21
90
2200 LET A$=INKEY$:IF A$="" THEN
 GO TO 2200
2250 FOR J=1 TO LT
2300 IF A$=C$(J) THEN LET CM=J:L
ET J=LT:LET P=2
2350 NEXT J:NEXT P:IF A$="Q" THE
N RETURN
2400 PRINT O$(CM)
2450 FOR P=0 TO 1 STEP 0
2500 INPUT"HEX ADDRESS (X=QUIT)"
;A$
2550 GOSUB 5200 :REM CHK&ADJ
2600 NEXT P:IF A$="X" THEN LET C
M=0
2650 RETURN
3000 REM****HEX BYTE S/R****
3010 LET HB=INT(N/16):LET LB=N-H
B*16
3020 LET B$=X$(HB+1)+X$(LB+1)
3030 RETURN
3100 REM*****D-H   S/R******
3110 IF NM<256 THEN LET N=NM:GOS
UB 3000:LET H$="00"+B$:RETURN
3120 LET HI=INT(NM/256):LET LO=N
M-256*HI
3130 LET N=HI:GOSUB 3000:LET H$=
B$
3140 LET N=LO:GOSUB 3000:LET H$=
H$+B$
3150 RETURN
4000 REM*****H-D   S/R******
4050 LET RX=1:LET DN=0:LET HL=LE
```

```
N(H$):IF (HL<1) OR (HL>4) THEN L
ET DN=-1:RETURN
4100 FOR H=HL TO 1 STEP -1
4150 LET D$=H$(H)
4200 LET V=CODE(D$)+C1*(D$>="0"
AND D$<="9") + C2*(D$>="A" AND D
$<="F")
4250 IF V>15 THEN LET DN=-1:LET
H=1:NEXT H:RETURN
4300 LET DN=DN+V*RX:LET RX=RX*16
4350 NEXT H:RETURN
4500 REM****DUMMY S/R*****
4550 RETURN
5000 REM****ALTER S/R*****
5020 FOR P=0 TO 1 STEP 0
5040 PRINT A$;:INPUT"NEW HEX VAL
UE (X=EXIT) ?";V$
5050 PRINT V$
5060 GOSUB 5340 :REM CHK&OBY
5080 NEXT P:RETURN
5200 REM*CHECK&ADJUST S/R**
5220 IF A$="X" THEN LET P=2:RETU
RN
5240 LET LL=LEN(A$):IF LL>4 THEN
 RETURN
5260 LET H$=A$:GOSUB 4000
5280 IF DN>=0 THEN LET P=2:LET N
M=DN
5300 LET A$=A$+"   ":IF LL<4 THEN
 LET A$="0000"(TO 4-LL)+A$
5320 RETURN
5340 REM**CHECK & OBEY S/R*
5360 IF V$="X" THEN LET P=2:RETU
RN
5380 LET H$=V$:GOSUB 4000
5400 IF (DN<0) OR (DN>255) THEN
RETURN
5420 POKE NM,DN
5440 LET NM=NM+1:IF NM>65535 THE
N LET P=2:RETURN
5460 GOSUB 3100    :REM D-H S/R
5480 LET A$=H$+"  ":RETURN
5500 REM****DISPLAY S/R******
5520 FOR P=0 TO 1 STEP 0
5540 INPUT"DEC.NO.OF BYTES(X=QUI
T)";N$:IF N$="X" THEN LET P=2:NE
XT P:RETURN
5560 LET BN=VAL(N$):IF (BN>0) AN
D (BN+NM<65536) THEN LET P=2
5580 NEXT P
5600 FOR B=NM TO (NM+BN-1) STEP
4
5620 LET L$="":LET NM=B:GOSUB 31
00
5640 PRINT H$;TAB(6);
5660 FOR C=0 TO 3
5680 LET N=PEEK(B+C):LET K$="."
5700 GOSUB 3000 :REM D-H S/R
5720 PRINT TAB(6+4*C);B$;
5740 IF N=0 THEN LET K$="■"
5760 IF (N>31) AND (N<128) THEN
LET K$=CHR$(N)
5780 LET L$=L$+K$
5800 NEXT C
5820 PRINT TAB(26);L$
5840 NEXT B:RETURN
6000 REM*****EXECUTE S/R****
6050 RANDOMIZE USR(NM):RETURN
6500 REM*****EXIT S/R******
6550 PRINT TAB(5);"■■■■END OF PR
OGRAM■■■"
6600 LET Z=2:RETURN
```

BBC Micro

```
39 REM********************
40 REM*   HCAC MONITOR 1   *
41 REM* ---------BBC------- *
42 REM* CHANGE THE SPECTRUM *
43 REM*  VERSION AS FOLLOWS: *
44 REM*                     *
45 REM*  REPLACE CODE( BY ASC( *
47 REM*                     *
50 REM* ADD,CHANGE,OR DELETE *
51 REM*      AS DIRECTED:    *
52 REM*                     *
53 REM********************
60 *TV 255
70 MODE 7
200 CLS
600 ON CM GOSUB 5000,5500,6000,6500
1050 LT=4:DIM C$(LT),O$(LT)
1150 C$(1)="A":C$(2)="D":C$(3)="G":C$(4)
="Q":C1=48:C2=ASC(C$(1))-10
2190 ----------DELETE----------
3020 B$=MID$(X$,HB+1,1)+MID$(X$,LB+1,1)
4150 D$=MID$(H$,H,1)
4500 ----------DELETE----------
4550 ----------DELETE----------
5050 ----------DELETE----------
5300 A$=A$+"   ":IF LL<4 THEN A$=LEFT$("0
000",4-LL)+A$
5420 ?(NM)=DN
5680 N=?(B+C):K$="."
5740 IF N=13 THEN K$=CHR$(255)
6050 CALL NM:RETURN
6600 Z=2:RETURN
```

Commodore 64

```
49 REM********************
50 REM*   HCAC MONITOR 1   *
51 REM* ---------CBM------- *
52 REM* CHANGE THE SPECTRUM *
53 REM*  VERSION AS FOLLOWS: *
54 REM*                     *
55 REM*  REPLACE ALL INSTANCES *
56 REM*  OF:"LET P=2" BY "P=1" *
57 REM*                     *
58 REM*  REPLACE CODE( BY ASC( *
59 REM*                     *
60 REM*  AND CHANGE OR DELETE *
61 REM*      AS DIRECTED:    *
62 REM*                     *
63 REM********************
200 PRINT CHR$(147);CHR$(142)
600 ON CM GOSUB 5000,5500,6000,6500
1050 LT=4:DIM C$(LT),O$(LT)
1150 C$(1)="A":C$(2)="D":C$(3)="G":C$(4)
="Q":C1=48:C2=ASC(C$(1))-10
2190 ----------DELETE----------
3020 B$=MID$(X$,HB+1,1)+MID$(X$,LB+1,1)
4150 D$=MID$(H$,H,1)
4500 ----------DELETE----------
4550 ----------DELETE----------
5050 ----------DELETE----------
5300 A$=A$+"   ":IF LL<4 THEN A$=LEFT$("0
000",4-LL)+A$
5740 IF N=0 THEN K$=CHR$(122)
6050 SYS(NM):RETURN
6600 Z=2:RETURN
```

This program will enable you to display the contents of memory, alter the contents of memory and execute a stored machine code program

MEMORY SPACE

At this stage in the course, we look at ways of finding or reserving space in memory to store our machine code programs. We also take our first look at how we can perform a simple arithmetic task by using machine code instructions to manipulate the contents of the accumulator register in the Central Processing Unit.

In the last instalment of the Machine Code course, we developed a very simple Assembly language program, translated (assembled) it into machine code, loaded it into memory and executed it. We used the Monitor program on page 139 for the latter two tasks. If the program was a more sophisticated package containing an assembler, we could have used it for assembling our machine code program as well. At this stage in the course, it's no great hardship to do the assembly by hand — indeed, it's very educational. But once you've grasped the principles of the process, and as your Assembly language programs get longer, there won't be any point in concerning yourself with the actual machine code translation. In fact, with larger programs, assembling by hand gets very tedious, and is prone to error. Consequently, when you reach this stage in learning machine code, you may want to acquire an assembler program suitable for your machine.

There were many significant points about using the short machine code program that we gave (see page 138). We used one of the CPU registers to manipulate memory, we had to decide where in memory to store the machine code, and we caused the microprocessor to execute it. These are all aspects of Assembly language programming that particularly puzzle a beginner, and it's worth looking at them more closely. Let's start with the question of where to store the machine code.

To the CPU the only difference between one byte of memory and the next is whether they're read-write memory (RAM), or read-only memory (ROM). ROM chips contain system programs and data that must be protected from accidental or deliberate overwriting, and therefore can only be read. ROM can't be written to, so we can't load a machine code program into ROM. Those areas of memory apart, there's theoretically nothing to stop us loading a program into any other part of memory, but there are practical considerations that prevent us using some areas.

The CPU uses certain sections of RAM for temporary storage in the course of its operations, and if we load a program there, then either it will simply be corrupted by the CPU's overwriting it, or (and this is more likely) the CPU will read our machine code as if it were some of its own data. The operating system also uses large parts of RAM for storing its working data, and for running the computer system. Loading machine code programs (or anything else for that matter) into any of these areas would be unwise or impossible for the same reasons that prohibit use of the CPU's workspace. Furthermore, BASIC programs can take up all the remaining RAM — partly as program text and partly as variable storage areas. Once again, it's unwise to tamper with these areas, and so the programmer

KEVIN JONES

Small System Architecture

A typical computer system, in its most schematic form, comprises memory and a CPU. The former is made up of ROM chips (containing system programs), RAM chips, and specialist chips dedicated to input/output operations.

Data and control signals flow into and out of the CPU and around the system along *buses*. These are routes — very similar to ribbon cables — which can carry a byte or more of data at a time. These buses may be uni-directional like the *address bus*, which only transmits in one direction, or bi-directional like the *data bus*, which can transmit in either direction. The *control bus* carries switching information around the system, opening and closing logic gates to direct the flow of data. The *address bus* carries a 16-bit address from the CPU to select one byte of memory, allowing data to flow along the eight-bit *data bus* into or out of the byte is faced with an apparently insoluble dilemma.

One answer is not to use BASIC at all, freeing areas like the BASIC Program Text Area. But it's usually convenient to write at least part of a program in BASIC, using machine code subroutines only where BASIC is too slow — animating screen displays, for instance. If BASIC and machine code programs are to coexist in RAM, then we must steal some space and designate it for machine code. We can move the boundaries of the BASIC Program Text Area, or we can find temporarily unused sections of it or of the operating system RAM.

Moving BASIC's boundaries is very easy on the BBC Micro, since these addresses are held in the system variables PAGE, TOP, LOMEM and HIMEM. PAGE, for example, points to the start of the BASIC Program Text Area — which is usually at address $1200. If we execute the instruction:

    PAGE=PAGE+500

then the operating system will store BASIC programs 500 bytes higher in memory, leaving a 500-byte area free for our machine code programs. The same effect on the other machines is achieved by POKEing higher addresses into the system pointers (see the memory maps on page 58). Alternatively, we could reserve space by lowering the address of the top of the BASIC Program Text Area. On the Spectrum, the command CLEAR followed by an address does exactly that. The only constraint on the amount of space stolen from BASIC in this way is that there will be enough space left for our BASIC program.

Small blocks of free space can be found in the operating system RAM, a typical example of which is the cassette buffer of the Commodore 64. This consists of 192 bytes of RAM (from $033C to $03FB) and is used by the operating system only when the cassette drive is employed. Many programmers find that this space alone meets all their machine code needs.

Even smaller blocks of space can be found within BASIC programs — REM lines, for example.

CPU Internal Organisation

The Z80 has a more complicated structure than the 6502. Registers are used as work space RAM in the CPU's operations, or for specific tasks such as controlling the stack, holding the address of the next program instruction, showing the effects of the last CPU operation, or holding addresses.

Both CPUs have an eight-bit accumulator connected to the ALU where arithmetic and logic operations are performed, but the Z80 also supports some 16-bit arithmetic in its paired registers (known as BC, DE, and HL).

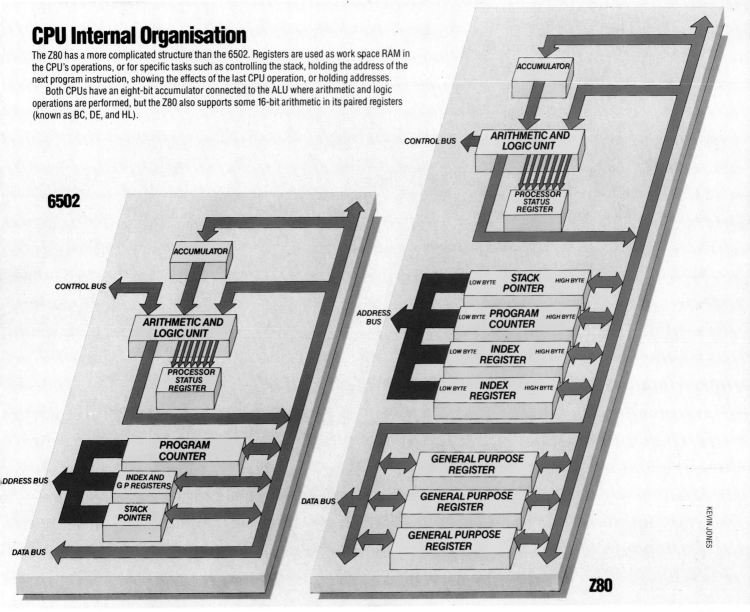

KEVIN JONES

In the BASIC Program Text Area this line:

    10 REM************************

has 25 consecutive bytes containing $2A, the ASCII code for '*'. These bytes are never inspected by the operating system or the BASIC interpreter because to them the command REM means 'ignore the rest of this line'. Once the line has been entered into a program in this form, a machine code subroutine can be loaded into the asterisk bytes, where it will reside untroubled by the interpreter. The big advantage of this apparently messy method (often used in programs for the expanded ZX81) is that when you SAVE, and subsequently LOAD, the BASIC program, then the machine code subroutine goes along with it. Using the other methods described usually means having to save the machine code separately from the BASIC program. The trouble with this method is that LISTing the line causes the operating system to interpret the machine code bytes as ASCII character data, which may corrupt the screen display. This explains why there were warnings embedded in the Demonstration programs on page 19 for the BBC Micro and the Spectrum. The Commodore 64 version of that program loads the machine code subroutine into the cassette buffer, whereas the BBC and Spectrum versions load it into their opening REM line — hence the warnings about not LISTing these versions of the program.

Once you've written an Assembly language program, assembled it into machine code, and LOADed it into the RAM of your choice, then you can proceed to execute it. This is done through the BASIC commands CALL (BBC only), SYS (Commodore 64 only) or USR (all three machines). Each of these commands is followed by the address of the first byte of the machine code program, wherever it's stored. All three commands mean the same thing to the interpreter: 'execute the machine code program starting at the address given, and return to execute the next BASIC instruction when the RET or RTS op-code is executed'. It is similar to the GOSUB command in BASIC.

In the last instalment we wrote a program to copy one byte's contents into another byte by loading the accumulator with the contents from one address, and then storing the accumulator's contents in the other address. This illustrates the centrality of the CPU's role in the entire system: data and control must flow from memory, through the CPU, and back to memory. Whereas in BASIC we can write LET X=Y (meaning 'copy the contents of Y directly into X'), in Assembly language we have to copy into the CPU from memory, then out of the CPU back into memory. The CPU registers (see the accompanying panel) are the bytes of RAM inside the CPU itself where data from memory is stored or manipulated. Both the Z80 and the 6502 have a register called the *accumulator*, which is referred to by a majority of the Assembly language instructions, and is the register in which arithmetic is chiefly done.

Suppose we want to add the two numbers $42 and $07 (remember that the symbol $ means the number is hexadecimal). We simply put one of them into the accumulator, and add the other in on top of the first — their sum will literally 'accumulate' in the register. Here are the instructions to perform this:

Z80		6502	
LD	A,$42	LDA	#$42
ADC	A,$07	ADC	#$07

Here the Z80 instructions both refer to the numbers to be loaded and added, whereas in the 6502 version the numbers are preceded by #, which shows that they are actual numbers rather than addresses. Thus, LDA #$65 means 'load the number $65 into the accumulator', whereas LDA $65 means 'load the contents of the byte whose address is $65 into the accumulator'. Similarly, the add instruction, ADC (it happens to be the same mnemonic in both Z80 and 6502) means in this case: 'add an actual number into the accumulator'. The numbers $42 and $07 are said to be 'immediate data', and LDA #$42 may be read as 'load the accumulator with the immediate data #$42'.

After these two instructions have been executed, the sum of the numbers will be contained in the accumulator. It is 'invisible' to us there, so we must store the accumulator contents in a byte of RAM where it can be inspected. The program must end with a return instruction, and must begin with an instruction to put an associated CPU register into the correct state, so the full programs read as:

Z80	
Machine Code	**Assembly Language**
A7	AND A
3E 42	LD A,$42
CE 07	ADC A,$07
32 ?? ??	LD BYTE1,A
C9	RET
6502	
18	CLC
A9 42	LDA #$42
69 07	ADC #$07
8D ?? ??	STA BYTE1
60	RTS

We won't bother about the meaning of the first instruction in either program at the moment, but notice that the fourth instruction contains the symbol BYTE1, rather than an actual address. The value of BYTE1 will be different from machine to machine, so we'll just use the symbol here, and replace it by a real hex number when we come to assemble the code.

Now we must decide where to locate the machine code, and what address BYTE1 represents. Choose a place to store the machine code and then make BYTE1 equal to the address of the byte after the end of the program, and put that address in lo-hi form into the machine code. After that use the Monitor program on page 139 to load and execute the machine code, and to inspect the byte where the result — $49 — should be stored.

STARTING ORDERS

When a program has been written in its Assembly language form, the machine code programmer must provide directives for the assembler at the beginning of the assembly. We look at several of these 'assembler directives' to see what functions they perform. These instructions may be used with both processors.

In the last instalment of the course, we wrote a simple machine code program that added two numbers into the accumulator and stored the result in memory. There was nothing very startling about what the program did, but, in writing it, we covered many points of significance to the machine code programmer. Let's look at the program again, with location addresses included, as if it were to be loaded at $0000, and the accumulated result to be stored at address $0009. (This is purely for example's sake: any attempt to use these particular locations would almost certainly result in an unrecoverable crash). The two versions of the program are:

Location Address	Machine Code	Assembly Language	
Z80			
0000	A7	AND	A
0001	3E 42	LD	A,$42
0003	CE 07	ADC	A,$07
0005	32 09 00	LD	BYTE1,A
0008	C9	RET	
6502			
0000	18	CLC	
0001	A9 42	LDA	#$42
0003	69 07	ADC	#$07
0005	8D 09 00	STA	BYTE1
0008	60	RTS	

Note that the fourth instruction (which stores the accumulator contents at $0009) in both programs does not specify a destination address in the Assembly language column. Instead, it uses a symbolic address, BYTE1. In the machine code version of the instruction, however, we see the op-code for 'transfer the accumulator contents' followed by 09 00, the two-byte lo-hi form of the address $0009.

This is another aspect of the translation (or assembly) process from Assembly language to machine code. Just as we use reasonably meaningful instruction mnemonics (STA and RET, for example, instead of hex codes such as 8D and C9) because they make the programs easier for us to read and write, so we will often use symbols such as BYTE1 instead of unfriendly hex addresses or numbers like $0009. This is no different from

initialising variables with constants in a BASIC program, and the reasoning is exactly the same in both cases — the program is made more readable, the possibility of errors occurring when writing such numbers is reduced, and the program is made more easily manipulable. For example, changing the statement in which the constant value is assigned to the variable in the first place will cause the new value to be used throughout the program automatically, needing no further editing on the programmer's part.

This is easy to understand when talking about BASIC programming, but where in our Assembly language program is the equivalent of the BASIC statement LET BYTE1=$0009? At present there isn't any such instruction. When we actually come to assemble the Assembly language into machine code we must remember to do this ourselves. If, however, we were using an assembler program to do the assembly for us, then we could make such an assignment statement at the beginning of the program (we give the Z80 version of the program here, although these assembler directives may be used with both processors):

Z80				
0000		BYTE1	EQU	$0009
0000	A7		AND	A
0001	3E 42		LD	A,$42
0003	CE 07		ADC	A,$07
0005	32 09 00		LD	BYTE1,A
0008	C9		RET	

BYTE1 is placed in a column of its own, known as the label field, which we will say more about later. In the op-code field, a new mnemonic (EQU, standing for 'equate' or 'is to be set equal to...') is used; and, in the operand field, the value that is to be assigned to BYTE1 is given (in this case, $0009).

It is important to note that although EQU appears in the op-code field, and looks like a mnemonic, it isn't an Assembly language mnemonic and doesn't belong in either the Z80 or 6502 instruction sets. Such a mnemonic is called a *pseudo-op* or an *assembler directive*. EQU tells the assembler program that "whenever it finds the preceding alphanumeric symbol (BYTE1 in this case), it must replace it by the value that follows the directive ($0009 here)'. Remember that when we use an assembler program we write only the Assembly language program, either as a tape/disk file or directly at the keyboard, and then call the assembler program to turn it into a machine code program. The output of an assembler is usually a full Assembly listing like those we've been producing, plus the machine code program consisting simply of a string of hex

Where To Locate Machine Code Instructions

BBC Micro
In direct mode enter:
PRINT.~PAGE
this gives the hex address of the start of your reserved space. Then enter:
PAGE=PAGE+N
where N is the decimal number of bytes you wish to reserve

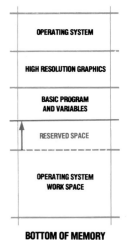

TOP OF MEMORY

OPERATING SYSTEM
HIGH RESOLUTION GRAPHICS
BASIC PROGRAM AND VARIABLES
RESERVED SPACE
OPERATING SYSTEM WORK SPACE

BOTTOM OF MEMORY

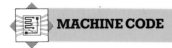

Spectrum

In direct mode enter:
LET RTOP=PEEK (23730) +
256*PEEK (23731)
LET RTOP=RTOP-N
PRINT "RTOP= ";RTOP
where N is the number of
bytes you wish to reserve for
your program. Your reserved
space starts at 1+RTOP

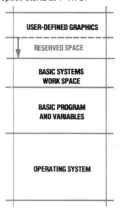

Commodore 64

Use the cassette buffer at
$033C to $03FB

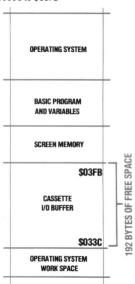

Warning
You must adjust these
memory pointers immediately
after turning on your machine
when there is no BASIC
program in memory

bytes. The machine code can be saved as a file for later use, or loaded immediately into memory for execution.

In performing the assembly for us, the assembler can be made to perform other tasks that we've been doing by hand — attaching the location addresses to each line of the program, for example. Another pseudo-op, ORG, does this for us. It is added to the program like this:

Z80				
0000			ORG	$A000
A000		BYTE1	EQU	$0009
A000	A7		AND	A
A001	3E 42		LD	A,$42
A003	CE 07		ADC	A,$07
A005	32 09 00		LD	BYTE1,A
A008	C9		RET	

Notice that the location address attached to the first line of the program is $0000, but the address of the following line is $A000, which reflects the effect of the ORG statement. Furthermore, notice that no machine code bytes appear on the lines containing pseudo-ops, precisely because they are not parts of the program and are not to be translated into machine code. Because they are features of the assembler program rather than elements of the CPU instruction set, pseudo-ops do differ from one assembler program to another. EQU, for example, is sometimes replaced by '=', and ORG by '.='. The effect is the same, however, and we shall continue to use ORG and EQU as if they were standard.

It may have occurred to you, while reading about assembler directives, that we've been using a pseudo-op almost from the start of the series: '$', the hex marker. This is no more than a directive to the assembler that what follows is to be treated as a hexadecimal number. Similarly, '#', introduced in the last instalment, is the 'immediate data' marker, signifying that what follows is an absolute quantity rather than a pointer or a symbol. Taking this a little further we could in fact regard Assembly language itself as no more than a series of pseudo-ops. Indeed, there's nothing to stop you inventing your own mnemonics for the machine code instruction set, provided they correspond one-to-one with that set. One very popular assembler program for the Vic-20 does just that: it uses a non-standard version of 6502 Assembly language, largely for the sake of formatting the Vic's 22-column screen.

In this course, we shall continue to use what we've been using so far — the Assembly language mnemonics published by the chip manufacturers — but it does no harm to be reminded from time to time that everything that we call machine code is symbolic. The CPU is indifferent to everything except voltage patterns on its input/output pins, so how we describe those patterns is entirely a matter of convention.

Having finished with pseudo-ops for the moment, let's return to inspecting our program for other points of interest. In particular, let's compare the translations here to the LDA and LD A

instructions with their translations in our earlier programs. Previously we wrote:

AD ?? ??	LDA $????	(6502)
3A ?? ??	LD A,($????)	(Z80)

meaning 'load the accumulator from the byte whose address is ????'. The load-the-accumulator op-code in translation is $AD (6502) and $3A (Z80). Compare this with the second line of the current program, which incorporates the instruction 'load the accumulator with the immediate value $42'. Here the op-codes are $A9 and $3E, for the 6502 and Z80 respectively. But why are they different? Possibly you've figured it out for yourself. Although we're doing the same class of operation (transferring data into the accumulator) in both programs, the source of that data differs. Therefore, to the CPU, they're different operations, and have different op-codes.

In the first version, data is to be loaded from a byte whose address is given. Nothing is stated or implied about the contents of that byte; the CPU is instructed simply to copy those contents into the accumulator. The three machine code bytes, AD ?? ?? and 3A ?? ??, are decoded by the CPU to mean 'interpret the two bytes following this op-code as the absolute address of the data source'.

In the second version, the data to be loaded into the accumulator is actually in the byte following the op-code, so the two machine code bytes, A9 42 and 3E 42, are decoded by the CPU to mean 'interpret the byte following this op-code as the data source'. Something in the op-code (A9 or 3E) tells the CPU to load the accumulator from the next byte. Since its program counter always contains the address of the next instruction to be executed, the CPU can calculate the address of the source byte, and then do a simple 'load the accumulator from an addressed byte' operation.

This reinforces the point that the operations of the CPU are mostly very simple, uncomplicated procedures. One whole class of its operations (about a fifth of its entire repertoire) consists of operations that involve copying data from an addressed byte into one or other of its internal registers. These 'primitive' operations all involve one task — to transfer data from memory to a CPU register — and all that distinguishes one instruction from another is the format in which the address of the source byte is presented.

Digging this deep into CPU micro-operations is potentially confusing at first, but well worthwhile for the unifying insights it brings later. Such insights are unnecessary if all you want to do is write Assembly language programs for the sake of speed and efficiency. To do that you need only pick up the idea, learn the instruction set, get a few programming tips, and start right in. If you want to understand what you're doing, however, you'll want to do more than just add another programming language to your range, and you'll find that understanding how one processor works makes learning other Assembly languages enormously easier and more interesting.

Assembly Exercise

1) In the box on the right, we have given the Assembly language version of a simple program. Assemble the program into machine code and determine the location addresses

2) What instruction is missing from this program?

3) What is the effect of the program on the registers and RAM concerned?

4) What does the term 'immediate data' mean? What other kinds of data could there be?

5) If BYTE1 in the program is treated as an address, on which page of RAM does it appear?

N.B. The values given in this program are for example only: if you wish to execute it, then you must choose locations and values suitable to your machine

Location Address	Machine Code	Assembly Language		
6502				
		START	EQU	$A000
		BYTE1	EQU	$45
		BYTE2	EQU	$38
			ORG	START
			LDA	#BYTE1
			CLC	
			ADC	#BYTE1
			STA	BYTE1
			ADC	#BYTE2
			STA	BYTE2
Z80				
		START	EQU	$A000
		BYTE1	EQU	$45
		BYTE2	EQU	$38
			ORG	START
			LD	A,BYTE1
			AND	A
			ADC	A,BYTE1
			LD	(BYTE1),A
			ADC	A,BYTE2
			LD	(BYTE2),A

The Effect Of Machine Code Instructions

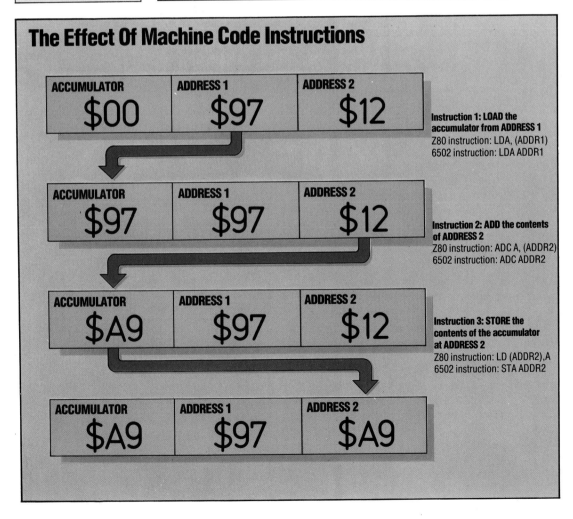

Instruction 1: LOAD the accumulator from ADDRESS 1
Z80 instruction: LDA, (ADDR1)
6502 instruction: LDA ADDR1

Instruction 2: ADD the contents of ADDRESS 2
Z80 instruction: ADC A, (ADDR2)
6502 instruction: ADC ADDR2

Instruction 3: STORE the contents of the accumulator at ADDRESS 2
Z80 instruction: LD (ADDR2),A
6502 instruction: STA ADDR2

The effect of data transfer instructions, such as LDA ADDR1 or LD (ADDR2),A, is always to copy the contents of the source location into the destination location. This location's contents are therefore overwritten; the source location is unaffected by the data transfer

STARTING FLAG

Having already used the add instruction in previous instalments of the course, we now begin to examine its implications in terms of methods of arithmetic, and the system architecture needed to support them. Here, we look more closely at the processor status register and its part in addition — in particular the role of the carry flag.

The add instruction in both Z80 and 6502 Assembly language is ADC — meaning 'Add With Carry' — a mnemonic of great importance for Assembly language programming. The concept of a 'carry' bit is of particular significance. Let's consider the addition of two hex numbers in the accumulator:

	A7	=		10100111
+	3E	=	+	00111110
	E5	=		11100101

Since the accumulator is an eight-bit register, both the numbers to be added and the sum itself must be in the range $00 to $FF (as they are here) or else they will not fit into the accumulator. Does this mean, therefore, that we are restricted to additions in which the sum is less than $100? Consider another addition in the accumulator, one which violates this restriction:

	FF	=		11111111
+	FF	=	+	11111111
	1FE	=		111111110

This shows the addition of the largest possible single-byte numbers, and seems to be an illegal addition. It requires a nine-bit accumulator. The solution to this dilemma is suggested in the statement of the problem — we need only an extra bit on the accumulator to contain the largest number that can be generated by the addition of single-byte numbers. That extra bit is required only in the sum, not in the addition operands, and it is required only when there is a 'carry' from the most significant bit of the accumulator.

PROCESSOR STATUS REGISTER

The extra bit is therefore known as the *carry bit*, and it is located in the eight-bit register associated with the accumulator known as the *processor status register* (PSR). This important register is connected to the accumulator and the ALU in such a way that individual bits of the PSR are set or cleared following any accumulator operation, depending on the results of that operation. The

contents of the process status register can be regarded as a simple number, but it is usually more informative to treat it as an eight-element array of binary flags, whose individual states show the particular effects of the last operation (a *flag* is any variable whose value indicates the state or truth-value of some condition, rather than being an absolute value. A flag variable usually has only two states or conditions: up or down, on or off, 0 or 1).

When any operation is performed on the accumulator that causes a carry out of the eighth bit, then the carry flag of the PSR will be set automatically to 1; an operation that does not cause a carry will reset (set to 0) the carry flag. This applies only to those operations that might legitimately cause a carry. Some operations, such as loading to or storing from the accumulator, do not affect the carry flag. Whenever we investigate a new Assembly language instruction in the course from now on, we shall want to know which of the PSR (or flag register) bits it affects. Naturally, we shall need to know more about the other PSR flags, but let's finish our discussion of the carry flag first.

In general, when adding two single-byte numbers we won't know in advance what they will be, so we have to be prepared for the sum of such an addition to exceed $FF; usually this will mean reserving two bytes of RAM to hold the result of an addition. Consider, again, the previous addition examples:

Hex Numbers		Carry Flag	Binary Numbers
A7	=		10100111
+ 3E	=		+ 00111110
00E5	=	0	11100101
		No Carry	
FF	=		11111111
+ FF	=		+ 11111111
01FE	=	1	111111110
		Carry	

The result of the addition is represented in both examples as a two-byte number. In the first case, the carry flag is reset to 0 because there is no carry out from the eighth bit of the sum (the two-byte result is $00E5, of which the hi-byte is $00). In the second case, however, there is a carry out from the eighth bit, so the carry flag is set, and the hi-byte of the result is $01.

To be sure of getting the correct result of an addition, therefore, we must store the accumulator contents in the lo-byte of the two-byte location, then store the carry flag as the hi-byte of that location. There is no single instruction for storing the carry flag, but the ADC op-code was formulated with precisely this operation in mind: ADC actually means 'add the instruction operand to the current contents of the carry flag, then add that result to the contents of the accumulator'. Addition is thus a two-stage process, in the first of which the current state of the carry flag is used, while in the second stage the state of the carry flag is updated.

This means, then, that before beginning an addition, we must consider the current state of the carry flag, since it will be added into the addition sum proper: hence the two unexplained instructions in previous instalments, CLC and AND A. The former, a 6502 instruction, means 'clear the carry flag', and does exactly that. The Z80 version, AND A, means 'logically AND the accumulator with itself'. While not designed solely to reset the carry flag it does have that effect and doesn't affect anything else, so is often used as a Z80 equivalent of the 6502's CLC.

Having cleared the carry flag before starting an addition, therefore, we must store its contents afterwards. This is achieved by adding the immediate value $00 to the hi-byte of the result. This won't affect the byte if the carry flag is clear, but will add 1 to it if the carry flag is set.

All of what we have said in this instalment leads to the first method for single-byte arithmetic:

1) Clear the carry flag
2) Load the accumulator with one number
3) Add in the second number
4) Store the contents of the accumulator in the lo-byte of a two-byte location
5) Load the accumulator with the contents of the hi-byte
6) Add in the immediate value $00
7) Store the contents of the accumulator in the hi-byte

When this procedure is turned into Assembly language we get:

COMMON TO BOTH PROCESSORS		
Label	Directive	Operand
BYTE1	EQU	$FF
BYTE2	EQU	$FF
LOBYTE	EQU	$A000
HIBYTE	EQU	$A001
	ORG	$A020

Z80		6502	
Op-code	Operand	Op-code	Operand
LD	A,$00	LDA	#$00
LD	(HIBYTE),A	STA	HIBYTE
AND	A	CLC	
LD	A,BYTE1	LDA	#BYTE1
ADC	A,BYTE2	ADC	#BYTE2
LD	(LOBYTE),A	STA	LOBYTE
LD	A,(HIBYTE)	LDA	HIBYTE
ADC	A,$00	ADC	#$00
LD	(HIBYTE),A	STA	HIBYTE
RET		RTS	

Remember that the values given for LOBYTE, HIBYTE and ORG are for example only — you must choose values appropriate to the machine that you use. Notice that the first two instructions of the program load $00 into HIBYTE, so that it's not corrupted by random data. We don't have to clear LOBYTE in the same way because its starting contents are overwritten with the lo-byte of the result.

It is worth remarking again about the differences of approach between Z80 and 6502 Assembly language as seen in the example. The 6502 code reads quite simply once you're used to it — the mnemonics themselves and the use of '#' to signal immediate data make the meaning of each instruction clear. The Z80 version is less straightforward because the LD mnemonic is used for all data transfers whether into or out of the accumulator. Also, there is no '#' symbol to signal immediate data, only the absence of brackets around the operand indicate this. Thus LD A,BYTE1 means 'load the accumulator with the immediate data BYTE1'; whereas LD A,(HIBYTE) means 'load the accumulator from the address HIBYTE'. In the full Assembly language listing there is no ambiguity in the meaning of such instructions, since the hex value of the op-code uniquely identifies the instruction. This may seem to beg the question, however — the op-code may be unique, but if there is a choice of unique op-codes, how does the assembler (or the person doing the assembly) choose between them? The answer lies in the Addressing Mode, which will be the topic of the next instalment.

Finally, we should take note that the processor status register contains other flags as well as the carry flag, which we'll examine briefly now, and return to in detail later in the course:

Z80 PSR:	S	Z		H		P/V	N	C
Bit Number	7	6	5	4	3	2	1	0
MSB								LSB
6502 PSR:	S	V		B	D	I	Z	C

PSR BIT	Z80	6502	PSR BIT
7	(S)=SIGN	(S)=SIGN	7
6	(Z)=ZERO	(V)=OVERFLOW	6
5	unused	unused	5
4	(H)=HALF-CARRY	(B)=BREAK	4
3	unused	(D)=BCD MODE	3
2	(P/V)=PARITY/OVERFLOW	(I)=INTERRUPT	2
1	(N)=SUBTRACT	(Z)=ZERO	1
0	(C)=CARRY	(C)=CARRY	0

For our present purposes the important flags are the carry, sign and zero flags. We have seen that after an addition the carry flag holds the value of the carry out of the eighth bit of the accumulator. The sign flag is always a copy of the eighth bit (bit 7) of the accumulator, and the zero flag is set to 1 if the accumulator contents are zero, and reset to 0 if the contents are non-zero.

Answers To Assembly Exercise On Page 145

1) The assembled programs are given in the box on the right.

Notice that the symbols BYTE1 and BYTE2 are used as both immediate symbolic data, and as symbolic addresses. When they are used as the latter, however, they need to be assembled in two-byte form.

2) The 'return from subroutine' instruction is missing from the end of both programs. In the 6502 version, the completed code would need to include the following line:

```
A00D              60              RTS
```

and the Z80 version needs this line:

```
A00D              C9              RET
```

3) The value $45 is first loaded into the accumulator register as immediate data, and then $45 is added on top of it, so that the accumulator contains the value $8A. This accumulated total is then stored in RAM at address $0045. The value $38 is then added into the accumulator as immediate data, so that the accumulator now contains the value $C2 ($45 + $45 + $38). This total is finally stored in RAM at location $0038.

4) 'Immediate data' is data that is actually stored in the instruction. In the instructions we gave in the exercise programs (such as LDA #$9C and LD A,$E4) the values $9C and $E4 are the data to be loaded into the accumulator. They are stored in the instructions of which they are operands, and comprise the contents of the byte immediately following the op-code. If data is not available, then it must be stored in some other part of memory, and be referred to by its address rather than its value.

5) The value of BYTE1 is given as $45, which properly written gives memory location $0045. Clearly, this address is on page zero of memory.

Exercise

We may wish to examine the contents of the processor status register (PSR), and it will be convenient to display this number as a binary rather than a hex byte. We include here the Spectrum version of a 'decimal-to-binary conversion subroutine'. This exercise asks you to patch this into the Monitor program on page 139.

```
7000 REM******BINARY BYTE S/R*******
7001 REM*CONVERTS A NUMBER N (<256)*
7002 REM*TO AN 8-CHARACTER BINARY  *
7003 REM*REPRESENTATION IN B$       *
7010 B$=""
7020 FOR D=8 TO 1 STEP-1
7030 LET N1=INT(N/2)
7040 LET R=N-2*N1
7050 LET B$=STR$(R)+B$
7060 LET N=N1
7070 NEXT D
7080 RETURN
```

Basic Flavours

On the Commodore 64, change line 7050 in the subroutine to:

```
7050 B$=MID$(STR$(R),2)+B$
```

Location Address	Machine Code	Assembly Language		
6502				
0000		START	EQU	$A000
0000		BYTE1	EQU	$45
0000		BYTE2	EQU	$38
0000			ORG	START
A000	A9 45		LDA	#BYTE1
A002	18		CLC	
A003	69 45		ADC	#BYTE1
A005	8D 45 00		STA	BYTE1
A008	69 38		ADC	#BYTE2
A00A	8D 38 00		STA	BYTE2
Z80				
0000		START	EQU	$A000
0000		BYTE1	EQU	$45
0000		BYTE2	EQU	$38
0000			ORG	START
A000	3E 45		LD	A,BYTE1
A002	A7		AND	A
A003	CE 45		ADC	A,BYTE1
A005	32 45 00		LD	(BYTE1),A
A008	CE 38		ADC	A,BYTE2
A00A	32 38 00		LD	(BYTE2),A

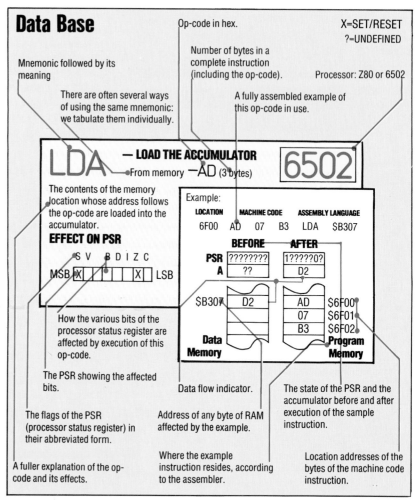

Data Base

Op-code in hex.

X=SET/RESET
?=UNDEFINED

Mnemonic followed by its meaning

Number of bytes in a complete instruction (including the op-code).

Processor: Z80 or 6502

There are often several ways of using the same mnemonic: we tabulate them individually.

A fully assembled example of this op-code in use.

LDA — LOAD THE ACCUMULATOR   6502

From memory —AD (3 bytes)

The contents of the memory location whose address follows the op-code are loaded into the accumulator.

Example:

LOCATION	MACHINE CODE	ASSEMBLY LANGUAGE
6F00	AD 07 B3	LDA $B307

EFFECT ON PSR

S V B D I Z C
MSB [X] [ ] [ ] [ ] [ ] [X] [ ] LSB

	BEFORE	AFTER
PSR	????????	1?????0?
A	??	D2

$B307 [D2] → [AD] $6F00
[07] $6F01
[B3] $6F02

Data Memory

Program Memory

How the various bits of the processor status register are affected by execution of this op-code.

The PSR showing the affected bits.

The flags of the PSR (processor status register) in their abbreviated form.

Data flow indicator.

Address of any byte of RAM affected by the example.

The state of the PSR and the accumulator before and after execution of the sample instruction.

A fuller explanation of the op-code and its effects.

Where the example instruction resides, according to the assembler.

Location addresses of the bytes of the machine code instruction.

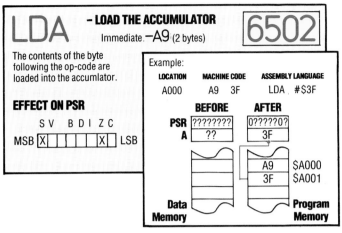

LDA — LOAD THE ACCUMULATOR
Immediate. —A9 (2 bytes) — 6502

The contents of the byte following the op-code are loaded into the accumulator.

EFFECT ON PSR

S V B D I Z C
MSB [X] [ ][ ][ ][ ][X][ ] LSB

Example:

LOCATION	MACHINE CODE	ASSEMBLY LANGUAGE
A000	A9 3F	LDA #$3F

BEFORE / AFTER
PSR ???????? → 0??????0?
A ?? → 3F

A9 $A000
3F $A001

Data Memory / Program Memory

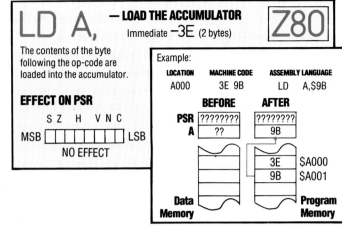

LD A, — LOAD THE ACCUMULATOR
Immediate —3E (2 bytes) — Z80

The contents of the byte following the op-code are loaded into the accumulator.

EFFECT ON PSR

S Z H V N C
MSB [ ][ ][ ][ ][ ][ ][ ][ ] LSB
NO EFFECT

Example:

LOCATION	MACHINE CODE	ASSEMBLY LANGUAGE
A000	3E 9B	LD A,$9B

BEFORE / AFTER
PSR ???????? → ????????
A ?? → 9B

3E $A000
9B $A001

Data Memory / Program Memory

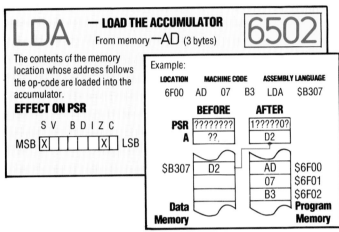

LDA — LOAD THE ACCUMULATOR
From memory —AD (3 bytes) — 6502

The contents of the memory location whose address follows the op-code are loaded into the accumulator.

EFFECT ON PSR

S V B D I Z C
MSB [X] [ ][ ][ ][ ][X][ ] LSB

Example:

LOCATION	MACHINE CODE	ASSEMBLY LANGUAGE
6F00	AD 07 B3	LDA $B307

BEFORE / AFTER
PSR ???????? → 1??????0?
A ?? → D2

$B307 D2

AD $6F00
07 $6F01
B3 $6F02

Data Memory / Program Memory

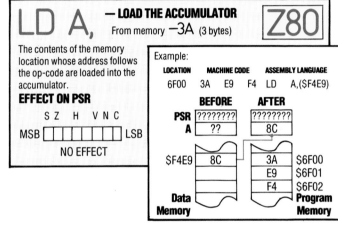

LD A, — LOAD THE ACCUMULATOR
From memory —3A (3 bytes) — Z80

The contents of the memory location whose address follows the op-code are loaded into the accumulator.

EFFECT ON PSR

S Z H V N C
MSB [ ][ ][ ][ ][ ][ ][ ][ ] LSB
NO EFFECT

Example:

LOCATION	MACHINE CODE	ASSEMBLY LANGUAGE
6F00	3A E9 F4	LD A,($F4E9)

BEFORE / AFTER
PSR ???????? → ????????
A ?? → 8C

$F4E9 8C

3A $6F00
E9 $6F01
F4 $6F02

Data Memory / Program Memory

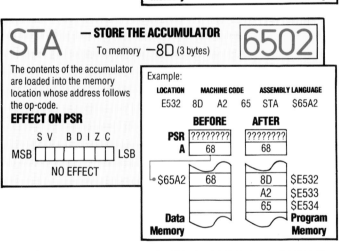

STA — STORE THE ACCUMULATOR
To memory —8D (3 bytes) — 6502

The contents of the accumulator are loaded into the memory location whose address follows the op-code.

EFFECT ON PSR

S V B D I Z C
MSB [ ][ ][ ][ ][ ][ ][ ] LSB
NO EFFECT

Example:

LOCATION	MACHINE CODE	ASSEMBLY LANGUAGE
E532	8D A2 65	STA $65A2

BEFORE / AFTER
PSR ???????? → ????????
A 68 → 68

$65A2 68 → 68

8D $E532
A2 $E533
65 $E534

Data Memory / Program Memory

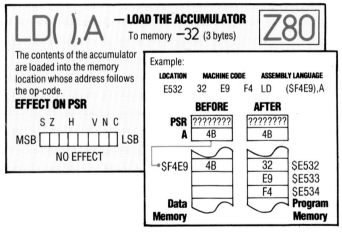

LD( ),A — LOAD THE ACCUMULATOR
To memory —32 (3 bytes) — Z80

The contents of the accumulator are loaded into the memory location whose address follows the op-code.

EFFECT ON PSR

S Z H V N C
MSB [ ][ ][ ][ ][ ][ ][ ][ ] LSB
NO EFFECT

Example:

LOCATION	MACHINE CODE	ASSEMBLY LANGUAGE
E532	32 E9 F4	LD ($F4E9),A

BEFORE / AFTER
PSR ???????? → ????????
A 4B → 4B

$F4E9 4B → 4B

32 $E532
E9 $E533
F4 $E534

Data Memory / Program Memory

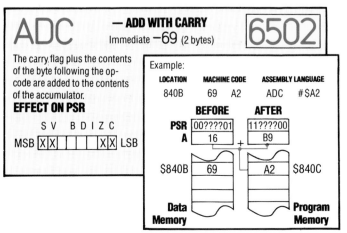

ADC — ADD WITH CARRY
Immediate —69 (2 bytes) — 6502

The carry flag plus the contents of the byte following the op-code are added to the contents of the accumulator.

EFFECT ON PSR

S V B D I Z C
MSB [X][X][ ][ ][ ][X][X] LSB

Example:

LOCATION	MACHINE CODE	ASSEMBLY LANGUAGE
840B	69 A2	ADC #$A2

BEFORE / AFTER
PSR 00???01 → 11????00
A 16 + → B9

$840B 69 → A2 $840C

Data Memory / Program Memory

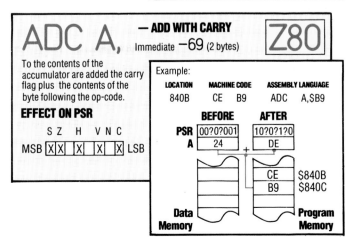

ADC A, — ADD WITH CARRY
Immediate —69 (2 bytes) — Z80

To the contents of the accumulator are added the carry flag plus the contents of the byte following the op-code.

EFFECT ON PSR

S Z H V N C
MSB [X][X][ ][X][ ][X][X] LSB

Example:

LOCATION	MACHINE CODE	ASSEMBLY LANGUAGE
840B	CE B9	ADC A,$B9

BEFORE / AFTER
PSR 00?0?001 → 10?0?1?0
A 24 + → DE

CE $840B
B9 $840C

Data Memory / Program Memory

MODES OF ADDRESS

The strength and versatility of Assembly language instructions is enhanced by the variety of ways in which these instructions can address memory. The different ways consist of direct, indirect and indexed addressing, and combinations of these. In this instalment we take a closer look at modes of addressing in machine code.

Every Assembly language instruction refers explicitly or implicitly to the contents of memory, and since one byte is distinguishable from another only by its address, every Assembly language instruction must, therefore, refer to at least one address. The manner in which an address is referred to may be direct and obvious, as in LDA $E349, which means 'load the accumulator with the contents of the address $E349'. In this case, both the accumulator (a byte with a name rather than a number for its address) and the address $E349 are mentioned unambiguously, and the nature of the relationship between them is clear.

On the other hand, the reference to an address may be much less obvious: RET, meaning 'return from a subroutine call', is a good example. This may not seem to refer to an address at all until you expand it into 'the location address of the next instruction to be executed is the place where the last subroutine call was made'. Here, the address whose contents are to be changed (i.e. the program counter — the register holding the address of the next instruction to be executed) is not mentioned, nor is the address at which its new contents (i.e. the new location address) are to be found. These two instructions can be seen as highly contrasting examples of addressing modes.

In the course so far we have seen instructions in two kinds of addressing mode: immediate mode, as in LD A,$45 or ADC #$31, and absolute direct mode, as in STA $58A7 or LD ($696C),A. These may seem like the 'natural' addressing modes, covering every possible case except the implicit modes such as RTS or RET, but there are other possibilities as well. We shall look at these separately.

ZERO PAGE ADDRESSING

Zero page addressing (also known as short addressing) is used whenever an instruction refers to an address in the range $0000 to $00FF. All addresses in this range have a hi-byte of $00, and therefore lie on page zero of memory. Such instructions need only two bytes — one byte for the op-code and one for the lo-byte of the address. When the CPU detects a single-byte

address at a point where it expects there to be two bytes, it assumes a hi-byte of $00, and so refers automatically to page zero. The advantage of this page zero mode is speed of execution: data on page zero is accessed significantly faster than data on any other page precisely because it requires only a single-byte address.

The Z80 and the 6502 microprocessors differ greatly in their use of the zero page mode. In 6502 Assembly language, any instruction that addresses RAM (such as LDA) can be used in the zero page mode, and all the 256 bytes of zero page are available to the CPU. In Z80 Assembly language, only one instruction — RST (the 'restart' or 'reset' instruction) — features the zero page mode, and it can address only eight specific page zero locations. Because the RST instruction is so specific in its addressing, it requires only a single-byte op-code (the address forming part of the op-code itself), which makes it very fast in execution. We will see more of the Z80 RST instruction later in the course because of the special uses to which it is put.

It may seem ridiculous to be comparing the speed of Assembly language instructions when the execution time of the slowest instruction is measured in microseconds anyway, but it isn't difficult to write Assembly language programs in which saving a microsecond per instruction execution can mean the difference between success and failure. Games programs featuring animated high-resolution three-dimensional colour graphics, for example, can involve millions of instructions per screen operation, and they must execute these commands as quickly as possible for the sake of smooth animation. Shaving a microsecond off one operation becomes very important when you put that operation inside a loop and execute it 64,000 times consecutively.

INDEXED ADDRESSING

Indexed mode is vital to Assembly language programming since it permits the construction of array-type data structures. Without such structures, programs are restricted to addressing memory locations individually by address: this is what we have done with all the programs so far in the course. Once indexing is possible, however, far more data can be handled, and more power is put at the programmer's disposal.

The essential elements of indexed mode are a base address and an index. Suppose we wish to keep a table of data — ASCII character codes, for example — in consecutive bytes. The base address of the table is the address of its first byte.

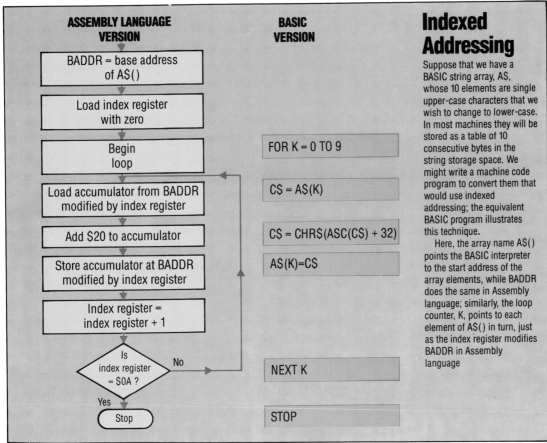

ASSEMBLY LANGUAGE VERSION

- BADDR = base address of A$( )
- Load index register with zero
- Begin loop
- Load accumulator from BADDR modified by index register
- Add $20 to accumulator
- Store accumulator at BADDR modified by index register
- Index register = index register + 1
- Is index register = $0A ? — No
- Yes
- Stop

BASIC VERSION

- FOR K = 0 TO 9
- C$ = A$(K)
- C$ = CHR$(ASC(C$) + 32)
- A$(K)=C$
- NEXT K
- STOP

Indexed Addressing

Suppose that we have a BASIC string array, A$, whose 10 elements are single upper-case characters that we wish to change to lower-case. In most machines they will be stored as a table of 10 consecutive bytes in the string storage space. We might write a machine code program to convert them that would use indexed addressing; the equivalent BASIC program illustrates this technique.

Here, the array name A$( ) points the BASIC interpreter to the start address of the array elements, while BADDR does the same in Assembly language; similarly, the loop counter, K, points to each element of A$( ) in turn, just as the index register modifies BADDR in Assembly language

LIZ DIXON

Given this, we can refer to every subsequent byte in the table by its position relative to the base address, so that the first byte is in position zero, the second byte is in position one, the third in position two, and so on. A byte's position relative to the table base address is called its index, and the absolute address of any byte in the table is calculated from the sum of the base address and the byte index. If we can construct a program loop in Assembly language, and use the loop counter as an index to the base address of the table, then we can address each byte of the table in sequence, just as we might access the elements of a BASIC array using a FOR..NEXT loop.

Once again, the Z80 and 6502 Assembly languages handle indexed addressing differently. The 6502 chip contains two single-byte registers called X and Y, each of which can hold an index that modifies a base address. This limits the length of a table to 256 bytes (the largest possible single-byte number). The Z80 chip contains two two-byte registers, IX and IY, which may hold the base address itself, and can then be incremented or decremented to point to successive bytes of the table. Since they are two-byte registers, IX and IY can address any byte addressable by the CPU itself. Their contents can also be modified by a single-byte index.

INDIRECT ADDRESSING

Indirect addressing involves the use of pointer addresses, a concept which was introduced early in the course, in relation to floating boundaries in memory (see page 128). Imagine that a group of people form a cinema club and that they meet every week to watch a film chosen by the club president. The film may be showing at any one of a dozen different cinemas, so when he has chosen the film for the week, the president writes details of the time and place on a postcard which he then sticks in the window of a shop in the centre of town. Club members don't know where the film will be from week to week, but they know where the shop is, and the shop 'points' them to the correct cinema. The address of the shop is, indirectly, the address of the cinema.

In indirect addressing mode it is possible to

IAN McKINNELL

Indicator Pointer
Examples of indirect addressing do not often appear in everyday life. However, in this photograph the train indicator board contains the actual data wanted by the traveller, so the sign telling him where to find the board indirectly addresses that data. Indirect addressing in an Assembly language instruction means that the address supplied in the operand contains the address of the byte where the data is stored; the operand address is a pointer

write instructions that contain the address of a pointer, and which operate on the contents of the location that the pointer indicates (not on the contents of the pointer itself). The advantages of this addressing mode are considerable, especially when combined with the indexed mode. Suppose, for example, that you write an Assembly language routine that searches a data table for a given character, and returns with the index position of the character. Suppose, also, that you want to keep several such tables in different places in memory, and that you want to use the same routine for searching any of them. If the routine is written so that it finds the base address of the search table indirectly via a given pointer location, then it can be used on any table provided that the contents of the pointer location are properly adjusted before the routine is called.

In general, programs require mixtures of these modes rather than pure examples of single modes. The 6502 instruction LDA, for example, can be used in the following modes:

Op-code	Operand	Mode
LDA	#$34	Immediate Mode
LDA	$A2	Zero Page Direct
LDA	$967F	Absolute Direct
LDA	$A2,X	Zero Page, Indexed by X
LDA	$967F,X	Absolute, Indexed with X
LDA	$967F,Y	Absolute, Indexed with Y
LDA	($A2,X)	Indirect, pre-indexed with X
LDA	($A2),Y	Indirect, post-indexed with Y

It is convenient to use a 6502 instruction in this example because it shows the combinations of addressing modes so clearly. Notice that the two indirect versions of the instruction are in zero page as well as indirect and indexed modes. A table such as this may seem confusing at first sight, but actually using the various modes soon makes their significance clear, and so far we have used both LDA and ADC in two modes — immediate and absolute — without confusion.

The table does answer the question posed in the last instalment of the course — how to tell the addressing mode of an instruction when the mnemonic is the same in every case? It can be seen that the format of the operand is different for every mode, and that the only ambiguity possible is whether an instruction such as LDA SYMB1 is zero page or absolute mode. An assembler program will resolve this for you, but if you are assembling the program by hand, you will have to determine whether SYMB1 has been defined as a single byte or as a two-byte quantity.

In general, once you start using an assembler,

you can forget about things like op-codes and the number of bytes per instruction, and concentrate on learning the programming techniques of Assembly language. It is important to understand the mechanics of machine code, but Assembly language used with a good symbolic assembler is a much better way of programming, combining the power of machine code with many of the facilities of high-level languages.

Answers to Exercise On Page 148

The Monitor program on page 139 was written in modules with expansion in mind, so adding a menu option is reasonably easy:

SPECTRUM VERSION
1) Adjust the initialisation by editing or adding the following lines:

```
1050 LET LT=5:DIM C$(LT):DIM O$(LT,24):DIM
     X$(16)
1150 LET C$="ADGQB":LET C1=-48:LET
     C2=10-CODE(C$(1))
1280 LET O$(5)="   B – BINARY DISPLAY"
```

2) The input routine at line 2000 has already elicited the start address, standardised it as a four-digit hex number in A$, and converted it to a decimal number in DN, so the binary display subroutine reads:

```
7000 REM**HEX&BIN DISP S/R**
7020 FOR P=DN TO (DN+15)
7040 LET NM=P:GOSUB 3100: PRINT H$,
7060 LET N=PEEK(P): LET NM=N
7080 GOSUB 3000: PRINT B$;" ";
7100 GOSUB 7300: PRINT B$
7120 IF P=65535 THEN LET P=DN+15
7140 NEXT P
7200 RETURN
7300 REM**BINARY BYTE S/R**
7310 LET B$=""
7320 FOR D=8 TO 1 STEP-1
7330 LET N1=INT(N/2)
7340 LET R=N-2*N1
7350 LET B$=STR$(R)+B$
7360 LET N=N1
7370 NEXT D
7380 RETURN
```

BBC/COMMODORE VERSION
Copy the Spectrum version, with the following amendments:
1) Change the initialisation of LT and O$() as in the Spectrum version above, and add C$(5)="B" to line 1150.
2) Line 600 transfers control to the command routine, so on the Commodore 64 and BBC Micro change this to:

```
600 ON CM GOSUB 5000,5500,6000,6500,7000
```

3) On the BBC change line 7060 above to

```
7060 N=?(P):NM=N
```

4) On the Commodore 64 change line 7350 above to:

```
7350 B$=MID$(STR$(R),2)+B$
```

COUNTER INSTRUCTIONS

Loops and conditional branches are implemented in Assembly language by using the processor status register flags to test the condition of the accumulator, and the relative jump instructions to change the flow of control in the program. These structures and the indexed addressing mode combine in creating data tables.

Before we can begin to use the various CPU addressing modes (especially indexed addresses) to advantage, we must first be able to write a loop. Without this fundamental structure we are in much the same position as a BASIC programmer who knows about arrays, but is ignorant of the FOR...NEXT command. There are no automatic structures like FOR...NEXT in Assembly language (though there is a Z80 instruction that is very close to it), but we can construct loops of the IF...THEN GOTO... type. These require instructions that make decisions or express conditions, and effectively change the order in which instructions are obeyed in the program.

Decision making in Assembly language centres on the flags in the processor status register. These flags show the effects on the accumulator of the last instruction executed, and are sometimes called *condition flags*. All these flags can be used in decision making, but we will need to consider only two of them at present — the zero (Z) and the carry (C) flags.

The state of these flags can be used to decide whether the processor executes the next instruction in the program, or whether it jumps to another instruction elsewhere in the program. The decision to continue or to jump is arrived at by the processor's either changing or accepting the address contained in its program counter. This register always contains the address of the next machine code instruction to be obeyed. When the processor begins to execute an instruction, it loads the op-code of the instruction from the byte pointed to by the address in the program counter. The address in the register is incremented by the number of bytes in the instruction so that the program counter then points to the op-code of the next instruction. If the current instruction causes the program counter to point to an address elsewhere in the program, then a jump is effectively generated.

On the 6502, the instruction BEQ causes the program counter to be changed if the zero flag is set. BCS is the equivalent instruction if the carry flag is set. On the Z80, these instructions are JR Z and JR C respectively. These four op-codes are called *branch instructions* because they represent a branch-point in the flow of program control. Their operand is a single-byte number, which is added to the address in the program counter to produce a new address. Consider what happens when the following program is executed:

ORG $5E00		
6502	**Z80**	
5E00 ADC #$34	ADC	A,$34
5E02 BEQ $03	JR	Z,$03
5E04 STA $5E20	LD	($5E20),A
5E07 RTS	RET	

If the ADC instruction at $5E00 produces a zero result in the accumulator (which is unlikely but, as we'll see later, possible), then the BEQ and JR Z instructions at $5E02 will cause $03 to be added to the contents of the program counter. The next instruction to be executed, therefore, will be the return instruction at $5E07, causing the instruction at $5E04 to be skipped over.

At first sight, this may seem wrong. After all, if the instruction at $5E02 causes $03 to be added to the program counter, surely the address stored there will become $5E05? But it is important to remember that the program counter always points to the *next* instruction to be executed and not the instruction currently being obeyed. Thus, when the instruction at $5E02 begins execution, the program counter will contain the address $5E04 — the location of the next instruction. If $03 is added to $5E04 the result will be $5E07, the address of the following instruction.

It's worth remarking here that the processor is not capable of checking whether the addresses pointed to are correct. If we inadvertently change the displacement in the instruction to $02, then the program counter will be increased (if the accumulator contains zero) by $02, and the processor will consider $5E06 to be the address of the op-code of the next instruction. In our correct program, $5E06 contains the value $5E, which is the hi-byte of the operand of the instruction at $5E04. The processor, however, cannot evaluate whether it is the right instruction or not. As far as it is concerned, $5E is a valid op-code and it will proceed to execute it, taking the bytes following $5E06 as the operands of the instruction. The program will probably crash as a result. Miscalculating displacements like this is one of the commonest errors in machine code programming.

In Assembly language programming, however, calculating jump displacements need not be a problem because the assembler program can do it for us. Therefore, instead of supplying a hex displacement as the operand of the branch instruction, we give the symbolic address of the instruction to be jumped to. This makes the Assembly language program far easier to follow. The assembler decodes the symbolic address into an absolute address, calculates the displacement necessary to get to the address, and writes that displacement into the machine code instruction. The symbolic address is called a *label*, and it's analogous to a BASIC program line number.

Let's take a closer look at how labels are used. A label is an alphanumeric string written at the start of an Assembly language instruction. It is treated by the assembler program as a two-byte symbol standing for the address of the first byte of the instruction. Therefore, we can re-write the program given in this way:

ORG $5E00				
	6502		**Z80**	
5E00	ADC	#$34	ADC	A,$34
5E02	BEQ	EXIT	JR	Z,EXIT
5E04	STA	$5E20	LD	($5E20),A
5E07 EXIT	RTS		RET	

The instruction at $5E02 can now be read as 'IF the value of the accumulator is zero THEN GOTO the address represented by the label EXIT'. This is an enormous improvement in readability over the previous version, and greatly decreases the chance of miscalculating the jump destination.

We can now use labels and the branch instructions to create a loop:

ORG $5E00				
	6502		**Z80**	
5E00 START	ADC	#$34	ADC	A,$34
5E02	BNE	START	JR	NZ,START
5E04	STA	$5E20	LD	($5E20),A
5E07 EXIT	RTS		RET	

Notice here the use of the new label, START, as well as the new branch instructions: BNE, meaning 'Branch if the accumulator is Not Equal to zero'; and JR NZ, meaning 'Jump if the accumulator is Not equal to Zero'. Let's consider what effect this code will have. The program will first add $34 to the accumulator. If the result is not equal to zero then the program branches back to $5E00 — the address represented by the label START. $34 will again be added to the accumulator, and the result will decide whether another branch occurs. This 'loop' will go on and on until the branch condition is met. When the contents of the accumulator do equal zero following an ADC instruction, then the branch at $5E02 will not occur, and the instruction at $5E04 will be executed next.

This is exactly like an IF...THEN GOTO... loop in BASIC, except that it's difficult to see how the accumulator could ever become zero. After all, it is being increased by $34 every time the loop is executed! How will it ever add up to zero? The answer lies in the fact that the accumulator is only a single-byte register, and if the addition results in a two-byte number, then the carry flag of the processor status register will be set, and the accumulator will hold the lo-byte of the result. If

the accumulator contains $CC, for example, then adding $34 will give the two-byte number $0100. The carry flag will be set, and the accumulator will hold the lo-byte of this result — $00. Thus, the contents of the accumulator would be zero, and the zero flag set as a result.

With this result in mind, we might re-write the program to use a different branch condition, incorporating the state of the carry flag rather than the state of the zero flag.

ORG $5E00				
	6502		**Z80**	
5E00 START	ADC	#$34	ADC	A,$34
5E02	BCC	START	JR	NC,START
5E04	STA	$5E20	LD	($5E20),A
5E07 EXIT	RTS		RET	

In this version, the instruction at $5E02 reads 'if the carry flag is clear, branch to START'. As soon as the result of adding $34 to the accumulator is greater than $FF, then the carry flag will be set, and the branch back to the START address will not occur.

LOOP COUNTERS

It may seem that branching according to the current condition of either the carry flag or the zero flag is a rather limited facility, but it permits a wide range of decision making, as we shall shortly see. What is definitely lacking from our repertoire now is the ability to keep a *loop counter*. We might wish, for example, to count the number of times that a loop is performed before the exit condition occurs, or we might want to cause an exit from the loop after a given number of iterations. The first objective is easily achieved by employing a CPU index register to hold the counter, and an increment instruction to update the counter:

6502		
0000	ORG	$5DFD
5DFD	LDX	#$00
5DFF START	INX	
5E00	ADC	#$34
5E02	BCC	START
5E04	STX	$5E20
5E07 EXIT	RTS	

Z80		
0000	ORG	$5DFA
5DFA	LD	IX,$0000
5DFE START	INC	IX
5E00	ADC	A,$34
5E02	JR	NC,START
5E04	LD	($5E20),IX
5E08 EXIT	RET	

The new structure has forced several changes in the program. Firstly, the instructions inserted at the beginning of the program require a new ORG address. These instructions have much the same effects on both the 6502 and the Z80 processors, but their lengths are different, so the location addresses are no longer the same in both versions of the program.

Secondly, new versions of the load (LDX, LD IX) and store (STX, LD( ),IX) instructions have been used to place an initial value of $00 in the CPU index register. The 6502 X register is a single-byte register, but the IX register of the Z80 has two bytes. The index registers have special functions, but they are essentially CPU RAM just like the accumulator, and here we use them as extra accumulators in which to keep the loop count. When the loop exit occurs, the contents of the 6502 X register will be stored at $5E20. In the Z80 version the lo-byte of the (two-byte) IX register will be stored at $5E20 and the hi-byte at $5E21.

Thirdly, a completely new instruction has taken the place of the ADC instruction as the START of the loop: INX and INC IX are both increment instructions, causing the contents of the index register to be increased (or incremented) by $01. This updates the value of the loop counter every time the loop is executed.

We can see the program as reading: 'make the loop counter zero, start the loop by incrementing the counter, add $34 to the accumulator, and branch back to the start of the loop if the carry flag is clear, otherwise store the loop counter contents at $5E20'. A further modification of the program will greatly increase its usefulness and scope:

6502		
0000	ORG	$5DFA
5DFA	LDX	#$00
5DFC START	STA	$5E22,X
5DFF	INX	
5E00	ADC	#$34
5E02	BCC	START
5E04	STX	$5E20
5E07 EXIT	RTS	

Z80		
0000	ORG	$5DF7
5DF7	LD	IX,$5E00
5DFB START	LD	(IX+$22),A
5DFE	INC	IX
5E00	ADC	A,$34
5E02	JR	NC,START
5E04	LD	($5E20),IX
5E08 EXIT	RET	

The 6502 and Z80 versions both have the same effect: they create at location $5E22 a storage table of the successive values of the accumulator as the program is executed, and eventually store at $5E20 the final value of the loop counter, which is also the number of bytes in the table starting at $5E22.

The 6502 version achieves this through the instruction STA $5E22,X, which means 'add the contents of the X register to the base address, $5E22, then store the contents of the accumulator at the address thus formed'. The STA instruction is here in the absolute direct indexed mode: that is to say, the X register is used as an index to modify the base address, $5E22. Since the X register is initialised to $00 and subsequently incremented every iteration, the starting value of the accumulator will be stored at $5E22, the next value at $5E23, and so on. After the loop exit occurs, STX will store the final value of the loop counter at location $5E20.

The Z80 version uses the IX register as a pointer to the current storage address, while still using the

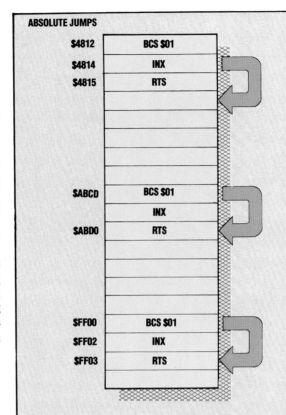

ABSOLUTE JUMPS

$4812	BCS $01
$4814	INX
$4815	RTS

$ABCD	BCS $01
	INX
$ABD0	RTS

$FF00	BCS $01
$FF02	INX
$FF03	RTS

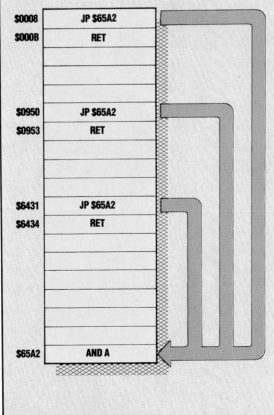

RELATIVE JUMPS

| $0008 | JP $65A2 |
| $000B | RET |

| $0950 | JP $65A2 |
| $0953 | RET |

| $6431 | JP $65A2 |
| $6434 | RET |

| $65A2 | AND A |

Relative Jumps
Most of the branch instructions, such as BCS (meaning 'branch if carry flag is set'), JR NZ (meaning 'branch if the accumulator is non-zero'), act according to the condition of the processor status register, and use the relative jump mode in redirecting the flow of control through the program. The alternative is the absolute jump.

In the example, the BCS $01 instruction always causes a relative jump of one byte forward (when it causes a jump at all, that is; it's conditional on the state of the carry flag) no matter what the location address at which the machine code resides. Here, the BCS $01 instruction is always followed by the INX instruction, itself only a single-byte instruction; when the carry flag is set, therefore, BCS will cause the INX instruction to be skipped.

Absolute Jumps
In this example, the JP $65A2 instruction causes an unconditional jump whenever it is encountered. Its effect is to redirect program execution to the address which forms its operand — $65A2 here. No testing is done, and the location address of the instruction at the time of execution is not significant; program execution always continues from the specified address.

Both jump modes have advantages and disadvantages, but the most important criterion in choosing between a relative jump or an absolute jump is relocatability: it's quite common in Assembly language programming to write a routine and assemble it at one ORG address, then re-use it in the same form but with a different ORG value. If all the jumps in the routine are relative, then changing the location addresses of the instructions will not matter at all, and the program will flow smoothly along its intended paths; if any of the jumps is absolute, however, when the routine is assembled at a different ORG, the jumps will still send control to the specified address, which may now have no significance for the routine. Relative jumps are relocatable, absolute jumps are not.

LIZ DIXON

lo-byte of IX as the loop counter. The instruction LD IX,$5E00 puts the base address, $5E00, into the IX register, so the lo-byte of IX will contain $00. The peculiar-looking instruction LD (IX+$22),A means 'add the address contained in IX to $22, and store the contents of the accumulator at the address thus formed'. Since IX is initalised to $5E00, and is subsequently incremented at every loop interation, the starting value of the accumulator· will be stored at $5E22, the next value at $5E23, and so on. Meanwhile the lo-byte of IX records the number of loop iterations, and is finally stored at $5E20 when the loop terminates. The LD (IX+$22),A instruction here is in the absolute indirect indexed addressing mode, which is rather more complicated than the 6502 version but much more powerful.

We have now looked at the Assembly language loop and array structures in some detail. These are both extremely helpful machine code programming techniques. In the next instalment of the course, we'll put them both to work.

Exercises

There are many important, and possibly puzzling, points in this instalment, and only experience of using the new addressing modes and instructions will make you fully understand them.

Use the CHAMP assembler package to assemble and SAVE the various program fragments in this instalment. When you execute a fragment, use the ‹debug› mode to examine the memory locations that should be affected. It's a good idea always to initialise these locations with a recognisable constant — $FF, for instance — before execution, so that afterwards you can tell whether memory has been affected by the program. You can use the ‹debug› Alter command to do this, or even the ‹debug› Move command.

Remember, as always, that the location addresses given in the program are for example only, and that you must choose addresses suitable for your machine.

Loading And Saving CHAMP

For convenience and security you should copy CHAMP onto another tape, and then remove the write-protect tabs from the original and the copy. In the following instructions, the LOAD instructions refer to the CHAMP tape, and SAVE refers to the copy tape:

BBC Model B
1) LOAD“CHAMP”
2) SAVE“CHAMP” : RUN : Quit to BASIC
3) *SAVE“CHAMP M/C” 1000 , 4600

Commodore 64
1) LOAD“CHAMP”
2) SAVE“CHAMP” : RUN : enter <debug> mode
3) Hit [w][ret], followed by [s] for SAVE
4) Start address 1000; end address 4600; filename “CHAMP M/C”

Spectrum
1) LOAD“CHAMP”
2) Quit to BASIC : SAVE “CHAMP” LINE 1
3) SAVE “CHAMP M/C” CODE 27000,9231

The conditional branch instructions, as we have seen, depend on the contents of the processor status register. One reason for adding the binary display option to the Monitor program (see pages 118 and 198) was to enable you to inspect the contents of the PSR before and after an instruction is executed, and observe the changes in the flags. There is no single instruction in either 6502 or Z80 Assembly language to store the PSR contents, so we must use these commands:

Z80	
3E00 F5	PUSH AF
3E01 F5	PUSH AF
3E02 E1	POP HL
3E03 22 lo hi	LD (STORE1),HL
3E06 F1	POP AF

6502	
3E00 48	PHA
3E01 08	PHP
3E02 48	PHA
3E03 08	PHP
3E04 68	PLA
3E05 8D lo hi	STA STORE1
3E08 68	PLA
3E09 8D lo’ hi’	STA (1+STORE1)
3E0C 28	PLP
3E0D 68	PLA

This sequence of instructions will cause the current contents of the PSR to be stored in the byte addressed by STORE1 (an address appropriate to your machine), while the accumulator contents will be stored at (1+STORE1). To use these instructions, simply insert them as a block before and after the program instruction whose effect you wish to observe. You must remember, however, to add two to the value of STORE1 every time you insert this block. When you've executed the program, you can use the Monitor to display the section of memory where you've stored the various contents of the PSR and the accumulator.

It may occur to you that this block should be treated as a subroutine rather than repeatedly entering it where it is required. There is an Assembly language equivalent of BASIC's GOSUB, but using it here would complicate matters since it uses the stack, and this would interfere with the block's use of the same list (PLA, PUSH, PHP, etc. are all stack manipulations, which will be more fully explained later). You may notice the difference in length between the Z80 and 6502 code: the Z80's two-byte registers and associated instructions are responsible for this variation.

GENERAL ROUTINE

Making machine code programs relocatable, so that their execution is independent of their locations, requires the use of symbols and labels rather than absolute addresses and values. We study some more assembler directives and their role in program structure, and take a first look at Assembly language subroutine calls.

Because Assembly language is essentially a simple programming language composed of the 'primitive' commands that the CPU can manage, you will find yourself constantly writing and re-writing fragments of program to do the same essential tasks that you take for granted as part of the instruction set of a high-level language — input/output handling, for example, or two-byte arithmetic routines. The sensible thing to do is to establish a library — on tape, disk or paper — of the most commonly used routines, and merge these into new programs as the need arises.

There are two major problems associated with this, however. The first is the difficulty of writing important, and often lengthy, routines in a sufficiently general way that they can be inserted in different programs without adjustment or re-writing. The second problem is in writing useful routines that are not rooted in one set of memory locations, so that they can be relocated in memory through a new assembly with a different ORG address, and perform exactly the same function there as in their original locations.

Both problems are aspects of the generality/portability problem familiar to BASIC programmers, and are solved in much the same way — by using variables to pass values from program to subroutine; by using local variables in subroutines to make them independent of the larger program context; and by avoiding the use of absolute quantities (both numerical or string constants) and program line numbers.

In Assembly language programming we have become used to the idea of memory locations as the equivalent of BASIC variables — programs operate on the contents of the locations, whatever those contents might be, in the same way that a BASIC program operates on the contents of its variables. Unfortunately, we have tended to refer to memory locations by their absolute addresses, a convenient habit at first, but one that must now be renounced in the name of generality. The answer is to use symbols instead of absolute addresses and values, and to use the range of symbolic forms offered by assembler pseudo-opcodes as the equivalents of both variables and program line

numbers. We have seen examples of both uses already. Consider this program, for example:

6502		Z80	
DATA1 EQU $12		DATA1	EQU $12
DATA2 EQU $79		DATA2	EQU $79
	LDA DATA1	LD	A,(DATA1)
LOOP	ADC DATA2	ADC	A,(DATA2)
	BNE LOOP	JR	NZ,LOOP
	RTS	RET	

Here we have two kinds of symbol, two values and a label, all used as the operands of the Assembly language instructions. Because of this, the program fragment is both general and able to be relocated. The only absolute quantities are the values of DATA1 and DATA2, and they can be initialised in the surrounding program, rather than at the start of the routine itself.

There are other pseudo-ops that we have not yet discussed. In particular, DB, DW and DS (though, like ORG and EQU, they may differ from one assembler program to another). These three directives, which stand for 'Define Byte', 'Define Word', and 'Define Storage', enable us to initialise and allocate memory locations, as in this example:

			ORG	$D3A0
D3A0	5F	LABL1	DB	$5F
D3A1	CE98	LABL2	DW	$98CE
D3B3		LABL3	DS	$10
D3B3		DATA1	EQU	LABL3

SYMBOL TABLE:
LABL1 = D3A0: LABL2 = D3A1: LABL3 = D3A3
DATA1 = D3A3
ASSEMBLY COMPLETE — NO ERRORS

In this full Assembly listing (the output of an assembler program) we see at the bottom for the first time a symbol table, consisting of the symbols defined in the program and the values they represent. There are several important things to notice in this fragment. First of all, in the line that begins LABL1, the DB pseudo-op is used. We can see from the listing that the ORG directive has given the address $D3A0 to LABL1, and the symbol table confirms this. The effect of DB here is to place the value $5F in the byte addressed by LABL1 — so memory location $D3A0 is initialised with the value $5F, as we can see in the machine code column of the listing.

Secondly, LABL2 represents the address $D3A1. However, DW has the effect of initialising a 'word' (two consecutive bytes) of storage, so the value $98CE is stored in locations $D3A1 and $D3A2 in lo-hi form — this can be seen clearly in the machine code column. Because DW automatically converts its operands into lo-hi form, it is most often used to initialise 'pointer' locations with addresses. LABL2, or location $D3A1, might be such an address — it points to location $98CE.

The third thing to consider is that the instruction DS $10 has the effect of adding $10 to the program counter. This is clearer in the symbol table than in the actual listing — LABL3 represents the location $D3A3 (the location following the previous instruction), though it appears from the listing that its value is $D3B3. This is actually the location address of the next instruction after the DS instruction, so DS $10 has reserved a block of 16 bytes (from $D3A3 to $D3B2 inclusive) between one instruction and the next. This is a process rather like putting long REM lines into a BASIC program to create unused space in the program text are that can then be POKEd and PEEKed as a machine code program area (see page 142).

Finally, the last instruction uses EQU to set one symbol equal to the value of another, so that DATA1 has the value $D3A3 (the value of LABL3). This is another source of possible confusion. LABL3 is the symbolic representation of the location address $D3A3, so DATA1 EQU LABL3 means 'the symbol DATA1 is to have the same meaning and value as the symbol LABL3'. The fact that the DB instruction has made the contents of $D3A3 equal to $5F has no significance for the meaning of the symbols LABL3 and DATA1. Keeping the distinction between a location and its contents clear in your mind is one of the most testing difficulties in the early stages of learning Assembly language programming. You may have had the same problem with BASIC program variables and their contents.

At first glance, the DB directive seems to duplicate EQU, but this is not the case. LABL1 means 'the location $D3A0', and DB $5F has initialised that byte with the value $5F, but, although the value of LABL1 is now fixed, the contents of the location it symbolises can be changed at any time (by storing the accumulator contents there later in the program, for example). Similarly, DATA1 is now a symbol whose value is fixed by the EQU instruction; its value cannot be changed by the program's execution. And again, LABL3 points to the start of a 16-byte data area, the contents of which can be changed in the program, but LABL3 is itself unchangeable.

This introduces, but does not exhaust, the possibilities of the new pseudo-ops. Consider this new version of the previous fragment:

				ORG $D3A0
D3A0	4D4553	LABL1	DB	'MESSAGE 1'
D3A9	CE98	LABL2	DW	$98CE
D3BB		LABL3	DS	$10
D3BB		DATA1	EQU	LABL3

SYMBOL TABLE:
LABL1 = D3A0: LABL2 = D3A9: LABL3 = D3AB
DATA1 = D3AB
ASSEMBLY COMPLETE — NO ERRORS

The DB instruction has a string, 'MESSAGE 1', as its operand, and the assembler has initialised the locations from $D3A0 to $D3A8 with the ASCII values of the characters within the single quotes. This can be inferred from inspection of the location address column in the listing, and is partly confirmed by the machine code column — the contents of the three bytes from $D3A0 to $D3A2 are shown to be $4D, $45, and $53, which are the hex ASCII codes for 'M', 'E', and 'S'.

This is a significant facility, not only because it relieves the programmer of the task of translating messages and character data into lists of ASCII codes, but also because it makes the listing much easier to read, and hints at the possibility of actually getting some screen output from our Assembly language programs. The latter is particularly significant because so far we have been restricted to storing results in memory and inspecting them using the Monitor program (see page 139). Naturally, we will be exploring screen-handling in this chapter, but there are aspects of Assembly language that we need to investigate before going onto that topic. If, however, you think about our habit of storing results in memory, and if you understand already that memory-mapped screen displays are, in effect, only areas of memory, then you may be able to see a way of addressing the screen from a program.

The most important aspect of this new DB facility is that it confers on LABL1 the status of a

Exercises

1) The first program fragment in the main text uses the DS pseudo-op to reserve $10 bytes of memory starting from the address represented by the label LABL1. Write an Assembly language program that will store the numbers $0F to $00 in descending order in this block, one number per byte. This should be done using a loop, and indexed addressing techniques, for which you will need to use the DEX (decrement the X register) or DEC (IX+0) (decrement IX) instructions. The loop should continue as long as decrementing the index register does not cause the zero flag to be set, so use the BNE or JR NZ branch instructions.

2) Using the techniques of the previous exercise, write a program to copy the message stored at LABL1 by the DB pseudo-op (see the second program fragment in the main text) to a block of memory starting at the address stored at LABL2 by the DW pseudo-op. The address $98CE may not be suitable for your computer, so change the initialisation, but the program should work for any address, and for any length of message. To implement this, your program must use either the number of characters in the message as a loop counter, or it must be able to recognise the end of the message — you might put an asterisk, for example, as the last character of any message.

BASIC string variable: When we write in BASIC:

```
200 LET A$="MESSAGE 1"
```

then we are actually creating a pointer to the start of a table of bytes containing the ASCII codes for 'M', 'E', 'S', and so on. Whenever the BASIC interpreter encounters a reference to A$, it looks in its own symbol table to find the location at which it points — that is, the starting location of the contents of A$. Similarly, in our Assembly language program we can treat LABL1 as the equivalent of A$, given that we have already written a program fragment that allows us to manipulate a table using indexed addressing.

The pseudo-ops, then, allow us to remove absolute addresses and values from our programs, and replace them with symbols. This has the effect of diminishing the problems of portability and relocatability. What we need now is to be able to access these portable, relocatable modules from the main program. In other words, we need a machine code equivalent of BASIC's GOSUB command.

There is such an instruction, of course: JSR and CALL in 6502 and Z80 respectively. Both require an absolute address (which can be a label) as operand, and both have the effect of replacing the contents of the program counter with the address that forms their operand. The next instruction to be executed, therefore, will be the first instruction of the subroutine so addressed. Execution continues from that instruction until the RETURN instruction — RTS and RET respectively — is encountered. This command has the effect of replacing the current contents of the program counter with its contents immediately prior to the JSR or CALL instruction was executed. The next instruction to be executed, therefore, is the instruction immediately following the JSR or CALL. This is exactly the mechanism used by the BASIC interpreter in executing and returning from GOSUBs. It's easily understood as such, but it raises the question of how the old contents of the program counter are restored when the RETURN instruction is executed. The simple answer is that the JSR and CALL instructions first 'push' the program counter contents onto the stack (see illustration on page 141) before replacing them with the subroutine address; and the RTS and RET instruction 'pop' or 'pull' that address from the stack back into the program counter. The questions of what the stack is, how you push or pop it, and why you'd want to do so, are the subject of the next instalment of the course.

Instruction Set

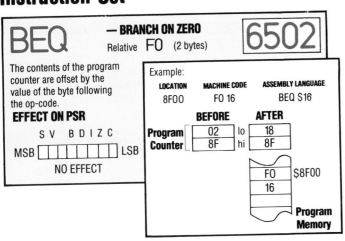

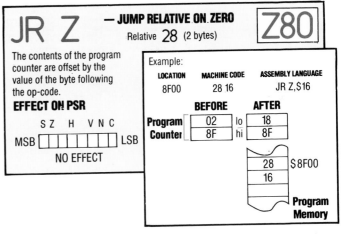

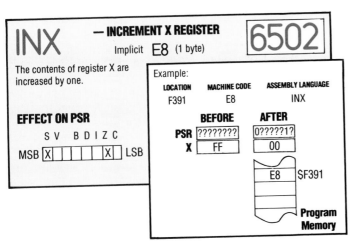

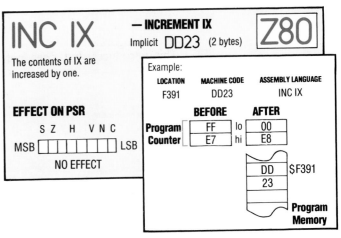

LAST IN FIRST OUT

The stack is a defined area of computer memory attached to the CPU that acts as a convenient workspace and takes a vital part in subroutine execution. It is easily accessed through the stack instructions, which permit the quick copying and restoring of register contents. We examine the stack and its operation in detail here.

Memory management is the essence of Assembly language programming, and most of the instructions we've studied so far in the course are concerned with simply loading data to or from memory locations. These locations have been accessed in a variety of ways — the addressing modes — but the instructions concerned have always taken a specific memory address as part of the operand. There is a class of instructions, however, that access a specific area of memory but do not take an address as operand. These instructions operate on the area of memory known as the *stack,* and they are known as the stack operations.

The stack is provided for both the central processing unit and the programmer to use as temporary workspace memory. It is a kind of 'scratch-pad', easily written to, read from and erased. The stack operations copy data from the CPU's registers into vacant areas of the stack, or copy data from the stack back into the CPU registers. These instructions require no address operand because a specified CPU register, the *stack pointer,* always contains the address of the next free stack location. Thus, anything written to the stack is automatically written to the byte pointed to by the stack pointer, and data loaded from the stack is always copied from the stack location last written to. Whenever a stack operation is executed, the stack pointer is adjusted as part of the operation.

In 6502 systems the stack is the 256 bytes of RAM from $0100 to $01FF; in Z80 systems the location and size of the stack are determined by the operating system, but may be changed by the programmer. This variation reflects the differences in the internal organisation of the two microprocessors (see the diagram on page 141): the 6502 has a single-byte stack pointer, while the Z80 stack pointer consists of two bytes.

The contents of the 6502 stack pointer are treated by the CPU as the lo-byte of the stack address, and a hi-byte of $01 is automatically added to this by means of a 'ninth bit' wired into the stack pointer. This extra bit is always set to one, so 6502 stack addresses are all on page one.

The Z80 stack pointer is a two-byte register capable of addressing any location between $0000 and $FFFF — the entire address space of the Z80 itself. The stack can thus be located anywhere in RAM, and its location can be changed by the programmer. This is not recommended, however, since the operating system initially sets the stack location and stores data on it. As the operating system may interrupt the execution of any machine code program at any time, and expect to find data relevant to its operation on the stack, any alteration of the location of the stack will mean that the data will not be available to it and the system may crash.

As an example of the use of the stack, consider the following routine to exchange the contents of two memory locations, LOC1 and LOC2:

6502		Z80	
LDA	LOC1	LD	A,(LOC1)
PHA		PUSH	AF
LDA	LOC2	LD	A,(LOC2)
STA	LOC1	LD	(LOC1),A
PLA		POP	AF
STA	LOC2	LD	(LOC2), A

The contents of LOC1 are loaded into the accumulator, and from there copied or 'pushed' onto the stack. The contents of LOC2 are then loaded to the accumulator, and stored in LOC1. The contents of the top byte of the stack are then copied or 'popped' into the accumulator, which restores the original contents of LOC1 to the accumulator. This is copied to LOC2, and the exchange is complete. Notice that the stack operations 'saved' the contents of LOC1 in memory as long as needed, but without the program specifying any memory location — except, by implication, the next free location on the stack.

This program fragment shows us a lot about stack operations. Primarily, they are reciprocal and sequential. The last item pushed onto the stack is retrieved by the next pop from the stack. Successive pushes with no intervening pops write data into successive stack locations, one 'above' the other, while pops without intervening pushes access successive locations 'downwards' from the current 'top' of the stack.

To visualise the stack, imagine writing notes on postcards and stacking them next to you on the desk, then reading and discarding cards until the stack is empty. The most recently written of the cards remaining in the stack is always the one on top. For this reason the stack is known as a Last In First Out (LIFO) data structure. Its converse, a First In First Out (FIFO) structure, is a queue. It is conventional to talk about the next free byte in the stack as the *top* of the stack, and to imagine the stack growing upwards. In both the Z80 and the 6502, however, the stack pointer is decremented by a push, so that the stack top is actually at the lower memory address than the stack bottom. This is less confusing if we describe the stack as 'rising towards zero'.

The first program fragment is also typical of programs using the stack in that the number of push instructions is exactly counterbalanced by the number of pops. This is not essential, but failure to observe this harmony of opposites when writing subroutines may result in an incorrect return from the subroutine and consequent program failure. This is one of the commonest bugs in Assembly language programs, but can be fairly easily traced by comparing the number of pop and push instructions in a program.

The Z80 version of the routine differs noticeably from the 6502 in one major respect: the 6502 pushes only single-byte registers onto the stack, while the Z80 always pushes a two-byte register. When you push or pop the Z80 accumulator, you also push or pop the contents of the processor status register, because the CPU treats these two single-byte registers as one two-byte register called the AF (accumulator-flag) register. The power of the Z80 derives greatly from its ability to handle two-byte registers.

It is a good programming habit to start subroutines by pushing the contents of all CPU registers onto the stack, and popping them off the stack immediately before returning from the subroutine. This ensures that the CPU after the subroutine call is in exactly the same state as it was before it, and means that any of the registers can be used in the subroutine with no fear of corrupting data essential to the main program. For example, consider this program subroutine:

	6502		Z80	
	LDA	LOC1	LD	A,LOC1
SUM	ADC	#$6C	ADC	A,$6C
GSUB	JSR	SUBR0	CALL	SUBR0
TEST	BNE	SUM	JR	NZ,SUM
EXIT	RTS		RET	
SUBR0	PHP		PUSH	AF
	PHA		PUSH	HL
	TXA		PUSH	DE
	PHA		PUSH	BC
	TYA		PUSH	IX
SUBR1	PHA		PUSH	IY
SUBR2	STA	LOC2	LD	(LOC2),A
	LDA	#$00	LD	A,$00
SUBR3	PLA		POP	IY
	TAY		POP	IX
	PLA		POP	DE
	TAX		POP	BC
	PLA		POP	HL
SUBR4	PLP		POP	AF
	RTS		RET	

Here, the effect of the instructions between SUBR0 and SUBR1 is to push the current register

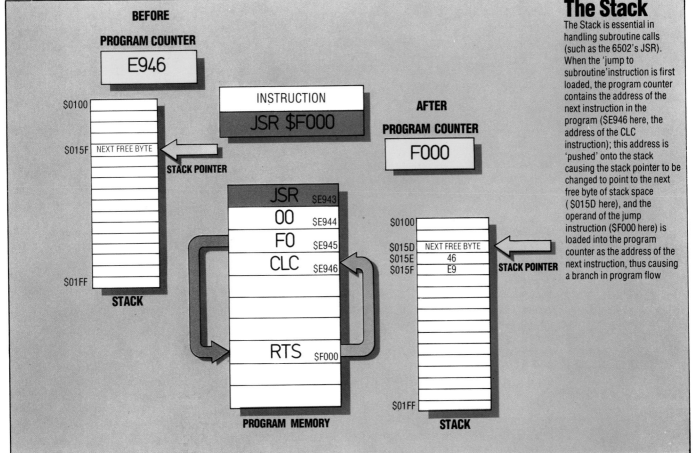

BEFORE

PROGRAM COUNTER

E946

INSTRUCTION

JSR $F000

AFTER

PROGRAM COUNTER

F000

$0100

$015F NEXT FREE BYTE ← STACK POINTER

$01FF

STACK

JSR	$E943
00	$E944
FO	$E945
CLC	$E946
RTS	$F000

PROGRAM MEMORY

$0100

$015D NEXT FREE BYTE
$015E 46
$015F E9 ← STACK POINTER

$01FF

STACK

The Stack

The Stack is essential in handling subroutine calls (such as the 6502's JSR). When the 'jump to subroutine' instruction is first loaded, the program counter contains the address of the next instruction in the program ($E946 here, the address of the CLC instruction); this address is 'pushed' onto the stack causing the stack pointer to be changed to point to the next free byte of stack space ($015D here), and the operand of the jump instruction ($F000 here) is loaded into the program counter as the address of the next instruction, thus causing a branch in program flow

KEVIN JONES

contents onto the stack, and the effect of the instructions between SUBR3 and SUBR4 is to restore those contents to the registers. The substantive instructions in the subroutine are the two starting at SUBR2, but the second of these is ineffective since the subsequent instructions completely change the state of the accumulator.

Notice that the Z80 PUSH and POP instructions can take any of the register pairs as an operand, but the 6502 can operate on only the accumulator (PHA and PLA) and the processor status register (PHP and PLP). Hence the need for the register-accumulator transfers (TXA, TAX, TYA, TAY) in the 6502 version. Notice also that we have made a deliberate mistake in the Z80 version in not 'popping' all of the registers in the reverse order to which they were 'pushed'. It illustrates the care needed in stack operations, but also demonstrates that you can push the stack from one register and then pop that value off the stack back into a different register — a laborious but sometimes convenient way of doing data transfers between registers.

The functions and uses of the CPU registers are the subjects of the next instalment, in which we conclude our general examination of the Assembly language instruction set. We also begin the study of machine code arithmetic.

Exercises

1) Rewrite the second routine given in the answers to the previous exercises so that the message at LABL1 is stored back at LABL1, but in reverse order, thus:

LABL1 EGASSEM A SI SIHT

Use the stack for this reversal.

2) Develop this routine so that the words of the message remain in their original order, but the characters of each word are reversed, thus:

LABL1 SIHT SI A EGASSEM

Answers To Exercises On Page 158

1) This subroutine stores the numbers $0F to $00 in descending order in the block of $10 bytes reserved by the DS pseudo-op at LABL1.

6502			Z80		
ORIGIN	ORG	$7000	ORIGIN	ORG	$C000
LABL1	DS	$10	LABL1	DS	$10
LABL2	DW	$7100	LABL2	DW	$C100
			OFFST	EQU	$0F
BEGIN	LDY	#$FF	BEGIN	LD	IX,LABL1
	LDX	#$10		LD	B,OFFST
LOOP0	INY		LOOP0	LD	(IX+0),B
	DEX			INC	IX
	TXA		ENDLP0	DJNZ	LOOP0
	STA	LABL1,Y		LD	(IX+0),B
ENDLP0	BNE	LOOP0		RET	
	RTS				

The differences in approach and instructions between the Z80 and 6502 are revealing. The 6502 uses the Y register as an index to the address LABL1, and the X register as a loop counter and source of the data to be stored. Notice that the X register is decremented two instructions before the BNE test at ENDLP0, but because TXA (Transfer X contents to the Accumulator) and the STA do not affect the processor status register, the test works on the effects of decrementing X.

The Z80 version uses IX indirect addressing mode to hold the storage address, and uses the B register as the counter and source of data. At ENDLP0 in the Z80 version we see DJNZ LOOP0, meaning 'decrement register B, and jump relative to LOOP0 if the result is non-zero'. This instruction is almost an Assembly language FOR...NEXT structure, and certainly makes writing Z80 loops easy and convenient.

2) This routine copies the message stored at LABL1 to the block starting at the address stored at LABL2. The value $0D (the ASCII code for Return or Enter) is stored at the end of the message as a terminator.

6502			Z80		
ORIGIN	ORG	$7000	ORIGIN	ORG	$C000
LABL1	DB	'THIS IS A MESSAGE'	LABL1	DB	'THIS IS A MESSAGE'
TERMN8	DB	$0D	TERMN8	DB	$0D
LABL2	DW	$7100	LABL2	DW	$C100
CR	EQU	$0D	CR	EQU	$0D
ZPLO	EQU	$FB			
BEGIN	LDA	LABL2	BEGIN	LD	IX,LABL1
	STA	ZPLO		LD	IY,(LABL2)
	LDA	LABL2+1	LOOP0	LD	A,(IX+0)
	STA	ZPLO+1		LD	(IY+0),A
	LDY	$FF		INC	IX
LOOP0	INY			INC	IY
	LDA	LABL1,Y		CP	CR
	STA	(ZPLO),Y	ENDLP0	JR	NZ,LOOP0
	CMP	CR		RET	
ENDLP0	BNE	LOOP0			
	RTS				

The 6502 version uses the Y register as an index to the indirect address ZPLO, in the post-indexed indirect mode. This mode is possible only with the Y register, and requires a zero page operand address — hence the initialisation of ZPLO and ZPLO+1 with the address stored at LABL2. The operating system in 6502 machines uses most of the zero page locations, but locations $FB to $FF on the Commodore 64, and $70 to $8F on the BBC Micro, are unused, so ZPLO is set to one of these locations. The Z80 version uses IX in indexed mode, and IY in indexed indirect mode.

Both routines use a 'compare the accumulator' instruction — CMP CR (6502) and CP CR (Z80) — in which the operand is subtracted from the accumulator contents, thus affecting the processor status register (PSR) flags. The accumulator contents are then restored, while the PSR shows the results of the comparison. When the accumulator contains $0D (the message terminator), the result of the comparison will be that the zero flag is set. Thus the ENDLP0 test will fail and control will pass to the return instruction.

REGISTERED ADDRESS

So far in the course we have taken a detailed look at how the CPU manipulates memory, using registers such as the accumulator and ALU. Now we can begin to look more closely at how simple procedures are performed in machine code. Here, we concentrate on the basic arithmetical operations of addition and subtraction.

The differences in operation between the Z80 and 6502 microprocessors in the way they go about performing these simple arithmetical tasks reveal the different philosophies behind their design. The Z80's many registers, with their sophisticated set of operation instructions, typify the processor itself — elegant, complex and powerful. The much simpler 6502 architecture and operation set seem to suggest an altogether humbler processor, which is robust and practical but apparently not quite in the Z80 class. This impression is accurate as far as it goes, but the 6502's wealth of addressing modes and its use of zero page as an extra index register, give it a subtlety and versatility that will enable it to dominate the home and business micro world for some time to come.

The great advantage of the Z80's registers is their flexibility — they can be treated simultaneously as both two-byte or single-byte registers, thus allowing enormous addressing scope. The 6502, on the other hand, has no two-byte registers, but is able — by way of its addressing modes — to treat zero page as an array of single-byte and two-byte registers.

ARITHMETICAL BASICS

We have seen that the CPU registers permit a variety of possible memory accesses, but manipulating memory usually requires something more than simply loading, storing and comparing its contents. The ability to perform the four operations of arithmetic is essential to a computer system, yet both the Z80 and the 6502 support only addition and subtraction. Multiplication and division must be programmed, as must the addition and subtraction of numbers larger than $FF. This is a limitation of both of the CPUs, though the educational value to the programmer of having to invent multiplication and division algorithms is enormous. On the 16-bit processors that succeeded the Z80 and 6502, however, both operations are supported, thanks to the greater speed and power of the CPUs.

We have used the ADC ('add with carry') instruction and a variety of INC ('increment') instructions, in doing single-byte arithmetic on

both CPUs. Here are the two ways of adding the contents of two two-byte memory locations:

6502		Z80	
ADDR1 DW	$7E60	ADDR1 DW	$7E60
ADDR2 DW	$4A51	ADDR2 DW	$4A51
SUM DS	$03	SUM DS	$03
BEGIN CLC		BEGIN LD	A,$00
LDA	ADDR1	AND A	
ADC	ADDR2	LD	HL,(ADDR1)
STA	SUM	LD	DE,(ADDR2)
LDA	ADDR1+1	ADD HL,DE	
ADC	ADDR2+1	LD	(SUM),HL
STA	SUM+1	ADC A,$00	
LDA	$00	LD	(SUM+2),A
ADC	$00	RET	
STA	SUM+2		
RTS			

The single-byte method employed on the 6502 can be used on the Z80, but the register-pair method used in the Z80 version has no 6502 equivalent. Notice the strategies used to handle the various carry possibilities, starting with the CLC (6502) and AND A (Z80) instructions that clear the carry flag prior to the addition, and ending with the modification of the third byte of SUM. Allowing for the maximum result is vital in all arithmetic.

Subtraction can be treated similarly to addition, both processors having a SBC ('subtract with carry') instruction although two-byte subtraction is supported on the Z80. Because of the possibility of generating a negative result in subtraction, however, we must now begin to investigate the binary representation of algebraic sign.

To start, we need say no more about negative numbers than is implied by this statement:

If $A+B = 0$ then it follows that $A = -B$

which implies that if A is a positive number, then its negation or complement is the number which when added to A gives a result of zero. For example, if A is the single-byte number $04, then its single-byte complement is $FC:

$04+$FC=$100

Remembering that $100=$00 (if we have only a single-byte register for holding the result), this complementary representation means that subtraction can be seen as addition with negative numbers. That is:

$A-B$ is the same as $A+(-B)$

Thus, $08-$05 is the same as $08+(-$05), and $(-$05)=$FB (as $FB+$05=$100), which means that our original subtraction problem can be re-

MACHINE CODE

Double Identity

The Z80's data registers can communicate as single-byte registers with every other single-byte register. They can each communicate with memory in direct, immediate, indirect, absolute, and indexed modes. When treated as BC, DE, HL – the two-byte register pairs – they can transfer 16-bit data to and from memory and the stack, and are effectively 16-bit accumulators for addition and subtraction. This combination of flexibility and resourcefulness is the key to the Z80's huge success

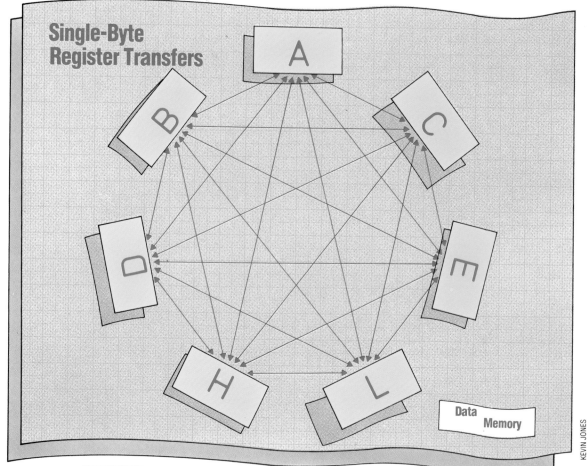

Single-Byte Register Transfers

KEVIN JONES

Plain And Simple

The 6502's internal communication is severely linear, and restricted to eight-bit data transfers. Only the accumulator can communicate directly with X and Y; only X can communicate with the stack pointer; and only the PSR and the accumulator access the stack. Memory transfers are possible in absolute, direct, indirect, indexed, immediate, and zero page modes. The 6502's inventive use of zero page mode compensates for the small size of its register set; zero page can be treated as 128 two-byte CPU registers

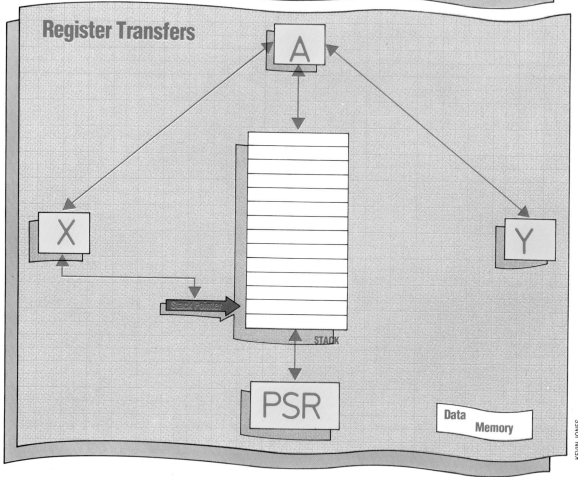

Register Transfers

KEVIN JONES

164

expressed as $08+$FB. The result of this sum is $103, which is $03 as a single-byte number.

This kind of representation is known as *two's complement*: the complement of a single-byte number is formed by subtracting it from $100. There is another representation known as *one's complement*, and the two are related in an interesting way. Consider this:

```
$05 = 00000101    binary
$FA = 11111010    one's complement
        +1
-----------------------
$FB = 11111011    two's complement
-----------------------
$05+$FA=$FF
$05+$FB=$00
```

The one's complement of a single-byte number is formed simply by complementing or negating each binary bit of the number. If one is added to this result, then the two's complement of the number is produced. A number and its one's complement always total $FF, while a number and its two's complement always total $00 (actually $100). It is conventional then, in signed integer arithmetic, to regard the numbers from $00 to $7F as the positive numbers, (0 to 127) and $80 to $FF as the negative numbers (-128 to -1). If you compare the binary representations of these numbers you will notice that all the negative integers have bit 7 set, while in the positive numbers bit 7 is always reset. Accordingly, bit 7 is known as the *sign bit* of a signed number, and the carry flag of the processor status register is set or reset as a copy of bit 7 of the result of the last arithmetic or logical operation.

There is no easy way round this potentially confusing subject, and it simply has to be approached when you start doing signed arithmetic. Fortunately, once its implications are understood, it can be handled mechanically by rule-of-thumb methods. These methods, and the multiplication and division alogrithms, are the subject of the next instalment of the course.

Answers To Exercises On Page 162

1) The following program reverses the order of the character string stored at LABL1:

6502

```
;
ORIGIN  ORG   $7000
LAST1   EQU   $0D
LABL1   DB    'THIS IS A MESSAGE'
TERMN8  DB    LAST1
;
BEGIN   LDX   #$FF
        LDA   #LAST1
        PHA
LOOP0   INX
        LDA   LABL1,X
        PHA
        CMP   #LAST1
ENDLP0  BNE   LOOP0
CLRSTK  PLA
;
BEGIN1  LDX   #$FF
LOOP1   INX
        PLA
        STA   LABL1,X
        CMP   #LAST1
ENDLP1  BNE   LOOP1
        RTS
```

Z80

```
        ORG   $C000
LAST1   EQU   $0D
LABL1   DB    'THIS IS A MESSAGE'
TERMN8  DB    LAST1
;
BEGIN   LD    IX,LABL1-1
        LD    A,LAST1
        PUSH  AF
LOOP0   INC   IX
        LD    A,(IX+0)
        PUSH  AF
        CP    LAST1
ENDLP0  JR    NZ,LOOP0
CLRSTK  POP   AF
;
BEGIN1  LD    IX,LABL1-1
LOOP1   INC   IX
        POP   AF
        LD    (IX+0),A
        CP    LAST1
ENDLP1  JR    NZ,LOOP1
        RET
```

In the 6502 version, the code between LOOP0 and ENDLOOP0 uses X-indexed addressing in a loop to load the characters one-by-one from LABL1, and push them onto the stack — having first pushed the ASCII value of the terminator character to mark the bottom of the stack. The last character pushed onto the stack is also the terminator, this time determined from its position as the last character in the string. This concludes the loop, and the terminate character on top of the stack is then cleared at CLRSTK.

The Z80 version uses IX in indirect addressing mode to load the accumulator from LABL1 onwards, and pushes not only the accumulator but also the flag register onto the stack. This means that the characters of the string at LABL1 are interspersed on the stack with successive values of the processor status register.

The code between BEGIN1 and ENDLP1 in both versions is a reflection of the previous loop and uses the same techniques, but this time pulling the character string off the stack in reverse order, and storing it at LABL1 onwards. The loop finishes when the terminator character is found at the bottom of the stack.

Notice how important it is to balance stack pushes and pulls, and that the most difficult part of the problem is deciding how to handle the extreme conditions — what to do at the start of the loops, how to terminate them, and what 'tidying-up' (if any) is then required.

The Z80 instruction at BEGIN and BEGIN1 (LD IX,LABL1−1) illustrates the usefulness of an assembler program. Here, it decodes the expression (LABL1 −1) to mean 'the address of the byte immediately before the byte whose address is LABL1', and assembles that address into the code. Most assemblers support some measure of expression evaluation, usually allowing one or two operands to be modified by a single arithmetic operator — normally '+' or '−'.

2) This program reverses the order of characters in each word of the string at LABL1, while maintaining the order of the words themselves:

6502

```
;
ORIGIN    ORG    $7000
LAST1     EQU    $0D
SPACE     EQU    $20
LABL1     DB     'THIS IS'
TERMN8    DB     LAST1
;
BEGIN     LDX    #$FF
LOOPO     JSR    RVSWRD
          CMP    #LAST1
ENDLPO    BNE    LOOPO
          RTS
;
;****REVERSE A WORD S/R****
LASTCH    DB     $00
LASTX     DB     $00
RVSWRD    TXA
          TAY
          INY
RVSLPO    INX
          LDA    LABL1,X
          PHA
          CMP    #SPACE
          BEQ    CLRSTK
          CMP    #LAST1
ENDRVO    BNE    RVSLPO
CLRSTK    PLA
          STA    LASTCH
          STX    LASTX
RVSLP1    PLA
          STA    LABL1,Y
          INY
          CPY    LASTX
ENDLP1    BNE    RVSLP1
          LDA    LASTCH
          RTS
```

There are several points of interest here: the use of JSR and CALL instructions, for example. The RVSWRD subroutine is similar in structure to the program given in Exercise 1, but it reverses only the characters of a word, not the whole string. In both the 6502 and Z80 versions, the index register (X and IX respectively) is used to pass the start address of the word to the subroutine, and the accumulator is used to pass back to the calling program the value of the character that terminated the work (either a space or the string terminator character). Passing values this way is a very common Assembly language technique, and must be used with care — especially if you are in the habit of pushing all CPU registers at the start of every

subroutine (as demonstrated on page 161).

Another significant feature is the use of the Y register in the 6502 version, first to hold the start address of the word while X is used as an index on the stacking loop, then as an index on the 'un-stacking' loop while X holds the end address of the word. 'Address' is used imprecisely here as X and Y are single-byte registers, so neither can hold a full address. Instead, in this case they hold an offset to the address LABL1. In contrast, the Z80 IX and IY index registers can hold a full two-byte address.

In the Z80 version, IX and IY are not used at all — the HL and DE register pairs are used instead. Like the 6502 X and Y registers, these hold the word start and

Z80

```
          ORG    $C000
LAST1     EQU    $0D
SPACE     EQU    $20
LABL1     DB     'THIS IS A MESSAGE'
TERMN8    DB     LAST1
;
BEGIN     LD     DE,LABL1-1
LOOPO     CALL   RVSWRD
          CP     LAST1
ENDLPO    JR     NZ,LOOPO
          RET
;
;***REVERSE A WORD S/R***
LASTCH    DB     $00
RVSWRD    PUSH   DE
          POP    HL
          INC    HL
RVSLPO    INC    DE
          LD     A,(DE)
          PUSH   AF
          CP     SPACE
          JR     Z,CLRSTK
          CP     LAST1
ENDRVO    JR     NZ,RVSLPO
CLRSTK    POP    AF
          LD     (LASTCH),A
;
RVSLP1    POP    AF
          LD     (HL),A
          INC    HL
          LD     A,L
          CP     E
          JR     NZ,RVSLP1
          LD     A,H
          CP     D
ENDRV1    JR     NZ,RVSLP1
          LD     A,(LASTCH)
          RET
```

end addresses, but instead of being indexes on a base address, they are used as indirect addresses (the instruction LD A,(DE) means 'load the accumulator from the byte whose address is held in DE'). All the Z80 register pairs can be used in this way. An odd limitation of the instruction set is the lack of any two-byte comparison instruction. Thus, comparing the contents of DE and HL involves comparing E with L, then D with H. Similarly, in the 6502 version, X and Y are compared indirectly using a memory location, since there is no instruction for comparing X with Y.

MULTIPLE CHOICE

As we continue our investigation of Assembly language arithmetic, we consider the problems associated with subtraction, and the various ways of dealing with them. We also begin to look at the programming of multiplication in machine code, and introduce a new class of logical operations — the Shift and Rotate op-codes.

Both the Z80 and 6502 support the SBC (SuBtract with Carry) instruction, but their implementations are quite different. On the 6502, the carry flag is used to handle the *borrow* facility, which is the equivalent in subtraction of the carry facility in addition. In Z80 Assembly language, SBC works in exactly the same way as the ADC instruction — the carry flag is set or reset to indicate the result of the operation.

Suppose that we add $E4 to $5F using ADC (having cleared the carry flag first). The result in the accumulator is $43, and the carry flag is set, showing that the true result is $0143. There has been an overflow into the carry flag because the accumulator cannot contain the full result.

Now suppose that on the Z80 we again clear the carry flag, and subtract $E4 from $5F: the result in the accumulator is $7B, and the carry flag is set. If we now add $7B to $E4 (having cleared the carry flag once again) we find the result in the

accumulator to be $5F, and the carry flag is set. This is entirely consistent, as can be seen:

$5F − $E4 = $7B   Carry Set
$5F = $E4 + $7B   Carry Set

If we take the carry flag's state as indicating that a negative result has occurred, then we can interpret $7B as a two's complement number:

$7B In Binary	= 01111011
Take Away One	− 1
Gives One's Complement	01111010
Negate	
Gives Two's Complement	10000101 = $85

We should expect to find, then, that $5F − $E4 results in the negative number −$85. Let's check this result in decimal:

$5F =	95 decimal
−$E4 =	228 decimal
$85 =	−133 decimal

Clearly, this all makes sense as far as it goes. Suppose now that the subtraction in question was actually a two-byte sum: $375F − $21E4.

HI	LO		
$37	5F	=	14175 decimal
−$21	E4	=	−8676 decimal
$15	7B	=	5499 decimal

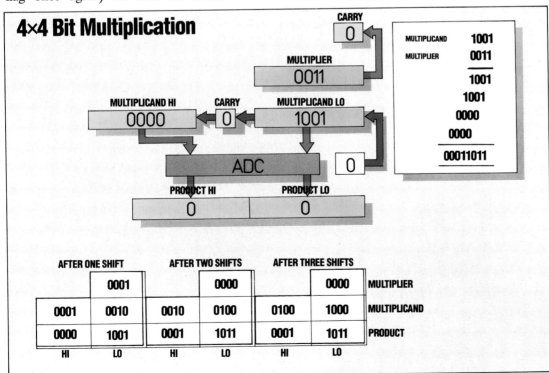

4×4 Bit Multiplication

AFTER ONE SHIFT		AFTER TWO SHIFTS		AFTER THREE SHIFTS		
	0001		0000		0000	MULTIPLIER
0001	0010	0010	0100	0100	1000	MULTIPLICAND
0000	1001	0001	1011	0001	1011	PRODUCT
HI	LO	HI	LO	HI	LO	

Shift Times
This example shows four-bit multiplication for the sake of clarity—the number of bits does not affect the algorithm. The worked example shows how the product is formed by the addition of zeros or shifted versions of the multiplicand, depending on whether each bit of the multiplier is zero or one. The multiplier bits are right-shifted through the carry flag, while the multiplicand bits are left-shifted from lo-byte to hi-byte through the carry flag

We know that if we do the lo-byte subtraction first the result is $7B, and a carry. That carry is then added by the SBC instruction to $21, making $22, which is then subtracted from $37, giving $15. The answer, $157B, can be seen to be correct by checking the decimal version.

Two-byte arithmetic on the Z80, therefore, follows this simple procedure:

1) Clear the carry flag.
2) Subtract the lo-bytes with carry.
3) Subtract the hi-bytes with carry.

The 6502 version of this sequence differs in the first particular — the carry flag must be set to permit a 'borrow' out of the lo-bytes from the hi-byte. If no borrow occurs, then the subtraction proceeds as normal, and the carry flag remains set for the subtraction of the hi-bytes, which should similarly proceed normally. If an underflow occurs in the lo-byte subtraction, however, the carry flag acts as the 'ninth bit' of the accumulator. This ensures that a correct result occurs there, and that the carry flag is then reset. When the hi-bytes are subtracted with a reset carry flag, the effect is the same as in the Z80 hi-byte subtraction with the carry flag set — the number to be subtracted is decremented before the subtraction takes place. Both methods of dealing with the subtraction borrow have their equivalent in the old-fashioned arithmetic methods of 'borrowing' here, and 'paying back' there. Let's consider the 6502 version in more detail.

If we clear the carry flag, and subtract $E4 from $5F, the result is $7A in the accumulator, and the carry flag remains clear. We have seen from the Z80 example that a 'true' result is $7B with the carry flag indicating a negative number. $7B is the two's complement of the 'real' answer (−$85). We can see that $7A is the one's complement of this number, and that the state of the carry flag, therefore, is a kind of switch on the accumulator's mode. That is to say, it is set for two's complement, and reset for one's complement.

If we do the subtraction on the 6502 with the carry flag set, then the accumulator contains $7B, and the carry flag is reset. If this is a two-byte subtraction, putting the carry flag into reset state will ensure that the hi-byte subtraction result is decremented, thus taking care of the 'borrow' from the lo-bytes.

MULTIPLICATION

Consider the decimal multiplication sum:

174	Multiplicand
×209	Multiplier
1566	1st Partial Product
000	2nd Partial Product
+348	3rd Partial product
36366	Final Product

You don't have to understand positional notation to use this method, you just have to be able to follow simple procedures and do single-digit multiplication. The heart of the method is the writing of each partial product one place to the left of the previous product (the empty columns are left blank here for emphasis). Once the necessity for this is accepted, then forming the partial products requires only a knowledge of the multiplication tables.

The combination of shifting partial products and rote learning of tables is what makes decimal long multiplication difficult for many people. There is only one real product in binary multiplication, and that is one times one; all other single-digit products result in zero. Consider this binary long multiplication sum:

1101	=	13 decimal
1001	=	9 decimal
1101		1st Partial Product
0000		2nd Partial Product
0000		3rd Partial Product
1101		4th Partial Product
1110101	=	117 decimal

The shifting of partial products is clearly seen in this example, as is the overall simplicity of multiplication in binary. A partial product is equal to either zero or to the shifted multiplicand, depending on whether the corresponding multiplier bit is one or zero. That immediately sounds like the sort of test we've become used to as

Logical Shift Right

ACCUMULATOR: 1 1 0 1 0 1 1 1 → PSR CARRY FLAG 0 BEFORE

ACCUMULATOR: 0 1 1 0 1 0 1 1 → 1 AFTER

Rotate Right With Branch

ACCUMULATOR: 0 1 1 1 0 0 1 1 → PSR CARRY FLAG 0 BEFORE

ACCUMULATOR: 1 0 1 1 1 0 0 1 → 1 AFTER

Rotate Left

ACCUMULATOR: 1 1 0 1 1 0 0 1 ← PSR CARRY FLAG 0 BEFORE

ACCUMULATOR: 1 0 1 1 0 0 1 0 ← 1 AFTER

an Assembly language control structure. To perform binary multiplication, examine each bit of the multiplier in turn, and add zero (if the bit is zero) or the shifted multiplicand (if the bit is one) to the total. How, then, do we examine a single bit of the multiplier, and how do we shift the multiplicand?

Testing the state of a particular bit in a byte can be done using the BIT instruction on both the Z80 and 6502 microprocessors. On the Z80, this instruction takes an address and a bit number as its operands, and the zero flag is set if that particular bit is zero and reset if the bit is one. On the 6502, the operand is an address. The contents of this address are ANDed with the accumulator, and the zero flag is set or reset, depending on whether the result is false or true.

These instructions permit subtle programming, but neither method is particularly convenient here. It would be much more convenient if the bit in question could be made to act as the carry or zero flag, so that program flow would branch automatically according to the state of each bit in turn. Needless to say, both processors' instruction sets make that possible through the use of the *shift* instructions. As the name implies, these will also solve the problem of shifting the multiplicand.

There are a variety of shift and *rotate* instructions in both instruction sets, although the Z80's are more complex than those of the 6502. In general, their effect is to shift each bit in a register one position to the right or to the left. They differ in detail in their treatment of the end bits of the register — a bit must be shifted out of the register at one end while another bit is shifted in at the other end. If bit 7 is shifted out of the register and put immediately back into bit 0, then the operation is a *rotate left*. If bit 0 is shifted into bit 7 the operation is a *rotate right*. If this is done, then the contents of the register change in order, no new values are introduced, and after eight such rotations the register will be restored to its original state.

If rotation is not employed, then a destination for the shifted-out bit is necessary, and a source must be found for the shifted-in bit. Both are most often supplied by the various condition flags of the processor status register (PSR), and in particular the carry flag. In constructing a multiplication subroutine to multiply two single-byte numbers, we need to shift the multiplicand left and the multiplier right. The multiplicand bits must be shifted out into the hi-byte of the multiplicand while zeros are shifted into the unoccupied bits. The multiplier bits have to be shifted through a PSR flag for testing, but their destination, and the state of the shifted-in multiplier bits, is unimportant unless we need to preserve the contents of the multiplier. All that concerns us about the multiplier during multiplication is whether the shifted-out bit is one or zero.

Given, therefore, that the multiplier is stored at address MPR, the multiplicand at MPDLO, and the product at PRODLO and PRODHI, we can write these subroutines as follows:

EIGHT-BIT MULTIPLICATION					
6502			**Z80**		
	ORG	$C100		ORG	$D000
START	LDA	#$00	START	LD	BC,(MPR)
	STA	PRODLO		LD	B,$08
	STA	PRODHI		LD	DE,(MPDLO)
	STA	MPDHI		LD	D,$00
	LDX	#8		LD	HL,$00
	CLC		LOOP0	SRL	C
LOOP0	ROR	MPR		JR	NC,CONT0
	BCC	CONT0		CALL	ADDIT
	JSR	ADDIT	CONT0	SLA	E
CONT0	ASL	MPDLO	ENDLP0	DJNZ	LOOP0
	ROL	MPDHI		LD	PRODLO
	DEX			RTS	
ENDLP0	BNE	LOOP0	MPR	DB	$E2
	RTS		MPDLO	DB	$7A
MPR	DB	$E2	MPDHI	DB	$00
MPDLO	DB	$7A	PRODLO	DW	$0000
MPDHI	DB	$00	ADDIT	ADD	HL,DE
PRODLO	DB	$00		RET	
PRODHI	DB	$00			
ADDIT	CLC				
	LDA	PRODLO			
	ADC	MPDLO			
	STA	PRODLO			
	LDA	PRODHI			
	ADC	MPDHI			
	STA	PRODHI			
	RTS				

As can be seen from this example, programming the Z80 is made much easier by its 16-bit registers and associated instructions. In particular, compare the ADDIT subroutine in the two programs. The 6502 version uses ROR to rotate the multiplier rightwards through the carry, and ASL and ROL to shift the multiplicand leftwards out of MPDLO into MPDHI through the carry. The loop is controlled by the X register as a counter.

The Z80 version uses SRL to shift the multiplier rightwards through the carry, and SLA and RL to shift the multiplicand leftwards in DE via the carry. The loop is controlled by register B as a counter. Notice that the ADD instruction not only supports 16-bit register arithmetic, but also is not affected by the carry flag — unlike ADC.

In the next instalment of the course, we will discuss methods of division, and consider various ways of controlling the screen display. This will complete the tutorial element of the course, and will be followed by 6502 and Z80 exercises and examples in future instalments.

Exercise 15

1) Write a multiplication subroutine using a 16-bit multiplicand and an eight-bit multiplier of your choice.
2) Multiplication is merely repeated addition: write an eight-bit by eight-bit multiplication subroutine that does not use the shift or rotate instructions.

THE GREAT DIVIDE

We conclude this series of machine code tutorials with a brief study of unsigned binary division and the use of operating system ROM routines in Assembly language screen display programming. In a summary of this introduction to machine code we review the major themes and topics — from BASIC to branching, from arrays to assemblers.

Just as we used the manual long multiplication method as an algorithm for binary multiplication (see page 168), so the manual long division method is a model for binary division. Consider this binary long division:

```
        00001110 r00              quotient
1011)10011010                     dividend
    −1011                         subtract divisor
     10000
     −1011                        subtract divisor
      1011
      −1011                       subtract divisor
        00                        no remainder
```

The essence of the method is the repeated subtraction of the divisor from the high order bits of the dividend. Depending on the result of this subtraction, a zero or a one is shifted into the quotient. The remainder is the result of the last subtraction of a divisor.

The various ways in which this algorithm may be implemented in Assembly language are not as apparent as they were for multiplication. However, as before, the Z80 version uses the power and flexibility of its 16-bit registers, while the 6502 must fetch and carry eight bits at a time. The divisor is in the address labelled DIVSR, the dividend in DVDND, the quotient in QUOT, and the remainder in RMNDR. The program in Z80 and 6502 Assembly language is given.

Notice in both cases that when the divisor is subtracted from the partial dividend with a negative result, the dividend must be restored by adding the divisor back in again. The 6502 version is noteworthy for its treatment of the processor status register after the divisor subtraction: the carry flag must be rotated into the quotient, but its state must also be preserved to indicate the result of the subtraction. Consequently, the PSR is pushed onto the stack before the rotation, and pulled off it afterwards, thus restoring the carry to its immediate post-subtraction state.

We have now considered the four rules of arithmetic — this is plainly worth doing as a

16-BIT BY 8-BIT DIVISION					
Z80			**6502**		
START	LD	A,(DIVSR)	START	LDA	#$00
	LD	D,A		STA	QUOT
	LD	E,$00		STA	RMNDR
	LD	HL,(DVDND)		LDX	#$08
	LD	B,$08		LDA	DVDHI
LOOP0	AND	A		SEC	
	SBC	HL,DE		SBC	DIVSR
	INC	HL	LOOP0	PHP	
	JP	P,POSRES		ROL	QUOT
NEGRES	ADD	HL,DE		ASL	DVDLO
	DEC	HL		ROL	A
POSRES	ADD	HL,HL		PLP	
	DJNZ	LOOP0		BCC	CONT1
	LD	(QUOT),HL		SBC	DIVSR
	RET			JMP	CONT2
DIVSR	DB	$F9	CONT1	ADC	DIVSR
DVDND	DW	$FDE8	CONT2	DEX	
QUOT	DB	$00		BNE	LOOP0
RMNDR	DB	$00		BCS	EXIT
				ADC	DIVSR
				CLC	
			EXIT	ROL	QUOT
				STA	RMNDR
				RTS	
			DIVSR	DB	$F9
			DVDLO	DB	$E8
			DVDHI	DB	$FD
			QUOT	DB	$00
			RMNDR	DB	$00

programming exercise for the insight it brings to machine processes, but inventing all the various combinations of single- and multiple-byte arithmetic is unnecessary, given that programmers have been writing these routines in textbooks and magazines for years. When the need arises for variations of the routines that we have developed, they will be supplied or set as exercises.

SCREEN OUTPUT

So far in the course we have used RAM memory and the CPU as a calculating system, and left the results of our efforts somewhere in RAM to be inspected manually using a monitor program. This is obviously unsatisfactory, but until arithmetic and subroutine calls had been studied there was simply no point in considering the screen output from machine code.

Most micros have a memory-mapped display. This means that an area of RAM is dedicated to holding an image of the screen. The screen display is composed of dots, or pixels, which are either on or off. These can, therefore, be represented by binary ones (on) or zeros (off), and the entire contents of the screen can be regarded as a 'mapping' into dots of the bits that comprise those bytes of screen RAM. Unfortunately, although the BBC Micro, the Spectrum and the Commodore 64 all use this mapping technique, none of them does so in a straightforward manner. For our purposes, the simplest method would be to divide each row of the screen into pixel bytes numbered consecutively from left to right, the leftmost byte in a row following the rightmost in the preceding row. For a variety of reasons this is not the case on any of these machines. Let's consider each case separately.

The Spectrum screen is always in high resolution mode, and a fixed area of memory is set aside for mapping the screen. The mapping is complex, however, as the screen is divided horizontally into three blocks of eight PRINT rows, and each print row is divided horizontally into eight pixel rows. The addressing of the bytes that comprise these rows is sequential within the rows, but not between the rows. The BBC Micro and the Commodore 64 do not follow this pattern, but are equally devious. For the moment, it is considerably easier to understand if we confine ourselves to outputting ASCII characters to the screen.

This is something that the machine does all the time, and there are, therefore, machine code routines in ROM for the purpose. Given a suitably detailed description of their operation, we can call these routines from our own Assembly language programs. What we need to know is the call address, the communication registers, and any necessary preliminaries.

On the Spectrum there are no preliminaries to observe, and the communicating register is the accumulator, which must contain the ASCII code of the character to be printed. We need only issue the instruction RST $10 and the character whose code is in the accumulator will be printed on the screen at the current cursor position. This is very much the pattern of the other two systems, but the RST (ReSTart) op-code is peculiar to the Z80 command set: it is a single-byte zero-page branch instruction that must take one of only eight possible operands—$00,$08,$10,$18, etc. to $38. Each of these locations points to the start address of a ROM routine, somewhere in zero page. These routines are typically dedicated to handling input and output, and we call them through the RST instruction rather than directly by address. This is partly for speed (it is quicker to use RST than CALL, although only the CPU would notice the difference), and partly for the sake of the program's portability. If every Z80 programmer knows that RST $10 calls the PRINT routine on every Z80 machine, then nobody is going to bother about where a particular systems software engineer actually locates the PRINT routine, and the engineer is free to locate it anywhere, provided that zero page is arranged in such a way that the RST locations direct programs to the start

addresses of the commonly-agreed routines.

On the BBC Micro the procedure is similar: an ASCII code in the accumulator combined with a JSR $FFEE command will cause the character to be PRINTed on the screen at the current cursor position. This is the OSWRCH routine, much referred to in BBC literature and well documented in the Advanced User Guide.

The Commodore 64 follows the pattern of the other two machines. An ASCII code in the accumulator and a JSR $FFD2 command causes the character to be PRINTed at the current cursor position. This is the CHKOUT routine, and is documented in the Programmer's Reference Guide.

This, therefore, is the general pattern of use of ROM routines and demonstrates the principle of communication registers. A communication between the calling program and a subroutine may pass either way — an input routine, for example, might pass a character from an external device to the CPU via the accumulator. Even when there is no substantive information passed like this, an error code may well be returned from the subroutine through one of the registers. This sort of protocol is documented in the many machine-specific works of reference now available.

Input from the keyboard and other devices will be dealt with in later instalments, as will high resolution plotting from machine code. We conclude this instalment of the course with a summary of the various aspects of Assembly language and machine code programming.

IN SUMMARY

We began the course with a wide-ranging look at machine code from a very non-specific point of view, trying to dispel some of its mystique and place it in context as just one kind of code among all the others that we (and computers) use. We have seen how the same sequence of bytes in RAM can be interpreted at one moment as a string of ASCII data, at the next as a BASIC program line, at the next as a string of two-byte addresses, and then again as a sequence of machine code instructions. A few minutes spent playing with a machine code monitor program should convince you that some sequences of bytes can be disassembled as three quite different, but valid, sequences of instructions — depending on whether you start the disassembly at the first, second or third byte in the sequence. Nothing intrinsic to the code prevents this happening, and the CPU itself cannot tell whether it's executing the code that you wrote, or some garbled version of it, accidentally transposed in memory.

We went on to consider the organisation of memory, and the common conventions of addressing. To make any sense of this we had to begin the study of binary arithmetic, which immediately delineated the horizons on our view from the CPU — in eight-bit processors we are confined, except in particular circumstances, to the limits of a byte (in other words, the range of decimal numbers 0-255). Once we encountered the meaning and appropriateness of binary arithmetic, the limitations of the decimal system for dealing with the world of Assembly language became apparent. In exploring the idea of paged memory we saw how the size of the logical pages must be a function of the number base, and in a binary system that means that the page size must be a power of two. Two to the power of eight gives 256 — the magic number in an eight-bit microprocessor system.

Binary very quickly became too unwieldy and too prone to error for use as a numbering system, and we passed on to hexadecimal (number base 16) arithmetic. We saw how the eight-bit byte can be fully represented by two hex digits, from $00 to $FF, one digit representing the state of the lower four bits, and the other standing for the upper four bits of the byte.

STORING AND ADDRESSING

The way that BASIC programs are stored in the program area was exhaustively examined. By describing tokenisation as another form of machine code, we gave a useful insight into the operating system. Our discussion of end-of-line markers showed how the BASIC interpreter handles the difficulty of telling where one piece of code ends and another starts, and the Commodore's link addressing introduced both the lo-hi address convention and the idea of indirect addressing.

From there we moved directly into Assembly language itself. We started from the primitive operations of the CPU as directed by the eight-bit op-codes that constitute its program instructions. With the idea of coding so thoroughly explored, it was a short step to Assembly language mnemonics. Once we had made that step it became clearer that programming in machine code or Assembly language or BASIC was still just programming, and that what counted was solving the logical problem before worrying about how to code the solution. Problem-solving has been the central theme of the course. But the obscurity of some of Assembly language's concepts forced our attention first to clearing the haze of confusion that besets most people on first contact with low-level languages.

The course proceeded to spend some time on the practicalities of loading and running machine code programs on computers that were more or less dedicated to running BASIC programs. We looked at system variables and operating system pointers on the BBC Micro, Spectrum, and Commodore 64, and learned how to 'steal' space from BASIC.

We glanced at the architecture of small computer systems and the Z80 and 6502 CPUs, and moved on to begin writing Assembly language programs that manipulated memory and the accumulator. Assembler directives or pseudo-ops were introduced here, a step towards practicality and the real world, but also a step away

from machine code, manual assembly, and the laborious detail of low-level programming.

The need for the logical constructs of a programming language was now obvious, and we turned to considering the processor status register (PSR). Its role as a recorder of the results of CPU operations was immediately illustrated in an introduction to binary arithmetic, using the 'add with carry' instruction. The central role of the PSR and, in arithmetic, of the carry flag, was obvious as soon as it was seen. The course has concentrated on the processor status register and the associated instructions since then.

CHANGING THE FLOW

We briefly examined the various addressing modes; indexed addressing was given most attention because of its importance in handling loops, lists and tables. The need for a class of instruction to change the flow of control in a program is evident once these structures are introduced, so we began to examine the conditional branch instructions while still exploring the potential of indexed and indirect addressing. With conditional branching, primitive arithmetic and array-type structures, we have almost all the bones of any programming language. Fleshing out the form through practice and systematic investigation is the remaining task.

The Assembly language subroutine call and return was examined both for itself and as a way of introducing the last unexplored area of the operating system — the stack. Seeing how it works, what it is for, and how we might use it introduced some new ploys to the repertoire of machine code programming, while a more searching look at the CPU registers and their interactions introduced new possibilities in the manipulation of memory and the microprocessor.

Finally, with a working knowledge of the architecture of the microprocessor and a vocabulary of op-code instructions, we approached binary arithmetic. The oddities of subtraction and two's complement, and the complexities of multiplication and division have all been covered in detail.

Answers To Exercises On Page 169

1) The fastest-running solution is certainly a routine written specifically for 16-bit multiplicands, on the same lines as the eight-bit routine in the last instalment. On the other hand, if you split 16-bit multiplication into two separate eight-bit multiplications (multiplier by lo-byte, followed by multiplier by hi-byte), then you can call the existing eight-bit routine twice, adjust for a carry out of the lo-byte, and store the results in the product bytes.

2) A multiplication routine using repeated addition consists simply of a loop whose counter is the value of the multiplier; each time the loop is executed, the multiplicand is added into the product.

ROR — ROTATE RIGHT
Register — 6A (1 byte) `6502`

The contents of the byte are rotated one bit right through the carry.

EFFECT ON PSR

S V B D I Z C
MSB [X][ ][ ][ ][ ][X][X] LSB

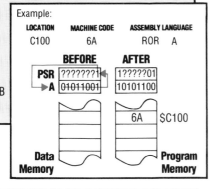

RR — ROTATE RIGHT
Register CB (2 bytes) `Z80`

The contents of the byte are rotated one bit right through the carry.

EFFECT ON PSR

S Z H V N C
MSB [X][X][ ][0][ ][X][0][X] LSB

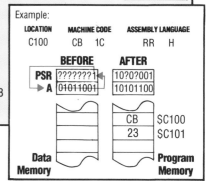

SBC — SUBTRACT WITH BORROW
Absolute -ED (3 bytes) `6502`

The contents of the memory location are subtracted from the accumulator; carry shows borrow status.

EFFECT ON PSR

S V B D I Z C
MSB [X][X][ ][ ][ ][X][X] LSB

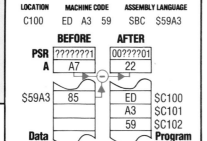

SBC — SUBTRACT WITH BORROW
Immediate — DE (2 bytes) `Z80`

The contents of the byte following the op-codes are subtracted from the accumulator.

EFFECT ON PSR

S Z H V N C
MSB [X][X][ ][X][ ][ ][X][X] LSB

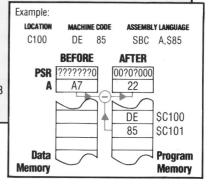

ASL — ARITHMETIC SHIFT LEFT
Register —0A (1 byte) `6502`

The contents of the byte are shifted one bit left through the carry; zero is shifted into lsb.

EFFECT ON PSR

S V B D I Z C
MSB [X][ ][ ][ ][ ][X][X] LSB

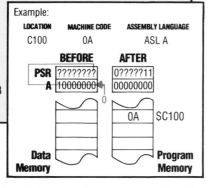

SLA — SHIFT LEFT ARITHMETIC
Register —CB (2 bytes) `Z80`

The contents of the byte are shifted one bit left through the carry; zero is shifted into lsb.

EFFECT ON PSR

S Z H V N C
MSB [X][X][ ][0][ ][X][0][X] LSB

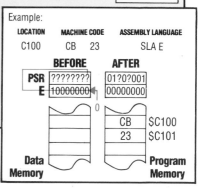

CMP — COMPARE THE ACCUMULATOR
Absolute -CD (3 bytes) `6502`

The contents of the memory location are compared with the accumulator.

EFFECT ON PSR

S V B D I Z C
MSB [X][ ][ ][ ][ ][X][X] LSB

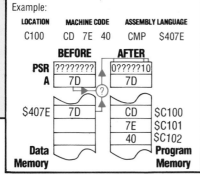

CP — COMPARE THE ACCUMULATOR
Immediate — FE (2 bytes) `Z80`

The contents of the byte following the op-code are compared with the accumulator.

EFFECT ON PSR

S Z H V N C
MSB [X][X][ ][X][ ][X][1][X] LSB

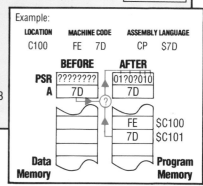

5 SOFTWARE

Word processing, databases and spreadsheets are by far
the most common 'serious' software applications on the
micro. Although these tend to be dismissed by home
computer users as suitable purely for business, they have
many facilities that are rarely explored.

WRITING FOR THE SCREEN

Many home programmers dream of writing a best seller. But they rarely realise what they are up against. Professional software companies have enormous resources behind them to help produce their chart-toppers. One UK software house has over £250,000 worth of minicomputers dedicated to creating packages for home micros.

Expensive equipment doesn't necessarily mean successful programs; some amateur writers have managed to make a small fortune with software they've produced on a Spectrum at home. All the same, home programming whizzkids are becoming an endangered species, especially with the development of the big software houses over the past few years. Their powerful computers and sophisticated programming aids give them a real advantage over the home computer owner and allow their programmers to be more productive.

One of the most important attributes of serious software for home machines is the speed of operation; and this means that programs need to be written (at least in part) in machine code. But machine code is extremely difficult to work with — in particular, machine code programmers need other pieces of software to help write their programs. At the very least, an assembler program will be required to translate the programmer's source code into the object code that the machine understands, and this can be quite a challenging job if a big program is involved. Many software writers work in this way. To write a program for the Spectrum, for example, they will use an assembler program running on the same machine. This method has its limitations.

Primarily, the quality of assembler programs available for home machines is poor. Even the simplest of these packages will use up considerable amounts of memory, and therefore limit the size of the programs that can be written with it. Many home machines are also extremely unpleasant to work with for long periods of time: poor keyboards, poor displays and, in some cases, a lack of disk drives, can make using such equipment a tortuous task.

For these reasons most professional companies don't use the micro that the program is intended for (called the 'target machine'), but use business computers with special software (known as 'development systems') instead. Programmers using these machines often write in languages such as PASCAL and C. They use versions of these

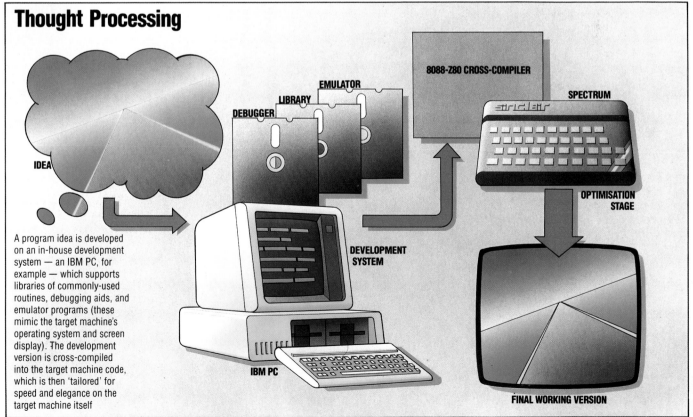

Thought Processing

IDEA

DEBUGGER

LIBRARY

EMULATOR

8088-Z80 CROSS-COMPILER

SPECTRUM

OPTIMISATION STAGE

DEVELOPMENT SYSTEM

IBM PC

A program idea is developed on an in-house development system — an IBM PC, for example — which supports libraries of commonly-used routines, debugging aids, and emulator programs (these mimic the target machine's operating system and screen display). The development version is cross-compiled into the target machine code, which is then 'tailored' for speed and elegance on the target machine itself

FINAL WORKING VERSION

KEVIN JONES

Intelligent Software
Specialising in strategy games
such as chess, IS uses IBMs
and Apples, with its own
specially-developed interfaces,
to develop software. Dividing
programs into their machine-
dependent and universal
segments makes it easier for IS
to support a range of
computers and dedicated
chess-playing machines

languages known as cross-compilers or cross-assemblers, which permit the work to be done on a micro that uses an 8086 processor, for example, while the programs that are produced will work on machines with Z80 processors. These cross-compilers are high-level languages (like BASIC), which makes them easy for the programmer to use, but the programs they create are written in machine code. Skilled machine code programmers scrutinise the programs that are developed, and often succeed in further optimising them.

Clearly, a development system has an enormous advantage over the home micro. A disk-based assembler, or one making use of expanded RAM space to store larger tables, will work more efficiently than an assembler that has to be wound in off tape and operates in the confines of a home micro. Debugging routines can be added into the development version of the code, with no worries about the code being too big for memory. It is also far better to work on a business computer that has a good keyboard, sharp display and disk drives.

A firm that makes use of this technique of program development is Intelligent Software (IS), founded in 1981 out of a pooling of experience between David Levy, the chess specialist, and Robert Madge's ANT Microware. The company specialises in strategy games, mostly written on contract for all the popular home micros. They also develop the software side of dedicated chess machines. Although there are no rapid combat displays in games like chess and bridge, a great deal of computation goes on behind the scenes. So, like arcade games, strategy games also need the speed of assembler-written software.

As well as using the target machines themselves for development, IS uses IBM PCs and Apples with specially developed interfaces to allow code to be exchanged across its range of machines. The company is often involved in conversion projects — transferring a chess game, say, from one computer to another — so its programmers have

TONY SLEEP

learned to write code in a form that is easily segmented. One level of segmentation that proves useful when the time comes to hand code from one processor to another is the division of the program into playing code and input/output code. The I/O code on the new machine will have different port or memory addresses, and will perhaps be strategically different too (polling replaced by interrupts, and so forth). Ingenuity may well be required to get round the hardware limitations, but there won't be a forbidding quantity of input/output. Playing code, on the other hand, will be there in abundance, but because it is isolated from the hardware (except, of course, the processor) its conversion will be straightforward.

IS wants to avoid restricting programmers' inventiveness, so there are very few 'house rules' to govern the writing of code. One important point that it insists on, though, is that source code includes numerous comments, so it is always clear what the routines are doing.

Where programmers are working at home for a software house, each developing his or her own project, there is little pooling of resources. In this case, individuality is preserved at the cost of a great deal of duplicated effort, because the code for similar routines has to be reinvented by each separate programmer.

One software company, Psion, is making use of computers even larger than the IBM PC. Among British software houses writing for the home computer games market, Psion is unique in doing the bulk of its development on minicomputers. The company's hardware installation alone is worth a quarter of a million pounds.

Psion began as a company by developing software for the ZX81 — and used ZX81s to do it.

BOB BROMIDE

Visions
Programmers working from
home on the target machines
provide the bulk of Visions'
programming effort. After the
game concept and scenarios
have been decided, the
component routines are
developed in native Assembly
language (Z80 or 6502) using
assemblers such as HiSoft
DevPak on the Spectrum

When it went on to create the Horizons tape issued with every Spectrum, Psion bought a TRS-80 with disks, a machine that uses the same Z80 processor, and built a special interface between the two machines. But by August 1982, the company decided that it couldn't go on knocking up a completely different development system every time a new home computer went on the market. So it ploughed back profits into buying heavyweight hardware with plenty of spare processing power. In principle, this hardware should be flexible enough to cope with whatever computers the future might bring. The machines chosen were a pair of Vax 750s, running the DEC operating system VMS.

The Vax 750s brought two advantages to Psion: the quality of the software provided by DEC, with the opportunity it provides to create specially designed software aids, and the sheer 'muscle-power' of the operating system and hardware combination. There is plenty of room for a collection of software aids like compilers, libraries of common subroutines, and debugging programs, all shared between the 16 to 20 programmers who may be logged on to a single machine at the same time. The two machines allow software to be easily transferred from one to the other when needed.

Libraries of common subroutines had already been part of Psion's philosophy in the TRS-80 days, but on a dual floppy system swapping the data between disks became tedious. The new Vax machines allow teams of writers to work together, sharing common project libraries from which modules can be called up almost instantly, and libraries can even be shared between teams working on different projects. This is the big advantage of a timesharing system — and as an added bonus it will also take care of their administrative work without having to interrupt the programmers. Psion plans to add a third Vax to shoulder the administration tasks, leaving two machines free for software production.

Even if you could afford it, you would be wrong to think that going out and buying a Vax would instantly put you on a par with Psion. Very little of this well-developed work environment has been handed to Psion on a plate by DEC. It has taken a lot of hard slog, both to get simple tasks performed efficiently and reliably, and in the large number of hand-wrought software aids and utilities (written in C) that Psion has added.

Psion uses C, an 'intermediate-level' language that can produce reasonably compact and fast object code for 16-bit chips like the 8086, although this is far from the case for eight-bit C compilers. So in writing for target machines like the Spectrum it has been necessary for Psion to develop its own special techniques. Psion is not keen to disclose its secrets, but it is known the company used C to write its own compiler, which in default of a name gets called 'our table language'. This looks a little like C, is portable between different processors, and creates

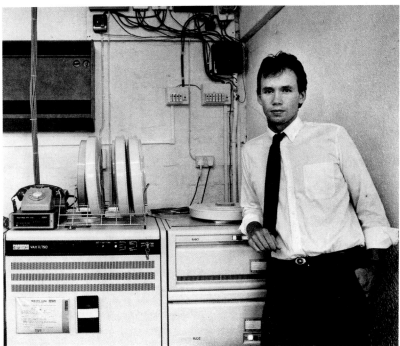

TONY SLEEP

Psion
In 1982 this company bought a pair of Vax 750 minicomputers as the basis of their software development system. Each machine allows up to 20 programmers at a time to use the range of cross-compilers, software libraries and debuggers for creating and translating programs

extremely efficient code.

There is a universal rule that system maintenance and writing in-house programming aids like the table language generally takes 30 per cent of the entire programming effort, but Psion finds the extra time well worth while. Having the source code developed in-house means total ownership: you can take it to pieces and improve or adapt it in a way completely impossible with commercially acquired software. If a bug turns up in bought-in software it is difficult or impossible to get it fixed, and there is usually no question of making internal changes.

The special software bought by Psion includes programs that are exact simulations of popular microprocessors, such as the Z80 and 6502. Thus, the DEC Vax computers can be made to behave just as if they were Commodore 64s or Spectrums. Despite the power of the Vax computers, the simulators run at a fraction of the speed of the target machine. The advantage is that they allow the programmer to look at the contents of every register inside the microprocessor at any stage of the program. This is particularly useful for tracking down bugs in programs. Normally, when a machine code program goes wrong and crashes, the programmer can't tell what went wrong. Psion can thus save many hours of debugging.

Much of Psion's recent development effort has gone into producing the suite of four standard business programs that are provided with the Sinclair QL. The Motorola 68000 family of chips, one of which powers the QL, was designed around high-level languages, and C programs compile down so efficiently on these chips that writing in assembler becomes unnecessary. If all home computers followed the QL lead, C could replace assembler completely, and Psion and the smaller software houses could leave the Dickensian work of hand-coded translation behind forever.

SUM OF THE PARTS

'Integrated software' has become one of the fashionable expressions of the software business. Here we discuss exactly what is meant by integration and look at the advantages and disadvantages such a system offers.

Integration represents one of the most exciting trends in software ever. And while for the moment it applies mainly to business systems, its techniques have begun to filter down to home micros. An example of this is the Sinclair QL, whose four software packages encompass the main principles of integration.

The main achievement of integration is to enable the programmer to switch between different packages quickly and simply. In an ideal system it should not be necessary to quit one program, return to the operating system, swap disks and then start up another program. To be effective, the change of application has to be almost at the push of a key and some programs, such as the Lotus 1-2-3 and Ashton Tate's Framework achieve this.

It is also useful to be able to transfer data between packages easily. For example, you might create a column of yearly sales figures for your business in the spreadsheet program, then transfer that whole column to the word processing program where you might be writing the annual report. You could use the names and addresses in a database file with the word processor to write a personalised letter to all the people on file. On the

Lisa and Macintosh, this facility is extended to the point where you can create a freehand drawing with the graphics program and then move it straight to a word-processed document.

In addition, all the different programs should work in the same way and feel the same in use. Screen layouts, command keys, prompts, error messages — all the aspects of the 'user interface' — should be identical or comparable. If they are not, the user cannot confidently go from one area to another without having to stop and adjust to the change in operating procedures. This interrupts the flow with which the software can be used and does not allow it to be exploited to the full.

A handy side effect is that the package becomes easier to learn. Having to learn to use five new application programs — some menu-driven, others command-driven, all with different command formats — is a daunting task for anyone. But if they all work in the same way, you need to learn one only. This feature is known as 'commonality' and is often referred to when integrated software is discussed.

We have established then that integrated software involves three design principles: the ease of switching from one application to another; freely interchangable data; and commonality of format. This contributes to making the computer more accessible to the average user whose needs can be met with two or three software applications. It will also undoubtedly increase the popularity of the personal computer as it becomes more efficient and easier to use.

However, integrated software also has its disadvantages. Primary among these is the fact that integrated software packages need large amounts of RAM to operate. Imagine trying to fit a word processor, spreadsheet, and database — the three applications that are most commonly integrated — into 16 or 32 Kbytes. It can probably be done, but there would not be much, if any, room left to store data. It is this problem that restricts integrated software to machines with large memories: in general, to computers with 128 Kbytes or more. Of course, programs that are integrated can share some routines, so disk storage operations and other housekeeping activities need only to be written once. Nevertheless, each application has its own special requirements, and these take up space in RAM.

A second weakness of integrated software is an offshoot of the same problem of storage. To save on the amount of memory a program requires, software writers take shortcuts with the individual applications. A word processor that is built into an integrated package with two or three other

COURTESY OF MICROSCOPE

IAN McKINNELL

applications cannot be as thorough and as complete as a word processor that stands on its own. The main reason for this is that a stand-alone program can take up as much memory by itself as the integrated programs take together.

One example can be found with two programs that run on the IBM PC and similar computers. Multimate is a program designed around the software that is used in Wang dedicated word processing equipment. It has many options for creating and formatting text that are not found in smaller programs, which makes creating very large and complex documents fairly simple. Multimate by itself requires 192 Kbytes of RAM to operate. Lotus 1-2-3, an integrated word processor, spreadsheet and database program, also requires 192 Kbytes. Yet the same space used by Multimate for one application must now handle all the software required for three complete programs in Lotus. As a result, the word processor in Lotus 1-2-3 is limited to simple memo writing.

A third disadvantage of integration also arises from one of its strengths. It is important, as we have seen, for integrated programs to look alike, so they are easy to learn and operate. Unfortunately, certain compromises have to be made by the software writers for this to be possible. The best way to operate a spreadsheet might not be the best way to use a database or word processor, so elements of the optimum design for each tend to be blended into a usable mixture. Microsoft found this to be a problem when designing a stand-alone word processor, Microsoft Word. The company wanted the screen display and the program's operation to be compatible with their hugely successful spreadsheet, Multiplan, so it would be easy to integrate the two programs. Microsoft included the same on-screen menu in Word that Multiplan users found so helpful, only to discover that the writers who needed a program like Word disliked having a menu on the screen all the time.

The point to remember about all software is that it has to do what the user wants. If a person has several tasks to do, like letter writing, simple accounts, and mailing lists, integrated software can make the job much easier. But there are sacrifices, and someone who wants to write a novel or very lengthy company reports on his microcomputer may have to continue to use separate, stand-alone word processors, spreadsheets, and database programs. Nevertheless, as software writers learn more about compressing computer instructions into smaller and smaller spaces in memory, and the memory in home machines starts to inch its way upward, integrated software will become more and more important to the home user as well as the business user. As a hint of things to come, two under-£500 computers are being sold with integrated software: Sinclair's QL, and the Commodore Plus/4.

To illustrate this approach, we will take a closer look at some of the integrated programs that are having a large effect on software development.

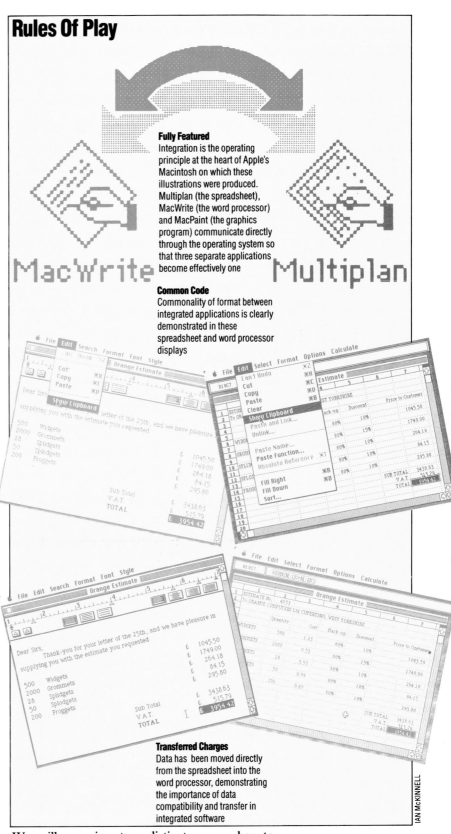

Rules Of Play

Fully Featured
Integration is the operating principle at the heart of Apple's Macintosh on which these illustrations were produced. Multiplan (the spreadsheet), MacWrite (the word processor) and MacPaint (the graphics program) communicate directly through the operating system so that three separate applications become effectively one

Common Code
Commonality of format between integrated applications is clearly demonstrated in these spreadsheet and word processor displays

Transferred Charges
Data has been moved directly from the spreadsheet into the word processor, demonstrating the importance of data compatibility and transfer in integrated software

We will examine two distinct approaches to integration: one exemplified by Lotus 1-2-3 and similar programs, in which the applications, although working together, look very much like typical computer programs have always looked and the second type found on machines like Lisa and Macintosh, where the whole operating environment is designed for integration.

IAN McKINNELL

SYMPHONY
IN SOFTWARE

We now examine in detail Lotus's 1-2-3 and Symphony, and Psion's Xchange, three packages that are designed for large business systems but whose techniques will soon be applied to lower-priced machines.

As we have already seen, integrated software requires an environment in which the user has instant access to all the different tasks that may be required, where operating procedures remain the same no matter which application is being used, and where information may be moved freely between different applications. There are many different ways of achieving these aims.

Lotus 1-2-3 uses the familiar spreadsheet format, in which figures and formulae are entered into a matrix of 'cells' and can be freely amended and instantly recalculated. However, 1-2-3 offers many extra facilities and can be used for much more than just financial forecasting and analysis. The spreadsheet cells may be used to store information such as names and telephone numbers as well as numeric data, so a specific area of the grid may be used as a table containing relevant details — for example, a list of clients and

their associated account numbers. As 1-2-3 offers functions for searching for and reorganising such information, this grid area may in effect be used as a small database. It is also possible to take a set of cells containing numeric data and use 1-2-3 to display this information in the form of different types of graph, thus removing the need for a separate business graphics program. Finally, 1-2-3's text-handling capabilities mean that it can be used for memo writing, although memory limitations preclude its use as a true word processor.

This combination of different facilities means that 1-2-3 is the only program that many users ever need. Because all the information for different applications is contained in a single spreadsheet, it is easy to achieve results that would be impossible with traditional programs. For example, let's assume that a 1-2-3 user operates several different news-stands in different parts of a large city, and needs to record weekly, monthly, quarterly and annual sales figures for each location. This is best done by placing the location of each stand and its sales figures into a spreadsheet. Formulae are written in such a way that the only figures that must be changed by the

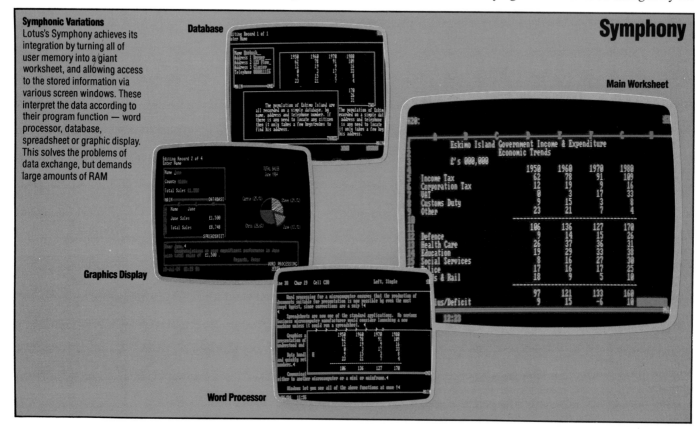

Symphonic Variations
Lotus's Symphony achieves its integration by turning all of user memory into a giant worksheet, and allowing access to the stored information via various screen windows. These interpret the data according to their program function — word processor, database, spreadsheet or graphic display. This solves the problems of data exchange, but demands large amounts of RAM

user are the weekly receipts for each stand — other figures are then adjusted automatically.

So far, this is all standard spreadsheet material, but what if the owner wishes to put the stands in order of sales, so that the location with the highest sales is at the top of the list? These stands would initially be entered in alphabetical order, but will need re-sorting each week on receipt of the new sales figures. With Lotus 1-2-3 this may be done quickly and easily. The newsstand owner may require a weekly chart that shows how each stand has performed; a sequence of keypresses will allow this information to be retrieved for the spreadsheet/database, displayed in graph form, and printed out.

LOTUS SYMPHONY

Lotus's follow-up to 1-2-3 is called Symphony, and follows the same principle of basing applications on the spreadsheet format. However, Symphony allows the user to divide the screen display into separate windows, each of which focuses on a different part of the spreadsheet. Each window is formatted in a manner appropriate to the information it displays.

If the information to be displayed is held as text, the window takes the form of a small word processor screen, with margins and tab stops clearly marked. If a graph display is required, the window will show the labelled and scaled axes. Database information is displayed with each entry having its own screen; this looks like a card-index record. So, although Symphony is really an overgrown spreadsheet, it gives the impression of having four major applications all onscreen and working at the same time.

Like 1-2-3, Symphony can 'learn' particular sequences of keystrokes so that the user can automate any operations that are carried out frequently. The small programs that activate the sequence are called 'keyboard macros'. Symphony also includes its own high-level programming language. Programs are stored on the worksheet in the same way as all other data, and have access to all the operations available: so, if you have a task such as an invoicing or stock control system, you can write the program in Symphony's programming language and it will automatically be part of all the applications in the Symphony 'environment'. Once you are familiar with Symphony, you will find it easier to write programs in its command language than it is to use a separate programming language such as BASIC because Symphony already deals with such tasks as drawing graphs or searching for and organising data.

Symphony is just one of several similar systems that are now on the market. Ashton Tate's Framework is a strong competitor — this provides a similar range of functions but hides its underlying data structures to an even greater extent. Both Symphony and Framework are expensive (around £400 each) and require large amounts of memory. Symphony will work with

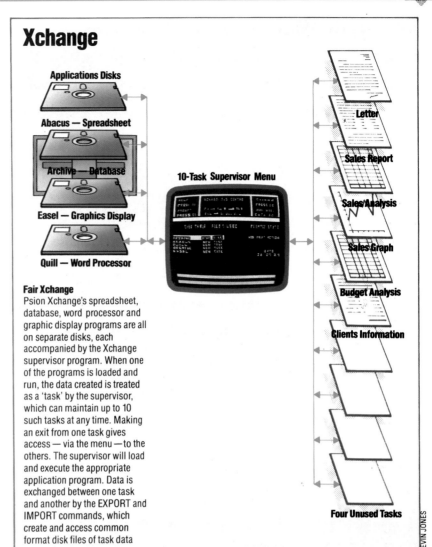

Xchange

Applications Disks

Abacus — Spreadsheet

Archive — Database

Easel — Graphics Display

Quill — Word Processor

10-Task Supervisor Menu

Fair Xchange
Psion Xchange's spreadsheet, database, word processor and graphic display programs are all on separate disks, each accompanied by the Xchange supervisor program. When one of the programs is loaded and run, the data created is treated as a 'task' by the supervisor, which can maintain up to 10 such tasks at any time. Making an exit from one task gives access — via the menu — to the others. The supervisor will load and execute the appropriate application program. Data is exchanged between one task and another by the EXPORT and IMPORT commands, which create and access common format disk files of task data

Letter

Sales Report

Sales Analysis

Sales Graph

Budget Analysis

Clients Information

Four Unused Tasks

KEVIN JONES

320 Kbytes of RAM but really requires 512 Kbytes to make the most of its facilities, while Framework needs a minimum of 256 Kbytes. As a result of these demands, the packages will run on 16-bit microcomputers only.

Interestingly, neither Symphony nor Framework requires information or portions of program to be swapped between disks and main memory, as is the case with most business programs. In theory, of course, computer memory continues to become cheaper and cheaper, so it is not unreasonable for software developers to assume that most users will have large amounts available. In practice, however, this is not yet the case and it will be some time before such memory-intensive integration becomes commonplace. Although a program such as Symphony sets new standards of performance, such software is still constrained by hardware limitations — it's only by being such a large, carefully crafted program that Symphony manages the things it does.

An alternative method of providing integrated software has been developed over the last 20 years, and packages that use this method are now starting to appear on the market. It is this different approach to integrated software that we shall be considering next.

COMPLETE CONTROL

So far we have been looking at the most common approach to integrated software, that of producing all-in-one programs covering all the functions that you need. However, this is not the best system, as such programs are huge and wasteful of memory. Now we look at a more versatile method.

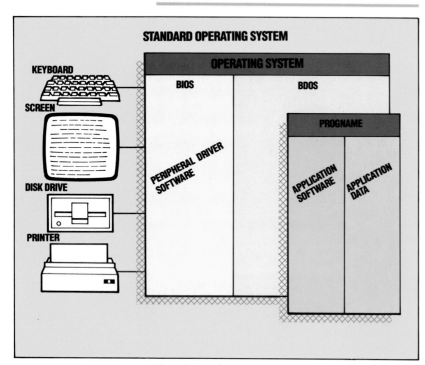

STANDARD OPERATING SYSTEM

KEYBOARD

SCREEN

DISK DRIVE

PRINTER

OPERATING SYSTEM

BIOS

BDOS

PERIPHERAL DRIVER SOFTWARE

PROGNAME

APPLICATION SOFTWARE

APPLICATION DATA

Operating Under Orders
With the traditional operating system the program currently running has complete charge. Its logic determines what appears on the screen, when the disk drive is to be accessed and how to interrogate the keyboard. Its general instructions are passed to the operating system, which manages the detailed driving of the particular hardware in use. The program's execution is paramount, and the operating system's subordination is taken for granted

The alternative approach to integrated software is based on a completely different principle. This relies on the computer's operating system to provide the basic facilities of integration, and individual programs written to work with that system will automatically fit and work together.

Creating such an operating system has been no easy task, since it requires the computer's hardware and software to be more sophisticated than in traditional designs. Apple has led the field with its custom-designed Lisa and Macintosh computers, although several other companies, notably Microsoft, are preparing systems to run on other popular computers such as the IBM PC.

Programs for these new operating systems are very different from programs for traditional systems. A large part of most programs deals with the user interface – the routines that receive commands and information from the user and present the results. Opinions differ on how programs should be operated, so nearly every package has its own unique operating procedures

and needs to be learnt from scratch.

An integrated operating system provides a built-in set of user interface routines for every application program to use. When the program wants to display a list of options on the screen for the user to choose from, there's a ready-made routine to do it in the operating system. The advantage of this, of course, is that all the programs written to work with the operating system will have roughly the same operating procedures. Once you've learnt one program on the system, you're well on the way to using all of the others available!

One particular user interface provided for these programs is the mouse. This is a pointing device used to choose options from the screen via a corresponding cursor. An alternative is the 'touch-screen', in which a matrix of light beams responds to the touch of a finger. The display is divided into separate 'windows', each containing a different option or task. Technically, such a user interface demands a fast processor, lots of memory and very high-resolution graphics. But it is worth these extra costs because the system is generally applicable to almost any program available, it is very easy to learn and it provides the simplest possible way for the user to be able to see and switch between several applications at a time.

OPERATION CONTROL

It is important to appreciate the way this system integrates programs. The program and user are never in direct contact – everything has to be done through the operating system and the operating system is in control the whole time. In effect, each application program becomes an extension of the operating system, and the computer is a single integrated 'environment'.

This brings us onto the second major difference in the way such systems function. In a traditional system, communication between program and operating system is very much one-way. The program asks for a specific task to be carried out and the operating system subsequently does it.

In an integrated system, the operating system is in control and make demands of the program. For example, the operating system may send a message to the program that says 'Could you redraw your display because the user has just moved it to the other side of the screen' or 'Hold everything, the user has moved the mouse to a different application' or 'Here's some data for you taken from a spreadsheet.' In other words, the program has to be able to respond to the requests and demands of the operating system as well as the other way round.

Once you have this degree of co-operation between all the software on a machine, it is easy to build an integrated environment. Each program has its own window on the screen. When the user puts the mouse inside the window and chooses an option, the operating system notifies that particular program and the relevant operation is carried out.

For example, if the user moves to the corner of the window and selects the option to pick up that window and move it to a new position, routines in the operating system carry out the task and then, if necessary, inform the program of the changes so that it can amend its display appropriately. If the user takes the mouse to a different window, the original program is temporarily dormant and the operating system starts working with the new program – switching between applications is as simple as moving the mouse.

Like large all-in-one programs, such systems suggest that all the programs and information on the screen at any one time are in memory and available for use. To facilitate this, many systems have massive memories – one Megabyte on the Apple Lisa, for example, and 512 Kbytes on the Macintosh. Even then, it is usually necessary for the operating system occasionally to swap information and programs on and off disks to accommodate everything. To make the system acceptably fast, it is generally necessary for it to operate on a hard disk.

In order for data to be exchanged easily between programs, the operating system has a built-in set of formats and routines for transferring data. When you 'export' some data from one program and ask to 'import' it to another, the operating system will suspend the first program and start the second, then ask the current application to read in and process information coming from another program. These pathways can be set up automatically so that when you change information in a spreadsheet, for example, a graph of the same spreadsheet will automatically change also. The two programs don't run at the same time – the operating system merely juggles between the two of them as it needs to.

A slightly more sophisticated concept is demonstrated by Apple's Lisa, where information can be 'cut' to a clipboard window from any program and then 'pasted' into any other. Formatting information is carried with the data so that a graph produced with the business graphics software will be transferred as a graph into another program.

This then is the most sensible way to create integrated software. It enables you to mix and match any programs on the system, switch between them and move information between them easily. The drawback is that it requires sophisticated hardware that for the moment is quite expensive, and there is very little software available for you to integrate.

However, any technological innovation of this scale will take time to become commonplace. The mouse and windows interface was, for example, developed by Xerox's research teams over 10 years ago but it's taken until now for such a system to appear in the shops!

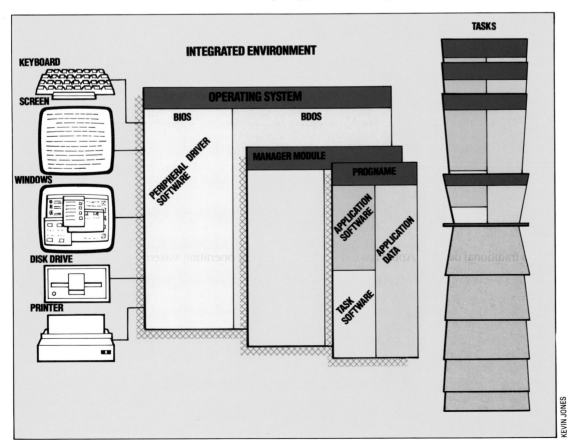

INTEGRATED ENVIRONMENT

KEYBOARD

SCREEN

WINDOWS

DISK DRIVE

PRINTER

OPERATING SYSTEM

BIOS

BDOS

PERIPHERAL DRIVER SOFTWARE

MANAGER MODULE

PROGNAME

APPLICATION SOFTWARE

APPLICATION DATA

TASK SOFTWARE

TASKS

KEVIN JONES

Combined Operations
In an integrated system the operating system is enhanced by the addition of a manager module, which treats all current programs and data as 'tasks' to be scheduled and processed, and handles the underlying detailed operating system as simple system support software. This module moves tasks in and out of main memory and on and off disk according to user's requests and current task's needs. It is equipped to pass information to and from applications in standard forms, and so enables the transfer of data among the tasks. In effect the manager is a high-priority task itself, and its relationship with the other tasks is symbiotic rather than servile

IN FORMATION

The spreadsheet was one of the first major applications for microcomputers. Its use in the home, however, has been hampered by the assumption that it is strictly for business use. But the spreadsheet has a range of useful possibilities, serving as an 'ideas generator' as well as a valuable aid in the collation and display of information.

Like a word processor or database, the spreadsheet has many facilities that are rarely explored by its users. Most people with a word processing system seldom use its more sophisticated commands, while database programs tend to be used as file management and index systems to the exclusion of their data processing abilities. The majority of home micro owners, however, don't own a spreadsheet program and can't see the need for one. Many believe they would find such a program boring and of little practical use, and are generally intimidated by its association with financial and business uses. This view of spreadsheets underestimates the importance of financial management in the home, and overlooks the fact that spreadsheets are simply ideas processors that have become stuck with the accountancy image. In fact, as word processing is to text, spreadsheets can be to concepts.

A spreadsheet is really a text editor and calculator in one. It is called a spreadsheet because it is divided into rows and columns like an accounting spreadsheet, with data shown in cells, or boxes. These are like the cells of a paper spreadsheet in that they can be used in a number of different ways: text can be entered into a cell where it will remain on display, numerical data can be entered for display and calculation, or mathematical formulae operating on the contents of other cells can be entered. Once some formulae are in place, the spreadsheet becomes a user-generated program waiting for input. Whenever new data — text, numeric, or algebraic — is entered, all the formulae cells are recalculated in turn, thus keeping the spreadsheet constantly up to date with data input. The spreadsheet can, therefore, be used for simple screen/printer layout tasks, making it easy to format and to print not only calculations you could do yourself (if they weren't so tedious), but calculations you would never otherwise have thought of.

In many cases, using a spreadsheet will help to reveal needs the user was unaware of — such as keeping inventories, analysing sports results, designing forms, producing timed synchronisation charts for theatre sound and lighting cues, generating tax returns, deciding whether to rent or buy a television, and so on. All these things could be programmed by someone with a working knowledge of BASIC, but each would take hours to develop, and most of this time would be spent on working out and debugging the endless PRINT TAB, PRINT AT, and INPUT commands needed for formatting the screen display. The great advantage of the spreadsheet is that you format the display as you work out the relationships between your variables. This is done as naturally as you would lay out a sheet of paper, by writing the text, data and the results of calculations wherever you want them to be on the display.

Spreadsheets support a variety of commands to make layout easy: you can copy, move or delete blocks of cells, insert and delete rows and columns, and define the format of a cell or block in terms of size, justification (alignment with other items in the same column), and position of the decimal point. These are exactly the details that are so difficult to handle in most dialects of BASIC, but which are vital to the appearance and ease of use of any report.

Analogous to these formatting facilities are the calculating functions. With a single command you can calculate the mean value of a row or column of data, count the non-zero entries in a table, work out the sum of an array of values, find the maximum and minimum values in a list, and use these facilities in mathematical expressions with more familiar operators and functions such as '+' and '/', SQR and ABS. Not all spreadsheets support all of these facilities, however. The options offered depend upon the available computer memory and how much you are prepared to pay for the program. Prices range from around £5 to several hundred pounds.

Perhaps the most useful single spreadsheet command is REPLICATE. Using this allows a calculation or value typed into one cell to be duplicated in any number of other cells, so that the setting-up of accumulating tables of data — such as mortgage interest from month to month, or household spending week by week — can be achieved in a dozen key-strokes. Spreadsheet programming very quickly becomes a natural extension of arithmetic BASIC, enabling complicated mathematical expressions to be expressed in a more straightforward way than BASIC allows.

Completed spreadsheets can be SAVEd to and LOADed from tape and disk, and many versions offer the option of saving just the text and data in a file format that can be used by word processing

Marking Time

Format
The FORMAT command has been used to set the width of column D, left-justify all text cells, and display all numbers to two decimal places

Copy
Any block of cells can be copied to any part of the sheet by the COPY command

Scaling Factor
Multiplied by an actual mark to produce a corresponding scaled mark

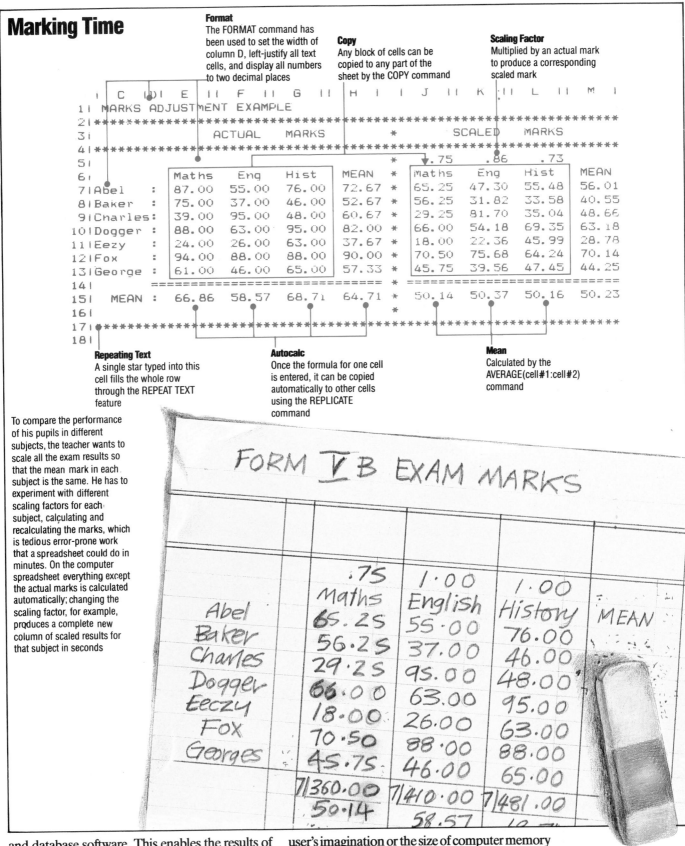

```
     I  C  I(D)I  E   II   F   II   G   II   H   I   I   J   II   K  .II   L   II   M   I
  1 I MARKS ADJUSTMENT EXAMPLE
  2 I*********************************************************************************
  3 I            ACTUAL    MARKS          *       SCALED     MARKS
  4 I*********************************************************************************
  5 I                                     *  ▼.75     .86      .73
  6 I       Maths   Eng    Hist    MEAN   *  Maths   Eng    Hist    MEAN
  7 IAbel   : 87.00  55.00  76.00   72.67  *  65.25  47.30  55.48   56.01
  8 IBaker  : 75.00  37.00  46.00   52.67  *  56.25  31.82  33.58   40.55
  9 ICharles: 39.00  95.00  48.00   60.67  *  29.25  81.70  35.04   48.66
 10 IDogger : 88.00  63.00  95.00   82.00  *  66.00  54.18  69.35   63.18
 11 IEezy   : 24.00  26.00  63.00   37.67  *  18.00  22.36  45.99   28.78
 12 IFox    : 94.00  88.00  88.00   90.00  *  70.50  75.68  64.24   70.14
 13 IGeorge : 61.00  46.00  65.00   57.33  *  45.75  39.56  47.45   44.25
 14 I        =============================     =============================
 15 I  MEAN : 66.86  58.57  68.71   64.71  *  50.14  50.37  50.16   50.23
 16 I                                     *
 17 I*********************************************************************************
 18 I
```

Repeating Text
A single star typed into this cell fills the whole row through the REPEAT TEXT feature

Autocalc
Once the formula for one cell is entered, it can be copied automatically to other cells using the REPLICATE command

Mean
Calculated by the AVERAGE(cell#1:cell#2) command

To compare the performance of his pupils in different subjects, the teacher wants to scale all the exam results so that the mean mark in each subject is the same. He has to experiment with different scaling factors for each subject, calculating and recalculating the marks, which is tedious error-prone work that a spreadsheet could do in minutes. On the computer spreadsheet everything except the actual marks is calculated automatically; changing the scaling factor, for example, produces a complete new column of scaled results for that subject in seconds

and database software. This enables the results of calculations and projections to be incorporated *en bloc* into a text or data file, and is a valuable step towards integrated software. This usually applies only to the more expensive packages.

Given a reasonable set of commands, a spreadsheet program is limited mainly by the user's imagination or the size of computer memory available. The programs themselves are usually extensive, and applications with large tables and sophisticated data processing facilities can quickly fill the rest of memory. Complicated calculations, moreover, can appreciably slow the program's calculating response.

POWER PACKS

We look at four spreadsheet-based programs for home micros — Micro Swift, Practicalc II, PS and Vizastar — packages that some believe prove that 'the ordinary home micro has enough power to compete with the bigger business systems'.

Micro Swift, Practicalc II, PS and Vizastar belong to a new breed of enhanced spreadsheet-based packages, which have clearly had their inspiration from Lotus's integrated 1-2-3 package and its successor, Symphony (see page 644). But whereas the Lotus 1-2-3 and Symphony packages were written for the IBM PC and compatible machines (1-2-3 requires 296 Kbytes of user memory to run, and Symphony demands at least 320 Kbytes), the new packages are designed for home micros. In some respects, the four packages we look at here have wrought miracles in compressing many of the features available on the larger packages into the 30 Kbytes or so of memory available to the user of micros such as the Commodore 64.

However, as yet, these 'mini-Symphony' packages can offer only two of the four options that make the more powerful (and expensive) packages so attractive. Given current hardware limitations, to try to incorporate all four options — spreadsheet, database, word processor and programmability — would undoubtedly necessitate the sort of compromises that have made the Three-Plus-One ROM-based software of the Commodore Plus/4 something of a disappointment.

RELATIVE STRENGTHS

Let's consider some of the options offered by these four programs, to compare their relative strengths. PS, Micro Swift and Vizastar are all programmable, to a greater or lesser extent. This is an extremely valuable facility, since it allows the user to automate functions that would otherwise require many keystrokes to carry out — in the same way that keyboard macros are used with Lotus 1-2-3 (see page 181). The three programs do this in different ways, and we will consider their separate approaches in turn.

Modules are programmed on the PS package using familiar BASIC commands. These modules are then saved by pressing <f3> and executed using <U>, or, alternatively, they can be auto-executed on loading by SAVEing them to disk with a full stop after the program name. The package has a range of helpful programming facilities: for example, it can GOSUB to a subroutine in a program from a formula within a cell, simply by inserting the GOSUB command within the formula. Functions can be defined using the FN function, and the program also has the facility to pass string, row and column, and numeric values.

Micro Swift can be programmed by simply placing a list of commands in column Z — the first command giving the name of the program, preceded by a hash sign (#), and the last line containing the command @QUIT. Let's consider a simple example:

```
Z1 #SUM
Z2 @SUM(A1,A3)
Z3 @ASSIGN(Z2,A4)
Z4 @QUIT
```

This program will add the values contained in cells A1, A2 and A3, and then assign the value, now found in cell Z2, to cell A4. The program is called with the instruction #SUM.

Of all the packages considered here, perhaps the simplest to program is Vizastar, since the commands consist of the initial letters that would be pressed to execute them manually. Thus, to use a specific database, you would press the CBM key followed by D(ata), U(se), D(atabase) and the name of the database. Finally, you would press <RETURN>. In programming, the slash sign (/) is used in place of the CBM key, so that / DUDname[RET] will execute the action if <f8> is pressed. Function and editing keys are programmed by pressing <CTRL> plus the appropriate key, and this letter is printed out when the function is used in a program. However, when the cursor keys are programmed in this way, they are printed as [up], [down], [left] or [right].

Vizastar's database is a powerful implementation, actually using a section of the notional sheet (rows 1,000-plus) not otherwise available to the user, to store record formats. Each record can consist of up to nine screens, and they can be accessed by the Key or Next, Prior, First, Last or Current commands (each utilising the initial letter from a command menu). Records may also be Added, Replaced (modified) or Deleted.

The fields have letter names, starting with A and finishing with BK, which relate to the columns of that name in the spreadsheet. Therefore, as an example, search criteria can be set up on a blank line of the spreadsheet. A is always the key field — the field on which data is sorted.

Practicalc II is a spreadsheet that uses a 'long label' facility, which allows text to spill over from one cell across any blank adjacent cells. This facility allows the program to operate as a word processor with a maximum line length of 100

Lorry Load

According to transport consultant Terry Palmer, most of the truck fleets in this country consist of around five vehicles. But most of the computer packages available for managing them are designed for a larger number of lorries, and cost over £1,000. The MEM Computing fleet management package, for example, costs £1,200, plus another £850 each for vehicle costing and tachygraph analysis modules — the program can handle fleets of 1,000 vehicles or more.

It's not surprising that, with those sort of costs, few small fleet owners have felt able to justify computerising their operations, as Terry Palmer found when he conducted a survey sponsored by the Science and Engineering Research Council. As a result, Palmer set about devising a system that would make more commercial sense.

Although he started developing it using Lotus 1-2-3, he ended up fitting it into the memory of one of the most popular micros on the market — the Commodore 64. Palmer used Vizastar, a programmable spreadsheet-cum-database that costs less than £100. He estimates a total cost including software and hardware of £1,000 — about a fifth of the total cost of the larger systems.

Palmer's research was conducted as part of a project he is carrying out in association with the Polytechnic of Central London to see if small truckers would find the information provided by such a system useful, and if they would be prepared to invest in it. He started with the familiar log sheet that all truckers use, and came up with report forms on which the truckers record all the jobs done, their journeys, destinations, mileage, fuel costs, cash expenses and operational costs. At the end of each week, the data from the sheets is transferred into the spreadsheet.

At the end of data entry, the sheet has already calculated whether a profit or loss has been sustained, and produces a complete analysis of the week's business. The weeks can be further consolidated in monthly analyses, and the months into an annual return.

Since Vizastar also treats a part of the sheet as a database, saving records and retrieving them from disk in exactly the same way as dedicated database programs (using a key field, or allowing browsing through the list by the use of Next, Prior or Current, First or Last commands), a permanent customer record can be maintained. The sheet can also be used for quotations.

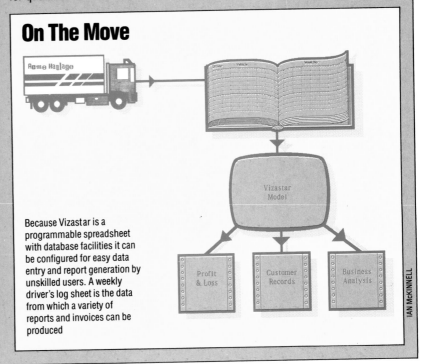

On The Move

Because Vizastar is a programmable spreadsheet with database facilities it can be configured for easy data entry and report generation by unskilled users. A weekly driver's log sheet is the data from which a variety of reports and invoices can be produced

IAN McKINNELL

characters. This option has most of the common word processing facilities, including word-wrap, block move, insert and delete.

It is also possible to LOAD a spreadsheet into part of such a document. The spreadsheet would still be 'active' — meaning that its formulae, values or other contents may be modified for the purpose of the main document, without, of course, affecting the sheet on disk.

Though memory limitations prevent more than a couple of required options to be accessible within any one program, all four of these programs can access word processing or database files produced by other programs from the same publisher. For example, Vizastar can handle word processor files generated by Vizawrite; Micro Swift can access database files produced by Micro Magpie; and Practicalc and PS can use files from Practicorp's Practifile. Indeed, since they all utilise sequential formats, they can all access and manipulate files from each other, as well as completely unrelated programs, like the Easy Script word processor. If this isn't exactly complete software integration, it's taking us very close to it.

Micro Swift: For the Commodore 64
Price: £19.95
Publisher: Audiogenic, PO Box 88, Reading, Berks.
Format: Disk

Practicalc II: For the 48K Apple II, BBC Micro and Commodore 64
Price: £69.95
Publisher: Practicorp, Goddard Road, Whitehouse Ind Est, Ipswich, Suffolk IP1 5NP
Format: Disk

PS: For the Commodore 64
Price: £69.95
Publisher: Practicorp, Goddard Road, Whitehouse Ind Est, Ipswich, Suffolk IP1 5NP
Format: Disk

Vizastar: For the Commodore 64
Price: £99.95
Publisher: Viza Software, 9 Mansion Row, Brompton, Gillingham, Kent ME7 5SE
Format: Disk with 4Kbyte cartridge

DATA ORGANISATION

A properly constructed database will organise information, whether large or small amounts, and allow the quick and easy access to any one item or combination of data. To begin our detailed look at databases, we illustrate the thinking behind setting up an efficient and well structured system.

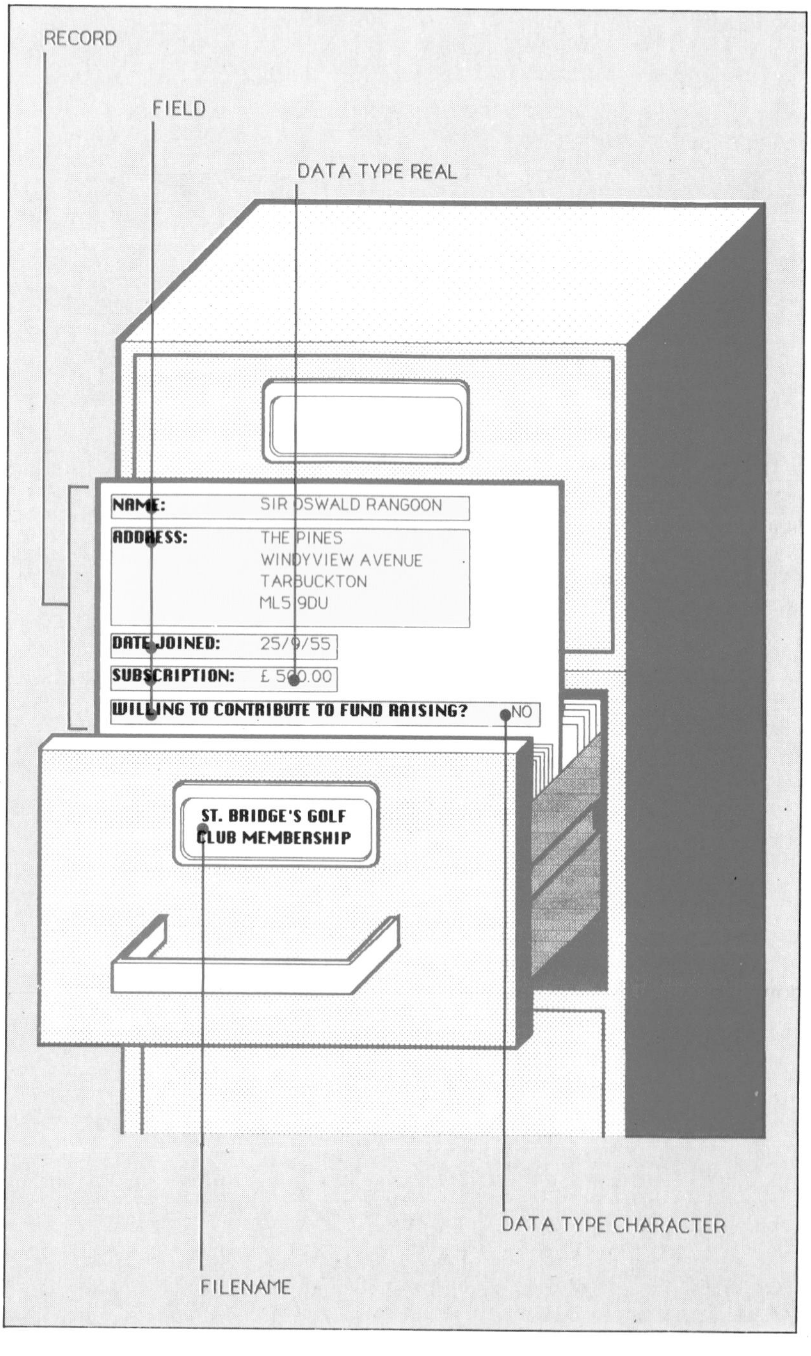

People who have to manipulate large bodies of structured data range from club secretaries to newsagents, estate agents to hospital administrative staff. A computer and a database manager program can help keep data organised and up to date. But before it is practical to talk about how database programs are used, it is important to review some of the fundamental concepts involved.

To the computer programmer, data can be viewed as being either structured or unstructured. Unstructured data are isolated units, usually stored in variables or constants. Examples might include NUMBER_OF_GOES:= NUMBER_OF_GOES +1 or IF HIT = 1 THEN PROCEDURE INCREMENT. In these two examples, NUMBER_OF_GOES and HIT are variables; in the first case, the value of the variable is being changed, and in the second, it is being tested (with a possible branch to a procedure). It is clear that the objects NUMBER_OF_GOES and HIT can have only one value at a time.

Computer programmers, especially those familiar only with BASIC, are accustomed to thinking of data as being unstructured in this way, but in real life we are used to thinking of structured data and take such structures for granted. Think of all your friends, for example. You certainly have your own 'data structure' in this respect. You know their names, you know their sex, you know their age (approximately), you probably know their jobs, and you may know their salaries and other things as well. We call a related set of facts such as this (about one person, concept or object) a record. Each record consists of one or more fields (which may be of similar or dissimilar data types) and where we have put the whole set of records together, it is called a file.

To put this into context, consider a golf club secretary who has to administer 500 members. To keep things in order, he maintains a card index — one card for each member. Each card contains various sorts (types) of information (data) about a single member. The information might include NAME, FORENAME, SEX, AGE, YEAR JOINED, SUBSCRIPTION PAID?, SALARY, MEMBER NUMBER, and so on. In computer terminology, each of these pieces of data within the record is known as a field, and the various fields contain different types of data. NAME and FORENAME will obviously be character strings, so 1374662 would not be an appropriate piece of data for a member's name. SEX input will be a Boolean type, capable of taking only one of two binary values. AGE will be an integer type (assuming that we do not need to know that a member is 37.624 years old.). YEAR JOINED will be an integer value

RECORD

FIELD

DATA TYPE REAL

NAME:　　　SIR OSWALD RANGOON

ADDRESS:　　THE PINES
　　　　　　WINDYVIEW AVENUE
　　　　　　TARBUCKTON
　　　　　　ML5 9DU

DATE JOINED:　25/9/55

SUBSCRIPTION:　£ 500.00

WILLING TO CONTRIBUTE TO FUND RAISING?　NO

ST. BRIDGE'S GOLF
CLUB MEMBERSHIP

DATA TYPE CHARACTER

FILENAME

IAN McKINNELL

with a restricted range. We'll assume that YEAR_JOINED = 1066 is inappropriate, even if the file contains records of past members Also, YEAR JOINED = 2001 is unlikely unless the club rules allow children to put their names down for future membership. SALARY would be data of type real; someone might earn a salary of £12,345.67.

Programmers need to be keenly aware of the data types available in the chosen programming language. Some languages, including BASIC and C, are weakly typed, while others such as PASCAL insist on all data items conforming to strictly defined types.

If it's not clear how this is relevant, let's first look at how BASIC and PASCAL deal with data before we define a database. BASIC recognises only two data structures — variables and files. If further structuring of data is required in a BASIC program, the programmer will have to impose it because the language does not provide it. BASIC variables may be of a number of different types, including integer values (SCORE% = 7 for example), single precision reals (SALARY! = 1234.56), double precision reals (GARETH'S SALARY = 123456.66666666666) and string variables (WONDERFUL$ = 'The Home Computer Advanced Course'). There is no such thing in BASIC as a constant type, such as PI = 3.141592 — of course, you can always set that value to the variable PI, but you can just as easily include the statement PI = 6.2 later in the program.

Other programming languages — PASCAL is probably the best known example — provide several pre-defined types and allow programmers to define other, new ones in terms of the existing types. The pre-defined types in PASCAL are constants (non-variables) and variables of type char (characters), integer (whole numbers), real (real numbers such as 12.71) and boolean (binary data that is either true or false). Sets, arrays, records and files are built in, and new data types can be easily defined by the programmer. Here's how you would create the data type DAYS.

```
TYPE
    DAY=(MONDAY, TUESDAY, WEDNESDAY,
        THURSDAY, FRIDAY, SATURDAY, SUNDAY);
```

Any variable used in the program of type DAY could only have one of the values specified, so if DAY_OFF was defined as being of type DAY, DAY_OFF :=NOVEMBER would be illegal, but DAY_OFF := SUNDAY would be acceptable.

From the computer programmer's point of view, there are pros and cons to the subject of strong typing; sometimes it gets in the way, sometimes it helps prevent programming errors. We have covered a few of the concepts of defining types of data, so now let's look at the relevance of data structures to databases.

WHAT IS A DATABASE?

A database is any collection of structurally related data. Conventionally, the data will be organised as a file (with its own filename), the file will consist of records (each with its own record number), and the records will consist of one or more fields of data, the fields containing one or more data types.

Supposing your database is organised as a card index in a box, the primary key to each entry will almost certainly be a name, arranged alphabetically. If there is a need to look for any member called Svensen, you will flick through the cards until you find the S file, then slow down until you find any names beginning with Sv until you finally locate any entries for Svensen. If, however, you were asked to find how many female members you have, finding the answer would be more tedious. The task of finding the data would be even more time consuming if someone wanted to know how many members are over 36 years old and earn £11,000 a year.

But this is exactly the sort of thing a database program can do at the touch of a few computer keys. Strictly speaking, the database is the information, and the program that helps you enter and manipulate it should be called a 'database manager'. To maintain this distinction between the collection of data and the program that manipulates it, we'll stick to the convention of calling the program a database manager, or DBM for short.

DATABASE MANAGERS

DBMs vary in their capabilities considerably. The simplest ones are little more than electronic address books able to retrieve a record when given a simple parameter such as NAME = ? The more sophisticated DBMs have their own built-in programming languages that allow the information in the database to be manipulated in highly complex ways, including exporting data fields to other programs (such as payrolls, invoicing software or word processors). In this series, we will look at DBMs, from the cheap and cheerful to the very advanced, and learn how to use them properly. Before we do that, however, let's review the preamble about data typing. A good DBM will allow the user to define the type of data allowable for each field, and will reject an entry such as NAME = 143326 or YEAR JOINED = 1066. It would also report an error if you tried to find records conforming to IF NOT (MALE OR FEMALE) AND SALARY<0. Good DBMs, unlike programming languages, need to have strong type checking to prevent erroneous data from being input when the records are created or modified.

In further instalments of this series, we'll look at how various DBMs organise their records. We'll consider relational and multi-file databases, fixed length versus variable length fields and records, creating databases and extracting data from databases. To illustrate the concepts involved, we'll concentrate on three DBMs — Psion's Archive, Ashton Tate's dBase II and Caxton Software's Card Box, with quick glances at various other packages. Programming examples will use the syntax of the products considered, though general examples will be written in BASCAL, a pseudo-language hybridised from BASIC and PASCAL.

NAMING NAMES

We have seen how databases can manipulate large bodies of related data given the fundamentals of proper structuring. Continuing our exploration of databases, we will construct a simple system based on the idea of an address book, highlighting the importance of careful planning in the design stage.

One of the major advantages of an old-fashioned address book is that very little structure is imposed beyond basic alphabetic ordering. It is flexible in the sense that you can have entries such as:

> PETER GLOVER, 16 Rhiwbinal Cresent, Cardiff (0222-601227)
> — his girlfriend's called Clair — office: 0222 680545 Ext 160
> — call after 4 — moves to new flat in Jan.

Followed by:

> GODFREY — 696-1949

Followed by:

> GREG — see Ashton-Tate

Using an address book, you are free to list people under their first names, their surnames or even by 'indirect addressing' with 'pointers' to other entries. As soon as a database such as this gets transferred to a computer, however, a more systematic approach is usually called for.

Given that a computerised address book has some disadvantages compared with the original, let's design a format for one that will be flexible enough to cater for most circumstances. We'll consider each field in turn, starting with the name.

Names come in two parts: the generic half, called the surname, and the specific half, called the forename. In most countries, the forename(s) are followed by the surname, whereas in China, Japan, Hungary and some other countries, the surname precedes the forename. In Japan, there is only ever a single forename (except that it follows the surname), while in a Chinese community in England, it is customary to have an English forename as well as a Chinese forename. Thus, Li (surname) Yu Chow (forenames) will be known to most of his English friends as Paul.

Already, we have plenty of opportunity for confusion, and we're only considering the name field. Clearly, we will have to impose some discipline, and decide whether forenames or surnames are to come first, and how long an 'allowable' name may be. Names may be as short as Ng or as long as Cholmondley-Smythe, possibly even shorter or longer, so we must always allow for extreme examples. If the database manager (DBM) uses fixed length fields, we will have to choose a field length more than adequate for the longest name we are likely to encounter. (The disadvantages of fixed length fields will be discussed later in the series.)

If we have to impose a format, as indeed we do when designing a database, it is probably simplest to use the surname field as the primary key field, so we will start with the surname and follow it with one or more forenames. The address also poses problems. Doubtless, you have seen clip-out forms in American magazines that ask for your City, State and Zip Code. British addresses simply don't fit into that format. A further complication arises when you consider that even the 'Name, House Number, Street, City, County, Country' format is not always appropriate. In Japan, for example, the city is listed first in an address, followed by the district within the city, followed by the lot number of the building plot within the district, with the addressee's name coming last.

A BASIC SPECIFICATION

In this simple database example, as in more complex ones, it is probably not possible to cater for every conceivable combination, so we will have to settle for a compromise. Assuming you are never likely to be communicating with someone having 16 forenames, let's see how well the following basic skeleton would work:

- Surname Field — up to 40 characters
- Forename Field — up to 60 characters
- Address Field 1st Line — up to 80 characters
- Address Field 2nd Line — up to 80 characters
- Address Field 3rd Line — up to 80 characters
- Address Field 4th Line — up to 80 characters
- Address Field 5th Line — up to 80 characters
- Telephone Field — up to 20 characters
- Note Field — up to 80 characters

This basic specification should cover most eventualities, though there may still be problems. One potential difficulty is the limited length of the Note field. Another problem is that Country is not specified as a separate field. Depending on the length of the address, the country could be found in the third, fourth or fifth address fields, or not at all. This would not normally be a problem until we wanted to search our database using Country as a key. If your database application had to deal with many foreign correspondents, it might be better to design the database with a separate Country field. Decisions such as these will always be needed at the design stage.

The DBM you run on your computer will determine the ease with which you can implement a specific database on your system. One of the very simplest DBMs is Caxton's Card Box. The program has limited facilities for extracting and manipulating data, but if your requirements are straightforward, it will give you the results you need with the minimum of fuss. Card Box does not give you a sophisticated programming language to manipulate fields or records. It does, however, allow you to extract specific records by entering simple commands at the keyboard. Using Card Box to create the database outlined above, you need only to load the program and follow a simple sequence of entries.

USING CARD BOX

The first thing you have to do is decide on a format for the record. This format determines what information will be stored, how it will be indexed (that is, which fields will be designated as 'key' fields) and how the records will actually appear on the computer screen or printouts. If we call the database file ADBOOK, Card Box will create a format file called ADBOOK.FMT. This can be edited if required to alter the way the information is displayed. Alternative format files can also be created to display the database information in different ways.

As with most DBMs Card Box allows you to enter 'permanent' text in each of the fields. In the case of an address book, it is pretty obvious what the significance of each field is: John Smith is clearly a name and not part of an address; similarly, 0222-680545 is obviously a telephone number. In other databases, you might need to be reminded what the significance of each field is. This is where 'permanent' text comes in handy. Compare these two records:

```
06116
3995
86
34.75
Dongle with widget nozzle
```

and

MAKER'S PART NUMBER	06116
OUR PART NUMBER	3995
NUMBER LEFT IN STOCK	86
PRICE	34.75
DESCRIPTION	Dongle with widget nozzle

The information is identical in both cases, but the second example, with permanent text that appears in every record, makes mistakes much less likely.

Card Box allows each field to be given one of four possible indexing attributes: NONE, MAN(ual), AUTO or ALL. In a stock database, it is unlikely that we would ever need to use PRICE as a key field; you are not likely to ask: 'Do you have any parts that cost less than £40 and more than £30?' It is quite possible, however, that we would need to know how many #06116 items are still in stock, so that

MAKER'S PART NUMBER would need to be made a key field.

Returning to our address book example, we are sure to want to search the database by Name, and probably by Forename too. Both of these would need to be made key fields. If we were running a business, we might also need to search records by City and possibly even by telephone area dialling code. It is important to remember that you cannot create an efficient database until you have worked out how you are going to use it. Unlike the old card indexes, databases require that you anticipate beforehand how you are likely to use them.

Design Elements
Megafinder allows you to design your own forms. This one was derived from the same form, supplied ready-made with the program, used in our other screen display

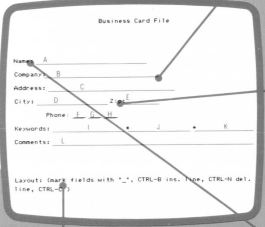

FIELD LENGTH
These are indicated by underline characters (_). The total length of all the fields in a form determines how many forms may be stored in a file. Therefore, it makes sense to keep fields as short as is practical, bearing in mind the nature of the data that will be entered

FIELD LABELS
These are entered by the user when designing the form and, in this program, are entirely for the user's convenience. The program uses them when displaying information on the screen but takes no account of field labels when sorting data, which it does using FIELD IDENTIFIERS

FIELD IDENTIFIERS
Not to be confused with the FIELD LABELS, the identifiers determine the order in which fields will be accessed when entering information. Identifiers also enable fields to be sorted separately or in groups. Using Megafinder's INDEX option, allocating field D to Index 1 would allow the user to sort quickly through the different records according to the alphabetical arrangement of cities

COMMAND LINE
This shows some of the commands that may be used when editing a design. Lines and characters may be inserted and deleted, and the finished design can be saved to disk by pressing CTRL-C

Allow Us To Show You Our Card
Database management systems may offer several different methods of manipulating information. This screen dump of Megafinder, a DBM running on the Apple computer, shows a selected record from a file named 'Business Card' and, below this, a list of command options. Data held by the program can be sorted into up to four different INDEXes to speed information recovery. The DBM will also search for a MATCH between input data and stored data, JUMP to specified sections of the database (e.g. to the section holding company names starting with M), CHANGE and DELETE information, and PRINT a record or report, either to the screen or a printer

KEYING IN

We have already seen how database managers can organise information into complex structures called records that contain fields of data of various types. But to extract these data we have to make use of 'keys'. We consider this vital concept here.

A *key* is a tool built into the database manager software that helps you to locate a specific record. Consider a car maintenance manual. If you want to adjust the carburettor, the information on how to do it will be tucked away somewhere in the manual. It might be on page 36 (for example), so this page number could be considered as the key to the information you need. Chances are, however, that you will not know that carburettors are dealt with on page 36, so you would turn instead to the index. This will give you the page number you need, enabling you to turn to the right part of the manual without having to leaf through every page.

And so it is with a DBM. Every record in a database file will have a unique record number (known as the *primary key*), but to find a specific record you have the choice of looking at each record in sequence until you find the right one, or, if you know the record number already, going straight to the appropriate record. You also have the choice of using one of the fields as a key (technically known as a *secondary key*). If we had a database on car servicing, we would use the PARTNAME field as the key.

Most DBMs allow specific fields to be designated as 'key fields'. When a field (PARTNAME in this case) has been designated as a key field, the DBM will maintain an internal table of words (character strings) in the specified field, together with the appropriate record number (primary key). When you search for the record dealing with carburettors, the DBM searches through the PARTNAME table until it encounters the character string 'carburettor', sees what the corresponding record number is, and then extracts that record. Here's how you might implement such a scheme in a simple DBM written in BASIC:

```
INPUT 'ENTER KEY FIELD';KEYF$
INPUT 'ENTER WORD TO SEARCH';WRD$
GOSUB 20000 : REM SEARCH SUBROUTINE
PRINT RESULTREC
```

All that is happening here is that one of several arrays has been selected, using KEYF$, and has been searched by the subroutine using the string WRD$ as a search key. If the search subroutine is powerful enough, it will be able to allow for small typing errors and still pick out a likely record. A simple routine like this need not depend on keeping a table of key entries — ordinary searching procedures through all the records will work.

In the past, DBMs that have operated microcomputers have been fairly simple affairs, such as one you could write in BASIC in a reasonably short time. However, a major breakthrough came with the advent of the Sinclair QL, with its 68000 processor. Psion Ltd, using powerful VAX minicomputers, developed Archive for the QL and brought advanced database management capabilities within the reach of the home micro user. To see how Archive works, let's create a trivially simple database on car maintenance with just four records. Each will consist of just two fields, PARTNAME and SERVICE:

Carburettor
Remove top and twiddle knob

Oil tank
Lift cap and fill with oil

Battery
Open cap and fill with distilled water

Washer
Open cap and fill with water

When running Archive on the QL, you are presented with a screen divided into three areas: a command prompt area at the top of the screen, a work area in the centre and a display area at the bottom of the screen. To start a new database file, select the CREATE command. To create our car maintenance database, type CREATE 'CAR' <CR> ('CAR' is the name given to the file). Then enter the names of the fields:

```
PARTNAME$ <CR>
SERVICE$ <CR>
<CR>
```

The $ sign appended to the field names indicates that the field consists of a character string. The final <CR> terminates the process.

To add records to the database, you type the command INSERT<CR>. This displays the field names in the work area and allows you to enter the data for each field. Pressing F5 after a record has been entered correctly adds it to the database file. When all the records you want to enter have been typed in, you can exit the INSERT mode by hitting the Escape key. The file can then be left by typing the CLOSE command.

To search an Archive file for a record, it must first be opened. This can be done by typing either the LOOK command, which allows records to be

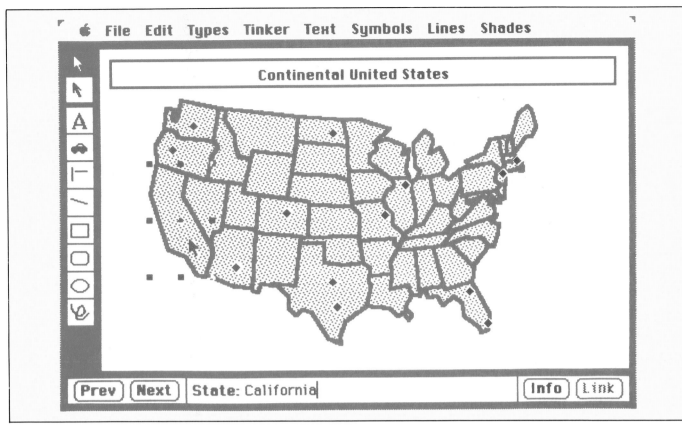

 File   Edit   Types   Tinker   Text   Symbols   Lines   Shades

Continental United States

Prev   Next   State: California   Info   Link

examined only, or OPEN, which allows records to be searched and modified. Having OPENed or LOOKed a file, you can enter simple commands such as FIRST (to show the first record in the file), LAST (to show the last record), NEXT (to show the next record) or BACK (to show the previous record).

Searching for a record involves adding an argument to a command, as in FIND 'CARBURETTOR'. This command will search all fields until an entry matching the part in quotes is located. Logical operators can also be used, as in SEARCH PARTNAME$='CARBURETTOR' AND SERVICE$='TWIDDLE'. This will search the file until a record containing the string CARBURETTOR is found in the PARTNAME$ field *and* a string containing TWIDDLE is found in the SERVICE$ field of the same record. The OR operator can be used in the same way, so that a record will be located if the string specified for one field OR the string specified for the other field can be matched.

Records will generally be entered into a database in a haphazard way, but it is frequently necessary to access them or print them out in some kind of order. Suppose, for example, that you have been given the task of entering into a database all the books in a library by author, title, publisher and ISBN (International Standard Book Number). The simplest way to do this would be to work along the shelves, entering the data for each book as you encountered it. By using the sorting capabilities built into your DBM, you could then sort the records alphabetically (by author, title, etc.), or even numerically by ISBN.

It is even possible to combine a primary sort

with a secondary sort. Suppose you wanted the file to be printed out in alphabetical order by author, with each author's entries further sorted alphabetically by title. This would enable printouts like this:

ADAMS, D. M.
    Duck Rearing for Profit and Pleasure
    Groves Publishing Co.
    0-85527-435-2
ADAMS, D. M.
    Migration Atlas of Ducks and Geese
    Clerihew Books Ltd.
    0-7195-1332-4
ADAMS, D. M.
    Preparing Ducks for the Table
    Groves Publishing Co.
    0-85527-438-6
ADAMS, E.
    Vowel Harmony in Altaic Languages
    University of Chicago Press
    226-52719-0

If the field names in Archive were AUTHOR$, TITLE$, PUBLISHER$ and ISBN, sorting the records first by author and then by title would be as simple as:

ORDER AUTHOR$;A,TITLE$;A

The A in this example stands for 'list by ascending alphabetic order'.

Already, it should be clear that DBMs can make light work of time-consuming tasks such as locating records and re–ordering them in specific ways. We will next look at some of the more advanced facilities built into many DBMs.

The US At Your Fingertips
Filevision was originally developed for the Apple II and III computers, but had to wait until the greater processing power of the Macintosh allowed its remarkable and unique features to be fully appreciated. The program uses the Macintosh's mouse interface to access the database by 'pointing and clicking'. At the 'front' of the program is a sophisticated drawing package that allows you to create a graphics framework for your database. The shapes and symbols you draw are linked into the fields of the database.

We show the main screen for a database of information about the USA. If we point the mouse to indicate California, a simple click gives a brief amount of data about that state; a double click opens a text field that can store a far greater amount of information. The stored data can be linked and sorted in the same way as any normal database. For example, by choosing 'Highlight Some' from the 'Tinker' menu, the program will allow you to specify a search criteria — say, all those states with populations exceeding 10 million — and then display the results by drawing thicker outlines around those states on the map. This information could also be printed out simply by selecting 'Print' after entering the specified criteria

M
MAKING RECORDS

Many database managers possess a built-in language allowing you to set up searches and access information with the minimum of effort. Using examples from Ashton Tate's dBase II, we will see how powerful and efficient a DBM can really be as we create and enter data into simple files.

There's more to databases than just organising data as a collection of records in a file. Accessing records is possible using simple commands, but the better DBMs allow users to write procedures using a built-in programming language. This can extend the power and usefulness of a database considerably.

To understand the use of user-written procedures in databases, we should first review the way most DBMs use commands. A command, such as SEARCH, LOCATE, DISPLAY, NEXT, LAST and so on, is processed by the DBM to find out what the user wants. Having done that, it opens the database file and goes through it sequentially, starting with the first record and working its way through to the last record, extracting en route the records that meet the requirements. Such commands are sometimes said to belong to a 'query language'.

In contrast to direct commands or queries, many DBMs — Psion's Archive (see page 192) and Ashton Tate's dBase II are two good examples — allow programs or procedures to be written by the user to simplify the process of extracting or collating information. These procedures are more than just collections of standard commands or queries. They are written in complete (if limited) programming languages that are built in as part of the DBM. Some of these DBM programming languages are quite similar to ordinary programming languages, and are quite easy to learn. Psion's Archive incorporates a language that is, to all intents and purposes, identical to Sinclair's SuperBASIC. Writing procedures to use with Archive is perfectly straightforward for anyone familiar with SuperBASIC.

Although the dBase II language is not quite like any other language, it is sufficiently like a structured BASIC with a few reserved words to be easy to learn and use. Its structures are fairly simple, and include DO WHILE . . . ENDDO, DO CASE . . . ENDCASE and IF . . . ENDIF. In addition, there are about a hundred commands — some familiar and some tailored specifically for use within a database environment. Familiar-looking commands include CALL (to call a machine language), NOTE (equivalent to REM in BASIC),

STORE <expression> to <variable> (equivalent to LET <variable> = <expression> in BASIC) and many others. Less familiar commands include SKIP (to move forward or backward through records in the file), PACK (to remove unwanted records from the file) and FIND <character string>.

Several functions are also provided, including familiar, BASIC-like functions and more unusual ones. Examples include CHR <expression> (equivalent to CHR$(x)), LEN <character string expression> (equivalent to LEN in BASIC), TYPE <expression> (returns the type of expression) and DATE() (a system variable containing, naturally enough, the date).

To see how useful a custom-written procedure can be, compared with simply using a sequence of commands from the keyboard to extract information, we'll use dBase II to create a stock and inventory database, and then write a simple procedure in the dBase II language to extract some information. The records in the file will be quite simple, with four numeric fields and one character field. A typical record (also used in previous instalment) looks like this·

MAKERSPART NUMBER	06116
OUR PART NUMBER	3995
NUMBER LEFT IN STOCK	86
PRICE	34.75
DESCRIPTION	Dongle with widget nozzle

First we need to find a one-word name for each field, and to decide on the lengths of the fields, and whether they are to be 'character', 'numeric' or 'logical' fields. This should be sufficient:

MAKERSPART	: 5 characters; numeric
OURPART	: 5 characters; numeric
REMAINING	: 3 characters, numeric
PRICE	: 6 characters; numeric
DESCRIPTION	: 40 characters; character

Once dBase II is running, it responds with a full stop (period) prompt on the screen that tells you it is waiting for input. The command that starts a new file is CREATE, and we will also have to supply a name for the file as a whole (we'll use PARTS as the filename). The process would look like this:

```
. create parts <CR>
ENTER RECORD STRUCTURE AS FOLLOWS:
FIELD    NAME, TYPE, WIDTH, DECIMAL PLACES
001      makerspart,n,5,0
002      ourpart,n,5,0
003      remaining,n,3,0
004      price,n,6,2
005      description,c,40
006      <CR>
```

Our input has been given in lower case letters and dBase II's response has been printed in upper case letters. Notice that numeric fields require the number of decimal places to be specified as well as the width of the field. Pressing the Return key without entering any information, as in field 006, terminates the initial phase of file creation.

Next we need to enter some data. This is done by using the APPEND command. This causes the screen to clear and a 'skeleton' of the record to appear, waiting for data to be entered.

```
MAKERSPART :            :
OURPART    :            :
REMAINING  :        :
PRICE      :            :
DESCRIPTION :
```

Data can now be typed in at the keyboard and will be fed to each field in turn. A carriage return signals that entry to a field has finished; as soon as Return is pressed for the final field, all the data will be accepted and the skeleton record will reappear, waiting for details of the next record. Terminating data entry is done by pressing Return at the start of an empty record.

Having entered data into the file, you will want to use it. Suppose that, for auditing purposes, you needed to know the retail value of your entire stock. One way this could be done would be to look at each record in turn on the screen and make a note of the number of parts remaining in stock for each item, record the price of each and multiply the two figures. After looking at all the records and noting all the prices and numbers of each item in stock, you could then get the total value by multiplying each price by the number of parts and then adding all the subtotals. If you were using a conventional card index, this would indeed be the only way of arriving at a solution.

Most DBMs allow this sort of information to be retrieved far more simply. Here's how you would do it with dBase II:

```
. use parts
. sum remaining * price
37870.58
```

The first line is a command instructing dBase II to work with the file called PARTS. The second line is a command meaning 'add together for all records the result of multiplying the REMAINING field by the PRICE field of each record'. The third line is the sort of response that might be returned after the total value, in pounds, of the entire stock. Beats card indexes, doesn't it?

This example clearly illustrates how powerful a good DBM can be, even using nothing more than

a simple command. But the real power comes from storing sequences of commands as a program. To store our simple stock valuation commands as a program called VALUE, the following dialogue would be needed:

```
. modify command
ENTER FILE NAME: value
set talk off
use parts
sum remaining * price
set talk on
cancel
```

This short program will be stored on disk and can be used from within dBase II at any time by typing in the command:

```
. do value
```

The program will be automatically read in and executed, and as soon as it has finished, control will be returned to dBase II.

Accounting Procedure

```
* Display Accountants
SET TALK OFF
USE MEMBERS
DO WHILE .NOT. EOF
   IF JOB="ACCOUNTANT"
      DISPLAY NAME
   ENDIF
   SKIP
ENDDO
```

The program we give here, which extracts the names of club members who are accountants, is written in Ashton-Tate's dBase II command language. The first line, beginning with an asterisk, indicates that this is a comment line. We do not require that all the record numbers be displayed, as dBase II carrys out the search, so we SET TALK OFF.

There may be a number of different files held on the database, and so we must specify which file (in this case MEMBERS) is to be searched. As we wish dBase II to search through all available records, we construct a loop around the DO WHILE . . . ENDDO structure.

Within the loop we set a condition that states whenever the job field contains the string 'ACCOUNTANT', the program should display the record's name field. Note that the IF condition must, of course, be terminated by ENDIF. The program then drops through to the SKIP command which tells dBase II to go on to the next record

GOOD RELATIONS

Database managers implemented on home micros generally incorporate 'relational organisation' methods as a means of arranging the input data. We look at the structure and functioning of this type of system, as well as its two alternatives – hierarchical and network systems.

Most of the DBMs available on home computers are of the type known as 'relational' database management systems. At its simplest, this means that each record in a DBM file takes the form of a table, made up of rows and columns, after the fashion of a spreadsheet. The various ways in which the information can be presented might suggest a more complex structure, but it is basically nothing more than a straightforward table or grid. The database is organised in much the same way as you might yourself put the information down on paper. Each record is structurally the same and each field within the record is of a fixed length.

The term 'relational' comes from the fact that each 'row' in the database is clearly related, in a fixed and rigid way, to each 'column'. This is not a very flexible way of organising data, but it does make for relatively simple database manager programs. Because home computers — even the new 16-bit machines with 128 Kbytes of memory or more — have comparatively small memories, slow processing speeds, and limited data storage capacities, the restrictions of a relational system are part of the price that must be paid for combining affordable computing with database management.

An altogether different approach to this tabular organisation of data is to order it in a hierarchical form. We can think of the data being organised as if it were a tree, with each branch having sub-branches, the sub-branches having twigs, even leaves. To illustrate this, we'll create a database of the stock in a newsagent's shop. First, we'll present it in a relational way, then show how it would be

Tree Surgery
Whereas a 'relational' DBM stores information in tabular form, a 'hierarchical' DBM organises its data in 'tree' form. In the example shown, the single category 'medicine' holds pointers to the different types of medicine available, each of which will hold pointers to the different brand names, and so on. Hierarchical DBMs can be very efficient in their use of memory, but are more complicated in structure, than their relational counterparts

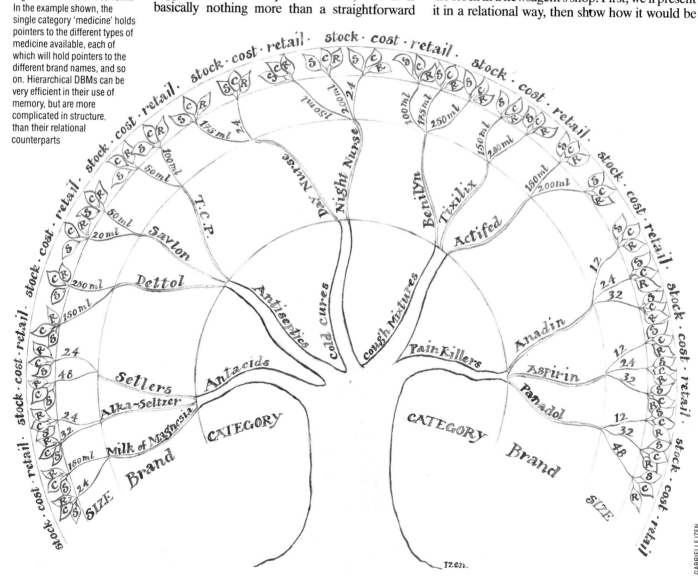

GABRIELLE IZEN

organised hierarchically.

CATEGORY	BRAND	SIZE	STOCK	COST	RETAIL
CIGARETTE	EMBASSY	20	350	98	105
CIGARETTE	EMBASSY	10	140	50	56
CIGARETTE	DUNHILL INT	20	85	108	125
CIGARETTE	SILK CUT MILD	20	105	106	126
SWEETS	BOUNTY	1	106	14	17
SWEETS	TWIX	1	95	12	16
SWEETS	MARATHON	1	25	15	19
MAGAZINE	YOUR SPECTRUM	1	35	85	95
MAGAZINE	NEW STATESMAN	1	12	60	80
MAGAZINE	CITY LIMITS	1	86	50	60
DRINKS	LUCOZADE	150	35	25	37
DRINKS	TIZER	150	40	18	27
DRINKS	QUOSH	150	20	16	25

When represented hierarchically, this newsagent's stock database could look like this:

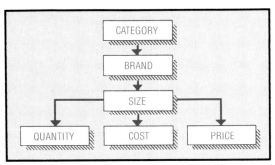

The record, instead of being organised into fields, is organised as 'segments' of data, where each segment might contain more than one field. Organised hierarchically, instead of relationally, the entries corresponding to CIGARETTE in the relational database would look like this:

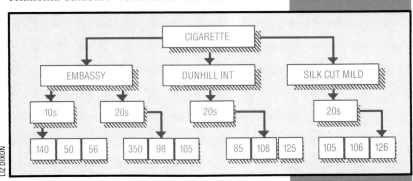

When it is represented in this way, each item of information can clearly be seen as being either superior or subordinate to another item of data. All that is required is a 'pointer' from one data segment to another. In this example, we need only one CIGARETTE segment, with pointers to the various types of cigarette held in stock, and further pointers to the sizes, cost, price and so on.

Suppose the newsagent has just one hundred 'categories' of stock, but a thousand lines on sale; with a relational database, one thousand records would be required — one for each line. With a hierarchical database, only one hundred segments would be needed to cover the entire stock. It saves a lot of duplication but makes the database much

more complicated structurally.

There is a further type of database organisation known as the CODASYL or network system, a standard database organisation specified by the database task group of the Conference on Data Systems Languages — hence CODASYL. The problem with a hierarchical database is that the data can only be organised to flow in one 'direction'; to use the tree analogy, one branch cannot be attached to two trunks. But, to return to our newsagent, EMBASSY PANATELLAS, for example, could be a 'branch' of both EMBASSY and CIGARS. The problem particularly comes to the fore whenever a single 'component' can have more than one 'maker'. If you sell auto spares, a single 'big end linking gasket' for a BL Marina could be made by British Leyland, BL Bargain Parts Ltd, or Taiwan Carbits Corporation. As we can see, the relationship between goods supplied and parts suppliers can become very complicated.

In the CODASYL system, a network of sets is used in which each set consists of a collection of records. Unlike a record in a relational database system, the record length need not be fixed, and any record can belong to more than one set. The CODASYL system allows a set to consist of only one record, and a record cannot belong to more than one occurrence of the same set type. Structures of the following type are therefore not allowed:

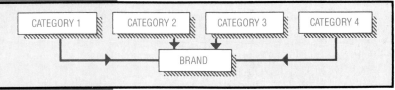

This is a serious limitation. Although we might not have CIGARETTEs, MAGAZINEs and DRINKs all with a brand name of, say, FABULAN, it is easy to conceive of a situation where a company called Supercars Ltd. could be part of a structure like:

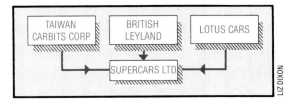

Although hierarchical and CODASYL databases are more flexible than relational ones, they are more complex and really need the power of mainframe or minicomputers. Home computers almost invariably use relational systems. The commonest problem to arise from this limitation is in situations where, for example, you have an inventory of parts (or books, or other goods) that you sell, and each part (book, etc.) has more than one supplier. Therefore, you need a record of parts, and a linked set of records for related suppliers for each part. Multi-file DBMs allow more than one file to be open at a time, and for an active file to refer to a subsidiary file.

DOUBLE-ENTRY DATABASE

It is important to recognise when considering DBMs that certain types of files require different approaches to the organising, cross-referencing and retrieval of data. We present a number of examples illustrating these different approaches, from the straightforward 'flat' database to the complex and powerful dBase II.

Any record held in a 'flat' database will be completely self-contained; that is, any given record will hold all the information required, without the need to refer to another record. Traditional card-box files are flat in this sense. We can think of a library database, for example: each record consists simply of the fields TITLE, AUTHOR, PUBLISHER and ISBN (International Standard Book Number), and no cross-referencing is required.

Sometimes a field will contain an entry that can have a record in its own right. In a club membership file, for example, a CHILDREN field can refer to other records in the same file; if the children of a member are also club members they will have records of their own. But a field can refer to records that might not fit into the general structure of the database file. Consider a parts inventory database, containing the fields PART NUMBER, PRICE, NUMBER IN STOCK and SUPPLIER. It's highly likely in this case that the SUPPLIER field will also refer to other records that do not fit into the structure defined for the PARTS database.

To illustrate this, here, first of all, is the CLUB MEMBERSHIP file:

MEMBER'S NAME	Sue Gomez
YEAR JOINED	1979
SUBSCRIPTION?	Paid
OCCUPATION	Teacher
SALARY	8900
CHILDREN	Jill Gomez, Philip Gomez

In this example, the field CHILDREN contains two entries; both of these could have similar entries in the CLUB MEMBERSHIP file, if they were also members. Compare this with a PARTS database record:

PART NUMBER	3995
NUMBER IN STOCK	86
PRICE	34.75
DESCRIPTION	Dongle with widget nozzle
SUPPLIER	Widgerama Ltd; Dongle Corp of Taiwan

There are two entries in the SUPPLIER field; neither of these could have records that could fit into the

structure of the PARTS database. So, a parts inventory such as this would probably have a second database file for suppliers, in which each entry might look something like this:

SUPPLIER	Dongle Corp of Taiwan
ADDRESS	57 Kau Moo Road, Taipei, Taiwan, R.O.C.
TELEPHONE	010-886-2-223-4478
SUPPLIES1	Dongle with widget nozzle
PRICE1($US)	34.75
SUPLIES2	Valve paste ($\frac{1}{2}$ litre can)
PRICE2($US)	6.00
SUPPLIES3	Dazzlebrite polish (small can)
PRICE3($US)	2.30
SUPPLIES4	Dazzlebrite polish (large can)
PRICE4($US)	4.00
SUPPLIES5	—

It is perfectly obvious that the information we need about each of the suppliers is quite different in structure from the information we need about the parts the company sells. The solution is to have two different database files — one for the parts themselves, and another, separate file, for each of the suppliers.

If separate but related files are to be usefully implemented, it is obviously necessary for the DBM to be able to handle more than one file at a time. Less sophisticated DBMs, such as Card Box (see page **190**), can work only on a single file at a time, but DBMs such as dBase II (see page **194**) can use one file (such as PARTS) as a primary file and another (such as SUPPLIERS) as a secondary file. A really good DBM will allow a sort to be run on a primary file (to extract selected records) as well as the extraction of relevant records (such as SUPPLIERS) from related files.

The dBase II package allows two related files to be used at the same time, and associates them by using common key fields. Two commands allow reference to be switched from one to the other:

Stock Order

Using our own index card filing system, entries can be as complex (or untidy) as we wish. DBMs have to adopt a more structured approach to data entry, but sophisticated programs will allow the user to call up related files and, when entering data, to skip certain fields if they have been made redundant by other entries in the record. Taking the illustrated record as an example, the field labelled 'Re-order sent' is relevant only if the stock approaches or falls to zero. Consequently some DBMs, such as 'Rescue', enable the user to set up fields to be dependent on, or calculated by, previous fields

KEVIN JONES

SELECT PRIMARY and SELECT SECONDARY. If the primary file is PARTS and the secondary file is SUPPLIER, and we were working on the PARTS file, we would issue the command USE PARTS. If we then wanted to cross-refer to the suppliers file we would issue the commands: SELECT SECONDARY, and then on the next line, USE SUPPLIER. All the usual dBase II commands are available for use, and they will operate on the file that was most recently selected.

There are times when the contents of a field (such as SUPPLIER in the PARTS file previously mentioned) do not require the facilities of completely dependent records (in independent files), so that dependent fields within the same record would suffice. As an example, suppose you are keeping a database on the latest automobile technology, storing records of press cuttings and references in books that you have seen, relating to things as diverse as injection-moulded plastic bodies and electronically controlled fuel injection. You might design a database format like this:

```
TOPIC:_____
SYNOPSIS1:_____
SYNOPSIS2:_____
SYNOPSIS3:_____
SOURCE:_____  ISBN:_____
TITLE:_____
DATE:_____
PAGE*NO:_____
```

If the source of an entry is a magazine, such as *Autocar* or *Off Road Rider*, the ISBN field will be irrelevant, since magazines do not have International Standard Book Numbers. If, however, the source of the entry is a book called *Programming ROM Chips for In-car Computers*, there will be an ISBN. Similarly, if the source is a book or a magazine, there will be a page number. But if the source was the BBC television programme *Wheelbase*, the PAGE NO field would not be needed. Some DBMs, such as Rescue, by Microcomputer Business Systems, allow the

presence or absence of any particular field within a record to be either calculated or dependent upon other, previous fields.

Thus, if the SOURCE is not a book, the ISBN field will not be prompted for entry and will not be displayed (either on the screen or in printouts). If the source is neither a book nor a magazine, the PAGE NO field will not be required and will not be displayed. A DBM able to do this can save on memory by eliminating unnecessary fields, and helps to improve the presentation of information. It is still, however, less versatile than a DBM able to relate records in one file to records in another file.

In databases where there may be some root information that remains constant for every record, and some branch information that may or may not be required, we have what is known as a 'two-level hierarchy'. As a general rule, multi-file DBMs can treat two-level hierarchical data as a subset or special case of a multi-file database. For example, a SOURCE reference to a book could relate to a BOOKS file and a SOURCE reference to a programme could relate to a PROGRAMMES file.

There is one final thing to bear in mind. A hand-written card-index file of your own design can be as complex as you care to make it. But there will be serious limitations among the different, commercially available DBMs as to what they can and cannot handle structurally. So before purchasing a DBM for your micro, think hard about what exactly you want it to do and look carefully at the specifications for any product you are considering.

Databases Detailed

NAME	MANUFACTURER	MACHINE	FORMAT	PRICE	COMMENTS
Betabase	Clares	BBC	disk	£25.00	Max record length 2048. Max fields 200. Max file size 99K (40T), 199K (80T)
Database	Gemini Marketing	Spectrum	cassette	£19.95	Card index system. User-defined records.
DFM Database	Dialog	C64	disk	£24.00	15 fields/record. 36-character alphanumeric field. 9-figure numeric field.
Practifile	Computer Software Associates	C64	disk	£44.50	3800 rec/file. Rearranges data for mailing list. Batch entry.
MicroPen	AMSoft	Amstrad	disk	£49.95	Contains built-in word processor and spreadsheet. Max record length 1024. Max no of records in file 32750.

THE MIGHTY PEN

Using Archive, Card Box and dBase II, we have illustrated thus far many of the fundamental concepts of database management. We now turn our attention to MicroPen, designed for the Amstrad CPC 464, which is just one of many DBMs now available at relatively low cost for most home micro users.

Described as a 'database filing system for the CPC 464', MicroPen is published by the Amsoft division of Amstrad, but is the work of the software house, Intelligence Ireland. MicroPen forms part of a triptych of programs comprising a DBM, word processor and spreadsheet. The package has conceptual similarities to suites such as the Lotus 1–2–3 and Sord's PIPS. The DBM component includes a word processor called Penform. This is used to create the on-screen format of the records to be used within a DBM file. The DBM itself is called, simply, Pen.

The Amstrad version of MicroPen runs under CP/M-80, and therefore requires at least one DDI-1 disk drive. Although this might seem like an unfortunate extra expense, you will quickly realise that the speed and capacity of disks is essential — cassette-based DBMs can be painfully slow and frustrating.

Before a database file can be created, you must first create the layout or format for the records that will go into the file. This is done by running Penform. Although referred to in the documentation as a word processor, this is really just a screen editor. That is to say, it allows characters to be entered or modified on the screen, moving the cursor around using the cursor keys. Simple editing commands, such as [CTRL]Y to delete a line or [ESC]E to save to disk, augment the cursor keys. Penform is not a full word processor, as it cannot be used to create and edit full-length documents such as letters or articles.

There are a few restrictions on how much information can go into a MicroPen database file. A record (called a 'layout' in the documentation) may have up to 100 fields in it, but no record may contain more than 1,024 characters. Theoretically, a file may contain up to 32,750 records, but in practice such a large number of records is not feasible on a floppy disk-based system. The full complement of 32,750 records, each containing the maximum allowable 1,024 characters, would require more than 33 megabytes of disk storage just for the raw data alone (assuming that data-

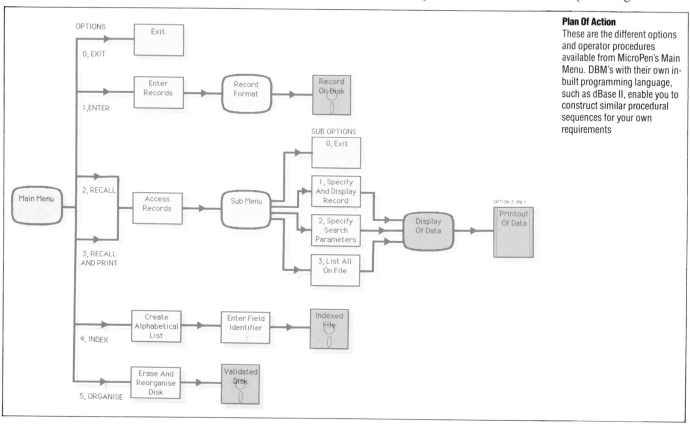

Plan Of Action
These are the different options and operator procedures available from MicroPen's Main Menu. DBM's with their own in-built programming language, such as dBase II, enable you to construct similar procedural sequences for your own requirements

compression techniques are not used).

An unusual feature of the MicroPen DBM is that each field in a record has to be given a unique identifier on-screen. These identifiers are called 'field markers' and may be any printable character except the square bracket, which is unavailable because it has a special role as a field delimiter.

If we were using MicroPen as the DBM for our PARTS database, a record layout created by Penform might look like this:

```
Maker's Part Number:    [A             ]
Our Part Number:   [B             ]
Price:   [C    ]    No. In Stock: [D         ]
Description:   [E             ]
Supplier:   [F             ]
Supplier's Phone Number:   [G         ]
Who To Speak To:   [H             ]
```

Having created a format such as this, it is saved to disk using a filename such as PARTS.INP (the .INP 'extension' to the filename is required by the Pen DBM program).

RUNNING PEN

When it is run, Pen displays a prompt on the screen that asks which database file is to be used. To use our inventory database, we would answer PARTS (the .INP extension to the filename is not required). Pen then displays a menu, known as the 'main menu', which provides five options:

```
Database: PARTS, per record 328, records on file 0.

0=Exit, 1=Enter, 2=Recall, 3=Recall & Print, 4=Index,
5=Organise
```

Option 1 is needed to enter records. The top line — the statistics line — shows that there are 382 characters per record, but no records (as yet) are in the file. Selecting option 1 displays the record format on the screen with instructions. In our example, the screen would look like this:

```
Press {ESC} when data entry completed for record 1
Press ^C to clear field

Maker's Part Number:
Our Part Number:
Price:                     No. In Stock:
Description:
Supplier:
Supplier's Phone Number:
Who To Speak To:
```

The data is typed in the usual way. After the data for a field has been input, pressing ENTER ends entry for that field and moves the cursor to the next field. Errors within a field can be corrected by using the Delete key. When the entire record has been entered correctly, a sub-menu will be displayed using the Escape key:

```
0=Exit
1=Continue
2=Write Record to File
```

Option 2 writes the record to disk and displays the format for the next record.

The main menu option 2 allows records to be accessed, or recalled. This option brings up another sub-menu:

```
Recall by:     0=Exit
               1=Record number
               2=Search
               3=List all on file
```

Options 0 and 1 are fairly self-explanatory; option 1 allows you to specify and display a relevant record — it assumes, however, that you know the number of the record you want, although it is unlikely that you will remember this if there are many records in the file. Option 2 allows various search parameters to be specified so that a certain record can be located that conforms to the specification. The search sub-menu is:

```
Press Escape when search profile complete. To set
search mode:
^Q=Contains,^W=Not contains,^E=Equals,^R=Not
equals,^T=Greater,^Y=Less
```

You will already have noticed that there is a great inconsistency in the commands and menu options for the various parts of the package: sometimes the Escape key must be pressed, sometimes a CTRL - letter combination, sometimes a menu number. The CTRL - letter combinations seldom have real mnemonic values — ^E to find a record with matching fields during a search, ^Q to specify Contains and so on. Be that as it may, the 'search' options allow reasonable flexibility in specifying the records to be searched for.

Having given the parameters that define the record required, CTRL - letter combinations allow records to be located that contain the specified data; do not contain the specified data; have matching field data; do not have matching field data; or have a field value less than the specified field value. If you wanted, for example, to locate records of parts with a PRICE less than 37.50, this could easily be achieved.

MicroPen has the useful facility of being able to create an index of all the entries in a database file. Indexing is done by field, and the maximum number of records must also be known. The field is specified by its identifier, not by our name for the field. To get an index of Our Part Number, and assuming that there were 500 records in the file, we would specify B=#500 (B being the identifier for the Our Part Number field).

MicroPen offers reasonably advanced search and indexing capabilities and, at around £50, will be affordable to many home computer users. It does not, however, offer the advantage of a built-in programming language, such as those included with Archive and dBase II. Although dBase II is an expensive package designed for expensive computers, Archive comes 'free' with the Sinclair QL at an all-inclusive price comparable to an Amstrad CPC 464 plus disk drive and MicroPen software. These are the kinds of considerations you should bear in mind before buying a computer system and the DBM software to go with it.

WORKING WITH WORDS

Word processing packages, which now abound for almost every computer, represent by far the most widespread 'serious' application for home micro users. An exploration of some of the more popular packages begins here with an overview of word processing in general.

Word processing is essentially a combination of different operations, some of which are user-dependent and some performed entirely by the computer. These operations are the entry of text into the computer, the creation of a file in RAM or on disk to hold the text (usually in ASCII format), the display of all or part of a file on a VDU in readable form, the manipulation of the data in that file and, finally, the manipulation of the various created files themselves.

It is necessary to spell this out, because any word processor must be judged according to the success with which it performs, or enables the user to perform, these operations. Some word processing programs are, for example, particularly good at displaying text (MacWrite, for example, shows a variety of exotic founts on screen), while others excel at file manipulation. In addition to the performance of these relatively

CHRIS STEVENS

low-level tasks, word processing software must also be judged on the power and extent of the high-level facilities it offers.

Word processing has now become so familiar that the complex programming it requires is often taken for granted. Furthermore, it is an area of programming that is of fairly recent origin. There are a variety of reasons for this. First, a VDU is essential to display the text, and these have only become standard output devices on computers in the last ten years. Secondly, computers are designed to handle numbers, not text. The introduction of the ASCII code obviously solves this problem, but the code holds 255 different characters, and as such is not at all efficient in its use of memory. A standard typewriter keyboard holds just over 100 characters (counting shifted keys), so it's easy to see that a 255-character code has considerable inbuilt redundancy. For this reason, word processing is not only complex, but also very demanding of memory.

This complexity leads to the problem of text manipulation having to be tackled in many different ways. Word processors come in many different shapes, sizes and forms, ranging from a £6,000 dedicated machine down to a £5.95 program designed to run on a home computer. In this section, we will be examining examples from each main category.

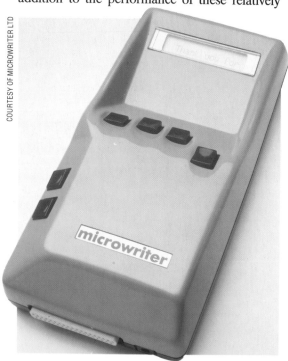

COURTESY OF MICROWRITER LTD

Real Dedication
The Amstrad PCW 8256 is the latest in the range of low priced products from the company. Packaged as a dedicated word processor and based around the Z80 chip with 256 Kbytes of RAM available, the PCW provides a computer, monitor, integrated disk drive, printer and bundled word processing software

Finger Language
The Microwriter offers a completely different concept in word processing from other machines on the market. Disposing of the standard QWERTY keyboard altogether, individual characters are entered by pressing different combinations of the pads. When the text of a document has been entered, the Microwriter is then connected to a printer to obtain 'hard copy'

DEDICATED WORD PROCESSORS

Dedicated word processors, such as those made by Wang and IBM, have become very popular in the business market. They consist of a display terminal, a keyboard with a number of keys specifically used for word processing functions (a Paste key, for example), and a means of storing text files on hard or floppy disk. With the exception of the Amstrad PCW 8256 at around £400, such machines are expensive — often costing over £5,000. Nevertheless they do offer a number of advantages that come from specialisation — purpose-built keyboards, networking facilities and ergonomically designed displays. Word processing involves a lot of staring at the screen, so a wide (80-column plus) and clear display is essential.

By contrast, word processing software falls into many different categories. At the lowest level, some form of text manipulation can be accomplished using a simple screen editor, as provided by most operating systems. You can use this facility to print out short paragraphs in direct mode, but obviously this isn't going to suffice for anything except the very briefest memo.

Further up the scale is the 'text handling program', which enables the user to set up a text file and edit it directly on screen. This is much closer to the concept of a proper word processor, and some text handlers even offer search routines (to locate a particular string) and cut/paste functions, which enable the user to manipulate small blocks of text within a file. A good example of such a program is the TEXT facility offered on the Kyocera range of portable computers, badge-marketed on the Olivetti M10 and the Tandy Model 100. This program offers cut, paste, copy, search and print functions, storing text as a file in CMOS RAM, with a battery back-up so that it will still be there next time the machine is used.

WORD PROCESSING PROGRAMS

Finally, we have the programs that can properly claim the title of word processor. These fall into two categories — RAM-based and disk-based. The former category was really introduced for the benefit of home computer users who lacked disk storage and therefore required a program that loaded wholly into RAM and, because cassette storage is so slow, held the entire document in RAM as well. Only when the document has been edited to a final version is it saved to tape. RAM-based programs are limited in the scope of the facilities they can offer for obvious reasons. In particular, document size is severely limited, and the size of blocks of text that can be shuffled around may also be restricted.

RAM-based programs do, however, have one big advantage over their disk-based relatives — they tend to be much faster in operation, since the different facilities do not rely on numerous disk accesses to function. A good example of a RAM-based word processor is Tasword, which allows the user to create a document of up to 13,000

characters, or just over 2,000 words.

Disk-based programs tend to allow you to work on far larger documents and in theory the document size is limited only by the area of storage available on the data disk itself. The program loads portions of the relevant file as required, though this can often lead to considerable delays, especially if you're at the end of a long document and want to return to the beginning. Typical examples of disk-based systems are WordStar and PerfectWriter. Such programs are often bundled with business systems, but otherwise they tend to be expensive — WordStar 2000, for example, is over £300. One advantage of disk-based programs is that they tend to make greater use of the disk-operating system they run under (CP/M, MS-DOS and so on) and will therefore tend to have greater file compatibility than their home computer equivalents.

We are going to be examining a number of different types of word processor and assessing their various strengths and weaknesses. Starting with WordStar, a program that has succeeded in establishing an industry standard by which all other programs are judged, we will go on to look at MacWrite, as an example of a program that excels with its display. We will also be discussing various RAM-based programs, such as Tasword and Mini-Office.

Computer Companion
Lap-held portable computers are gradually gaining an increasing share of the market. The advantage of these machines is that the user can perform 'computing on the move'. Most of the lap-held computers, like the Olivetti M10 shown here, that are currently available have a word processing capability held in ROM. Although the word processing facilities and the amount of free memory on these computers is restricted due to the limited power that is available, they are useful tools for letters, memos and so on

WHAT'S ON THE MENU?

We continue our look at word processing by assessing MicroPro's WordStar system, which although released in the late 1970s is still the industry leader. Based largely on the CP/M operating system, WordStar's enormous range of capabilities makes it an extremely powerful tool.

Literally hundreds of word processing programs have been written over the last decade, and each one has claimed to be an improvement over the rest. Yet the market leader remains one of the oldest word processors around. WordStar, from MicroPro, was originally written for CP/M machines, and made its first appearance in 1978, shortly after the company was founded. It has since been rewritten to run under PC-DOS/MS-DOS, and was chosen for the IBM PC and, consequently, for its compatibles, which now dominate the business market. WordStar's staying power is due to its almost unrivalled word processing facilities. This is in spite of the fact that the system is not particularly user-friendly, although it did pioneer the use of on-screen 'help' menus.

As we've just noted, the roots of WordStar lie in CP/M, the highly successful operating system which is virtually standard for business micros, and as such, it carries many of that system's best and worst features. To begin with, when WordStar is loaded, it is added to the list of CP/M's 'transient' programs, which lets WordStar take advantage of CP/M's disk operating facilities. And like CP/M, WordStar makes use of a wide range of control characters.

THE OPENING MENU

After loading and running the program, WordStar users are confronted with the Opening Menu, which displays all the options available, as well as the contents of the currently logged disk drive. If you haven't changed the disk, this will consist of the programs that make up WordStar. It's worthwhile noting here that WordStar filenames use the same format as CP/M filenames — a name of eight characters or less followed by a full stop and a three-letter extension if required.

On the Opening Menu is a list of 13 commands, which are divided into five sections. Under Preliminary Commands, you have the choice of changing the logged drive, turning the File Directory on and off, and setting the Help level. The Help level is defaulted to level 3 on booting up, and displays all the available commands at the top of the screen. By moving down to level 0, the screen will be clear

Essential Abilities

Listed here are 11 features available on many word processing programs. In this and the following instalments, we'll be looking at whether the packages examined contain these features and how well they are implemented.

Wordwrap
The ability of a program to move a word from one line to the next if there is insufficient space.

Block Movement
Allows the user to define a 'block' of text that can be manipulated independently of the rest of the document.

On-Screen Help
Provides assistance, in the form of messages, informing the user how to access the features available.

80-Column Screen
A word processing package should allow the user as much view of the document as possible. An 80-column screen is considered the minimum for this.

Word Count
This gives the user an indication of how much has been written so far.

Find/Replace
Searches for letters, words or phrases and changes them to something else.

except for the status line.

You have the choice at this stage of opening or editing a document or non-document file. The former is text that can be edited with WordStar while the latter refers to programs that can be run from your computer. A list of File Commands follows including the options to print, rename, copy and delete.

The last two sections in the Opening Menu are System Commands and WordStar Options. The first provide you with an interface to CP/M, allowing you to run one of the programs on disk, or else exiting to the operating system. The second give you the choice of using either MailMerge or SpellStar. MailMerge is a mailing list program ideal for printing out personalised letters, addresses for envolopes, and other business-orientated mailing activities. SpellStar is a spelling checker that checks each input word in a document file against a dictionary held in memory. Any words that don't correspond with those in the dictionary will be pointed out to the user for confirmation.

Using the D option at this point will result in a document file being opened (or one being created if it is a new file), and the screen will switch back to the Main menu. Indicated on the top line is the currently logged drive, and the name of the document file to be edited. This is followed by the current cursor position and a prompt informing you whether or not the Insert facilitiy is ON or OFF.

WYSIWYG
This is an acronym for 'what you see is what you get' and refers to the process whereby the user can view text on the VDU in the form in which it will appear on the printed page.

Mailshot Facility
Installed either integrally or as an associated program, mailshot programs can 'customise' standard letters or documents by inserting specific names and addresses at the required points and printing the address labels.

Spelling Checker
Provided in a similar format to mailshot programs, spelling checkers will read each word in a document and compare it with a dictionary of words held in memory. Words that do not match with those in the dictionary will be pointed out to the user.

Founts Available
Although a lot will depend on the printer, many word processors will support different founts, such as bold and italic.

File Linking
Documents are necessarily limited by the amount of available memory. Thus, when producing long documents, it is useful to be able to link the files together for printing or Search/Replace functions.

A Galaxy Of Stars
As WordStar has become so popular, it is not surprising to discover that its manufacturer, MicroPro, has released several versions of the original CP/M program. Over the past few years, one of the most popular versions of WordStar has been WordStar Professional, which has been translated to run under the MS-DOS system used on the Apricot range and the IBM PC. As an added incentive, MicroPro has included SpellStar and MailMerge.

More recently, the company has launched WordStar 2000, also for the IBM PC. This program, although superficially similar to its ancestor has been described as 'the Rolls Royce of word processors'. Provided on five disks, the programs and files that constitute WordStar 2000 add up to two Mbytes! But this kind of power is not cheap — WordStar 2000 is priced at £300 or £400

Finally, as an indication of the future of the CP/M WordStar, MicroPro has written a version of the program known as Pocket WordStar intended for users of the Amstrad CPC 464 and 664. Because these computers maintain a high-resolution screen display, there is insufficient memory remaining from the 64 Kbytes available to be able to run WordStar adequately. Therefore, MicroPro has developed a smaller version for these machines, which will be marketed by Cumana

Below this, assuming that the Help level is still set at 3, is another list of available commands, once again divided into sections. The first displays a summary of the cursor movements, amply illustrating WordStar's attachments to CP/M. Early CP/M machines didn't have cursor control keys, and so movements were performed by pressing the Control key plus another key simultaneously. These keys are concentrated on the left-hand side of the keyboard, the core being the S, E, D and X keys, which correspond to cursor left, up, right and down, respectively.

Among the miscellaneous items, you will notice B (CTRL B), which is listed as Reform. This will rejustify a paragraph on screen after editing and corrections have made a mess of the original. (Incidentally, the format appearing on screen corresponds exactly to how it will appear on hard copy, providing, of course, that your printer accommodates whatever margins have been set in WordStar.)

On the far right of the Main menu help screen are a series of other menu titles, giving you access to a number of additional functions. The Help menu, for example, provides detailed descriptions of how each WordStar command works. The Quick menu, on the other hand, contains a number of miscellaneous 'quick' commands, including, among others, the various Find and Replace options.

The On-screen menu provides the means to format the screen to any size and shape, letting you set the tabs, margins, line spacing and so on. One very useful function allows you to set the page length, appearing as a dotted line in the text. With this, you can see where the page breaks will occur when printing and so enabling you to arrange the document accordingly.

Also available on the On-screen menu is the Wordwrap toggle. Once set, this takes any word that will not fit onto the end of a line and places it at the beginning of the next, thereby removing the worry and bother of hyphenating words.

The third of the additional menus contains some of the most useful and powerful commands available on WordStar. Although the Block menu can perform a number of operations, its principal function is to manipulate blocks of text within a document. The range of operations is listed under the Block Operations section.

By performing CTRL commands at the beginning and end of required text, blocks can be created and will be displayed in 'reverse video' (the blocked text will be significantly less bright than the rest for easy recognition). Once the block has been created, it becomes possible to move or copy the text to another area of the document, delete it or even save it to a separate file on disk. But you're not confined to moving only paragraphs. It's also possible under WordStar to move columns, which is very handy if you are writing tables or letters with two or more rows of text. In this case, it is merely a question of demarcating for blocks columns instead of lines.

Included in the Block menu are the three save

Wordwrap

★★★☆

Although WordStar wordwraps when text is being written, it does not automatically reformat text when margins are changed.

Block Movement

★★★★★

WordStar allows the definition of blocks of any size and permits the full range of block manipulations.

On-Screen Help

★★★★★

On-screen Help menus are characteristic of WordStar and helped establish its popularity.

80-Column Screen

★★★★★

The program not only supports an 80-column screen, but also permits margins of up to 255 characters across.

Word Count

There is no word-counting facility in WordStar.

Find/Replace

★★★

WordStar supports several versions of this feature, enabling strings of up to 30 characters to be searched for.

WYSIWYG

★★★★★

More than any other word processing package, WordStar is acclaimed for its ability to format text on screen.

Mailshot Facility

★★★★

WordStar was one of the first programs to feature a mailshot program, and MailMerge is still the standard by which others are judged.

Spelling Checker

★★★★

Advanced versions of SpellStar have a dictionary of around 20,000 words to use for spelling verification.

Founts Available

★★★

Bold Strike and italics are included in the additional founts.

File Linking

★★

Separate files can be printed continuously using MailMerge, but facilities such as Find/Replace through several files at once are not supported.

À La Carte

WordStar is characterised by the Help menus, which are displayed at the top of the screen. Although experienced users tend to dispense with the Help menus, they are extremely useful to beginners, as they provide an easy reference to the commands that are available.

Each of the three screens shown here provides a different range of commands. The opening screen, which is the one presented to the user when WordStar is loaded, contains mostly DOS commands to enable the user to access files. The Main menu contains commands that are most likely to be used when keying in the text, while the Block menu contains a number of editing commands

This prompt tells the user the current logged drive and the file that is being edited

This is the Main menu under Help level three, giving full explanations of the available commands

Page, line and column numbers indicate the cursor position

This prompt reminds you that INSERT mode is ON

IBM versions of WordStar allow a number of commands to be entered via the function keys. This line shows the current function key settings

This line shows the number of columns currently set, although these can be altered. The ! signs indicate the default TAB settings, which can also be changed

commands, offering the options of returning to the text, going to the main menu or exiting WordStar. You should bear in mind that when using commands listed under the separate menus, it's not necessary to recall the menu to the screen. To save and exit the system, for instance, you merely have to type CTRL KX, which will perform the command automatically.

Let's conclude this brief overview of WordStar with a look at the 'dot commands'. These are embedded in the text on separate lines, each beginning, naturally enough, with a full stop, and concern print formatting and adding extra features to the hard copy, such as top and bottom margin widths and page numbers. The command .pl (followed by a number), for example, sets the number of lines to be printed on a page. Because these commands are not acted upon by WordStar until the software is processing the document for printing, they in fact act as CTRL characters to the printer.

WordStar's power has managed to keep this program at the top of it's field for almost a decade. As CP/M moves 'down market' towards home machines such as the Amstrad range, it seems very likely that WordStar will follow and become the leader in the home computer market as well.

A Popular Bundle

WordStar is an interesting example of how the recognised popularity of a program generates its own momentum to make it even more popular. Once WordStar established itself as the leading word processing software for CP/M micros, many manufacturers began bundling it with their machine, resulting in an even larger user base for the package.

An early example of this kind of marketing was the Osborne 1, which not only bundled WordStar with the machine, but also included the SuperCalc spreadsheet. The fact that both of these programs run under CP/M meant that it was possible for them to share common files. This kind of idea proved so popular that other software programmers began to incorporate the idea of data passing and file sharing, which eventually led to the development of integrated software packages, such as Lotus 1-2-3.

Nowadays, almost all micros come with bundled software, particularly word processors. These range from the highly sophisticated and very expensive Perfect Software from Thorn EMI (for the Advance and Wren) to the budget-priced Tasword II, which was bundled in the 'six-pack' provided with early versions of the Spectrum+

SQUEEZED IN

Word processing packages for home micros are invariably shaped by the potential of each individual machine. In particular, the range of features provided in any given program will depend on the amount of memory available. We look at three of the more successful packages for the most popular home computers.

Word processing is undoubtedly one of the most popular applications for home microcomputers. Programs range from simple text editors priced at a few pounds to sophisticated and expensive disk or ROM-based word processing packages. However, any program is only as good as the hardware it's designed for, and the packages written for most home micros don't have many of the more complex features provided on programs for business computers.

The primary restriction imposed on a word processor for an eight-bit computer is the limitations of memory. Thus every additional feature included in the software will take up space that would otherwise be available for storing text. This has proved to be a major stumbling block in the implementation of WordStar on the Amstrad CPC 464 and 664. Although these machines can use the CP/M operating system, there is insufficient memory available adequately to implement the full WordStar program. However, a scaled down version of the program — called Pocket WordStar — has been developed.

Another problem confronting word processor programmers of home micros is the method of back-up storage. Most home micros still rely on cassettes for back-up storage; thus, all of the program and text has to be held within the computer, placing even greater demands on the available memory.

EASY SCRIPT

A very large number of word processing packages have been written for the Commodore 64, but by far the most popular of these is Easy Script (mainly because Commodore bundles it with the disk drive).

The main problem for anyone wishing to write a word processing package for the Commodore 64 is the screen display, which can only produce a maximum character resolution of 40 by 25. The programmer is therefore forced to make the best of 40 columns, meaning that Easy Script doesn't have the luxury of help screens, which would otherwise occupy too much room on the screen. Furthermore, screen limitations prevent Easy

Script from having any wordwrap facility, although it is possible to view the text wordwrapped prior to it being sent to the printer.

In order to overcome this problem, the programmers of Easy Script have chosen to use the screen as a 'window' on the document. The margins can be set up to 240 columns across, and when a line reaches the 40-column limit, the screen will scroll sideways until the margin limitation is reached. At this point, the screen will abruptly return to the beginning of the next line. Although this method isn't ideal, you can get used to it or, alternatively, write in 40 columns and then reformat the text before it is sent to the printer.

The various print formatting and editing commands essential to a word processing program are accessed via the Commodore 64's function keys. Pressing one will get you into a particular mode, and if followed by a keypress, will select the appropriate option. Thus editing commands are accessed by pressing F1, which is shown by Edit flashing at the top of the screen. Text and page layout are selected by pressing F3, which produces an inverse star at the cursor position. The codes to set the margins, justify the text and so on can then follow. Easy Script makes great use of these and other commands embedded in the text, which are only acted upon when the document is sent to the printer. This means that a number of the functions won't be seen on screen, reducing the ability to see what the final printed document will look like.

Easy Script contains almost all of the features you'd expect from a word processing package, such as full block manipulations, which includes copying, transferring and separate filing of the blocks, although you should note that some features work a lot better than others. The Find/Replace function, for instance, is notoriously slow, particularly when using linked files that have to be loaded separately and then searched.

TASWORD II

A word processing program that is widely used on the Amstrad range and the Spectrum+ is Tasword II. On loading, this program bears a striking resemblance to WordStar. At the top of the screen is a Help menu containing a list of the commands (and their control characters), divided into logical sections. Beneath this menu is the 16 by 80 character area set aside for writing text.

Tasword II is a powerful word processing package. The program contains a large number of commands that enable the user to format the text on the screen. Text can be moved right, left or centred on screen, and the margins set to a maximum of 128 columns. If the margins are reset, it's possible to rejustify the text to fit in with the new format. Wordwrap is implemented within Tasword, automatically rejustifying the line if a word is taken over to the next. The program is unusual in that the additional spaces are included only on the second half of the line.

The program also facilitates block commands, although the list is not extensive. Once defined, blocks can be moved, copied or deleted, but the commands suffer from a problem that occurs in a number of features of Tasword II — the program delimits blocks in terms of lines. Thus when the user defines a block as starting midway through a line, the program will move the entire line, including the words that were meant to be outside the block area.

A similar problem is encountered when using the insert mode. Many word processors will automatically insert the text at the cursor position and move the remainder of the text to the right. Unfortunately, Tasword will either allow a single character to be inserted or provide an entire line. Furthermore, this extra line will appear under the present one, again ignoring the fact that the cursor may be in the middle of a line rather than at the end of it.

Where Tasword II really scores is in the wide number of printer control features it offers. To begin with, users are able to customise, or 'install', their own version of Tasword. This is possible by defining the page layout — setting the number of lines on a page and so on — and redefining both the print and the printer control characters.

Tasword has a wide range of printer control characters based around the Epson standard codes. They are accessed by pressing CTRL and the Space bar together, followed by the appropriate letter, with upper case turning the option on and lower case switching it off. There are 20 codes available through the program, ranging from variable line spacing to various forms of emphasised printing — such as underline, bold strike and italics.

Additional founts such as Lectura Light and Compacta are catered for by the Tasword printer control characters, but are not available under the program itself. In order to access these, the manufacturer, Tasman, has introduced a second program that can be run with Tasword called Tasprint, which can be configured for a wide range of dot matrix printers. Once configured, Tasprint can be loaded before Tasword and will assign itself an area of memory that will not be overwritten by Tasword, after which you are able to access the five additional founts. Naturally, you pay the price for these additional founts with a reduced text area; Tasprint takes up around five of the 13 Kbytes that would otherwise be available.

VIEW

The BBC Micro has a somewhat different problem to overcome than that of the Commodore 64. Its screen display uses a large quantity of memory which, on the standard Model B, is in short supply. Like a number of other companies, AcornSoft has chosen to supply its word processing package, View, on ROM to fit into one of the BBC Micro's sideways sockets. This doesn't take up any of the available memory space and yet avoids the problem encountered by a number of large word processing systems, which continually have to read extra programs from disk.

This is an important consideration. Should you choose to have an 80-column display, the best that can be hoped for is just under 10,000 characters in memory. If an eight-Kbyte program was included in this, the text area would be considerably reduced, but you don't have to use 80-column mode with View. The screen can be used as a window on the document, as with Easy Script and most other good packages.

View is undoubtedly one of the better word

VARIATIONS ON A TURTLE

Our examination of the LOGO language has already shown us how procedures can be defined to carry out sequences of commands. Such procedures are more flexible if the user is able to input different values that will alter the effect achieved when the procedure is called.

In LOGO, a word — here we'll take SIZE as an example — may be used in three different ways. To distinguish between these, LOGO uses three different notations: SIZE,:SIZE (pronounced 'dots size'), and "SIZE ('quotes size'). As we have already seen, if LOGO meets the word SIZE, with no preceding punctuation, it takes it to be a procedure name and will carry out the sequence of commands in the SIZE definition. :SIZE is used to indicate the *value* held in the variable name — if LOGO encounters :SIZE it will retrieve the value associated with the name. "SIZE is used to refer to variable names and procedures, but indicates that we are referring to the *name* itself, and not to any value that might be associated with it. Thus, "SIZE might be used to refer to a variable, while :SIZE would refer to the value that has been allocated to that variable. (Note that quotes are required before, but not after, the word. The end of the name is indicated by a space.)

MIT LOGO is not totally consistent in its use of this notation. After the commands EDIT, ERASE and PO, a procedure name should be written without quotes. Thus, the correct syntax is EDIT SQUARE, even though SQUARE is not a call to the procedure SQUARE, but is merely the name of that procedure and should logically be preceded by quotes. LCSI LOGO is more logical and demands that quotes are used with these commands.

To use any of the procedures we have defined so far we simply type the procedure name, in exactly the same way as we would use LOGO commands such as DRAW or HIDETURTLE. However, other commands — FORWARD, for example — need extra information before they can be used. The word FORWARD on its own is meaningless — a value must be assigned to it before LOGO can carry out the command. If variable names are included in our procedures, we can input any required value and thus vary the effect obtained when the procedure is called.

Let's consider the procedure we defined in a previous instalment to draw a square:

```
TO SQUARE
   REPEAT 4 [FD 50 RT 90]
END
```

As it stands, this procedure will draw a square with sides of 50 units in length. However, it would be far more useful if the square could be drawn to any chosen size — to do this, we must input the desired value. To change SQUARE to accept an input, use the editor to replace the fixed value of 50 with the variable "SIDE and add :SIDE to the title line. Our procedure will now look like this:

```
TO SQUARE :SIDE
   REPEAT 4 [FD :SIDE RT 90]
END
```

When the procedure is called, it is now necessary to give the variable "SIDE a value. Try SQUARE 40, SQUARE 10, and so on to see how the size of the square will vary.

Let's see exactly what happens when you type SQUARE 30. LOGO first looks up the definition of SQUARE. The title line tells it that one input is required, and that this is to be named "SIDE. The value on the input line (in this case 30) is allocated to the variable "SIDE and the commands in the procedure definition are then obeyed. The best way of visualising this is to imagine that each variable name refers to a box containing its value. When LOGO reaches the line FORWARD :SIDE it goes to the box labelled "SIDE, retrieves the value found there and uses this as the input to FORWARD. The box labelled "SIDE is used only in the procedure that refers to it. If another procedure also uses "SIDE as the name for an input, it will use a different box. "SIDE is therefore referred to as a *local* variable.

We can also use inputs with subprocedures. The HOUSE procedure we give here is our solution to the problem that we set previously (your answer may be different) can be modified so that different values may be input:

```
TO HOUSE :BIG
   SQUARE :BIG
   FD :BIG RT 30
   TRI :BIG
   LT 30 BK :BIG
END

TO SQUARE :SIZE
   REPEAT 4 [FD :SIZE RT 90]
END

TO TRI :SIDE
   REPEAT 3 [FD :SIDE RT 120]
END
```

Here, we have used three different variable names — "BIG, "SIZE and "SIDE. We could have used the same name for all three, as variables are local to the procedures in which they are used, but this could have been confusing.

To see how these procedures work, let's see what happens if we type HOUSE 30. Logo reads the input line and assigns the value 30 to the variable "BIG in HOUSE. The first line of HOUSE is therefore now equivalent to SQUARE 30. The variable "SIZE in SQUARE is, in turn, assigned the value 30. SQUARE is now run, with FD :SIZE becoming FD 30. A similar procedure is followed when TRI is called.

Now try adapting the procedures for drawing the five-by five board so that BOARD takes the size of the square as an input.

Here's a procedure that draws polygons, with the number of sides given as an input:

```
TO POLY :SIDES
    REPEAT :SIDES [FD 50 RT 360 / :SIDES]
END
```

Using this procedure with one input, POLY 3 will draw a triangle, POLY 4 a square, and so on. However, in all the polygons drawn by this procedure, the sides will be 50 units in length. A more general procedure that draws polygons of any size requires two inputs — one for the number of sides, and one for the required length. To do this, all that is needed is to adapt the POLY procedure to replace the 50 with a variable name and add that name to the title line:

```
TO POLY :SIDES :SIZE
    REPEAT :SIDES [FD :SIZE RT 360/ :SIDES]
END
```

Now POLY 5 30 will draw a pentagon with sides of 30 units in length. You might like to try adapting your new version of the board-drawing procedure so that it will draw any square board (not just five-by-five). There will now be two inputs — the number of squares in each direction, and their size.

GLOBAL VARIABLES

So far we have considered variables that are local to the procedures that use them. But variables may be defined that are available for use by all procedures. These are known as *global* variables and are useful for communicating information between different procedures. However, their use makes debugging more difficult and so they should be used sparingly.

The command MAKE is used to assign values to global variables. MAKE "SIDE 3 assigns 3 as the value of the variable "INSIDE. MAKE "SIDE :SIDE + 1 increases the value of "SIDE by one. The exact meaning of the notation in this second example is: find the value of the variable "SIDE, add one, then assign the result back to the variable named "SIDE. In each case, MAKE requires two inputs — the name of the variable, and the value to be assigned to that variable.

To sum up the programming features we have covered in this instalment of the Logo course, we've designed some procedures for drawing spirals. The main procedure is named EQSPI. This requires three inputs: the initial length of the line to be drawn, the angle that must be turned at each 'corner' of the spiral, and a scale factor by which

the initial length must be multiplied to produce the spiral effect. Different sets of inputs may be used to achieve different effects — we tried 70 283 0.95, 70 143 0.95, and 20 243 1.05. Try other sets of numbers and see what happens.

NOWRAP is a new command. This stops the turtle 'wrapping around' the screen — when the turtle reaches the screen boundary the procedure will stop with an 'out of bounds' error message. In many cases, the wrap-around effect can give interesting results. In this procedure it spoils the spiral effect, so NOWRAP is used to turn it off.

The main procedure EQSPI repeatedly draws a line (the length of which is determined by the scale factor), then turns through a fixed angle, and finally alters the scale factor. The length of the lines drawn either increases or decreases, depending on whether the scale factor is greater than or less than 1. The large number after REPEAT is simply to keep the procedure going for a long time. If you've seen enough, press Control-G (or Break) to stop the procedure running. Most of the variables are local, with the exception of "SCALE. This is global because "GROW changes its value, and this new value must be made available to S.FORWARD. Thus, "SCALE is used to communicate between the two procedures.

Spiral Procedure

```
TO EQSPI :SIZE :ANGLE :FACT
    SETUP
    REPEAT 1000 [S.FORWARD :SIZE RIGHT :ANGLE
        GROW :FACT]
END
TO SETUP
    DRAW NOWRAP MAKE "SCALE 1
END
TO GROW : NUMB
    MAKE "SCALE :SCALE 1 :NUMB
END
TO S.FORWARD :DIST
    FORWARD :SCALE 1:DIST
END
```

Logo Flavours

LCSI versions use the command FENCE rather than NOWRAP to stop automatic wrapping.

The Atari version doesn't have FENCE, so use WINDOW instead. This stops the turtle from wrapping around, but, unlike FENCE, it doesn't halt the procedure when the turtle reaches the screen boundary.

In the Spiral procedure on the Spectrum, replace DRAW in the SETUP subprocedure with CS.

Procedure Problems

1) Write a procedure to draw a circle of radius 50. Modify the procedure so that the radius is given as an input to the procedure.

2) Write a procedure that draws a 'target' consisting of five concentric circles.

Exercise Answers

1) Tangram Puzzles

The man sitting, the man bowing, and the cat shapes, all use the other side of the parallelogram piece from that used by the dog in last week's example. In order to turn a piece over in LOGO, you simply change all RIGHT turns to LEFT turns. So instead of:

```
TO PAR
   REPEAT 2 [FD 25 RT 45 FD 35 RT 135]
END
```

we will sometimes need its 'other side' given by:

```
TO PAR1
   REPEAT 2 [FD 25 LT 45 FD 35 LT 135]
END
```

All the other piece procedures are exactly as given in the last part of this course

Man Running

```
TO RUNNING
   MOVE1 TRI1 MOVE2 PAR MOVE3 TRI3 MOVE4
   TRI3 MOVE5 SQUARE MOVE6 TRI1 MOVE7 TRI2
   MOVE8
END

TO MOVE1
   LT 45
END

TO MOVE2
   PU FD 25 RT 135 FD 17.5 LT 45 PD
END

TO MOVE3
   PU FD 75 RT 90 PD
END

TO MOVE4
   PU RT 90 FD 25 RT 90 PD
END

TO MOVE5
   PU FD 50 RT 135 FD 50 LT 135 PD
END

TO MOVE6
   PU RT 135 FD 21 RT 135 FD 25 LT 90 FD 50
   LT 90 FD 25 RT 90 PD
END

TO MOVE7
   PU FD 25 RT 135 FD 71 RT 45 BK 35 PD
END

TO MOVE8
   PU FD 35 LT 90 FD 25 RT 45 FD 17.5 LT 45
   FD 25 RT 135 PD
END
```

Man Sitting

```
TO SITTING
   MOVE1 TRI1 MOVE2 TRI2 MOVE3 TRI3 MOVE4
   TRI1 PAR1 MOVE5 SQUARE MOVE6 TRI3 MOVE7
END

TO MOVE1
   LT45
END

TO MOVE2
   PU FD 25 LT 45 FD 17.5 RT 90 PD
END

TO MOVE3
   PU BK 15 LT 90 PD
END

TO MOVE4
   PU FD 50 RT 45 FD 25 RT 90 PD
END

TO MOVE5
   PU FD 25 LT 45 FD 35 LT 45 PD
END

TO MOVE 6
   PU BK 50 LT 90 PD
END

TO MOVE7
   PU BK 21 RT 135 BK 50 RT 90 FD 35 LT 90
   PD
END
```

Man Bowing

```
TO BOWING
   MOVE1 TRI1 MOVE2 PAR1 MOVE3 TRI3 MOVE4
   TRI3 MOVE5 TRI1 MOVE6 TRI2 MOVE7 SQUARE
   MOVE8
END

TO MOVE1
   LT 90
END

TO MOVE2
   PU FD 25 RT 135 FD 30 PD
END

TO MOVE3
   PU LT 45 FD 35 LT 135 BK 50 PD
END

TO MOVE4
   PU RT 90 FD 50 LT 135 PD
END

TO MOVE5
   PU RT 90 FD 50 LT 135 FD 5 RT 90 PD
END

TO MOVE6
   PU RT 90 FD 25 RT 45 FD 7.5 RT 45 BK 35
   PD
END

TO MOVE7
   PU FD 35 RT 135 FD 7.5 LT 45 FD 55 RT 45
   PD
END

TO MOVE8
   PU LT 45 FD 36 RT 45 FD 56 LT 135 FD 5
   LT 45 BK 25 PD
END
```

Cat

```
TO CAT
   MOVE1 TRI3 MOVE2 SQUARE MOVE3 TRI1 MOVE4
   TRI1 MOVE5 TRI3 MOVE6 PAR1 MOVE7 TRI2
   MOVE8
END

TO MOVE1
   PU FD 50 RT 90 PD
END

TO MOVE2
   RT 170
END

TO MOVE3
   PU RT 90 FD 25 LT 90 PD
END

TO MOVE4
   RT 180
END

TO MOVE5
   PU RT 90 FD 25 LT 80 FD 50 RT 45 FD 50
   RT 90 PD
END

TO MOVE6
   LT 155
END

TO MOVE7
   PU LT 160 FD 35 PD
END

TO MOVE8
   PU FD 35 LT 45 FD 21 RT 135 PD
END
```

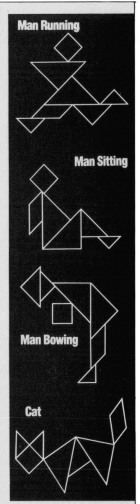

Man Running

Man Sitting

Man Bowing

Cat

These are our suggested answers to the Procedure Problems on page 565:

2)
```
TO HOUSE
   SQUARE FD 50 RT 30
   TRI LT 30 BK 50
END
TO SQUARE
   REPEAT 4 [FD 50 RT
   90]
END
TO TRI
   REPEAT 3 [FD 50 RT
   120]
END
```

3)
```
TO BOARD
   REPEAT 5 [LINE FD
   10] BK 50
END
TO LINE
   REPEAT 5 [SQUARE RT
   90 FD 10 LT 90] LT
   90 FD 50 RT 90
END
TO SQUARE
   REPEAT 4 [FD 10
   RT 90]
END
```

4)
```
TO SIX.STAR
   TRI MOVE TRI MOVE.
   BACK
END
TO TRI
   RT 30 REPEAT 3
   [FD 50 RT 120]
END
TO MOVE
   PU FD 29 RT 60 PD
END
TO MOVE.BACK
   PU LT 60 BK 29 PD
END
```

REPEAT PERFORMANCE

The LOGO language uses the mathematical technique of recursion (an instruction that refers to itself) to great effect. Coupled with variable inputs, the use of recursion in procedures can produce some extremely interesting results.

One of the first programs we defined in the course was a procedure to draw a square. The definition instructed the turtle to move forward a certain distance, turn right 90 degrees and repeat those two steps three more times. Here is another way to draw a square:

```
TO SQUARE
  FD 50
  RT 90
  SQUARE
END
```

If you were to try this out, the turtle would draw a square and then carry on moving around the perimeter of the square until you pressed Control-G or BREAK. The most noticeable thing about this new SQUARE procedure is that it calls itself — in other words, it is 'recursive'.

When this procedure is run, LOGO fetches the definition of SQUARE and begins to obey the instructions. The turtle is moved FORWARD 50 and then turned RIGHT 90. The next instruction is SQUARE, so LOGO fetches the definition of SQUARE and begins to obey it. This will go on *ad infinitum* if the program is not interrupted.

It is also possible to use recursive calls in procedures that require inputs:

```
TO POLY :SIDE :ANGLE
  FD :SIDE
  RT :ANGLE
  POLY :SIDE :ANGLE
END
```

This procedure can produce all the polygons we have defined so far in this chapter (see page 222) as well as many we haven't looked at (you might like to try using the procedure with an angle value of 89). It is also possible to change the value of the input in the recursive call. Thus:

```
TO POLYSPI :SIDE :ANGLE
  FD :SIDE
  RT :ANGLE
  POLYSPI (:SIDE + 5) :ANGLE
END
```

The only difference between this procedure and

POLY is that five is added to the value of SIDE each time it is called. So if you began with POLYSPI 10 90, then the first call would draw a line of length 10, the second would be 15, then 20, and so on. The result is a spiral. You might like to experiment with different inputs: 10 90, 10 95, 10 120, 10 117, 10 144 and 10 142 are interesting starters. You could also try modifying the procedure — one possibility is to change addition to subtraction or multiplication.

Here's a similar procedure that increments the angle rather than the side value:

```
TO INSPI :SIDE :ANGLE :INC
  FD :SIDE
  RT :ANGLE
  INSPI :SIDE (:ANGLE + :INC) :INC
END
```

Try various inputs: 5 0 7, 10 40 30, 15 2 20, 5 30 20 will do initially. Why do some shapes close and others not? Can you find a rule?

The simple repetition of a piece of code is referred to as *iteration*. LOGO uses REPEAT for this purpose, while other languages use a variety of constructs, such as FOR...NEXT, REPEAT...UNTIL, and WHILE...WEND. However, LOGO relies much more on recursion than it does on iteration. If you've programmed in other languages you may have difficulty in breaking away from using iteration, but turtle graphics is ideal for experimenting with recursive calls.

STOP RULES

All of the recursive procedures we have looked at so far continue repeating indefinitely. Clearly, we need a way to make a procedure stop at some point. Taking the SQUARE procedure as our example, a possible place to stop it would be after it has drawn a complete square and the turtle's heading is back to 0. This can be done by adding a 'stop rule' to the procedure:

```
TO SQUARE :SIDE
  FD :SIDE
  RT 90
  IF HEADING = 0 THEN STOP
  SQUARE :SIDE
END
```

The new primitives are STOP and IF. The first of these commands causes a procedure to stop running and returns control to the calling procedure. An IF statement is LOGO's way of making decisions. IF is followed by a condition, and THEN by an action that is carried out if the condition is true.

Let's look at a version of POLYSPI with a stop rule and consider exactly what happens when it is run:

```
TO POLYSPI :LENGTH
    IF :LENGTH > 15 THEN STOP
    FD :LENGTH
    RT 90
    POLYSPI (:LENGTH + 5)
END
```

This is what happens when we run POLYSPI 10. The POLYSPI procedure is called and a local variable is defined with its value set at 10. Since this value is not greater than 15, LOGO proceeds to carry out the movement FD 10 RT 90, and then makes a new call to POLYSPI, but this time with an input value of 15. This causes a copy of the procedure to be called again. Because LENGTH is not greater than 15, the turtle is made to move FD 15 RT 90, and another call to POLYSPI is made. But this time, the local variable has been increased to 20, so the procedure stops and returns control to the procedure that called it (POLYSPI 15). This procedure in turn has come to its final line, and returns control to its calling procedure. This also stops, at which point the program has come to its end.

We have shown how recursion in LOGO involves procedures calling copies of themselves. It is important to keep in mind that the recursive calls are copies that exist alongside the original procedure, working as if they were completely different from it. When finished, such a procedure always returns control to the procedure that called it. To illustrate more clearly the process of returning from procedure calls, we can rearrange POLYSPI in this way:

```
TO POLYSPI :LENGTH
    IF :LENGTH > 15 THEN STOP
    POLYSPI (:LENGTH + 15)
    FD :LENGTH
    RT 90
END
```

If you run this you will see that the program does its drawing 'backwards': the lines are drawn spiralling inwards rather than outwards. (This will be shown more clearly if you use a larger value in the condition statement — for example, using 50 instead of 15.) What is significant here is that LOGO draws each line as control is returned from the procedure calls. In our previous example, a line was drawn and control was then passed to another procedure. But here, all the procedures are called before any drawing begins, and the last created value of LENGTH is the one used first.

Finally, we should note that recursion is a technique that uses up a lot of memory. Procedures in which the recursive call is in the last line are the most efficiently implemented, however, as they don't take up any extra memory no matter how many times they're called. If a procedure can be written so it is 'end recursive' then this is usually worth doing.

Logo Flavours

In all LCSI versions the action part of an IF statement is written as a list within square brackets and without the THEN. For example:

    IF HEADING = 0 [STOP]

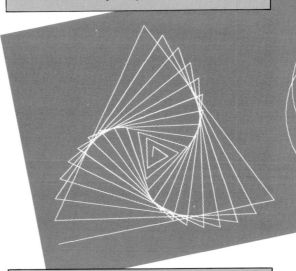

Exercise Answers

A procedure to draw a circle, given the radius as input, with the present position as a point on the circumference:

```
TO CIRCLE :RADIUS
    REPEAT 36 [FD ( 2 * :PI * :RADIUS / 36 )
    RT  10]
END
MAKE "PI (3.14159)
```

If we adapt this procedure so that the centre of the circle is at the present position we get:

```
TO C.CIRCLE :RADIUS
    PU LT 90 FD :RADIUS RT 90 PD
    CIRCLE :RADIUS
    PU LT 90 BK :RADIUS RT 90 PD
END
```

TARGET uses C.CIRCLE to draw 5 concentric circles:

```
TO TARGET
    C.CIRCLE 10 C.CIRCLE 20 C.CIRCLE 30
    C.CIRCLE 40 C.CIRCLE 50
END
```

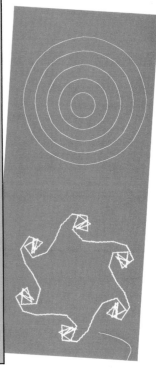

229

DO THE LOGOMOTION

In this part of our look at LOGO, we will develop a simple game in which the turtle gets lost in space. To do this, we will first need to look more closely at various input and output methods.

ın our 'Space Turtle' game, the turtle is stranded in the depths of space, a long distance from its base, to which it must return. The game will require us to print various messages on the screen. The necessary command for this is, not surprisingly, PRINT. Once a message has been printed, the cursor is moved to the beginning of the next line.

To print a single word, PRINT is followed by the word itself — thus, PRINT "HELLO prints the word 'HELLO' on the screen. PRINT " is used to print the 'null word' (a 'word' that has no characters). The effect of this command is simply to print a blank line. If more than one word is to be printed, the text is enclosed in square brackets to indicate that it forms a *list* :

PRINT [YOUR TIME HAS RUN OUT]

PRINT is also used to display the contents of a variable, so PRINT :SCORE will take the value held in the variable "SCORE and display it. Messages and variable values may be combined in the same PRINT statement by enclosing the complete instruction in *round* brackets, as in:

(PRINT [YOUR SCORE WAS] :SCORE)

PRINT1 behaves in exactly the same fashion as PRINT does, except that in this case the cursor will remain at the end of the printed text and will not be moved to the next line. This can be demonstrated by entering:

PRINT1 [WHAT IS YOUR NAME?]

OUTPUT OPERATIONS

LOGO commands, such as HIDETURTLE or PRINT, cause something to happen — they may be said to have an effect on the turtle. However, other LOGO primitives — XCOR, for example — do not have an effect, but instead output a value. This value is then normally used as the input to a command. So, for example, typing:

PRINT XCOR

would cause XCOR to output the value corresponding to the turtle's current x co-ordinate to the command PRINT, which then displays the result. Thus, if the current value of XCOR is 20, PRINT XCOR will cause the number 20 to appear on the screen. If XCOR is typed on its own, the message RESULT: 20 will appear. This is actually an error message (LCSI versions are somewhat less polite and would print YOU DON'T SAY WHAT TO DO WITH 20).

The procedures we have so far written have all been commands. To create *operations* we must make use of the primitive OUTPUT. As a simple example, here's a procedure that outputs the distance of the turtle from the origin; this procedure uses SQRT to return the square root of a number:

```
TO DISTANCE
    OUTPUT SQRT (XCOR*XCOR + YCOR*YCOR)
END
```

Try moving the turtle to different screen positions and use DISTANCE to determine how far it is from the origin. For example, SETXY 30 40 PRINT DISTANCE should give the answer 50.

When LOGO executes an OUTPUT instruction it stops running the current procedure, returning control to the procedure that called it. This can be seen in the procedure MAX, which outputs the larger of two numbers:

```
TO MAX :X :Y
    IF :X > :Y THEN OUTPUT :X
    OUTPUT :Y
END
```

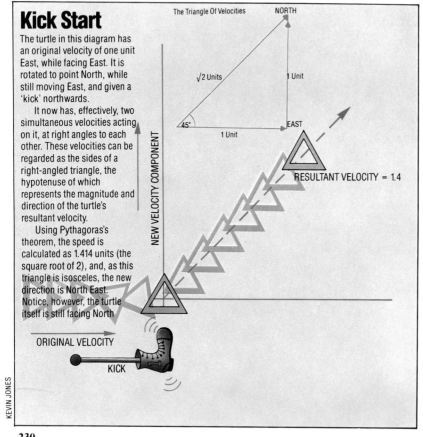

Kick Start
The turtle in this diagram has an original velocity of one unit East, while facing East. It is rotated to point North, while still moving East, and given a 'kick' northwards.

It now has, effectively, two simultaneous velocities acting on it, at right angles to each other. These velocities can be regarded as the sides of a right-angled triangle, the hypotenuse of which represents the magnitude and direction of the turtle's resultant velocity.

Using Pythagoras's theorem, the speed is calculated as 1.414 units (the square root of 2), and, as this triangle is isosceles, the new direction is North East. Notice, however, the turtle itself is still facing North.

KEVIN JONES

PRINT MAX 6 2 will give 6 as a result. Try writing a procedure to give the absolute value of a number, so that PRINT ABS 4 and PRINT ABS (-4) will both return the value 4.

Our game will ask you to type in your name and press Return. Here is a procedure to do this:

```
TO GET.NAME
   SPLITSCREEN
   PRINT1 [WHAT IS YOUR NAME?]
   MAKE "NAME FIRST REQUEST
   (PRINT "HELLO :NAME)
END
```

REQUEST waits for a line to be typed in and terminated with a Return. It then outputs the line as a list. FIRST outputs the first element of a list. Try the GET.NAME procedure and type in 'Holly' as the name. Now see what happens if 'Holly Johnson' is used as an input.

The game will control the turtle's onscreen movement by using the keys R, L and K. R will turn the turtle clockwise (right) through 30 degrees; L will turn it anticlockwise (left) by the same amount; while K is used to 'kick' the turtle — increasing its speed in whatever direction it is currently facing. The turtle will be moving around the screen, and we will require it to respond immediately to these keys. It would be a help if there was a LOGO primitive — READKEY, perhaps — that would output the last key that was pressed. If this was the case, we could write:

```
TO COMMAND
   MAKE "COM READKEY
   IF:COM = "R THEN RIGHT 30
   IF:COM = "L THEN LEFT 30
   IF:COM = "K THEN KICK
END
```

Unfortunately, this primitive does not exist! However, we can write it as a procedure, thus:

```
TO READKEY
   IF RC? THEN OUTPUT READCHARACTER
   OUTPUT"
END
```

When a key is pressed it is stored in the keyboard buffer. READCHARACTER simply outputs the last character from the buffer — if the buffer is empty READCHARACTER will wait for a key to be pressed and then output the relevant character. RC? is true if the buffer contains any characters and is false if the buffer is empty. So READKEY will now output the last character in the buffer, or will output a null word if the buffer is empty.

THE DYNATURTLE

Our space-going turtle is in fact a *dynaturtle*. This is a turtle that has a velocity, as well as a position and a heading like any normal earthbound turtle. The dynaturtle is in space, so there is no friction and no gravity. The dynaturtle will obey Newton's laws of motion. Our illustration will make this clearer, but as an example, let us assume that the dynaturtle is moving left to right across the screen with a velocity of 1. If the L key is pressed, the

dynaturtle will turn to face the top of the screen, but the turtle's momentum will keep it moving on its horizontal course. If K is then pressed, the dynaturtle will get a 'kick' in the direction in which it is facing. This results in a push up the screen of velocity 1, and the dynaturtle will move diagonally across the screen with a velocity of 1.4. The dynaturtle will allow you to experiment with a body that obeys Newton's laws; it is designed to allow you to develop an intuitive understanding of these laws without you needing to understand all the relevant equations.

In the program, the dynaturtle's velocity is considered in terms of two components along the x and y axes. These components are found by using the SIN and COS functions. The only game controls are the three already mentioned. To begin the game, just type START. You have a fixed time in which to reach your goal, and the program keeps a record of the best score to date.

Logo Flavours

MIT LOGO	LCSI LOGO
DRAW	CS
PRINT1	TYPE
RC?	KEYP
READCHARACTER	RC
REQUEST	RL
SETHEADING	SETH
SETXY	SETPOS (followed by a list)
FULLSCREEN	FS (Not available on the Spectrum)
SPLITSCREEN	SS (Not available on the Spectrum)

IF has a slightly different syntax in LCSI LOGO, e.g:

IF DISTANCE < 5 [DONE STOP]

Extraterrestrial Turtle
The program as printed will generate the turtle and the target (its home base) only. The stars and planets shown here were added using some simple circle procedures

Abbreviations

OUTPUT	OP
PRINT	PR
READCHARACTER	RC
REQUEST	RQ
SETHEADING	SETH

Space Turtle Program

```
TO START
    MAKE "MAX 0
    MAKE "BEST "
    DRAW
    HT
    TARGET
    PLAY
END

TO TARGET
    PU SETXY 0 5 PD
    RT 90
    REPEAT 36 [FD 31.4/36 RT 10]
    PU
END

TO PLAY
    GET.NAME
    INIT
    DRIVE
END

TO GET.NAME
    SPLITSCREEN
    PRINT1 [WHAT IS YOUR NAME?]
    MAKE "NAME FIRST REQUEST
END

TO INIT
    MAKE "SCORE 200
    SETXY 100 100
    SETH 270
    MAKE "XVEL 0
    MAKE "YVEL 0
    FULLSCREEN
    ST
END

TO DRIVE
    COMMAND
    DYNA.MOVE
    IF DISTANCE <5 THEN DONE STOP
    MAKE "SCORE :SCORE – 1
    IF :SCORE = 0 THEN OUT.OF.TIME
    STOP
    DRIVE
END

TO COMMAND
    MAKE "COM READKEY
    IF :COM = "R THEN RIGHT 30
    IF :COM = "L THEN LEFT 30
    IF :COM = "K THEN KICK
END

TO READKEY
    IF RC? THEN OUTPUT
    READCHARACTER
```

```
    OUTPUT "
END

TO KICK
    MAKE "XVEL + 3 * SIN HEADING
    MAKE "YVEL + 3 * COS HEADING
END

TO DYNA.MOVE
    SETXY XCOR + :XVEL
    YCOR + :YVEL
END

TO DISTANCE
    OUTPUT SORT
    (XCOR * XCOR + YCOR * YCOR)
END

TO DONE
    PRINT"
    SPLITSCREEN
    (PRINT [WELL DONE] :NAME)
    (PRINT [YOUR SCORE WAS]
    :SCORE)
    REPORT
    AGAIN
END

TO REPORT
    IF :SCORE > :MAX THEN MAKE
    "MAX :SCORE MAKE "BEST :NAME
    PRINT "
    (PRINT [HIGH SCORER IS] :BEST
    [WITH] : MAX [POINTS])
END

TO AGAIN
    PRINT1 [ANOTHER GO?]
    MAKE "ANS FIRST REQUEST
    IF :ANS = "YES THEN REPLAY
    STOP
    IF :ANS = "NO THEN STOP
    PRINT [MAKE YOUR MIND UP, YES
    OR NO?]
    AGAIN
END

TO OUT.OF.TIME
    PRINT "
    SPLITSCREEN
    PRINT [YOUR TIME HAS RUN OUT]
    AGAIN
END

TO REPLAY
    HT
    GET.NAME
    INIT
    DRIVE
END
```

FIGURE IT OUT

In this part of our LOGO tutorial, we look at the facilities the language offers for working with numbers. LOGO would probably not be the first choice of language for applications that require a lot of calculation, but it does offer an impressive array of numerical primitives.

Almost all LOGO implementations support both integer and real (decimal) arithmetic, using the infix operators + - * / . These operators are called 'infix' because they are written between the numbers they work on — for example, 3+4. Some LOGOs also include 'prefix' arithmetic, in which our example would be written as SUM 3 4. One advantage of this notation is that it is consistent with the way in which other LOGO operations and commands are written.

MIT LOGO supports infix arithmetic only, but it is simple to program prefix forms if they are required. Define SUM and PRODUCT and try them:

```
TO SUM :A :B
   OUTPUT :A + :B
END

TO PRODUCT :A :B
   OUTPUT :A * :B
END
```

The 'precedence' of operations (the order in which they are carried out) follows the usual mathematical rules. Anything within brackets is done first, followed by multiplications and divisions, and finally additions and subtractions:

```
PRINT (3 + 4) * 5
PRINT 3 + 4 * 5
```

Now try the prefix forms:

```
PRINT PRODUCT 5 SUM 3 4
PRINT SUM 3 PRODUCT 4 5
```

This demonstrates another advantage of the prefix forms — there is no need for rules of precedence and the line is evaluated in the same way as any other line of LOGO commands.

The usual division operation (/) gives the result as a real number. Two other operations, QUOTIENT and REMAINDER, are often useful for working with integers.

```
QUOTIENT 47 5 is 9
REMAINDER 47 5 is 2
```

A standard method for converting a number in base 10 to binary is to keep dividing the number by two until the result is zero. The binary number is found by writing the remainders found at each

stage in reverse order. For example, to convert 12 to binary:

```
12/2 = 6; remainder = 0
6/2  = 3; remainder = 0
3/2  = 1; remainder = 1
1/2  = 0; remainder = 1
```

So, reading the remainders upwards, we find that decimal 12 is 1100 in binary.

Using QUOTIENT and REMAINDER we can implement this technique easily in LOGO. By putting the print statement *after* the recursive call we get the remainders printed in the correct (reverse) order.

```
TO BIN :X
   IF :X = 0 THEN STOP
   BIN QUOTIENT :X 2
   PRINT1 REMAINDER :X2
END
```

Two operations exist for rounding numbers — INTEGER and ROUND. INTEGER outputs the whole number part of a number, simply ignoring any figure after the decimal point, and ROUND rounds a number up or down to the nearest whole number.

The following procedures calculate the compound interest on an investment at a given rate of interest. In PRETTY.PRINT, INTEGER is used to get the pounds, and ROUND is used to round the pennies to the nearest whole number.

```
TO COMPOUND :PRINCIPAL :RATE :YEARS
   IF :YEARS = 0 THEN PRETTY.PRINT
   :PRINCIPAL STOP
   COMPOUND :PRINCIPAL * (1 + :RATE / 100)
      :RATE :YEARS — 1
END

TO PRETTY.PRINT :MONEY
   MAKE "POUNDS INTEGER :MONEY
   MAKE "PENCE ROUND (:MONEY —
      :POUNDS) * 100
   (PRINT :POUNDS "POUNDS :PENCE
      "PENCE)
END
```

TESTING TIME

We have already used =, <, and > as logical tests in a number of procedures. The logical operations ALLOF, ANYOF and NOT can be used to combine other tests. ALLOF is true if both its inputs are true, ANYOF is true if either of its inputs is true, and NOT is true if its input is false. So we get:

```
IF ANYOF :X > 0 :X = 0 THEN PRINT "POSITIVE
IF NOT :X < 0 THEN PRINT "POSITIVE
IF ALLOF :X > 0 :X < 100 THEN PRINT
   [BETWEEN 0 AND 100]
```

LISSAJOUS FIGURES

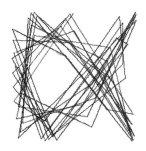

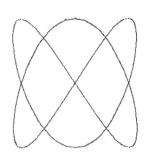

LISSAJOUS FIGURES

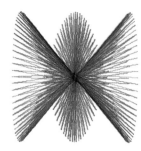

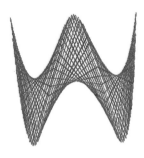

One Step Over The Line

The Drunkard's Walk theorem states that after N steps in completely random directions the probability is better than 0.5 that the drunkard's distance from the starting place will be less than SQR(N) steps. This is a statistical prediction based on a large number of steps, LOGO lets you test it for yourself:

```
TO DRUNKWALK :STEPNO
   :STEP
   CS REPEAT :STEPNO [RT
   (RANDOM 361) FD
   :STEP]
END
```

PI COMES TO MONTE CARLO

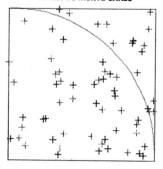

The operation NUMBER? outputs TRUE if the input is a number, otherwise FALSE is returned. We use this in the procedure PRIME?, which outputs TRUE if its input is a prime, and FALSE otherwise. It begins by checking that the input is indeed a number, and that it is greater than two. PRIME.TEST then checks to see if any integer between the square root of the number and two will divide into it exactly, leaving no remainder.

```
TO PRIME? :NO
   IF NOT NUMBER? :NO THEN PRINT [NOT A
      NUMBER DUMMY] STOP
   IF :NO < 2 THEN OUTPUT "FALSE
   OUTPUT PRIME.TEST :NO INTEGER SQRT :NO
END
```

```
TO PRIME.TEST :NO :FACT
   IF :FACT = 1 THEN OUTPUT "TRUE
   IF (REMAINDER :NO :FACT) = 0 THEN OUTPUT
      "FALSE
   OUTPUT PRIME.TEST :NO :FACT — 1
END
```

RANDOM NUMBERS

RANDOM n outputs a random integer between 0 and n−1. The procedure DRUNK makes the turtle stagger across the screen, turning a random angle at each step. The input A gives the maximum size of the turn that can be made at any time. If you run this procedure you will find that the turtle turns in vague circles, moving to the left or to the right depending on the value assigned to A.

```
TO DRUNK :A
   FORWARD 1
   RIGHT (— :A/2 + RANDOM :A)
   DRUNK :A
END
```

The so-called 'Monte Carlo method' is a technique for solving mathematical problems through the use of random numbers.

We'll demonstrate by finding an approximation to pi by using this method. Our illustration shows a quarter-circle drawn within a square. The area of the square is 100×100 square units, and the area of the quarter-circle is $(1 \div 4) \times pi \times 100 \times 100$ square units. The ratio of the areas circle ÷ square is equal to pi ÷ 4. Now drop a pin at random on the square 1,000 times and count how many times the pin falls within the quarter-circle; call this number IN. The value of IN/1000 should be approximately the same as the result of : circle ÷ square — i.e. pi ÷ 4. So if we do the experiment, multiply IN by four and divide by 1,000, then the result should be an approximation to pi. That is precisely what the following procedures do:

```
TO MC
   DRAW
   PU
   MAKE "IN 0
   MC1 1000 100 100
   (PRINT [VALUE OF PI IS] 0.004 * (:IN))
END
```

```
TO MC1 :NO :XNO :YNO
   IF :NO = 0 THEN STOP
   RANDOM.POINT :XNO :YNO
   IF INSIDE? THEN MAKE "IN :IN + 1
   MC1 :NO — 1 :XNO :YNO
END
```

The procedure MC simply sets the conditions, calls MC1 and prints the results. MC1 does most of the work, calls RANDOM.POINT to position the turtle, and then increments IN if the point is inside the circle. This continues until the procedure has been carried out the correct number of times.

```
TO RANDOM.POINT :XNO :YNO
   SETXY RANDOM :XNO RANDOM :YNO
END
```

```
TO INSIDE?
   IF (XCOR * XCOR + YCOR * YCOR) < 10000
      THEN OUTPUT "TRUE
   OUTPUT "FALSE
END
```

RANDOM.POINT sets the turtle at a random position within the square, while INSIDE? checks to see if the turtle lies within the circle. It will take some time to run this, but eventually a value for pi of 3.15999 will be obtained.

LISSAJOUS CURVES

Lissajous curves are an interesting family of curves in which the x co-ordinate of each point is determined by the sine function and the y co-ordinate by the cosine:

```
TO LJ: COEFF1 :COEFF2 :STEP
   DRAW PU HT
   POS :COEFF1 :COEFF2 0 PD
   LJ1 :COEFF1 :COEFF2 0 :STEP
END
```

```
TO POS :COEFF1 :COEFF2 :ANGLE
   MAKE "X 100 * SIN (:COEFF1 * :ANGLE)
   MAKE "Y 100 * COS(:COEFF2 * :ANGLE)
   SETXY :X :Y
END
```

```
TO LJ1 :COEFF1 :COEFF2 :ANGLE :STEP
   POS :COEFF1 :COEFF2 :ANGLE
   LJ1 :COEFF1 :COEFF2 (:ANGLE + :STEP) :STEP
END
```

Logo Exercises

1. Write a procedure to output the nth power of a number, so POWER 4 2 would output 16.
2. Write a set of procedures to convert a decimal number to hexadecimal (use a similar technique to the binary example, but this time divide by 16).
3. Write a procedure EVEN? that will output TRUE if a number is even and FALSE if it is not.
4. Use the Monte Carlo method to find the area under the curve $y=x^2$ between x=0 and x=10.

POETRY IN MOTION

In this article in our LOGO series, we turn our attention to list processing, which is central to the way the language works. We also take another look at recursion (and revisit the psychoanalyst) before using LOGO to write a little poetry.

A list is a collection of objects in order, and is identified in LOGO by using square brackets; so that [CEYLON MADRAS VINDALOO] is a list. We have encountered lists several times in this series. In fact, we can't escape from them in LOGO, because the language is based on lists. We've already seen how a definition for a square — REPEAT 4 [FD 50 RT 90] — has a list of instructions (within the square brackets) as its second input. Similarly, MAKE "INP REQUEST assigns to INP a list consisting of the input from the keyboard.

Lists can be assigned to global variables — for example, MAKE "CURRY [CEYLON MADRAS VINDALOO]. The command PRINT :CURRY prints the list without the square brackets: that is, CEYLON MADRAS VINDALOO.

A LOGO object can be a number, a word or a list; and a list is defined as simply a collection of objects. This is, of course, a recursive definition; a list can contain another list, or a list of lists, and so on. [[CHICKEN TIKKA] NAN SALAD] is a valid list, with a list as its first element ([CHICKEN TIKKA]). Recursive procedures are often needed to process lists, precisely because lists are recursive objects.

The majority of our programming in LOGO has until now been concerned with one number or one word at a time. When we want to process groups of objects at the same time, we need to organise these simple objects into a single unit. LOGO takes the list as its basic method of grouping simple objects. The list is chosen because it is extremely versatile — you can construct any complex data organisation by starting from a list.

The two fundamental list operations are FIRST and BUTFIRST. FIRST [CEYLON MADRAS VINDALOO] outputs CEYLON — that is, it gives us the first element of the list. BUTFIRST [CEYLON MADRAS VINDALOO] outputs MADRAS VINDALOO; in other words, it gives us the list without its first element.

Here's a procedure that prints the elements of the list, one below the other:

```
TO PRINTOUT :LIST
    PRINT FIRST :LIST
    PRINTOUT BUTFIRST :LIST
END
```

So PRINTOUT [CEYLON MADRAS VINDALOO] gives:

```
CEYLON
MADRAS
VINDALOO
```

The first command prints the first element of the list and then passes the task of printing the rest of the input list to another copy of PRINTOUT. When you run this procedure you'll get an error message when it runs out of data. Here's a more elegant way of finishing:

```
TO PRINTOUT :LIST
    IF EMPTY? :LIST THEN STOP
    PRINT FIRST :LIST
    PRINTOUT BUTFIRST :LIST
END
```

EMPTY? checks to see if its input is the 'empty list' — []. Some MIT versions do not have the primitive EMPTY?, but you can always define it as follows:

```
TO EMPTY? :LIST
    IF :LIST = [] THEN OUTPUT "TRUE
    OUTPUT "FALSE
END
```

Similar to FIRST and BUTFIRST are LAST and BUTLAST. LAST [CEYLON MADRAS VINDALOO] outputs VINDALOO, and BUTLAST [CEYLON MADRAS VINDALOO] outputs CEYLON MADRAS.

BABBLING

For our first exploration in list processing, we'll try to mimic some random babblings on the psychoanalyst's couch. First we'll assign all the words we know to the variable WORDS:

```
MAKE "WORDS [MOTHER FATHER SEX MURDER
JEALOUSY FIRE SEA DEATH DREAM]
```

We want to produce a constant random stream of these words, for experience has shown us that these are the words that are always successful in attracting our psychoanalyst's attention. To get a random element of the list we need to select a random number, n, between one and the length of the list (nine in this case) and then select the nth element of the list.

```
TO NTH :NO :LIST
    IF :N = 1 THEN OUTPUT FIRST :LIST
    OUTPUT NTH :NO – 1 BUTFIRST :LIST
END
```

Let's use this procedure with a few examples to see how it works. Say you type NTH 1 :WORDS. The condition in the first line is true, so the procedure outputs FIRST :WORDS, which in our example is MOTHER.

Try NTH 2 :WORDS — now the condition is false

Abbreviations

BUTFIRST	BF
BUTLAST	BL
SENTENCE	SE

so the procedure outputs NTH 1 BUTFIRST :WORDS. This ignores the first list element and takes the first word from the remainder of the list — FATHER.

So our procedure to print a random word from our limited vocabulary would be:

```
TO GETRANDOM :LIST
    OUTPUT NTH ( ( RANDOM 9 ) + 1 ) :LIST
END
```

To use this, type GETRANDOM :WORDS.

Our procedure is restricted to lists of nine items. We could improve on this if we could determine how many items there are in a given list. Here is a procedure that does this:

```
TO LENGTH :LIST
    IF EMPTY? :LIST THEN OUTPUT 0
```

Mock Turtle Sings
An extract from the Mock Turtle's song from 'Alice in Wonderland' by Lewis Carroll. The metric pattern, a little difficult to duplicate in a computer poem, is adapted from an old folk song, and is also utilised by Mary Howitt in the classic poem, 'The Spider and the Fly'

SIR JOHN TENNIEL

'Will you walk a little faster?' said a whiting to a snail,
'There's a porpoise close behind us, and he's treading
    on my tail.
See how eagerly the lobsters and the turtles all
    advance!
They are waiting on the shingle — will you come and
    join the dance?
    Will you, won't you, will you, won't you,
        will you join the dance?
    Will you, won't you, will you, won't you,
        won't you join the dance?'

'You can really have no notion how delightful it will be
When they take us up and throw us, to the lobsters, out
    to sea!'
But the snail replied 'Too far, too far! and gave a look
    askance —
Said he thanked the whiting kindly, but he would not
    join the dance.
    Would not, could not, would not, could not,
        would not join the dance.
    Would not, could not, would not, could not,
        could not join the dance.

```
    OUTPUT 1 + LENGTH BUTFIRST :LIST
END
```

To see how this works try: LENGTH [SCIENCE FICTION]. As the list contains some words the first condition fails, so the procedure outputs 1 + LENGTH [FICTION]. Now LENGTH [FICTION] outputs 1 + LENGTH []. On calling LENGTH with an input of [], the condition in line 1 is true, so the procedure outputs 0. Now LENGTH [FICTION] outputs 0 + 1 = 1 and, finally, LENGTH [SCIENCE FICTION] outputs 1 + 1 = 2. So a more general procedure for getting random words from a list of any length is:

```
TO GETRANDOM :LIST
    OUTPUT NTH ( ( RANDOM LENGTH :LIST ) + 1 )
    :LIST
END
```

In many versions of LOGO there is a primitive, ITEM, which does precisely what NTH does, and a primitive called COUNT that does the same as LENGTH. Using these we can rewrite the procedure:

```
TO GETRANDOM :LIST
    OUTPUT ITEM ( ( RANDOM COUNT :LIST ) + 1 )
    :LIST
END
```

To print a selection of 10 comments to keep your psychoanalyst listening attentively, simply type:

```
REPEAT 10 [PRINT GETRANDOM :WORDS]
```

There is a pattern to these list processing programs that was shared by many of our recursive turtle graphics procedures. The pattern is:

● If the task to be performed is extremely simple then do it and stop.
● Otherwise do a small part of the task.
● Then pass the rest of the task onto another procedure (often a copy of the original procedure).

This is a highly successful strategy, which we will encounter repeatedly in list processing programs. Compare this polygon drawing program:

```
TO POLY :N
    IF :N = 0 THEN STOP
    FD 30 RT ( 360 / :N )
    POLY :N — 1
END
```

with the version of PRINTOUT given earlier. The structure of the two procedures is identical.

RANDOM POETRY

Having failed to impress our psychoanalyst, we now turn our hand to poetry. Here, we will want to produce whole sentences rather than single words.

```
TO POEM1 :LENGTH
    IF :LENGTH = 0 THEN PRINT "STOP
    ( PRINT1 " ' GETRANDOM :WORDS )
    POEM1 :LENGTH – 1
END
```

PRINT1 " ' is included to print a space between words. To use this procedure, type POEM1 6 for a six-word sentence.

It would be useful to be able to extend our original list of words without having to go to the trouble of writing it all out again. One way of extending a list is to use the operation SENTENCE, which takes two inputs and makes a list from them. So SENTENCE "JAM [HONEY JAR] outputs [JAM HONEY JAR].

```
TO ADDWORDS1 :LIST
    MAKE "WORDS SENTENCE :LIST :WORDS
END
```

So we can now extend WORDS with ADDWORDS [ANXIETY REPRESSION [FEAR OF FLYING]]. The problem with this is if the variable WORDS has not previously been assigned a value. The primitive THING? is used to overcome this by testing if a variable has been assigned a value; it outputs true if its input has a value associated with it. We can now improve our list of extra words with ADDWORDS1:

```
TO ADDWORDS1 :LIST
    IF NOT THING? "WORDS THEN MAKE "WORDS []
    MAKE "WORDS SENTENCE :LIST :WORDS
END
```

Using a different list of words, we obtained the following piece of 'poetry' using this procedure:

APPARITION LOUDLY SPOKE SPLENDID PARANOID PLANET TERRIFIED THE WITH GREEN APPARITION FLOATING PARANOID ROBOT MAN FLEW SPOKE FLOATING LOUDLY

One of the more obvious failings of our computerised poetry is its total disregard for English grammar. The poems might make more sense if we could constrain them to some simple syntactical patterns — such as: noun, verb, noun. One way to do this is to have a number of lists, one for each part of speech. We could then choose one word from each list according to our desired sentence structure.

We leave this problem for you to explore and investigate. In the next instalment of the course, we will show you some ways of how to improve the turtle's poetry-writing abilities.

Logo Flavours

Some versions of MIT LOGO do not have EMPTY?, ITEM and COUNT. In all LCSI versions, use:

EMPTYP for EMPTY?
LISTP for LIST?
TYPE for PRINT1

There is a primitive, EQUALP, which tests whether its two inputs are the same. Use this for comparing lists and words in place of the equals sign (=). (The equals sign works for lists on some LCSI versions, but not on others.)

Remember the different IF syntax:
IF EMPTYP :LIST [OUTPUT 0]
On Atari LOGO use SE for SENTENCE, and note that ITEM is not implemented

Exercise Answers

Answers to the exercises on page 234:

1. Calculation powers:

```
TO POWER :A :N
    IF NOT ((INTEGER :N) = :N) THEN PRINT
    [WHOLE NUMBER INDICES ONLY] STOP
    IF :N = 0 THEN OUTPUT 1
    OUTPUT :A * POWER :A :N – 1
END
```

2. Converting to hexadecimal:

```
TO HEX.PRINT :NO
    IF :NO < 10 THEN OUTPUT :NO
    IF :NO = 10 THEN OUTPUT "A
    IF :NO = 11 THEN OUTPUT "B
    IF :NO = 12 THEN OUTPUT "C
    IF :NO = 13 THEN OUTPUT "D
    IF :NO = 14 THEN OUTPUT "E
    IF :NO = 15 THEN OUTPUT "F
END

TO HEX :NO
    IF :NO = 0 THEN STOP
    HEX QUOTIENT :NO 16
    PRINT1 HEX.PRINT REMAINDER :NO 16
END
```

3. Testing if a number is even:

```
TO EVEN? :NO
    IF ((REMAINDER :NO 2) = 0) THEN OUTPUT
    "TRUE OUTPUT "FALSE
END
```

4. Finding an area using the Monte Carlo method:

```
TO MC
    DRAW PU MAKE "IN 0
    MC1 1000 10 100
    (PRINT [AREA IS] (:N))
END

TO MC1 :NO :XNO :YNO
    IF :NO = 0 THEN STOP
    RANDOM.POINT :XNO :YNO
    IF INSIDE? THEN MAKE "IN :IN + 1
    MC1 :NO – 1 :XNO :YNO
END

TO RANDOM.POINT :XNO :YNO
    SETXY RANDOM :XNO RANDOM :YNO
END

TO INSIDE?
    IF YCOR < XCOR * XCOR THEN OUTPUT "TRUE
    OUTPUT "FALSE
END
```

WHO DUNNIT?

As part of our tutorial we examine LOGO's list processing facilities with a look at how to set up a simple database. We use the example of a murder investigation, in which a list of suspects is created and then analysed to ascertain who the murderer was.

A terrible murder has been committed in a small community in the Ozark Mountains. Zachariah has been viciously attacked with an axe and killed. We know that Matthew and Joshua both own axes, James and Ebenezer own guns, and cousin Jane has a knife. Matthew and James both had blood on their hands when they were questioned by the local sheriff.

Our LOGO database of information about this crime will consist of a list of *facts* — each of which consists of a *relation,* together with one or more nouns. When represented in LOGO, one fact is [OWNS MATTHEW AXE] or, in English, 'Matthew owns an axe'. To represent the fact that James had blood on his hands, we use [BLOODY JAMES].

We begin our investigation with an empty database:

```
TO SET UP
   MAKE "DATABASE []
END
```

We then add facts to our database as we discover them (providing they are not already in the database). For example, we would input ADD [OWNS JANE KNIFE] using the following ADD procedure:

```
TO ADD :FACT
   IF NOT MEMBER? :FACT :DATABASE THEN
      MAKE "DATABASE FPUT :FACT :DATABASE
END
```

The database will eventually fill up:

```
[ [BLOODY MATTHEW][BLOODY JAMES][KILLED
   ZACHARIAH AXE] [OWNS MATTHEW AXE]
   [OWNS JOSHUA AXE] [OWNS JAMES GUN]
   [OWNS EBENEZER GUN] [OWNS JANE KNIFE] ]
```

To print out the database use SHOW. This can be followed by either "ALL, in which case the whole database will be printed, or by the name of a relation, in which case only the facts for that relation are printed. So, SHOW "OWNS will show us who owns what.

```
TO SHOW :S
   IF :S = "ALL THEN LIST.ALL:DATABASE
   LIST.REL :S:DATABASE
END
TO LIST.ALL :LIST
```

```
   IF EMPTY? :LIST THEN STOP
   PRINT FIRST :LIST
   LIST.ALL BUTFIRST :LIST
END
TO LIST. REL :S: LIST
   IF EMPTY? :LIST THEN STOP
   IF :S = FIRST FIRST :LIST THEN PRINT FIRST
      :LIST
   LIST.REL:S BUTFIRST:LIST
END
```

Now we must devise ways of querying the database. The simplest kind of query we might make of our database is to check whether a fact is known to be true. This we do with a procedure called DOES, which checks whether a fact is in the database. For example, DOES [OWNS JANE KNIFE] should give the answer YES.

```
TO DOES :FACT
   IF MEMBER? :FACT :DATABASE PRINT "YES
      ELSE PRINT "NO
END
```

It would be much more useful for our investigation into this terrible murder if we could ask questions such as 'Who owns an axe?'. The way we will deal with this is to use 'variables'. Any word whose first character is ? will be assumed to be a variable. We can then paraphrase the question as:

```
WHICH [OWNS ?SOMEONE AXE]
```

The reply to this will be a list of all possible values of the variable ?SOMEONE that are consistent with the information in the database.

```
[?SOMEONE MATTHEW]
[?SOMEONE JOSHUA]
NO (MORE) ANSWERS
```

We can have multiple variables. For example:

```
WHICH [KILLED ?MAN ?IMPLEMENT]
```

will give the answer:

```
[?MAN ZACHARIAH] [?IMPLEMENT AXE]
NO (MORE) ANSWERS
```

Let's consider the procedures that enable this analysis of the database, individually. WHICH passes the job over to FIND, indicating DATABASE as the source of facts.

```
TO WHICH :QUERY
   FIND: QUERY :DATABASE
   PRINT [NO (MORE) ANSWERS]
END
```

FIND sets up two global variables, VARS and ANS: VARS is used to hold each possible set of values of the variables in the question, and these are collected together in the list ANS.

```
TO FIND :QUERIES :DATA
   MAKE "VARS []
   MAKE "ANS []
   COMPARE :QUERY :DATA
   PRINTL :ANS
END
```

COMPARE looks at each fact in the database in turn. If there is a match then the new set of values in VARS are added to ANS before setting VARS back to the empty list. COMPARE then continues working through the DATABASE to see if there are any other possible matches.

```
TO COMPARE :QUERY :DATA
   IF EMPTY? :DATA THEN STOP
   IF MATCH? :QUERY FIRST :DATA THEN MAKE
      "ANS FPUT :VARS :ANS
   MAKE :VARS[]
   COMPARE :QUERY BUTFIRST :DATA
END
```

To see what MATCH? does, consider the case where the inputs are [OWNS ?SOMEONE AXE] and [OWNS JOSHUA AXE] in response to which MATCH? outputs TRUE and sets VARS to [?SOMEONE JOSHUA]. If the inputs are [OWNS ?SOMEONE AXE] and [KILLED ZACHARIAH AXE], then MATCH? outputs FALSE.

The real difficulties arise, however, if there is more than one variable involved. VALUE? is used to check if the variable has already been assigned a value for that fact in the database.

We have used here an alternative notation for conditionals in LOGO. TEST evaluates a condition. If the result is true then the actions following IFTRUE will be performed, otherwise the actions following IFFALSE will be carried out.

```
TO MATCH? :QUERY :FACT
   IF ALLOF EMPTY? :QUERY EMPTY? :FACT THEN
      OUTPUT "TRUE
   TEST FIRST FIRST :QUERY ="?
   IF TRUE IF NOT VALUE? FIRST :QUERY FIRST
      :FACT :VARS THEN OUTPUT "FALSE
   IFFALSE IF NOT (FIRST :QUERY = FIRST :FACT)
      THEN OUTPUT "FALSE
   OUTPUT MATCH? BUTFIRST :QUERY BUTFIRST
      :FACT
END
```

To see how VALUE? works, let's first consider the case where the inputs are ?IMPLEMENT, AXE, and [?MAN ZACHARIAH]. VALUE? tries to ascertain whether the variable ?IMPLEMENT could have the value AXE. There are three possibilities: ?IMPLEMENT already has a value, which is not AXE, and VALUE? outputs FALSE; ?IMPLEMENT already has the value AXE, and VALUE outputs TRUE; or ?IMPLEMENT does not have a value, so it is given the value AXE, and this information is added to VARS and TRUE is output.

```
TO VALUE? :NAME :VALUE :VLIST
   IF EMPTY? :VLIST THEN MAKE "VARS LPUT LIST
      :NAME :VALUE :VARS OUTPUT "TRUE
   TEST :NAME = FIRST FIRST :VLIST
   IFTRUE IF :VALUE = LAST FIRST :VLIST THEN
      OUTPUT "TRUE ELSE OUTPUT "FALSE
   OUTPUT VALUE? :NAME :VALUE BUTFIRST
      :VLIST
END
```

PRINTL simply arranges for the components of ANS to be printed out below each other.

```
TO PRINT :LIST
   IF EMPTY? :LIST STOP
   PRINT FIRST :LIST
   PRINTL BUTFIRST :LIST
END
```

MORE COMPLEX ENQUIRIES

Our investigation will not go far, however, unless we can ask more complex questions, such as 'What implement killed Zachariah, and who owns such an implement?' In LOGO, this reads:

```
WHICH [ [KILLED ZACHARIAH ?IMPLEMENT]
   [OWNS ?SUSPECT ?IMPLEMENT] ]
```

WHICH now takes a list of queries as input and the values found will be those that make all of the queries true. If you then wish to ask a single query with this new form of WHICH the syntax we use is:

```
WHICH [ [OWNS ?ANY KNIFE] ]
```

We need make only minor alterations to these procedures:

```
TO WHICH :QUERIES
   FIND :QUERIES :DATABASE
   PRINT [NO (MORE) ANSWERS]
END
```

```
TO FIND :QUERIES :DATA
   MAKE "VARS []
   MAKE "ANS []
   COMPARE :QUERIES :DATA
   PRINTL :ANS
END
```

COMPARE now has a rather difficult job to do. Let's take [[KILLED ZACHARIAH ?IMPLEMENT][OWNS ?SUSPECT ?IMPLEMENT]] as an example input. COMPARE goes through the database, one fact at a time, to find a match for the first query, and ends up matching ?IMPLEMENT with AXE. The routine then considers the second query ([OWNS ?SUSPECT ?IMPLEMENT]), starting again from the beginning of the database. A match is found for the second condition, with the value of ?IMPLEMENT as AXE and ?SUSPECT as MATTHEW. There are no more queries, so this is a possible solution.

But we have not finished yet; there may be other values that satisfy the second query, while keeping ?IMPLEMENT as AXE. So COMPARE now proceeds through the database from the point it left off, and indeed finds a second solution with ?SUSPECT as JOSHUA. Of course, the procedure does not stop there, but continues searching the DATABASE. This time it reaches the end without finding any new matching values.

It is possible, however, that there is another solution to the first query — other than ?IMPLEMENT as AXE — so we must go back to the point where we found that match in the database and carry on from there. This process is called *backtracking*. In this case, there are in fact no other solutions.

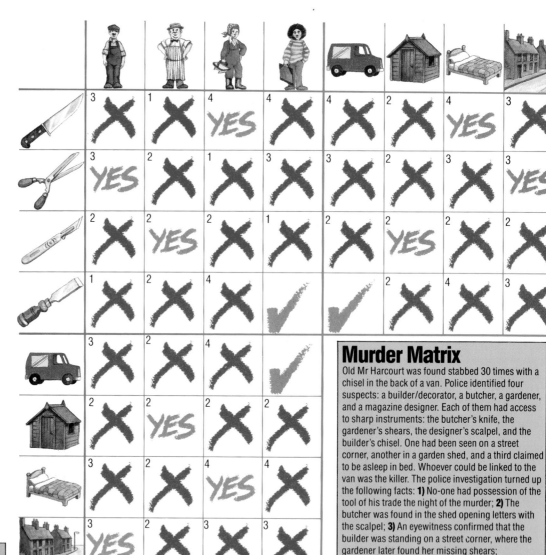

DAVID HIGHAM

Murder Matrix

Old Mr Harcourt was found stabbed 30 times with a chisel in the back of a van. Police identified four suspects: a builder/decorator, a butcher, a gardener, and a magazine designer. Each of them had access to sharp instruments: the butcher's knife, the gardener's shears, the designer's scalpel, and the builder's chisel. One had been seen on a street corner, another in a garden shed, and a third claimed to be asleep in bed. Whoever could be linked to the van was the killer. The police investigation turned up the following facts: **1)** No-one had possession of the tool of his trade the night of the murder; **2)** The butcher was found in the shed opening letters with the scalpel; **3)** An eyewitness confirmed that the builder was standing on a street corner, where the gardener later found her missing shears; **4)** The gardener was in bed using a butcher's knife to make herself a roast beef sandwich.

Logo Flavours

Some versions of MIT LOGO do not have EMPTY? or MEMBER?. Definitions for these have been given previously (see page 237).

In all LCSI versions use EMPTYP for EMPTY? and MEMBERP for MEMBER?. There is a primitive, EQUALP, which tests whether its two inputs are the same. Use it for comparing lists and words instead of an equals sign (which works for lists on some LCSI versions, but not on others).
The IF syntax in LCSI LOGO is demonstrated by:

IF EMPTYP :CONTENTS
[PRINT [NOTHING
SPECIAL]] [PRINT
:CONTENTS]

The first list after the condition is performed if the condition is true, and the second if it is false.
LCSI LOGO also supports the TEST, IFTRUE, IFFALSE syntax for conditionals

In order not to lose track of where it is up to in its assignment of variables, COMPARE puts the present values on a *stack* before MATCH? is used (since MATCH? may alter these assignments), and then recovers these values afterwards. Here is the full procedure:

```
TO COMPARE :QUERIES :DATA
    IF EMPTY? :QUERIES THEN MAKE "ANS FPUT
       :VARS :ANS STOP
    IF EMPTY? :DATA THEN STOP
    PUSH :VARS
    TEST MATCH? FIRST :QUERIES FIRST :DATA
    IF TRUE COMPARE BUTFIRST :QUERIES
       :DATABASE
    PULL "VARS
    COMPARE :QUERIES BUTFIRST :DATA
END
```

In COMPARE we use a stack to keep track of the value of VARS, instead of using a temporary variable, because COMPARE could call itself between the time we want to save the values and the time we want to restore them. Therefore, any such temporary variable could be overwritten by the next call and the original values lost. The stack prevents this from happening.

PUSH puts a value on 'top' of the stack, first creating the variable STACK if it does not already exist.

```
TO PUSH :DATA
    IF NOT THING? :STACK THEN MAKE "STACK []
    MAKE "STACK FPUT :DATA :STACK
END
```

PULL takes an item from the stack, and assigns it as the value of a variable.

```
TO PULL :NAME
    MAKE :NAME FIRST :STACK
    MAKE "STACK BUTFIRST :STACK
END
```

What we have then are the rudiments of a 'logic programming' language. That is a language in which we simply add facts and rules to a database and then query that database by means of logical descriptions of the data we require. The best example to date of a logic programming language is PROLOG — but that's another story!

processing programs available on any home micro. Instead of having the help screen, you are provided with an overlay that fits over the function keys, since almost all of the word processing commands are accessed via these keys, either singly or in conjunction with the Shift or Control keys.

Among the additional features included in View is the facility allowing you to define your own 'macros'. These are short programs (created using View commands and text), which can be used to provide you with additional commands by way of a user-defined two-letter code.

The program also includes commands that perform such functions as word counting and formatting, continuous processing (which allows you to edit a document from disk or tape and then pass it directly to another file), and a full set of Find/Replace commands. These not only perform the usual functions but also permit 'wildcard' characters.

Pocket Money

It is a measure of the seriousness with which the Amstrad range of computers is now being regarded that a number of software companies which had previously only manufactured programs for business applications are now 'customising' their CP/M programs to run on the Amstrad machines. One of the greatest coups for Alan Sugar's company is that MicroPro has developed a version of WordStar, the leading professional word processing package, to run on the CPC 464 and 664 computers.

Although Pocket WordStar runs with less memory than the original package, this does not mean that it has lost many of the features of its parent program. On the contrary, almost all the facilities provided on the full WordStar package are also implemented on Pocket WordStar. The only features that are missing from the customised Amstrad version are those which require more memory than the computer has available — for example, the facility that allows the user to Print a File and Edit at the same time.

MicroPro has managed to achieve this by retaining a number of the submenus on disk, which are loaded as required. This, of course, means that Pocket WordStar is somewhat slower than its predecessor, but this is a small price to pay for an excellent word processing package on such a low-cost machine

EASY SCRIPT

Wordwrap

Easy Script only supports wordwrap when the document is being sent to the printer.

Block Movement

The program allows transfer, copy and separate filing.

On-Screen Help
Not available.

80-Column Screen
Easy Script has a 40-column screen.

Word Count
Easy Script has no word count facility.

Find/Replace

Up to 32 characters can be searched for, although the facility is extremely slow.

WYSIWYG

Although Easy Script allows the user to examine the page layout, the low-screen resolution limits its usefulness.

Mailshot Facility

The package incorporates a simple Mail Merge facility but does not permit the printing of address labels.

Spelling Checker

A sister package, known as Easy Spell, is available from the manufacurers.

Founts Available

Easy Script supports enlarged, condensed, reversed and bold print.

File Linking

The program supports commands to link files, either from cassette or disk, for editing or printing.

TASWORD II

Wordwrap

Wordwrap is fully supported, with automatic justification.

Block Movement

Tasword II permits transfer, copy and deletion functions, but not separate filing.

On-Screen Help

On-screen help is provided by a window at the top of the screen, which can be scrolled to display all of the available commands.

80-Column Screen

The program displays a full 80-column screen with a maximum right margin value of 128.

Word Count

Constantly available.

Find/Replace

TasWord II allows single word search only.

WYSIWYG

A number of print format options are recognised as control characters only by the printer, and these cannot be displayed on the screen.

Mailshot Facility
Not available.

Spelling Checker
Not available.

Founts Available

Tasword II implements several different founts, with additional styles provided on Tasprint.

File Linking

The program only allows a file to be added to the bottom of another.

VIEW

Wordwrap

Full wordwrap is supported, although there is no command to turn off this function.

Block Movement

The block operations permitted by View include deletion, move and copy.

On-Screen Help

View offers no on-screen help, but does provide an overlay for the function keys.

80-Column Screen

View supports a 76-column screen. However, this drastically reduces the amount of memory left for text.

Word Count

Although View has a word count facility (which actually counts spaces) this is not a constant display.

Find/Replace

View can only find and replace single words, although it also supports wildcard characters.

WYSIWYG

The program allows full display of the document as it will appear on the page, except for the 'highlight' facilities (underlining the bold print).

Mailshot Facility
Not available.

Spelling Checker
Not available, but AcornSoft have promised that one will be provided in the future.

Founts Available

Bold is the only additional character emphasis available.

File Linking

The Macro commands allow a wide range of file linking facilities.

WORDS WITH A MOUSE

Every Picture Tells A Story
Like all packages written for the Macintosh, MacWrite makes extensive use of icons to execute commands positioned around the periphery of the screen. Many of these — such as the scroll bar — are commonly used on a number of Macintosh programs, whereas others are unique to MacWrite

It's Written All Over It
Apple has met a great deal of resistance to the idea of the Macintosh as a serious business machine. Part of the problem has undoubtedly been the lack of a comprehensive word processing package, which is a prerequisite for business use. However, a number of word processing programs have appeared, although they are only a handful compared with the hundreds that are available for the IBM PC

The Apple Macintosh supports a wide variety of graphics capabilities under its WIMP environment, but it also accommodates a very efficient word processing system. MacWrite's methods of manipulating text are handled entirely by mouse control, doing away with the usual control characters.

In contrast to the packages we've looked at in the previous instalments of this series, which are based on menus and control characters, MacWrite, the word processing package bundled with the Macintosh, relies heavily on the mouse-based pull-down windows and icons now expected from a Macintosh program.

On booting MacWrite, you are presented with the opening screen, consisting of a large window on which the document will be displayed. Above that is a series of icons and a ruler, and at the top is a menu bar consisting of six titles. Below this is the title bar where the name of the current document is shown.

Unlike most other packages, on which the cursor is moved with the aid of control keys, MacWrite manipulates it with the mouse controller. On other word processors, the cursor is used to set a position in the text that indicates where a particular option is to be performed. It can be positioned, for example, to insert text or create a block. The cursor is used identically in MacWrite, but it is also used to move the icons,

which alter the Tab and margin controls, as well as pull down and select items on the menus.

Pulling down a menu displays a number of different options, but not all of them are immediately usable. Those available are shown in black print while the others are shaded grey. The menu will often consist of a number of preset options, with the currently selected one having a tick next to it. Selecting another preset option will move the tick to that selection, indicating that this is the current default option.

The File menu contains the DOS commands that allow you to open and close files, as well as save them under the current, or a different, filename Also included in this menu is the Print command.

The second of the menus listed is Edit, which provides a number of commands for manipulating the text. Perhaps the most important of these for the beginner is the Undo command, which will erase all of the actions performed since the mouse button was last pressed. This might seem drastic, but many errors will occur due to incorrect selections with the mouse. Thus very little valuable work will actually be lost using Undo. Also included in this menu are the block movement commands.

BLOCK COMMANDS

As with WordStar, blocks are created by delimiting the required text. After placing the cursor at either the beginning or end of the block and pressing the mouse, the cursor will change to

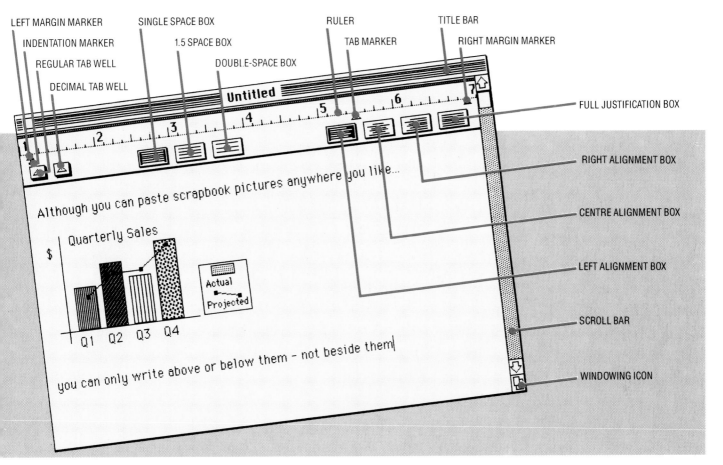

LEFT MARGIN MARKER
INDENTATION MARKER
REGULAR TAB WELL
DECIMAL TAB WELL

SINGLE SPACE BOX
1.5 SPACE BOX
DOUBLE-SPACE BOX

RULER
TAB MARKER

TITLE BAR
RIGHT MARGIN MARKER

FULL JUSTIFICATION BOX
RIGHT ALIGNMENT BOX
CENTRE ALIGNMENT BOX
LEFT ALIGNMENT BOX
SCROLL BAR
WINDOWING ICON

Untitled

Although you can paste scrapbook pictures anywhere you like...

Quarterly Sales
$
Actual
Projected
Q1 Q2 Q3 Q4

you can only write above or below them - not beside them

an icon known as the 'insertion point', which will allow you to insert text from that position. If you move the cursor up or down from this point, however, the corresponding text will be shown in inverse video, which in effect marks the block. A second press on the mouse will then set the other end of the block.

Once marked, a number of different operations can be performed on the block. By returning to the Edit menu, for example, you can select the Cut option, which places the block in a 'clipboard'. This is a buffer that stores the block before operations are performed on it. To view the contents of this buffer, you select the Show Clipboard option in the Edit menu. By setting another insert point and returning to the Edit menu, you can select the Copy or Paste options, which allow you either to copy or transfer blocks into that position. Note that any blocks involved in these operations will automatically be reformed.

The Search menu contains the Find/Replace commands and is identical to that implemented on most other word processing software.

A RANGE OF FOUNTS

Many word processors allow different founts to be used within a particular document, but most of these are limited to those used for emphasising, such as italics and bold face. Furthermore, because most packages confine themselves to using the character matrices already held within the computer's operating system ROM, it's usually impossible to see exactly how the document will

appear until it has been printed.

MacWrite, however, contains many different founts, with more being added as each new version of the software appears. Also, because the Macintosh text screen is bit-mapped, rather than having the usual character cell arrangement, these founts can actually be displayed on screen. Despite this facility, however, the system is not perfect. Many of the founts, such as London (a Gothic style) are almost illegible on screen.

This bit-mapping facility is used to somewhat better effect within the Style menu, a series of options providing the more usual forms of emphasis and effect, such as underline and bold face print. These can be printed on screen in order to gauge their effect before sending the document to the printer.

Most of MacWrite's page layout functions are held under the Format menu, although the actual page size formats are held in the File menu. Headers and footers (standard titles that will appear on the top and bottom of each printed page) can be set, as well as the page number, time and date. The last three are displayed as icons that can be 'dragged' from their own menu bar and placed anywhere in the header or footer area.

Underneath the ruler at the top of the screen is a series of small arrow icons that can be dragged along to set the margins, paragraph indentations and Tab settings. The document will be reset automatically when any parameters are changed. Two boxes below and to the right of the ruler are 'Tab wells', from which you can obtain further

MACWRITE

Wordwrap

★★★★★

Wordwrap and automatic justification are fully implemented in MacWrite.

Block Movement

★★★★★

Text and graphics can be moved and positioned anywhere within a MacWrite document.

On-Screen Help

Not implemented.

80-Column Screen

★★★

MacWrite supports only a 60-column screen in default mode, although 9 point text (the smallest print size) will allow 80 columns.

Word Count

No word count facility is provided in MacWrite.

Find/Replace

★★★

MacWrite enables up to 44 characters to be found and altered in the current window.

WYSIWYG

★★★★★

The ability to show various founts and diagrams on-screen is one of the major features of MacWrite.

Mailshot Facility

Not implemented.

Spelling Checker

Not implemented, although utilities from third party manufacturers are available.

Founts Available

★★★★★

MacWrite implements a wide variety of founts, although the actual number varies between different versions.

File Linking

★

Although some features — such as Cut and Paste — can be transported between documents, there is no file linking facility as such.

---

icons and set them on the ruler. To the right of these are a number of page icons, each having lines to indicate their functions. The first three correspond to single, one-and-a-half and double line spacing, while the remaining four at the far end of the bar indicate justification.

TEXT AND GRAPHICS

The Apple Macintosh allows text and graphics to be combined on the page and displayed on screen. MacWrite supports this facility, although pictures and images have to be drawn with MacPaint and MacDraw, the art packages bundled with the Macintosh. Pictures can be accessed by means of the Scrapbook facility, which is part of the Macintosh's built-in desktop. The Scrapbook is an area of memory set aside to store and transfer both text and graphics anywhere within a document. Furthermore, because of the machine's flexibility, the pictures can be adjusted to any size required.

Although MacWrite is an extremely easy package to learn and use, it nevertheless has its drawbacks. To begin with, the program leaves little memory space available for text on the standard Macintosh. This might be difficult to believe considering the machine has 128 Kbytes, but the operating system and bit-mapped screen use up a lot of space. Also, the fact that MacWrite's text resides entirely in the computer's memory (as opposed to some other advanced word processors that continually save the text to disk) means that only about five pages or so can be written into the machine before it runs out of memory.

For all of that, though, MacWrite is an unusual package based around an unusual operating system. The way in which the WIMP format has been adapted for an application that has previously relied entirely on keyboard entry is both intriguing and ingenious.

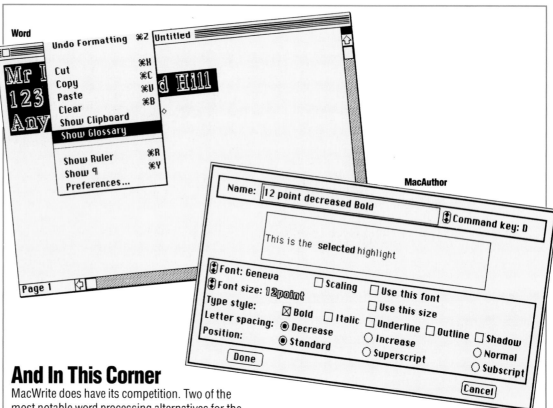

And In This Corner

MacWrite does have its competition. Two of the most notable word processing alternatives for the Macintosh are Word from Microsoft and MacAuthor from Icon Technology. Both address the central problem with MacWrite — it is unable to handle more than a few pages of text. At first glance, both packages appear similar to MacWrite, with icon-driven commands and a screen surrounded by the scroll and title bars. However, they contain additional features that make the Macintosh a much more serious proposition for attempting professional word processing.

Word contains a number of features intended to allow greater flexibility and power, enabling up to four documents to be manipulated on screen at once. It also offers an improved type of Glossary, rather than relying in the Scrapbook facility, which has its limitations.

While Word is intended as a business word processing system for the Macintosh, MacAuthor, as the name suggests, is aimed at writers. It has been developed to enable the greatest possible flexibility in the use of characters. The user can create new characters, for example, by combining those within the existing character set and altering the 'style' of the text at will. Because of this greater flexibility, MacAuthor is somewhat harder to get to grips with than Word or MacWrite. Despite this, many professional writers may find the extra effort worthwhile

6 LANGUAGES

Even if we rarely need to go beyond BASIC, a knowledge of
the qualities and applications of other computer languages
can be very worthwhile. PASCAL and LOGO are both
powerful, expressive and influential languages and working
with them will improve your overall programming
technique and help you to grasp more advanced concepts.

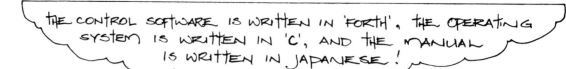

LANGUAGE ASSESSMENT

For many of us, making use of the BASIC built into our micros is sufficient for most of our programming requirements, but certain applications require more appropriate languages. The choice may seem daunting, but a short assessment of your needs and the languages' capabilities will make the task much easier.

Until recently, the owners of small microcomputers had only BASIC or assembly language available. Now, most of the common languages are available on even the smallest machines, and you only have to go up as far as an IBM PC-compatible or any other MS-DOS machine to have virtually a complete range. Since compilers and interpreters can be quite expensive, and very few people will therefore want to have more than three or four (if that), the problem of choice remains despite increased availability.

Efficiency, in terms of memory used and execution times, can become an important factor, particularly with programs that are interacting with the external environment. In BASIC, for example, some programs would take so long to write and debug that it would be quicker to learn a more appropriate language and write it in that. A program to interrogate and update a file of stock

The Good, The Bad And The Usage

Language: BASIC
Good points: Easy to learn and use, widely available. Cheap. Good provision of arithmetic functions. Good string handling
Bad points: Most versions do not have a good module facility or control structures. Non-standardised. Execution is often inefficient and slow. Poor file handling. Restricted range of data types and structures. Easy to write bad, unclear code
Use: Short, straightforward one-off programs involving arithmetic or string handling

Language: LOGO
Good points: Sound mathematical basis, easy to learn at a basic level. Turtle graphics. Good list-processing facilities, good provision for modules, data types and structures. Widely and cheaply available
Bad points: Programming beyond the initial stage can get very complicated and cryptic. Many incompatible versions. Often inefficient in execution
Use: Graphics, list-processing, learning about mathematics and advanced programming concepts

Language: PASCAL
Good points: Well-structured. Good range of data types. Fairly standard. Widely available. Easy to produce high-quality code
Bad points: Input/output not clearly defined, file handling in particular is bad
Use: Learning good programming techniques. General small-scale semi-mathematical programming

items on-line, for instance, would be a simple task in COBOL using indexed files. Written in BASIC, it would have to use sequential files or a hashing algorithm and direct access files that would make it far more complicated than necessary.

Design features that make a language easy to learn and use also tend to create problems when program size increases, where one of the major requirements is the facility to decompose the program into reasonably self-contained modules that can be programmed independently.

Some languages, like COBOL and FORTRAN, are rigidly defined by international committees, making any change to reflect new hardware and types of processing a slow procedure. However, a program written on one machine should only need recompiling, or at most a few minor changes, to run on a different machine.

Languages like PASCAL and C have a *de facto* standard defined by the inventor(s). Most versions of these languages are fairly consistent with the standard but, particularly in languages like PASCAL where input/output is not clearly defined, each implementor is free to make alterations and additions, although programs using these features will not be very portable. Finally, we have languages like BASIC, where there is no standard.

Yet another factor is the type of translator program used. Interpreters tend to be easy to use and better for program development, but slower and less efficient at running the programs. Compilers are more complicated to use but produce a more efficient final product. This is now being reduced, though, by the introduction of incremental compilers and animated debuggers.

Some languages have spawned hardware developments to enable them to run more efficiently. For example, a lot of work has been put into producing a processor that runs FORTH directly; similarly, there exists a processor that runs PASCAL P-code. It may be possible in the near future to produce a hardware-based compiler, which will make the process of using a compiled language much easier.

The major factor remains, however, the type of application the language is being used for. Let's look now at a few languages and list their strong and weak points. Then we can look at a few typical applications and consider what language might be most suitable.

Language: FORTH
Good points: Efficient execution, extendable by the user. Good structures
Bad points: Too low a level for much serious work. Difficult to understand. Many different versions
Use: Low-level work in preference to assembler, particularly controlling hardware

Language: FORTRAN
Good points: Highly standardised. Large libraries of software available. Exceptional range of mathematical and scientific functions
Bad points: Old-fashioned. Poor structures. Easy to write cryptic code. Input/output designed around punched-cards. Strict program layout
Use: General scientific, engineering and mathematical programming

Language: COBOL
Good points: Highly standardised, available on a very large range of machines. Fairly easy to read. Excellent file-handling
Bad points: Verbose, difficult to learn. Compilers are large and expensive. Badly structured with a poor range of data types
Use: Commercial data processing

Language: C
Good points: Good range of data types and structures. Good modular structure. Provides access to hardware. Produces fast, efficient code
Bad points: Easy to produce cryptic code. Level too low for much serious work. Not properly standardised, relying too much on libraries
Use: Systems software as a replacement for assembler. Anywhere where maximum efficiency is required

Language: LISP
Good points: Good list processing, mathematically sound. A lot of software and support available. Widely used on larger machines
Bad points: Difficult to learn, understand and use
Use: Artificial intelligence and general list-processing

Language: PROLOG
Good points: Sound mathematical basis. Easy and fun to use. Supposedly closer to human reasoning
Bad points: Not a 'pure' relational language — it has some procedural aspects and needs some awkward features, such as the cut, to run efficiently
Use: Artificial intelligence, database applications

Language: Assembler
Good points: Complete control of all aspects of the machine. Potentially, at least, the most efficient
Bad points: Completely non-standard. Difficult to learn and use
Use: Maximum efficiency, but only if all else fails

Applied Linguistics

The table shows a list of applications, followed by the languages most suited, in order of preference:

Application	Languages
Statistical analysis	FORTRAN, BASIC, PASCAL,
Stock control	COBOL, PASCAL, BASIC
Controlling robot arm	FORTH, C, Assembler
Adventure game	PROLOG, C, BASIC
Expert system	LISP, PROLOG, LOGO
Education	LOGO, PROLOG, PASCAL

ADVANCE TO LOGO

We begin a comprehensive look at LOGO, a programming language designed primarily with education in mind. We look at the history of its development, the basic structural philosophy behind the language and the types of users it may appeal to.

Having examined BASIC and machine code programming in detail, we begin our course on other popular computer languages with a series of articles about LOGO. You may wonder why we have chosen this language as a subject for an extended learning programme. After all, there are many other languages that perform certain functions extremely well, and home computers are rarely supplied with LOGO. Nevertheless, LOGO does offer some very attractive features to the home computer user.

First of all, LOGO is one the best introductory languages available on any computer today. Of course, if you have been programming in BASIC, you may feel little need to know about an introductory language. Yet, even for the experienced BASIC programmer, LOGO can serve as an excellent introduction to 'structured' programming and to the use of procedures instead of statements. Secondly, LOGO is available on cartridge or cassette for most home computers. In fact, one of the best versions of LOGO available is written for the Spectrum and distributed by Sinclair. Finally, LOGO is a very powerful learning system. Though not an easy language to master by any means, LOGO is one of the few programming languages that is easy to start working with.

Meet LOGO

LOGO has two fundamental characteristics that make it such a powerful educational language. The first is that it is interactive: when you type in a command, you immediately see the results on the screen. This means it is easy to make progress (particularly for children and beginners) because you can check yourself at every step.

The second vital feature is that LOGO is extendable: complete operations are handled by lists of elemental LOGO instructions. These lists are called procedures. Once a procedure has been defined as a set of particular instructions, the name of that procedure takes on the status of a new LOGO command. From then on, the entire procedure can be executed simply by typing in its name. In this way, you can actually create your own commands in addition to those 'primitives' that are an inherent part of the language.

In programming with LOGO, most people tend to be more exploratory than with other languages. Sometimes they will take a fairly strict approach and define a specific outline from the very beginning. Sometimes they will start with a core problem and write a procedure to solve it, and then build a program around that procedure. It is possible to take a flexible approach to LOGO programming because there are usually several ways to arrive at a particular result.

LOGO's origins lie in the artificial intelligence language LISP, which was invented in the early 1960s to make it easier for computers to deal with complex data structures. Its name derives from the fact that it is a 'list processing' language, which means that its basic data structure is a list, rather than a character string or numeric array, as in BASIC. LISP's essential functions manipulate the data within a list. List elements can be simple symbols or whole lists. The advantage of this approach is that non-numeric data (such as a sentence) is more easily processed in this manner.

LISP relies heavily on the principle of recursion, whereby something (usually a function or procedure) is defined in terms of itself. In the case of LISP, the item being defined is always a list. These are not accidental characteristics of LISP, but arise from its origins in computer-based investigations of natural language and human intelligence. However, the language is not an easy one to learn, and in 1968 a group of people associated with the Massachusetts Institute of Technology (MIT) set about devising a language for children based on LISP.

The charismatic leader of the group at MIT was Seymour Papert. He had previously spent a number of years studying cognitive (learning)

Founding Father
Seymour Papert, the founding father of LOGO, is shown here at a conference sponsored by Commodore in 1983. Papert is now associated with LOGO Computer Systems, Inc, (LCSI), which provides LOGO programs for the Sinclair Spectrum, Atari computers, and others

development among young children with Jean Piaget (1896–1980), the leading educational psychologist of his generation. On moving to MIT, Papert began to work closely with an artificial intelligence expert, Marvin Minsky. In his work with LOGO, Papert attempted to bring the ideas of both his colleagues together, uniting theories of cognitive learning and artificial intelligence.

Work on LOGO continued throughout the 1970s, and other groups were set up to experiment with the new language. The most notable of these was based in Edinburgh. All of this development work was carried out in university research departments using mainframes or minicomputers. It was only with the arrival of microcomputers that LOGO became more widely available.

LOGO is a sophisticated language that needs a lot of memory, both for the code and as working space. The LOGO interpreters found on micros typically require around 30 Kbytes of memory, and another eight Kbytes or more for the graphics display. All of this before you even start programming! So, although it was possible to implement simple BASIC interpreters on home micros from the moment they were marketed, it was not until home computers with over 48 Kbytes of RAM were widely available that LOGO on micros became a feasible proposition.

But it was Seymour Papert's *Mindstorms* (Basic Books, 1980) that took LOGO out of the research departments and brought it to the attention of a much larger group of people. In his book, Papert develops a vision of how computers might be used in education. This is a result of the synthesis of three sets of ideas: theories of cognitive development, artificial intelligence and the movement in education towards child-centred learning. Papert wants to see children programming computers, rather than computers programming children (which, he argues, happens in most 'computer aided instruction').

The book looks forward to the emergence of a new 'computer culture', in which 'formal' ideas previously considered beyond the capabilities of children will be easily handled by them. They will be able to do this because of the way they have used computers to explore formal ideas. It is this active, co-operative (pupil-to-pupil and pupil-to-teacher) and unstructured exploration of ideas that constitutes the 'LOGO philosophy' underlying the language's use in education.

Papert writes and convinces by the sheer power of his rhetoric. However, there are a number of serious problems with the theory. There is very little experimental evidence to back it up, despite a number of studies; Piaget's theories of cognitive development are turned into a prescription for education in a way that Piaget never intended; and there are problem-solving areas (even in mathematics!) that LOGO doesn't cover.

As teachers use LOGO more widely in the classroom, they are finding that not everything works in the way that Papert describes, and they aren't getting the results they had hoped for. There

Authorised Versions
Shown here are the most comprehensive and well-documented versions of LOGO for the Commodore 64 (Terrapin-MIT), Sinclair Spectrum, and Atari computers (LCSI). Although expensive, these are the manufacturers' authorised versions of LOGO and will most closely resemble the original MIT language. Commodore 64 LOGO is available on disk for £34.95; Atari LOGO comes on cartridge for £59.95; and Sinclair LOGO is a cassette-based version for £39.95. There are less expensive LOGO programs on the market. Some, particularly for the Spectrum, cost as little as £8.95

is a danger of disillusionment, but once we set aside the over-enthusiastic claims of what the language can do, LOGO still remains an excellent way of introducing computer concepts, of exploring certain kinds of ideas and developing problem-solving skills.

LOGO on present day micros has too little workspace and runs too slowly. To some extent it is a language that is waiting for the hardware to catch up with it. But as a language for learning it has no serious rivals.

Who Is LOGO For?

Who can benefit from learning to program in LOGO? We feel that many people, even experienced programmers, can learn a great deal from LOGO programming, including:

- Anyone who is new to computing, or new to programming;
- Anyone who likes playing with computers, and thinks computers ought to be fun to use;
- Anyone frustrated by a lack of expressive power in another programming language;
- Anyone who has an interest in thinking about thinking, learning, or teaching;
- Anyone who wants an insight into more advanced areas of computing, especially those that are related to the study of artificial intelligence.

Having said this, we must remind you that, like BASIC and machine code programming, LOGO is not for everyone. Specifically, LOGO might not be the best language for:

- Anyone who thinks using computers is 'work'. Some languages are designed for work, as are cart horses. But a cart horse is hardly the one you would choose for an afternoon ride in the countryside;
- Anyone who needs or expects a great deal of speed from the computer as it processes instructions. LOGO uses a lot of memory, and runs slowly on the present generation of microcomputers. (On comparable programs, LOGO can run at half the speed of BASIC.)

Even for these groups, however, a knowledge of LOGO can be very valuable. LOGO can be used to sketch out a solution to a problem and prepare it for translation into another language.

TURNING TURTLE

Developed by Seymour Papert as an educational aid, as we have seen, LOGO is a powerful and sophisticated language. Many versions of LOGO are now available and here we discuss ways in which the language's turtle graphics can be used to draw complex shapes with the minimum effort.

The first version of LOGO to appear on microcomputers was MIT LOGO; this is now regarded as the 'standard' version and is produced by Terrapin Inc for the Apple and Commodore 64 machines. Logo Computer Systems Inc (LCSI) produces another version for the Apple, Atari and Spectrum computers, and LCSI LOGO for the BBC Micro should soon be available. There are other versions, but these two are the most widely available. Our example programs all use MIT LOGO; where there are differences between MIT and LCSI versions, these will be explained in the 'Flavours' box.

There is only one way to learn LOGO — by experimenting! We will suggest certain things for you to try, but the best thing to do is to solve problems that you have set for yourself.

Once loaded, LOGO is in 'immediate' mode and is ready to receive and obey commands. In most versions, these commands must be entered in upper case letters. Type DRAW and you will see that the screen is divided into two sections (this is called 'splitscreen' mode). The upper section is

for the graphics; this takes up most of the display area and in the centre is the 'turtle', represented by a small triangle. The lower section is for text, and at the moment will simply contain the prompt '?'.

The turtle is an object that we can communicate with by giving it commands. Thinking of the turtle as an 'object' will make programming with it easier to understand. The most important things to be considered are the turtle's position, its heading (direction), and whether the 'pen' it carries is down (in which case it will draw a line as it moves) or up (in which case the turtle will move without leaving a trace). Typing DRAW positions the turtle in the centre of the screen, facing straight upwards with the pen down.

Now let's try giving the turtle a command:

FORWARD 40

The turtle will move 40 units up the screen, drawing a line as it goes. FORWARD is a turtle command, and the number 40 is its 'input'. Some commands need inputs, while others do not — DRAW, for example, does not require an input.

A second turtle command is BACK. BACK 10 instructs the turtle to move back 10 units. So FORWARD and BACK (each with a number of units as inputs) change the turtle's position on the screen. RIGHT and LEFT, on the other hand, do not change the turtle's position but simply rotate it — that is, they change its heading (direction). These two commands require an angle of between zero

Abbreviations

Many LOGO commands have abbreviations: here are the ones for commands introduced in this part.

Command	Abbreviation
FORWARD	FD
BACK	BK
RIGHT	RT
LEFT	LT
PENUP	PU
PENDOWN	PD
PRINT	PR
FULLSCREEN	FS
TEXTSCREEN	TS
SPLITSCREEN	SS

Meet The Turtle

A turtle is a robot drawing tool. It has wheels, controlled by stepper motors, and a retractable pen. It can be instructed to move forward, back, left and right, and can lift or lower its pen. When lowered, the pen produces a drawing on the surface where the turtle is placed. When they were first developed, turtles were dome shaped, like the Edinburgh turtle shown here, and controlled from a computer keyboard. This turtle connects to the computer via a parallel cable and costs about £192. Newer turtles are remote controlled. A radio-controlled version of the Edinburgh turtle is now available for just over £200. And there is a turtle-shaped robot, the Valiant Turtle, also shown, which has an infrared connection to the computer. The Valiant Turtle costs about £229. By extension, the name turtle is also used to refer to the drawing cursor on the computer screen in LOGO. Most screen turtles are simple triangular shapes, although Atari LOGO displays a tiny turtle-shaped cursor

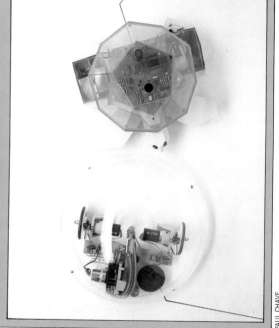

PAUL CHAVE

and 360 degrees as inputs. Experiment by using these commands — try drawing some simple shapes; see what happens if you instruct the turtle to move a greater distance than the screen size permits; try using negative numbers as inputs. To start again with a clear screen, type DRAW.

When trying out commands, you may find that the turtle moves into the text section of the screen, and thus appears to be 'behind' the text so that it can't be seen. These commands may help:

FULLSCREEN — allows the full screen area to be used for graphics;

TEXTSCREEN — removes all graphics and leaves you with text only;

SPLITSCREEN — returns you to splitscreen mode;

PENUP — allows the turtle to move without drawing a line;

PENDOWN — the turtle leaves a 'trail' as it moves.

The commands we have discussed so far are all instructions to make the turtle do your bidding. But you can also use LOGO to get information back from the turtle. The turtle's heading is measured in degrees; a heading of 0 indicates that the turtle is facing straight upwards, and the heading is measured clockwise through 360 degrees. To find the turtle's heading, type:

PRINT HEADING

The turtle's position on the screen is defined in terms of a co-ordinate system, with its origin at the centre of the screen (i.e. the turtle begins at a point with x and y co-ordinates of 0). You can find the turtle's position at any time by typing:

PRINT XCOR PRINT YCOR

Try out these commands by drawing a shape and then ascertaining the turtle's position and the direction in which it is facing. Use this data to return the turtle to its starting point.

You may have found that error messages have appeared in the text area during your experiments with LOGO commands. If not, then make a deliberate mistake to see what happens. For example, type:

FORWARD50

You will see the message:

THERE IS NO PROCEDURE NAMED FORWARD50

The reason for this is that LOGO requires a space between the command FORWARD and the input 50 so as to avoid confusion with a possible command called FORWARD50. You may also get an error message if you have typed a command in lower case.

LOGO is equipped with a line editor that enables you to correct instructions if you notice an error before you press Return. Use the cursor keys to move along the line to the incorrect text. To insert characters, simply type them in — the text to the right of the mistake will move

automatically to accommodate any extra characters. The delete key removes the character to the left of the cursor. Once the line is correct, pressing Return will allow LOGO to accept the new instruction. If you have already pressed Return before noticing a mistake, typing Control-P will retrieve the last line for editing. This feature is equally useful for repeating commands.

Now we can try something a little more mathematical — for example, a square. Remember that a square has four equal sides and that its corners are right angles (90 degrees), so something like this will produce the desired result:

FD 50 RT 90
FD 50 RT 90
FD 50 RT 90
FD 50 RT 90

Notice that we can abbreviate the commands, and can put more than one command on a single line.

Unfortunately, you may hit a technical problem at this point — your square may look more like a rectangle. This is because of the 'aspect ratio' of your screen — that is, the ratio of the vertical step size to the horizontal step size. There is a LOGO command to deal with this: use .ASPECT followed by a number (the default is 0.8) to change the aspect ratio until your shape really is a square. Now try the following exercises: draw an equilateral triangle; a pentagon; a hexagon; various rectangles; a rhombus; a parallelogram — indeed, anything that takes your fancy!

You may simplify some of the commands and reduce the amount of typing by using REPEAT. To draw the square again, simply type:

REPEAT 4[FD 50 RT 90]

REPEAT is a command with two inputs. The first is a number that indicates the number of times LOGO must do something, and the second is a 'list' of the commands to be obeyed. This list must always be enclosed in square brackets. So our square example tells LOGO that it must repeat the FORWARD 50 RIGHT 90 sequence four times. Now try using REPEAT to simplify construction of the shapes you have already created, and see if you can produce the star shapes shown in some of our illustrations.

Logo Flavours

On the Atari, the turtle looks like a turtle, not a triangle!

All LCSI versions:

Use CLEARSCREEN (abbreviation CS) to begin drawing.

Use Control-Y to recall the last line (except Spectrum, which does not have this feature).

To change the aspect ratio:

Apple LCSI — SETSCRUNCH followed by new ratio

Atari — .SETSCR followed by new ratio

Spectrum — SETSCRUNCH followed by two co-ordinate numbers [x y] (the norm is [100 100])

LOGO Exercises
Can you write procedures to create these shapes? The samples shown were drawn with LCSI LOGO on an Atari 600XL

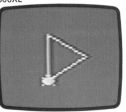
Equilateral Triangle

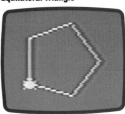
Pentagon

Hexagon

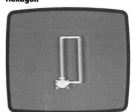
Rectangle

Five-Pointed Star

Ten-Pointed Star

Parallelogram

IAN McKINNELL

219

PLAYING TURTLE

Abbreviations

EDIT	ED
HIDETURTLE	HT
SHOWTURTLE	ST

So far we have concentrated on using the language LOGO in its immediate mode, in which each command is obeyed as it is entered. An alternative mode allows LOGO users to define a sequence of commands as a 'procedure' that is given a specific name. The commands in the procedure will be carried out only when it is called by name.

Procedures may be unfamiliar to many micro programmers, but the concept is found in everyday 'instruction procedures' such as cooking recipes and knitting patterns. Here we'll create a LOGO procedure that we will call SQUARE. (Unlike LOGO commands, which must always be typed in upper case letters, procedure names may be in either upper or lower case.) We begin by typing:

    EDIT SQUARE

The screen will clear, then the message TO SQUARE will appear at the top of the display as a reminder of the procedure name, and EDIT CTRL-C TO DEFINE CTRL-G TO ABORT will be printed at the bottom. This somewhat cryptic message helps to guide your actions while in 'edit' mode. EDIT simply tells you that LOGO is no longer in immediate mode but expects a procedure to be created. Once this is done and you are ready to store your procedure, pressing Control-C will define (record) the listing,

while Control-G will allow you to abort the procedure and start again.

You may type whatever you wish in edit mode, but none of the commands will be obeyed at this time. LOGO simply makes a note of your instructions and stores them in its 'dictionary' under the name you have given your procedure. Complete the SQUARE procedure definition by typing the following commands:

    TO SQUARE
      REPEAT 4 [FD 50 RT 90]
    END

Now you can tell LOGO to define this procedure (i.e. remember it) by typing Control-C; you will then receive the message SQUARE DEFINED. If you have made a mistake in your definition you can abort the whole process by typing Control-G, in which case you must begin again, or you may use the edit mode's full screen editor to make corrections. This allows you to use the cursor keys to move anywhere within the procedure and insert or delete characters where desired. (The immediate mode's line editor permits corrections to be made only on the last line entered). LOGO has many more commands that make editing long procedures simple; we will consider these later.

Now your procedure has been successfully defined, let's see how it works. Type DRAW to access the graphics screen, then type SQUARE — the commands in the procedure definition will now be obeyed and the turtle will draw the square. As you can see, procedures are used in exactly the same way as the basic LOGO commands — simply type the procedure name and it will carry out the instructions you have defined. The original commands that are present when LOGO is loaded are called 'primitives'. Once you have 'taught' the language a new procedure it can then be used in just the same way as a primitive. In other words, LOGO is an 'extensible' language, so it may be tailored to suit your own particular requirements.

If your procedure does not do what you expected, it is a simple matter to change the definition. As we have defined it, SQUARE draws a square with sides of 50 units in length. Let's assume that you would prefer a smaller square — say, 30 units each side. Return to the editor by typing in:

    EDIT SQUARE

The text making up the procedure is now displayed, and the screen editor can be used to change the 50 to 30. Once this has been done, redefine the procedure with Control-C and type SQUARE to ensure that it is now the size you

PENTAGON

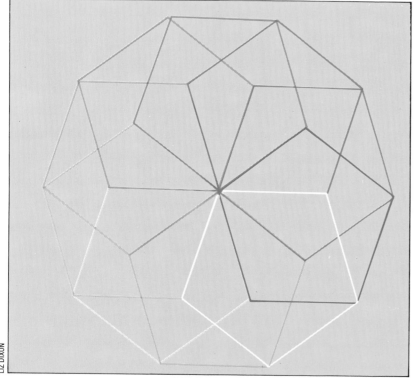

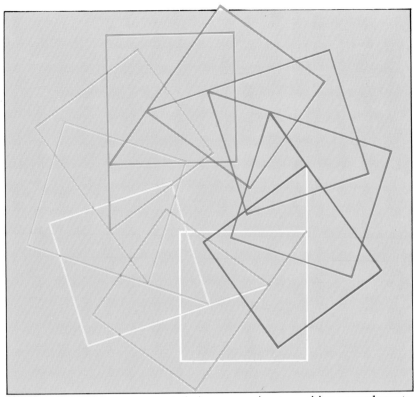

SQUARE

---

designed for you to experiment with; your attempts at drawing the various shapes may well have led to some unexpected results. To draw a triangle, you may first have tried something like this:

REPEAT 3 [FD 50 RT 60]

and then discovered that you have created half a hexagon! If you tried to draw the six-pointed star, you will certainly have found it much harder than you expected. When dealing with such problems, it is often helpful to 'play turtle' by imagining that *you* are the turtle moving around. Indeed, it is said that you can tell the difference between BASIC and LOGO programmers by watching their shoulders move while they program! Imagine drawing any closed shape from the turtle's point of view. The turtle has to go completely around the shape, and must end up back in the same place, facing in the original direction. So it must turn through a multiple of 360 degrees. If the shape is 'convex' (none of its internal angles is greater than 180 degrees), then the turtle will have turned through exactly 360 degrees. In the case of the triangle, there are three turns to be made — so each must be 360/3 = 120 degrees. From this, you should be able to deduce that the correct command for drawing a triangle is:

REPEAT 3 [FD 50 RT 120]

Even for non-convex polygons, such as the star shapes we have already investigated, the same principle applies — the only difference is that now the total angle turned is a whole-number multiple of 360 degrees (because you are creating more than one complete shape).

These principles are general (they don't apply simply to polygons) and they make up what is known as the 'total turtle trip theorem'. If you examine the six-pointed star from the turtle's point of view, you will see that the shape cannot be drawn by the turtle simply moving forward and turning through the same angle each time. Instead, a more complex procedure is required.

TURTLE CO-ORDINATE GEOMETRY

Turtle geometry is concerned with the properties of shapes themselves, rather than the relationship of shapes to an external point of reference, as is the case with co-ordinate geometry. Turtle geometry is relative — movements are made in a specified number of units from the turtle's current position on the screen. Co-ordinate geometry uses absolute values — the screen is imagined as a grid, with a defined number of units extending vertically and horizontally from the centre. Each point on the grid has a specific numeric value, and movement is defined in relation to these grid references. However, it is possible to use co-ordinate geometry with the turtle.

For example, the command SETXY 20 30 moves the turtle from its current position to the point (20,30). If PENDOWN has been specified, the turtle will draw a line as it moves; conversely, the PENUP

wanted. As an exercise, try writing procedures to draw the shapes you created in the last section: triangles, rectangles, pentagons, stars and so on.

Now try using your procedures with the REPEAT command. For example, define PENT as:

REPEAT 5 [FD 50 RT 72]

and then try:

REPEAT 10 [PENT RT 36]

You can experiment with other shapes in the same way, and you should soon discover that complex shapes can be built up quickly and easily by using REPEAT. Try this one:

REPEAT 10 [SQUARE RT 36 FD 25]

We show what results are given by the turtle in the diagrams on the following page. The examples we gave in the last section (see page 218) were

Cogito Ergo LOGO
The turtle can be addressed in terms of Cartesian or 'Turtle' geometry. In the former, turtle positions are expressed absolutely — they are measured from the imaginary X and Y axes whose origin [0,0] is the CS position; in turtle geometry, commands are expressed relative to the turtle's current position and heading, whatever they may be

PU SETXY [0,0]
PD SETXY [20,20]
Y
(20,20)
45°
−X
(0,0)
X
−Y

CARTESIAN GEOMETRY

45°
CS RT 45 FD 30

45°
RT 45 FD 30

TURTLE GEOMETRY

ALAN COODE COURTESY OF VALIANT DESIGNS LTD.

LOGO Demo
Anthony Ginn's Demolition
Turtle game introduces the floor
turtle and helps to encourage
spatial awareness in young
children. One player places a toy
tower somewhere on the board,
and chooses the turtle's start
position and heading. The other
player then programs the turtle
to hit the tower, using as few
commands as possible

command will cause the turtle to move without
leaving a trace. The origin (0,0) is in the centre of
the screen.

The following procedures perform the same
task, and illustrate the difference between turtle
and co-ordinate geometry:

```
TO SQUARE1
    REPEAT 4 [FD 50 RT 90]
END

TO SQUARE2
    SETXY 0 50
    SETXY 50 50
    SETXY 50 0
    SETXY 0 0
END
```

Typing SQUARE1 or SQUARE2 after returning to
DRAW will give exactly the same result. But what
happens if you wish to rotate the two squares
through 30 degrees? RT 30 SQUARE1 works
correctly in the first case, but the second
procedure needs to be completely rewritten
(because it specifies absolute screen co-
ordinates), and this is not a trivial task. But there
are times when the use of co-ordinates in LOGO is
helpful: as you will see from these examples,
SETXY is considerably faster at drawing lines than
FORWARD is.

Another feature of turtle geometry is its 'short-
sightedness'. The turtle concerns itself only with a
single movement at a time; it builds up shapes by
taking a series of short 'steps'. Let's play turtle and
consider how a circle is constructed. Imagine that
you are the turtle — what would you need to do to
produce a circle shape? You would move forward
for a short distance and turn a little — and you
would repeat this sequence many times. In LOGO
terms, this translates into something like:

```
TO CIRCLE
    REPEAT 360 [FD 1 RT 1]
```

```
END
```

This procedure works, but it runs very slowly. It
can be made to run faster if the turtle is not drawn
at every step. The LOGO command HIDETURTLE is
used to make the turtle invisible — SHOWTURTLE
draws it again. Our example is really drawing a
360-sided polygon: the lines that form it are so
short that they give the appearance of a smooth
curve. In fact, 360 sides are more than enough to
give the illusion of a circle — a 36-sided polygon is
sufficient. So the following procedure draws an
acceptable circle, and draws it at a considerably
greater speed:

```
TO CIRCLE
    REPEAT 36 [FD 10 RT 10]
END
```

Now try writing procedures that will result in a
semi-circle, a quarter-circle, and a sixth of a circle;
and combine two of these to make a petal shape.

Playing turtle again, how would you move if
you wished to spiral in towards a point, rather than
travelling in a circle around it? You would still
move a short distance before turning, but in this
case you would turn more and more each time (or
travel a shorter distance for each turn, which
comes to the same thing). The spiral procedure
here is a little long-winded, as we have restricted it
to use only the commands we have introduced to
date, but it will demonstrate that principle:

```
TO SPIRAL
    FD 10 RT 10 FD 10 RT 20 FD 10 RT 30
    FD 10 RT 40 FD 10 RT 50 FD 10 RT 60
    FD 10 RT 70 FD 10 RT 80 FD 10 RT 90
END
```

Logo Flavours

LOGO editors are very similar, but each has its own
peculiarities because of the particular keyboard of
the machine. Consult the LOGO manual for your
machine.

For all LCSI versions the command to edit the
procedure SQUARE is EDIT "SQUARE (quotation
mark before but not after the name of the
procedure).

To set the turtle at (20,30) use SETPOS [2 30] on all
LCSI versions.

Exercise Answers

Triangle	REPEAT 3 [FD 50 RT 120]
Pentagon	REPEAT 5 [FD 50 RT 72]
Hexagon	REPEAT 6 [FD 60 RT 60]
Rectangle	REPEAT 2 [FD 25 RT 90 FD 50 RT 90]
Parallelogram	REPEAT 2 [FD 25 RT 70 FD 50 RT 110]
Rhombus	REPEAT 2 [FD 50 RT 70 FD 50 RT 110]

Stars:

1. REPEAT 5 [FD 50 RT 144]
2. REPEAT 8 [FD 50 RT 135]
3. RT 30 REPEAT 3 [FD 50 RT 120]
   PU LT 30 FD 29 RT 90 PD
   REPEAT 3 [FD 50 RT 120]
4. REPEAT 10 [FD 50 RT 108]

PIECE WORK

We have already seen that the LOGO user can define procedures to carry out sequences of commands. Procedures, once defined, may be used in exactly the same way as LOGO 'primitives' (the basic commands of the language). It follows, therefore, that we can use procedures in the definition of further procedures. We show you how.

As an illustration of this principle, let's consider the tangram puzzle. This is a square that has been divided up into seven geometric pieces, which are combined in various ways to form different shapes. In our example, we will use the seven basic pieces to create a shape that resembles a dog. We start by defining LOGO procedures for each basic

piece; these 'piece procedures' are then incorporated into a further procedure, which is given the name DOG. As the turtle must be correctly positioned before each piece is drawn, other procedures — MOVE1 to MOVE7 — must also be used.

It would be just as easy to produce this drawing by simply stringing one command after the other in one long procedure. Our method uses the principles of 'top-down' design. We have covered this subject in some detail (see page 56), but, very roughly, it simply means breaking a problem up into a number of parts and then proceeding to solve each part in turn. The great advantage of this approach is that the LOGO programmer may define a procedure containing subprocedures that have yet to be defined. The main procedure cannot be

Shaping Up

The tangram puzzle is a collection of seven shapes that can be mixed in various combinations to create simple designs. Here we list LOGO procedures to draw the seven basic tangram pieces, as well as a sample program that draws the figure of a dog. The DOG procedure begins drawing with the triangle for the dog's hind leg

Tangram Procedures
```
TO SQUARE
    REPEAT 4 [FD 25 RT 90]
END
TO PAR
    REPEAT 2 [FD 25 RT 45 FD 35 RT 135]
END
TO TRI1
    FD 25 RT 135 FD 35 RT 135 FD 25 RT 90
END
(There are two triangles of this size)
TO TRI2
    FD 35 RT 135 FD 50 RT 135 FD 35 RT 90
END
TO TRI3
    FD 50 RT 135 FD 71 RT 135 FD 50 RT 90
END
(There are two triangles of this size as well)
```

Dog Program
```
TO DOG
    TRI3 MOVE1 PAR MOVE2 TRI2 MOVE3
    TRI1 MOVE4 TRI3 MOVE5 TRI1 MOVE 6
    SQUARE MOVE7
END
TO MOVE1
    PU FD 15 LT 45 PD
END
TO MOVE2
    PU RT 45 FD 35 LT 45 BK 35 PD
END
TO MOVE3
    PU LT 45 BK 25 PD
END
TO MOVE4
    PU RT 90 BK 25 PD
END
TO MOVE5
    PU FD 50 RT 45 PD
END
TO MOVE6
    PU FD 25 RT 135 FD 5 LT 90 PD
END
TO MOVE7
    PU LT 90 FD 5 RT 45 BK 25 RT 45
    BK 50 LT 90 BK 50 PD
END
```

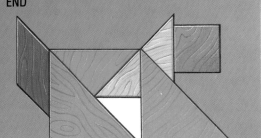

KEVIN JONES

Abbreviations

ERASE	ER
PRINTOUT	PO
PRINTOUT TITLES	POTS

run, of course, until the subprocedures have been written or dummy routines provided in their place. To show how this works, let's consider how the dog-drawing program was constructed.

The DOG procedure was written first, even though none of its component procedures yet existed. We then wrote each of the shape-drawing procedures separately. These were followed by the positioning procedures. Each time a new procedure was written, DOG was run to ensure that everything fitted together properly. When LOGO came to a MOVE procedure that had not been written it stopped with an error message. However, it was easy to tell from the drawing whether everything up to this point was correct, or if there was an error in the last MOVE procedure.

Our set of procedures demonstrates another important point — each of the shape procedures, and the DOG procedure itself, leaves the turtle state unaltered. That is, the turtle is at the same position with the same heading at the end of the procedure as it was before the procedure was run. Such procedures are said to be *state transparent*. Making procedures state transparent eases the task of putting procedures together to construct more complex drawings. Take the DOG procedure, for example: once the turtle is positioned we know that after drawing a piece the turtle will return to the position it was in when it started that piece. So we need know nothing about the internal workings of the procedures in order to put the pieces together. By making DOG state transparent, we make it easier to use this procedure as part of another — for example, we could draw a whole screenful of dogs.

LOGO WORKSPACE

By now you will have a fair number of procedures in the computer's memory — so let's take a closer look at LOGO memory organisation. LOGO's working memory consists of a list of *nodes* (each of five bytes). Once LOGO is loaded, you will have between 1,000 and 3,000 of these, depending on the machine you use. As procedures are defined, these nodes are used up. Other nodes may be used as procedures are run or if variables (to be discussed later in the course) are used.

The procedures you have defined constitute your *workspace*. You can see which procedures are held in the workspace by entering POTS (for PRINTOUT TITLES). To look at an individual procedure, use PO (for PRINTOUT) — for example, PO SQUARE. If a procedure is no longer required, workspace can be freed by using ERASE — the command ERASE SQUARE would remove the procedure called SQUARE from memory. Erasing a procedure releases the nodes used. LOGO will mark these nodes, but will not yet add them to the list of free nodes; instead it will continue working with its present free nodes list until all of these have been used up. It will then go through its memory, gathering up all the nodes that have been released and using these to form a new list of free nodes. This process is referred to as *garbage collection* and is the reason why LOGO seems to hesitate for a second or two from time to time.

SAVING PROCEDURES

In order to make permanent records of your procedures on disk, you must save the workspace as a file. Using MYPROCS as an example file name, you would type SAVE "MYPROCS (note the quotation marks before, but not after, the file name). The workspace itself will not be affected by this. The file may be loaded with READ "MYPROCS. This causes the procedures in the file to be defined and added to the current workspace. If a procedure is defined with the same name as a procedure already held in the workspace, then the new definition replaces the earlier one.

Other useful disk-handling commands are CATALOG and ERASEFILE. CATALOG gives a list of all the files on the disk, and ERASEFILE "MYPROCS would erase the MYPROCS file from the disk. Cassette-based versions of LOGO use different commands — the relevant manual should be consulted for these.

Procedure Problems

1) Write procedures for the other tangram shapes shown. (You will first have to solve the puzzle of how to construct the shape from the different pieces,

of course!)
2) Write a procedure to draw a 'house' (simply an equilateral triangle above a square).
3) Write a procedure to

draw a five-by-five board of squares.
4) Rewrite the procedure used earlier to draw a six-pointed star so that it uses subprocedures.

LIZ DIXON

Logo Flavours

In all LCSI versions, procedure names must be prefixed by a quotation mark if they are inputs to PO or ERASE: for example, PO "SQUARE and ERASE "SQUARE.

To read a disk file use LOAD "MYPROCS.

Versions supporting cassette tapes or microdrives have somewhat different commands from those for disks. You should consult the relevant technical manual.

REPEAT PERFORMANCE

This is the final part of our tutorial stream on programming in LOGO language. Here we show you how to add new control structures to the language, and explain how to write procedures that can themselves write procedures.

The LOGO primitive RUN takes a list as its input, and causes this list to be executed just as if it were a line of a procedure. This can be used to add new control structures to the language as and when they are required. So we could define a WHILE procedure as follows:

```
TO WHILE :CONDITION :ACTION
    IF NOT ( RUN :CONDITION ) THEN STOP
    RUN :ACTION
    WHILE :CONDITION :ACTION
END
```

Here's an example of how we could use it. POWER prints all the powers of its input below 1000:

```
TO POWER :X
    MAKE "P :X
    WHILE [:P < 1000] [PRINT :P MAKE "P :P * :X]
END
```

Control structures, such as WHILE, REPEAT and FOR, are common in other languages, but they are not really necessary in LOGO. A more natural way to write POWER in LOGO would be:

```
TO POWER :P
    IF NOT :P < 1000 THEN STOP
    PRINT :P
    POWER P * :P
END
```

REPEAT is provided in all versions of LOGO, but it is not strictly necessary, since you could define an equivalent word, REPT, in the following way:

```
TO REPT :NO :LIST
    IF :NO = 0 THEN STOP
    RUN :LIST
    REPT :NO – 1 :LIST
END
```

RUN is an extremely useful primitive for more advanced LOGO work. A program can assemble a list and then pass it to RUN to have it obeyed. We'll see an example of this shortly.

TAKING PROCEDURES APART

First of all we must define a procedure to draw a triangle in the usual way:

```
TO TRI
    FD 50 RT 120 FD 50
```

```
    RT 120 FD 50 RT 120
END
```

Now type PRINT TEXT "TRI. The result should be:

The text of the procedure is given as a list of lists, where each 'inner' list is one line of the procedure. To see why there is an empty list at the start, define this replacement for addition:

```
TO ADD :A :B
    PRINT :A + :B
END
```

Now PRINT TEXT "ADD will give:

```
[:A :B][PRINT :A + :B]
```

Clearly, the first list contains the inputs for the procedure. So TEXT enables us to get inside a procedure and find out what is there. DEFINE, on the other hand, does the opposite: it lets us define a procedure as a list of lists without having to go into the editor. Now try DEFINE "L [[:A] [FD :A] [RT 90] [FD :A / 2]] and then run L using, for example, L 30. Using DEFINE in immediate mode in this way has no advantages over using the editor. The advantage that DEFINE gives us is the ability of one procedure to create another procedure.

GROWING

We are now going to develop a small system for investigating growth. The basic commands in our system are ASK, which selects the shape we will deal with, and GROW, which changes the size of the chosen shape. For example, ASK "SQUARE will draw a square, and then GROW [* 10] will erase the square and then redraw it with each of its sides increased by a factor of 10.

To keep the programs simple we will have to accept a few restrictions on what we can do with these commands. Firstly, the shape procedures given as inputs to ASK may not contain REPEAT or call subprocedures. Secondly, the system will break down if you get negative results. Neither of these problems is very difficult to deal with if you should wish to improve on what we give here.

ASK works by assigning the name of the shape to the global variable "CURRENT and then running the procedure. It does this by creating a list of one item — the procedure name — and then using RUN to execute it.

```
TO ASK :OBJECT
    HIDETURTLE
    MAKE "CURRENT :OBJECT
    RUN ( LIST :OBJECT )
END
```

Draw Me A Turtle

One cannot progress far in LOGO without coming across recursion, something defined in terms of itself. We have seen such examples as procedures that call themselves, lists defined in terms of lists, and now procedures to write procedures. With a little imagination, it would be easy in LOGO to create a drawing in the style of MC Escher, using the turtle to generate a turtle that draws a turtle...

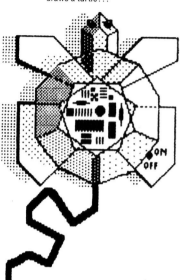

GROW first wipes out the original drawing (Commodore LOGO uses PENCOLOR-1 for erasing), then uses DEFINE to define the current procedure as a rewritten one. The pen colour is then returned to normal and the new shape drawn. Note that the input to GROW is stored in the variable OPLIST — which we will need to use later.

```
TO GROW :OPLIST
    PENCOLOR -1
    RUN ( LIST :CURRENT )
    DEFINE :CURRENT REWRITE.PROC TEXT
        :CURRENT
    PENCOLOR 1
    RUN ( LIST :CURRENT )
END
```

REWRITE.PROC splits the text up into lines and passes them one at a time to REWRITE.LINE:

```
TO REWRITE.PROC :TEXT
    IF EMPTY? :TEXT THEN OUTPUT []
    OUTPUT FPUT REWRITE.LINE FIRST :TEXT
        REWRITE.PROC BUTFIRST :TEXT
END
```

REWRITE.LINE checks along a line looking for a FD or FORWARD. If one is found, it passes the rest of the line over to CHANGE to deal with it.

```
TO REWRITE.LINE :LINE
```

```
    IF EMPTY? :LINE THEN OUTPUT []
    IF ANYOF FIRST :LINE = "FD FIRST :LINE =
        "FORWARD THEN OUTPUT CHANGE BUTFIRST
        :LINE
    OUTPUT FPUT FIRST :LINE REWRITE.LINE
        BUTFIRST :LINE
END
```

CHANGE constructs the 'rewritten' line. The first item of LIST — the input to CHANGE — would have been the input to FORWARD in the original procedure. Say this is 50, and if OPLIST contains [* 2], then SENTENCE FIRST :LIST :OPLIST would be [50 * 2]. CHANGE now uses RUN to evaluate this list (obtaining a result of 100). Finally, a list is constructed consisting of FD, the newly evaluated quantity and then the rewrite of the rest of the line.

```
TO CHANGE :LIST
    OUTPUT ( SENTENCE "FD ( RUN SENTENCE
        FIRST :LIST :OPLIST ) REWRITE.LINE
        BUTFIRST :LIST )
END
```

COPYCAT

It is sometimes useful to be able to make a copy of a procedure. So let's define a procedure — COPYDEF — so that COPYDEF "NEWNAME "OLDNAME would define NEWNAME as a copy of OLDNAME (OLDNAME would itself remain unaffected). An

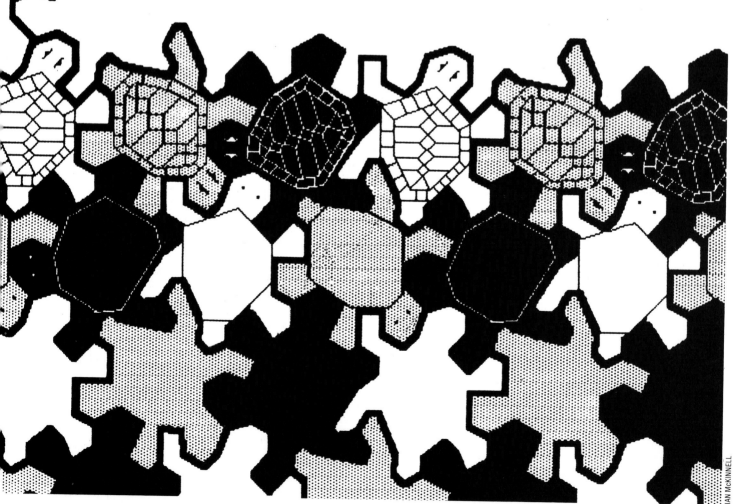

obvious definition is:

```
TO COPYDEF :NEW :OLD
    DEFINE :NEW TEXT :OLD
END
```

The trouble with this definition is that if OLD does not exist then the procedure simply goes ahead and defines NEW as nothing. It would be better to pick up this problem and report on it. So a better definition of COPYDEF would be:

```
TO COPYDEF :NEW :OLD
    IF NOT PROCEDURE? :OLD THEN ( PRINT
        [THERE IS NO PROCEDURE] :OLD ) STOP
    DEFINE :NEW TEXT :OLD
END
```

This uses a procedure called PROCEDURE?, which outputs TRUE if its input is a procedure, and FALSE otherwise. PROCEDURE? and its counterpart, PRIMITIVE?, are very useful tests, but unfortunately they do not exist in MIT LOGO. So we've developed versions of PROCEDURE? and PRIMITIVE? that will work on both the Apple and the Commodore versions of LOGO:

```
TO PROCEDURE? :NAME
    IF NUMBER? :NAME THEN OUTPUT "FALSE
    IF LIST? :NAME THEN OUTPUT "FALSE
    TEST WORD? :NAME
    IFTRUE IF WORD? TEXT :NAME THEN OUTPUT
        "FALSE ELSE  IF NOT ( TEXT :NAME = [] ) THEN
        OUTPUT "TRUE
    OUTPUT "FALSE
END
```

```
TO PRIMITIVE? :NAME
    IF NUMBER? :NAME THEN OUTPUT "FALSE
    IF LIST?:NAME THEN OUTPUT "FALSE
    TEST WORD? :NAME
    IFTRUE IF WORD? TEST :NAME THEN OUTPUT
        "TRUE ELSE OUTPUT "FALSE
END
```

AFTERWORD

We have now dealt with all the major features of standard LOGO, and have covered a wide area of possible applications. If you want to read more about the language, here are four suggested books:

• *Learning with Logo* by Daniel Watt (McGraw-Hill) is a wonderful introductory book, and is ideal for using with children.
• *Logo* by Harold Abelson (McGraw-Hill) is the 'standard' book on the language.
• *Turtle Geometry* by Harold Abelson and Andrea diSessa (MIT Press) takes a serious look at turtle geometry. The maths involved is at sixth form and college level — one of the later chapters develops a simulator for General Relativity in LOGO!
• *Thinking about [TLC] Logo* by John R. Allen, Ruth E. Davis and John F. Johnson (Holt Sanders International Editions) uses the rather idiosyncratic TLC LOGO, but the book is valuable for its investigation of artificial intelligence themes using LOGO.

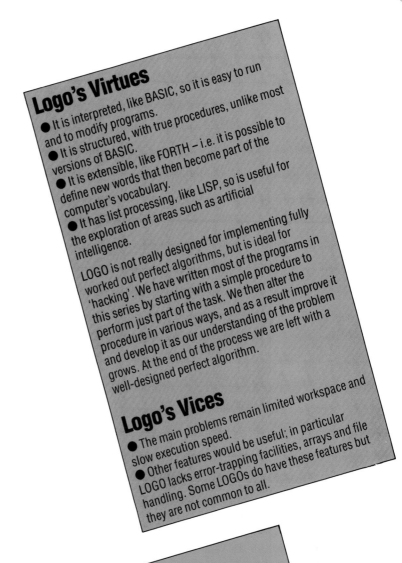

Logo's Virtues

● It is interpreted, like BASIC, so it is easy to run and to modify programs.
● It is structured, with true procedures, unlike most versions of BASIC.
● It is extensible, like FORTH – i.e. it is possible to define new words that then become part of the computer's vocabulary.
● It has list processing, like LISP, so is useful for the exploration of areas such as artificial intelligence.

LOGO is not really designed for implementing fully worked out perfect algorithms, but is ideal for 'hacking'. We have written most of the programs in this series by starting with a simple procedure to perform just part of the task. We then alter the procedure in various ways, and as a result improve it and develop it as our understanding of the problem grows. At the end of the process we are left with a well-designed perfect algorithm.

Logo's Vices

● The main problems remain limited workspace and slow execution speed.
● Other features would be useful; in particular LOGO lacks error-trapping facilities, arrays and file handling. Some LOGOs do have these features but they are not common to all.

Logo Flavours

On all LCSI versions use:
    NUMBERP for NUMBER?
    LISTP for LIST?
    WORDP for WORD?
    EMPTYP for EMPTY?

For the different IF syntax, see page 240

Spectrum LOGO has COPYDEF as a primitive, as well as PRIMITIVEP (corresponding to our PRIMITIVE?) and DEFINEDP (corresponding to our PROCEDURE?)

On the Atari use: PC for PENCOLOR, SE for SENTENCE, and HT for HIDETURTLE. DEFINE and TEXT do not exist in Atari LOGO, though the manual gives a way of defining them.

The pen colours used will differ from machine to machine. PC –1 is used here to erase lines, but some LOGO versions have this as a primitive PE (standing for 'Pen Erase')

A STRICT DISCIPLINARIAN

We begin a detailed examination of PASCAL, the most influential of the high-level programming languages. Here, we discuss the language's origins and the principles behind its development. Often characterised as a 'strict disciplinarian', PASCAL is designed to encourage good programming technique.

The PASCAL programming language was originated by Professor Niklaus Wirth of Zurich around 1970. It is named after the 17th century French mathematician and philosopher, Blaise Pascal, who invented the first four–function calculator. The PASCAL language was mainly influenced by ALGOL 60, and was a direct response by Wirth to the oversized and complex ALGOL 68. He intended that PASCAL would:

●Allow precise expression of programming concepts and structures.
●Demonstrate that a small machine-independent language with a rich and flexible set of data, statement and program structuring features could be used as a general purpose problem–solving tool.
●Help gain insight into methods of organising large programs and managing complex software projects with safety and security.
●Have extensive error checking capabilities, especially during compilation, thus minimising programming errors and providing an excellent vehicle for teaching computer programming.
●Be able to be implemented efficiently on microcomputers.

All the design objectives have been realised with great success — a small PASCAL compiler typically occupies 24 Kbytes, and is twice as efficient as FORTRAN (itself noted for speed). Although PASCAL has a small vocabulary and is easily learnt (it has only 35 'key' or 'reserved' words as opposed to over a hundred in most variations of BASIC), it is nevertheless much more powerful. More importantly, PASCAL is much more expressive in both the way that algorithms can be written and the ease with which data can be described simply and coherently, no matter how complicated that data might be.

Perhaps the greatest single benefit of PASCAL is that it provides a simple and coherent way of expressing extremely powerful algorithms. Above all, it's the *way* that one thinks about computing problems that most directly influences the ease with which we can solve them. PASCAL's natural freedom of expression means that the language is a marvellous tool for solving problems, rather than being part of the problem itself. The language has many other advantages, as well. PASCAL is a compiled language, which not only means that programs execute many times faster, but that precious memory is not used up by the presence of the source program text and a language interpreter — all you need is the compiled 'object' code.

The whole philosophy of the language is to protect you from your own folly and to prevent an error-laden program from running at all. This may seem very strange at first, particularly to BASIC programmers. Often, however, in BASIC, the quicker we get to run a program, the longer it is before we get it to work.

In fact, especially for a large program, it is actually much easier to program in PASCAL than in BASIC. Sometimes PASCAL is characterised as a 'strict disciplinarian' and, although this is often voiced as a criticism, it in fact indicates the excellence of PASCAL's error diagnosis and reporting. We all need an occasional slap on the wrists to remind us that it takes thought and care to write robust error-free programs. After all, these imposed disciplines are no more than those required to organise any program effectively and securely. The resulting reduction of the time taken to debug programs that 'almost work' is a real bonus. In short, PASCAL helps you find solutions — it's not a part of the problem itself.

To the programmer coming to PASCAL from BASIC, the most striking difference about PASCAL programs of any size is the abundance of peculiar-looking definitions and declarations that may seem rather pointless, if not totally useless. The first yard and a half of any large PASCAL program doesn't seem to actually do anything. This is partly because, although you can effectively add your own words to the language, this must be done before you can use them if PASCAL is to understand what they mean. So, whereas in BASIC a program is stated first (using statements like GOSUB 5000) and the subroutines defined *after* the main program, PASCAL enables you to define new commands like ClearScreen or Pause (so many seconds) at the start of the program and use these in the main procedure. For example:

```
begin
    ClearScreen;
    Write ('Hello!');
    Pause (3);
    ...etc.
```

PASCAL encourages a methodical, but very practical approach to computer programming. It

---

PASCAL's Major Programming Features
●Completely free format and layout of the program text
●Flexible requirements in the naming of program objects
●The ability to define new command 'words'
●Simple and consistent syntax
●Data typing
●Modular programming structure
●Flexible control of data and processes
●Natural recursion
●Excellent compile–time error diagnosis
●A small, highly efficient compiler

Blaise Pascal, 1623-1662
Mathematician, scientist and philosopher, Blaise Pascal designed the world's first mechanical calculator in 1642. The PASCAL language was named in honour of this contribution to the science of computing

presents the user with a very high-level conceptualised view of a computer system, so that data and processes can be defined and expressed in a natural, logical way. This ensures a high degree of inherent portability and safety, and both the error detection and diagnostics are excellent. In general, PASCAL has had a greater influence on other computer languages — and software design — than any other programming language.

Our diagram showing the genealogy of high-level languages features only the main influences of most of the important compiled imperative languages, and so does not include LISP, PROLOG or any other functional language. Nor is FORTH shown — it's almost unclassifiable! The mainstream of influence starts with ALGOL 60, and there is hardly a single modern language of any note that has not been derived, either directly or indirectly, from PASCAL. This in turn means that a sound knowledge of PASCAL will be an enormous advantage in understanding the languages of the next decade — such as MODULA-2, OCCAM or ADA.

Besides being used extensively for teaching purposes, PASCAL has been widely adopted for many commercial and systems applications. It has been used for writing software as diverse as financial packages and language compilers. The 'p-system', the famous portable operating system designed at UCSD (University of California at San Diego) in the late 1970s, was both developed and written in PASCAL. The software for Apple's Lisa and Macintosh, including their operating systems, was mainly written in either PASCAL or its derivative, CLASCAL. Many thousands of professional programmers were weaned on PASCAL, either on the University's DEC or VAX, or possibly on an Apple II running the p-system version known as Apple PASCAL. Members of the original UCSD team can now be found busily writing MODULA-2 compilers or other systems and applications software for many of the leading software houses — all in PASCAL or a derivative.

The most remarkable thing about all this is that it has happened despite the almost complete lack of sponsorship from any major commercial interests. PASCAL succeeds purely on its own merits, and not because any large manufacturers have vested interests in selling it. Our PASCAL programming stream will concentrate on the standard language (ISO PASCAL), but some machine specific examples will be given where graphics or operating system calls are required.

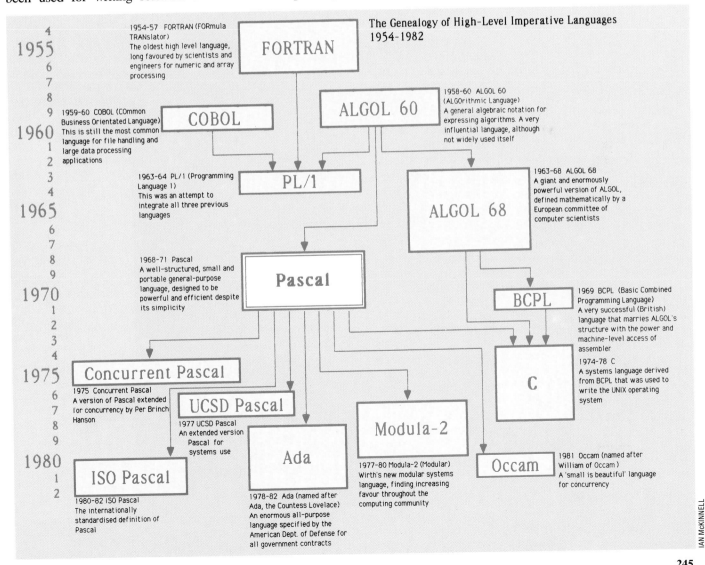

The Genealogy of High-Level Imperative Languages 1954-1982

1954-57 FORTRAN (FORmula TRANslator)
The oldest high level language, long favoured by scientists and engineers for numeric and array processing

1959-60 COBOL (COmmon Business Orientated Language) This is still the most common language for file handling and large data processing applications

1958-60 ALGOL 60 (ALGOrithmic Language) A general algebraic notation for expressing algorithms. A very influential language, although not widely used itself

1963-64 PL/1 (Programming Language 1) This was an attempt to integrate all three previous languages

1963-68 ALGOL 68 A giant and enormously powerful version of ALGOL, defined mathematically by a European committee of computer scientists

1968-71 Pascal A well-structured, small and portable general-purpose language, designed to be powerful and efficient despite its simplicity

1969 BCPL (Basic Combined Programming Language) A very successful (British) language that marries ALGOL's structure with the power and machine-level access of assembler

1974-78 C A systems language derived from BCPL that was used to write the UNIX operating system

1975 Concurrent Pascal A version of Pascal extended for concurrency by Per Brinch Hanson

1977 UCSD Pascal An extended version Pascal for systems use

1977-80 Modula-2 (Modular) Wirth's new modular systems language, finding increasing favour throughout the computing community

1981 Occam (named after William of Occam) A 'small is beautiful' language for concurrency

1980-82 ISO Pascal The internationally standardised definition of Pascal

1978-82 Ada (named after Ada, the Countess Lovelace) An enormous all-purpose language specified by the American Dept. of Defense for all government contracts

IAN McKINNELL

FIRST WORDS

Having discussed the origins and development of PASCAL we run through some of the fundamentals of its syntax and vocabulary. Programmers are weaned off the familiar but less efficient characteristics of BASIC with examples that demonstrate the structure and economy of the language.

The problem normally encountered first when using a compiled language is learning to cope with the multi-stage process required to obtain even a small executable program. First, the source text has to be entered via some form of text editor or word processor. Then, having saved the source on tape or disk, the language compiler must be loaded and instructed to compile the source to some form of machine code (often with a complex string of command line options). Lastly, this 'object' file must be re-located and linked with any run-time library routines needed. Possibly the program can be loaded and run without further effort, but should the compiler use a 'pseudo-code' or intermediate code, then a run-time interpreter must be used to execute the program.

If all this sounds a little too formidable, take comfort from the fact that all the PASCAL packages available for home computers avoid these problems to a large extent. At the very least during program development your source text, compiler and object program can be co-resident in memory. PASCAL's efficiency and small size makes this possible, and the resulting system is often no more complicated in use than a resident BASIC package. It's only when we start writing programs of any significant size that we need to resort to the more complicated processes described above.

Each system will have its own set of commands to control the editor and compiler, and you must refer to the relevant documentation for help with these. Very often, a simple E for edit, C for compile and R for run will be all that is required. What concerns us is the correct syntax to be entered for every program, no matter how trivial or complex. Fortunately, PASCAL is so well standardised that there will be little or no need for the many programming 'flavours' that we have given in the past to deal with the different dialects of BASIC (although later in the course we will have to deal with some minor exceptions). So let's look at our first complete PASCAL program:

```
Program First (output);
Const
        Message = 'Pascal Programming';
Begin
```

Popular Compilation
A full professional implementation of PASCAL can often cost more than the price of a home computer, but recently there has been a wave of reasonably priced compilers for popular home micros. We show a selection of packages now available

```
        write (Message)
End.
```

Before we study this example in depth, try entering, compiling and running it. If you get any complaints from the compiler, read the error message carefully and see if you can spot what's wrong. Every symbol must be presented exactly as shown. Take special care with the semi-colon at the end of the first and third lines and the full stop at the end of the program. When you have successfully executed this program you will see the following message displayed on the screen:

Pascal Programming

The program may be trivial but it demonstrates the overall form that every PASCAL module (program, procedure or function) will have. There are three separate parts:

1. The heading, in this case a program heading.
2. Declarations and definitions, here a single constant definition.
3. The 'body', which contains all the executable statements.

The syntax requirements of PASCAL, at least for the fundamentals of the language, may best be defined by means of 'syntax diagrams'. These are like the road map of a one-way system. A legal route through the diagram proceeds from top left to bottom right, and every box that we pass through is either a 'syntactic entity' (that is, it

Package: HISOFT PASCAL
For: Spectrum, Amstrad, MSX machines
Price: Spectrum (£25) Amstrad and MSX (£29.95)
Description: A slightly non-standard implementation, but a bargain nonetheless. The package comes with its own editor and a turtle graphics library

Package: Acorn ISO PASCAL
For: BBC Model B, Electron
Price: £69
Description: Excellent value. There are two compilers: one in ROM, with a semi-intelligent editor and memory-to-memory compilation; the other a disk-based system for second (6502) processor owners

Package: Oxford PASCAL
For: Commodore 64
Price: £49.95 (disk) £19.95 (cassette)
Description: Another bargain. Limbic Systems, which produces the package, is expected to release versions for the BBC Micro in February, 1985 and the Spectrum in April, 1985

represents itself) contained in a round-edged box, or another item described elsewhere by a separate syntax diagram, indicated by the rectangular box in which it is enclosed.

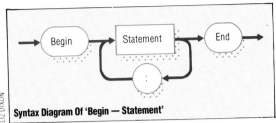

Syntax Diagram Of 'Begin — Statement'

Referring first to the overall diagram of a program, it can be seen that the words Begin and End are defined to be part of PASCAL's vocabulary, and require no further diagrams to elaborate their meaning. In fact, PASCAL recognises only 35 words as having a fixed meaning, and for the sake of completeness we list all of them here. Our first program makes use of only four of them — Program, Const (short for constant), Begin and End. The word following Program is an 'identifier' that identifies the program's name and can be any legal identifier you choose.

If we start with a letter and use only letters or digits there are an almost infinitely large number of names we could use. Predictably, however, it is impossible to use a reserved word. For example:

```
Name
PASCAL
Program One
N
XYZ123
Address 12
FloraMacDonald
AVeryLongIdentifierIndeed
```

are all legal, whereas:

```
Prog-1
TEN%
Lumber.Jack
and
Time$Square
IDon'tKnow
1001Dalmatians
It figures
```

are illegal, either because they contain symbols which are not alphanumeric, start with a number or (in the case of and) duplicate one of PASCAL's reserved words. The last example is illegal because a space is used to separate the words, each component word (It and figures) being quite legal. In PASCAL, as in English, there is no difference in meaning between lower-case letters and capitals, though some non-standard versions may insist on reserved words being in upper case.

Apart from spaces and the end of a line, there is another item of PASCAL syntax that can be used as a separator — a comment. This may appear anywhere in the text except, of course, in the middle of words. Comments are delimited by 'brace' (curly bracket) symbols.

Let's be a little more adventurous and enter something that looks like a real PASCAL program:

```
Program Program Two (input, output);
            {Gives the square of a number}

Const
            Prompt ='Enter a number:';
Var
            number :integer;

Begin
    WriteLn;
    WriteLn;
    write (Prompt);
    read (number);
    WriteLn (number, 'squared is', number * number)
End.
```

Notice that we now include the identifier input in the heading. Input and output are required in PASCAL, and they identify the external files with which the program will communicate. Normally on a micro they will be the keyboard and VDU screen respectively. By including input, we can now read from the keyboard using the standard PASCAL procedure read. As with write, any 'parameters' must be listed in brackets.

The memory used to store these parameters is reserved by the Var declaration, in this case for a single whole number. Unlike BASIC, which can usually distinguish only between numbers and strings (by using a dollar sign after the identifier), PASCAL has an almost unlimited range of data types available. It therefore becomes important to let the compiler know how much memory to reserve for storage of each data item. You must always declare every single variable in a Var declaration.

The cursor will remain positioned immediately after the prompt as if we had used a BASIC PRINT statement with a final semi-colon. This is not a bug but exactly what we asked for by using PASCAL's built-in write procedure. Whenever a new line is required, we must use the alternative procedure WriteLn. The Ln is a contraction of the word Line, and it is helpful to use a capital W and L to indicate the start of each of the component words. A simple WriteLn statement without parameters will merely create a new line.

PASCAL enables us to differentiate between data that varies and items that will remain constant throughout the execution of the program. Notice, therefore, that the Const definition uses an equals sign, whereas the Var declaration uses a colon.

PASCAL's 35 Reserved Words									
And	Case	Do	End	Function	In	Not	Procedure	Set	Until
Array	Const	Downto	File	Goto	Label	Of	Program	Then	Var
Begin	Div	Else	For	If	Mod	Or	Record	To	While
					Nil	Packed	Repeat	Type	With

LANGUAGES

VARIABLE TYPES

Symbolic Shapes
These three shapes are the symbols commonly used in PASCAL syntax diagrams:

● The rounded, or lozenge-shaped, symbol represents PASCAL reserved words, or characters that need no further explanation (such as `letter`' or `digit`')

● A circle represents a PASCAL operator (+, —, *, ., etc)

● The rectangular symbol stands for a word or phrase that has its own separate syntax diagram

PASCAL uses four simple data types in its variable declaration statements. Here we discuss the differences between integer, real, character and boolean variables, giving examples of how these are used, and look at compound statements.

PASCAL provides four simple data types that are pre-defined for us, and given the identifiers Integer, Real, Char and Boolean. Numbers are classified according to whether they may have a fractional part (real numbers) or are natural whole numbers (integers). Of course, the actual range of numbers available is determined by how many bytes are used to store a given value of either type. Design decisions like this are taken by the compiler writer (the 'implementer') and such features are said to be 'implementation dependent'. All these implementation dependencies must be specified in the documentation for a compiler to be validated by the ISO (International Standards Organisation) standard for PASCAL.

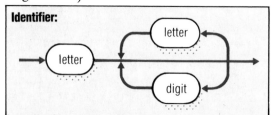

Identifier:

The range of integers on your compiler will almost certainly be either from −32,768 to 32,767 or from −2,147,483,648 to 2,147,483,647, depending on whether a two or four byte representation is used. PASCAL names the value of the maximum integer, represented by the predefined constant identifier, MaxInt. You can therefore easily find this value with the statement:

    WriteLn ('MaxInt is :',MaxInt)

Real numbers will also be held to a limited range and accuracy — usually from about 1.7E+38 — with six or seven digit precision at worst. This form of writing real numbers, known as 'scientific notation', is the default in PASCAL, but you may use the more usual form of writing them with a decimal point (e.g.123.456) if appropriate.

Be warned, however, that a real number *always* has a decimal point separating the whole and fractional parts, *both* of which *must* be present. So 0.1 and 1.0E−1 are acceptable, but .1 or 1E−1 are illegal. Fortunately, these strict rules only apply to numbers that must be recognised as real in the program text. If you are entering data from the keyboard, for example, an integer will be read and

converted automatically if a real value is expected.

Char is short for character, of course, and a value of this type will be one of the members of the character set (usually ASCII) available on the computer. PASCAL ensures its own portability by assuming that:

●The characters A to Z will be alphabetically ordered, which means A is less in character value than B, and B less than C, etc.
● The digit characters 0 to 9 will be ordered and contiguous, meaning that whatever the value of 0 , 1 will be the next, and so on.

ASCII character sets also have a contiguous alphabet, but this is not essential to PASCAL — merely convenient for PASCAL programmers! Each character value will have a numeric code, which is one value of a sub-range of the integer type. ASCII codes are defined over the range 0 to 127, and many machines will extend this to 225 for extra codes for graphics characters. We can easily map any ordered character set onto the scale of 'ordinal' values used internally by the computer. PASCAL provides the predefined function Ord: this returns the integer code of its argument — so Ord (A) is the equivalent of 65 in the ASCII character set. Another function, chr, gives the reverse mapping — chr (65) giving the character A (notice that a dollar sign is *not* used with chr).

The range of both character values and integers is defined for every implementation, and they exist on an ordered scale of known constants. For this reason they are termed 'ordinal' or 'scalar' types. Whatever the value, we always know what the previous and next values are, if any. These adjacent values can be obtained by the two scalar functions:

    pred (item) (predecessor)
    succ (item) (successor)

Thus succ (3) will always be the character value 4, but pred (Z) will only be Y on some character sets, such as ASCII. Pred (MaxInt) will be either 32,766 or 2,147,483,646. The chr function may only be used with an argument that is a character code. All the other scalar functions may be used with any scalar type, though if ord is used with integers, it just returns the value of its argument.

Boolean variables are the simplest of all the scalar types, as there are only two values in the scale — false and true (in that order). As they are simple scalar types, the scalar functions may be applied to any boolean value — the ordinal value of false is 0 and ord (true) is 1. The other scalar functions, pred and succ, however, aren't very useful here. Your PASCAL compiler should object

248

strongly if you try something like WriteLn (pred(false)) — it is hardly suprising to learn that it is an error to attempt to evaluate a nonexistent value.

The following constant definition part of a program shows all the simple ordinal types as they may appear in PASCAL source text.

```
CONST
    VAT        = 0.15;
    columns    = 40;
    space      = ' ';
    debugging = false;
```

EQUALITY AND ASSIGNMENT

The equals symbol (=) *always* means equals in PASCAL, and is used for equating constant identifiers to the values they will retain. When we declare variables in the VAR declaration section, the colon (:) separates the newly declared variable identifier from its type. For example:

```
VAR
    ratio    : real;
    number   : integer;
    symbol   : char;
    done     : boolean;
```

When we wish to assign values to these variables, the composite 'assignment operator' (:=) is used. This helps to distinguish clearly between the three

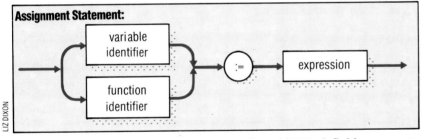

Assignment Statement:

classes of operation. CONST definitions equate permanent values, VAR declarations only reserve memory space, and assignment gives a (possibly temporary) value to the identifier.

THE COMPOUND STATEMENT

When two or more statements must be executed as part of a single process, we can bracket them between the words BEGIN and END as a 'compound' statement. Remember that each constituent statement must be separated from any following statement with a semi-colon. We have already seen a compound statement of course, since every program's body of executable statements takes this form. Here is a complete program that uses many of the features we have already considered. We will adopt the convention of writing the reserved words in upper case letters to help distinguish them from identifiers. Notice the blank lines left between each part of the program structure to aid readability:

```
PROGRAM Circle (input, output);

CONST
    pi       = 3.1415926536;
```

```
    prompt   = 'Enter the radius:';

VAR
    radius
    area        : real;

BEGIN
    WriteLn;
    write (prompt);
    read (radius);
    area := pi * radius * radius;
    WriteLn;
    WriteLn ('The area of a circle',
        'of radius', radius : 8 : 3);
    Write Ln ('is: ', area : 10 : 3)
END.
```

There are two aspects of syntax worth noting in this example. Firstly, the VAR part declares two identifiers of the same type — both real. Two separate declarations are not necessary, however, since lists of items are simply separated by a comma; this is universal in PASCAL. So, when we specify more than one argument to a procedure — as in the WriteLn statements — the same syntax applies. The second new feature is the output formatting used to override the default scientific notation of real values. We may optionally specify two integers, separated by colons, to force a certain field width for the entire number and its fractional part.

In our Circle program, three decimal places will be given in each case for both the radius and area. Because the area will be a larger (and therefore longer) number, we allow a total of 10 character positions instead of only eight for the radius. These integer values must exceed zero, allow for a possible sign, have at least one digit, and accommodate the decimal point to be written before the fractional part. Illegal values will cause errors at run time, or (at best) revert the format to scientific notation; WriteLn (X : 6 : 2) would not allow room for numbers greater than 99.99, for instance.

More valuable still, PASCAL will automatically round off the last digit for us to give the best accuracy within any requested numeric field. Further, any variable or expression may be used, not just a constant. This allows enormous flexibility, including tabulation facilities. With all other data types, only one integer value is needed — or indeed allowed — to specify the field width. To specify a width of one will cause integers to be written in the minimum size field, with no spaces. Therefore, we must remember to put them in ourselves if results are to be tabulated. For example:

```
WriteLn ('Total: ' : 20, weight : 1, 'tons.')
```

PASCAL will normally refuse to give a misleading or inaccurate output, but the ability to suppress all spaces means that we must be careful not to print two consecutive numbers with a field of one. For example, if 12 and 34 were written this way, 1234 would be the output.

CONSTRUCTIVE DECISIONS

Our PASCAL stream now turns to the subject of decision-making constructs. We consider the IF statement, which is familiar to BASIC programmers, and the CASE statement, a structure that allows multiple choices to be made within one construct.

The IF statement in PASCAL is similar to that in most languages. Because the end of a line does not terminate a statement, we can use PASCAL's free format to show the possible paths through the structure of the IF statement with logical indentation. Here are two IF statements:

```
IF count = limit
    THEN
        WriteLn ('No room')
    ELSE
        write ('Next?');
IF number > maximum THEN
    maximum := number
```

In the second example, the absence of an ELSE clause implies:

```
ELSE
    {do nothing}
```

The alignment of the reserved words THEN and ELSE (when present) helps your eye to follow the flow of control through the 'construct'. A semicolon is used to separate statements, as shown in the example, and so they can *never* appear before an ELSE. Remember that there is no ELSE statement in PASCAL only an IF statement; THEN and ELSE are used to delimit the boolean condition and the statements in the two clauses. In fact, every time we use an IF statement, we are testing a boolean value. The THEN 'clause' is executed only if the expression evaluates to true and, if an ELSE clause follows, the statement(s) there will be performed when the boolean value is false.

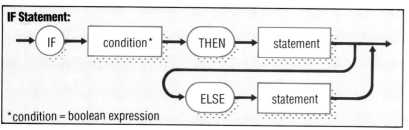

IF Statement:

IF → condition* → THEN → statement

ELSE → statement

*condition = boolean expression

PASCAL was the first language to introduce the conceptual data type known as enumerated scalars. These are extremely helpful in enabling us to retain a high level view of data classification, without continually having to mentally translate data into numeric codes. (Numbers are the computer's language, not ours — unless we happen to be solving a specifically mathematical problem.) We have already seen how a simple constant definition can help us here:

```
CONST
    width = 80;
```

The constant identifier width may then be used throughout the program to reference the number of columns across the width of the screen or printer. Rewriting the program for a 40-column VDU is then a simple matter of changing one line in the definition at the start of the program; all the calculations for print formatting and so on will be automatically altered accordingly. A complete scale of constants could then be defined in this way.

If we were using colour graphics, the colours available could be mapped onto an appropriate scale of numbers (red = 1, green = 2, for example), but this would theoretically accommodate taking the square root of green, or multiplying blue and yellow! This is not only illogical, it is also a potential source of error when we are reasoning about problems that do not in themselves deal with numeric data. The TYPE definition part of a PASCAL program can be used to define an entirely new conceptual scalar type by simply enumerating a list of identifiers representing all the constant values of the scale. For example:

```
TYPE
    hue = (red, green, yellow, blue, magenta, cyan);
```

Because it is a definition (of the new type) and not a declaration, the syntax uses the equals sign to define the type identifier (hue) to refer to the ordered values of the type enclosed in brackets. Analogously, the pre-defined type integer refers to all the whole numbers available on the PASCAL implementation.

As always in PASCAL, successive identifiers in a list (in this case, colour values) are separated from each other with commas. These values are, of course, internally mapped onto integer values with the ordinal numbering starting at zero. This numeric representation is automatically organised by the compiler, and is much the same as the underlying codes for the computer's character set. Just as the character A has an ASCII code of 65, each value of hue will have an ordinal number that we can obtain with the scalar function ord. So, in this example, ord (red) is 0 and ord (cyan) would be 5. Having now defined this new scalar type, we could declare a variable in the usual way:

```
VAR
    colour : hue;
```

This declares an identifier (colour) to be a data item of the type hue, just as the declaration:

```
VAR
    letter :char;
```

indicates the character nature of the data object named letter. The only operations defined on enumerated types are relational tests and the use of the scalar functions. For example, we could write:

```
if colour < cyan then
    colour := succ (colour)
```

Remember that pred (red) and succ (cyan) don't exist! The variable colour is incompatible with variables of any other type, scalar or otherwise. This means that we can no longer perform illegal functions like taking square roots or saying:

```
colour := colour + 1
```

This does lead to one obvious restriction. Characters and numbers can be used as parameters for write and WriteLn statements, but

```
WriteLn (colour)
```

would be illegal. This is because the values of the type are purely conceptual, and if we want to print their names, we must map the colour values on character strings. This is an ideal application for the other PASCAL choice construct, the CASE statement.

We have seen how the IF statement in PASCAL looks entirely familiar, and benefits in readability from PASCAL's free format conventions. There are times, however, when multiple option decisions have to be taken that would need something like:

```
IF N = 1
    THEN
        write ('st.')
    ELSE
        IF N = 2
        THEN
            write ('nd.')
        ELSE
            IF N = 3
                THEN
                    write ('rd.')
                ELSE
                    write ('th.')
```

Whenever the statement to be executed depends on the value of a simple scalar being in a certain limited range, we can use the CASE statement to advantage. In this instance:

```
CASE N OF
    1         : write ('st.');
    2         : write ('nd.');
    3         : write ('rd.');
    4,5,6,
    7,8,9,    : write ('th.')
END {CASE}
```

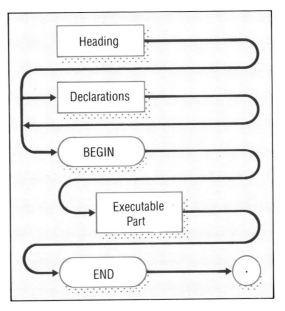

Skeleton Program
This is simplified syntax diagram of a PASCAL program, showing all the major elements. Note that PASCAL reserved words appear in upper case. This is a convention developed to set them apart from non-reserved words. Most versions of PASCAL, however, will accept reserved words in lower case

Notice that this is satisfactory only for values of N in the range of 'case labels' specified in the 'body' of the CASE statement — 1 to 9 in this example. All the values that N might have at execution time *must* be listed individually, and it would be illegal, for example, if N = 0 were entered.

Many PASCAL compilers possess the additional reserved word OTHERWISE or OTHERS, which may be used to list a default action. Refer to your manual for the extended syntax necessary here.

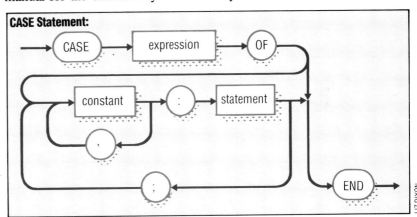

CASE Statement:

This is the only statement in PASCAL that uses END to delimit a structure that was not entered via a BEGIN, so it is common practice, and good style, to qualify every CASE statement's END as shown.

The construct works by evaluating the scalar expression delimited by (or between) the reserved words CASE and OF. A simple variable name is a minimal expression that does not require calculation. The value obtained is then compared with each constant listed in the case label lists, and when a match is found the statement following the colon, and *only* this statement, is executed. The flow of control does not 'drop through', therefore, so that the structural integrity of the construct is preserved. If several operations need to be performed, a compound statement enclosed between a BEGIN/END pair may of course be used.

In certain circumstances, some values might

require no action to be taken, in which case the simplest of all PASCAL statements can be used. This is the 'null' statement, which means 'do nothing', and it consists of absolutely no syntax at all! Here is an example:

```
CASE N MOD 4 OF
    0 :{do nothing};
    1,3 : begin
        write (N MOD 4 : 1, 'quarter');
        if N MOD 4 > 1 then
            write ('s')
        end;
    2:write ('a half')
END {CASE}
```

Notice that a semicolon is still needed to separate this non-existent statement from what follows. The last label's statement doesn't need one because it is followed by a reserved word (END); not another label or statement. The use of the MOD operator in the expression ensures that the value must be within the range 0 to 3. MOD gives the remainder from integer division, as in BBC and other BASICS.

In the next part of our look at PASCAL, we will examine these and all the other PASCAL operators, as well as in-built functions. In the meantime, here's the solution to the problem of how to print the character strings for each value of our own colour type and hue:

```
CASE colour OF
    red      : write ('Red');
    green    : write ('Green');
    yellow   : write ('Yellow');
    blue     : write ('Blue');
    magenta  : write ('Magenta');
    cyan     : write ('Cyan');
END {CASE}
```

Choice Constructs

The IF . . . THEN construct will execute the 'process' if the condition is found to be true. If the condition is false, the program simply drops through to the next statement.

Whereas the IF . . . THEN construct presents an 'option', IF . . . THEN . . . ELSE presents a 'choice'. Depending on the outcome of the test performed at the beginning of the construct, either one of two processes will be executed

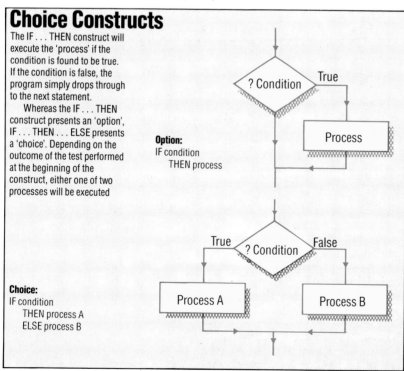

Option:
IF condition
    THEN process

Choice:
IF condition
    THEN process A
    ELSE process B

Monthly Statements

This program, which simply calculates the number of days between a date input by the user and the end of the month, provides some useful examples of PASCAL programming principles.

The CASE statement is used to map numeric input data on to PASCAL enumerated types, using these for internal processing and then mapping back on to string output data. Notice the use of the dummy char variable (symbol) to read whatever delimiting character separates the input numbers

```
PROGRAM          Date     ( input, output);

CONST
    FullStop = '.';

TYPE
    Calendar = ( Jan, Feb, Mar, Apr, May,
        Jun, Jul, Aug, Sep, Oct, Nov, Dec );

VAR
    Monthname      : Calendar;
    day,
    month,
    year,
    Left           : integer;
    symbol         : char;
    LeapYear       : boolean;

BEGIN
    WriteLn ( 'Enter the date in the form :' );
    WriteLn ( 'DD/MM/YY' : 40 );
    WriteLn;
    write ( 'Date ? ' );
    read ( day, symbol, month, symbol, year );
    LeapYear := year MOD 4 = 0;
                ( neglecting centuries )

    IF ( month > 0 ) AND ( month <= 12 )
        THEN
            CASE month OF

            1        : MonthName := Jan;
            2        : MonthName := Feb;
            3        : MonthName := Mar;
            4        : MonthName := Apr;
            5        : MonthName := May;
            6        : MonthName := Jun;
            7        : MonthName := Jul;
            8        : MonthName := Aug;
            9        : MonthName := Sep;
            10       : MonthName := Oct;
            11       : MonthName := Nov;
            12       : MonthName := Dec

            END      ( CASE )
        ELSE
            BEGIN
                WriteLn ( 'Eh ?');
                WriteLn ( '     - the program is ',
                          'about to CRASH !' )
            END;     ( MonthName is uninitialised )

    CASE MonthName OF

    Jan, Mar,
    May, Jul  : Left := 31 - day;

    Apr, Jun,
    Sep, Nov  : Left := 30 - day;

    Feb       : IF LeapYear
                    THEN
                        Left := 29 - day
                    ELSE
                        Left := 28 - day

    END; ( CASE )

    WriteLn;
    write ( 'There are ', Left : 1,
            'days left in ' );

    CASE MonthName OF

        Jan    : write ( 'January' );
        Feb    : write ( 'February' );
        Mar    : write ( 'March' );
        Apr    : write ( 'April' );
        May    : write ( 'May' );
        Jun    : write ( 'June' );
        Jul    : write ( 'July' );
        Aug    : write ( 'August' );
        Sep    : write ( 'September' );
        Oct    : write ( 'October' );
        Nov    : write ( 'November' );
        Dec    : write ( 'December' );

    END; ( CASE )

    WriteLn ( FullStop )

END .
```

1+2=20?

The discipline of PASCAL's data classification and the great variety of possible data types are features that make the language ideally suited to the clear-cut logic of mathematics. We look at aspects of PASCAL's arithmetic abilities.

What is one plus two? Without further information we might reasonably venture the answer: three, of course. The implicit assumption is that we are dealing with pure natural numbers, but suppose we put one 10p coin and two 5p coins in a vending machine? The result could be 20 pence — or, viewed from a different angle, a cup of coffee and two pence change. This sort of data classification is fundamental to any problem description, and PASCAL helps us to organise and describe our data in a clear and logical manner.

As we have already seen, we can create new and special categories of data so that we can think about the solution to the problem and design algorithms based on the processing of each data object in a manner appropriate to its type. If we inadvertently try to do something silly, like reading a Boolean truth value from the keyboard, the PASCAL compiler will trap this logical error immediately. You can appreciate the hours of frustrating debugging that can be saved if a language compiler won't even let you execute a single instruction until every error has been purged from the source program! The incompatibility between different data types and the richness of the ways in which we can describe them is one of the most valuable qualities in PASCAL. Far from feeling restricted in what we can do, we shall very often wish to take further advantage of PASCAL's 'strongly typed' data descriptions, and deliberately impose some additional constraints of our own on variables.

Now that we have used all the simple types of variables (those that may only have one value), we can fully summarise the rules for manipulating them. None of the scalars are 'compatible' with a variable of any other scalar type, though the two numeric types have many characteristics in common, and are allowed to 'rub shoulders' on occasion. As a real number can approximate a whole number, assignment is possible from integers to reals, but never vice versa. Here are some examples:

```
Program Compatibility (input, output);

VAR
   intA,
   intB :integer;
   Xreal,
   Yreal :real;

BEGIN
   read (intA, Xreal); {read an integer, then any legal
      number}
   Yreal := intA; {real := integer is OK}
   intB := Xreal; {** ERROR : illegal **}
   {. . etc.
```

Arithmetic operations are, not altogether surprisingly, defined only on the numeric types. For both integers and reals, the usual four symbolic 'operators' may be used:

+ addition
− subtraction
* multiplication
/ floating point division

In this context, they are 'dyadic' or binary operators, as they always require two 'operands' of either numeric type. Whenever one of the operands is real, the result of the expression will be real—so that: $2+2.0$ is 4.0 (not 4). In the case of the division symbol, the expression evaluates to a real even when both operands are integers: $3/5$ is 0.6, $8/4$ is 2.0.

When we are dividing integral values, a 'real' answer often makes no sense. Twelve chocolates divided among ten people gives one each with two chocolates left over, for example. The integer result and remainder can be obtained with the two integer division operators, DIV and MOD (both of which are reserved word systems in PASCAL): 15 DIV 5 = 3 and 15 MOD 5 = 0; 31 DIV 7 = 4 and 31 MOD 7 = 3. Be careful if your data is likely to be negative, as integer division is not defined for any negative values of denominator. With both types of division, real and integer, any attempt to divide by zero will result in a run-time error—at least until someone invents a way to evaluate infinity.

Multiplication and division operations are, of course, evaluated before addition and subtraction in an expression. The usual bracket notation must be used to override this logical 'precedence'. For example: (8 + 4) DIV 2 = 6, but 8 + 4 DIV 2 = 10.

TRANSFER FUNCTIONS
Although we cannot make direct assignment of a real value to an integer, PASCAL provides very useful 'transfer functions' with the identifiers trunc and round, which may be used to perform this mapping. Trunc simply truncates a real number disregarding its fractional part, whatever it may be, so that trunc (3.999) = 3 and trunc (−123.456) = −123. The function round performs intelligent rounding, towards zero if the fractional part is below 0.5 in

The Golden Section

There is only one point on a line which bisects it so that the ratio of the length of the smaller section to the larger is the same as the ratio of the larger section to the length of the whole line. This ratio is called 'sectio aurea', or the 'golden section', and like pi is an irrational number with an infinite number of digits

The golden section was used by Greek artists and architects (notably in the design of the Parthenon) and is often revived in theories of proportion. However, some of its most familiar manifestations are to be found in nature. The 'sea-shell' spiral is based on the golden section, since its radius vectors, separated by 90°, are in this section ratio

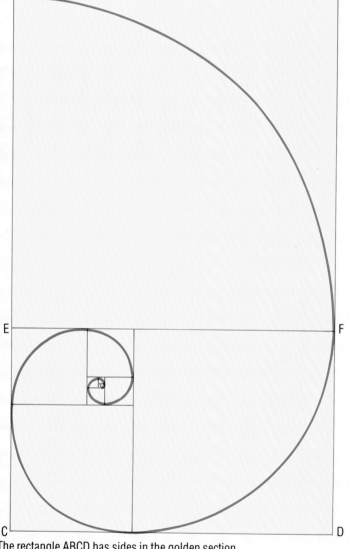

The rectangle ABCD has sides in the golden section ratio. A square ABEF can be delineated within this, such that a rectangle with the same ratio of sides as ABCD is formed (EFDC). The process can be continued ad infinitum and the corners of the squares are points on the 'golden section spiral'

value and away from zero otherwise: thus, round (1234.5) = 1235 and round (−0.49237) = 0. Naturally, an error will occur if the real argument to either of these functions would give an integer result that lies outside the scale of the type integer (−MaxInt to MaxInt), so always check with an IF statement first. Also, the argument *must* be real, not integer (they are already truncated and rounded, after all).

There is one nicety that will be unfamiliar to programmers who have agonised over expressions using the INT function in BASIC. PASCAL has a predefined function that returns a Boolean result: false if its integer argument is an even number and true if it's odd. The identifier used is, not surprisingly, called odd.

```
IF odd (N)
    THEN
        WriteLn ('That's odd!')
    ELSE
        WriteLn ('That makes us even.')
```

or:

```
IF odd (N) THEN
    IF N MOD 2 = 0 THEN
        Write Ln ('Zap the compiler!')
```

The table shows all of PASCAL's arithmetic functions. They may all take any single numeric argument, real or integer, and the first two, abs and sqr, will return a value compatible in type with their argument. Thus: abs (− 19.372) is 19.372, and abs (255) is 255. The other functions will, however, *always* give a real result, so that sqrt (16) is 4.0, not 4. This is because the algorithms used to evaluate them are modelled on the summation of a series of terms, all of which are fractional.

There is an important lesson in style here with regard to the comparison of reals. Notice that we used the word 'is' rather than an equals sign when referring to the real results of the arithmetic functions. We mean 'is the same as' rather than equal to, because it is *never* safe to compare real values for exact equality. The slightest error in calculations will mean that two nominally 'equal' reals may in fact differ by, say, 1.0E-27. Insignificant, of course, but the computer doesn't know that. Instead of using IF X = Y THEN .. we can use PASCAL's predefined abs function:

```
IF abs (X - Y) < SmallestSignificant THEN {etc.}
```

Here we test for when the difference between X and Y is extremely small. Exactly how close we regard as insignificant could usefully be specified in a CONST definition at the head of the program. Logarithms are given to the natural base (e), not 10, and exp raises e to the power of its argument (that is, it 'exponentiates'). There is no actual exponentiation operator in PASCAL, which was a deliberate design decision by Wirth. How often have you seen BASIC programs doing silly things like saying:

```
500 LET D = B^2 + 4 * A * C
```

which uses the slowest and most inaccurate way

possible of evaluating the square of a number? B * B is far better, of course. Notice that PASCAL's sqr (N) returns the square of N directly as a true integer (assuming N is an integer); sqr (X/3) would give a real. Notice also another BASIC habit to start breaking: sqrt (it) *not* sqr (it) if you want the square root of a number.

Function	Returned Value
abs (K)	absolute value of K
sqr (K)	square of K
sqrt (K)	square root of K
sin (A)	sine of A radians
cos (A)	cosine of A radians
arctan (T)	angle (in radians) with tangent T
ln (K)	natural logarithm of K
exp (L)	e raised to the power L ('anti-ln' of L)

SUBRANGE TYPES

All the scalar types have a defined and ordered range of values, and they may be used as a 'host' type from which we can derive new subrange types. These are composed, as the name suggests, of a contiguous portion of the host type. The lower and upper bounds required to delimit the subrange are listed between the 'ellipsis' symbol (..) in the definition of the subrange type identifier; for example:

```
TYPE
    byte = 0 .. 255 {subrange of integer}
    alpha = 'A' .. 'z'; {subrange of char}
    suit = (club, diamond, heart, spade); {a new type}
    major = heart .. spade; {subrange of suit}
```

Apart from the advantages we discussed earlier, a good optimising PASCAL compiler will store variables of the type byte, for instance, in eight bits instead of a possible 32 (if four-byte integer representation is used). Thus a large array of this type will take up only 25 per cent of the memory that would be used with unqualified integer elements. Notice that the type major has two possible values, rather like thinking of Boolean values being defined as:

```
TYPE
    boolean = (false, true);
```

All subrange types inherit both the data classification and the operations defined on their host type.

The previous definition of alpha may allow more than just letters of the alphabet, of course. In particular, the ASCII character set has six other symbols in the gap between 'Z' and 'a', including the square bracket symbols ('[' and ']'). These are also among PASCAL's 23 reserved symbols, and are used to delimit the components of some structured data types, as in many languages. BASIC also used these symbols originally for enclosing array indices, but the syntax was changed to round brackets because older computers sometimes had 'half-ASCII' character sets that did not include lower case letters, square brackets, the braces used for delimiting comments in PASCAL, and some other symbols. The unmodified Apple II also suffered from this restriction. PASCAL provides the following optional alternatives for cases where this problem arises: (. and .) are allowed in place of [and], and (* and *) may be used instead of { and }. The second alternative, for comment delimiters, is quite common; however, only ISO-validated compilers are likely to support the square bracket alternatives. Either, or both, substitutions may be made, so that: (* this is a legal comment}.

Band Of Gold

The program Golden, given here, generates Fibonacci terms and prints them together with their ratio. Using the program, it can be seen that one of the interesting properties of the Fibonacci series (1, 1, 2, 3, 5, 8, 13, etc.) is that the ratio of each successive pair of terms increasingly approximates to the value of the golden section.

The program demonstrates some of the principles already discussed in the course, including further examples of PASCAL's REPEAT structure. As an exercise, you could try to alter the loop's terminating condition so that it stops when the next Fibonacci term to be calculated exceeds MaxInt

```
PROGRAM     Golden      ( output );

CONST
        Epsilon      = 1.0E-08;

TYPE
        Fibonacci    = 1 .. MaxInt;

VAR
        first,
        second,
        next     : Fibonacci;
        ratio,
        Gold     : real;
        count    : integer;
BEGIN
  WriteLn ( 'The Golden Section' : 30 );
  WriteLn;
  WriteLn ( 'Fibonacci Series :' );
  first := 1;    { by definition }
  second := 1;
  ratio := first/second;
  count := 0;

  REPEAT
    IF count MOD 10 = 0 THEN
      BEGIN { Heading every 10 lines }
        WriteLn;
        WriteLn ( 'First' : 10,
          'Second' : 10, 'Ratio' : 14 );
        WriteLn
      END;

    WriteLn ( first : 10, second : 10,
            ratio : 16 : 8 );
    count := count + 1;
    Gold := ratio;    { remember old GS }
    next := first + second;
    first := second;     { move up . . }
    second := next;      { the series }
    ratio := first / second

  UNTIL abs ( ratio - Gold ) < Epsilon;

  WriteLn;
  WriteLn ( 'The Golden Mean is : ',
      100 * ratio : 10 : 5, '%' )
END .
```

PLAY IT AGAIN, RAM

Thus far in our PASCAL series, we have looked at most of the language's rich set of structured statements, enabling us to write programs to solve most types of problems. Here we examine the three different 'iteration' — or repetition — constructs, which allow us to control program loops.

We have already looked at two of PASCAL's three statement structuring methods: sequential structures using the 'word brackets' BEGIN and END (see page 248), and choice, or selection, using IF and CASE constructs (see page 250). The third type of statement structure is 'iteration', or repetition, for which PASCAL provides three different constructs. The FOR statement gives a 'counter-driven' loop, whereas both WHILE and REPEAT statements are 'condition-driven'.

The Boolean expression delimited by the reserved words WHILE and DO is evaluated first, and if the result is true, the following statement (which can be any PASCAL statement including a

within the current balance of the account, the WHILE loop will not be performed at all. If the body is executed, looping will stop when the expression becomes false. The flow of control reverts to sequential operation, and the first statement after the WHILE construct will then be executed. The appearance of the Boolean expression at the head of this construct indicates syntactically the security of the PASCAL 'semantics' (or the precise meaning and behaviour of the statements). If you want to iterate only if a condition is true, the WHILE loop should be used.

There are often situations when we need to perform the body of a loop at least once in order to set up the condition that stops it, as with the Golden program example (see page 255). Under these circumstances the REPEAT . . UNTIL construct more accurately expresses the algorithm, and provides a natural high-level syntax.

Notice that the terminating condition now appears at the end of the structure, and that it is logically opposite to the condition used to code the WHILE construct. That is to say, the REPEAT loop terminates when the Boolean expression evaluates to true, whereas a WHILE construct stops (if indeed it ever started) on the condition being false. If the body of the REPEAT statement contains several statements, they should really be enclosed within BEGIN . . END word brackets as a compound statement, but PASCAL relaxes this rule because the reserved words REPEAT and UNTIL will sufficiently

REPEAT Statement:

WHILE Statement:

condition::=
boolean
expression

LIZ DIXON

structured statement of any degree of complexity) will be repeatedly executed as long as the condition remains true. This Boolean condition is re-evaluated after every execution of the statement in the 'body' of the WHILE construct. Obviously, this implies that at least one of the items evaluated in the expression must be changed in some way by the actions within the loop. As an example:

```
WHILE MaxInt > 1 DO
    WriteLn ('Looping!')
```

would have great difficulty in terminating. Here's a more realistic (and safer) example:

```
read ( withdrawal );
WHILE withdrawal > BankBalance DO
    BEGIN
    WriteLn ('Insufficient funds — try again:');
    write ('Amount?');
    read (withdrawal)
    END
```

The most valuable asset of the WHILE construct is well illustrated by the previous program segment. If, when the withdrawal amount is first read, it is

delimit the loop's body. It's perfectly legal to put the superfluous BEGIN and END words in, however, rather like using an extra semi-colon before a reserved word except that no null statement is created.

The following segment will count the number of occurrences of the letter 'e' in a sentence entered from the keyboard. You must complete the sentence with a full stop when the REPEAT loop terminates and the result is printed.

```
count := 0;
REPEAT
    read (symbol);
    IF symbol = 'e' THEN
    count := count + 1
UNTIL symbol = '.';
WriteLn ('There were', count : 1,
    '''e''s in the sentence.')
```

In this case, there is no obvious preference for either construct, and we could just as well have used a WHILE loop:

```
count := 0;
read (symbol);
```

Golden Exercise Answer
On page 255, we set an exercise with our Golden program, which generated Fibonacci terms and the ratios of successive pairs. We asked you to try to alter the loop so that the terminating condition stops when the next Fibonacci term to be calculated exceeds MaxInt.

With two's complement representation, if an integer result exceeds MaxInt, the sign bit gets 'clobbered'. The number then looks negative, so our Golden program would crash, as the type Fibonacci excludes negative values. Even with integers, the loop would never stop. We can't say:

UNTIL first + second > MaxInt

because there is no number greater than MaxInt, by definition. However, a little cunning rearrangement to do subtraction rather than addition provides the solution:

UNTIL second > MaxInt—first

Now, of course, the real arithmetic and the constant Epsilon are no longer required

```
WHILE symbol <> '.' DO
   BEGIN
      IF symbol = 'e' THEN
         count := succ (count);
      read (symbol)
   END;
   write ('There were', count : 1,);
   writeLn ('''e''s in the sentence.')
```

The difference between the two structures can clearly be seen, however. The action required to set up the terminating condition (the read statement in this example) will often occur twice when a WHILE construct is used, once immediately before entry to the construct and again as the last statement in the body of the WHILE loop.

Although the WHILE loop is the only essential construct in any language, it is sometimes convenient to have a means of repeating something a specified number of times, perhaps over a certain range of values within a scale. PASCAL provides a third construct for creating such 'counter-driven' loops. The BASIC programmer may feel on familiar territory here, but there are a number of important differences between the PASCAL construct and BASIC's FOR loop that should be borne in mind. First, any scalar variable may be used as the loop controller, not just integers. Secondly, and more importantly, the PASCAL FOR . . DO statement is completely secure; like the WHILE loop, it may not be executed at all (if, for instance, the starting value is greater then the final one) and there are severe restrictions placed upon the use of the controlling variable in PASCAL. In particular, it is illegal to change this value anywhere in the body of the loop. Moreover it is an error in PASCAL merely to threaten to change it! We'll see the real benefit of these safety precautions when we deal with procedures and functions, but meanwhile, here is an illegal example:

```
FOR N := 1 TO 10 DO
   IF N = 10 THEN
      N := 1
```

Sheer silliness, of course. Having requested the loop to be performed ten times, the IF statement would reset the value of N back to 1 and create an infinite loop.

Notice that the syntax of the FOR . . DO construct has an assignment statement between the first two delimiters (FOR and TO) which assigns the initial value to the loop control variable, and the final value of the scale is given by the expression enclosed by the reserved words TO and DO. Both these values must, of course, be the same simple scalar type as the controller. Some further examples:

- FOR letter := 'A' TO 'Z' DO { etc }
- FOR month := Jan TO Dec Do { etc }
- FOR N := N TO succ (MaxInt DIV 1000) DO { etc }

The last example assumes that N has been given a suitable value some time previously, and remember that if this were to exceed the specified

FOR Statement:

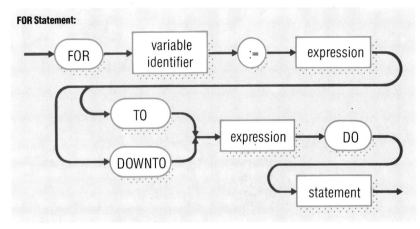

final value, the loop would not be performed at all. For the occasions when we wish to descend a scale of values, the reserved word DOWNTO is used in place of TO. So, for example, NASA might be able to use:

```
FOR CountDown := 10 DOWNTO 0 DO
   WriteLn (Countdown : 32 — 3 * CountDown );

WriteLn ('We have LIFT OFF !')
```

PASCAL maintains rigorous control over the FOR loop, and does not allow any equivalent of BASIC's optional STEP increment or decrement.

Real Ale Program

```
PROGRAM        RealAle   ( output );

TYPE
  beer = ( Mild, Bitter, Special, Warmer );
VAR
    price,
    pints   : real;
    ale     : beer;
BEGIN
  WriteLn ( 'Pints' : 6,
      'Mild' :9, 'Bitter' :8,
       'Special' :8, 'Warmer' :8 );
  WriteLn;
  pints := 0.5; { start at half a pint }

  REPEAT
    IF pints — trunc ( pints ) > 0.4
      THEN { write as ##.# }
        write ( pints : 6 : 1, ' ' )
      ELSE { write as an integer }
        write ( round ( pints ) :4, ' ':3 );

    FOR ale := Mild TO Warmer DO
      BEGIN
        CASE ale OF
         Mild    : price := 65;
         Bitter  : price := 69;
         Special : price := 74;
         Warmer  : price := 79
        END;   { CASE }
          { round and convert to pounds : }
          write ( round ( price * pints )
                      / 100 : 8 : 2 )

      END;
        { now start a new line }
      WriteLn;
      pints := pints + 0.5

  UNTIL pints > 10
END .
```

What's Yours?
The program Real Ale prints a price list of four different types of beer for a range of quantities in half pint increments. Each class of ale is represented by a conceptual constant identifier enumerated in the TYPE definition of beer. The selection of the associated price is naturally made with a CASE statement. Whole pints are printed as integers, padded out with two extra spaces, while the formatting of real amounts suppresses unwanted decimal places

ON THE SET

In addition to PASCAL's familiar data structures, such as arrays and files, the language also includes sets and records. We examine the first of these structured types, as well as summarising the levels of precedence for the PASCAL operators we have examined so far.

We often talk about a computer's character set. But what precisely is meant by a set and how does it differ from an array? The main characteristic of a set is that it is a collection of objects that can be processed as a single entity, rather than each element having to be accessed individually. A practical example would be the set of all people who program in PASCAL, or the letters of the alphabet that are vowels. There is often no particular ordering involved, with the only question of interest being: is this particular object a member of the set or not?

For reasons of efficient implementation, PASCAL places some restrictions on sets. They can only have simple scalar types as their members — not arrays or other structured data — and there will be an (implementation-defined) upper limit on the range allowed for this 'base' type. The syntax is straightforward, for example:

```
TYPE
    Numbers   = SET OF 0 . . 127;
    Alphabet  = SET OF 'A' . . 'Z';
    ColourMix = SET OF ( Red, Green, Blue );
```

The range of possible values of the ordinal base type of the set may be expressed with the same syntax as for subrange types.

Set variables are declared in the VAR declaration part, in exactly the same way as all variables in PASCAL, and may appear in statements literally (i.e: as 'literals') enclosed within square brackets, thus:

```
VAR
    codes : Numbers;
    palette : ColourMix;
BEGIN
    codes := [0 . . 2, 4, 8, 16, 32, 64];
    palette := [Red . . Blue ]; { etc. }
```

This segment would initialise the set codes to contain only the numbers 0 to 2 inclusive and 4, 8 and so on, as listed. Because there is no inherent order in the set itself (as opposed to its base type), we could equally well express this set as [64, 32, 16, 8, 4, 0 . . 2] but notice that the subrange 2 . . 0 (illegal in an actual subrange definition) would merely indicate an empty range. In fact, any set can be initialised to an empty set of its type with the statement: AnySet :=[ ], which gives rise to the only exception to the general rule in PASCAL, namely, the type of any literal is known by inspection. Without at least one member of the set appearing literally, neither we nor the compiler can determine its type. Fortunately, the empty set can only occur in assignments (as in the example) or expressions in which the other identifiers will have already had their types declared. This does mean, however, that the empty set is a subset of every set type, but that's only natural.

SET OPERATORS

One of the most useful operators PASCAL provides for set structures is, like DIV and MOD, a reserved word: IN. It enables us to test for membership of a set, and is a relational operator that takes two operands. The left-hand side must be an expression evaluating to one of the possible members of the set — in other words, a value of the set's base type — and the right-hand side may be a set variable or set literal. The whole expression will give a Boolean result — true if the value is a member of the set and false otherwise.

So: N IN codes and Green IN palette are legal Boolean expressions. The usual test for a character being a digit could be written as:

```
IF (c >= '0' ) AND (c <= '9' ) THEN . . .
```

How much less confusing to test for c's value being a member of the set of characters we're interested in, using:

```
IF c IN ( '0' . . '9' ) THEN . . .
```

Or perhaps, if we are writing a program to play a card game:

```
TYPE
    rank =(deuce, three, four, five, six, seven, eight,
            nine, ten, Jack, Queen, King, Ace );
    CardSet = SET OF rank;
VAR
    card : rank;
    pictures: CardSet;
BEGIN
    pictures :=( Jack . . Ace );
    IF card IN pictures THEN { etc. }
```

Contrast this last example with:

```
IF (card = Jack) OR (card = Queen) OR (card = King)
OR . . .
```

There are also operations defined on sets as a whole in PASCAL. These are set intersection, union and difference. If B is the set of all BASIC programmers and P represents PASCAL people, then the intersection of the two sets is the set of programmers using *both* BASIC and PASCAL. The union of P and B is the set of people who program in either PASCAL or BASIC — that is, the *combination* of the two sets.

Set difference is, as it suggests, the result of removing or subtracting all members of one set from the other. Thus, in PASCAL notation,

Snookered?

The game of snooker is played with 15 red balls (all of which score one point if 'potted'), a white 'cue' ball and the six 'colours' which score the points shown:

yellow	2
green	3
brown	4
blue	5
pink	6
black	7

After each red ball is potted, the player is allowed to try his hand at potting one of the colours. Potted colours are then removed from the pocket and replaced on the table. After the last red and colour combination, all the colours must be potted in ascending order of value.

A 'break' in snooker is a series of legal shots terminated either by the player's failure to pot a ball, by a foul shot or by the end of the game (no more balls). Write a program to calculate the maximum possible 'break', but — and here's the catch — ensuring that the only number appearing in the program is 15. Snookered? The solution will be found on page 262

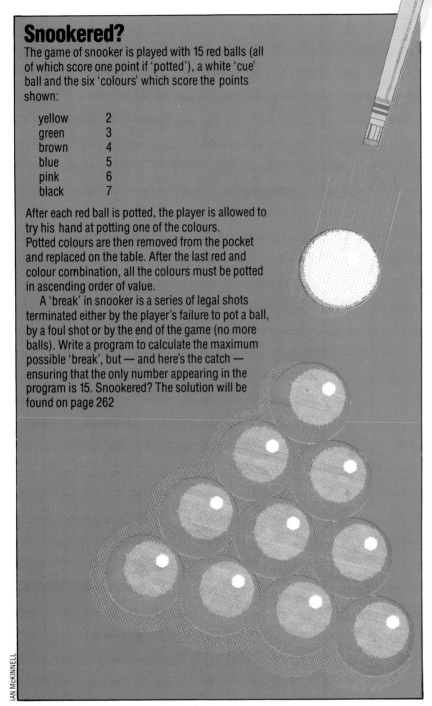

IAN McKINNELL

P — B represents all those who program in PASCAL but not in BASIC. Similarly, the notation used for union is P + B, and for intersection P * B. These operator symbols happen to be the same as the well-known arithmetic operators, but the different class of operations should not be confused. Actually, the reason they appear so naturally in the context of set operations is that they represent the bit testing that is involved here.

Imagine a set of eight elements. The presence of a particular member could be indicated by setting the appropriate bit in an 8-bit pattern (one byte); absence from the set can be set similarly by a zero. Membership tests, then, just require a mask or bit test, a set union becomes an OR operation and intersection will be a simple AND. These operations are invariably available at machine code level, so that the PASCAL compiler is able to provide set data structures and their associated operations very efficiently. The memory overhead is also minimal, and especially when the size of sets can be kept within a computer's word size (on 32-bit and over machines, for example), set operations can be the most efficiently implemented ones in PASCAL.

ORDER OF PRECEDENCE

We can now conveniently summarise all the operators in PASCAL. Those we haven't dealt with explicitly are all familiar from other languages, and PASCAL keeps things extremely simple by only having four levels of operator precedence. Naturally, the 'unary' or 'monadic' operators take precedence over all the others. These are the symbols + and —, which indicate the sign of a number and the Boolean negation operator NOT. The second precedence level has all the 'multiplication' operators (including the division symbols) followed by addition/subtraction and, at the lowest level of precedence, all the relational operators including IN.

Notice that the other two Boolean operators (AND and OR) are treated correctly as multiplying and adding operators, respectively. This faithfully echoes the actual Boolean algebra involved, and means that many relational tests are bracketed to override this precedence. Otherwise, for instance: IF N > 0 AND N < 10 THEN . . will give a compile time error, because the expression 0 AND N (which should be evaluated first) attempts to combine two integer operands with a Boolean operator.

Perhaps this is another habit you've acquired from BASIC? If so, now is the time to start breaking it! Naturally, any operators of the same precedence level are evaluated from left to right, as usual. The symbol used for assignment (:=) has a lower precedence than any of the above operators, as the expression on the right-hand side of an assignment must be fully evaluated before the assignment is made. One word of caution: you can never assume that any part of an expression won't be evaluated, so that: IF (N > 0) AND (K/N < 10) THEN . . . could crash a program if N was zero (creating a division by zero error !).

Operator Precedence

The table below shows the order of precedence of PASCAL operators. The use of round brackets forces an enclosed expression to be evaluated separately, hence overriding the normal order of precedence (shown here) if required

Precedence	Operators	Type
Highest	NOT +−	{unary}
	AND */ DIV MOD	{multiplying}
	OR +−	{adding}
Lowest	< <= <> >= > IN	{relational}

Bingo!!

A Bingo card may best be represented by a set. Although the base elements (integers in the range one to 90) are ordered, the only vital consideration is whether or not a called number is on the card. In PASCAL parlance: 'number IN Card' is either true or false.

The program simulates a game of Bingo by first reading the card numbers from the keyboard and then, as each number is 'called', testing for the set of called numbers being a superset of the card. The expression Card—Called will become the empty set when every member of Card is also in the set Called.

Adding a member to a set that already contains it leaves the set unchanged, as does 'removing' a non-member. Notice that we cannot add a member to a set directly; but by creating a one-element set by enclosing the number within square brackets, we can obtain the union of two sets.

As it stands, the program will allow duplicated card entries, and will accept an illegal number outside the range one to 90, causing a run-time error. As an exercise, can you think of a simple way of adding loop constructs to prevent both these anomalies and to reject numbers that have already been called?

```
PROGRAM          Bingo    ( input, output );

CONST
        Columns = 40;    {  to suit VDU  }
        HalfWay = 25;    {       "       }

TYPE
        Bingo   = SET OF 1 .. 90;

VAR
        count   : 1 .. 15;
        Allowed,
        Called,
        Empty,
        Card    : Bingo;
        number  : integer;
        House   : boolean;

BEGIN

  Empty := [ ];
  Allowed := [ 1 .. 90 ];
  WriteLn ( '*** BINGO ***' : HalfWay );
  WriteLn;
  WriteLn ( 'Enter the 15 card numbers,' );
  WriteLn ( '(each followed by RETURN) :' );
  Card := Empty;

  FOR count := 1 TO 15 DO
    BEGIN
      write ( count : 10, ': ? ' );
      ReadLn ( number );
      Card := Card + [ number ]
    END;

  WriteLn;
  WriteLn ( 'EYES DOWN !' : HalfWay );
  WriteLn;
  WriteLn ( 'Now call each number : ' );
  Called := Empty;

  REPEAT
    write ( '? ' : HalfWay );
    ReadLn ( number );
    Called := Called + [ number ];
    House := Card - Called = Empty

  UNTIL House;

  WriteLn;
  WriteLn ( 'Congratulations !' : HalfWay );
  WriteLn ( 'Your numbers were :' );
  WriteLn;

  FOR number := 1 TO 90 DO
    IF number IN Card THEN
      write ( number : Columns DIV 8 )

END.
```

IAN McKINNELL

RECORD TIME

Continuing our look at PASCAL's varied data structuring methods, we consider further operations on sets and examine another structured type — the 'record'. Records are the most useful way of packaging data of differing data types together.

We have now examined the ways in which sets can be extremely useful to the PASCAL programmer, and are able to be implemented efficiently at machine level because the operations defined on them have direct equivalents in most processors' native instruction sets. They are always constructed by collecting a group of elements that can be any true scalar type (not real). Apart from being able to test for membership with the operator IN, however, all operations on sets are defined on the whole structure. Although there is no selection mechanism for extracting a particular element, we can use the set inclusion operators (<=>=), and check for set equivalence ('equality') with = and <>.

When sets are manipulated by mathematicians, they can not only contain unbounded objects, but may also be considered theoretically infinite (such are the advantages of problem-solving on a piece of paper rather than on physically constrained hardware). Your implementation will place some limit on both the size and range of sets, so don't try to define ambitious types such as:

```
HugeSet = SET OF integers;
```

The lower bound of the set membership must have an ordinal value of zero or above, and the upper bound will be restricted to some absolute value — between 255 and 4,095 on microcomputer implementations. Notice that the empty set (represented literally by []) is a member of all possible sets — whatever their type. This may appear to be a hole in PASCAL's strongly typed armour, but in practice, the type of the empty set can always be deduced from the type of other sets in any expression.

Strict inclusion of true subsets cannot be obtained directly, and the operators < and > are not defined for set structures. This is for implementation reasons — most restrictions in PASCAL make good sense from the point of view of efficiency or sheer logic. Should you wish to test for strict inclusion, a dual test is needed, for example:

```
(A>=B) AND (A<>B)
```

This was not required in the test for House in our Bingo program, on the facing page, as a set of called numbers may either be equivalent ('equal') or, more likely, a superset of the numbers on the card. So, for instance, this Boolean expression could have been expressed as:

```
House := Called>=Card
```

which becomes true when all the members of Card are included in the set of Called numbers. This is

exactly the sort of fundamental property of sets that makes them valuable data structures for problem-solving. For now, probably the most useful application of sets will be for testing subsets of the type char. The following scheme (in PASCAL/ English) would be helpful for programming any interactive application such as a game.

```
Negative := [ 'N', 'n' ];
Affirmative := [ 'Y', 'y' ];

REPEAT
    { Play the game }
    { display the score(s) }
    write ( 'Again ? ' );
    ReadLn ( reply );

    WHILE NOT ( reply IN Affirmative + Negative ) DO
        BEGIN
            Write Ln ( 'Y(es) or N(o)' :Columns );
            write ( 'Another game ?' );
            ReadLn ( reply )
        END

UNTIL reply IN Negative
```

When we wish to access individual elements of a structure, the choice open to us falls between arrays (familiar enough), files and records. The latter have the exceptionally powerful ability to mirror real-life records of data, with mixed 'fields' of any data type — simple or structured.

PASCAL'S USE OF RECORDS

The most common form of data record used in business contains fields for names, addresses, telephone numbers, account codes and so on. The important thing is to be able to handle this data as one lump of information and *also* to be able to access any individual field and process the data appropriately. PASCAL allows such objects to be assigned (and manipulated in other ways) as a whole, yet enables access to any component fields for comparison or processing according to their individual data type. The definition of a mixed record is quite straightforward:

```
TYPE
    room = RECORD
            number   : 1 .. 999;
            wing     : (North, East, South, West );
            occupied : boolean
          END; { room }
VAR
    office : room;
```

Just as the CASE statement was exceptional in using the reserved word END as a delimiter, the definition of a record is the only exception in the declaration part of a block to the rule that BEGINs and ENDs are used in pairs. For this reason it is helpful to comment a record's END with its identifier, as in our example. Any variable of type room will contain three component fields. In this case, each field is of a different scalar type, but they could just as well be the same type — simple or structured. There are no restrictions whatsoever on the types allowed within record fields, so we can have one field that might be an array of files of records containing sets!

Within the delimiting words RECORD and END, the defining syntax is exactly the same as for a VAR declaration. Here, however, we are declaring field identifiers that are an integral part of the record structure. Hence the names number, wing and occupied do not exist outside the 'scope' of the record's identifier. These field names are local identifiers, and they could duplicate the names of variables in the program. They can only be accessed via PASCAL's two selection mechanisms for records: 'dot' notation and the WITH statement.

To select a particular field using dot notation, the whole record's identifier is separated from the following field identifier by a dot ('.').
For example:

    office . number

would refer to the integer subrange field only. We could initialise the contents of the record with statements such as:

    read (office . number);
    'office . wing := East;'
    'office . occupied := people <> [ ]'

and so on. Notice that we sneaked in an empty set with a type that depends on whatever type people is — we haven't actually declared it!

THE WITH STATEMENT
Dot notation can become somewhat cumbersome with cases in which we want to access most or all of a record's fields. An alternative structured statement is available that 'uncovers' the field identifiers. The WITH statement's semantics mean, roughly: 'I want to do something with this record, so I wish to specify only the field names'. The syntax of the WITH statement has exactly the same form as the WHILE loop (see page 256), and the sequence of initialising assignments we have given could be better expressed as:

    WITH office DO
       BEGIN
          number := 123;
          wing := East;
          occupied := true
       END

Throughout the extent of the WITH statement (from the BEGIN to its END in this case), the field identifiers do not have to be qualified with the record's identifier and dot and may be referred to directly, as shown. There is no confusion here

should another program variable be named Number, for example. The local scope always takes precedence. Using dot notation, however, we can communicate values across these scope boundaries. As an example:

    office . number := Number

would assign an external variable's value (Number) to the record field (number). Remember that

PASCAL Set Operations
This is a list of all the set operations available in PASCAL (with corresponding Venn diagrams where appropriate)
1. Union (S1 + S2): This is the superset comprising all the objects in both set S1 and set S2 combined (diagram 1)
2. Difference (S1 — S2): The subset of the members of S1 that do not also belong to S2 (diagram 2)
3. Intersection (S1 * S2): The subset of objects common to both sets (diagram 3)
4. Equivalence (S1 = S2): Where the membership of S1 and S2 is identical (diagram 4)
5. Non-equivalence (S1 <> S2): This is true when every member of S1 is not a member of S2, and vice versa (diagram 5)
6. Inclusion (S1 <= S2): This is true if every member of S1 is also a member of S2
7. Inclusion (S1 >= S2): This is true if every member of S2 is also a member of S1
8. Membership (m IN S1): This is true if the single element set ([m]) is a subset of S1

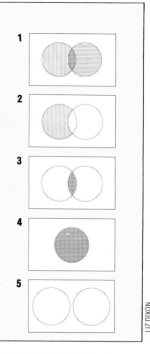

Give Us A Break
Here is our solution to the problem we set to create a program that would calculate the maximum possible break in a snooker game

```
PROGRAM     MaxBreak    ( output );

CONST
     RedBalls  = 15;

TYPE
     snooker   = ( white, red, yellow, green,
                     brown, blue, pink, black );
VAR
     ball   : snooker;
     score  : RedBalls .. MaxInt;
BEGIN
   score := RedBalls * ( ord ( red ) + ord ( black ) );

   FOR ball := yellow TO black DO
      score := score + ord ( ball );

   WriteLn ( 'The maximum break is : ', score :3 )
END.
```

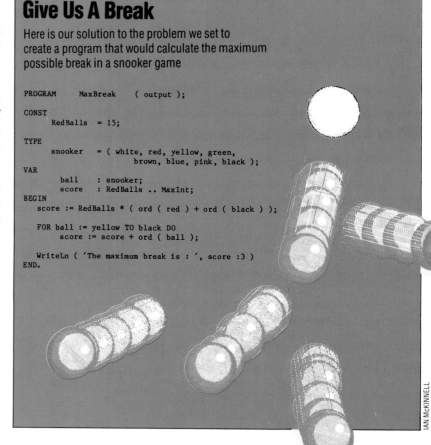

PASCAL is not case-sensitive (it doesn't distinguish between small or capital letters), and the unqualified identifier number would refer to an external variable unless it was within a WITH statement. In any case, it would be essential to use dot notation if we had an assignment between two variables of the same record type, say:

    parcels . wing := reception . wing

Here, the WITH statement could only be used to uncover one of the variable's fields, otherwise there would be a confusing ambiguity, which the compiler would disallow. The best we could do would be:

    WITH parcels DO
        wing := reception . wing

Consequently, both forms of notation have their uses. Which form to use will usually be obvious from the application.

The next area we shall look at is the use of arrays and files in PASCAL, and begin to investigate the full potential of these exceptionally powerful data structuring methods.

Data Protection

We set an exercise with our Bingo program on page 260 for you to add loop constructs to the program to prevent the repetition of a called number and detect an illegal number outside the range one to 90. The best way to protect the Bingo program from erroneous data entry is to add a WHILE construct after both ReadLn statements. The structure will be the same in each case:

    WHILE the number is unacceptable DO
        give a suitable error message
        write another prompt
        read the date again

In the case of the initial card entries, we must ensure that the entered number is not outside the range allowed (one to 90) and also prevent the repetition of a previous entry. Thus:

    WHILE NOT (number IN Allowed) OR (number IN Card) DO
        BEGIN
            WriteLn (number: 20, 'is not valid');
            write ('Re-enter:' :14);
            ReadLn (number)
        END;
        {etc.}

When calling the numbers, the same strategy applies but with the condition for entering the validation loop altered to:

    WHILE NOT (number IN Allowed) OR (number IN Called) DO
        {etc.}

A Long Distance Run

The program Distances reads two lengths expressed in yards, feet and inches from the keyboard. A record type definition is used to allocate a separate field for each value of the differing units of measurement. The program then adds the lengths together, carrying any inches over into the field 'ft' and surplus feet into the 'yds' field by using the DIV and MOD integer operators to give the sum and remainder respectively. The results are assigned to the fields of 'Total' and then printed. Direct assignment of whole records would be straightforward (e.g: Alength := Blength) but any processing or manipulation must be applied to each component field, so that Total :=Alength + Blength is illegal. Notice the use of dot notation and the WITH statement to read the values for Alength and Blength

```
PROGRAM    Distances    ( input, output );
CONST
        MaxByte  = 255;
TYPE
        byte     = 0 .. MaxByte;
        distance = RECORD
                        ins  : 0 .. 11;
                        ft   : 0 .. 2;
                        yds  : byte;
                   END; ( distance )
VAR
        inches,
        feet   : byte;
        Alength,
        Blength,
        Total  : distance;
BEGIN
    WriteLn ( 'Enter lengths as yds ft and ins,' );
    WriteLn ( 'separated by  SPACE  or RETURN.' );
    WriteLn;
    write ( 'First : ' : 15 );
    read ( Alength . yds, Alength . ft, Alength . ins );
    write ( 'Second : ' : 15 );
    WITH Blength DO
        read ( yds, ft, ins );
    inches := Alength . ins + Blength . ins;
    feet := Alength . ft + Blength . ft + inches DIV 12;
    WriteLn;
    WITH Total DO
        BEGIN
            ins := inches MOD 12;
            ft := feet MOD 3;
            yds := Alength . yds + Blength . yds
                   + feet DIV 3;
            WriteLn ( 'The total length is :' );
            WriteLn ( yds : 25, ' yds. ', ft : 1,
                      ' ft. and ', ins : 1, ' ins.')
        END
END
```

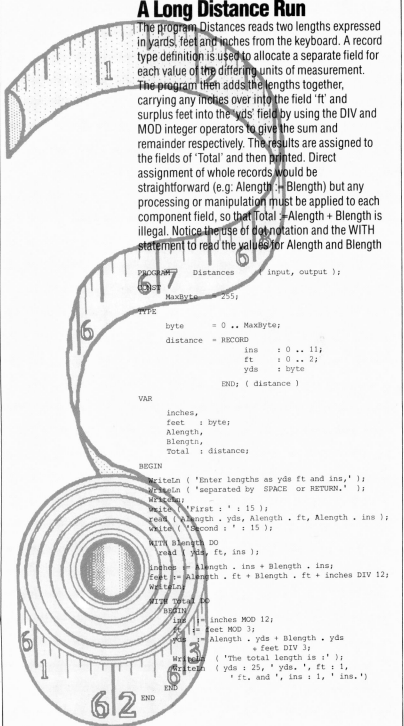

'ZAPPING KLINGONS IN 17 DIMENSIONS'

Because of PASCAL's enormous power and flexibility with regard to its data structures, such as records and sets, it needs to make much less use of arrays than other languages. In this section, we look at the use that PASCAL does make of arrays, including such aspects as packing, indices and the constraints made on dimensions.

In many programming languages, we may find that the array is a very natural means of mapping real-world data such as lists, tables and matrices onto a computer data structure, and an efficient way of providing access to individual elements for processing. However, the main reason for their almost universal use is out of sheer habit. Quite simply, no data structuring method other than the array was available in most of the earlier languages. The earliest high-level language, FORTRAN, only had complex numbers and arrays, and its descendant, BASIC, omitted complex numbers. This is why the FOR .. NEXT loop is the only defined iteration structure.

That was fine in the days when FORTRAN was used only to perform matrix operations on every element of an array, and when BASIC was used only to introduce students to the rigours of programming in FORTRAN. We have already seen some examples of the extra flexibility of control that condition-driven loops (WHILE and REPEAT) bring to PASCAL. Perhaps even more importantly, we're beginning to glimpse some of the tremendous power and ease of expression that some of PASCAL's other data structures, such as sets and records, offer. The dominance of the array as a universal 'data tool' for programming is therefore considerably reduced in PASCAL.

ARRAY FLEXIBILITY IN PASCAL

So although most programmers will feel on familiar ground when dealing with arrays in PASCAL, there are two significant points that should be kept in mind. Because PASCAL enables such a vast choice of data structuring methods, many programming problems may well be solved more effectively in terms of other structures. Secondly, arrays are entirely unconstrained in the structural complexity of their elements, so that much greater flexibility can be achieved in PASCAL.

The definition of an array type reserves storage for a certain fixed size of array, and defines both the base type of its index (subscript) and the type of each component. So, for example:

```
TYPE
    CharCounts = ARRAY [ 'A' .. 'Z' ] OF integer;
```

```
VAR
    list : CharCounts;
```

would reserve storage for 26 integers that would be referenced by specifying the array identifier followed by a bracketed indexing expression. Square brackets are always used with arrays, as they were originally in BASIC (the subsequent usage of round subscript brackets was intended to cater only for some limited character sets that lacked square brackets). To access a particular integer in the list just mentioned, we can write :

```
list [ 'M' ] or list [ pred (symbol) ]
```

In the second example, the expression pred (symbol) must, of course, evaluate to a char value in the subrange 'A' through 'Z'. Any true scalar type may be used to index an array dimension, but not reals or structured types. This disallows nonsensical attempts to refer to list ['second'] or flag [3.75], for example. Using the illustrated type definition, we can initialise every counter element to zero in an array of type CharCounts with:

```
VAR
    letter   : char;
    counter : CharCounts;
BEGIN
    FOR letter :='A' TO 'Z' DO
        counter [letter] := 0
```

and so on. Obviously, counter [1] is illegal for this structure (it's the wrong index type) and counter ['a'] doesn't exist (the subscript is outside the defined subrange), so it's always good practice to define type identifiers for the indexing variables. In any case, we shall find that we invariably need them when defining our own procedures and functions.

If these subranges are in turn defined on values given in a CONST definition, the whole program may be rewritten to deal with different sized structures by the alteration of one line. For example, although there is no pre-declared type string in PASCAL, one way to model them (though not necessarily the best) would be :

```
CONST
    StringLength = 25;
TYPE
    StringSize = 1 .. StringLength;
    string = PACKED ARRAY [ StringSize ] OF char;
```

Notice that the reserved word PACKED can precede any structured type reserved word (SET, ARRAY, RECORD or FILE). By 'packing' data structures, we can gain considerable benefits in memory usage, particularly on computers with long word sizes (16/32 bits or more).

Data Types In Pascal

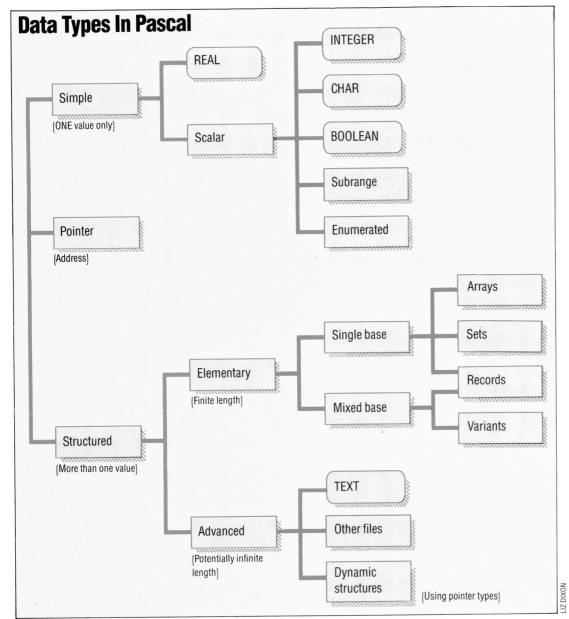

That's Typical!
PASCAL's disciplined data structuring forces the programmer to adopt a more methodical approach to program construction. Only two of the three basic data types, shown here, can be subdivided into other categories. But the range of possible simple and structured data requires strict definitions of all the data used in a program. This extra effort often rewards the PASCAL programmer with more elegant solutions to programming problems than other languages can provide

THE STRING TYPE

The only time you actually need to be aware of packing is when using literal string constants. A string of characters enclosed in quotes is taken to be indexed from one (not zero) and therefore declared implicitly as :

```
PACKED ARRAY [ 1 .. N ] OF char
```

in which N is the number of chars in the string. Consider this program:

```
PROGRAM PackString;
CONST
    Pascal ='Pascal';
TYPE
    string = PACKED ARRAY [ 1 .. 10 ] OF char;
VAR
    S        :string;
BEGIN
S := Pascal;
S := 'Too many characters';
S := 'Pascal '
END.
```

In the body of the program, the first two statements are illegal because of the incompatibility in lengths, but the third is acceptable (four spaces being used as padding characters). If the definition of the type string were not packed, all assignments to literals would be incompatible. In practice, these restrictions are not a great problem, however. Although PASCAL officially only supports the use of the read and write procedures for I/O of whole structures from and to files on backing storage, we can write literal or variable string types like these directly to the VDU. Try writing a program using a similar string declaration to the last example, and incorporate the statement:

```
REPEAT
    write ('String (Q to quit):');
    ReadLn ( S );
    WriteLn ('The string was :''',s,'''')
```

UNTIL S [1] IN ['Q', 'q']

Once you've got this running, test the program and check the following points:

- Are leading spaces or tabs ignored?
- What happens if the line is longer than the string length?
- What does s contain if only one character is entered?
- What if just Return is pressed?
- Can you include suitable code to pad out any insignificant elements with spaces?

MEMORY CONSTRAINTS

As far as PASCAL is concerned, there are no limits at all to either the size or the number of dimensions you may specify for an array. If you can envisage zapping Klingons in a space-time continuum of 17 dimensions, then you can create a suitable data structure in PASCAL! Your computer may be excused for not taking kindly to the following type definitions, however:

```
HugeType = ARRAY [ integer ] OF SET OF char;
    { a request for at least 64K x 128 bytes!}
EvenBigger = ARRAY [ 1 . . 1000 ] OF
    RECORD
      surname,
      forename : string;
      address  : ARRAY [ 1 . . 5 ] OF string;
      present  : SET OF attendances;
      {etc.}
    END: { EvenBigger }
```

The physical memory size will inevitably limit such ambitious programming. Again, this reinforces the value of being able to specify subranges of the scalar types, thus minimising any storage overhead.

In the next few pages we shall see how, when dealing with files, only one or two components of the structure are required to reside in memory at any one time. This can free us from all constraints in memory size, and is yet another example of the powerful tools available to the PASCAL programmer.

Eratosthenes' Sieve

This well-known benchmark program for finding primes is optimised for speed of execution by ignoring even numbers and using an array of 'flags' (8,192 elements for primes up to 16,384). Therefore, at least eight Kbytes of storage is required; perhaps 32K in languages lacking single-byte Booleans and four-byte integers. This is why it won't run unaltered on BBC BASIC. In PASCAL, however, the full set would require only 16,384 bits (2K) and enable us to model Eratosthenes' original algorithm more accurately and clearly:

```
Put all the numbers (1 . . max) into a sieve
Take out the number one (prime by definition)
{ print it if required }

REPEAT
    Take out the lowest number in the sieve
    { print this prime }
    remove all its multiples from the sieve
UNTIL the sieve is empty
```

Such a large set will only be available on mainframes, but we can simulate one by using an array of smaller sets (100 or 1,000 elements, say, depending on your compiler). Each set's array index is found from the integer division of the number, and its membership of the set is represented by N modulo 100 or 1,000. Unless you have a 100-bit computer, however, the speed will probably be somewhat slower than the array version

```
PROGRAM    SieveList  ( output );
{ Find prime numbers by Eratosthenes' algorithm }
CONST
  SetSize        =   100; { ~ implementation }
  PredSetSize    =    99; { SetSize - 1 }
  MaxPrime       = 16383; { for MaxInts = 32767 }
  ListMax        =   163; { MaxPrime DIV SetSize }

TYPE
  PrimeRange     = 1 .. MaxPrime;
  dimension      = 0 .. ListMax;
  SetRange       = 0 .. PredSetSize;
  Siv            = SET OF SetRange;
  Eratosthenes   = ARRAY [ dimension ] OF Siv;
  cardinal       = 0 .. MaxInt;

VAR
  Sieves         : Eratosthenes;
  count,
  multiple       : cardinal;
  index          : dimension;
  N              : PrimeRange;
  number         : 0 .. PredSetSize;

BEGIN
  WriteLn;
  WriteLn ( 'Eratosthenes'' Sieve' : 50 );
  WriteLn ( '===================' : 50 );
  WriteLn;
  WriteLn;

  FOR index := 0 TO ListMax DO
    Sieves [ index ] := [ 0 .. PredSetSize ];
        { put every number in the sieves }

  Sieves [ 0 ] := [ 2 .. PredSetSize ];
{ WriteLn ( 1 ); }{ prime number by definition }
  count := 1;

  FOR N := 2 TO MaxPrime DO
    BEGIN
      index := N DIV SetSize;
      number := N MOD SetSize;

      IF number IN Sieves [ index ] THEN
        BEGIN
          count := succ ( count );
        { WriteLn ( N ); }
          Sieves [ index ] := Sieves [ index ]
                            - [ number ];

          multiple := N + N;

          WHILE multiple <= MaxPrime DO
            BEGIN
              index := multiple DIV SetSize;
              Sieves [ index ] := Sieves [ index ]
                            - [ multiple MOD SetSize ];
              multiple := multiple + N
            END
        END
    END;

  WriteLn;
  WriteLn ( count : 25, ' primes found.' )
END .
```

STRUCTURAL LINGUISTICS

In PASCAL, we can define our own procedures and functions to supplement those already built into the language. This means, however, that we must fully understand the differences between the two in order to structure our programs efficiently. Here, we look at this aspect, as well as the important concepts of 'scope' and 'parameter passing'.

Before completing our survey of data structures in PASCAL, we'll take a look at some mechanisms for structuring programs. This is done by defining our own procedures and functions to supplement those already built into the PASCAL language, such as the procedure write and the sqrt function. But before defining any of our own, let's review why write is a procedure and not a function, and why sqrt is a function and not a procedure. When we say, for example:

```
write ('Hello!')
```

we expect the character string supplied as the single parameter to appear on the standard output file. In other words, write identifies a subprogram that knows how to send data in the form of a character stream to the output device (VDU). But what would the following 'statement' do?

```
sqrt (256)
```

The answer, of course, is that it would generate a compile-time error message — it isn't a legal statement. On the other hand:

```
write (sqrt (256) )
```

would not only be legal, but it should produce something like 1.60000E+01 on the screen. Ask yourself why this is so, and why it does seem so inevitable and obvious — if you can appreciate the reasons, you will not be in any doubt as to the fundamental difference between a procedure and a function.

The identifier write invokes a process that sends data to an output stream and is a procedure that can be called by its name. Another PASCAL procedure is page (F), which is used to start a new page on the text file F. The sqrt identifier, however, must always be supplied with a single numeric 'argument' and it merely returns a result — the real number that is the square root of its argument. So the first distinction between procedures and functions is that there is no such thing as a function statement. Just as writing 16 in isolation means nothing (it's only a value), expressions such as sqrt (X/3) or odd (N) have no meaning on their own. The function identifiers behave rather like variables

that are never initialised, but are computed every time their name is used in a program statement. The single value result that is returned is evaluated from an inspection of the current value (or values) of the argument(s) to the function — that is, the result is a function of the argument(s).

Procedures, on the contrary, do not return a value and thus cannot be used in expressions. This again is not surprising. The statement:

```
N: = WriteLn
```

clearly demonstrates its illegality, just as LET N = PRINT would in BASIC.

Writing large programs in PASCAL is made much easier by having the ability to name our own procedures and functions and control their accessibility and the linkage between them. Just as with the naming of variables, the relative lack of restrictions on identifiers means that we can choose helpful and meaningful names for our own subprograms. Consider the following problem:

```
PROGRAM Incomplete (input, output, datafile);
                    {declarations . .}
BEGIN
   Open (datafile);
   WHILE NOT EoF (datafile) DO
      BEGIN
         read (datafile, item);
         Process (item)
      END
END.
```

Even though we have not yet dealt with file handling, you should have no difficulty in understanding what the program does. In the declaration part of the program, we would declare one procedure to locate a file of data on backing storage and open it for reading (Open), and another to manipulate each item of data appropriately (Process). The program also uses two of PASCAL's predefined identifiers. The procedure read (which we have used thus far to read textual input) can be used as shown to read any data, structured or not, from a file of the appropriate type. The Boolean function EoF (End of File) returns the value true when the last record of the file supplied as its argument has been read. Again, by omitting the file identifier, this defaults to the standard file input. For text files only, the function EoLn (End of Line) returns true when the last character on a line has been read. Let's see how this applies when defining our own subprograms.

In essence, there is little difference between programs, procedures and functions — they are all modules that may have their own local data descriptions and bodies of statements. The only change in the syntax is for the heading. A program heading, as we have seen, consists of the reserved word PROGRAM, a user identifier naming the program and a parameter list identifying the files with which the program will communicate. The heading of a procedure substitutes the reversed word PROCEDURE and extends the 'formal parameter list' to include the type identifiers of each data parameter. So, for example:

```
PROCEDURE Lines (NumLines : integer);
    VAR
        N : integer;
    FOR N := 1 TO NumLines DO
            WriteLn
END;
```

The procedure's END is followed by a semicolon, not a full stop as at the end of a program. NumLines, the formal parameter identifier, is passed the actual value in the calling statement:

```
Lines (5)
```

This admittedly trivial procedure is nonetheless useful if we frequently wish to leave several blank lines (five in this case) for clarity of output, and saves us (and the compiler) from having rather boring sequences of WriteLn statements separated by semicolons. This general purpose procedure will allow you to leave as many blank lines as you need, so that Lines(10) will produce 10 blank lines, Lines(20) gives 20 lines, and so on.

SCOPE

This example is also a good illustration of PASCAL's security. The FOR loop control variable *must* always be declared as a true local variable. We could not have said, for instance:

```
For NumLines := 1 TO NumLines DO . . .
```

A Lot Of Scope

```
PROGRAM Scope;

VAR
    N   : integer;
    X   : real;
PROCEDURE A ( Y : real);

    TYPE
        X = SET OF char;
        {etc.}

PROCEDURE B ( N: integer );
    {etc.}

BEGIN {Main program —
    Scope}

    . . .
    A (succ (N)/ 3);
    B (N);
    A (X)
        {etc.}
END.
```

In the program Scope, outlined here, the regions and scopes of the different variables and procedures are shown in the following table:

Proc/Var	Region	Scope
A	main	A,B,main
B	main	B,main
N (global)	main	A,main
X (real)	main	B,main
X (in proc A)	A	A
N (in proc B)	B	B

Although this would be acceptable in a main program, the loop security cannot be guaranteed if a loop controller is non-local, or 'relatively global'. (For more information on 'local' and 'global' variables, refer to LOGO, page 226.) Have you ever spent hours debugging a BASIC program that contained a statement like:

```
300 FOR N = 1 TO T
400 GOSUB 2000
500 NEXT N
```

only to find that a remote subroutine, perhaps called indirectly and conditionally, used N for some other purpose? PASCAL expressly forbids such uncontrolled behaviour, and helps save wasted development time. Any identifier declared within a block has a defined 'region' that extends throughout that block. However, its 'scope' (that part of the block from within which it is accessible) ony extends from the point of its declaration to the end of that block, and this may be limited further by redefinition. In the previous example, the N referred to within the procedure Lines is, naturally, the locally declared integer, and this declaration temporarily overrides any relatively global one throughout each activation of the procedure.

Referring to the main program outline (Scope) in the example, the region of the global variables N and X is the whole of the program. The scope of X is from its declaration to the end of the program excluding anywhere within procedure A. This is because another X (SET OF char) is defined as a type identifier and its region is the block of A. Similarly, within B, N refers to B's formal parameter, not the global variable.

Although the region of both A and B is the entire program, the scope of B only commences at its defining point, and so while you could use A in procedure B, B is invisible to A. This reinforces PASCAL's trenchant logic: no program can be executed until it has been written! This also explains why the definitions and declarations *must* be in the order CONST, TYPE, VAR, followed by procedure and function definitions ordered according to the structural requirements of the program. Many PASCAL compilers are 'one-pass' (they read the source code only once), and this would not be possible if this logical ordering were not insisted upon.

The extra effort of having to declare data local to any procedure is amply repaid. Modularity is achieved by the passing of all data values as parameters to procedures, and although you may see PASCAL programs that use procedures without any parameter lists, accessing all data globally, this practice should be strictly avoided. In fact, it can be seen as one of PASCAL's weaknesses insofar as it will permit this sort of abuse. Notice that, just as any reference to X within A means the type X, using N within B refers to its local formal parameter and the global integer N is temporarily inaccessible. Apart from the inherent security, this enables a team of programmers to work on a large project without having to worry about identifier clashes.

The call to B passes the value of the global N as an actual parameter, which happens to be called the same name in B but is an entirely separate variable. This implies several important points:

● A local copy of the passed value is made on entry to a block.
● Any change to this 'value parameter' within its block does not affect the actual parameter passed from the calling point.
● The value passed may be any expression of the correct type.

Naturally, any procedure statement must list the actual parameters of the call, and they must match the formal parameter list in the heading in number, position and type. The mechanism for parameter value passing may be envisaged as initialising the formal parameter identifier to whatever value is specified in the calling statement. Thus:

```
Lines (succ(N+gap)DIV 2)
```

implies the following assignment statement upon entry to Lines:

```
NumLines := succ (N+gap) DIV 2
```

Bearing in mind this secure way of passing values, you might like to figure out how we can possibly write a procedure to process some data when it is required to alter that data's values.

From Base To Base

The program BaseValue illustrates the use of procedures with value parameters. Any base from 2 (binary) to 16 (hexadecimal) may be selected, and decimal numbers entered from the keyboard will be displayed in the appropriate notation. For example, 32767 — MaxInt on several small PASCAL compilers — would become 7FFF in hexadecimal, 111111111111111 binary or 77777 in octal.

Try implementing the following modifications:

●   To cope with negative representation, we must convert the number to its two's complement. At machine level, this is done by negating it and adding one. Can you think of an easy way to do this in PASCAL?
●   Maybe you would like to perform conversions the other way round? If so, you could use the program as a model for one to take a number in any base (2 to 16) and to output the result in decimal form. Perhaps you could incorporate this as a procedure in the program above?
A clue: think about the data and linkage

```
PROGRAM        BaseValue   ( input, output );
        { converts decimal numbers to ANY base
          in the range binary to hexadecimal }
CONST
        Columns = 79;  { per screen/printer }

TYPE
        byte    = 0 .. 255;
        cardinal = 0 .. MaxInt;

VAR
        number,
        base    : integer;
        FedUp,
        legal   : boolean;

        {1111111111111111111111111111111}

PROCEDURE   WriteDigit ( digit : byte );
    { value of list [ count ] passed to digit }
  BEGIN
    IF digit IN [ 0 .. 9 ]
      THEN
        write ( digit : 1 )
      ELSE       { represent as A .. F }
        CASE digit OF
          10   : write ( 'A' );
          11   : write ( 'B' );
          12   : write ( 'C' );
          13   : write ( 'D' );
          14   : write ( 'E' );
          15   : write ( 'F' )
        END     { CASE }

  END;  { WriteDigit }
        {1111111111111111111111111111111}

PROCEDURE      Print   ( N       : cardinal;
                         base    : byte );
    CONST { all this data is local to Print }
        MaxDigits = 32;
    TYPE
        bounds     = 1 .. MaxDigits;
    VAR
        list    : ARRAY [ bounds ] OF byte;
        index   : bounds;
        count   : byte;
  BEGIN
    count := 0;

    REPEAT
        count := succ ( count );
        list [ count ] := N MOD base;
        N := N DIV base

    UNTIL N = 0;
              { print starting with MSB : }
    FOR count := count DOWNTO 1 DO
        WriteDigit ( list [ count ] )

  END;  { Print }
        {1111111111111111111111111111111}
BEGIN  { BaseValue - Main program }

  REPEAT
    WriteLn ( 'Choose a number base : ' );
    WriteLn ( '    2 .. 16      ' : Columns );
    WriteLn ( '(any other quits)' : Columns );
    write ( 'Base ? ' );
    read ( base );
    legal := base IN [ 2 .. 16 ];

    IF legal THEN
      BEGIN
        write ( 'Number (0 changes base) ? ' );
        read ( number );
        FedUp := number <= 0;

        WHILE NOT FedUp DO
          BEGIN
            write ( number : Columns DIV 2,
              ' to base ', base : 1, ' is ' );
            Print ( number, base );
            WriteLn;
            write ( 'Number ? ' );
            read ( number );
            FedUp := number <= 0;
          END
      END

  UNTIL NOT legal

END .
```

VALUABLE VARIABLES

PASCAL allows no such thing as a function statement — functions compute values rather than invoke procedures for them. Here, we look at the use of functions within parameters and provide several examples that illustrate PASCAL's strict, and therefore concise, structural integrity.

Just as procedures may be defined and called by name, functions may also be called, but only in expressions — not as statements. Whereas procedure calls invoke the execution of subprograms to perform some process, function calls *compute* a value. The result returned may be of any simple type, real or scalar, or a 'pointer' type (which we have yet to deal with). The only difference in the heading, besides using the reserved word FUNCTION, is that the type identifier of the returned result must be specified. Suppose that PASCAL did not have the predefined function odd — we could easily define our own:

```
FUNCTION Odd (number : integer) : boolean;
   BEGIN
      Odd := number MOD 2 > 0
   END; {Odd}
```

The value is returned in the function identifier, and therefore must be assigned to it in the body of the function, as shown. In this respect, function names are like variables which are never initialised, but their values are computed whenever they appear in an expression. They can only appear on the LHS (left-hand side) of an assignment, so if we were careless (and long-winded) and programmed the assignment as:

```
IF number MOD 2 > 0 THEN
   Odd := true
```

(forgetting the necessary clause ELSE Odd := false), a path through the construct exists leaving the result undefined.

As with the procedure parameters we have considered so far, the value of the actual parameter is passed to the local integer identifier, number, from the 'activation' point. So:

```
WriteLn ( Odd ( sqr ( N DIV 100 ) ) )
```

which would always print False, performs four operations :
1. the expression N DIV 100 is calculated
2. this temporary integer value is passed to sqr as an actual value parameter
3. its square is returned and passed to Odd
4. the Boolean result is now evaluated and passed

to the WriteLn procedure as another value parameter

If N had the value 17 when the statement above was executed, what would its value be afterwards? This may seem like a ridiculous question, of course. There is no possible reason for N's value to be changed during evaluation of any function involving N as a parameter. The results of all functions should merely depend on the 'state of the world' as it exists. That is, the returned value is a 'function' (sic) of the value(s) of their 'arguments' or parameters. PASCAL's mechanism for passing only the value of variables ensures that even if the parameters are changed locally by a function or procedure, and because they are in fact local copies, the actual parameters will not be altered at the activation point.

GLOBAL DATA VS PARAMETERS

For these same reasons, although PASCAL does not forbid it, data should not be accessed globally. All data linkage between procedure and function calls should be controlled by parameter lists — even though the data is within the subprogram's scope. The only exception to this general rule is for the access of global constants. Because of their very nature, no harm can befall them in PASCAL, as it is impossible to alter their values. If a constant value were passed as a parameter, however, it would become a local variable and therefore no longer secure.

```
FUNCTION Lower (character :char)           :char;
      {returns the lower case of any upper case
argument}
      CONST
         offset = 32; { ASCII ord ('a') — ord ('A')}
      BEGIN
      IF character IN [ 'A' . . 'Z' ]
         THEN
            Lower := chr ( ord (character ) + offset )
         ELSE
            Lower := character
   END; { Lower }
```

When we are defining procedures, it is sometimes essential that they *should* alter the values of their parameters — otherwise they would not perform the task for which they were designed. An obvious example is PASCAL's own read procedure. It would not be very helpful if read (N) merely gave a value to an integer that was local to read and the value of N were unchanged. In such cases, we need to pass the address of a variable parameter (rather than its value) in order that the procedure may refer directly to it rather than a local copy. This mechanism is called 'passing by address' or 'by reference', and should normally be used only with procedures, not functions.

Passing of variable parameters is achieved simply by including the reserved word VAR before any item (or items) in the procedure's parameter list. The syntax of a parameter list can be seen to be identical to the VAR declaration of a block; but instead of VAR appearing once as a delimiter, it only appears before an item that needs to be VARied by a procedure. For instance:

```
PROCEDURE Process (VAR counter: CountList);
```

APPLICATION DEVELOPMENT

Let's illustrate this powerful technique by developing a program to read some names from the keyboard and, associated with each name, an amount of money that each person owes us. For simplicity, we'll just use one string per name and express the debts as integer amounts in pounds sterling. Once the program is tested, we could add further details such as addresses, telephone numbers and so on. We would like to print out the list of names either in ascending alphabetical order or possibly in order of largest amounts owing. The natural data structure will be a list of records containing fields of the appropriate type that can easily be added to later. We can handle each record as a single piece of data, but use any of the fields we choose as a 'key' for sorting. (For more information on 'keys' see page 192.) First, let's design the full data representation:

```
CONST
    StringLength = 20;
    ListLength   = 50;
TYPE
    Cardinal   = 0 .. MaxInt;
    StringSize = 1 .. StringLength;
    string     = PACKED ARRAY [ StringSize ]
                        OF char;
    data       = RECORD
                            name : string;
{other fields to suit}      debt : Cardinal;
                        END;{data}
    bounds     =1 .. ListLength;
    RecordList = ARRAY [ bounds ] OF data;
```

This allows for fifty names and assumes (for now) that no name will exceed twenty characters, but by using definitions we can easily alter this.

We have expressed all the subranges and structures in a TYPE definition part for several reasons:

1. security — an index of type bounds can never exceed the defined limits of the array, for example
2. tracing bugs — should such a 'range error' occur during testing, the error message will help locate the trouble
3. convenience and efficiency — local variables can have existing types, avoiding duplication and saving memory
4. necessity — PASCAL insists that parameter type 'denoters' must be identifiers, not 'literals' (0 .. 255, for example)

Next, we have to think about a few essential variables and an algorithm, all of which will be discussed in the next part of the series. In the meantime, try to develop your own 'informal algorithm' for the program and make a list of any procedures that you feel may be necessary.

Positive Advantage

The program CardReader handles positive numbers in a fully 'bomb-proof' way by reading the data as characters. Conversion to the equivalent numeric value is performed simply by subtracting the original value of the digit character from that of the digit '0'. This will work for all character sets, as the characters '0' ... '9' are defined to be contiguous. Notice that the program has only two global variables (at 'level 0').

The data for processing the numbers and the function Value which performs the mapping is used only by ReadCard, and therefore all this is declared and defined within this procedure.

There is only one bug in the program as it stands — if a value greater than the cardinality of the compiler's integers (MaxInt) is entered, the assignment statement in the WHILE loop will crash.

What about writing another procedure ReadInt to cope with negative numbers?

```
PROGRAM         CardReader    ( input, output );

TYPE
        cardinal        = 0 .. MaxInt;

VAR
        PosNum  : cardinal;
        okay    : boolean;

    {1111111111111111111111111111111}

PROCEDURE   ReadCard ( VAR   N   : cardinal;
                       VAR   OK  : boolean );
    CONST
        space   = ' ';
    TYPE
        single  = 0 .. 9;
    VAR
        symbol  : char;
        digits  : SET OF char;
            {22222222222222222222222}
            { level 2 }
    FUNCTION Value ( digit   : char )   : single;
        { returns the numeric value of
          a digit on any character set }
        BEGIN
        Value := ord ( digit ) - ord ( '0' )
        END;    { Value }
            {22222222222222222222222}
            { back to level 1 }
    BEGIN { ReadCard }

        REPEAT
        read ( symbol )

        UNTIL symbol > space;

        digits := [ '0' .. '9' ];

        OK := symbol IN digits;

        IF OK THEN
        BEGIN
            N := 0;

            WHILE symbol IN digits  DO
            BEGIN { compute to base 10 }
                N := 10 * N + Value ( symbol );
                read ( symbol )
            END { any delimiting char or 'EoLn' }
        END     { after the number is discarded }

    END; { ReadCard }
    {1111111111111111111111111111111}
BEGIN   { CardReader - Level 0 Main program }

    page ( output );
    WriteLn;
    WriteLn ( '  This program reads positive' );
    WriteLn ( 'integers (in the range 0 .. ',
                    MaxInt : 1, ')' );
    WriteLn ( ' Termination of the program is' );
    WriteLn ( 'controlled by error detection.' );
    WriteLn;
    write ( 'Enter a number : ' );
    ReadCard ( PosNum, okay );

    WHILE okay DO
        BEGIN
            WriteLn;
            write ( 'The number entered was : ' );
            WriteLn ( PosNum : 1 );
            write ( 'Number ? ' );
            ReadCard ( PosNum, okay )
        END;

    WriteLn ( '--- ERROR DETECTED ---' : 40 )

END .
```

DYNAMIC STRUCTURES

As we continue to create a 'database', we move from the use of functions within parameters to the development of an 'informal' algorithm. And since the heart of any database is the organisation of its files, we present several programs illustrating PASCAL's insistence on precise programming techniques when dealing with files.

We can now continue the development of our 'database' by thinking about a few essential variables and an 'informal' algorithm.

```
VAR
    list  : RecordList;
    size : Cardinal;
BEGIN
    size := 0; { active size of the list }
    { read the data into the list, updating size }
    { sort size items into the correct order }
    {print size items of the list }
END.
```

To translate this informal algorithm into something more tangible, we need to express the three main stages of processing as calls to procedures (with appropriate names) and to list any known data that each will require in the form of a parameter list. When this simple step is done, we can then write all the procedure blocks as a skeleton. For example, the last statement in the program will become:

```
Print (list, size)
```

The procedure will have all the information it needs if we pass it the list of data values and the number of elements, so the heading will not need any VARs in this case:

```
PROCEDURE Print (items : RecordList;
                 high :bounds);
```

We could go on to code the procedure in full, but it is best to leave it as a BEGIN . . . END 'stub' for now and deal with the other 'level 1' procedures. We must choose a name for each one, decide which data items need to be passed as parameters to which procedures, and determine whether any of these items need to be passed as 'VAR' (address) parameters.

All the data structuring methods we have discussed so far have been fixed in size. This is specified in the TYPE definitions and therefore is known at compile time. PASCAL provides advanced data structures which can vary their size (and even their type within certain constraints) during execution of a program. The size of an advanced structure is only limited by the physical memory or backing storage available, and the most familiar advanced structure is the sequential file.

Like an array, each element of a file may be of any type, simple or structured, with the exception that you can't have a file of files. Using our previous record type definition, we could add the following declarations:

```
TYPE
        FileType = FILE OF data;
VAR
        DataFile :FileType;
```

which would enable us to create and process a file containing an infinite number of components, each one of which was a record of a name, debt and any other fields we wish. Just as we say read (symbol), meaning read a single char from the file input, we can say: read (DataFile, item) or, write (DataFile, item) and handle a whole record structure as one data object. If these files are required only during the execution of the program, the only other requirement is to open them for reading from or writing to with the predefined procedures reset and rewrite, respectively.

Should you wish to make them permanent, which is more likely, then the file identifiers must be listed in the program header parameter list. In this case, for instance:

```
PROGRAM DataHandler (input, output, DataFile );
```

Every time we use read or write statements, we call PASCAL's predefined file I/O procedures. The only two files we know about so far, in fact, are the standard I/O devices on our computer. The file input is normally a keyboard and output will invariably be a VDU screen on microcomputer systems. By pretending that these devices are files, the handling of all I/O becomes extremely consistent in PASCAL. Remember that when we say write (N), omitting any file name, the value of N is printed in character form on the file output. Leaving a file name out in read or ReadLn statements defaults to the file input. Both these files are text files — that is to say, each 'record' of the file is a single char value.

TEXT FILES

Unlike other files, however, text files may have (as well as an end of file marker) special end of line markers embedded anywhere within them. These markers will vary with different operating systems, and may consist of a single control character, two characters (CR and LF for example) or possibly no characters at all, the length of each line being

Reading From A File

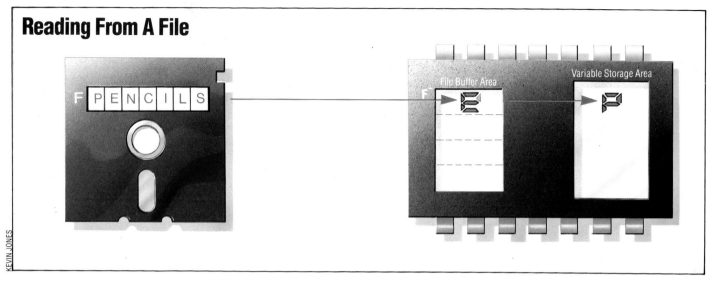

stored instead.

In order to preserve portability, PASCAL provides the function EoLn (F) and the two predefined procedures ReadLn (F) and WriteLn (F) — all of which can only be used with files of type text. The EoF (F) function can, of course, be used with any file type. As the end of line marker may or may not be a single char, reading a char value when EoLn is true will return a Space character. Consequently, we should normally check with EoLn beforehand. As both input and output exist before and after any program is executed, they are permanently open, and do not need to be explicitly located or created.

With files other than input and output we must assign them to an external system name and then either open them for reading with a call to the reset procedure — i.e. reset (SomeFile)—or create a directory entry preparatory to writing to them by rewrite (AnotherFile). A general scheme for processing a text file is thus simply:

```
{ open the file}

WHILE { not reached the end of the source file} DO
    WHILE {not at the end of a line} DO
        { read a character }
        { process the character }
    { skip the end of line }
```

PUT AND GET

The procedures read and write are in fact implemented using file buffers and the I/O primitives put (for output) and get (for input from files). When a file is rewritten, no information is placed in the buffer until a write is performed. This actually consists of the two operations:

```
F^ := data;
put ( F )
```

Similarly, the statement read (F, data) can also be expressed:

```
data := F^ ;
get ( F )
```

Thus the I/O statements in our Copy procedure:

```
read ( source, character );
write ( destination, character )
```

could equally well have been coded as:

```
destination^ := source^ ;
put (destination );
get ( source )
```

We would then not require the local char variable, character. A better understanding of the operation of ReadLn (F) may be obtained, perhaps, if we express it in terms of these primitives:

```
WHILE NOT EoLn ( F ) DO
    get ( F );{ throw away the rest of the line, if any }

get ( F ) { . . and skip the EoLn character(s) }
```

Thus after a ReadLn the file buffer will always contain the first item on the next line to be read. This could be a space if EoLn (F) is true or be undefined if EoF (F) is true. It is obviously illegal to attempt to read from a file when EoF is true, but it is also an error to perform any operation, including testing the file buffer. This means you need to be careful when dealing with files other than input and output. But by the same token, having to be aware of potential error conditions such as these will encourage the writing of extremely robust software.

Now that we know how to 'look ahead' at an incoming data stream, we can formulate the SkipBlanks procedure that we postulated earlier on.

```
PROCEDURE SkipBlanks ( VAR F : text );
    CONST
        space = ' ';
    VAR
        done : boolean;
    BEGIN
        done := EoF ( F );

        IF NOT done THEN
            done := input^ > space;

        WHILE NOT done DO
            BEGIN
```

In A File's Shadow

The process of opening a file F in PASCAL sets up an associated buffer area, F^, into which the first character from the file is read. When a read is performed, the character in the buffer area is assigned to a variable and the next character from the file is transferred to the buffer area. If the first few characters of F are PENCILS, then, on opening the file, P will be read into F^. Following the first read operation, P will be assigned to a PASCAL variable, and be replaced by E in the buffer, F^

```
        get ( F );
        done := EoF ( F );

        IF NOT done THEN
            done := F^ > space
        END

    END; { SkipBlanks }
```

Notice that this will skip all white space on a text file, including end of line characters. If we just wish to skip space on any one line, we can alter the conditional assignment to:

```
    done := EoLn ( F ) OR ( F^ > space)
```

Should we subsequently wish to skip all white space:

```
    REPEAT
        SkipBlanks ( F );

        IF NOT EoF ( F ) THEN
            TextFound := NOT EoLn ( F )

    UNTIL TextFound OR EoF ( F )
```

With this last modification it becomes a simple matter to write interactive programs checking for null inputs. For instance:

```
    REPEAT
        write ('Enter data :');
        SkipBlanks ( input )

    UNTIL NOT EoLn ( input )
```

This will fail if you happen to enter the control character used by the system to indicate the end of file, but we could always use the previous scheme if we wish to make our program absolutely safe.

The procedure assign has come to be regarded as a 'standard extension' and may well be officially adopted soon, along with open and seek for random access files. Other essential extensions in common use are:

```
    FUNCTION Fstat ( FileName )
```

which returns a boolean result — true if a file already exists — and a

```
    PROCEDURE Rename ( OldName, NewName)
```

facility.

Pascal Flavours

As far as PASCAL is concerned, there is no restriction on how many files you can have open at any one time. However, because files require using the computer's operating system, we find one area in which there are divergences from its strict rules. For example, some versions of the language, such as Hisoft PASCAL, do not support files.

The operating system file naming conventions may therefore pose a problem. Many mainframe PASCALs will take the first 10 or so characters of any file identifier and connect it with a file of that name, so our permanent file example would create one called DATAFILE. On many systems, the naming conventions are such that this is not possible. Some examples would be: A CP/M-FIL.DAT, #4:APPLEFOR.MAT and O:P.BBCFILE. The 'standard extension' for connecting a PASCAL file identifier is the assign procedure, used before resetting or rewriting:

```
    assign ( FileIdentifier, NameString )
```

So for our present purposes, assign (DataFile, D:OurFile.dat) would suffice

CopyText Program

PASCAL provides the identifier 'text' for the most common type of file, and this is used when we declare any text file variables in the program header parameter list. Here, we provide a text file copying facility. In order to make the program the most generally useful, we have formulated the whole of the copying process as a separate procedure called Copy, which can process any two text files.

Remember that non-standard compilers will require you to use reset (F1, 'Source') and so on in the main program. Notice that both files are passed as VAR parameters to the Copy procedure. This is because not only is the destination file updated, but the source file will also be read and so the status of the file will change. For this reason, file variables are always passed by address, never by value. Apart from any other consideration, a value parameter implies a local copy — a tall order with files that are always potentially bigger than the available memory! Passing of large structures such as arrays of records may also be made an exception for reasons of memory conservation

```
PROGRAM   CopyText ( F1, F2 );

VAR
     F1,
     F2    : text;

{11111111111111111111111111111111}

PROCEDURE  Copy ( VAR  source,
                       destination : text );
    VAR
       character    : char;
    BEGIN
       WHILE NOT EoF ( source ) DO
         BEGIN { copy a line : }
            WHILE NOT EoLn ( source ) DO
              BEGIN
                 read ( source, character );
                 write ( destination, character )
              END;
                 { now copy the end of line : }
            ReadLn ( source );
            WriteLn ( destination )
         END

    END;  { Copy }
{11111111111111111111111111111111}

BEGIN    { CopyText - Main program }

   assign ( F1, 'Source' );
   reset ( F1 );    { locate and open for reading }
   assign ( F2, 'Destination' );
   rewrite ( F2 );    { create it }
   Copy ( F1, F2 )

END .
```

DYNAMIC DUO

In this part we break away from the limitations thus far imposed on our files by implementing dynamic allocation. We look at concepts such as de-allocation, pointers, heaps and linked structures, which provide us with the freedom necessary to process files of unspecified size.

PASCAL provides two standard procedures (new and dispose) and a special data type, which together offer extraordinary power and flexibility in the 'dynamic allocation' and de-allocation of memory. A 'pointer' type is simply a variable which, instead of containing a data value such as an integer, is a 'pointer to' an integer or any other data object, structured or otherwise. The notation used is similar to that when we denote a file look-ahead buffer (which effectively points to the next record on the file, though in a totally different way). A pointer type is defined by preceding the identifier (of the data type we wish to point to) with an up-arrow:

```
TYPE
    LongArray  = ARRAY  1 . . 100  OF real;
    indirect   = ↑LongArray;
```

The same alternative symbol ('@') is supported by all ISO ̠PASCAL compilers. The type definition reserves a single memory location that will be used to hold the address of a large array only when it should be created with the procedure new. In the meantime, the pointer's value is undefined, just as any other variable would be, so that:

```
VAR
    address  : indirect;
    number   : integer;
```

would reserve space for one machine address (16 bits on an eight-bit micro) and one integer, with neither being initialised to any particular value.

Just as we might want to initialise the integer to zero before use, the pointer may be specifically assigned the special value NIL. This is a reserved word in PASCAL, merely signifying that the pointer doesn't point to anywhere useful, and is the equivalent of the numeric value zero (signifying the absence of any actual number). The two variables in the example could therefore be assigned thus:

```
    address := NIL
    number :=0;
```

As NIL is a constant value belonging to a generic type, it would perhaps be preferable to define it as an identifier in a language. Wirth obviously changed his mind on this aspect because in MODULA-2 the same word is in fact a predefined identifier, not a reserved word. In order to demonstrate the use of new and dispose we'll just use integers for simplicity.

When a pointer variable is needed to point to a new item, we call the PASCAL procedure new, which allocates space for the item and puts its address

into the pointer. The data item is then referred to by 'de-referencing' the pointer, p, with the notation p↑. Notice that the up-arrow now follows the pointer identifier, as with file – buffer notation, and may be thought of as 'the item that p is pointing to'. Needless to say, it is an error to de-reference a pointer that is undefined or one that points nowhere.

DYNAMIC DE-ALLOCATION

When we have finished with any data created by newing pointers, PASCAL's dispose procedure may be called. This is the opposite of new, in that the memory is returned to the dynamic pool and the pointer value becomes undefined. The program TwoPlusTwo illustrates these points:

```
PROGRAM TwoPlusTwo (output);

TYPE
    pointer   = ↑ integer;

VAR
    p1,
    p2        : pointer;
    answer    : integer;
BEGIN
    new (p1);
    p1 ↑ :=2;
    new (p2);
    p2 ↑ := p1 ↑;
    answer := p1 ↑ + p2 ↑;
    WriteLn (p1 ↑, '+', p2 ↑, '=', answer );
    dispose (p1);
    dispose (p2);
END.
```

This extremely peculiar method of adding two and two illustrates two important points:

● Dynamic variables are anonymous — there is no variable identifier (like N) that holds the value 2 anywhere in the program; these items are referred to indirectly.

● After the second dispose the only memory used is the single integer (answer); all the dynamic data no longer exists.

If you have followed our Assembly language series, you will have already appreciated that the indirection implicit in the use of pointers is analogous to indirect addressing at machine level. There are, however, big differences in the use of indirection in such a high-level language as PASCAL. First, we never know (or need to know) what the actual addresses are. The only 'absolute address' available to the PASCAL programmer is NIL.

Pointer Symbols

——————?

An undefined pointer (after a declaration, before an assignment or after dispose)

A pointer pointing 'nowhere' (after an assignment to NIL)

A record node with one data field and one pointer

Linked Lists

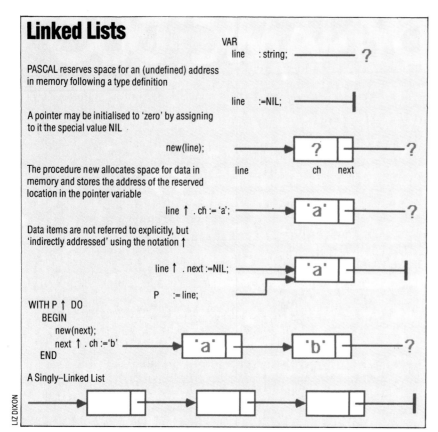

PASCAL reserves space for an (undefined) address in memory following a type definition

```
VAR
    line  : string; ────────── ?
```

A pointer may be initialised to 'zero' by assigning to it the special value NIL

```
    line  :=NIL; ──────────┤
```

The procedure new allocates space for data in memory and stores the address of the reserved location in the pointer variable

```
    new(line);
         line    ch  next
```

Data items are not referred to explicitly, but 'indirectly addressed' using the notation ↑

```
    line ↑ . ch := 'a';
```

```
    line ↑ . next :=NIL;

    P  := line;
```

```
WITH P ↑ DO
   BEGIN
      new(next);
      next ↑ . ch :='b'
   END
```

A Singly–Linked List

LIZ DIXON

In Succession

PASCAL offers the programmer the possibility of implementing 'linked lists' — powerful data structures in which each item points to the next item on the list. Lists may be singly-linked (between successive items), doubly-linked (i.e. each element has pointers to both the next and last item in the list), or circular (where the last item in a singly-linked list points back to the first item in the list)

Also, we are free to use, reclaim and subsequently re-use any of the memory available without the need to organise 'garbage collection' ourselves. The memory management is taken care of by PASCAL, and the only information we may require is how much memory is left. This is obtained by the non-standard function MemAvail or, in some implementations such as Acorn ISO PASCAL, the function Free. This returns the number of bytes remaining in memory.

Another useful extension is the function SizeOf (TypeIdentifier) which returns the size in bytes of any particular type. The user RAM is divided into two internal structures — the stack and the 'heap'.

The stack is used for procedure and function calls, storing their return addresses, local data and returned values. All dynamic data is allocated on the heap. This operates in a similar way to the stack

except that it is not a LIFO (meaning Last In First Out) data structure and the heap starts at the opposite end of user memory, growing towards the stack. With over-ambitious use of new and/or recursion, a 'stack-heap collision' could occur, but this can be avoided with:

```
IF SizeOf (thing) > PerCent * MemAvail THEN . .
```

where thing is the type identifier of the data about to be created and PerCent is a value in the region of 0.7, allowing 30 per cent of the memory for the stack and 70 per cent for the heap. If, as is usually the case, MemAvail/Free operates as a 'high water mark', an additional 'garbage count' of disposed items may be maintained.

LINKED STRUCTURES

The real power of pointers is realised when we create linked structures such as trees, singly- or doubly-linked lists, circular structures and so on. If we consider the problem of character strings, we can, and often do, use an array of some fixed size, say 80 characters. If we have an array of strings to store a document, for instance, each blank line will still take up 80 bytes of storage. Equally, we can't represent lines longer than 80 characters — the whole data structure is simply too rigid.

A PASCAL compiler has to distinguish between identifiers of any length. So, for example, how can we accurately model this real-world characteristic of varying size? The natural structure to use would be a record containing two fields : a field for each data item (chars in this case) and a second pointer field which points to the next record, if any, in the list.

```
TYPE
    string    =↑character;
    character =RECORD
                   ch   : char;
                   next  : string
                   END;
VAR
    line      : string;
BEGIN
    line := NIL;
         etc.
```

An empty string is represented simply by assigning the value NIL to the string. Any other sequence of characters will require a new record to contain each char and another pointer to point to the next record. The last record will have its next field initialised to NIL so that the end of the string may be detected. A procedure to print the string would then be:

```
WHILE line < >NIL DO
   BEGIN
      write (line ↑. ch);
      line := line ↑. next
   END
```

Notice that the data structure is a recursive one as it is defined in terms of itself. The pointer field cannot be given a type that has been fully defined, so a 'forward' reference is allowed.

The Circle Line

This program allows you to insert records containing mixed data into a dynamically allocated circular list. Data is placed in order of a key alphabetic field (Name), and therefore sorting algorithms are unnecessary

Circular List Program

```
PROGRAM   CircList ( input, output );
(
──
──  Intent : TO insert records containing
──  mixed data into a dynamically allocated
──  circular list. Data is placed IN order
──  OF a key alphabetic field (Name) thus
──  sorting algorithms are unnecessary.
                                              )

CONST
      StringLength  =  25;
      space         = ' ';

TYPE
      Cardinal      = 0 .. MaxInt;
      StringSize    = 1 .. StringLength;
      string        = PACKED ARRAY [ StringSize ]
                               OF char;
      thing         = RECORD
                          Name  : string;
                          ( . . other fields )
                          debt  : Cardinal
                          END; ( thing )

      pointer       = ↑ node;
```

```pascal
          node           = RECORD
                            item    : thing;
                            next    : pointer
                          END;  { node }
      VAR

          list           : pointer;

      {1111111111111111111111111111111111111111111}
      PROCEDURE  ReadThings   ( head : pointer );

          VAR

              data    : thing;
              OK      : boolean;

          {22222222222222222222222222222222}
          PROCEDURE  SkipBlanks ( VAR  F : text );
              { ignore leading white space }
              VAR
                  done    : boolean;
              BEGIN
                done := EoF ( F );

                WHILE NOT done DO
                  BEGIN
                    done := ( F↑ = space ) OR EoLn ( F );

                    IF NOT done THEN
                      BEGIN
                        get ( F );
                        done := EoF ( F )
                      END
                  END
              END;  { SkipBlanks }
          {22222222222222222222222222222222222}
          PROCEDURE  ReadCard   ( VAR F : text;
                                  VAR N : Cardinal;
                                  VAR OK : boolean );
              { collect a non-negative number }
              TYPE
                  single  = 0 .. 9;
              VAR
                  digits : SET OF char;
                  done   : boolean;

              {333333333333333333333333}

              FUNCTION  Value ( digit    : char )      : single;
                  { convert char TO numeric value }
                  BEGIN
                    Value := ord ( digit ) - ord ( '0' )
                  END;    { Value }
              {33333333333333333333333333}
              FUNCTION  Legal ( N      : Cardinal;
                                digit  : char )        : boolean;
                  { are we about TO overflow MaxInt ? }
                  BEGIN
                    IF N = MaxInt DIV 10
                      THEN
                        Legal := Value ( digit ) <= MaxInt MOD 10
                      ELSE
                        Legal := N < MaxInt DIV 10
                  END;    { Legal }
                  {33333333333333222222222222222}
              BEGIN  { ReadCard }

                digits := [ '0' .. '9' ];
                OK := NOT EoF ( F );

                IF OK THEN  { found a digit ? }
                  OK := F↑ IN digits;

                N := 0;
                done := NOT OK;

                WHILE OK AND NOT done DO
                  BEGIN  { build N TO base 10 : }
                    N := 10 * N + Value ( F↑ );
                    get ( F );
                    done := EoF ( F );

                    IF NOT done THEN
                      done := NOT ( F↑ IN digits );

                    IF NOT done THEN
                      OK := Legal ( N, F↑ )
                  END;

                IF NOT EoF ( F ) THEN
                  ReadLn ( F )

              END;    { ReadCard }
              {222222222222222222222222222222222222}
          PROCEDURE  ReadLine ( VAR  S  : string );
              { read a line OF chars from the keyboard }
              VAR

                  index  : 0 .. StringLength;
                  symbol : char;
              BEGIN
                SkipBlanks ( input );
                index := 0;

                WHILE NOT EoLn AND ( index < StringLength ) DO
                  BEGIN  { put a char into the string }
                    index := succ ( index );
                    read ( symbol );
                    S [ index ] := symbol
                  END;

                IF index < StringLength
                  THEN  { pad WITH NULs }
                    FOR index := index + 1 TO StringLength DO
                      S [ index ] := chr ( 0 )
                  ELSE
                    IF NOT EoLn THEN  { too many chars }
                      WriteLn ( 'WARNING - input truncated' );

                ReadLn

              END;  { ReadLine }
          {22222222222222222222222222222222222}
          PROCEDURE  Insert  ( list    : pointer;
                               data    : thing );
              VAR
                  scout,
                  link    : pointer;
                  alpha   : string;
              BEGIN  { put data into the head node : }
                list ↑ . item := data;
                scout := list;
                alpha := scout ↑ . next . item . Name;

                WHILE data . Name < alpha DO
                  BEGIN  { walk round the list }
                    scout := scout ↑ . next;
                    alpha := scout ↑ . next ↑ . item . Name
                  END;
                    { no check FOR duplicates }
                new ( link );           { create another node }
                link ↑ . item := data;  { insert the data, }
                link ↑ . next := scout ↑ . next;  { & link }
                scout ↑ . next := link         { into the list }

              END;   { Insert }
              {22222222222222222211111111111111111}

      BEGIN   { ReadThings }

        write ( 'Name ? ' );
        ReadLine ( data . Name );
            { stop on a null entry : }
        WHILE data . Name [ 1 ] <> chr ( 0 ) DO
          BEGIN
            REPEAT
              REPEAT
                write ( 'Amount owing ? ' : 20 ) ;

                IF EoLn ( input ) THEN
                  ReadLn ( input );

                SkipBlanks ( input )

              UNTIL NOT EoLn ( input );

              ReadCard ( input, data . debt. OK );

              IF NOT OK THEN  { no digits }
                WriteLn ( '*** ERROR - ' : 20,
                          'please re-enter ***' )

            UNTIL OK;

            Insert ( head, data );
            WriteLn ( '(RETURN when done)' : 40 );
            write ( 'Name ? ' );
            ReadLine ( data . Name )
          END

      END;   { ReadThings }
      {111111111111111111111111111111111111111111}
      PROCEDURE Display ( list  : pointer );

          VAR
              print   : pointer;
      BEGIN  { first skip the dummy head node : }
        print := list ↑ . next;
        page ( output );
        WriteLn ( 'Ordered list:' );
        WriteLn;
            { any (more) data TO print ? }
        WHILE NOT ( print = list ) DO
          BEGIN
            WITH print ↑ . item DO
              WriteLn ( debt : 8, Name : 30 );

            WriteLn;
            print := print ↑ . next
          END

      END;   { Display }
      {1111111111111111111111111111111111111111111}

BEGIN   { CircList - Main PROGRAM }

  new ( list );          { create a dummy head node }
  list ↑ . next := list; { point it TO itself }
  page ( output );
  WriteLn ( 'Enter data :    surname first, then' );
  WriteLn ( 'the amount owed in (whole) pounds :' );
  WriteLn;
  ReadThings ( list );   { put data into the list }
  Display ( list );      { now print it IN order }
  WriteLn ( '--- done ---' : 40 )

END .
```

GOTO END

Take, for example, the simple task of finding the length of a string, when this is unknown. Remember that we have padded out any 'spare' array elements of the array representation with ASCII NUL characters, chr (0), or terminated the dynamic list with the pointer value NIL. The array version would seem to be easy enough:

In concluding our exploratory look at PASCAL, we discuss the all important necessity of properly describing data, as well as touch on several aspects of the language we have not yet covered.

The designer of PASCAL, Niklaus Wirth, entitled one of his books *Data Structures + Algorithms = Programs,* which reflects the importance the description of data has on formulating the algorithms that process that data. If we use an array of chars to represent a character string, for instance, the functions and procedures needed to process them (find their length, concatenate them, and so on) will be vastly different from those required if a linked list is used.

```
FUNCTION Length (S :string):Cardinal;
   VAR
   N              :0..StringLength;
   found       :boolean;
   BEGIN
     N :=0;
     found := false;
     REPEAT
        N := N+1;
        found :=S[N]=chr (0)
     UNTIL found OR (N=StringLength);
     IF found
        THEN
           Length := N−1
        ELSE
           Length := StringLength
END; {Length}
```

TreeSorter Program

This program uses some procedures from the previous CircList program, and these are referenced at the appropriate point. Data consisting of names, the amounts of debt owing and any other fields you care to add are entered from the keyboard and inserted in ascending alphabetic order into a 'binary tree'.

Each node of the tree has two pointers for linking to 'lesser' or 'greater' items. Traversal of the tree is accomplished by comparing the new data with the Name field in each node and taking the appropriate link field (LoBranch or HighBranch). When we find an empty node (that is, one with a NIL value branch) the item is inserted. Writing the data to the file is then achieved simply and naturally by means of a recursive procedure.

You could use these examples as a basis for a very neat database manager — a suite of programs, perhaps, tailored to your own use. Just one word of caution: if you read a sorted file into a binary tree, every insertion will be on the same branch and the tree will become a singly-linked list.

For simpler applications, the circular list is probably the most versatile. There are no NIL pointers in it whatsoever, thus sparing us a double test on each comparison, whereas the binary tree will have (Number of Nodes+1) NILs.

```
PROGRAM   TreeSorter  ( input, output, DataFile );

CONST
        FileName        = 'Treedata';
        StringLength    = 25;

TYPE
   Cardinal     = 0 .. MaxInt;
   StringSize   = 1 .. StringLength;
   string       = PACKED ARRAY [ StringSize ]
                        OF char;
   thing        = RECORD
                        Name    : string;
                        { other fields . . }
                        debt    : Cardinal
                  END;  { thing }

   FileType     = FILE OF thing;
   tree         = ↑ bough;
                  {** forward reference to : }
   bough        = RECORD
                        item       : thing;
                        LowBranch,
                        HighBranch : tree
                  END;  { bough }

VAR
   data         : thing;
   DataFile     : FileType;
   trunk        : tree;

INCLUDE 'Utils.src' {** source file containing :
              SkipBlanks, ReadCard and ReadLine
                   - see  CircList  program **}
   {111111111111111111111111111111111111111111}

PROCEDURE  ReadAmount ( VAR amount : Cardinal );
            {** Validate a legal Cardinal value **}
   VAR
        OK         : boolean;
   BEGIN
     REPEAT
        REPEAT
           write ( 'Amount ? ' : 20 );

           IF EoLn ( input ) THEN
             ReadLn ( input );

           SkipBlanks ( input )
           {** prompt again if at end of line **}
        UNTIL NOT EoLn ( input );

        ReadCard ( input, amount, OK );

        IF NOT OK THEN
           WriteLn ( '--- ERROR ---' : 20,
                         ' please reenter' )
        UNTIL OK    {** insist on a valid number **}

     END; { ReadAmount }
        {111111111111111111111111111111111111111111}

PROCEDURE        Grow    ( VAR   leaf   : tree;
        {** graft on to tree **}    data   : thing );
   BEGIN
     new ( leaf );

     WITH leaf ↑ DO
        BEGIN
           item := data;
```

There is some room here for both error and confusion. Why do we need the local Boolean variable found? And why must we assign the value N–1 to Length? These are minor irritations, but formulating more complicated algorithms can become very error-prone and confusing if we have to resort to artificial devices like this.

Using 'bit flags' (which we know as Boolean types) is the oldest trick in the programmer's book, but they are often introduced simply for the sake of the computer, not as a natural part of the algorithm. The local variable N must be used, not Length, as this is a function identifier, not a variable. Function identifiers on the right-hand side of a statement like:

```
Length := Length+1
```

would attempt to invoke a recursive call to the function Length itself.

Contrast this with the Length function needed for strings using a linked list. With the dynamic representation, remember that the TYPE definition of string is very different, allowing any length of string to be created. Data descriptions such as these will often be defined recursively.

RECURSION

Many trivial examples used to illustrate recursion could equally well be expressed (if not better) as iterative algorithms; but let's look at the Length function for the recursive string type:

```
FUNCTION Length (S :string)    :Cardinal;
   BEGIN
      IF S=NIL
         THEN
            Length :=0
         ELSE
            Length := succ(Length(S↑. next))
   END;   {Length}
```

The head of the list is S and the expression S↑.next selects the pointer field of the next record in the list. Alternatively, it can be thought of as being a list starting with the next record (ButFirst). Whenever we do not find a NIL, we call for an evaluation of the length of ButFirst and increment it with the succ function.

There are many more problems that can only be solved efficiently by the natural use of recursion. The previous example is fairly trivial, and will allow you to write Length without using recursion

```
         LowBranch := NIL; {** No more data yet, }
         HighBranch := NIL { beyond this bough  **}
      END

   END; { Grow }
      {11111111111111111111111111111111111111111111}

   PROCEDURE       Climb        ( shoot   : tree;
   {** find place to insert **} data    : thing );
   VAR
         stem    : tree;
         larger  : boolean;
   BEGIN
      WHILE shoot <> NIL DO
         BEGIN        {** find an empty bough **}
         stem := shoot;
         larger := data . Name  >
                           stem ↑ . item . Name;
         IF larger
            THEN {** climb upwards **}
               shoot := shoot ↑ . HighBranch
            ELSE {** climb downwards **}
               shoot := shoot ↑ . LowBranch
         END;

      Grow ( shoot, data );

      IF larger
         THEN        {** insert above **}
            stem ↑ . HighBranch := shoot
         ELSE        {** insert below **}
            stem ↑ . LowBranch := shoot

   END; { Climb }
      {11111111111111111111111111111111111111111111}

   PROCEDURE       Print ( VAR    F      : FileType;
   {** write data to a file **} root   : tree );
   BEGIN
      IF root <> NIL THEN
         WITH root ↑ DO    {** recursion : }
            BEGIN  {** write out in order : }
            Print ( F, LowBranch ); {** low first,}
            write ( F, item ); { the root itself, }
            Print ( F, HighBranch ) { high last **}
            END

   END; { Print }
      {11111111111111111111111111111111111111111111}

   PROCEDURE       Reclaim ( VAR root   : tree );
   {** recover allocated memory for further use **}
   BEGIN
      IF root <> NIL THEN {** recurse **}
         BEGIN    {** reclaim branches first - }
         Reclaim ( root ↑ . LowBranch );
         Reclaim ( root ↑ . HighBranch );
         dispose ( root ) { - then the root **}
         END

   END; { Reclaim }
      {11111111111111111111111111111111111111111111}


BEGIN   { TreeSorter - Main program }

   assign ( DataFile, FileName );
   page ( output );
   WriteLn ( '=== Tree Sort ===' : 25 );
   WriteLn;
   WriteLn ( 'Enter some data (surname first)' );
   write ( 'Name ? ' );
   ReadLine ( data . Name );
   ReadAmount ( data . debt );
   Grow ( trunk, data ); {* plant the tree trunk *}
   write ( 'Name ? ' );
   ReadLine ( data . Name );

   WHILE data . Name [ 1 ] <> chr ( 0 ) DO
      BEGIN
         ReadAmount ( data . debt );
         Climb ( trunk, data );
         WriteLn ( 'RETURN when done' : 40 );
         write ( 'Name ? ' );
         ReadLine ( data . Name )
      END;
   {** other processing, then write the file : }
   WriteLn ( 'Writing data to : ', FileName );
   rewrite ( DataFile );
   Print ( DataFile, trunk );
   WriteLn;
   WriteLn ( 'Debt' : 8, 'Name' : StringLength );
   WriteLn;
   reset ( DataFile ); {** read the file, }
      { and print the ordered data : }
   WHILE NOT EoF ( DataFile ) DO
      BEGIN      {** read each record **}
         read ( DataFile, data );
         {** write the fields to the VDU : }
         WITH data DO
            WriteLn ( debt : 8, ' : ', Name )
      END;

   Reclaim ( trunk );    {** dispose memory }
   { for other processing etc. **}
END .
```

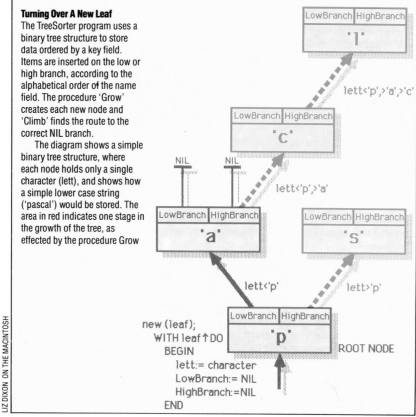

Turning Over A New Leaf
The TreeSorter program uses a binary tree structure to store data ordered by a key field. Items are inserted on the low or high branch, according to the alphabetical order of the name field. The procedure 'Grow' creates each new node and 'Climb' finds the route to the correct NIL branch.

The diagram shows a simple binary tree structure, where each node holds only a single character (lett), and shows how a simple lower case string ('pascal') would be stored. The area in red indicates one stage in the growth of the tree, as effected by the procedure Grow

```
new (leaf);
   WITH leaf↑DO
   BEGIN
   lett:= character
   LowBranch:= NIL
   HighBranch:=NIL
   END
```

LIZ DIXON ON THE MACINTOSH

with little difficulty. The code is larger, and a local counter must be used (as with the array version) specifically to avoid recursion.

```
FUNCTION Length(S :string)    : Cardinal;
   VAR
      N    : Cardinal;
   BEGIN
      N := 0;
      WHILE S < > NIL DO
         BEGIN
            N := N+1;
            S := S↑.next
         END;
      Length := N
   END;   {Length}
```

Even with this iterative algorithm, the clarity and concision are apparent and are due to the simple recursive nature of the data structure.

Many PASCAL compilers support 'directives', which are instructions to the compiler — *not* declarations or statements. The only directive actually required by the ISO Standard is Forward. Should two procedures or functions need to call each other, they are said to be 'mutually recursive'. This occurs only rarely, but it does pose a problem: we can't use any PASCAL object until it has been declared or defined.

The solution is to declare only the heading of one sub-program, replacing its block with the compiler directive FORWARD. After the full definition of the other module, the heading is given in abbreviated form (omitting the parameter list) and the block is defined at that point. Other directives are often available to control compile-

time options, but should not be used liberally if you wish to retain portability. This means, besides a special symbol (usually $) having to appear as the first character in the comment, non-portable options may not be flagged by a different compiler.

MORE FLAVOURS

A few non-standard implementations (notably HiSoft) will require slightly different syntax for forward pointer declarations. In this instance, you should refer to your manual. There are very few 'flavours' of this sort, and none whatsoever with PASCAL compilers that conform to the ISO definition of the language.

One other difference that you will find with UCSD, TCL/RML/Oxford and HiSoft versions is the lack of a dispose procedure. In lieu of this, the non-standard procedures mark and release are provided.

There is one more important advanced data description in PASCAL that we have not mentioned – the 'variant'. When we have wanted to store items of different types, we have used a record with appropriately typed fields. But supposing the description of a part or even the whole record needed to be flexible? Typically, we may wish to store different personal information about so-called 'data subjects' depending on, say, whether or not they were married. A variant record has its 'fixed part' defined first, then the variant part is specified by introducing a variant selector (of any simple type) and using the reserved words CASE and OR. For instance:

```
TYPE
   gender = (male, female);
   variant = RECORD
      {any common fields}
      CASE married : boolean OF
         false : ( );
         true  :DateWed :string;
            CASE sex: gender OF
               male : ( );
               female : (MaidenName :string))
   END: {variant}
```

Notice that empty field lists must still have brackets. Space on a file will be fixed (for the largest variant), but memory may be saved with pointers to variants, such as new (p, true, male).

The few weaknesses in PASCAL have been largely eliminated by the efforts of PASCAL experts (and by Wirth in MODULA-2). The language is tremendously powerful and yet small, efficient, general-purpose and easily learnt. Of course, if you don't stray outside the ISO definition, there will be some system-level operations that you cannot implement. But writing these routines in assembler or BCPL and linking them to a PASCAL program is just one possible solution. The benefits of having all your PASCAL source code portable across any micro, mini or mainframe in the world are irresistible. PASCAL is the closest approach we have to a computing *lingua franca*.

7 PERIPHERALS

Buying your micro is usually just the first step in building
up a complete system. From joysticks for enhanced games
playing to modems for telecommunication links, a vast
range of add-ons and attachments is available to upgrade
and expand your computer and the tasks it can accomplish.

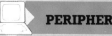

PERIPHERAL VISION

CHRIS STEVENS

Buying a home computer is often only the first step in setting up a complete system. The basic machine may be augmented or adapted by purchasing one or more of the many peripherals on the market. Here we examine some popular add-ons, and give some tips on what to look for when buying.

Until recently, the most important peripheral for the home user was a plug-in module containing extra memory. Memory was expensive, and machines like the ZX-81 and Vic-20 were designed to keep costs to a minimum — indeed, the unexpanded ZX-81 offered the user a mere 700-odd bytes with which to write programs. Today's machines come ready-equipped with up to 64 Kbytes of RAM — 128K is rapidly becoming the norm — and thus add-on 'RAM packs' are now rarely required. Today's user has a plethora of peripherals to choose from — modems allow communication between owners who may live hundreds of miles apart, motorised vehicles or robot arms can be controlled by using a suitable interface, and speech synthesisers may be used for fun or for educational purposes.

Although there are many different peripheral devices on the market, most of these are manufactured for the more popular machines only. This is a consideration that must be borne in mind when you decide on which machine to buy — Spectrum, Commodore and Acorn owners will always have more choice than those who opt for Orics or Sords. Newer machines take time to build up a peripheral market, although the recently introduced MSX standard will make things easier by allowing the same add-ons to be used with all machines that conform to the MSX specification.

A major consideration for the peripheral buyer is the question of compatibility — any purchase must work with any other devices that may be bought in the future. The classic example of this concerns the Sinclair Spectrum. Many Spectrum owners will have bought the Interface One and a Microdrive or two, only to find that some of their existing peripherals — and even some of their software — will not work with the Interface One in place.

However, if compatibility between devices is maintained, choosing add-ons for your machine can greatly increase the fun of computing. Suitable peripherals can allow you to design a computer system that suits your own particular requirements, and this system can then be added to as your needs change.

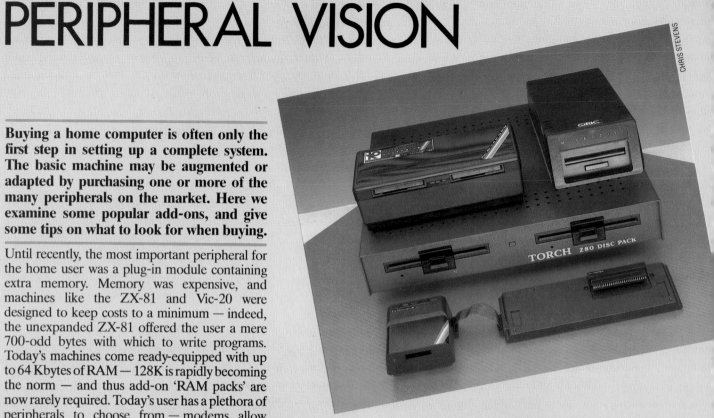

Storage Systems

The most common storage device for use with a microcomputer is the ordinary tape recorder. This has the benefit of being easy to use and relatively cheap, but its drawbacks soon become apparent. Programs take a long time to load, and it is difficult to keep an accurate record of what is on any particular tape. Disk drives are faster and more reliable, but cost more. Most home computers are restricted to one type of disk drive, and some of these — notably Commodore models — are notoriously slow in operation. Most home machines still use $5\frac{1}{4}$in drives, but 3in or $3\frac{1}{2}$in drives are now becoming more popular. The Oric/Atmos drive, for example, uses 3in disks with a capacity of 160 Kbytes per side. The BBC Micro is extremely flexible, allowing many different disk systems to be connected. The Torch Disk Pack effectively turns the BBC into a new computer, with a Z80 microprocessor to complement the computer's 6502 and an additional 64 Kbytes of memory. The Torch also provides four 'business' programs and comes with a version of BBC BASIC that is designed to run on the Z80 processor.

The Sinclair Spectrum, on the other hand, has no provision for the connection of standard disk drives, although some independent companies have produced special disk interfaces. Sinclair has produced the Interface One/Microdrive system, which uses a loop of tape that can hold around 85 Kbytes of data. The tape is completely under computer control, and any single item can be located within 10 seconds or so. This gives a performance that is midway between that of a tape recorder and a disk drive, at a price considerably less than the cheapest disk drive system. The Interface One has the added advantage of supplying a (non-standard) RS232 interface, and can be used for 'networking' — linking up to 64 Spectrums or QLs.

A rival to the Interface One system is the Rotronics Wafadrive. This also uses loops of tape to hold data, but includes RS232 and Centronics interfaces and a word processor program in the price. Tapes are supplied in three different sizes — 16, 64 and 128 Kbytes — with the smallest capacity tape giving the fastest working speed. A Wafadrive for the Commodore 64 is now available and versions for other micros are also planned.

Shown here are the Rotronics Wafadrive, the Oric/Atmos disk drive, the Torch Disk Pack and the Sinclair Interface One with Microdrive.

Graphic Devices

Producing graphics on a home computer is made considerably easier if one of the many different types of graphics devices is used. The cheapest of these are light pens, which can be used to 'draw' directly onto the display screen by using a photoelectric cell to detect the position of the light pen's tip as it touches the screen. A development of this is the Stack Light Rifle, which can be used as an alternative to a joystick in game-playing. pages 230-231).

Many people find it difficult to draw 'freehand' on a display screen. Tracing lines on a flat surface is considerably easier, and many devices are manufactured to allow users to do this. Graphics tablets use a special pen that transfers any movement made on the tablet's surface to the computer; this means that they may be used to draw images freehand or to trace over printed images. Other 'drawing' devices are digital tracers, which make use of variable resistors held in a mechanical arm to detect the position of the stylus that is fixed at the tip of the arm.

Here we show British Micro's Grafpad graphics tablet, the Robot Plotter digital tracer and the Stack light pen and Light Rifle.

Modems

The development of cheap modems for home computers allows users to communicate with each other via the telephone network. A large number of modems have been produced for machines equipped with a standard RS232 interface; with the right software, these can access the Prestel database, which has many pages devoted entirely to the home user. Modems can also be used to communicate with other users via 'bulletin boards' — databases that are often run on an amateur basis by micro enthusiasts. However, the question of compatibility arises once again — different baud rates are used by different bulletin boards, and a modem that can use Prestel is often unsuitable for communication with a bulletin board.

Neither the Spectrum nor the Commodore 64 has a built-in RS232 interface, and thus cannot use standard modems. For the Spectrum, the best-selling modem is the Prism VTX5000, which has built-in software to enable the user to access Prestel. Software on tape allows two Spectrums equipped with Prism modems to exchange data programs. Commodore supplies its own modem for use with the 64, and has set up its own system, Compunet, to link Commodore 64 owners in a network.

Modem users should keep a careful eye on the clock, as enthusiasts can soon run up huge telephone bills. Fixed annual charges for Prestel and Compunet users are also high.

Our picture shows the Prism VTX5000 and the Commodore modem.

Speech Synthesisers

Many popular home machines can produce speech with the addition of a speech synthesis unit. The units available may be grouped under two headings — one type is supplied with a fixed vocabulary of 100 or so different words (the Acorn speech synthesiser for the BBC Micro uses the voice of Richard Baker), while the other uses 'allophones' — a set of different sounds and pauses from which words are constructed.

The Currah range of speech units uses the allophone system, and the company produces modules for both the Spectrum (Microspeech) and the Commodore 64 (Speech 64). Some Spectrum and Commodore 64 games, notably those produced by Ultimate, have speech built in — this is produced automatically if a Currah unit is connected. Our picture shows the Currah Speech 64, and the Cheetah Sweetalker for the Spectrum.

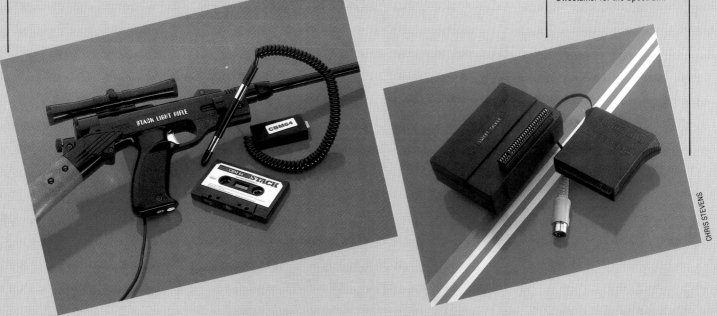

CHRIS STEVENS

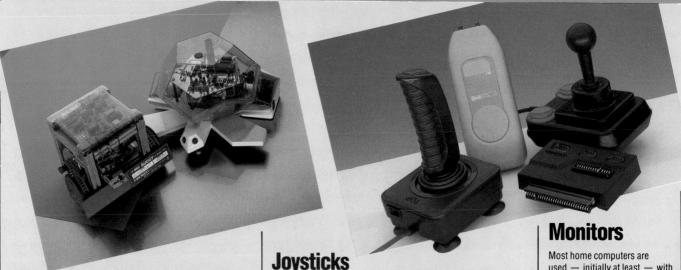

Computer-Controlled Devices

Computers can easily be used to control devices in the 'real' world. The application usually quoted is the control of a home central heating system — this is quite possible, although hardly worth the effort as a perfectly effective time-switch is fitted to such systems anyway. Much more fun are the various wheeled vehicles that may be controlled by the computer. The Valiant Turtle is a wheeled vehicle that looks slightly like a turtle and which can produce the graphics used by the LOGO language. This can be fitted to the Spectrum, Commodore 64 and BBC Micro, and uses an infrared beam to communicate with the computer. The BBC Buggy is a similar type of device, but is linked to the computer by trailing wires. It can also be used to draw lines, and is fitted with sensors.

Our picture shows both the Valiant Turtle and the BBC Buggy.

Printer/Plotters

For anyone who uses a home computer for program development or for word processing, a printer soon becomes a vital acquisition. Most printers are either dot matrix or daisywheel in format. Dot matrix types use a grid of small dots to build up each letter, allowing graphics to be printed, and are fast in operation but produce a poorer print quality than the daisywheel, which is basically a computer-controlled typewriter.

An alternative system is the small printer/plotter that is marketed for the Tandy, Atari, Commodore and Oric computers. This uses paper that is just over four inches in width, and is fitted with four small ballpoint pens to allow multi-coloured text or graphics to be produced. The text is 'drawn' in the same way as the graphics, and a full set of characters is programmed into the device. A further alternative is provided by the Epson P40 thermal printer, which uses a column of heating elements to burn an impression on special paper. This is extremely cheap, yet gives a reasonable quality of print and runs on rechargeable batteries. Again, the paper used is fairly narrow, but the P40 can produce an 80-column printout if the condensed mode is used.

Shown here are the printer/plotter (in its Tandy/Radio Shack guise) and the Epson P40 thermal printer.

Joysticks

The first peripheral that a home computer owner buys is usually a joystick. Many computers are fitted with suitable interfaces, and some of the newer machines have joysticks supplied as standard. The most common joysticks use the nine-pin 'D'-connectors first adopted by Commodore and Atari micros, and since followed by many independent companies. BBC joysticks are decidedly non-standard, so the choice here is more limited, and Commodore has inexplicably ignored its own standard on its Plus/4 and 16 micros, restricting buyers of these machines to the Commodore-designed joysticks.

Sinclair has marketed the Interface Two, a joystick interface and ROM cartridge port for the Spectrum. Until this was produced, no 'official' joystick interface had been provided for this machine, and the *de facto* standard has been the Kempston interface, the specifications of which have been adopted by many other companies. Unfortunately, the two are incompatible and many best-selling games will work quite happily with the Kempston interface but will not work at all with the Interface Two, so Kempston has now produced an interface that is compatible with software written for both Interface Two and the old Kempston format. One possible alternative is to buy a 'programmable' interface, which allows the user to run any software, whether or not it was originally designed for joystick use. This works by using the joystick to mimic the action of the keyboard and is probably the best buy for any Spectrum owner who has a large software collection.

Of the many joysticks on the market, the most unusual is the remote-controlled Cheetah RAT joypad. This has no cable to link it to the computer, but uses an infrared beam to send and receive signals. As yet, this is available only for the Spectrum. The Amstrad system is also somewhat unusual. The Amstrad micro has a single joystick socket, but a second joystick may be connected to the first, enabling two-player games to be run.

Our joystick photograph shows (from left to right): the Amstrad joystick, the Cheetah RAT, the Kempston PRO 5000, and (front) the Kempston interface for the ZX Spectrum.

Monitors

Most home computers are used — initially at least — with an ordinary television set as the display screen. This often poses problems, as other members of the household may want to watch television while the computer owner is playing Pacman, and, anyway, the picture quality is often poor. The answer is to use a monitor, which provides a better quality picture. The user must ensure that the correct monitor is bought, as there are two main standards — RGB and composite video.

Composite video monitors are used with Atari and Commodore micros, while the BBC, Oric/Atmos and Sinclair QL machines require the RGB format, which provides the best picture quality of all. Some micros rely on the television speaker to produce sound, so these will require monitors with built-in speakers. Several television manufacturers now produce sets that are fitted with monitor interfaces; these are ideal purchases if the user requires both a television set and a high-quality display. Shown here is the Microvitec Cub.

GOING DOTTY

Most home computer owners eventually decide that the one thing they need to make life complete is a printer. Even if it is used solely for listings, a printer makes a programmer's tasks much simpler — debugging a program is considerably easier if 'hard copy' is available — and a printer is obviously a necessity for word processing.

An inexperienced computer owner is likely to be bewildered by the choice of printers available, as there are almost as many different machines as there are makes of home computer. A decision must first be made as to the type of printer required; this will usually be either a dot matrix or daisy wheel model, although there are other varieties, such as thermal or ink-jet printers. A daisy wheel model produces the highest quality results (generally at a correspondingly high price) and is therefore best for word processing; whereas a dot matrix printer is usually cheaper, faster in operation and ideal for listings and general programming tasks. Here, we will concentrate on dot matrix printers.

A dot matrix printer may be purchased for less than £200, although very sophisticated models can cost £1,000 or more. Important points to consider are the printing speed and the quality of the text produced; more expensive models have extra features such as proportional spacing (i.e. narrow characters such as 'i' are allocated less space than wide ones like 'm') and different character sets. In general, you get what you pay for — you must decide whether such features are worth the extra money.

Printing speed is important as use of the printer 'ties up' the computer because text must be stored in the computer's memory until the printer is ready for it. Therefore, the computer cannot be used for other tasks while printing is taking place. Printer speeds are quoted as 'characters per second' (cps), so whereas an expensive model running at 200 cps might take one minute to print out a long program listing, a cheaper model with a print speed of 30 cps would take more than six minutes to produce the same listing — and during that six minutes the computer cannot be used for any other tasks. This problem may be overcome by using a printer *buffer*. This is simply a circuit board containing RAM chips, which is connected between the printer and the computer and stores the data while

Printer Artistry
These print-outs show the kind of graphics that can be produced by certain dot matrix printers. Each pin on the print head is controlled individually, and it is possible to produce some complex and satisfying patterns. Details on how to do this will be given in future instalments of the course. These images were created using Paintbox from Print'n'Plotter Products

the printer works on it, thus freeing the computer for other operations. More expensive printers have large buffers built in.

The print speeds quoted by the manufacturers should, however, be taken with a pinch of salt. As with car fuel consumption figures, these are always given for ideal conditions and often bear little resemblance to real life! Printer speeds are calculated for the production of a single line of text composed of the same character. Normal text, with its different characters, spaces, line feeds and carriage returns, slows down the print head. Thus, a printer with a quoted speed of 160 cps would probably average only about 100 cps when printing out a program listing.

The quality of the characters produced on the paper varies considerably from printer to printer. It depends mainly on how many pins are used in the print head — the mechanism that forms the characters on the paper. The cheapest models use just seven pins in the print head, whereas the more expensive machines can have 16 or more. On the Commodore printer, which has only seven pins, the characters are produced as a seven by six matrix of dots. The Canon PW1080, however, uses a 16 by 23 matrix to produce its characters. Consequently, the individual dots cannot be seen and the characters have a clearly defined, 'solid' appearance. For program listings, the quality of the print is not really important; whereas for word processing it obviously is.

A dot matrix printer is really a dedicated microcomputer; it uses ROM and RAM memory chips and has a microprocessor. As such, it can be programmed to do other things apart from printing text. This is done by sending special control codes from your micro to the printer, or by setting small switches — known as DIP (Dual In-line Package) switches — inside the printer case. For example, the standard ASCII character set, which is stored in the printer's memory, can be altered to suit different alphabets. In Britain, the hash sign (#) is often changed to print as a pound sign (£).

Other special effects include double-width characters, emphasised (darker, heavier) text, and different line spacings. The Epson FX80 is one of the more versatile dot matrix printers and has over 70 of these printing features. It can print in italic characters, underline text automatically and allows proportional spacing.

The Epson range of printers has become something of an 'industry standard'. This means that much of the software that requires a printer — word processing packages, invoice programs, etc. — assumes you have an Epson. This is an important point, for the different makes of printer are by no means compatible.

Other considerations may well influence the choice of printer; certainly, reliability is an important factor. A cheap £200 printer might be all right for producing the occasional listing but it is unlikely to stand up to the continual daily use that an office printer would suffer. Similarly, noise is one factor that is often overlooked: if you like to burn the midnight oil, some printers can be positively deafening at one o'clock in the morning. Does it have a friction feed? All dot matrix printers come with a 'tractor' feed, which will work only with continuous paper — the type with sprocket holes up the sides. If single sheets of paper must be printed, however, a friction feed is necessary.

Finally, perhaps the most important factor — will it work with your micro? Most dot matrix printers come with either a Centronics parallel socket or an RS232 serial interface. If a printer does not have the right one for your micro, then sometimes an alternative interface can be fitted, although this can add over £50 to the price. Even with the right interface, the correct cable is needed to connect the printer to the computer.

Pinprick Details
These print samples show the difference in quality between several dot matrix printers. The main reason for the variation is the number of 'pins' in the print head; those with the most pins have the most detailed characters. The first sample uses only seven pins, and can't produce the 'tails' of the letters g, p, q and y below the line. It is said to lack 'true descenders'

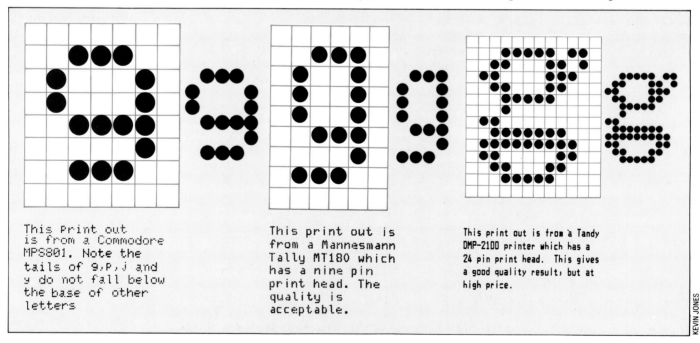

This Print out is from a Commodore MPS801. Note the tails of 9,p,j and y do not fall below the base of other letters

This print out is from a Mannesmann Tally MT180 which has a nine pin print head. The quality is acceptable.

This print out is from a Tandy DMP-2100 printer which has a 24 pin print head. This gives a good quality result, but at high price.

KEVIN JONES

ALL UNDER CONTROL

Even the cheapest dot matrix printers incorporate a range of 'special effects', such as the ability to print in large characters, which can make a print-out a far more exciting document visually. Here, we show you how such effects are obtained — and how to get your computer and printer 'talking' to each other in the first place!

A dot matrix printer can do far more than simply produce program listings. A quick leaf through the pages of the printer's user manual will show you that a variety of 'special effects' can be produced on paper. Even the cheapest dot matrix printers will let you alter the size of the characters printed on the paper. Normally, the text is printed out at 80 characters per line, but this number can be increased by selecting the 'condensed print' mode (which uses smaller characters), or decreased by selecting 'enlarged print'. In a similar way, the line spacing — the gap between the lines of text — can be altered. A large spacing given by four lines per inch, for example, could be reduced to, say, eight lines per inch, giving a heavier density print-out.

The printer that we will look at in detail here, the Epson FX-80, is a fine example of a machine that has a wide range of printing features. The emphasised mode, which prints out text in darker type, and the alternative mode, which switches from the normal typeface to *italic* characters, are two of its standard facilities. But perhaps its most interesting feature is its ability to change any of the characters stored in the printer's memory, an extremely useful facility for foreign alphabets or for printing scientific symbols. Before going on to investigate how these features are produced, however, let's consider how a printer goes about the simple task of printing out a program listing.

The way that a computer 'talks' to a printer varies from machine to machine. The Dragon, for example, uses a simple variation of the LIST command — LLIST — to instruct the printer to produce a copy of a program. Other machines require the opening of 'channels' or 'streams' to gain access to the printer. As the exact method varies so much, it is best to consult your computer's user manual — the printer manual is unlikely to be of much use here.

Having established communication between the two machines, your first print-out may be a little disappointing. The most likely problems are that all the text has been printed out in one indecipherable black line, or there are blank lines between each line of the program. The explanation for both these faults lies in the difference between a 'line feed'

character and a 'carriage return' character. After your computer has sent a line of text to the printer, it also sends a carriage return character, which moves the print head back to the left margin ready to print a new line. Some computers also send a line feed character to move the paper up one line; others assume that the printer does this automatically. To further complicate matters, most printers have an internal switch that decides whether the printer generates its own line feeds or not. If either of these problems occurs, find this switch — by consulting the printer manual — and flick it to the alternative position.

Apart from producing program listings, a printer can also be used as an output device — instead of characters being displayed on the screen, they are printed out on paper. Again, the exact method of doing this varies from computer to computer — the 'standard' BASIC command is LPRINT and this is used by the Spectrum and Oric. On a Commodore 64, OPEN1,4 followed by PRINT#1,"HELLO" would print the word 'HELLO'. With a Dragon micro the same task is accomplished using PRINT#−2,"HELLO". The BBC Micro uses VDU2 followed by PRINT "HELLO" and the VDU3 command. The programming examples that we give here use LPRINT, so you might have to alter this for your machine.

ADDRESS LABELS

```
10 LPRINT "MR JOHN SMITH"
20 LPRINT "7 THE PARADE"
30 LPRINT "ANYTOWN"
40 LPRINT "ABC 123"
50 FOR I=1 TO 7
60 LPRINT
70 NEXT I
100 GOTO 10
```

This listing is a simple program to produce address labels. These can be purchased on a roll with sprocket holes on both sides, so that they can be used with the tractor feed on the printer. Because it does not use any special control codes, the program will work with any make of printer. As it stands, the program will print the same name and address repeatedly. You might want to alter it so that you can input different names and addresses, or even have it read them from a data file. The FOR...NEXT loop between lines 50 and 70 prints seven blank lines, and is used to position the print head at the beginning of each label correctly. The exact number of blank lines may need to be adjusted for your machine.

Our program is quite adequate for simply printing labels, but to print something more complex, like an invoice or letterhead, we are going to have to use some of the special effects that we mentioned earlier. These are produced by sending

ELITE
```
ABCDEFGHIJKLMNOP
QRSTUVWXYZabcdef
ghijklmnopqrstuv
wxyz0123456789 !
"£$%&'()*+,-./:;
<=>?@[\]^_`{|}~
```

PICA
```
ABCDEFGHIJKLM
NOPQRSTUVWXYZ
abcdefghijklm
nopqrstuvwxyz
0123456789 !"
£$%&'()*+,-./
:;<=>?@[\]^_`
{|}~
```

EMPHASISED PICA ITALIC
```
ABCDEFGHIJKLM
NOPQRSTUVWXYZ
abcdefghijklm
nopqrstuvwxyz
0123456789 !"
#$%&'()*+,-./
:;<=>?@[¥]^_`
{|}~
```

ENLARGED ELITE
```
ABCDEFGH
IJKLMNOP
QRSTUVWX
YZabcdef
ghijklmn
opqrstuv
wxyz0123
456789 !
"£$%&'()
*+,-./:;
<=>?@[\]
^_`{|}~
```

DOUBLE-STRIKE CONDENSED PICA
```
ABCDEFGHIJKLMNOPQRSTUVW
XYZabcdefghijklmnopqrst
uvwxyz0123456789 !"£$%&
'()*+,-./:;<=>?@[\]^_`{
|}~
```

Dotted Around
Dot matrix printers offer a range of typefaces such as Pica, Elite, and Italic, and typestyles such as condensed, enlarged and emphasised. All the examples shown here were produced by the Epson FX-80

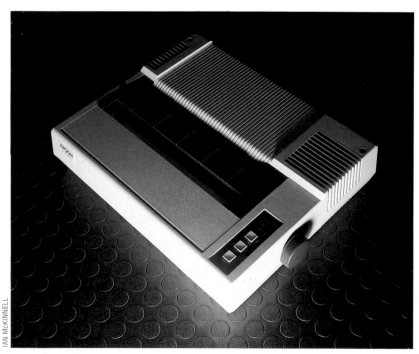

Epson FX-80
A popular printer among business and home micro owners, though expensive at £300-400. The FX-80 has a nine-pin head, and maximum print speed of 160 characters per second. Most software packages (word processors, for example) support Epson and Epson-type printers

IAN McKINNELL

control codes to the printer as well as to the normal text characters.

In addition to having a code for each character on the keyboard, the ASCII character set (see page 131) has a group of 'invisible' characters that do not print anything on the screen or paper. It is these codes that are used to turn on the printer's special effects: in the standard ASCII set there are four codes (17, 18, 19 and 20) that are reserved as device control commands. Unfortunately, the ASCII character set does not have enough reserved control characters for the 70-odd features of an Epson FX-80, and in order to overcome this, most effects are produced by sending 'escape codes' to the printer. These consist of two or more character codes, starting with an ESC character (ASCII code 27). For example, to turn on the proportional spacing feature on an Epson you send ESC-p — i.e. the Escape character followed by the lower-case 'p' character.

In BASIC, this is written as:
LPRINT CHR$(27);"p"
The ESC character cannot normally be produced by pressing the Escape key on your keyboard, and consequently the CHR$ function is used.

On the BBC, you would use:
VDU2
VDU1,27,1,112
VDU3
The VDU2 command turns on ('enables') the printer; VDU1 means 'send the following character to the printer only' (PRINT would send the following ESC character to the screen as well, with undesirable results). VDU3 turns off ('disables') the printer.

These command sequences apply only to the Epson FX-80. If you try to send the same code sequence to a different printer, it will either have no effect, do something unexpected, or cause the printer to 'hang up' (i.e. refuse to respond to the computer).

CREATING AN INVOICE

Our second listing demonstrates the use of some of the Epson's features to create an invoice heading, as might be used by a small garage. The codes we have used here are those used by the Epson FX-80. The Epson range of printers is one of the most popular; so much so that other manufacturers make models that are 'Epson-compatible'. If your printer is incompatible with the Epson, however, you must alter the control codes accordingly.

```
999 REM INVOICE HEADING
1000 LPRINT CHR$(12)
1010 LPRINT CHR$(14);TAB(12);"HCAC
MOTORS LTD."
1020 LPRINT CHR$(13);CHR$(13)
1030 LPRINT CHR$(27);"E";
1040 LPRINT TAB(36);
1050 LPRINT CHR$(27);"-";CHR$(1);
1060 LPRINT "INVOICE";
1070 LPRINT CHR$(27);"-";CHR$(0);
1080 LPRINT CHR$(27);"F";
1090 LPRINT CHR$(13);CHR$(13);CHR$(13)
1100 REM INVOICE DETAILS PRINTED
```

To begin, line 1000 sends the character with code 12 to the printer. This is the 'form feed' character, which instructs the printer to roll the paper to the start of a new sheet. Then we have ASCII code 14; this is called the 'shift out' (SO) character, and on the Epson it causes all subsequent text to be printed in enlarged letters. In our program it is used for the heading, giving the name of the garage in large letters. The TAB function is used to centre the heading.

CHR$(13) is the carriage return character, which produces a single blank line when printed on its own. Several are used in lines 1020 to 1090 to space out the top of the invoice. ESC-E in line 1030 turns on the emphasised mode, and all subsequent text is printed in darker type (caused by printing the same letters several times over). Line 1050 turns on the 'underlining' feature, and line 1070 turns it off, after printing and underlining the word 'Invoice'. ESC-F disables the emphasising mode. The print-out will look like this:

```
HCAC  MOTORS  LTD.



          INVOICE
```

We have shown only the initial part of the program here; a completed invoice program would include lines to print out customer details — name, make of car, money owed, etc. These details would have been obtained from a series of questions at the beginning of the program, and the answers would have been stored as variables.

The two programs that we have given here are simple examples of the sorts of alternative uses that a dot matrix printer can be put to. Many people are now exploring the use of a printer beyond simply using it to make program listings. In fact, programming your printer can be just as enjoyable as programming the computer itself.

FIRST IMPRESSIONS

The graphics capabilities of dot matrix printers often tend to be overlooked, simply because users don't know they exist. In this section we show how to set up a printer to produce attractive graphics, and how to construct a screen dump program that will do the work for you.

Most home computers have a low resolution graphics mode in which pictures are built up from graphics characters, each the same size as a conventional text character. These 'block' characters have character codes greater than 127, as the numbers 0 to 127 are reserved for the ASCII character set. So PRINT CHR$(90) would print an ASCII character on the screen — 'Z' in this case — whereas PRINT CHR$(128) displays a graphic character — a black rectangle if you are using a Dragon micro.

To print the letter 'Z' on a printer, we would type LPRINT CHR$(90), so you might think that LPRINT CHR$(128) would similarly print a black rectangle on paper. Unfortunately this is not the case. This is because the characters above code 127 vary enormously between different makes of micro, and obviously printer manufacturers cannot produce a special printer for each computer on the market. What they tend to do is either copy the standard ASCII set into the codes 128 to 255, or alternatively program in their own graphics characters.

The Epson range of printers does not come with any graphics characters. Instead you can change any of the standard ASCII characters to produce your own graphics characters. This is achieved by sending suitable 'escape codes' to the printer as discussed in the last two pages.

High resolution computer graphics are constructed from small dots, or pixels, rather than from whole characters. In a similar way, high resolution printing uses small dots of ink. The print head in a dot matrix printer has a number of pins arranged in a vertical line that moves across the paper as it prints. Usually, characters are made up from a grid of dots (perhaps eight by eight dots). It is possible, however, to produce graphics by controlling the pins individually.

The first step is to switch your printer into its graphics mode. As with any other printing exercise, this is done by sending an escape code that is specific to the type of printer being used. On the Epson FX-80 for example, the necessary instructions are:

LPRINT CHR$ (27); "K";CHR$ (N1);(N2);

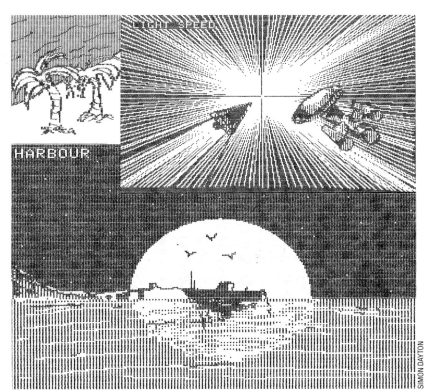

The letter "K" indicates graphics mode and the numbers (N1) and (N2) set the width of each line of graphics — in other words the number of dots that will fit across the page.

When in standard graphics mode, the FX-80 can print a maximum of 480 dots in one line. Other modes allow resolutions in the range of 576 to 1920 dots per line. If we wish to use the full width, therefore, 480 will be the required line length. Two numbers are required in our code to set the width, because the maximum size of each number is 255. The second number (N2) is therefore multiplied by 256 and added to the first, (N1). So for 480, the numbers are 1 and 224 (480=256×1+224). Therefore, on the Epson FX-80 printer we need the following instruction:

LPRINT CHR$ (27);"K";CHR$ (224);CHR$ (1);

Having programmed the printer with the graphics line length we need to send the graphics data. Even though there are nine pins in the print head of an Epson FX-80, only the top eight can be used in most graphics modes. Starting from the bottom pin we number them 1,2,4,8,16,32,64 and 128. The data for all eight pins can then be represented by a single number, between 0 and 255, and this is sent to the printer using LPRINT CHR$(X), where X is the number. So if we wanted only the bottom pin to 'fire' we would send CHR$(1) to the printer; to trigger the top pin alone we would send CHR$(128). For a combination of pins we simply add up the

Screen Print
These designs were drawn on-screen using a graphics tablet. The screen contents were then dumped to an Epson FX-80 printer, showing the graphic possibilities of the dot matrix printer

Pin Point
The pattern was produced on a dot matrix printer by sending alternate pairs of the decimal numbers 195 and 60 to the print head. The chart (below) shows how these numbers in binary are interpreted by the print head pins, (illustrated on the right). Controlled paper feed causes the next line to overprint the gap left by Pin 1

PIN NUMBER	PIN VALUE		
9	128	●	○
8	64	●	○
7	32	○	●
6	16	○	●
5	8	○	●
4	4	○	●
3	2	●	○
2	1	●	○
		195	60

● PIN FIRES
○ PIN DOES NOT FIRE

PRINT HEAD

USED FOR TEXT, NOT FOR GRAPHICS MODE

PRINT HEAD MOVES ACROSS PAPER

STEVE CROSS

numbers of each pin. This process is then repeated for each of the 480 dots across the page.

In the illustration there are two pin patterns: CHR$(195) and CHR$(60). So to print the first four columns of the line pattern we type:

LPRINT CHR$(195);CHR$(195);CHR$(60); CHR$(60);

After four columns the pattern repeats, so a FOR...NEXT loop takes care of the rest of the line.

It is important to realise that CHR$(60) in the example does not instruct the printer to print the ASCII character with code 60 — it is a way of representing the data for the pins in the print head. The printer recognises it as such because we have previously transmitted the CHR$(27);"K" sequence to turn on the graphics mode.

This method of printing, known as *bit image*

Splash Of Colour
This picture of the Spectrum keyboard was produced on a colour ink-jet printer — in effect this is a dot matrix printer in which the pins are replaced by ink jets

printing, is described for an Epson FX-80 printer; other printers use a similar method, but the exact details will vary. Producing graphics in this way is quite laborious, and only really suitable for patterns. A much better way of printing graphics is by means of a *screen dump*. This is a program that copies what is displayed on the monitor screen onto the paper.

By scanning across and down the screen display, the program tests to see if the pixel is on at each position. If it is, then we want a pin in the print head to fire at the corresponding position on the paper. The scanning is done by using the POINT(x,y) function, or similar commands that are available on most micros; if a pixel is lit then the function POINT(x,y) will be 1; if it is unlit, the function is 0. The different screen resolutions of different micros mean that some adjustment might be necessary.

One problem that might have occurred to you is: how does a screen dump program handle colour displays? The usual solution is to use different dot patterns for each colour. A screen pixel that is black might be printed using four dots in the form of a square; one that is red might be represented by a two dots; and one that is white would not use any dots. The POINT(x,y) function produces a different number dependng on the colour of the pixel, and so can still be used.

Screen dump programs are usually added to the end of the program producing the picture, in the form of subroutines. To 'dump' the picture to the printer you might press the key 'P', and the program would then jump to the subroutine. A screen dump program written in BASIC tends to be quite slow, taking perhaps five minutes to print out a small picture. Machine code versions are slightly quicker.

As you can see, the graphics capabilities of dot matrix printers are reasonably advanced — if a little cumbersome to use. Once mastered however, the printed page can be as attractive as the screen display.

SCREEN DUMP BY DIMENSION GRAPHICS

GRAPHICS BY IAN McKINNELL

FLOWER POWER

Daisy wheel printers produce print of a far higher quality than their dot matrix rivals, and allow useful features such as proportional letter-spacing. For a home computer owner, however, the need for quality print-outs may be overshadowed by the comparative expense and slow speeds of these printers.

At first sight, a daisy wheel printer might seem a strange buy for a home computer owner. It is not really suitable for listing programs, it is slow, and it costs more than a dot matrix printer. Nevertheless, for some applications it is a good choice. The area in which a daisy wheel printer wins hands down is in the quality of the print. A dot matrix printer builds up each character by printing a pattern of dots: no matter how many pins are used in the print head, the individual dots can still be seen in the printed text.

With a daisy wheel, on the other hand, the characters are produced by a type block hitting an inked ribbon — just like a typewriter. These type blocks, one for each character, are arranged in a circle rather like the petals in a flower — hence the name *daisy wheel*. The resulting print is easier to read and also looks more 'professional'.

The penalty to be paid for this higher quality print is in the printer's speed: daisy wheel printers are much slower than comparably-priced dot matrix printers. The reason for this lies in their different printing methods. To print a character using a daisy wheel printer, the print wheel is first spun until the required 'petal' is at the top, then the print hammer hits the type block, and the carriage is moved on to produce the next character.

Compare this with a dot matrix printer, where the dots are printed as the carriage moves across the paper, and the difference in speed between the two types of printer is understandable. A £400 daisy wheel prints about 20 characters per second (cps); an Epson FX-80 dot matrix printer costs about the same, yet can print at a speed of 160 cps. Some daisy wheel printers are faster, but they cost more — as much as £1,000 for an 80 cps model.

To increase the print speed, both daisy wheel and dot matrix printers often have two extra features: bi-directional printing and logic seeking. *Bi-directional* simply means that one line of text is printed from left to right, and the next line is printed from right to left. The printer does not have to wait for the carriage to return and it can therefore print faster. *Logic seeking* means that the carriage skips spaces to reach the next word in the text — less sophisticated printers take the same time to 'print' a space as any other character.

Dot matrix printers have their character shapes stored in ROM memory inside the printer; daisy wheel printers have the character stored as type blocks on the print wheel. Each method has its advantages: with a dot matrix printer, the character shapes can be re-defined by sending suitable escape codes to the printer from your micro. With a daisy wheel printer the process is much easier: simply swap the current daisy wheel for a different one.

Daisy wheels come in a variety of type styles and pitches; the *type style* refers to the design of the characters, and the *pitch* refers to their width. Some of the more common type styles are Courier, Roman, Gothic and Italic. The pitch is normally 10 or 12 characters per inch. A plastic daisy wheel costs about £5, whereas a metal version costs over £20; metal wheels have the advantage over plastic of lasting much longer.

The one problem with all these different type styles is that few of them are exactly the same as the character set used by a micro. This means that some of the characters on your micro keyboard will be printed out as something completely different. Often the 'hash' character ('#') prints as a pound sign ('£'), or a square bracket ('[') prints as a fraction ('½'). With many type styles the number '0' (zero) is indistinguishable from the capital letter 'O' and similarly the lower case letter 'l' may be mistaken for the number '1'. While the more expensive daisy wheel printers have 127-character print wheels, most can only print 92 or 96 characters, and it's these that suffer most from this type of problem.

As you can imagine, trying to debug a program is not made any easier if you are not sure which characters are 1's and which are l's. For this reason, and also because of its slowness, a daisy wheel printer is not recommended if you use your computer mainly for programming.

SPECIAL EFFECTS

A daisy wheel printer can be programmed to produce a variety of special effects, just like a dot matrix printer. Although the number of these effects is limited, the method of programming the printer is identical to that used for a dot matrix printer, namely by sending escape codes (see page 288). For example, on a Diablo daisy wheel printer the ESC-E code turns on the automatic underlining, and ESC-R turns it off again. Using standard Microsoft BASIC, you would type LPRINT CHR$(27);"E"; and LPRINT CHR$(27);"R"; to send the above codes to the printer. Other codes include ESC-1 to set a tab stop; ESC-9 to set the left margin;

Quality At A Price

```
Print sample with 10 characters per inch
Print sample with 12 characters per inch
Print sample with 15 characters per inch

A half-line feed is used for subscripts:-
          H₂O

ESC-E turns on the automatic underlining
and ESC-R turns it off.

Bold print makes text stand out from the
rest of the text.

The ESC= code is used to centre text:-

              A Centred Heading

These lines of text were printed without
the proportional spacing feature.  Note
especially how the numbers 0123456789
are spaced out. Without proportional
spacing, the width of each character
is the same.  For example, a 'W' is the
same width as an 'i':-
WWWWWWWWWWWW
iiiiiiiiiiii

These lines of text were printed using
the proportional spacing feature.  Note
especially how the numbers 0123456789
are spaced out.  Using proportional
spacing, the width of each character
varies.  For example, a 'W' is much
wider than an 'i':-
WWWWWWWWWWWW
iiiiiiiiiiii
The overall effect is to make the text
more attractive.
```

More expensive and less flexible than a dot matrix printer, the daisy wheel produces typewriter-quality printing and proportional spacing. The wheel itself (distinctly flower-like) is easily replaced by another in a different typeface or style

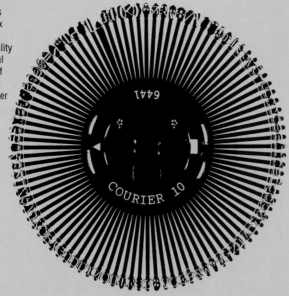

and ESC-U to feed the paper up half a line — useful for subscripts. The daisy wheel equivalent of emphasised text on a dot matrix is called *emboldening* — where each character is printed four times to make it stand out. The Diablo code for this feature is ESC-O. Emboldening script, however, drastically reduces the print speed.

Some daisy wheel printers allow you to vary both the distance moved between characters and the line spacing. If this is so, then the printer can be used to create graphic images or screen dumps, just like a dot matrix printer (see page 289). If a screen pixel is 'on' then the daisy wheel prints a full stop, if it's 'off' then a space is printed. By reducing the distance moved between characters, a whole horizontal line of the screen can fit across the paper. Similarly, the line spacing is reduced so as not to leave a gap between the lines. The process is, however, very slow.

One feature not seen on dot matrix printers is the ability to centre headings automatically. Sending ESC = to a Diablo printer will centre the rest of that line between the margins. Another novel feature is the decimal tab: ESC-H will cause all numbers to be printed with the decimal points aligned, which is a useful feature for sums of money.

The more expensive daisy wheel printers can usually perform proportional spacing. With this feature the pitch is not a standard 10 or 12 characters per inch. Instead, it varies depending on the width of the character being printed. For example, the character 'w' is much wider than the character 'i', so with proportional spacing the carriage would not advance as far for an 'i' as it would for a 'w'. What this means is that characters in successive lines of text do not fall exactly underneath each other, and the overall effect is more pleasing to the eye. The lines of text that you are now reading are proportionally spaced. Often a special daisy wheel is necessary to use this feature correctly, but it is turned on and off using escape codes — like any other printer effect. On a Silver-Reed EXP 770 printer, the codes ESC-P and ESC-Q turn the proportional spacing on and off.

For a business, a daisy wheel printer can easily be justified; for most home computer owners it probably can not. There is an alternative though, and that is to adapt an electronic typewriter. Daisy wheel printers cost more than electronic typewriters, even though they both use the same print method. Until recently, however, typewriters could not easily be connected to a computer — they had no interface circuitry or RS232 socket. But now every electronic typewriter on the market either comes with a built-in computer interface, or can be fitted with an interface kit for about £100. The great advantage in adapting an electronic typewriter, apart from saving about £200 over a comparable daisy wheel printer, is that it can still be used as a conventional typewriter. So you have both a typewriter, for typing a short letter or addressing envelopes, and a daisy wheel printer for word processing.

ON THE BLOWER

One of the great strengths of the BBC Micro is its facility for EPROM chips (priced at around £5 each), which allow the user to keep important programs permanently on board the computer. The Micron EPROM programmer — or 'blower' as it is popularly termed — is an inexpensive device for programming EPROM chips.

One of the biggest advantages of the BBC Micro is its flexibility. In designing the machine, Acorn chose to include four empty ROM slots, allowing the user to place extra ROMs for specific applications in the machine, and these can be 'paged' by use of the * command. The provision of these slots has been one of the greatest successes of the machine, since it enables users to have programs fitted on-board that can be accessed much faster than having to LOAD them from tape or disk.

There is now an enormous selection of these applications ROMs available, covering a wide range of programs, including word processing, databases, and languages such as LOGO. However, it is also possible for users to write their own programs and then transfer them to an EPROM (erasable programmable read only memory), allowing them to be permanently stored within the machine. This is done by programming the EPROM with a device known as, naturally enough, an 'EPROM programmer', which is popularly known as an 'EPROM blower'.

Like all ROMs, an EPROM consists of a matrix of electrical lines in columns and rows, each intersection of which is known as a cell. If there is a connection between a line in a column and one in a row, then the logic state at that point will be one, otherwise it is zero. When a series of electrical impulses, corresponding to an address, arrives on the address bus, the electricity will pass down eight of these lines (these eight pulses represent a byte). Depending on whether or not there is a connection on the appropriate cross lines, the electrical charge will pass through to the cross lines and cause a charge to be sent, via the data bus, back to the processor. In this way, data held at an address is transferred to the CPU.

Typically, the logic states in an EPROM memory array are all set at one — each address holds the value &FF. If a large voltage is passed through a cell, the connection will break, thus producing the complementary logical state of zero. To program a particular address of an EPROM, we have to first set up the necessary bit pattern on the address pins, to specify the address

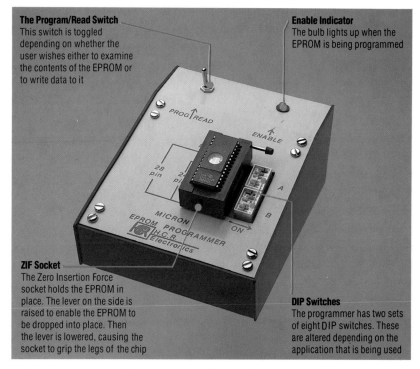

The Program/Read Switch
This switch is toggled depending on whether the user wishes either to examine the contents of the EPROM or to write data to it

Enable Indicator
The bulb lights up when the EPROM is being programmed

ZIF Socket
The Zero Insertion Force socket holds the EPROM in place. The lever on the side is raised to enable the EPROM to be dropped into place. Then the lever is lowered, causing the socket to grip the legs of the chip

DIP Switches
The programmer has two sets of eight DIP switches. These are altered depending on the application that is being used

to be programmed. Then we send the required code down the data bus. A pulse of 50 microseconds is applied to the appropriate data pins at 25v — and the address is programmed. By incrementing the address and sending another bit pattern to the data pins, it is possible to program the entire EPROM. However, unlike some other types of programmable ROMs in which this process is irreversible, an EPROM, as its name suggests, can be wiped clean.

An EPROM is characterised by a small quartz window above the chip. When strong ultraviolet light is shone through this window, the atoms in the chip are ionised to a higher electrical state and the bonds between the atoms will be re-established. This allows current to pass once more between the cross lines on the matrix, and the logical state will again be one. Ultraviolet light is not strictly necessary, however, since the EPROM programmer can write a software routine to reset all the memory locations to &FF.

The Micron EPROM programmer from HCR Electronics enables the user to program up to 16 Kbytes of machine code onto an EPROM. The programmer is a small box, the most prominent feature of which is a ZIF (zero insertion force) socket. This enables EPROMs to be inserted without damaging the pins which, once broken, render the chip useless. The ZIF socket is designed to accommodate either 24-pin or 28-pin chips. Two sets of DIP switches, which are altered

Blower Parts
An EPROM programmer allows users to keep their programs permanently in memory. Programs are loaded into the computer and then transferred to the programmer via the user port where they are 'blown' onto the chip

Close Examination
The chip within the EPROM housing can be easily viewed through the quartz window in the centre. Careful examination of the chip will show the thin pieces of wire that join the chip I/O connections to the pins. A closer look will show the arrays that make up the EPROM

depending on which of the various options one uses, are beside the ZIF socket. On the top left-hand side of the programmer is a switch that needs to be set according to whether you want to program or read the EPROM. Obviously, care has to be taken when using the programmer to ensure that the switch is on the correct setting — otherwise the EPROM may be reblown, thus losing the program held on the chip.

The device has a ribbon cable that is connected to the BBC's user port from the power supply. You can LOAD and SAVE programs into a buffer area, and then transfer the programs onto the EPROM with the menu-driven software provided with the machine. The software is held on cassette and, naturally, the first thing the new user is advised to do is dump it onto an EPROM.

Once loaded, the software presents a menu on the screen giving the available options. To copy a program onto an EPROM, the program must first be loaded into memory using the (L)oad option. This command has the effect of placing the program into a buffer area, set aside by the EPROM software, starting at location &2000. After this has been done, the user then selects the (P)rogram option from the main menu. The screen then displays the list of EPROM types that can be programmed using the device. After choosing an EPROM the screen will display the 16 DIP switches and their settings; switches needing to be altered from the previous program will flash. The program prompts the user to flick the read/write switch to PROG. Pressing any key will initiate the programming of the EPROM, with each memory address being displayed as it is programmed.

The length of time taken by the 'blowing' process depends on how many of the addresses within the EPROM will stay set at &FF. This can take anywhere between 74 seconds for a short program, to a maximum of 14 minutes for a 16 Kbyte EPROM. By using the (V)erify command, you can check whether the EPROM has been programmed correctly. The software computes a checksum, and any faulty addresses are listed on the screen. If there are no errors, the EPROM can then be safely fitted into one of the ROM sockets of the BBC Micro.

Standard headers can be fixed to a program. Using the G command, a routine can be added to the beginning of the program, attaching a name, which can later be called with the * prefix, and a CALL command. When loading BASIC programs onto the EPROM, this command is used in conjunction with the (F)ill option. This command ensures that addresses not used by the BASIC program are left set at &FF and are hence still programmable. Headers can also be affixed to machine code programs but these can only be loaded from address &2000.

Considering how useful these devices are, it is perhaps surprising that EPROM programmers have not become more popular with BBC Micro owners. It is likely that many users feel these programmers belong to the realm of 'serious'

Interface Connections
The EPROM programmer connects, through a 12-way ribbon cable, to the BBC Micro's user port

electronics enthusiasts and beyond the scope of most home computer users. This is simply not so. EPROM programmers are easy to use, no knowledge of electonics is assumed, nor necessary, and the machines offer a number of advantages. Primary among these is speed of access — a program can be called instantly via the operating system without the need to LOAD from disk or cassette. Furthermore, once the programs are incorporated into the computer, the applications held on the EPROM can be called from within BASIC programs. Finally, users are given the immense satisfaction of seeing their custom-built programs taking their places among the BBC Micro's own on-board programs.

Pin Points

Pin Names	
A_0-A_{13}	Addresses
CE	Chip Enable
OE	Output Enable
O_0-O_7	Outputs
PGM	Program
Vpp Vcc	Supply Voltages
Gnd	Earth

This is a diagrammatic representation of the TMS27128 16 Kbyte EPROM, one of the chips that can be 'blown' using the HCR programmer. This is a 28-pin device (although it will also accept 24-pin chips). The chip has 14 address pins that allow it to address the 16 Kbytes of memory. The TMS27128 also has eight pins to provide an eight-bit output

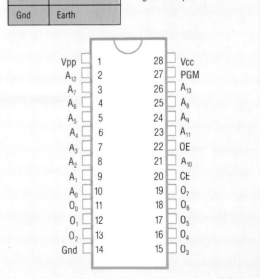

A SLICE OF MEMORY

The initial lack of a reliable, fast storage medium has meant that the Sinclair Spectrum has generally been overlooked as a machine for serious applications. The introduction of Sinclair's own Microdrive system, however, did not deter independent companies from producing storage systems such as the Rotronics Wafadrive.

Although the Sinclair Spectrum has become one of the most popular home microcomputers, it has been criticised in many quarters as being unsuitable for the 'serious' user. This has led to the Spectrum being dismissed as merely a games machine. Part of the problem has centred around the keyboard, which has not allowed the user to seriously consider using the machine for applications such as word processing and database management. Sinclair Research did attempt to defuse some of this criticism when it launched the Spectrum+, which is fitted with a QL-style keyboard.

However, this is only part of the problem. Other difficulties hounding the supporters of the Spectrum as a serious machine are the computer's lack of standard interfaces and, more importantly, a fast and reliable mass storage system — vital to any business or serious application for the hobbyist. Of course, with the introduction of Interface 1 and the Microdrive, the Spectrum could at least claim to have these facilities

available. But the suspicion remained that the Microdrive was slow and unreliable. Furthermore, although the software base on cassette for the Spectrum is enormous, very little software has made the transition to the medium used by the Microdrive. In a situation like this, third party suppliers tend to step into the gap and produce alternatives. Here we look at the first of two contenders in the race to dominate the Spectrum mass storage market — the Wafadrive from Rotronics. In the next instalment we will look at the Discovery 1 from Opus Supplies.

Unlike Interface 1 and the accompanying Microdrive units, the Rotronics Wafadrive is an 'all-in-one' unit. That is to say that both the peripheral interfaces and the mass storage units are enclosed in a single box. The advantage of this system is that the units do not have the trailing leads necessary for the Sinclair system, but it does mean that they lack something of the flexibility of the Microdrives, which can be daisy-chained together to expand storage space.

THE LOOK OF THE MACHINE

The Wafadrive is encased in black plastic with a 35-way ribbon cable ending in a cartridge slot fitted onto the Spectrum's expansion bus. On the front of the unit there is a pair of wafer cartridge drive slots. Between the slots are three light emitting diodes (LEDs). The central light is the power-on indicator, while the other two indicate drive activity.

On the rear of the drive unit are three edge connectors. On the left is a parallel expansion bus to allow Interface 2 to be connected. The centre edge connector is a Centronics-compatible interface to allow the drive to be attached to a parallel printer. The third is an RS232 serial port that enables the device to be interfaced with modems and other serial devices. These interfaces are an improvement over those provided on the Sinclair Interface 1, where, for example, one still has to connect a second Centronics interface to the unit's edge connector in order for it to run parallel printers. Unfortunately, however, users will still have to shop around for Centronics printers or modems with Wafadrive-compatible cartridge connectors.

The stringy floppy wafers specifically designed for the Wafadrive are in many ways similar to those used on the Sinclair equivalents. Inside each wafer is a continuous loop of video-type cassette tape with a width of 1.8mm. This tape is used instead of the more conventional audio tape because of its improved endurance and information storage capabilities. Once formatted,

Room In The Back
Unlike Sinclair's own system of mass storage for the Spectrum, the Rotronics Wafadrive comes in a single box containing twin drives, an RS232 port and a Centronics interface. The ribbon cable fits into the Spectrum's edge connector, and this positions the drives conveniently above the keyboard for easy access

CHRIS STEVENS

this tape can contain approximately 128 Kbytes of data, although Rotronics has also made 64 and 16 Kbyte cartridges available.

The cartridges themselves are approximately twice the width of the Sinclair wafers, although they are of similar length and breadth in their protective boxes. This gives the Rotronics cartridges an appearance of miniature cassettes. The Wafadrive cartridges do not need protective casings, as the delicate tape is protected by an automatic sliding cover, similar in design to that on the Sony 3½in microfloppy disks, although the Rotronics protection is made out of plastic instead of metal. On the left side of the wafer is a write protect tab, which can be snapped off. Of course, this tab cannot be replaced once it is broken off and users will have to find some other method of re-enabling their cartridges.

The commands used by the Wafadrive are more or less identical to those used on the Sinclair Microdrives. In both systems the command is followed by a *, indicating that the external storage device is to be accessed. Examples of this usage are SAVE *, LOAD * and VERIFY *. However, the Wafadrive system does have slight differences because there are always two Wafadrives present, as opposed to the numerous Microdrives that could be in the system. For example, when formatting a Sinclair wafer one uses the command FORMAT 'm' ;0;"name", where 'm' ;0 refers to the number of the Microdrive being used. When using the Wafadrive, the command is altered to FORMAT * 'a:name', with the a: referring to the name of the drive in use. Note that with the Wafadrive, there can only be a section a: or b:, whereas on the Microdrive the number can be from zero to seven.

THE 'STREAM' SYSTEM

The Wafadrive also takes advantage of the 'stream' system used on the Spectrum, in which there are 16 streams set aside for input/output management. Some of these are reserved for use by the screen and printer. However, channels four to 15 are available to other peripheral devices, and output streams to the Wafadrive are accessed by use of the OPEN # command. The Wafadrive also adds two extra streams to the system. Channels r and c (these letters can also be capitalised) are reserved for the RS232 and Centronics interfaces, respectively, and their usages are similar to the t and b channels — used when accessing the RS232 port on Interface 1.

There is an eight Kbyte ROM on board containing the extended BASIC commands used in controlling the system. This Wafadrive Operating System (WOS) is able to function by 'paging out' the lower eight Kbytes from the Spectrum's ROM, in much the same way that Interface 1 does. For example, the command LOAD * actually generates an error on the Spectrum; thus, when the BASIC interpreter encounters this command on the screen, it will call the error-handling routine. However, this call command will be intercepted by the WOS, which will then page in the Wafadrive

ROM. This in turn will take over the error handling and interpret LOAD * as a command.

Compared with the Microdrives, the Rotronics Wafadrive is somewhat slower. For example, a 100 Kbyte Microdrive requires an average of 3½ seconds to locate a piece of information, which is then transferred to the computer at a rate of up to 19.2 Kbaud. The Wafadrive, on the other hand, can only manage a maximum transfer rate of 18 Kbaud, with a maximum access time of 45 seconds on a 128 Kbyte wafer. This is significantly slower, although this relative sluggishness is partially compensated for by its increased reliability. However, it must be noted that the

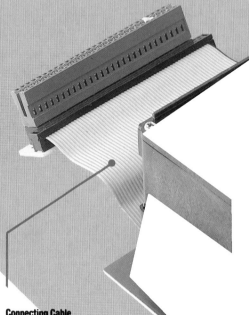

Drive Enable Lights
These LEDs tell the user which drive is currently being accessed

Connecting Cable
The 54-way cable connects to the Spectrum's own edge connector. The Wafadrive not only receives its controlling data through this bus, but also its power supply

ROM Chip
This 8 Kbyte EPROM contains the Wafadrive operating system (WOS)

Parallel Through Connector
This edge connector allows further Spectrum-compatible interfaces to be added to the system

Sinclair Microdrives were consistently faster than the Wafadrive in benchtest timings.

Although these access times are much faster than could possibly be achieved on cassette, they are still slower than comparable disk drive times. However, the Wafadrive, like the Microdrives, incorporates a handy procedure when accessing the tape's catalogue. The catalogue is held on the first sector of the cartridge after the splice joining both ends of the tape together. Thus, to CATalogue a wafer, the drive has to wind the tape until it discovers the splice and can read the next suitable sector. After several seconds, the tape head will be past the catalogue sector. However, should the CAT command be entered again, instead of winding the

Wafer Drives
The Wafadrive has two tape drives, which are both self contained units. At present, Rotronics provides 16, 64 and 128 Kbyte cartridges to fit these

Motors
Each drive has its own electric motor to turn the tape in the cartridges

RS232 Port
This serial port enables the Spectrum to be connected to standard communications equipment

Centronics Interface
The Wafadrive is fitted with a Centronics port to allow a printer to be attached — a necessary addition for word processing

Spectrum's Symbol Shift key in conjunction with other keys. Other functions that access files held on wafer can be obtained by means of the options command: these include SAVE and LOAD text files from cassette or from Wafadrive. Spectral Writer is a fine word processor, although it does not enable you to set the line length on the screen. It is perhaps unfortunate that even when using a Spectrum+, the quality of the keyboard somewhat diminishes the Spectral Writer's efficiency.

Of course, what makes or breaks any storage medium on a computer is the willingness of software houses to support it. At the moment this seems to be a serious drawback to the Wafadrive's success, since none of the major software houses are producing their programs on Wafadrive cartridges (this is also a problem that has been encountered by Sinclair itself). However, all is not lost for the Wafadrive user. At least one company is now producing a program that enables you to dump commercial software onto Wafadrive cartridges. This means that users will be forced to buy both the commercial cassette and a wafer to transfer it to, but it may be a small price to pay for the vastly improved access times that are produced.

Another minor difficulty of the Wafadrive is the edge connectors on the back of the machine. Because they are non-standard, users must be willing to convert the interfaces themselves, or else they will have to look hard for peripherals with suitable connections. But although the Wafadrive does have its drawbacks, it is a finely made machine, and certainly a viable alternative to the Interface 1 and Microdrive provided by Sinclair Research.

ROTRONICS WAFADRIVE	
DIMENSIONS	
230×110×80mm	
INTERFACES	
RS232 serial port, Centronics parallel interfaces, Spectrum edge connector	
FORMAT	
Continuous loop stringy floppy wafers	
CAPACITY	
16, 64 and 128 Kbyte wafers available	
SPEED	
Transfer rate: 16 Kbaud; maximum access time: 6.5 sec (16K), 45 sec (128K)	

whole of the tape round again, the drive will move for only a fraction of a second before displaying the catalogue again — it will be held in RAM once it has been called. Thereafter, the WOS merely checks to see whether the same wafer is inserted by looking at the next sector. If it is, the WOS will display the catalogue it already holds in RAM.

In keeping with the idea of implementing a mass storage system allowing the Spectrum to be used for more serious applications, Rotronics has included the Spectral Writer word processing program in the package. This is a relatively comprehensive system making full use of the Wafadrive. Functions such as reform paragraph, insert words and delete lines are called by using the

Wafadrive Cartridge
The Wafadrive cartridge is roughly twice the size of the Sinclair Mircodrive's equivalent. The wafer resembles a conventional cassette in its proportions, but the tape inside, is fixed in a continual loop. This means that the tape does not have to be rewound to access data that has gone past the read/write head

CHRIS STEVENS

Discovering New Worlds
The Discovery 1 is intended to
be an all-in-one expansion
system for the Spectrum user.
The machine comes complete
with a disk drive, operating
system and connections to
allow printers, joysticks,
composite video monitors and
other peripherals to be fitted
without the need for further
interfaces

OPUS SESAME!

Sinclair Research has provided the Microdrive for the Spectrum, but a need has remained for a more reliable and accommodating disk drive system. We conclude our two part series on alternatives to the Sinclair Microdrive by examining the Discovery 1 from Opus, following our look at Rotronics' Wafadrive.

In the previous Hardware article we looked at the Rotronics Wafadrive. Although this device proved to be somewhat more reliable than the Microdrive, it turned out to be slower in comparison, and still based around the rather suspect continuous tape system. In this article we turn our attention to a more conventional approach to mass storage: a disk-based system from Opus Supplies.

A disk drive for the Spectrum does not represent a new idea. Over the past couple of years there have been a number of disk operating systems and interfaces available for the machine; however, none of these systems have become particularly popular. This is partly because the interfaces have been advertised solely in the specialist press, which has given the devices an air of being intended only for the devout Spectrum enthusiast and machine code programmers, and partly because they have been available only through mail order houses and have not been given the kind of mass marketing needed to push them into the public consciousness.

The Discovery 1 is encased in sheet metal, extending the front of the machine to support the Spectrum that plugs into a cartridge slot via the expansion port. Although this seems a comparatively easy operation, users may find some difficulty in attaching the Discovery to the edge connector. This is because the cassette and aerial leads tend to get in the way and prevent the cartridge slot from being attached correctly. Bearing in mind that a badly attached edge connector could severely damage the Spectrum, this is a serious problem. The difficulty is not as pronounced with the original Spectrum (for which the Discovery was originally designed), but the new Spectrum+, with its larger casing, may have users struggling for several minutes before they are satisfied that the device is correctly fitted. Once the Spectrum has been fitted to Discovery 1, the machine effectively blocks off the computer's own power supply input. The Discovery has therefore been designed to power both itself and the Spectrum, thus making the micro's own external power supply redundant.

DUAL DRIVE UPGRADE

Above the cartridge slot on the left is a single $3\frac{1}{2}$in disk drive, with space on the right for a second drive. (Opus intends to launch a dual drive version of the machine called the Discovery 2.) Discovery 1 users wishing to upgrade their systems to dual drive configurations can expect an external additional disk drive called Discovery+ to be launched. However, users will not be limited only to Opus drives since the company claims that standard $5\frac{1}{4}$in disk drives can also be added in the same manner.

In common with Rotronics, Opus's philosophy in designing the machine is to provide not only a

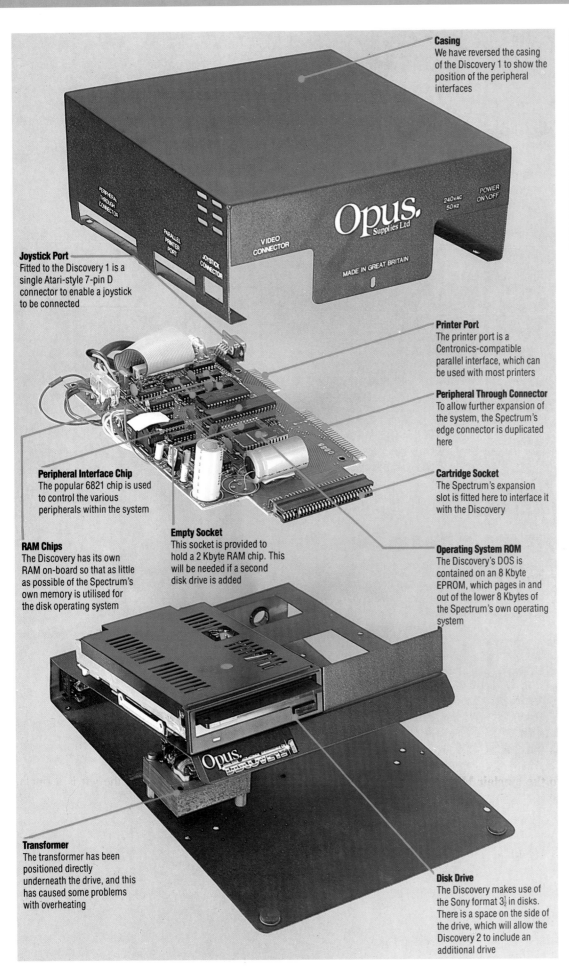

Casing
We have reversed the casing of the Discovery 1 to show the position of the peripheral interfaces

Joystick Port
Fitted to the Discovery 1 is a single Atari-style 7-pin D connector to enable a joystick to be connected

Peripheral Interface Chip
The popular 6821 chip is used to control the various peripherals within the system

RAM Chips
The Discovery has its own RAM on-board so that as little as possible of the Spectrum's own memory is utilised for the disk operating system

Empty Socket
This socket is provided to hold a 2 Kbyte RAM chip. This will be needed if a second disk drive is added

Printer Port
The printer port is a Centronics-compatible parallel interface, which can be used with most printers

Peripheral Through Connector
To allow further expansion of the system, the Spectrum's edge connector is duplicated here

Cartridge Socket
The Spectrum's expansion slot is fitted here to interface it with the Discovery

Operating System ROM
The Discovery's DOS is contained on an 8 Kbyte EPROM, which pages in and out of the lower 8 Kbytes of the Spectrum's own operating system

Transformer
The transformer has been positioned directly underneath the drive, and this has caused some problems with overheating

Disk Drive
The Discovery makes use of the Sony format 3½in disks. There is a space on the side of the drive, which will allow the Discovery 2 to include an additional drive

DISCOVERY 1	
DIMENSIONS	300×210×75mm
INTERFACES	Parallel through connector, Centronics parallel interface, joystick port, composite video jack
FORMAT	Single-sided double-density 3½in Sony standard disks
CAPACITY	250 Kbytes total, 180 Kbytes formatted
SPEED	Transfer rate 15 Kbaud, track to track access time 3 milliseconds

mass storage system for the Spectrum, but also to add extra peripheral interfaces allowing users to run printers and other devices. A composite video monitor socket on the back of Discovery 1 has been provided, according to an Opus spokesman, for business users wishing to attach a monochrome monitor (although of course composite video does produce a colour signal) for lengthy periods of word processing. However, on a machine noted for its colourful games programs, it is a pity that Opus could not have provided an RGB interface to produce a much clearer picture.

On the right side of the Discovery is a single Kempston—compatible, Atari—standard joystick port, next to which is a bi-directional Centronics parallel printer port. Finally, there is a peripheral through connector to enable other Spectrum-compatible interfaces, such as an RGB monitor, to be connected.

Like the Wafadrive, the Discovery disk operating system closely follows that of the Interface 1; for example, issuing a command requires <COMMAND> *. When the BASIC interpreter reaches the *, it does not recognise it as being a BASIC command and attempts to generate a syntax error. However, the DOS intercepts it and pages its own eight Kbyte operating system into the position of the lower eight Kbytes of the Spectrum's ROM, and then interprets the command. It should be noted that if the user has made a syntax error, even the DOS won't recognise it and an error message will be generated, although this will still be via the DOS ROM.

In designing its DOS system, Opus has gone further than Rotronics in providing compatibility — all of the commands available to the Microdrive have been retained. There are several reasons for this. Because of the Spectrum's single keyword entry system, it is obviously easier to write an operating system using inherent commands, rather than going to the trouble of writing your own. This also means that users who are already familiar with the Microdrive operating system will be able to use the Discovery immediately, since all the syntax is the same. Furthermore, tinkering with an operating system can lead to all kinds of unforeseen problems with the memory map. This means that programs compatible with Interface 1 may not necessarily be compatible with your revamped operating system, a problem that has plagued many other third party peripherals.

The way in which Opus has closely followed the Sinclair Microdrive command system is most noticeable when looking at the way the streams have been organised. On the Spectrum, output channels are organised into 16 streams numbered 0 to 15. Three of these are set aside for the screen, keyboard and printer, the others are free for use by any other peripheral. In the Sinclair list of Interface 1 commands, there are a number of single characters that open channels to specific devices; for example 'm' for Microdrive. The Discovery has adapted these to its own use, thus

the command LOAD * 'm';1;'name' will work just as well on Discovery 1 as on a Microdrive, although in this case 'm' refers to the disk drive. However, for added convenience, Opus has adapted the command format so that 'm' can be omitted, thereby shortening the somewhat long-winded Sinclair system. Other commands have also been adapted. The character 't' in a command on the Microdrive opens a channel to the RS232 interface, whereas on the Discovery it opens the channel to the parallel printer.

THE DISKS IN OPERATION

The disk drive supplied with the system uses the double—density Sony format $3\frac{1}{2}$in disks that are becoming increasingly popular on microcomputers. The disks themselves each have a total capacity of 250 Kbytes, which, when formatted, provide 180 Kbytes of available storage space. The disk operating system supports random access when searching for a file, which is considerably faster than the serial search methods used on some other disk systems. Also, there is no limit to the number of files that can be held on a disk, which can be important when one wishes to save a number of short files. If the directory is quickly filled, there may be a large amount of space on the disk that cannot be used.

When comparing the time it takes to SAVE and LOAD a file using the Discovery and Microdrive, the former proved to be somewhat faster in actually finding a file but considerably slower in SAVEing and LOADing it. Finding a file is faster on the disk system because the files are organised by random access whereas the Microdrives, by their nature, are serial access devices. Why accessing a file into memory is much slower is more difficult to explain, but it is a fact that the transfer rate of the Discovery 1 is much slower than that of the Microdrives — 15 Kbaud compared to 19.2 Kbaud. The real advantage of the Discovery lies in having a mass storage system more robust than the Microdrive's, and a storage medium having a wider range of manufacturers to choose from.

Opus appears to have given some thought to the problematic aspect of software support for the Discovery. Obviously, having a large company like Boots selling the product in their chain of stores is an advantage, since software houses will be able to offer their products alongside the machine itself. The company has also indicated that many software houses, including Melbourne House and Legend, have already agreed to transfer some of their existing programs onto the $3\frac{1}{2}$in disks.

The launch of the Discovery series of disk drives has clearly been well planned and Opus has obviously attempted to provide its new line with as much chance of success as it possibly could. For the company, the major task before it is convincing Spectrum owners that the Discovery is a more worthwhile investment for their machine than the Sinclair alternative. If the time is right and the Spectrum owner is ready for a disk—based system, Opus and its Discovery 1 could well be a success.

FAST MOVER

Commodore 64 owners have had to use, for the most part, Commodore's own storage devices, which lack both performance and storage capacity. With the introduction of the Phonemark 8500 Quick Data Drive, which uses stringy floppy wafers, the situation has dramatically improved.

Front Runner
There have been few 'third party' suppliers of alternative storage systems to the Commodore cassette deck and disk drive, despite the criticisms of these machines. The Quick Data Drive is a 'stringy floppy disk' system that uses continuous loops of tape identical to those in the Rotronics Wafadrive. At around £100, the system is not particularly cheap, but it is half the price of the Commodore disk drive, and in many applications is considerably faster

storage devices. When Commodore turned its attention to providing back-up storage for the PET series, it decided to provide its own cassette drive and incorporate a complex series of checks to ensure that the data being loaded was correct. While this increased the reliability of LOADing, it was at the expense of access speed. This system was carried over to the Vic-20 and later the Commodore 64.

Nowadays, the quality of cassette tape has greatly improved and the need for the long and complicated data checking on the Commodore machines has become unnecessary. Many commercial software packages now contain their own loading techniques, which remove many of the checks and make loading much faster, without any loss of reliability.

However, when LOADing their own programs, most users do not have access to these high-speed techniques and must still put up with the delays imposed by the Commodore operating system. The Quick Data Drive, which claims to load 15 times faster than normal cassettes and faster than the 1541 disk drive, can be seen as a commercial alternative to the Commodore peripherals.

The Quick Data Drive is quite a small device — just over half the size of the Commodore 1530 cassette deck. The drive is connected to the Vic-20 or Commodore 64 via the cassette edge connector. Unlike the Rotronics Wafadrive, the Quick Data Drive has only a single drive. While it would be preferable to have two drives when a system wafer and a data wafer need to be running simultaneously, most users will find the single-drive adequate. If absolutely necessary, a second drive can always be purchased and connected to provide dual-drive capability.

Because many home computer enthusiasts are considering purchasing faster and more efficient methods of accessing their programs, manufacturers are producing a wide range of mass storage devices aimed at the most popular home micros. Among these is the Phonemark 8500 Quick Data Drive from Dean Electronics, made for the Commodore 64 and Vic-20.

This device is a close relative of the Rotronics Wafadrive (shown earlier) designed for the Sinclair Spectrum. The drives for both were produced by BSR Electronics and each uses identical 'wafers'.

The standard Commodore 1541 disk drive, like the cassette drive, is notoriously slow. This is due not to the disk drive itself but the method by which the computer loads data. Much of the Commodore 64's operating system is inherited from the PET business machines of the mid-1970s, when mass storage systems, particularly cassette drives, were extremely unreliable as data

THE OPERATING SYSTEM

The fact that the drive plugs into the cassette port does not mean that you cannot have a cassette deck running at the same time. There is a cassette edge connector on the back of the Data Drive allowing cassette drives, or a second Quick Data Drive, to be daisy-chained together.

Although the Rotronics Wafadrive and the Quick Data Drive have similar appearances, they have very different methods of operation, reflecting the differences in the computers for which they were designed. Whereas the Wafadrive has its operating system held in ROM (emulating the ROMs on the Interface 1), the Quick Data Drive Operating System (QOS) is held on a wafer. In order to LOAD the QOS into the computer, you must press Shift/Run (as you would when LOADing a normal cassette). When the screen prompt PRESS PLAY ON TAPE appears, you then press a small button on the back of the drive that autoboots the system. Once this has been done, the QOS will perform it automatically for subsequent accesses.

The programs that make up the QOS are loaded into two separate areas of memory. First, the machine code routines for LOADing, SAVEing and searching programs are stored between addresses C000 and CFFF towards the top of memory (normally used for machine code programs). It is this module of the QOS that results in the increased LOADing speed of the drive.

Although the QOS does not implement any commands of its own (using instead those already available in the Commodore Operating System ROM), it will intercept the routines that deal with

QUICK DATA DRIVE	
DIMENSIONS	
147×118×49mm	
INTERFACES	
Socket to connect to the Commodore 64/Vic-20 cassette port	
FORMAT	
Continuous loop, stringy floppy wafers	
CAPACITY	
16, 64 and 128 Kbyte wafers available	
SPEED	
Average access time: 8 secs/ 15 Kbyte file; 43 secs/120 Kbyte file	

cassette and one and a half minutes from disk, took a mere 30 seconds to LOAD from the Quick Data Drive — a considerable improvement. However, as with all tape loop-based systems, much depends upon where the drive's read/write head is in relation to the beginning of the program.

The Quick Operating System finds the required data files by checking each of the heading blocks on the tape. When a wafer is formatted, the operating system will divide the tape into blocks, each with its own filename section. When it is required to load a file into the computer, it will search until it finds the block containing the first part of the file, load it and then find the second.

Similarly, when asked to display a directory of the wafer, the QOS will read each of the filenames as the read/write head passes over the tape, and register the blocks that contain files and those which are empty. When all the filenames have been read, the system will display the list of files plus the total amount of available space in bytes.

FILE MANAGEMENT UTILITY

The File Management Utility is a menu-driven set of routines covering such applications as formatting and reading the directory of the wafer. It also contains copying routines that allow data to be transferred from disk, cassette or wafer onto a back-up wafer. This is obviously an important feature of the Quick Data Drive system as few programmers would consider buying a storage system, no matter how good, that could not transfer existing programs onto the new medium.

Of course, there are drawbacks to the system. While the copying routines work fine for BASIC programs and sequential files, certain routines (machine code in particular) which are loaded to a specific area of memory will cause problems. This is because the two areas used by the QOS and FMU are also the areas in which machine code is kept. Thus when machine code programs are loaded, they will overwrite the Quick Data Drive operating system and crash the program.

This design feature means that while it is possible to copy your own programs, it is not, as yet, possible to transfer commercial software. If the Quick Data Drive sells in sufficient quantities, however, there will doubtless be a program produced to do so.

Until then, much depends on Dean Electronics' ability to persuade software houses to sell their games and applications on wafers. In this respect, they may find that the Rotronics Wafadrive will prove a valuable ally — software companies will thus be able to purchase larger quantities of wafers at larger discounts when they find that they can place both their Commodore 64 and Sinclair Spectrum software on the same storage medium.

Although it is still early, the company has had a measure of success. Some games, such as Epyx's highly rated 'platform' game Impossible Mission, are already available on wafer, but a much wider software base will be necessary.

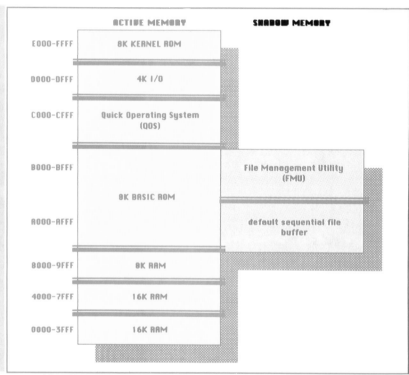

normal loading and insert its own.

The other part of the Quick Operating System is the File Management Utility (FMU), which contains a number of useful routines. This is kept in the top half of the eight Kbytes of Shadow Memory underneath the BASIC ROM — between addresses B000 and AFFF. The bottom four Kbytes between A000 and AFFF are used as a sequential file buffer that is used by the FMU.

Because the FMU is stored in the area of memory under the BASIC ROM, you cannot use both at the same time. In order to call it from memory, the command LOAD 'FMU' must be executed. This simply 'banks' out the BASIC ROM and enters the FMU.

Undoubtedly, the Quick Data Drive's operations are much faster than standard cassette methods. To compare loading times between the two media, we took a popular adventure game and used it as a benchtest. The complete 25 Kbyte program, requiring over nine minutes to load from

A Quick Memory
The Quick Data Drive does not keep its operating system in ROM but has to LOAD it from a systems wafer. The various components are installed in two separate areas of memory. The first, the Quick Operating System (QOS) is LOADed into the area usually reserved for machine code programs. The other part of the system, the File Management Utility (FMU) is held in the 'shadow RAM' behind the BASIC ROM. Also contained here is a file buffer where programs are loaded before they are SAVEd onto another medium

INDEX